D1557673

A Century of Russian Agriculture:
From Alexander II to Khrushchev

Russian Research Center Studies   63

A Century of Russian Agriculture

by Lazar Volin

From Alexander II
to Khrushchev

Harvard University Press
Cambridge, Massachusetts, 1970

© Copyright 1970 by the President and Fellows of Harvard College
All rights reserved

The Russian Research Center of Harvard University is supported by a grant from the Ford Foundation. The Center carries out interdisciplinary study of Russian institutions and behavior and related subjects.

Distributed in Great Britain by Oxford University Press, London

Library of Congress Catalog Card Number 72-119075
SBN 674-10621-0

Printed in the United States of America

Foreword   by Abram Bergson

Lazar Volin (1896–1966) was born in the Minsk province of Russia. His childhood was spent in Berlin and in Poland near Warsaw. Finally, the family moved to Harbin, where he completed the course of studies at the Russian gymnasium. After his immigration to the United States in 1915, he earned first his A.B. and then his Ph.D. in economics at the University of Michigan, and in 1926 joined the staff of the United States Department of Agriculture. He thus began to devote himself to what was to become a lifelong pursuit: the study of Russian agriculture. To that pursuit Volin would bring the advantages not only of a firm grasp of the Russian language and culture and advanced Western training in economics, but an ever deepening knowledge of Russian history. With a humanist's compassion for the Russian peasant under tsarist autocracy and Soviet dictatorship he combined an unwavering concern for scholarly objectivity.

That a remarkable career resulted goes without saying. In due time, Volin became chief of the East European Branch of the Department of Agriculture, a post he retained until his retirement in 1965. Universally recognized as one of the foremost Western authorities on Russian agriculture, he was the author of, or contributor to, hundreds of reports, essays, and other writings in the field. Many of these publications, including a monograph, were issued by the Department of Agriculture; others appeared in professional journals. If in respect to agriculture Russia is by now far from the Churchillian enigma, that is in no small part because of the pioneering efforts of Lazar Volin.

In undertaking this volume, Volin clearly was seeking to set down summarily a lifetime's researches and reflections. The result is an outstanding achievement. In one volume a distinguished scholar recounts the story of Russian agriculture over the century extending from the eve of the Emancipation to the post-Stalinian USSR, from Alexander II to Khrushchev and Brezhnev and Kosygin; a distinguished scholar, furthermore, who properly sees Russia's "agrarian problem" in the perspective of the historical relations between agriculture and the whole economy, and is able to bring to bear on its study an immense learning, extending from the thought of the narodniks of the last century to the misfortunes of Soviet agronomy under Stalin's Lysenko.

When he died on December 6, 1966, Volin had nearly completed a final revision of the draft of his manuscript which had previously been accepted by Harvard University Press. As far as possible, the revised manuscript has been subjected to only the usual press editing for style and clarity of exposition, though here and there the deletion of a dated passage was unavoidable. In a few cases, a clearly inadvertent factual or other lapse had also to be repaired.

The editing of so large a manuscript without the author's collaboration was a formidable task. Warmest thanks are due to Mrs. Joyce Lebowitz and Mrs. Margaretta Fulton, of the Harvard University Press, for the skill and diligence that they exercised in carrying it out. We must be deeply grateful also to Harry Walters, a former associate of Dr. Volin's, for reviewing the editing and counseling on the innumerable queries that were inevitably encountered. Dr. Edward L. Keenan was kind enough to check the transliteration of Russian words throughout.

In preparing a final revision, Dr. Volin apparently intended to bring up all strands of his story to the advent of Brezhnev and Kosygin. This he did not always succeed in doing and, as might be expected, the shortfall is to be noted especially in the final chapters, that is, from Chapter 19 on. Volin himself wrote elsewhere, however, of later developments in respect to the matters discussed there, and the reader seeking his views on them may wish to refer to his "Khrushchev and the Soviet Agricultural Scene" in *Soviet and East European Agriculture,* edited by Jerzy F. Karcz, University of California Press, 1967. Also useful are two reports of the Economic Research Service, U.S. Department of Agriculture, to which Dr. Volin contributed: *Soviet Grain Imports,* ERS–Foreign–135, September 1965, and *The USSR and Eastern Europe: Agricultural Situation,* ERS–Foreign–151, March, 1966.

Contents

Contents

A Century of Russian Agriculture:
From Alexander II to Khrushchev

Introduction

With a huge area of over 540 million acres sown to crops and about 40 percent of the population depending on the land for its livelihood, the Soviet Union continues to be one of the leading agricultural countries of the world, as well as an important participant in international agricultural trade. This agricultural pre-eminence has lasted despite the obstacles of severe climate and rapid, if lopsided, industrialization. Industrial development naturally resulted in a declining share of agriculture in the gross national product and in occupational distribution; but, because of the persistent problem of food supply, agriculture continues to play a disproportionately large part in the economic life of the Soviet Union. The failure of the annual harvest is still an event of greater importance in the lives of the Russian people than, say, what happens to steel production. The latter affects guns and missiles, which, to paraphrase Khrushchev, cannot be put into soup.

These facts alone should be sufficient justification for a full-scale analysis of the development of Soviet agrarian policy and practice. But there are additional reasons. The British economic historian J. H. Clapham approvingly quotes the dictum of Gustav Schmoller that "from 1500 to

1850 the great social question of the day in Europe was the peasant question." [1] What Schmoller said of the mid-nineteenth century is still true of the Soviet Union in the 1960s. It is evidenced by a series of agrarian revolutions, counterrevolutions, and far-reaching reforms which took place during the century following Schmoller's terminal date. In shaping these events, and indeed the whole Russian agrarian structure, policy has played a crucial role. That the agricultural problem has remained an explosive political and economic issue is attested by numerous public pronouncements of Russian leaders—prerevolutionary and postrevolutionary alike, including Khrushchev and his successors. In this persistence of the problem we have a clear manifestation of the historical continuity between the two periods. It therefore seemed that a better, more balanced, perspective would be gained by a historical review which stops not at the "great divide" of 1917 but penetrates as deeply as necessary into the recesses of the prerevolutionary past, utilizing the rich Russian literature and some excellent foreign works on the subject.

The first two parts of this study are devoted to such historical analysis, centering principally on the period between the 1850s and the 1950s. The last part attempts to give a systematic account of contemporary collectivized agriculture, its structure and the manner in which it functions or malfunctions—or, to borrow biological terminology, its anatomy, physiology, and pathology. Readers who are interested primarily in learning in some depth how collective agriculture is currently organized and what makes it tick can turn directly to Part Three.

Part One. Peasant and Landlord

1

Serfdom: Origins and Development

A little over a century ago, one day before Abraham Lincoln's inaugura-
tion and months before his Emancipation Proclamation, a manifesto was
signed by Alexander II in which the Autocrat of All the Russias announced the abolition of serfdom in his country "forever." Although
serfdom in Russia, like slavery in the American South, was a relatively
recent phenomenon, it cast a long shadow over subsequent agrarian developments. The century after emancipation is the chief object of interest
in this study, but it seems desirable to round out the picture with a short
account of serfdom since it loomed so large in the agrarian policy of the
Russian state.

The Rise of Serfdom

Serfdom reached its pinnacle in Russia relatively late, when it was already
on the decline or being abolished in the West. Whereas this has been
generally recognized by Russian scholars, considerable uncertainty and
difference of opinion exist concerning the genesis of serfdom. In fact,

the subject has provoked a long and lively controversy among Russian historians, giving rise to a voluminous literature.[1] I shall try to distill this debate with a few comments of my own.

Before dealing with the controversial matters, several important points must be noted on which there is general agreement among scholars. It is agreed, first of all, that chattel slavery, as distinguished from serfdom, existed in Russia since time immemorial but that it did not affect the majority of the population. It is also not disputed that the institution of serfdom became entrenched between the middle of the sixteenth and seventeenth centuries, in the process assuming many features of slavery. Most scholars hold that the peasants of Muscovite Russia, who were not slaves, were predominantly tenant farmers on the estates of private landlords or monasteries whose landholdings were very extensive; or they were settled on lands belonging legally to the Moscow rulers. Actually these lands were administered by the peasant communities, which assumed the responsibility for collecting taxes.

There were various types of tenancies, distinguished by differing degrees of dependence on the landlords, who came to wield considerable power over the peasants even before any legal loss of freedom. This resulted in oppression, though in some cases also in protection of individuals by powerful landlords, since the legal position of the peasantry in Russian society was very weak.[2] For those peasants who settled on crown lands, the regime was less oppressive because the master's power was more remote and the relationship less direct.[3]

Another important aspect of the agrarian situation in Muscovite Russia on which there is general agreement among scholars is the difficulty experienced by landlords in holding or attracting an adequate labor supply. This was accentuated in the sixteenth century by several interrelated factors. One was the acquisition of a considerable fertile and sparsely populated territory in the east and southeast as a result of successful wars against the Tatar khanates. This additional territory, which still had to be defended, the Moscow government was anxious to colonize. An impetus to such migration was also given by the agrarian revolution that the Moscow tsars, particularly Ivan the Terrible, were promoting. It had a double object: to destroy the old princely aristocracy, which was considered an adversary, and to create instead a new military class of gentry (*sluzhilye liudi*) loyal to the regime, which was required for the continuous wars. This military class was paid with land, the only abundant resource at the government's disposal. For this purpose both the confiscated estate land of the old aristocracy and the crown land settled by peasants were used. The gentry held the land granted to it only on condition that it would serve the tsar. This conditional tenure (*pomestie*) must be distinguished from the absolute property rights of the old aristocracy to their estates (*votchina*).

The abrupt and rapid changes in the structure of landholding, especially during the latter part of the reign of Ivan the Terrible, imposed heavy burdens and exerted a disturbing effect on the peasant-tenants. This was aggravated by long wars with Poland, Sweden, and Turkey and brought on a serious economic crisis in the 1670s and 1680s. Hence the urge to migrate, for which the newly acquired territory provided favorable opportunities. The Russian historian S. F. Platonov considered this large-scale peasant emigration the principal cause of the critical decline of population and agricultural production in the older central and western regions of the Moscow state during the last quarter of the sixteenth century. All other causes, such as failure of crops and consequent famines, epidemics and the devastation caused by the invasion of the Crimean Tatars, he considered secondary.[4] Although this runs counter to the generally accepted view, there is no dispute that the crisis brought to a focus the problem of securing adequate labor to cultivate the soil on the estates upon which the livelihood of the military class, as well as the tax revenue of the government, depended. It is worth noting that the small gentry suffered much more from the flight of the peasants than did the large landlords—nobles or monasteries—who were much better equipped to attract, hold, or reclaim the fleeing peasants. The peasants' flight to the frontier and the problem of reclaiming them long continued to preoccupy the landlords and the state; Soviet historians have brought to light much interesting material on this subject.[5] But what concerns us at this juncture is that an important, some would say crucial, change took place in the status of the peasants.

Until the last decades of the sixteenth century, peasant-tenants, unlike the slaves (*kholopy*), possessed the right sanctioned by the codes of 1497 and 1550 to change their masters each year during a short period after the end of the agricultural season in the autumn: namely, a week before and a week after St. George's Day. There is a question as to the extent to which this legal right of departure was actually exercised by the peasants. Some authorities do not think that it was. But B. D. Grekov, on the basis of more recently published monastery records, has come to an opposite conclusion.[6] In many cases the departure of tenants was assisted by other landlords who were anxious to secure workers. But there were also unassisted departures. Peasants were frequently leaving their holdings or "fleeing," as the Russian terminology of the time had it, with or without assistance of other landlords, and at other than the legally prescribed periods. This is, however, another problem. So long as a limited legal right to leave did remain, it is not possible to speak of a tight servile system, even though the prevailing farm tenancy might have had many of its earmarks. By the end of the sixteenth century, the peasants apparently lost the right to leave their masters even during the one period of the year. This signaled the beginning of full-fledged serfdom and is also the starting point of the celebrated controversy over how the loss of the right to move occurred.

Some Russian historians of the eighteenth and early nineteenth centuries considered, on the basis of inferential evidence, that a general law repealing tenants' right to move was enacted in 1592. The text of this law has never been discovered, and there are no references to it in subsequent legislation, as was customary in old Russia. The existence of such a law was inferred from a discovery by an eighteenth-century historian, Tatishchev, of another law passed in 1597, which restricted the right of landlords to bring civil suits to reclaim their fleeing peasants to a five-year period preceding the law. Those who fled prior to this period could not be claimed, unless such suits had already been originated by 1597. Hence the hypothesis that five years earlier, in 1592, a law was enacted which abolished the right of free movement and thus sanctioned bondage. This seemed more plausible since 1592 was the terminal year of a prolonged land census, which is considered by some authorities as having played a seminal role in binding the peasants. But this hypothesis was challenged by M. P. Pogodin in 1858.[7] Thus started a century ago the debate over the origin of serfdom in which some of the most illustrious figures in Russian historiography have participated.

The debate, which began with the rather simple question of the existence or lack of a general law binding peasants, shifted to a broader plane. Was serfdom created through positive action of the state, or was it essentially a product of gradual development through custom? It should be pointed out that this discussion had to be waged on a rather slender basis of historical evidence, which greatly complicated the task of analysis and made for an indeterminateness in much of the theorizing.[8] The weakness of the old "state" theory of the origin of serfdom was, as Pogodin pointed out, the very lack of any direct evidence of the existence of a specific law. A more serious blow to this theory was dealt by Vasilii Kliuchevskii, who in 1885 advanced a rival theory.[9] According to him and his followers, serfdom developed from the existing types of dependence and particularly as a result of an adaptation in the ancient institution of slavery. A common type of dependence resulted from long tenancies, which by custom established an indissoluble bond between the peasant and the holding he leased.

But there was even a more clear-cut form of legal dependence, known as *kabala,* in which indebtedness was a key factor. It was a type of indentured service, entered into voluntarily by people in strained circumstances who borrowed money from their masters; this was to be repaid with interest by service. The kabala servant's position was little different from that of a slave, but once the master was repaid the servant was again legally free. In many cases, no doubt, repayment of such debts, especially without assistance, was difficult. The master often did not want the loan repaid, preferring to continue the service indefinitely. It is interesting that the Code of 1550 tried to protect such debtors by limiting the amount of the loan to fifteen rubles—a rather large sum at that time. The Code of 1649 decreased it to three rubles. But this changed during the latter part of the century, as the position of the working population generally deteriorated. The regaining of freedom upon repayment of the debt was abolished by a decree of April 25, 1597 (not to be confused with the celebrated November 1597 decree discussed above) and probably also by a law passed in 1586, to which only references and not the actual text have been found. Yet this servitude, which was now called *kabal'noe kholopstvo,* was still limited to the lifetime of the master; unlike full-fledged slavery, it was not hereditary.[10] What made the kabala type of servitude so important to Kliuchevskii was that it clearly showed a line of causation from indebtedness to bondage, albeit in an incomplete form. But this was by no means the sole manifestation. It was customary for landlords generally to loan money and goods to their tenants. The indebtedness precluded even those tenants who had the legal right to leave their masters from exercising it, and in time it atrophied. Thus serfdom, according to this theory, developed gradually as a result of custom and the working of economic forces and not by a fiat of the state—certainly not by virtue of some one specific law. As Kliuchevskii put it: "Without bringing into peasant relations unexpected changes and allowing them to develop in accordance with the existing custom, legislation merely set the limits which these relations could not overstep in their development . . . Serfdom in Russia was created not by the state but only with the participation of the state; the latter was responsible not for the creation of serfdom, but for its boundaries."[11]

This theory clearly attributes to the state a passive or at least a subordinate or neutral role in the origin of serfdom. Kliuchevskii, as Struve points out, had a predecessor in F. I. Leontovich, who emphasized the indebtedness factor more than twenty years earlier: "The poor peasant, settling on someone else's land, almost without any means to carry on farming independently, imperceptibly was drawn into debt; the landlord became his creditor, extending his power over the peasant's person and labor . . . Apart from a few cases, the binding of peasants was always founded on an unchangeable principle of indebtedness or better to say, economic dependence . . . In this economic dependence of peasants on landlords must be sought the basic cause or, more precisely, the soil on which the bondage of the rural population originated in southwestern as in eastern Russia." [12]

Support for Kliuchevskii's thesis that serfdom has its roots in the institution of slavery is found in the writings of the Soviet historian S. Veselovskii: "In the history of northeastern Russia, as in the countries of western Europe, a transformation of a rather considerable number of slaves into peasant-serfs took place during certain stages of development. The slaves on arable land adopted the customs and the legal and production conditions of peasant life, acquired similar economic and social characteristics, and, in the end, merged with the mass of the peasantry, forming within it the first category of peasant-serfs. In the fourteenth and fifteenth centuries, the princes settled large groups of slaves, whole villages, on the arable land. The monasteries did not lag behind the princes in this matter, and perhaps were even ahead of them." [13] Conversely, as Iakovlev pointed out, "The development of serfdom in Russia proceeded along lines of growth of features which brought it nearer to actual slavery." [14]

By the beginning of the present century, Kliuchevskii's indebtedness theory had gained wide acceptance among Russian historians, though it also had its critics. The emphasis on economic causes, on the gradual development of bondage and on the importance of transitional stages between the two poles of slavery and freedom, constitutes the strength of this theory. Its weakness lies in minimizing the role of the state, which during the last quarter of the sixteenth and early part of the seventeenth century appears to have been less passive than represented by the theory. To that extent its critics were right. In the first place, as Kliuchevskii himself observed, the state was vitally concerned with the peasant as a taxpayer.[15] Miliukov gave first priority to taxation among the factors responsible for the development of bondage.[16] The government, undoubtedly, was interested from a fiscal point of view in a stable agrarian structure, based on a rural population firmly settled on the land. This generally coincided with support of the small gentry, on which the armed strength of the Muscovite state depended during a period of almost continuous warfare. But the government was also concerned with colonizing and defending an expanding southern frontier. This was helped by the migration of peasants from the older regions. The government was thus caught in a basic conflict between the interests of the landowning class, particularly the small gentry in the older regions, and the need to recruit colonists and defenders for the new frontier. Under such conditions the government often displayed contradictory, zigzagging tendencies and at times violated its own regulations regarding the flight of peasants to frontier regions. It is a far cry from such ambivalence to a negative conception of the state as simply standing aside, refraining from active participation in the solution of a problem so vital to the very social class it had helped to create and on which it depended to such an extent. A priori this seems unlikely, and documentary evidence unearthed since the end of the last century, though still meager, tends to confirm the doubt regarding the neutrality of the state.

Although new material has not indicated the existence of a general law establishing serfdom, it has shown that in the last two decades of the sixteenth century the right of the tenants to leave or change their masters during the St. George period was suspended by the government for certain so-called forbidden years (*zapovednye leta*). It is true that the original decree, presumably issued in 1580, has not been discovered. We do know, however, the texts of two decrees of 1601 and 1602 which lifted the suspensions of the forbidden years to a limited degree and only for the estates of the lower strata of the landowning class. Russian scholars at first regarded the forbidden years either as exceptions to the general rule or as temporary, perhaps enacted to aid in taking the population and land census that began in 1582. This was the view of Samokvasov, the editor of the new archive material.[17] After the 1920s the conception gained ground that the forbidden years were at the very root of the crystallization of bondage. Thus Platonov, who originally leaned toward Kliuchevskii's doctrine, wrote in 1922:

> However varied the interpretation of the forbidden years, the consensus is that they constituted a prohibition against moving and "assisted" moving (*vykhod i vyvoz*) of peasants and that they took place during the reign of Ivan the Terrible. Adopted at first as a temporary measure, it was applied for a long period of time and resulted, to cite the words of Diakonov, "in the dying out of peasant mobility and of the regulations concerning it contained in the Code [of 1550], without their being specifically abolished by legislation." The aim of further research regarding the question of the time and the methods of binding peasants is to determine when and in what form the Moscow government enacted its decree concerning the "forbidden years."[18]

A later authority, Grekov, who devoted much time to the study of this question, is even more categorical: "The 'forbidden years' undoubtedly were a very active force throughout the country and became a basis for further development of tendencies existing in a concealed form . . .

The 'forbidden years' are not a myth, not an accidental, obscure social phenomenon, but an important turning point in the life of Russian society." [19]

There is still another theory which does not deny the positive intervention of the state but attributes to the forbidden years an auxiliary role. It assigns the main part in enforcing bondage to the registration of peasants in a sort of Domesday Book (*pistsovye knigi*) during a census survey undertaken for this purpose by the Moscow government in 1581–1592.[20] The recording in the census of a peasant as settled on the estate of a particular landlord, according to this theory, ipso facto bound him to this landed property in the eyes of the law. The forbidden years were merely an additional instrument for accomplishing such a purpose. These measures were reinforced by the strict requirements under the decree of April 25, 1597, and probably some earlier lost decrees, for obtaining proper documents for registering the ownership of slaves and kabal'nye servants.

The last word has not been said on the subject of forbidden years and the part played by the state in the genesis of serfdom. Discovery of new historical material may significantly affect the perspective. The weight of the evidence, it seems to me, points to a larger role of the state than was attributed to it by many nineteenth- and early twentieth-century historians. Yet this is not inconsistent with the theory that economic factors and custom also played an important role. The acceptance of such a view, which envisages the development of serfdom as a complex process of interplaying economic, social, and political forces, does away with the antithesis that lies at the root of the famous controversy. The role of the different forces varied from time to time. For instance, the state apparently had a more active part in the development of serfdom during the last quarter of the sixteenth century, under the pressures of economic crisis and the political-military situation, than in the earlier periods.

What about the general reaction of Soviet historians to the controversy, as distinguished from the research contributions of individual scholars to specific problems like that of the forbidden years? They reject outright the whole problem as a creation of bourgeois-genteel historiography and identify serfdom with feudalism. "Without serfdom, there is no feudalism," writes a leading proponent of the doctrine, I. I. Smirnov.[21] Since feudalism in Russia, according to Soviet and some pre-Soviet historians, developed long before the sixteenth century, serfdom also originated considerably earlier. Smirnov cites approvingly Lenin's dictum that "serfdom in Russia has existed since the ninth century," that is, the

Kievan period.[22] According to this school, what happens in the sixteenth century is a new intensified stage of serfdom, the causes of which must be sought in the economic conditions and the relation of class forces during the period. The state is merely an instrument of the ruling class, serving its interests. That the state might have independent objectives, counter to the interests of the ruling class, was denied by Smirnov, who criticized the stress on the defense factor by earlier Russian historians.

But this thesis is contradicted by Grekov, another representative of the same school, who writes: "We should not forget that in this consequence of the class struggle for the peasants not only were the landowners interested, but also the feudal state which, besides the peasant question, was faced by many other problems of high importance, the most important among them being *the defense of its independence*. It is possible to understand correctly the history of the peasantry only by taking into account at least the more important facets of the highly complex life of the nation and of the state as a whole." [23] One can add little to this spirited refutation of narrowly mechanical and materialistic Soviet historical dogma by one of the leading scholars in the field. Although much emphasis is placed by Smirnov on the prohibition of peasant transfers in the development of bondage, for instance, he bypasses the earlier significance of these transfers in upholding the freedom of the peasants.

Whatever its genesis, the bondage system was de facto well established in Russia by the end of the sixteenth century. It is the consensus of Russian scholars that differences between various kinds of dependence were blurred and in practice disregarded by the landlords. M. A. Diakonov, referring to the seventeenth century, especially its second half, points out that the landlords were exchanging, mortgaging, and selling peasants, had unlimited control over their labor and the power of exaction, and severely punished them for disobedience. A. S. Lappo-Danilevskii points out that during the seventeenth century "the process of gradual rapprochement between the status of slaves and that of peasants was already quite clearly discernible." A similar opinion is expressed by A. A. Novoselskii.[24] Perhaps even more eloquent testimony to the peasants' loss of freedom was the silence of the new Code of 1649 regarding the St. George's Day rights. And equally silent on the matter were the landlords, the new landholding class that was opposed to peasant mobility. They had nothing to complain about on this score. Their real problem was the existence of statutory limitations on the right to reclaim the fleeing peasants. They therefore persistently petitioned the government to abandon the statute of limitations. In this the landlords were also completely successful. Their demands were granted in 1646 and confirmed by the Code of 1649. And so, by what it spelled out as well as by what it failed to mention, the Code of 1649 supported the tightening noose of serfdom.

If there are unresolved questions and disputed points regarding the development of serfdom prior to the eighteenth century, the course is clear from then on. It was marked by a legal consolidation of the bondage system. Curiously enough, this was a task largely accomplished by Peter the Great, who in other fields did so much to westernize Russia. A decree in 1714 abolished the distinction between hereditary tenure and conditional tenure and granted to the gentry full hereditary title to the estates. By a series of decrees issued between 1719 and 1723, toward the end of his reign, Peter ordered a population census as a basis for a poll tax to which all peasants were subject.[25] This also included slaves who formerly were not taxed. Thus Peter's fiscal legislation in effect eliminated the legal distinction between slaves and other categories of the peasant population, combining them in one class of serfs for whose taxes the landlord was responsible. Legislation during the next forty years under Peter's successors consistently downgraded the peasant's status in the community, and by mid-century it differed little from that of a chattel slave.

The position of the serf was characterized as follows by A. A. Kornilov:

> Although the noble landlords were themselves "slaves" of the Moscow tsars, nevertheless gradually each landlord also became a kind of tsar on his estate. While he did not possess the power of life or death over his subjects, it was entirely possible for him to dispose arbitrarily of the labor, property, and, to a considerable extent, person of his serfs. He could punish them in all sorts of ways: whip, beat, and even exile them to Siberia, draft them into the army, or sell them. Though the law provided some restrictions for the protection of peasants from abuses by landlords, still these restrictions could have only a very precarious application, because the law prohibited the serfs from complaining about their master.[26]

Intensification of Serfdom

What particularly brought the serfs close to the status of slaves was the wide latitude possessed by the landlords in the punishing, buying, and selling of peasants. Some legal restrictions on such dealings began to be imposed toward the end of the eighteenth century, but they were mild and were easily avoided by the landlords. It is necessary to bear in mind that the officials who were responsible for the enforcement of these and other modest legal safeguards themselves either belonged to the gentry or were dependent upon it for their jobs. Therefore they usually sided with the nobles.[27] What class bias, self-interest, or fear of offending the powerful and rich did not accomplish was completed by official corruption, which ran rampant. Nowhere is this better portrayed than in Gogol's *The Inspector General.*

The Russian peasant was delivered body and soul to the mercy of the master, to serve as the latter's "baptized property," in Alexander Herzen's caustic epithet. Whether the serf was treated cruelly or humanely, whether his working and living arrangements were favorable or unfavorable, depended entirely upon the decision of the lord. Kliuchevskii epitomized the situation: "The government and the gentry shared among them the serf; the government yielded to the gentry its rights to the person and labor of the serf in exchange for the obligation to pay his poll tax and to guard his farming insofar as it was necessary to maintain the productivity of the soil for fiscal purposes, 'so that land should not remain idle,' as a decree of 1734 expressed it." [28]

The ascendancy of the landowning class generally paralleled the degradation of peasantry, with one qualification: the exacting demands made on the gentry by Peter the Great. It is true that he abolished conditional land tenure; however, compulsory service to the state was exacted even more strictly. This became much less true under his successors, many of whom owed the throne to palace revolutions staged by guard regiments composed of the landed gentry. Finally, in 1762, during the short reign of Peter III, compulsory service to the state was entirely abolished, and any justification of national interest for the ownership of serfs completely disappeared. It could be argued that the peasants' "work for the landlord was something like a state duty imposed upon them in the interest of defending the state from enemies. The peasants had to feed the landlord, who in turn would defend the state and them from external enemies. But when the landlord gradually converted crown lands into his private property, then he began to look upon the peasants bound to the state as part of his real property." [29]

Under legislation instituted during the second quarter of the eighteenth century, only persons belonging to the gentry were permitted to own serfs. Members of the mercantile class or others who owned serfs were required by a decree of 1767 to divest themselves of their "property." A charter granted to the gentry in 1785 confirmed these privileges. The gentry became as absolute in the mastery of peasants as of the acres they cultivated. Thus the serf system in Russia reached its high mark during the reign of Catherine the Great (1762–1796), just about a century before its abolition.

Serfdom so far has been considered in its general and legal aspects. But there were important economic and social differences within the servile population. The serfs could be divided into three main categories: those discharging their obligations to the masters by paying a quitrent (*obrok*); those tilling the lords demesne (*barshchina* system), and those rendering service in the gentry households (manorial serfs, or *dvorovye*). There were also various combinations of these forms. Of the three principal types of servitude, the quitrent system was the most favorable from the peasant's standpoint. Although heavy tribute was often exacted, this system entailed less personal contact with the masters and less interference on their part with the life and work of the peasants. The serfs were therefore less subject to abuses. It was not merely poetic fancy on the part of Pushkin when he made Eugene Onegin, the hero of his *pièce du siècle,* shift the serfs he inherited from the *barshchina* to the quitrent basis in order to lighten the burden of servitude.

To the landlord, the quitrent system was advantageous where returns from agriculture were low, as in the less fertile, northern regions of the country. Here, because of inferior, podzol soil and less favorable growing conditions, a considerable area of estate land would have been needed to feed the serfs. But farming alone was as a rule insufficient to feed the peasants and enable them to pay the quitrent. They had to engage in various trades or seek employment in the cities, especially the capitals— Moscow and St. Petersburg. As was early noted by observers of Russian economic life, such nonagricultural occupations constituted an important source of quitrents.[30] This is the locus classicus of the quitrent system, as can be seen from Table 1. Exceptions are the similar soil areas of Belorussia and Lithuania, where the landowners were Polish and carried on more intensive farming. In the non-black-soil regions of Russia proper, various industries, at first handicrafts and later manufacturing (especially textiles), sprang up, using the surplus labor of the quitrent peasants.[31]

Although the peasants benefited from quitrent arrangements by gaining a certain measure of independence, their position was nevertheless precarious. For it was based not on a firm legal foundation but entirely on the convenience and whim of the lord, who could always shift the quitrent-paying peasant to a more onerous kind of servitude if he so desired. Moreover, for the vast majority of peasants life was a harsh struggle to eke out an existence and to pay the high and rising quitrents exacted by the landlords.[32] Yet a small minority of the peasants in this category had an opportunity to improve their lot, and a few even amassed fortunes with which they were able to purchase their freedom and to establish industrial dynasties. An example of this was the Morozov fam-

16

Table 1. Distribution of the peasant population between quitrent-paying and demesne serfs prior to 1861

Region	Demesne	Quitrent-paying
Non-black soil	41.1%	58.9%
Black soil	71.2	28.8
Volga	73.3	26.7
Eastern steppe	83.0	17.0
Belorussia	92.4	7.6
Ukraine		
West	97.4	2.6
East	99.3	0.7
South	99.9	0.1
Total (41 provinces of European Russia)	71.7	28.3

Source. I. I. Ignatovich, *Pomeshchichii krest'iane nakanune osvobozh-deniia* (Seigneurial Peasantry on the Eve of the Emancipation; 3rd ed., Moscow, 1925), pp. 70–76 and table 1 in the supplement. Cited in **P. I. Liashchenko**, *Istoriia narodnogo khoziaistva SSSR* (History of the National Economy of the USSR; 2nd ed., Moscow, 1950), I, 501.

ily of textile magnates, which, incidentally, later contributed in one of its scions a generous financial backer for the Bolsheviks in their struggling days. It was primarily under the quitrent system that traces were discernible of that economic differentiation or polarization of the peasantry into a small segment of rich and a great mass of poor peasants which characterizes, according to Marxist analysis, the development of nascent capitalism. But the extent of this class stratification should not be exaggerated, as it usually is by Soviet writers.

More prevalent on the eve of emancipation, as indicated by Table 1, was the barshchina system: it accounted as a whole for an estimated 72 percent of the serf population of European Russia, as against 28 percent of quitrent-paying serfs. The *barshchina* system was also much more onerous for the serfs, because they were more rigidly bound to the land than those on the quitrent basis. The demesne peasants usually divided their time between working the lord's land and their own. Forced plantation labor, requiring minute regulation and continuous supervision, naturally involved a great deal of interference on the part of the master. Moreover, it was in the interest of the masters in the fertile districts, where the barshchina system was largely concentrated, to reduce as far as possible the area of peasant landholdings in order to expand that of the demesne land. The landlords were not slow to act on this incentive. An extreme case was that of peasants who were entirely deprived of their own holdings and converted practically into slave workers, receiving a monthly ration from their masters—hence the term *mesiachnina* applied to this type of servile labor, derived from the Russian word *mesiats* (month). There is no statistical evidence to indicate how widespread *mesiachnina* really was, but in some provinces it was not insignificant.[33]

The tendency to expand the demesne area in the fertile zones became particularly pronounced after the nobility gained freedom from compulsory state service in the middle of the eighteenth century. Many of the nobles began to settle on their estates, exchanging the role of absentee landlord for that of gentleman farmer, with a predilection for what Russian scholars call "entrepreneurship," that is, commercial farming (production for the market).[34]

While the social and, to some extent, the intellectual life of the provinces gained as a result of the settlement of the nobility on the land, for the peasants it meant a tightening of the bondage system. For the technique of genteel entrepreneurship, in spite of much flirtation with the new agronomic science by the more advanced landlords, consisted primarily in a more intensive exploitation of serf labor, since only in this manner, as a rule, could larger returns be secured. A good deal of ingenuity, therefore, was exercised by the landlords in devising ways and means toward more profitable employment of serf labor. The net result was that the exactions from peasants, whether in the form of labor or quitrents, had increased in the nineteenth century.[35] The noble entrepreneurs did not confine their quest for profits to agriculture, but often also set up factories on their estates. However bad the lot of farm demesne labor, still more distressing was the position of those peasants who were forced to work in these veritable sweatshops.[36] The peasants, according to one observer, regarded the latter with the same horror as the plague.[37]

The third large category, manorial serfs, unlike the *mesiachniki* did not perform any field work; but they too were real pariahs. They were not allotted land for their own farming and were housed in the manor (in the cities as well as in the countryside), where their whole life was devoted to serving their masters. The number of manorial serfs had been increasing before 1860 because landlords considered that, by transferring peasant farmers into this category and forcing them off the land, they would save it for themselves during the forthcoming emancipation— which is precisely what happened. The manorial serf's entire existence depended completely upon the personality of the master, his character, tastes, and whims. There was obviously ample opportunity for the abuse of authority. In fact, from testimony of contemporaries with regard to manorial serfs there emerges a picture of slavery in its harshest aspects. Although the rod forever remained an emblem of the Russian bondage system, it was not the only or the most cruel method of punishment employed. One Russian historian says: "It is difficult to imagine what tortures some masters were able to invent." [38] Perhaps the worst excesses were exceptional, but it may also be true that many cases of cruelty never became a matter of record.

Grievous as was the fate of the male serf, that of the female manorial serf was even worse. Her whole life was regimented, down to the most intimate detail: marriage was hindered, and more often than not she became prey to her master's lust. This evil is much stressed in the literature on serfdom in Russia. It was not confined to the manorial women, although they were the greatest victims, but also affected the peasant women in the villages. Even the practices of *jus primae noctis* and manorial harems were not unknown.[39]

If the lot of the ordinary serf was difficult enough, it was often nothing short of tragic for the serf intelligentsia. Those who by virtue of special training as actors, artists, musicians, architects, and physicians, or who by exceptional native ability had succeeded in rising intellectually above the low cultural level of the gray peasant masses, were more sensitive to the brutality of the regime. The very tendency toward self-sufficiency characteristic of the manorial household—the effort to produce everything, even culture, with the help of serf labor, as described so well in the memoirs of Peter Kropotkin—led to the creation of this class of educated serfs.[40] Some few of these intellectuals, such as the famous actor Shchepkin and the Ukrainian poet Shevchenko, succeeded in gaining freedom through manumission, although it was often difficult because of the stubbornness of the masters. Most of the serf intellectuals ended their days as they had begun, in bondage, sometimes taking to drink or committing suicide. In spite of this generally sordid picture, not all masters were sadistic, tyrannical, or harsh with their peasants. Some, like the Decembrist Iakushkin and Princess Kropotkin, were humane and good to the peasants; others, because of their own weakness and lack of business ability, like the elder Count Rostov in *War and Peace,* permitted their serfs, especially the supervisory personnel, to take advantage of them and cheat them.

Such were the salient features of the different types of servitude in Russia. The aim was to maximize the economic exploitation of serfs and to take advantage of regional agricultural and economic conditions. An important aspect of Russian serfdom was its dynamic character. It steadily spread into new territory, encompassing additional elements of the population. In part this expansion was due to the colonizing efforts of the landowners themselves in settling their serfs on the new, cheaply acquired lands of the south and southeast. The process is reminiscent of the creation of the western cotton belt by the slaveholding planters of the American South.

But largely it was government policy that was responsible for the spread of serfdom. The periodic censuses of population introduced by Peter the Great for fiscal purposes, for example, were also used arbitrarily to drag into the net of bondage various unattached groups, such as illegitimate children, foundlings, and vagrants.[41] More important was the extension of the Great Russian form of bondage to large regions such as the Ukraine, where it had not existed before the second half of the eighteenth century. The custom of eighteenth-century Russian monarchs to reward their favorite courtiers and officials with "gifts" of inhabited villages also contributed. Some of these villages were confiscated from nobles who had fallen into disgrace. One of the worst offenders in this respect was that enlightened friend of Voltaire and Diderot and disciple of Montesquieu, Catherine the Great, who in her youth recorded her opposition to serfdom (as inconsistent with the principles of Christianity and justice) and scorned it in her comedies. This did not prevent her, however, from making gifts of some 800,000 peasants of both sexes.[42] Some of these were on estates confiscated from Polish landlords, and they were perhaps no worse off under their new Russian masters. But not without cause did her reign become known as the golden age of the serf-owning nobility: the noose of serfdom was knotted ever tighter around the peasant's neck.

Many large private estates, especially in eastern and southern Russia, were established in this period. In spite of subsequent subdivision as a result of inheritance, these latifundiae at the time of the abolition of serf-dom accounted for the lion's share of the nobles' holdings. In 1858 it was estimated that four out of five serfs were in estates of no less than 1,000 desiatinas (2,700 acres). Nearly half of all serfs (47 percent) belonged to nobles who possessed more than 500 male serfs each; 34 percent to those with 100 to 500; and less than 20 percent to nobles with fewer than 100.[43]

State Peasants

Important as the bondage system was and as much as it expanded during the eighteenth century, legally it never extended to the whole Russian rural population. In addition to the serfs of the landholding gentry and

Table 2. Peasant population according to the census of 1858

Category	Males	Both sexes
Privately owned serfs	9,803,000	20,173,000
State peasants	9,002,000	18,694,000
Serfs of imperial family	955,000	2,019,000
Private factory serfs	241,000	518,000
Workers in state mines and factories	114,000	230,000
Other	4,912,000	9,882,000
Total	25,027,000	51,516,000

Source. P. I. Liashchenko, *Istoriia narodnogo khoziaistva SSSR*, I, 325.

the imperial family, there was a large class of state peasants, *gosudarstven-nye krest'iane,* legally designated as "free rural inhabitants." This class was also created by the poll-tax and census legislation of Peter the Great. It tied together various elements of the unbound rural population just as it did the different categories of bound peasants. The category of state peasantry continued to serve as a catchall for additional elements of the free peasantry as Russia expanded geographically, as foreign colonists were induced to settle in the country, and as some groups were liberated from personal servitude. Among the latter must be mentioned the monastery serfs, who were freed after the secularization of the extensive church lands.

The state peasants constituted a substantial minority, accounting for more than a third of the total Russian peasant population by 1858 (see Table 2). These peasants, in fact, predominated in the less densely settled northern and a few of the southern provinces of European Russia. The rural population of Siberia consisted almost entirely of state peasants. In absolute numbers, the state peasants were a significant element also in some of the densely settled central and western provinces of European Russia: Moscow had over 500,000 males, or 31 percent of total peasant males, according to the 1835 census; Kiev, 594,000 or 15 percent; Kursk and Tambov, over 700,000 or close to a half.[44]

While state peasants were legally free, in reality their freedom was a tenuous affair. Until the Kiselev reforms of the 1840s, the government looked upon them as its property, to be exploited financially and disposed of as it deemed best. Peter the Great imposed on them, in addition to a poll tax, a quitrent, similar to that exacted from private serfs by their masters. During the eighteenth century and the first third of the nineteenth, the extraction of this tribute became the government's main responsibility. Characteristically, until 1838 the state peasants were under the jurisdiction of the Treasury (the Ministry of Finance in the nineteenth century). In line with the fluctuating fiscal requirements of the state, restrictions were imposed or relaxed on freedom of movement and choice of occupation. Fiscal considerations, buttressed by the prevailing doctrine of tutelage (*popechenie*) that was derived from the teachings of enlightened absolutism and the requirements of a police state, also dictated close supervision of the state peasants. In exercising it the *chinovniki* (bureaucrats) were aided by elected peasant officials, who were merely pawns.[45] Knowing the corruption and high-handedness of Russian officialdom of those days, it requires but little imagination to visualize the serious abuses to which the state peasants were subjected. The chinovniki saw the peasants primarily as a source of revenue for the state and themselves in which both shared, somewhat as the landlord and the state shared the private serf.

Besides the squeezing tactics of venal officials, the state peasants were also not free from the encroachment of landlords, aided and abetted by these same officials. The landlords strove by every means, legal or illegal, to acquire land from the public domain which was used or could be used by state peasants and to shift to the latter the brunt of the various labor services (corvée) required by the state, such as road repair or carting.[46] State peasants formed the main reservoir drawn upon for the imperial grants of "souls" and villages, thus easily converting supposedly free peasants into serfs. Even after the practice of imperial gifts of souls was stopped by Alexander I, at the beginning of the nineteenth century, grants of land from the public domain to private landowners continued.[47]

During the reign of his successor, Nicholas I, the transfer of state peasants to the ownership of the imperial family again reached considerable proportions. An exchange of land between the imperial estates and the public domain, undertaken in the 1830s, was particularly effective in reducing state peasants to bondage. In the province of Simbirsk alone, 350,000 became serfs.[48] State peasants were also used arbitrarily during the first half of the nineteenth century for pet government projects and experiments, such as Arakcheev's ill-reputed military settlements, where military service was combined with tilling of the soil.[49]

Enough has been said to make it clear that the legally free class of peasants was actually at the mercy of the government, which did with them as it saw fit. As these peasants themselves reportedly characterized their status: "We are not free; we belong to the state, to the tsar." [50] The picture was also somber on the economic side. Perhaps the best indicator of the depressed economic condition of most state peasants and of the heavy fiscal burden imposed upon them were the growing arrears in payment of taxes and quitrents—in spite of often ruthless methods of collection. Repeated cancellations could not stop the deficit. In 1814, arrears totaling 22 million rubles were canceled, but nine years later they more than doubled, to 47 million, and by 1826 reached 85 million. Once more a considerable part of the arrears was canceled, but by 1828 they again had grown to 45 million rubles; then to 51 million in 1831 and 68 million in 1835.[51] The situation was aggravated in the 1830s first by a virulent cholera epidemic, which raged in such regions as the Volga area, with their heavy concentrations of state peasants; and, second, by several successive years of poor crops, which weakened still further the already weak peasant economy.

The growing poverty of the state peasants was even confirmed by the general staff of the tsarist secret police. The Third Section of His Majesty's Chancery reported to the emperor that "state peasants, this considerable part of our population, are almost everywhere in the poorest condition." [52] That this must affect the fiscal interests of the state became obvious to the government of Nicholas I. Nor could it remain indifferent to the growing peasant unrest, which manifested itself in a number of local disorders, those in the Ural area in 1835 being the most serious.

The Striving for Freedom

It is generally true that the Russian peasant did not consent meekly to enslavement and oppression. In the opinion of Ignatovich, "Serfdom did not make out of the peasants timid, submissive slaves. In various ways, beginning with individual cases of disobedience and ending with formidable mass movements, putting the government on its mettle, they [the peasants] protested against serfdom." [53] Another authority writes: "The study of the peasant movement demonstrates patently that the striving of the peasants for freedom was continued by them through the whole history of 'enslavement' in Russia." [54] This thesis of prerevolutionary Russian historians has been further confirmed by a considerable volume of research carried on during the Soviet period.[55]

The peasant protest against serfdom only sporadically assumed the character of mass revolt. In this category is the wave of rebellions during the so-called period of troubles (smuta) at the beginning of the seventeenth century, which reached its zenith in a veritable peasant war against the Moscow government in 1606-07, led by Bolotnikov.[56] The celebrated Stenka Razin rebellion in the middle of the seventeenth century, originating along the southeastern frontier, was another example of mass revolt against the system. Both revolts, of course, were suppressed by the better-organized forces of the Moscow government. Though somewhat retarded, perhaps, by the peasant rebellions in the early seventeenth century, the development of the serf system continued unabated, reaching a high point during the reign of Catherine the Great. But her reign also witnessed another formidable revolt (1773–74), known in history as the Pugachev rebellion or the Pugachevshchina.

Emel'ian Pugachev was an adventurer and impostor who, in accordance with a time-honored Russian tradition, pretended to be Emperor Peter III (murdered more than a decade earlier), representing him as a champion of the peasants against the ruling class. Two factors helped to fan the discontent which ultimately burst into active revolt: first, the freeing of the landowning gentry in 1762 from compulsory service to the state; second, the liberation of monastery serfs and their transfer to the category of state peasants.[57] These steps were bound to arouse strong expectations among the serfs for their own liberation—which followed logically from the deep belief that the dependence of peasants was conditioned on the service of their masters to the tsar and should therefore cease with the discontinuation of that service. It is reflected, for instance, in the statement of the eighteenth-century publicist Pososhkov: "The landowners are not permanent proprietors of the peasants; they own them temporarily and their direct owner is the autocrat of all Russia." [58]

The Pugachev rebellion began as a local frontier mutiny, not unusual in the Cossack settlements in the southern Urals. But it spread like wildfire westward, toward the Volga, drawing into its vortex large masses of peasants. This was particularly true during the final stages, when the revolt extended into the more densely settled regions west of the Volga and when Pugachev himself was already in flight—"The Pugachevshchina without Pugachev," as it was characterized by a Soviet scholar.[59] The uprising had all the characteristics of other *jacqueries,* sowing panic among officials and the landowning class, many of whom were killed as their estates were pillaged by rebels. It required a powerful army to quell the rebellion. The nightmare of this "Russian mutiny, terrible and senseless," in the words of Pushkin, long haunted the Russian landowning gentry.[60]

Although the peasants were again decisively beaten in this major encounter with the state and the landowners, their hopes of freedom were not extinguished. It is true that a general revolt on the tremendous scale of the Pugachevshchina did not occur again for one hundred and thirty years, but unrest and disturbances were still plentiful. Every new accession to the throne or a major war, such as the Napoleonic invasion of 1812 or the Crimean War of 1854–55, was the signal for a fresh crop of rumors of impending freedom which led to scattered but numerous uprisings.[61] Tolstoy in *War and Peace* describes a peasant disturbance of this sort during the Napoleonic war. But he points out that the same peasants who were not above looting the estates were unwilling to supply forage for Napoleon's army and became guerrilla fighters. Napoleon did not touch serfdom in Russia. What the reaction of the Russian peasantry would have been if he had lived up to the traditions of the French Revolution, bringing liberty to the serfs, is an intriguing question.

The uprisings during the Crimean War were particularly serious. They were occasioned by the government's call for volunteers, which explicitly required the consent of the nobles for the enlistment of their serfs, such permission to be renewed every three months. The peasants rushed in droves to enlist, expecting to gain freedom. The government found it necessary to resort to military force to quell the disturbances. At this critical juncture it did not augur well for the regime. In 1856, after peace was concluded, new agitations were caused by rumors of a decree supposedly promising freedom to new settlers in the war-torn Crimea. This was enough to start a mass migration of serfs, and troops again had to be employed to halt it. We should note the power of a mere rumor to stir the peasant masses so deeply—a power grounded in the strong conviction of the peasant that he was being fooled by his master, who suppressed the true and favorable edicts of the "good tsar."

In addition to such major waves of peasant discontent, there were many reasons for disturbances on individual estates, such as excessive exactions in the form of increased quitrent work in the landlord's fields and workshops, cruel treatment, nonsupport during a famine, and so forth. Some of the reforms undertaken by the government in the 1840s regarding the status of state peasants were carried out in too arbitrary a fashion, which gave rise to disorders. Such were the "potato mutinies," caused by forcing state peasants to plant potatoes (just as Khrushchev a century later was pressuring Russian farmers to plant corn indiscriminately). A study made of the geographical distribution of the peasant mutinies reveals a curious fact.[62] Most of them occurred not, as might be expected, in the fertile black-soil zone, where the more oppressive *barshchina* system prevailed, but in the less fertile sections of the country, with their widespread quitrent system and greater development of rural trades. This paradox is attributed to the fact that it was not so much the actual degree of oppression that led to protests as it was the consciousness of oppression, which was likely to be keener among the relatively freer quitrent peasants (who often moved back and forth between town and village) than among those peasants bound to the demesne.

Many of these disturbances were simply strikes or collective "disobedience," as they were called, refusals to work and pay dues and taxes. However, peasant antagonism often took a more violent form, with calamitous results to the property and life of masters and overseers. Arson and murder were not uncommon. During the twenty years from 1834 to 1854, there were 144 cases of murder of landlords and their agents, not counting attempts at assassination. In 1835–1843, 416 peasants were deported to Siberia for the murder of landlords.[63] A milder method of revenge sometimes resorted to by the serfs was to subject the master to corporal punishment, previously so liberally applied to them. The number of such cases is probably larger than the few that actually have come to light, since it was to the advantage of both sides to keep the matter a secret.[64]

Statistical data from official sources on peasant disturbances for the period 1826–1861 have been published by Ignatovich, who indicates the incomplete character of the material but believes that the more important cases were probably covered.[65] The figures are as follows.

Years	Number of disturbances
1826–1829	85
1830–1834	60
1835–1839	78
1840–1844	138
1845–1849	207
1850–1854	141
1855	10
1856	25
1857	40
1858	170
1859	70
1860	100
1861 (Jan.–Feb.)	10

It will be noted that the number of peasant disturbances was trending upward during three consecutive five-year periods, reaching a peak in 1845–1849, followed by a considerable decline in 1850–1854. (I shall defer for the time being any consideration of the situation during the last years of serfdom.) The sharp increase in 1845–1849 is attributed by Ignatovich to special circumstances, such as the effects of adverse agrarian legislation enacted during that period and the echo of severe agrarian disorders in neighboring Galicia, then a part of Austria. It should be noted that the mass movement in connection with the call for military volunteers is not included in the figures for 1854 and 1855. Ignatovich also points out, particularly with respect to the next peak year, 1858, that the coverage of reported cases increased because of the demand of the Ministry of Interior for more detailed information. As a consequence, even insignificant disturbances, involving a few peasants and dealt with by local police officials, were now reported to the ministry. The figures for the last five years before the emancipation are, therefore, not fully comparable with the previous period. Unless the figures are greatly inflated, they point to increasing tension in the village. This is supported by specific data on the suppression of peasant disturbances by armed force, based on material from the Historical-Military Archive of the USSR.[66]

1841–1845	53
1846–1850	140
1851–1855	99
1856–1860	185
	477

In this connection one must not overlook the aggressive tactics employed by many landlords who, anticipating the emancipation, tried to gain every advantage with respect to landholdings. Transfer of peasant holdings to poorer land, resettlement of peasant families, depriving the peasant of his holding by moving him from demesne to manor, and other such practices were resorted to by some landlords in order to ensure the largest possible area of good land for themselves against the now inevitable day of partition between masters and serfs. The increasing rebelliousness of the peasants during the final stage of serfdom appears to have been in some measure a defensive reaction to the encroachments of the landlords.[67] Peasant disorders were always severely repressed, often by the military and with considerable bloodshed when the peasants resisted. The official attitude is perhaps best epitomized by an inscription on a common grave of the victims of one such "pacification," a particularly stubborn peasant uprising at the end of the eighteenth century: "Here lie those who committed crimes against God, the tsar, and the landlord, justly punished by fire and sword in accordance with the laws of God and the tsar." [68]

Pacification by military force frequently did not lead to the resumption of a normal state of affairs on the estate for a long period of time. Unrest, driven underground, often resulted in sabotage or flared up in repeated, sometimes more violent, uprisings. In some cases only a continuous quartering of troops ensured "law and order." In such instances the result was serious economic loss for the landowners; their estates greatly depreciated in value once they acquired the reputation of being "troublesome." [69] In general, peasant disturbances, isolated and scattered though they were, had important psychological and political effects. Continuously before the eyes of the landowning class and the government there was the terrifying specter of another Pugachev rebellion, "recalling like a menacing memento mori the necessity for ending serfdom, in the landowners' own interest." [70]

The peasant opposition to serfdom was not confined to individual or collective acts of violence, sabotage, and strikes. Flight was an even more important manifestation of such opposition during the earlier stages. There were no abolitionist societies in Russia to organize underground railways to freedom. But the dense forests in the north and northeast, and the vast steppes in the east and southeast, for centuries provided asylum for those who tried to escape from the oppression of the landlord, the government, and the church. It was in this manner that the unique institution of the Cossacks originated, the "most radical type of community known in Russian national history." [71] Even long after the Cossacks came under the controlling arm of the central government, the territory of these turbulent frontier settlers continued to be a refuge for runaway serfs and a breeding ground of insurrection. It was among the Cossacks in the Urals, it will be recalled, that the Pugachev rebellion was kindled. Not only individuals but whole villages, provoked by some wild rumor, sometimes fled en masse. According to Ignatovich, such escapist tendencies even during the second quarter of the nineteenth century constituted a greater menace to the system than mutinies, which were usually confined to single estates. "Hundreds and thousands of peasants would move in the same direction, influenced by a similar rumor and united by the same purpose." [72] Sometimes only the use of armed force could stop these flights.

We have already seen how this question of peasant flights was one of the chief preoccupations of the landowning class during the sixteenth and seventeenth centuries; but there was a conflict of interest between different sections—between the large and the small landowners, between those of the old regions and those of the new frontiers. The government also was torn by the dual need to protect the landowning military class and to colonize and defend the southern and eastern frontiers. But during the eighteenth and first half of the nineteenth century these conflicts disappeared. The landowners were no longer engaged in a kind of piracy of peasants, harboring on their estates refugee serfs fleeing from other masters, in order to augment their manpower. The government was no longer worrying about the defense of the frontiers. The fleeing serfs, therefore, became an unmitigated nuisance to the masters and to the state.

The Intelligentsia: The Peasants' Ally

As serfdom solidified toward the end of the eighteenth century, the restive peasantry acquired an ally in the young Russian intelligentsia. This small band of advanced spirits, nurtured on European liberal and humanitarian ideals, could not but recognize the moral evils of serfdom, despite their predominantly aristocratic origin. Thus there arose an ethical antagonism to serfdom within the landowning class. It was bolstered by arguments of the superior efficiency of free as compared with slave labor, derived from the teachings of Adam Smith.* The ideological cleavages within the Russian intelligentsia failed to affect its attitude toward serfdom. This was true of the different branches of the Decembrist revolutionary movement of the 1820s and of the divided intellectual movement in the 1840s: the relatively conservative Slavophiles and the more liberal Westerners were both unconditionally opposed to serfdom.[73] In fact, representatives of these two factions later worked hand in hand in the actual drafting of the emancipation legislation. Herzen felicitously characterized the situation when he compared the Slavophiles and Westerners to a double-headed eagle (the emblem of the Russian state), with the two heads turned in opposite directions and one heart beating in its breast.

The intelligentsia's opposition to serfdom could not express itself in an open legal form. Not only was freedom of political expression in the Western sense completely unknown under Nicholas I and his predecessors, but even the most elementary civil liberties were lacking. The government lived in constant fear that public criticism or attacks on serfdom, considered the cornerstone of the whole social edifice, would incite the peasants (though they were generally illiterate) or irritate the landlords.

* The Wealth of Nations was translated into Russian by order of the Minister of Finance in 1802–1806, and it became an essential part of the intellectual equipment of the educated class of the time. Even Pushkin's Eugene Onegin, who was a typical half-educated socialite, considered it necessary to read Smith. Although Smith and his disciples of the classical school of political economy exerted a strong influence on liberal abolitionist thought in Russia during the first quarter of the nineteenth century, the ideologists of the serfowning class also found the doctrine useful for their purposes, particularly to combat protectionism. For the Russian serfowners, like the southern slaveowners in the United States, were mostly freetraders. See I. Blumin, "Economic Views of the Decembrists," in Problemy ekonomiki, 5-6:204-220 (1940), and "Economic Ideology of the Russian Serfowning Class," Problemy ekonomiki, 2:174-193 (1937).

Hence the subject was taboo, and even official discussion of it was carried on behind a Chinese wall of secrecy.

The tragic fate of Alexander Radishchev, one of the earliest Russian abolitionists and a leading intellectual of his time, was an eloquent warning of what was in store for those who dared to break the taboo. In 1790, he published under his own imprint the celebrated *Journey from St. Petersburg to Moscow,* in which he denounced the horrors of serfdom and autocracy. The book, although it was passed by the censor, aroused the ire of Catherine the Great, who had long forgotten the liberal ideas of her youth and whose latter-day reactionary leanings were intensified by the outbreak of the French Revolution. The book was destroyed. Radishchev was sentenced to death, but the sentence was commuted to exile to Siberia when he recanted his views.

To enforce the ban against criticism of serfdom was thus the "first commandment" of censorship,[74] behind which lurked the threat of prison and Siberia. Its principal canon of operation, according to one authority, was *noli me tangere,*[75] meaning that its very existence was not to be mentioned in public. The "protective" hand of the censor did not stop at the frontiers but extended also to foreign literature on the forbidden subject. And so the Russian translation of *Uncle Tom's Cabin* was prohibited. But the designs of the censors were at least partly foiled. In the first place, the forbidden works were circulated over the length and breadth of the country, in many thousands of handwritten copies. The second part of Pushkin's celebrated poem *In the Village,* written in 1818 and strongly condemning serfdom, was well known among the educated classes, in spite of the fact that its publication was not permitted until half a century later. Another outstanding example of wide circulation in manuscript form was Belinsky's "Letter to Gogol," with its vigorous protest against the evils of serfdom, which by all accounts left a powerful impression on its readers.* It was possible on occasion for belles-lettres, with its special degree of social significance, to elude the censor by attacking serfdom only obliquely. The classic example is the collection of short stories by Turgenev known as *Diaries of a Huntsman.* The profound effect of this work on the reading public can be gauged from the admission of Alexander II, who told Turgenev that "since he read *Diaries of a Huntsman* the thought of the necessity of abolishing serfdom had not left him for a minute.[76]

Scholarship, like all other forms of intellectual life, experienced the

* The "Letter" was written in 1849 by Russia's foremost literary critic to the author of *The Inspector General* and *Dead Souls,* who toward the end of his life (when he suffered from mental depression), became an apologist for many of the social evils, including serfdom, which his earlier writings had helped to expose.

stifling effect of the reactionary political atmosphere. Few scholarly works that dealt critically with serfdom were permitted, and then for the most part in a foreign language. Thus the academician A. K. Storch, who taught political economy to members of the imperial family, was able to publish his treatise on the subject, in which he manifested his opposition to serfdom, in a French edition only. Even legally sanctioned publications in a foreign language did not necessarily exempt an author from subsequent persecution, as is exemplified by the sad case of Professor I. E. Schad who, on the recommendation of Goethe and Schiller, was appointed in 1804 to teach philosophy in the newly established University of Kharkov. Because of "dangerous ideas" discovered in his work on natural law, *Institutiones juris naturae,* published in 1814, he was dismissed from his post and deported in 1816, and all his books were ordered destroyed.[77]

If legal abolitionism was ruled out under Russian conditions, what about illegal underground activity? Such a movement, which resulted in the conspiracy of the Decembrists, developed in the early 1820s with the organization of a secret political society of young intellectual nobles, mainly officers in the imperial guard, patterned on similar societies in many countries of Western Europe. The Napoleonic Wars had brought these arisotcratic youths, through service in the Russian army abroad, into closer contact with the West and had thrown into sharp relief the contrast between European civilization and the semi-Asiatic backwardness of Russia. A new sense of national pride, evoked by the successful struggle with Bonaparte, whetted the appetite for reforms that would bring the internal progress of Russia more in line with its strong international position. Heading the list of such reforms were political freedom and abolition of serfdom—the cardinal twin tenet of the Decembrist faith.

Since the Decembrist opposition met only a blind and pointless reaction on the part of the government, it resorted to conspiracy, aiming at the establishment of a constitutional regime by way of a palace revolution. The death of Alexander I forced the conspirators to act, and they took advantage of the confusion created by the succession to stage a revolt among the guard regiments in St. Petersburg, on December 14, 1825. This revolt, as well as a mutiny in one of the regiments quartered in the Ukraine, was rapidly suppressed. Five of the leaders were executed, including Colonel P. N. Pestel, author of an interesting political tract entitled *Russkaia pravda* (Russian Truth). Another executed leader was the poet Kondrati Ryleev, an official of the Russian-American Company that controlled Alaska, then still a part of the Russian Empire. The rest of the Decembrists were deported to Siberia and the Caucasus.[78]

This abortive revolution, which decimated the flower of Russian intelligentsia, was staged by the intellectuals in "splendid isolation," without contact or support from the masses, from whom it was separated by high social barriers. There is evidence that the objectives of the Decembrists were frequently misunderstood in the peasant mind, in its dark distrust of the good intentions of the gentry. Hence the news of arrests of landowners implicated in the Decembrist plot was often welcomed by the peasants.[79] It was as if the intellectuals and the peasants, without knowing it, were simultaneously playing in the same drama on different stages.

After the suppression of the Decembrists, nearly a quarter of a century passed before a new weapon of attack on the system was fashioned, consisting of the émigré literature published abroad and smuggled into Russia. In 1847 there appeared in Paris a three-volume work entitled *La Russie et les Russes,* by N. I. Turgenev, who, as a political refugee in France, was settling old scores with his archenemy serfdom. More important was the fact that in the same year Alexander Herzen, who had already made a mark in the intellectual circles of Moscow, left his native land in order better to carry on his vendetta against serfdom and political despotism. He is the best representative of the "penitent nobleman," who was driven by remorse over "sins" against the people into the revolutionary camp and exile. Herzen combined a passionate devotion to freedom and justice with a clear, skeptical mind, a fighting spirit, encyclopedic erudition, and a remarkable literary talent for debunking. He was well equipped for intellectual leadership in the campaign against serfdom. In this task he was assisted by his friend, the poet Nicholas Ogarev, who joined him in self-exile to form a political-literary partnership, reminiscent of the more famous one of Marx and Engels.

In 1853, Herzen published a pamphlet entitled *Baptized Property,* which was probably the deadliest sortie against serfdom since Radishchev's. The most effective new weapon proved to be the periodicals he founded in London. In 1856, he began the publication of the magazines *Polar Star* and *Voices from Russia,* in which considerable attention was paid to the peasant question, and many articles and memoranda were printed that could not pass the censor in Russia. On July 1, 1857, the first number of Herzen's well-known paper, *Kolokol* (The Bell), left the printing press, and a "most powerful and rapidly shooting gun was set off." [80] The appearance of *Kolokol* marked the beginning of a period in which, following the defeat suffered by Russia in the Crimean War and the death of Nicholas I, the question of ending serfdom ceased to be academic and became one of practical politics. The subject was eagerly discussed by the educated public. Since the government was slow to relax censorship, *Kolokol* had a vital function to perform in guiding progressive Russian public opinion. The best evidence of and tribute to its influence was the fact that, although theoretically illegal, the journal was freely circulated in Russia and widely read not only by the intelligentsia but also in official circles, including, it was rumored, Alexander II himself.

The abolitionist intellectuals did not confine themselves merely to the task of arousing the sleeping moral conscience of the ruling classes. From Radishchev to Herzen, abolitionists also conducted a war of nerves by playing up the constant fear of another Pugachev rebellion. The strength of that fear was attested by the secrecy with which it was felt necessary to shroud all official deliberations on the peasant question. Herzen, writing from London in 1853, was quite outspoken when he called on the nobility to take a speedy initiative in the matter of emancipation: "A Pugachev revolt is terrible, but we shall say frankly that if the liberation of peasants cannot be bought otherwise, it still is not bought too dearly." [81] Thus the writings of intellectuals tended to bring the danger of peasant unrest, though not without some exaggeration, into the spotlight of public attention.

The intellectual opposition to serfdom was not in vain. In spite of all handicaps, by the middle of the nineteenth century it had succeeded in morally discrediting serfdom among the educated classes including the young tsar, by focusing public attention on its hideousness, cruel abuses, and general injustice and inhumanity, which brutalized and demoralized slave and slaveowner alike. Only a decade or two earlier, literary apologetics for serfdom were not uncommon. Their leitmotiv was the more favorable status of the Russian muzhik as compared with that of the peasant in Western Europe or the factory worker in England. Serious technical magazines were devoted to the discussion of the best method of utilizing serf labor, arguing the pros and cons of the quitrent and *barshchina* systems. After the Crimean War, this attitude changed. The only magazine that spoke for the serfowning class vigorously denied the charge of defending serfdom and resorted to various weak euphemisms to express its credo. When the proponents of serfdom decided to establish a similar magazine, they had no difficulty in raising the necessary capital but were not able to find an editor; the project lapsed.[82]

Besides propaganda, the abolitionist intellectuals also acquitted themselves well in helping the government of Alexander II (who, incidentally, never trusted the intelligentsia) to prepare and draft the emancipation legislation and regulations. The government profited from the stream of unpublished pamphlets, memoranda, and schemes dealing with the peasant question, which appeared after Alexander II's accession to the throne: "The government grasped at these memoranda and schemes with both hands." [83] Thus it fell to the intellectuals to represent the interests of the voiceless peasantry in drawing up the emancipation reforms.

The Landowners' Opposition to Emancipation

No matter how urgent emancipation appeared to the intelligentsia, no matter how restive the peasantry was under bondage or even how inevitable it seemed to Alexander II, who saw the handwriting on the wall, the attitude of the landowning class was still crucial. All the evidence points to the unabated fear and implacable hostility toward emancipation on the part of the majority of landowners. The landowners' hostility seems inconsistent with a widely held theory that serfdom was not only a stumbling block to national economic and cultural progress—an indisputable proposition—but that it was becoming increasingly disadvantageous to the landowners' economic interests. The use of serf labor, according to this theory, ceased to be profitable and serfdom had been ripe for abandonment by the middle of the eighteenth century; the Crimean War merely provided the *coup de grâce*.

The original ideological source of this doctrine was laissez-faire economic liberalism, which postulated the advantages of the free labor contract over any form of coercion. But it also fit neatly into what later developed as the materialistic or economic interpretation of history, associated largely with the names of Karl Marx and Friedrich Engels. Nothing could be more tempting than to explain the downfall of serfdom as motivated by the economic self-interest of the master class.

But the emphasis on economic factors in the abolition of serfdom was not peculiar to Marxist historians and economists; it influenced many others long before Marxist dogma had acquired a monopolistic position in Soviet Russia. Thus A. A. Kornilov wrote: "The landlords have been convinced for a long time that, no matter how harsh the discipline, serf labor can never compare in productivity with free labor. In the 1840s, this conviction was already an axiom for thinking and reading landlords . . . The landlords were becoming more and more convinced about the high cost and low productivity of serf labor, except in the industrial districts, where the serfs were permitted to engage in outside occupations on payment of a quitrent, which sometimes provided a considerable income to their masters." [84] Even the most zealous defenders of class interests, according to this authority, "essentially would not have objected to the abolition of serfdom on the condition that the landowning gentry retain most of its land and secure a good redemption payment for the personal liberation of serfs and for the right to use their labor gratis and in an arbitrary manner." [85]

Miliukov also thought that liberation of the serfs, if there were no land allotments, would not have been objectionable to the landlords.[86] He based his argument on the fact that nineteenth-century Russia was passing from a self-sufficient manorial economy to a money-exchange economy, with a growing domestic and foreign trade in agricultural products. This development tended to raise the value of land and made the use of inefficient serf labor (remunerated by holdings of land) less advantageous than the employment of more productive hired labor. But the landlords as well as the government realized, according to Miliukov, that the Russian peasant tenaciously adhered to the maxim, "we are yours but the land is ours." [87] They would never tolerate landless emancipation.

Official recognition of this fact and its adverse effect on the course of emancipation is contained in a memorandum from Prince Vasil'chikov (a high government official) to the secret committee set up in 1835 to consider the peasant question. It was necessary, wrote the prince, "to spread and assert at every convenient opportunity the basic rule that the land is the inseparable and inalienable property of the landlord and that the peasant can use it not otherwise than with the consent of the landlord and in consideration for performance of definite services. The unfortunate idea which exists nearly everywhere among the serfs, that they themselves belong to the master but the land belongs to them, is one of the principal obstacles to the achievement of the desired aims. For the introduction of the intended improvements in the position of the peasants can create unrest and give cause for serious disturbances." [88]

Since landless emancipation was impossible, the landlords preferred not to upset the applecart, not to tamper with the system even though it was allegedly becoming less and less advantageous. Among the evidence marshaled in support of this theory were: the growth of population, requiring more intensive cultivation of the land, which was considered incompatible with serfdom; low grain prices, presumably reflecting a chronic state of overproduction of estate agriculture; * the burdensome

* A Soviet statistician, P. I. Popov, criticized the overproduction theory on the ground that it was based on a statistical misconception. He showed that a theoretical estimate of the normal crop of some two billion poods, which could yield a surplus above normal requirements, was erroneously accepted by many students as the actual average production during the last two decades of serfdom. According to Popov's analysis, surpluses above normal requirements occurred only during years of good or average crops and constituted a reserve against the deficits during the frequent years of poor crops and famine. Such reserves were especially necessary in a country with primitive means of communication: in pre-railway Russia, scarcities and gluts coexisted in close geographical proximity. Popov has rightly rejected the notion that climatic surpluses, reflecting

mortgage debt from which emancipation might free the landlords. However, many of these factors need correction or are capable of an interpretation that is not in harmony with the abolitionist thesis. Such a task of re-examination has been performed by the well-known economist Peter Struve, who writes:

> With a limited market for agricultural products . . . the landlords had to keep their money expenses of production as low as possible. Payment in kind or forced labor conforms with this requirement of very low money expenses . . . The ownership of "baptized property" could have burdened the Russian landowners only in the overpopulated areas, in the estates having little land. But we have no indication that the landowners in such areas actually were so burdened by their peasants that they tried to get rid of them. Otherwise we would have witnessed a large-scale liberation of peasants . . . To receive quitrents was a pleasant privilege, and the landowners were not at all interested in its abolition. The landowners who utilized peasant labor in the form of the *barshchina* also were not interested in the abolition of serfdom. Moreover, as far as the demesne economy was concerned, the serf system was still closely integrated with the process of production and was conducive to its most advantageous organization.[89]

The crucial test, then, is this: if the bondage system had become really disadvantageous for the landlords, it would have been more profitable to operate with free labor. And, as Struve argues, if free labor were more profitable, the landlords would have tried to replace the serfs with free workers. This could have been done legally and was even encouraged, albeit very mildly, by legislation passed in 1803 and 1842. In any event, the government no doubt would have readily removed any existing legal obstacle if a significant abolitionist sentiment had developed among the influential landowning class. Far from this, however, the overwhelming majority of landlords not only vehemently resisted any government attempt to mitigate serfdom, but made every effort to extend it by settling serfs on new land and expanding the *barshchina* system in the more fertile regions of southern and central Russia. Also, the contention of Tugan-Baranovskii and other Russian economists that serf labor was rapidly disappearing in factories is shown by more recent historical research to require serious qualification.[90]

---

fluctuating weather conditions, represented overproduction, in the sense that the output systematically exceeded market and consumption requirements. See his article on grain-forage balance in *Komissiia SNK SSSR po izucheniiu sovremennoi derevni: Sel'skoe khoziaistvo na putiakh vosstanovleniia,* ed. L. Kritsman, P. Popov, and Ia. Iakovlev (Moscow, 1925).

In reality, free labor in agriculture was used only as a last resort in districts where the supply of serfs was limited, although much was made of such exceptional cases in later years. To argue that landlords were prevented from making a shift to free labor because of a shortage of capital is only to give an additional weighty reason for their attachment to serfdom. Perhaps the landlords were poor judges of their immediate economic interests. But much evidence to the contrary has been adduced by Struve, Liashchenko, and others. They exhibited, in any case, a keen understanding and skill in defending their economic interests during the emancipation. So there is strong ground for thinking that the economic motives of the landowning class, far from tending toward emancipation, were really aligned with a basic resistance to change; one should also think of such psychological factors as inertia, conservatism, and fear of the loss of social prestige and power, which made the abandonment of serfdom anathema to most landlords. And this notwithstanding the growing feeling that "to own serfs was dangerous." [91]

A better case could be made for the inevitability of emancipation after the Crimean War on the basis that the Russian autocracy could not maintain its international power position, could not provide domestic security in the face of the growing peasant discontent, and could not improve its weakened finances without increased economic growth, which was blocked by serfdom. These objectives required major revamping of the economic and administrative structure, which, it was generally agreed by thinking people, had to start with serfdom.

The Feeble Effort at Reform

The three Russian monarchs who followed Catherine the Great—Paul I, Alexander I, and Nicholas I—were more alert to the evils of serfdom and showed a somewhat greater inclination to grapple with the problem. But because of the hostility of the landowning nobility, which also included the higher echelons of the bureaucracy, no significant change took place in government policy, apart from a few mitigating gestures. Paul I (1796–1801) is known in history for his antagonistic attitude to Catherine and to the nobles his mother so greatly favored, and for his generally erratic, despotic behavior that suggested serious mental instability. He was assassinated after a short reign, during one of those familiar Russian palace revolts. Paul showed a surprising interest in the peasant question prior to his accession to the throne, when he was kept from active participation in state affairs.[92] Peasant disturbances that greeted the beginning of his reign, and the numerous petitions depicting the serfs' exceedingly harsh lot, heightened his concern with the problem. Paul's initial steps, which included some tax relief, cancellation of a previously announced draft of recruits for the army, restoration of the oath of allegiance to the sovereign on the part of the serfs and of the right to petition him, were certainly popular. His most important ameliorative measure was the edict of April 5, 1797, requiring strict observance of Sundays and holidays, and limiting in rather ambiguous language the work of demesne peasants to three days a week. With the exception of E. P. Trifiliev, Russian historians consider this law of little practical value because of continuing violations by the lords. Yet as a first attempt to impose a significant restriction on the powers of the landlords, it is regarded as something of a historic landmark. Paul's agrarian policy, however, was marked by contradictions, and some of his actions were contrary to peasant interests. Probably the worst offense was his distribution of peasants as gifts, which exceeded even Catherine's generous grants.[93]

Alexander I (1801–1825) began his reign as a liberal, by sponsoring in 1803 a law establishing a class of "free cultivators"; this encouraged the voluntary liberation of peasants (including whole villages), with land to be owned by each family separately. The masters were to be compensated by a single payment or in installments, or by a continuation of the services of the freemen. During the more than half century this law was on the statute books, only about 114,000 male souls and their families were freed. Thus a mountain bore a mouse. The later policy of Alexander is perhaps best expressed by the manifesto of 1814, in which the tsar, at the end of the Napoleonic struggle, thanked the various classes of his realm and bestowed privileges on them. The peasants, who expected an improvement of their lot, received but a single line for their heroism: "The peasants, our loyal people, will be recompensed by God." [94] One other measure was adopted during the latter part of Alexander's reign— the liberation of serfs in 1816–1819 in the Baltic provinces, where there was much conflict between the Lettish and Estonian peasantry and the German landlords. Unlike the free-cultivator law of 1803, the peasants of these provinces were liberated without land and became tenants of the German landlords, who continued to exploit them.

Nicholas I also realized that serfdom was both a powder magazine and a brake on national progress. He organized nine secret committees to study the question, but was afraid to disturb the status quo. He told his Council of State on March 30, 1842: "Doubtless serfdom as it exists at present in our country is an evil that is generally evident; but to tamper with it now would be, of course, an even more disastrous evil." [95] So another palliative was tried, with the adoption in 1842 of a law establishing a class of obligated (*obiazannye*) peasants; it permitted the voluntary liberation of serfs without ownership of land but with allotment of holdings, for which they paid dues to the landowners in money or in kind. The landowners also retained certain police powers over the freemen, but were not responsible for supporting them during famines or other emergencies. Under this law, only 25,000 male souls with their families were freed; altogether, under the laws of 1803 and 1842, less than 150,000 of more than 10 million male serfs gained freedom.

A different method of dealing with serfdom, familiar in Central Europe, was amelioration through regulation rather than outright abolition. It was tried in the western provinces, which until the partition of Poland in the late eighteenth century constituted a part of Russia and where the landlords were mostly Polish and Roman Catholic. The peasantry was Ukrainian, Belorussian, and Lithuanian, and the first two groups were Russian Orthodox with special claim to protection from a government which, under Nicholas I, adopted as a policy guide the trinitarian formula: Autocracy, Orthodoxy, and Nationality (which meant, of course, Russian nationalism). More important, political tension had developed between the Russian government and the Polish landowning class, with the government on the peasants' side. The relief method used was to fix and record, in so-called inventories, the holdings, dues, and services of peasants on each estate, hoping in this manner to prevent abuses on the part of the landlords. But even in the three southwestern Ukrainian provinces, where the measure was energetically pushed by Governor-General D. G. Bibikov, it was not considered by those who studied it of any great significance in improving the position of the peasantry.[96] The situation was, if anything, even less favorable in other western provinces. It is significant that Nicholas I, when he was not afraid of hurting the landowning class, was able to take some bold steps. He granted approval for one far-reaching reform to Count Kiselev, the only aide who was genuinely interested in the peasant question and who was called by Nicholas his "chief of staff for peasant affairs." In 1838 state peasants were transferred from the jurisdiction of the Ministry of Finance to the newly organized Ministry of Public Domain, entrusted to Kiselev. In principle they became the wards of the state, rather than objects to be mulcted and exploited. Although often impaired by poor administration and excessive paternalism, Kiselev's reform was the first large-scale measure for the improvement of peasant conditions. The disastrous Crimean War, however, made it necessary to take more radical steps.

2

Emancipation

Alexander II, who as heir to the throne manifested a strong conservatism
in peasant affairs, by the time the Crimean War ended was apparently
convinced that serfdom must be abolished. Shortly after peace was concluded in April 1856, addressing a delegation of noblemen in Moscow,
he pointed out that serfdom cannot "remain unchanged . . . It is better
to abolish serfdom from above than to wait until it will begin to abolish
itself from below. I ask you gentlemen to give thought to the question
of how it can be brought about." The government was determined at this
early stage that the initiative in the matter of emancipation should come
from the nobility. No progress was made for some time, until the ice was
broken by nobles in the Lithuanian provinces, who were threatened by
Governor-General Nazimov with a very stiff regulation of peasant duties,
the "inventories." The Lithuanian landlords thought that they might
lose less by a voluntary petition to the government for emancipation.
Permission was "graciously" granted by an imperial edict addressed to
Nazimov, on November 20, 1857, setting forth guiding principles for
general information. The nobility of other provinces, prodded by officials, willy-nilly had to follow suit with greater or lesser haste. The gov-

ernment won its point; it forced the landowning class to make the first move and, by the same token, committed itself publicly and irrevocably to emancipation. After this, the preparatory work for the reform went into high gear.

The Drafting of the Legislation

In each province there was established a committee consisting of members elected by local landowners (one for each *uezd,* or county) and two landlords appointed by the government. In accordance with detailed terms of reference issued by the central government, the committee dealt with the whole problem of emancipation, and not merely with its local aspects. The conclusions and supporting material were then embodied in a report. For the most part, there were separate majority and minority reports, reflecting the often heated conflict of opinion within the committee. In the capital, by 1857, a committee of high functionaries was formed, the Main Committee on Rural Organization, to deal with the emancipation question. But its members did not distinguish themselves by their zeal in prosecuting the task and were, for the most part, antagonistic to the cause. Therefore, in order to draft the complicated legislation and to review the reports of the provincial committees, lower echelons of officialdom had to be called in. Special drafting commissions (actually one commission consisting of several sections) were created, first under the chairmanship of Count Rostovtsev, an old collaborator of Alexander II's, who became a warm supporter of emancipation. Later, the unsympathetic Count Panin was appointed chairman. Here were gathered some outstanding experts, both bureaucrats and landowners, including a number of devoted supporters of emancipation. One was Nicholas Miliutin who, as Deputy Minister of Interior, played a highly influential role on the commission.[1]

After twenty months of arduous work, the commission completed its assignment, in October 1860, and the emancipation legislation was ready for the two final stages: approval by the Main Committee, under the chairmanship of the emperor's brother, the Grand Duke Konstantin Nikolaevich,* and by the Council of Empire. Opening the session of the

* When Alexander II undertook the momentous task of emancipation he had hardly anyone to lean on in his official entourage. Count Rostovtsev, a renegade Decembrist, was an exception, having become a convert to the cause after his appointment as chairman of the drafting commission. But he died in the middle of his task and was replaced, to the consternation of the liberals, by the reactionary Panin. (See A. Dzhivilegov, "Count V. N. Panin," *Velikaia reforma,* V, 147–155.) This curious appointment demonstrates how heavily Alexander relied on the small circle of the conservative court

council, Alexander II urged haste in the passage of the reform, pointing out that further delay after four years of preparation and consideration was dangerous. He went on to say: "I cannot but be surprised and rejoice, and am certain that you also rejoice, over the confidence and calm manifested by our good folk [the peasants] in this matter." The legislation was passed quickly: though the reform was more radical than originally contemplated, some revisions were made which were unfavorable to the peasants. Finally, on February 19, 1861, more than three years after work on the reform had seriously begun, the law, with an accompanying manifesto, was signed by Alexander II. It was published only on March 3, 1861, and did not go into effect until two years later. Thus serfdom was legally "abolished forever" in Russia with one stroke of the emperor's pen and not gradually, step by step, over a long period of time, as in most of Western Europe.

The act of 1861 applied only to the serfs of the landowning nobility. The land tenure and administrative organization of the two other important categories of peasants—imperial and state—were settled by separate acts on June 26, 1863, and November 24, 1866, which were modeled on the 1861 law, though with important differences (favoring the peasants). There was other legislation dealing with various minor groups of serfs. The peasants of the imperial family were personally liberated by decree on July 23, 1858.

To understand the character of the emancipation legislation, it is important to bear in mind that it was a compromise of conflicting pressures—the inevitability of emancipation with land had to be reconciled with powerful landowning interests. These interests were represented

---

aristocracy, even though he could have chosen for such a mission an able individual from among the more liberal strata of officialdom. But he distrusted such people as Miliutin and even Kiselev, who was appointed ambassador to Paris. It was fortunate in the circumstances that Alexander found warm support for the reform among members of his family. One was his aunt, the Grand Duchess Elena Pavlovna, a gifted woman known for her intellectual and artistic interests and her humanitarianism. She took an active interest in supporting the emancipation reform, influencing the emperor and inspiring, advising, prodding, and protecting those who toiled in that vineyard. (See A. F. Koni, "Grand Duchess Elena Pavlovna," *Velikaia reforma*, V, 34–51.) Among those she influenced was the Grand Duke Konstantin Nikolaevich, who played a highly influential role in championing the liberal reforms of Alexander II's reign. The Grand Duke rendered signal service to the cause of emancipation, as was publicly acknowledged by his brother. Konstantin tried to speed up the emancipation both in the conservative Main Committee and in the Council of Empire. It is symptomatic that Konstantin was dismissed from all his offices for being too liberal by the regime of Alexander III, under whom political reaction became intensified. See Koni, "Grand Duke Konstantin Nikolaevich," *Velikaia reforma*, V, 34–51; G. Dzhanshiev, *Iz epokhi velikikh reform* (From the Epoch of the Great Reforms; 3rd ed., Moscow, 1892), pp. xix–xxix.

not only by the provincial committees, but also in the Main Committee, in the Council of Empire, and at the imperial court. I used the plural "interests" advisedly since, apart from a general opposition to abolition per se, the landowning class was by no means monolithic. On the contrary, there was considerable divergence, even conflict, among the landowners as to the best or the least harmful terms for the emancipation. This divergence was largely caused by the differences in natural and economic conditions among various regions of the vast country and was reflected in the reports of the provincial committees. Broadly speaking, there were four important groups among the serfowning gentry. In the northern and north central provinces, which had inferior podzolic soils and relatively better developed trade and industry, the landowners derived their income largely from quitrents paid by their serfs. Although these landowners were quite willing to let the peasants have all the land they had been cultivating, and even more, they demanded compensation for the loss of the profitable quitrents. Since such landowners also needed capital if they were to start farming on their own, they insisted on immediate rather than gradual redemption.

By contrast, the landowners in the fertile black-soil area, where land was becoming increasingly more valuable and labor was plentiful, were interested primarily in retaining as much land as possible. Still another group consisted of the landowners in the steppe regions, where land was abundant but labor scarce. It was to their advantage to give their former serfs a certain amount of land which would bind them to their place of abode and thus provide a sufficient labor force to work the estates, until migration of free labor from other parts of the country could make itself felt. Finally, there were the landowners in the northwestern provinces, mostly Poles, whose estate agriculture was relatively highly developed. Their preference, as in the black-soil zone, was landless emancipation, or a system of so-called *Bauerland,* under which the peasants would become permanent tenants through periodically revised voluntary agreements; they also wanted to retain considerable police power.

I shall explain presently how the effort to appease this array of conflicting vested interests affected the emancipation legislation. But it is not my purpose to describe systematically and in detail this complicated law. It has been admirably done many times.[2] I shall instead address the central question of how the emancipation reform led to the agrarian revolutionary situation it was designed to forestall, according to the classical statement of Alexander II.

What, then, were the underlying principles on which the emancipation was based, and how were they implemented in legislation and administration? There were, broadly speaking, three cardinal principles. First, the liberated peasants were to become land proprietors. They were to be allotted holdings that would enable them to gain a livelihood and to pay taxes to the state, as well as to redeem the purchase price of the land. Thus, with some exceptions, a landless proletariat, an exclusively tenant class, was to be avoided. Second, the landlords were to be paid a fair price for the land they allotted to the liberated peasants. The government, on certain conditions, was to pay this compensation in a single operation and collect it from the peasants over a long-term period, in installments. The landlords were to receive no additional payments for liberating the person of the serf. These appeared to be sound principles. However, under pressures from the landowning class, the emancipation legislation and its implementation deviated more or less widely from the basic pattern. And from such deviations stemmed much of the difficulty that bedeviled the post-emancipation period of Russian agrarian history.

Land Allotment

The requirement of land for the liberated serfs was doubtless a strong point of the reform, not lessened by its inevitability in view of the expectations of the Russian peasantry. Although the principle of land allotment was settled rather early during the drafting stages of the legislation, the question of the extent to which it was to be carried out soon became one of the principal battlegrounds for the defenders of peasant interests and the landowners. The objective of the former was the maintenance of the status quo in the land allotment. Not that the status quo was ideal. The holdings originally allotted to the serfs bore no necessary relation either to labor power or to family needs. Much serf labor, in fact, was employed in cultivating the landlord's own fields, and the situation was accentuated in the important black-soil zone, with the growth of the *barshchina* system. There was also considerable divergence in the size of peasant holdings between the larger and smaller (but often more heavily populated) estates. And this was also true of the different regions since, with migration legally impossible, the distribution of the rural population corresponded very imperfectly to the available land resources.

Despite these and other difficulties, the maintenance of existing peasant landholdings seemed to the emancipation drafters the maximum that could be achieved. Yet even the status-quo principle was not adhered to consistently and was subjected to many qualifications designed to protect the landlords' properties. The result was diminished peasant holdings. It was provided in the emancipation law itself that the estate land retained by the landlord could not be decreased beyond a certain limit, set at one third of its area (in the steppe provinces it was one half). Furthermore, the area to be used for this calculation was restricted to farmland situated at a distance not to exceed 12 versts (7.95 miles) from the manor. All land in excess of a certain allotment norm established for each district—the higher one, if there were both a higher and a lower norm—was to revert to the landlord. Now even the higher norms, as they were finally set up, were by no means generous. They were, as a rule, either below the average size of what was supposed to be the existing peasant holding or coincided with it, and only rarely exceeded it.[3] I say "supposed to be" because the statistical data at the disposal of the emancipation drafters were far from precise. The figures on land held by peasants appear to have been underestimated, particularly with respect to pastures, meadows, and the unplowed fallow land in regions where continuous cropping prevailed. The rather tight norms based on such statistics, coupled with the other provisions of the law, resulted in a decreased allotment of land to the liberated peasants, whose former holdings were also for the most part small.

Another factor contributing to the diminution of peasant land was the provision in the law whereby the landlord could discharge the obligation to provide his serfs with land by granting a small free allotment, about one fourth of the normal size, to those willing to accept it. Not a few peasants, especially in the southeastern provinces where additional land could be cheaply leased, succumbed to the blandishments of these "gifts" or "quarter-size" holdings. They later became more appropriately known as poverty allotments, because they were responsible for some of the worst destitution that existed in Russian villages. Finally, over 700,000 manorial serfs and peasants in military service were not allotted any land. The number of manorial serfs had increased during the last years of the servile system, from 1,036,000 to 1,467,000, or 41.7 percent.[4] This increase was probably not unconnected with the expectation on the part of the landlords that it would not be necessary to allot any land to these peasants upon emancipation.

Thus, through various cracks in the wall built to guard the existing peasant land allotment, the landowners helped themselves to peasant-held land. The extent of such cut-off land, *otrezki*, as it later became known, was greatest of course in the fertile black-soil area. In some of these provinces the cut-off land ranged from more than 20 to close to 40 percent, even though the peasants now had more time to cultivate their own holdings.[5] On the other hand, in regions with poor soil, the area was reduced but little or even increased since it was to the advantage of the landowners to dispose of as much land as possible at a high price. Where the attitude of the government toward the landowning nobility was not friendly, the conditions of emancipation were more favorable to the peasants. Altogether, in thirty-six provinces of European Russia the peasant-land area decreased by about 18 percent.* In the non-black-soil provinces, however, the area was reduced by slightly less than 10 percent, while in the black-soil provinces the reduction reached 26 percent. In Samara and Saratov provinces, the reduction exceeded 40 percent; in Poltava and Ekaterinoslav, it was 40 percent; and in Kazan, Kharkov, and Simbirsk over 30 percent.[6] Conversely, in the western provinces, the peasant area increased after the emancipation: Grodno, 12 percent, and Minsk, 41 percent.[7]

It is only fair to point out that, if the landowning class could have had its way, even a larger proportion of peasant land would have been expropriated. For instance, it was estimated by Miliukov that in certain provinces the drafting commissions originally proposed to take away less than one seventh of the land held by serfs, as against the one half demanded by the provincial committees of landowners.[8] Eventually, a compromise was effected and the landowners got only one third of what they had originally demanded. Granting that it might have been much worse, we are still confronted here with a veritable enclosure movement, staged by the Russian landowning class. As a result of the emancipation, almost three fourths of the peasant households were allotted holdings not exceeding 10 desiatinas (27 acres), and about one fifth not exceeding 5 desiatinas (13.5 acres).[9] Considering the extensive character of Russian cultivation with its predominance of grain crops, it is clear that the former serfs began their emancipated existence with a modest and often niggardly allotment of land.

The imperial peasants were treated much better by the reform. Their land area was increased by 14 percent, but the increase was mostly in the sparsely populated northern and eastern provinces; in the central provinces the area remained the same or decreased. All in all this category of peasants was better provided with land, with more than one half of the households obtaining allotments of 10 desiatinas.[10] The state peasants fared best of all, retaining all their land: they were better endowed to begin with, thanks partly to the reforms introduced in the 1840s by Kiselev. The allotment per male adult (*revizskaia dusha*) of state peasants exceeded that of the freedmen by 88 percent and of the imperial peasants by 23 percent.[11]

* Serfdom practically did not exist in the then very sparsely settled Siberia and in the extreme north of European Russia; it had been abolished in the Baltic provinces at the beginning of the nineteenth century. Serfdom in the Caucasus was dealt with by separate legislation in the 1880s.

The holdings of the state peasants have been considered by one Russian authority, L. V. Khodskii, as the best criterion for judging the adequacy of the land allotment.[12] He proceeded on the assumption that the average area of land possessed by former state peasants represents a reasonable norm because the government, in its own interest as a landowner, would have tried to provide enough land to utilize fully the labor of its tenant families. On this basis Khodskii calculated that 43 percent of the former private serf families, exclusive of manorial serfs, and 14 percent of the former state and imperial peasant families received holdings below this norm; holdings above the norm were 14 and 36 percent, respectively. Of the whole peasant population, 33 percent were provided with land above the norm and 28 percent below the norm. The last group was considered by Khodskii as inadequately provided with land.

An unstated assumption of all such estimates is a certain amount of stability in agricultural technique. For a change in the latter is bound to affect the norms adopted for land allotment. With improved or more intensive cultivation, involving greater inputs of labor and capital, or a more efficient utilization of land and other factors, more output can usually be obtained from a unit of land and, consequently, less land is required. Unfortunately, the slow technical progress of nineteenth-century Russian agriculture justifies the assumption of considerable stability in agricultural technique, or very slow improvement. Whatever the situation at the time of the emancipation, however, it was aggravated by the subsequent rapid growth of the rural population. In the fifty provinces of European Russia, exclusive of Congress Poland and the North Caucasus, it probably did not exceed 50 million in the 1860s; by 1900 it had reached 86 million. As a result, the average allotted land area per male peasant, which was estimated at the time of emancipation at 13 acres, decreased by 1900 to 7 acres, or 47 percent. In a number of regions, there was an even greater reduction. The net effect was that the peasants at the end of the nineteenth century had, on the average, only a little more than half and in many regions less than half of the land allotted to them forty years earlier.[13]

The increased pressure of population on the allotted area made it difficult for the peasants to forget the loss of land, the *otrezki*, suffered during the emancipation settlement. In fact they did not forget it.[14] That it was a serious grievance is attested, among other things, by the fact that Lenin, who was always on the alert to exploit every discontent in his party's interest, advocated the inclusion in the early program of the Russian Social Democratic Party a demand for the restoration of this lost land to the peasants. This meant championing the small peasant proprietor, which is contrary to orthodox Marxist dogma; but such theoretical considerations never stopped Lenin when he was bent on achieving an important practical aim.

Whereas the adverse effect of land loss on the peasants' well-being became increasingly manifest with the rapid growth of population, other shortcomings of the emancipation reform began to be felt earlier. Often the peasants received poor treatment in the matter of the quality of land. The landlords retained the best land, while the peasants were given land of inferior quality. Forced to use every bit of such land in order to gain even a meager livelihood, they plowed up steep slopes of ravines and other land unsuitable for farming. This hastened the process of soil erosion and contributed to the spread of the devastating droughts that bedeviled Russian agriculture.[15] Holdings also were often inconveniently situated. In some cases they were at an exceedingly long distance from the village, a serious handicap when we recall that this was the age of the horse and not of the tractor and automobile. Other holdings, called "mousetraps," were accessible only by passage through the property of the landlord, which created a source of endless friction to plague future peasant-landlord relations. What was especially important, the peasant holdings frequently lacked the essential elements of a well-balanced farm, such as pasture, forest, and water. Shortage of pasture adversely affected livestock and, therefore, the supply of manure needed to fertilize the fields, particularly in the poorer northern and north central regions. Lack of forests meant that inadequate forage supply was diminished further by diversion of straw for use as fuel.[16] In order to remedy such situations, the peasants had to lease land from their former masters, often on onerous terms.

Here is an object lesson which is significant for our own times, when international attention is focused on the problem of land reform in the underdeveloped countries. Not only the size of the holding but also the quality of the land, and the location and balanced character of the holding, are important if a peasant is to be a really independent proprietor and if economic dependence on the large landowner is to be avoided.

To sum up: Although the conditions of the emancipation land settlement differed for various categories of the peasant population, land was allotted to all of them (excepting the manorial serfs). Nevertheless, a large segment of the peasantry began their free existence handicapped by inadequate or ill-balanced holdings—a condition aggravated by the subsequent rapid growth of rural population and by primitive techniques. Thus the seed of peasant land hunger and of a new agrarian crisis was planted early. It was helped along to maturity by the financial arrangements of the emancipation settlement and by the tax system.

Financial Aspects of Emancipation

The finanical arrangements of the emancipation settlement, also unfavorable to the peasants, began to pinch even earlier than the shortage of land. The former serfs had to compensate the landlords for the land allotted them, though not for the termination of their personal bondage. The compensation originally was to be in the form of quitrents or labor services, substantially as it was under serfdom, but the cash quitrent was considered the more normal form of compensation. The landlord had almost no control over the person of the peasant after the preliminary two-year period following emancipation, and could not arbitrarily change the type and rate of compensation once it was set. At the same time, his obligations toward the peasants, such as providing food in case of a harvest failure or responsibility for tax collection, also lapsed.

Provision was made in the law for the purchase or redemption by the peasant of his allotment, but originally no definite date or limit was set for this operation. Proposals of outright compulsory redemption of land, advanced during the drafting stage of the emancipation legislation and favored by many landowners in the non-black-soil area, were rejected by the government, on financial grounds. With the exception, again, of the western provinces, where the authorities were confronted with the Polish question, redemption was made optional with the landlord. He could compel the peasants to redeem their land, but peasants could not force the landlord's hand in this matter (though the two parties could voluntarily agree on it). Before redemption began, the liberated peasant continued to be tied by direct obligation to his former master. This stage, as its name, "temporarily obligated," implies, was to be a transitional one, though of indefinite duration.

To facilitate the process of redemption, the state extended financial aid by advancing to the landlord in cash and securities 80 percent of the total redemption sum of a full or standard allotment; 75 percent if it was less than standard size. It was calculated as capitalized value at 6 percent interest of the cash quitrent. These advances were to be repaid to the government, with interest, by the peasants in forty-nine annual installments. Such repayments were collected on the same basis as taxes. Despite its optional character as far as the landlord was concerned, on the whole the redemption operation proceeded fairly rapidly and, contrary to the fears of the government, was financially successful. By February 1, 1870, some 55 percent of all freedmen were already redeeming their land.[17] Landlords who, as a rule, were in need of cash and anxious to obtain government loans forced speedy redemption, forgoing for the most part the higher annual payments that they were otherwise able to exact and the 20 percent or more of the total peasant obligation not covered by the loan.[18] But twenty years after the emancipation, there still remained over 20 percent of the freedmen who had not begun to redeem their land. Finally, compulsory redemption was ordered by a law of December 28, 1881, to take place no later than January 1, 1883. Thus, more than two decades elapsed after the emancipation manifesto until the stage of temporary obligation to the landlord was ended. Now all had to pay redemption to the government.

A somewhat similar financial settlement was effected in the case of the state and imperial peasants though, as with the land allotment, they were treated more generously than the private serfs.[19] If the assessed redemption value per desiatina of land allotted to the imperial peasants is taken as 100 percent, then for the state peasants it was 127 percent; for the private serfs in the western provinces, 138; and for all other private serfs, 218. The latter had to pay for a desiatina more than double the amount paid by the imperial peasants and considerably more than the state peasants. Perhaps an exhaustive investigation (if the material were available) would reveal that variations in geographic distribution and quality of land among the three types of peasants played some part in this outcome. But it seems to me that Russian scholars have been right in emphasizing political-economic causes. For example, by a decree of March 1, 1863, liberalizing emancipation in the northwestern provinces after the Polish insurrection, the quitrents of the former serfs, which served as a basis for setting redemption payments, were reduced by 20 percent.

That redemption payments and taxes constituted a heavy and growing burden, the testimony of competent witnesses, official and unofficial, leaves no doubt. On few points of the Russian agrarian problem has there been so much agreement. It was the leitmotiv of several scholarly works and of numerous witnesses, some of them landlords, who gave evidence in the early 1870s before the Valuev Commission, the first of the many government commissions set up to inquire into conditions of Russian agriculture during the post-emancipation period. Thus one of the witnesses, Prince Vasil'chikov, author of a well-known work on the agrarian problem, stated that "peasant farming is declining, and if for no other the most important reason is that the land allotted to the peasants is burdened by taxes which exceed the returns from it. I consider this point so essential . . . that in my opinion it would be useless to attempt to seek others. I fully concur with the opinion expressed by the Provincial Marshal of Nobility of the Petersburg Province, Count Shuvalov, that the key to the improvement of agriculture in Russia lies in tax reforms." [20]

The Valuev Commission, in its report, put a stamp of approval on the thesis that peasant taxation, in which redemption payments played such a large role, was burdensome.[21] With varying argumentation and force, this thesis continued to be an essential element in the clinical diagnosis of the ills of Russian rural society. That the redemption payments were heavy is strongly suggested by the fact that they, for the most part, exceeded the prevailing market value of the land shortly before emancipation and during the following decade. It was estimated that, in the non-black-soil provinces, the redemption value of the allotted land exceeded by 90 percent its average market value during the years 1863–1872, and in the black-soil provinces by 20 percent.[22] As compared with the average market value of land during the period 1854–1858, redemption payments were 57 percent higher in the black-soil area and 127 percent in the non-black-soil area. Only in the western provinces where, as already noted, conditions of liberation were most favorable to the peasants, was the redemption value of the allotted land slightly below the market value for 1863–1872, but still nearly 8 percent higher than during 1854–1858. A special commission set up by the Ministry of Finance estimated that in twenty-three provinces redemption payments would have been decreased by more than 40 percent if they had been based on the market value of land.[23]

That the government realized during the drafting of the emancipation legislation that the compensation fixed for the land allotted to the peasants was too heavy, "considerably higher than the rent which the land was capable of yielding," was corroborated twenty years later by the Grand Duke Konstantin, who had played so signal a role in the reform.[24] The overevaluation was due to inclusion in the value of land additional compensation for the person or labor of the liberated serf. Since this was illegal, it was done in a veiled, though not too surreptitious, form through overevaluation of land.* This was admitted in high government circles as early as 1877, and again when the problem of redemption payments was reviewed in 1881.[25] Nearly a quarter of a century later, Count Witte had this to say in his report as chairman of a special conference to consider agricultural problems: "The redemption payment in most cases exceeded considerably the income [rent] of the land, and thus the landlord was receiving what amounted to a concealed compensation for being deprived of his rights over the person of the peasant." [26]

Another device by which such extra compensation was secured was through differentiation of redemption payments by geographic area and

---

* The great disparity between the redemption and market values of land in the non-black-soil provinces becomes intelligible when it is remembered that serf labor, which could be employed profitably in handicrafts or transportation, was more valuable than the poor agricultural land of these regions.

through gradation in inverse relation to the size of the holding. The first desiatina of the allotted land was usually assessed higher than the others for purposes of the redemption payment. In the non-black-soil provinces, for instance, half of the redemption payment for a full, or standard, allotment was assessed against the first desiatina, one quarter against the second, and one quarter against the rest. Therefore, the smaller the actual allotment, the greater the redemption payment per unit of land—an application, in a sense, of the principle of marginal utility. Needless to say, it was not this economic-psychological principle, and not even the official justification that the first desiatina of the allotment comprised the most valuable land because it was often better manured, which was responsible for this gradation. Rather, it was the desire to prevent peasants with small allotments from escaping payment for their personal liberation.

If any further evidence is needed of the heavy fiscal burden imposed on the Russian peasantry by redemption payments and taxes, which were collected jointly, it is provided by the fact that arrears accumulated almost continuously from the very beginning of emancipation. This was a problem with which the tsarist government was constantly preoccupied during the post-emancipation period. For the arrears kept piling up despite the collective responsibility of the whole peasant community, the mir, for taxes and the very severe measures adopted in their collection. Forced sales of the peasants' personal property, including livestock, were carried out ruthlessly. There was also corporal punishment of tax delinquents and their compulsory hiring out by the mir to work off tax debts, as well as forfeiture of allotted land. The excessive zeal and often illegal actions of local authorities in "knocking out" tax arrears, with consequent great economic losses to the peasant population, sometimes brought rebukes even from the government in St. Petersburg.[27] Livestock losses, due to the forced sale of animals at ridiculously low prices, were particularly detrimental to peasant agriculture since they weakened the very foundation of peasant farming by depriving it of draft power and of manure to fertilize the fields.[28]

The government gained little immediate benefit from the ruinous prices of these forced sales. In the long run it was the loser because of the deterioration of peasant agriculture and the inability to cope with frequent crop failures and famine. The very timing of the tax collections, which were sped up immediately following the harvest, was highly disadvantageous to the peasants. The need of cash to pay taxes forced many of them, and especially the poorer ones, to sell their grain quickly in the autumn; the large supplies thrown on the market depressed prices. Grain prices usually went up in the spring, when many peasants had no grain to sell and some even had to buy. This gap between the low autumn prices at which many peasants had to sell grain and the higher spring prices at which some of them had to buy it back was another evil to which the fiscal system contributed.

From time to time the government became alive to the need for tax relief. The most important move of this kind occurred in the early 1880s under Minister of Finance N. Kh. Bunge, a former professor of economics at Kiev University. The poll tax, which had existed since the days of Peter the Great in the early eighteenth century, was abolished in European Russia beginning in 1887.* Redemption of allotted land became compulsory instead of optional for landowners, and redemption payments decreased on the average by 20 percent and by a minimum of 16 percent; arrears due on January 1, 1883, were canceled. Despite the relief which this action afforded, arrears again began to accumulate. Peasant land continued to be much more heavily taxed than the privately owned estate land. In 1891, for instance, taxes of various kinds, including redemption payments, amounted to 1.33 rubles per desiatina of peasant land, whereas a desiatina of private land was assessed at only about 0.2 rubles. In 1899 the taxes per desiatina of peasant land increased to 1.5 rubles, while they remained practically the same for private land.[29]

To the direct taxes and redemption payments must be added indirect taxes, excise taxes, and customs duties. They were much heavier and increased more rapidly than direct taxes. During the last two decades of the nineteenth century, indirect taxes more than doubled, and by 1901 they were five times as large as direct taxes.[30] Since excise taxes, in order to produce revenue, must be imposed on articles of mass consumption, the peasant population naturally was bound to bear the brunt of indirect taxation.

And what did it get in return for this heavy fiscal burden? Precious little in terms of social and welfare services, or education, or technical aid to agriculture. The great bulk of state expenditures was for military and administrative purposes.† As one authority on Russian financial policy put it: "The spending of this money, obtained with such difficulty and with tremendous sacrifices on the part of the population, whose most urgent needs remained unsatisfied, was far from being always economical

---

* In Asiatic Russia the poll tax was abolished later and gradually. See I. K. Ozerov, *Osnovy finansovoi nauki* (Principles of Finance; 5th ed., Prague, 1923), I, 317.

† A qualification should be made here. Tax funds were also used to foster industrialization and railroad construction. This must have resulted in some benefits to the peasant population through increased employment and widening markets for farm products—if not immediately, then in the long run. I shall return to this matter in Chapter Three.

or rational." [31] It is not surprising that the analogy with overtaxed French peasants on the eve of the Great Revolution should suggest itself even to so moderate a student of Russian rural conditions as Prince Vasil'chikov, who prophetically viewed the French example as a "serious warning" to Russia. He observed, "the taxation system can undermine the favorable effects of freedom and equal rights and provoke the small farmers into the same violence against the large landowners as was manifested in France at the end of the last century." [32]

Strong as such statements may have seemed at the time, the significance of the fiscal aspect in the Russian agrarian problem cannot be exaggerated. High taxation further depressed the income and the standard of living of the peasants and their ability to accumulate the capital needed for farming. It also led to legal restrictions on land ownership and even to the curtailment of the peasants' civil rights. It was envisaged by the drafters of the emancipation reform that the freedmen would eventually become independent small proprietors once the redemption payments for the land were completed.[33] Article 165 of the emancipation law granted the peasant unlimited private ownership of his landholding immediately upon payment of the redemption in a lump sum, rather than in the forty-nine installments. However, the principle of small land proprietorship was gradually "replaced by a new and alien concept of a special peasant-allotted land tenure." [34] To protect the government's heavy stake in the collection of redemption payments and taxes, the peasant's allotted land was made a sort of mortgage-collateral and was encumbered by legal restrictions that distinguished it sharply from estate and other nonpeasant land held in fee simple. The legal differentiation between allotted and other land was tightened by a law passed on December 14, 1893, which added new restrictions and confined even more closely the ownership of the allotted land to the peasant class. Article 165 was repealed.[35]

The title to the allotted land was vested not in the individual peasant or his family, but in the mir or obshchina. The mir, too, was pressed by law into tax assessment and collection, under the principle of joint unlimited liability of all its members. That the principle of collective responsibility for tax delinquency acted as a disincentive on the improvement of peasant farming was attested by highly responsible witnesses before the Valuev Commission in the early 1870s. Thus, in the opinion of a former Marshal of Nobility, A. V. Sheremet'ev, there were two main causes of peasant destitution: excessive taxation and the collective responsibility of the peasant community for taxes. "The peasant has become convinced that no property in his possession is secure; he has no incentive to get an extra horse or a cow and, particularly, a good farm implement because, upon the first intensified campaign for collection of tax arrears, all his belongings will be sold, to pay not only his personal debt but also the debt of his fellow villagers.[36]

I shall have more to say about the mir as an economic and social institution in Chapter Four. Here I only want to point out that, largely in order to enforce its tax-collection authority, the mir was armed with broad police powers over its members, including even exile to Siberia, which were formerly exercised by the nobles. An important weapon was the famous Russian passport, which hung like the sword of Damocles over the head of any peasant who wanted to leave his native village. For, in order to receive or to renew the much coveted passport, which was issued only for a limited period, he had to obtain permission from both the mir and the head of his household.

The peasant household was legally strengthened by the fact that the courts, during the post-emancipation period, sanctioned the custom according to which peasant property in Russia was a joint family affair. Whereas this served to protect the interests of each member, it tended to subject him to strong family tutelage. For instance, all his earnings from whatever source, if he was not legally separated from the household, were supposed to go into the common pool—a serious matter, considering the prevalence of migratory work in the overpopulated Russian village. The earnings of women were excepted, but they were supposed to provide their own clothes and the dowry for their daughters. This explains the paradoxical fact that peasant women, with their notoriously inferior status, had personal property rights denied to men.[37] Even peasants who had long lived and worked away from the village were often forced to continue their contributions to the household of which they legally remained members.

Although fiscal reasons bore a heavy responsibility for the fact that the emancipated peasant was made neither a truly independent land proprietor nor a full-fledged citizen, an important share for this must also be attributed to the nature of the Russian police state. Its authoritarian paternalism became accentuated with the growth of political reaction after the emancipation reform, which intensified during the reign of Alexander III (1881–1894). The liberated Russian peasantry, instead of being drawn closer to the rest of the citizenry, was actually segregated into a "kind of caste," an oppressed caste, lorded over by the chinovniki.[38] The peasants, to be sure, had their own local communal administration in the mir and a higher unit, the *volost,* or township, consisting of several communes. They also had their own lower courts, which functioned in accordance with a rather ill-defined law that was often unfairly and arbitrarily administered. But the peasant officials and judges, though elected by their constituents, were in practice dominated by arbitrary and ruthless government officials. This was aggravated when an institution of special functionaries (rural chiefs, or *zemskie nachal'niki*), recruited from the local nobility and given wide authority over peasant affairs, was created by a law of 1889. Then, as the reign of Alexander III approached its end, the paternalism of the police state was reaching its pinnacle. But it could not ward off the gathering storm in agriculture.

3

Land Hunger and the Agrarian Crisis

Toward the end of the nineteenth century, it was quite clear that the Russian countryside was in the throes of a serious crisis. As a matter of fact, the idea that all was not well with emancipated rural Russia dates back to the early seventies, when the first official commission of inquiry, the Valuev Commission, was set up. In belles-lettres, which always reflected very accurately the pulse of social thought in pre-Soviet Russia, the theme of rural distress was taken up by outstanding writers of the period, such as Gleb Uspenskii and Zlatovratskii, and later Chekhov. Perhaps the best portrayal came from the pen of A. N. Engelhardt, who was exiled to his estate in Smolensk province and who, in the late seventies, depicted rural poverty in his celebrated *Iz derevni* (From the Countryside). What finally made the gloomy view of agrarian conditions a popular stereotype was the crop failure and catastrophic famine of 1891, which gave a severe jolt to any complacency that might have existed.

The Impoverishment of the Village

Whatever the differences as to the causes of impoverishment, there was remarkable agreement on its symptoms. To numerous observers of Russian rural conditions, the growing destitution of the village seemed so evident that it required no special demonstration. This motif runs through many of the reports of the local investigating committees set up by the Conference on Agriculture, established in 1902 under the chairmanship of Minister of Finance Witte.

The representatives of the *zemstvo* (local government assembly) declared in the Novgorod Provincial Committee, in northwestern Russia: "To prove . . . the impoverishment of the peasant population is unnecessary because this fact has become so sharply manifested that it has inevitably won general recognition." A member of the Kharkov Provincial Committee in the Ukraine, N. N. Kovalevskii, states in his interesting report:

> I suppose no one will require from me the proof that our countryside is deteriorating. This process did not begin today; it has been in plain view and has progressed rapidly. We who live in the countryside can observe directly how, on the one hand, peasant farming is becoming impoverished and declining . . . and how, on the other hand, estate agriculture is also declining . . . To the people who do not live in the village and cannot observe conditions directly, the picture of general impoverishment is disclosed clearly by official data concerning the regularly growing tax arrears, by the sharp increase in the number of peasants lacking horses and cows, by expenditures of the government and private charity for feeding those suffering from famine, and by the Red Cross efforts to combat scurvy and typhus. Finally, we see a sign of degeneration in the lowering of physical requirements for military service.

"If you were to observe," said a government official from the province of Ufa in eastern European Russia, "what a peasant eats, you will note that his food contains neither meat nor milk nor eggs; there is only, and then not always, black bread and brick tea. This food is especially hard on the children, among whom only the exceptionally strong survive. Millions of poods of grain and millions of eggs are shipped abroad while epidemics due to undernourishment are spreading like a village fire among the population. It cannot be that the peasants do not understand the nourishing qualities and tastiness of meat, milk, eggs, and similar foods, but this food is simply beyond their means." Note that these complaints, so strikingly similar in tenor, come from three widely separated points of the country—north, south, and east.[1] The theme recurs throughout reports and observations from all the regions of Russia.

Vymiraiushchaia derevnia (Dying Village) was the title given to a survey of two villages of Voronezh province in central Russia, made at the beginning of the present century by the health authority A. I. Shingarev. He emphasized in the preface to his second edition that "the picture of the physical and economic sickness of the population . . . was characteristic of the general condition of the rural population in a large area of Russia. Only in this case, it was sharply focused because of an especially unfavorable land-tenure situation." "Chronic undernourishment," writes a conservative student of rural conditions in the central regions of European Russia, "is a usual phenomenon in the peasant family; they eat better only when they have to do some heavy work." [2] Often so great was the poverty in the village that even the presence of cockroaches and bedbugs was considered a sign or relative prosperity: they were not to be found in the poorest peasant households since there was nothing to feed on.[3] And at least one investigator confirmed this by finding a high degree of correlation between the number of infested peasant houses and the size of the landholdings.[4] It is unnecessary to dwell on the primitive character of peasant houses (which in the winter also often lodged animals), their unsanitary condition and their meager furniture. Enough has been said to show that most Russian peasants lived close to the margin of subsistence or even in semistarvation; just keeping body and soul together was the central preoccupation of existence.

An important indicator of the deteriorating position of the peasantry was the decline in livestock. An illustration of this is provided by the Kromskoi district of Orel province, central Russia, where two agricultural censuses were taken in 1887 and in 1901. The first census showed 115 horses, 86 cows, and 554 sheep per 100 households. Fourteen years later there were 94 horses, 82 cows, and 523 sheep. In 1887, 30.6 percent of all households were without horses and, in 1901, 38.2 percent. The proportion of households with 2 horses decreased from 23.0 percent in 1887 to 18.1 percent in 1901. Households having more than 2 horses decreased from 9.2 percent to 3.7 percent during this period.[5] If the peasant could keep his head above the water in years of good harvests, he was faced with disaster when crops failed, as they often did under Russia's climate. Starvation, epidemics, increased mortality, a decrease in the number of livestock, including vital work horses, mark the process of the growing destitution of a famine-striken village.[6] The adverse effects of such conditions were felt long after the worst of a famine had passed.

A pathetic commentary on the situation is that, while the nineteenth century brought an end to famine in Western Europe, Russia witnessed, if anything, even more frequent visitations of this scourge.[7] The terrible famine of the early 1890s became a historical landmark, comparable to the Irish potato famine of the 1840s. It did more than anything else to focus public attention on rural destitution. There was another serious famine in 1897, and the twentieth century characteristically opened with one as well. The famine of 1901 provoked one of the young Lenin's bitter denunciations of the tsarist government, for its callousness to the victims of starvation [8] (it strongly resembles W. H. Chamberlin's attack on Lenin's heirs thirty years later, for the "man-made" famine of 1932–33). What Rudyard Kipling wrote about the Indian peasant, in the 1890s, can be applied as well to the Russian peasant:

> He eats and hath indigestion,
> He toils and he may not stop,
> His life is a long-drawn question,
> Between a crop and a crop.

The Russian poet Nekrasov wrote much in the same vein about the peasantry of his native country, notably in his famous "Who Lives Well in Russia?"

Such is the clinical picture of the chronic and acute rural distress in Russia of the late nineteenth century. In diagnosing this crisis, we should not confuse it with the type of depression that afflicted agriculture during the last quarter of the nineteenth century in many other countries. That depression was primarily a price phenomenon. When the price decline, which had begun in the mid-1870s, stopped and the price level began its upward climb in the late 1890s, the agricultural depression largely disappeared. Insofar as its causes lie in production, the depression was essentially a response to competition from new sources of low-cost supplies of grain and other farm products (often spoken of as overproduction), which the growing network of railways and steamships brought within the orbit of the world market.

Of course, Russia, which became a leading grain-exporting country during the last third of the nineteenth century, did not escape the adverse effect of the decline in grain prices. Those estate owners engaged in commercial farming felt the price decline most painfully. Obviously they could not be shielded by protective tariffs, as in a country like Germany, which relied on imports for its agricultural products.

The question of the effect of low grain prices on agriculture provoked considerable discussion in the Russian economic literature of the nineties. Perhaps the zenith was reached with the publication, in 1897, of the collective study edited by A. I. Chuprov and A. S. Posnikov.[9] It was estimated in this study that only from a fourth to a third of the grain crop was marketed—the remaining three fourths or two thirds was consumed on the farm. The conclusion was that, on the whole, low prices were advantageous to the majority of the peasant population, which was either self-sufficient or had to buy when grain prices were high (at the end of the harvest year). This view was hotly disputed, and it does seem to be too extreme. For instance, a special study of 82 peasant household budgets in the province of Kazan, brought out that for 11 peasant households, or 13 percent of the total number, low prices were advantageous; for 55 households, or 67 percent, high prices were profitable; and for the remaining 16 households, or 20 percent, the question of price was immaterial.[10] These results certainly throw serious doubt on the general applicability of the Chuprov-Posnikov conclusions. But a generalization that can be safely made is that, to the Russian peasant producer, the size of the crop was more important than prices. A large crop was an unmitigated boon and not an economic calamity, as it often proved to be for the farmer in Western Europe and America; conversely, a small crop was an unmitigated evil. In good crop years, the Russian peasant not only sold more grain but ate more, fed more to livestock, and built up his reserves. Russian peasant agriculture, unlike that of the West, suffered not from overproduction but from underproduction, as a result of the needs of the growing population and the export requirements of the national economy. The Russian agrarian crisis was a more elementary and a more deep-seated phenomenon than an agricultural depression in more advanced capitalist countries.

Combatting the Crisis

An effort to overcome the crisis in Russian agriculture could have taken two directions: an improvement of agricultural technique and increased capital input, which would have led to more intensive farming and a more productive use of the land; or an expansion of crop area. The first was the path followed by agriculture in Western Europe in the nineteenth century; the second is the traditional method of underdeveloped, sparsely settled countries, with their large tracts of uncultivated land suitable for cropping. Eventually, with the growth of population and the exhaustion of free land, the first method becomes the only means of increasing domestic agricultural output. But there were many obstacles to the intensification of peasant agriculture in nineteenth-century Russia. One of the outstanding champions of both agricultural improvement and the expansion of peasant land area, A. A. Kaufman, wrote: "The existing land allotments in the case of a considerable majority [of peasants] would have been entirely sufficient with a higher level of cultivation; but the masses of our population are still too ignorant and, therefore, very inert; they find it too difficult to adopt those fundamental improvements in farming which would be rational under existing conditions." [11] Actually, the problem is more complicated, since a process of intensification usually involves a change in the methods of farming and in the cropping system; this requires not only knowledge and initiative on the part of the farming population, but also some capital and the stimulus of a profitable market for the disposal of farm surplus. The peasants, for the most part, were unable to turn easily to more intensive farming as a way out of the crisis because of inadequate markets, a shortage of capital, lack of knowledge of improved methods, or a combination of all these factors.

Some capital is usually needed for the purchase of implements, livestock, and seed. If there is a shift in acreage from food to feed or industrial crops—from grain, let us say, to tame hay (clover or some other grass)—which cannot be expected to yield immediate benefits, it may be necessary to purchase bread to tide the family over during the transitional period.[12] But it is hardly necessary to dwell on how hard it would be for the peasant to incur such expenditures, in the light of what we have seen earlier of the heavy taxes and redemption payments that were draining the Russian village.

The point is neatly summed up by the Balashov District Committee (Saratov province) of the Witte Conference:

> The low productivity of peasant farming is an expression of the general economic sickness of the peasant, whose declining agriculture brings constant deficits which are covered only by chronic starvation. Under such conditions there can be no question of expenditures for any agricultural improvements. Taxes, year in and year out, suck out of the peasant population an enormous share of its income, contributing almost nothing in exchange toward agricultural progress and increased productivity of national labor.[13]

The situation would have been different if, as a result of rapid industrial expansion and a growth in nonagricultural population, there had developed a profitable market for such products of intensive agriculture as dairy products, poultry and eggs, meats, vegetables, fruits and fibers, items for which small farming is often particularly well adapted. This was actually the case in Western Europe and the United States during the second half of the nineteenth century, but much less so in Russia. The urban population, it is true, doubled between 1871 and 1901 in European Russia, from 7 to nearly 14 million; but the rural population had grown from 58 to 86 million and constituted more than four fifths of the total population in 1901.[14] Agriculture, therefore, experienced to a much lesser extent the beneficial stimulus of a strong domestic market.

In Russia, too, industrial development, closely linked with increased railroad construction, began in earnest during the last two decades of the nineteenth century, stimulated by the economic policies of powerful ministers of finance. Perhaps the best single indicator of this growth was the increase in the labor force employed by the manufacturing and mining industries—from 1.3 million in 1887 to over 2 million in 1897.[15] The number of railway employees increased from 215,000 in 1884 to 554,000 in 1900.[16] Some considered the industrialization to be overstimulated, wasteful, and too costly and burdensome to the peasantry. However valid such criticism might be from the standpoint of method and tactics, the fact is that industrialization did not get far enough by the end of the century to be of immediate help to the peasant. What can hardly be disputed is that the initial impact of industrialization on peasant agriculture would have been more beneficial, or less unfavorable, but for the neglect of the agrarian problem. Excessive sacrifices by the peasantry are not inevitable in industrial development though, as Alexander Gerschenkron shows, this was the traditional Russian pattern, from Peter the Great on.[17]

The principal economic policymakers, Vyshnegradskii and Witte, were quite unlike their predecessor, Bunge, in their indifference to the agricultural situation. Vyshnegradskii, a self-made man and an interesting combination of scientist, college professor, and financier before he became a high government official, did nothing for peasant agriculture during his five years as Minister of Finance (1887–1892), even though the end of his term coincided with the most critical period of famine and rural destitution. Yet the landowning nobility did obtain financial aid during his regime. Also, for balance-of-payments and foreign-exchange considerations, he was greatly concerned with promoting grain exports, then the principal Russian export commodity. To Vyshnegradskii is attributed the slogan: "We will be underfed, but we will export [*ne doedim, no vyvezem*]," which was not far from reality in those years.

Count Witte, perhaps the most colorful and brilliant figure in the bureaucracy of the last two Romanovs, was greatly influenced by German state-interventionist economists, particularly Friedrich List, who was a strong advocate of industrial protectionism. Witte worked with Vyshnegradskii in railroad matters and later succeeded him as Minister of Finance (1892–1903). He also vigorously championed industrialization and railroad construction, while manifesting little concern for agriculture during most of his tenure in office. As a strong believer in tsarist autocracy and in an enlightened paternalistic bureaucracy, Witte opposed local self-government and curtailed the zemstvo's financial powers, though it was the only government institution that was trying to do something for the peasants. It is only fair to add that his aggressive industrial policies and his introduction of the gold standard did not endear Witte to the landowning class. Toward the end of his term as minister, Witte became more interested in the peasant question, perhaps influenced by the industrial depression that brought home the importance of an expanded market, requiring a prosperous peasantry. Improvement in the collection of rural taxes and, particularly, the abolition in 1903 of the joint guarantee for payment of taxes by the whole peasant community were reforms instituted by Witte. The creation of a state monopoly for the sale of liquor, primarily a fiscal measure, was also motivated to some extent by the desire to combat alcoholism among the masses (it proved abortive). In 1902 Witte succeeded in organizing the Conference on Agriculture, which threw so much light on contemporary agricultural and rural conditions, but it was too late. Witte's days as Minister of Finance were numbered; he was dismissed in 1903, and his agricultural conference was suddenly closed in March 1905 without having completed its task.

Whatever the errors and faults of Vyshnegradskii and Witte, the industrialization of which they were the architects proved beneficial to the economic life of the country, including the peasantry. And the cost of this process in the late nineteenth century cannot even begin to compare with the sacrifices exacted from the peasantry during the socialist industrialization of the 1930s.

The government's economic and financial policies, inadequate markets, and lack of capital were not the only stumbling blocks to agricultural improvement. Knowledge is an essential prerequisite of agricultural as of every other kind of progress. This includes general literacy and technical know-how. The first hurdle to overcome was illiteracy. According to the census of 1897, 76 percent of the whole rural working population (aged twenty to fifty-nine) and 63 percent of the men were illiterate. Even among the local agricultural-improvement societies, which, in the words of an official publication, constituted the "cultural advance guard of the village," illiteracy reached 15–24 percent, according to an investigation by the Ministry of Agriculture in 1912.[18]

There is ample evidence to corroborate the statement that "nowhere is there exhibited a closer connection between elementary education and national prosperity than in agricultural improvement."[19] More specifically, a witness before the Serpukhov District Committee (Moscow province) of the Witte Conference stated that literate peasants were the first to be convinced of the advantages of the introduction of grasses in rotation. Conversely, illiterate peasants insisted that they wanted to live "in the old way, as their grandfathers did, and do not want any change." [20] A statistician who testified before the Nizhnii Novgorod District Committee pointed out that there was a direct correlation between the literacy of the populations and the use of fertilizer.[21] Many other examples of correlation between schooling and modernization could be given.

In the light of this situation, did the Russian government make an effort to foster education? Not at all—just the reverse. The government's attitude was well characterized by N. N. Kovalevskii, a member of the Kharkov District Committee of the Witte Conference: "The principal objective of the government was not to spread popular education as widely and as rapidly as possible, but to ward off some kind of danger to the nation because the people would acquire too much knowledge unnecessarily through schools and books, and would broaden their intellectual horizon. There are still a number who are convinced that popular ignorance is the best guarantee of social order." [22]

The well-known economist and educator A. A. Manuilov, who became Minister of Education in the Provisional Government in 1917, wrote in 1905: "The peasants' access to books was hindered to the utmost by the authorities; lectures and talks in the village, even when dealing with strictly specialized subjects, actually met with almost insurmountable obstacles." [23] And, if one seeks further evidence of obstruction, one will find more than enough in the memoirs of such distinguished workers in the field of popular education as I. I. Petrunkevich and A. A. Kizevetter, the future leaders of the liberal Constitutional Democratic (Kadet) Party.

As a matter of fact, to teach even the three Rs without government permission, which was not easy to obtain, was a crime punishable by a fine from five to two hundred rubles and, in the western provinces, by a fine of three hundred rubles or imprisonment for three months. Another impressive manifestation of the hostile official attitude toward the spread of education was the order of Count Delianov, the Minister of National Enlightenment (ironically enough, the official title of the Ministry of Education), to the effect that servants' children (literally cooks' children— *kukharkiny deti*) were not wanted in the secondary schools. It is hardly surprising, therefore, that the masses were not considered fit to commune with the great treasures of Russian literature. When the centenary of Pushkin's birth was celebrated only seven works of the greatest Russian poet were permitted to be read publicly in the villages.[24] The whole situation at the turn of the century may be summed up in the words of N. A. Khomiakov, the future president of the conservative Third Duma: "Nine tenths of the Russian population is culturally backward—but why? Because the peasantry was treated merely as living implements of a large farm . . . converting agricultural products into cash needed by the national economy." [25]

Obviously, no scheme of special agricultural education could be built on a foundation of wholesale illiteracy, even if the government had been inclined to do so. In 1890, there were only forty-three agricultural schools of all categories, with a total of 2,715 students and a budget of less than 700,000 rubles. In the whole Russian Empire, with its great preponderance of agriculture, until the end of the nineteenth century there were only three agricultural colleges. Not until the first decade of the twentieth century was a significant step forward taken in agricultural education. Decades that could have been devoted to agricultural progress were lost by standing pat.

All of this should prepare the reader to expect little along the lines of organized agronomic aid, known in the United States as the extension service, which performs the vital function of teaching the farmer practically and informally the ways of agricultural improvement. An official publication of the Ministry of Agriculture gave this as one of the most important reasons for the backwardness of Russian agriculture: "Almost until the end of the past [nineteenth] century, the population had not received agronomic aid to any serious extent, either from the government or from the organs of local self-government, and was left in this respect entirely to its own devices." [26]

Spurred on by the famine of 1891, which drew public attention to the primitive techniques of peasant agriculture, the Ministry of Agriculture and Public Domain was created in 1894, replacing the former Ministry of Public Domain, of which the Department of Agriculture had been merely a branch.* But expenditures to aid agriculture (agronomic assistance, agricultural education, research) still remained insignificant. In 1895 they amounted to the paltry sum of 2.5 million rubles; and by 1900 they had increased to 3 million rubles; by 1903 they rose to slightly over 4 million and remained at this level until 1907, when a spurt in such

---

* The negative attitude of the top layer of the St. Petersburg bureaucracy toward agricultural problems and improvement was related by Count Lamzdorf, then an official of the Ministry of Foreign Affairs, which he later headed. He recorded in his diary for November 24, 1890, an account of a dinner conversation reported by a colleague, in which Minister of Interior Durnovo, Minister of Finance Vyshnegradskii, and Minister of Public Domain Ostrovskii opposed the rumored creation of a ministry of agriculture and even ridiculed the idea. Vyshnegradskii told what he replied to a visiting land-owner who argued for the pressing need to establish such a ministry: "But the Minister of Agriculture will not have anything to do." F. A. Rotshtein, ed., *Dnevnik V. N. Lamzdorfa, 1886–1890* (The Diary of V. N. Lamzdorf; Moscow, 1926), p. 350.

expenditures began.[27] The chief sufferer from this neglect was, of course, the peasant: the landlords, with their superior education and financial resources, either did not need outside assistance or could more easily obtain and pay for it than the poverty-stricken peasants.

The central government, however, was not alone in this field of what might be broadly termed public-welfare functions, but shared it with the local zemstvoes, which were organized in 1864 in most of the provinces of European Russia. In general, what has been said about the inadequacy of agronomic aid applies to the zemstvo as well, but with two important qualifications. First, there was considerable variation between the practices of the zemstvo in different provinces, depending upon leadership, tradition, and such. Second, the zemstvoes were not free agents, but subject to growing administrative interference from the central authorities, who were suspicious of the zemstvo's liberal tendencies.

An excellent example of the differences in attitude toward agronomic aid is provided by the varying experience of the Moscow and St. Petersburg provinces. The peasants there, and in general throughout north-central Russia, were suffering from a chronic shortage of animal feed, which affected adversely not only livestock but crop yields as well, because of a deficiency of the manure needed by the poor soil in these areas. This strained feed situation was, to a large extent, the consequence of a shortage of meadows and pastures in the holdings allotted to peasants upon emancipation, and was further aggravated by using such land for food crops.[28] The best way out of the difficulty was to introduce into rotation tame hay, which has the additional merit of being a good predecessor for grain and flax. In Moscow province, the zemstvo assisted the peasants along these lines with credit for seed and machinery and with technical advice, under the leadership of agronomists Bazhaev and Zubrilin. As a result, between 1892 and 1904, nearly a thousand villages introduced a crop-rotation system based on tame hay. Marked economic gains followed. Not only were the peasants able to gather considerable quantities of hay, but their grain yields doubled or trebled; flax also grew well on clover land, which led to the expansion of the acreage under this crop. On the other hand, in St. Petersburg province, where the zemstvo was inactive, only five villages adopted a crop-rotation system with tame hay in the course of 30 years.[29]

Thus, with proper aid, even illiterate peasants could be persuaded to adopt improved farm practices. But, as observers stated, the task of persuasion was not an easy one, for it was difficult for the peasants to change their traditional three-field cropping system and make what amounted to a leap in the dark. That they did take this risk proves that inertia, the obstacle to agricultural progress stressed by no less an authority on the agrarian question in prerevolutionary Russia than A. A. Kaufman, was by no means insuperable—a point with which Kaufman would have agreed.

And what of the leaders of the successful Moscow campaign to abolish hunger and want among the rural population? Were they honored and rewarded by the government? Quite the contrary. Zubrilin, the agronomist who was largely responsible for the introduction of the new rotation system, was dismissed from his post and arrested in 1906. Herein lies a tale of the frequent, vexatious meddling with the zemstvo, considered a "foreign body in the bureaucratic centralized system" of the Russian state.[30] D. N. Shipov, the president of the Moscow zemstvo in the 1890s, a recognized national leader in this field and a man of very moderate political views, compared the zemstvo to a steam engine working under unfavorable conditions, when most of the power generated is wasted in friction caused by bureaucratic interference and only a small part is used for productive work.[31]

Despite the fact that representation in the zemstvo was heavily loaded in favor of the landowning classes, especially after a new electoral law was enacted in 1890, these bodies were constantly suspected of subversive tendencies. Since liberalism was broadly interpreted in high government circles as any activity on behalf of the masses, be it purely educational or strictly for welfare, it was not difficult to level such accusations. The cardinal sin of the zemstvo in the eyes of the reactionary adherents of the autocratic regime was that, as a representative institution, it smacked too much of the hated constitutionalism to which it was considered a logical stepping stone by liberals and even by some conservatives (Witte, for instance, presented to the emperor, in 1897, a strong anti-zemstvo memorandum). And, true enough, the members of the zemstvo did play a leading role in the constitutional movement of 1904–05 and in the short-lived liberal Russian parliaments of 1906–07. Moreover, it was as a rule the liberals who, in the missionary spirit, took an active interest in zemstvo work. This was especially true of the appointed experts and technicians—teachers, statisticians, physicians, agronomists. In this manner, the upper-class bias which the suffrage law imparted to the zemstvo was largely offset, and useful work was accomplished. But much more would have been done if the central authorities had not interfered.

Enough has been said to indicate how difficult was the path of improvement of agricultural technology during the forty years following emancipation, and how little the peasant was assisted by the government. Under such conditions technical progress could not overcome the backwardness that was at the root of the agrarian crisis. This is not to say that progress was entirely lacking. As Kaufman and other students pointed out, the pressure of population on land was, in itself, a factor that compelled improvement in technology, albeit a slow one. Kaufman concluded that peasants who were relatively better provided with land often suffered even more severely from primitive techniques than farmers with smaller holdings, who were forced by circumstances to intensify their cultivation, to adopt, let us say, a three-field system instead of continuous cropping or to introduce tame hay into rotation.[32] Improvement of yields on peasant land was recorded on the basis of an analysis of the grain yields reported by the Central Statistical Committee between 1883 and 1915, which indicated an unmistakable upward trend.[33] That greater progress could have been achieved is evidenced, as Kaufman correctly states, by the fact that on privately owned land average grain yields increased more rapidly than on peasant land, or from 33 to 47 poods per desiatina between the 1860s and the 1890s—a rise of 42 percent.[34] The generally higher yields on private land were due partly to the fact that it was better land. But Kaufman was on shaky ground when he asserted, "In Russia there are likewise no insuperable obstacles to the raising of the productivity of the soil to the level which has been reached in the West." [35] Actually, there are serious climatic obstacles which, with the exception of a few areas, militate against the increase of crop yields to the high Western level: the short growing season in Russia and its large, dry (semiarid) land area.

Although some progress was achieved, the typical picture of nineteenth-century Russian agriculture is one of general backwardness, low crop yields, and agricultural underproduction, of frequent famines and growing destitution, concentration on small grains, and the plowing up of meadows and pastures for food crops, with a consequent shortage of forage and adverse effect on livestock. Yet this dark picture cannot be painted in a uniform hue for the country as a whole. Different shades have to be used—from the darkest for the overpopulated south-central area of European Russia and the dry eastern regions, to lighter shades for the more industrialized and urbanized humid regions of the north and west, where diversification of agriculture had begun—sugar beets, potatoes, flax, grasses.

The Need for Land

The peasant naturally saw the root of all his difficulties in the shortage of land, his only salvation in an increase of land. Under existing conditions it was the path of least resistance, for it was easier to continue the same type of farming over a larger area than to reorganize the system of farming. Psychologically, and historically, this ubiquitous tendency toward "spreading out" rather than "digging in" becomes intelligible when it is considered that Russia, unlike Western Europe, is a country of relatively recent settlement of its eastern and southern regions. "The history of Russia is a history of a country in the process of continuous colonization," said Kliuchevskii.[36] There is a certain resemblance here to the United States.

To the landowners and conservatives generally, the process of migration to new frontiers often indicated the "vagabond" tendencies of the Russian peasant. It was feared that, with the emancipation, there would develop a shortage of labor on the estates. These fears proved to be greatly exaggerated, even though there was a spontaneous rush of settlers into the southern and eastern steppes. The danger to the landowners arose, instead, not so much from the wanderlust of the peasant as from his desire to stay at home and have more land. The peasant did not have to go into the wilderness to see land that he could cultivate when right near his own narrow strips were the broad acres of "nobles' nests," which he or his father had tilled as serfs. How to lay his hands on this land, of which he considered himself unjustly deprived, became the haunting preoccupation of the Russian peasant.

One method was purchase from the landowner. Estate land, in fact, began to slip into the hands of the peasant shortly after the emancipation. In 1883, a special financial institution, the so-called Peasant Land Bank, was created by the government to facilitate the purchase of land by peasants. But the bank was not very active until near the end of the century, when a new charter broadened its operations. Still, with little in the way of government assistance, the peasants of European Russia acquired some 43 million acres of estate land in the course of the forty years following the end of their bondage. This area constituted 16 percent of the total privately owned land, according to the census of 1905, and was equivalent to an addition of 11.5 percent to the allotted peasant land.[37] But this was an expensive bargain for the peasants, because it led to the inflation of land values despite the decline of agricultural prices. For instance, the price of land purchased with the aid of the Peasant Bank more than doubled during the twenty-year period, 1883–1903. Small plots of land were especially expensive. Unless it was purchased by the whole community, then, buying land was out of reach of the poorer peasants, who needed it most.

Despite substantial purchases by the peasants, private landowners (including the imperial family) still owned, in 1905, an area of 240 million acres, or more than one third of the total area in farmland.* It was a

* Public domain land is not included. The great bulk of it was situated in the five northern provinces and was mostly under forest or not suitable for agriculture.

Table 3. Distribution of private land in 1905, exclusive of land owned by peasants in holdings of 135 acres and less [a]

Size of holding		Holdings		Area in private holdings	
Desiatinas	Acres	Number	Percent	Million acres	Percent
50 and under	135 and under	172,652	56.3	6.1	2.8
50–100	135–270	44,877	14.6	8.7	4.0
100–500	270–1,350	61,188	20.0	38.1	17.3
500–1,000	1,350–2,700	13,982	4.6	26.5	12.0
1,000–2,000	2,700–5,400	7,766	2.5	29.1	13.2
2,000–5,000	5,400–13,500	4,288	1.4	35.1	15.9
5,000–10,000	13,500–27,000	1,098	.4	20.5	9.3
Over 10,000	Over 27,000	699	.2	56.1	25.5
Total		306,550	100.0	220.2	100.0

[a] Exclusive of land owned by the imperial family.

Source. Tsentral'nyi Statisticheskii Komitet MVD. *Statistika zemlevladeniia 1905 g. Svod dannykh po 50-ti guberniiam Evropeiskoi Rossii* (Statistics of Agriculture for 1905. Collection of Data for 50 Provinces of European Russia; St. Petersburg, 1907).

highly concentrated form of landownership, making the contrast with the petty peasant holdings even more glaring. Of the enormous privately held estate area, more than 60 percent was in less than 14,000 large properties, exceeding 2,700 acres each.† (See Tables 3, 4, and 5.)

Much of this large area was not farmed by the owners, but leased to the peasants who cultivated it in small plots. According to various estimates made before the First World War, from over a third to more than 40 percent of the peasant households leased land, which constituted an addition of 20 to 30 percent to the total allotted peasant area.[38] In some districts leasing was even more widespread. For instance, in three districts of Moscow province, over 80 percent of small farmers leased land, according to an investigation that covered the years 1898–1900. In Moscow province as a whole, the leased land was equivalent to an addition of approximately one fourth to the total allotted area and about one half to the allotted holdings of the lessees. Meadow and pasture constituted 95 percent of the total leased land in that province, pinpointing the serious

† A comparison with Imperial Germany is instructive because much prominence has been given to the political influence of large landowners, particularly the Junkers. But, according to the German agricultural census of 1907, there were in the whole of Germany only 334 farms of 2,500 acres or more (1,000 hectares and over), and these properties accounted for less than 1,500,000 acres (exclusive of leased land) out of a total area of over 106 million acres of farmland.

Table 4. Distribution of allotted peasant land, 1905

Size of holding		Holdings		Area held	
Desiatinas	Acres	Number	Percent	Million acres	Percent
5 and under	14	2,857,650	25.3	24.4	6.6
5–8	14–22	3,317,601	29.4	58.6	15.8
8–20	22–54	3,807,044	33.8	154.5	41.8
20–50	54–135	1,062,504	9.4	83.4	22.6
Over 50	Over 135	232,556	2.1	48.6	13.2
Total		11,277,355	100.0	369.5	100.0

Source. Tsentral'nyi Statisticheskii Komitet MVD. *Statistika zemlevladeniia 1905 g. Svod dannykh po 50-ti guberniiam Evropeiskoi Rossii.*

shortage of this type of land among peasant holdings.[39] These estimates, even though they cannot claim great precision, establish beyond doubt the wide prevalence of leasing. But it must be emphasized that the leasing of land by the peasant was, as a rule, supplementary to his own holding. Whereas the Russian farmer was often part-tenant and part-owner, he was seldom a full tenant (like the Irish farmer) prior to the land reforms of the late nineteenth century.

A small porportion of allotted land was rented out mainly by those peasants who were not able to continue their own farming. Most of the

Table 5. Distribution of land in fifty provinces of European Russia, 1905

Type of property	Acres (millions)	Percent of total
Public domain	372.8	34.9
Imperial estates	21.2	2.0
Privately owned [a]	274.7	25.7
Allotted peasant	374.6	35.1
Other	23.7	2.3
Total	1067.0	100.0

[a] Including 154.5 million acres of land privately owned by peasants.

Source. Tsentral'nyi Statisticheskii Komitet MVD. *Statistika zemlevladeniia 1905 g. Svod dannykh po 50-ti guberniiam Evropeiskoi Rossii.*

leased area consisted of estate land. The availability of land for leasing primarily determined the variation in peasant (partial) tenancy from region to region. Thus, in the southwestern provinces, a region of intensive commercial estate farming with an important sugar-beet industry, the landowners preferred to cultivate their land rather than to lease it. Tenancy, therefore, was unimportant despite dense population and small peasant holdings. On the other hand, in the southeast, a region of extensive grain farming, leasing was common despite relatively sparse population and large peasant holdings. The densely populated central provinces were also characterized by small peasant holdings and extensive leasing of estate land.

That the Russian peasants were eager to lease land if it were available in their neighborhood, all students and observers agree, but there has been considerable difference of opinion as to the underlying reasons. Was leasing dictated solely by the insufficiency of the allotted holdings to provide subsistence and full employment for the peasant family—subsistence leasing? Or was it a method of concentration of land in the hands of the economically stronger peasants who were engaged not in subsistence farming but in commercial or, as the Russians would say, capitalistic agriculture? At the time, such students of the question as Kablukov, Manuilov, Kosinskii, and Bazhaev upheld the subsistence theory, while Karyshev and, especially, Lenin defended the opposite view. Thus the leasing question, as we shall see later, became part and parcel of the great controversy over the penetration of capitalism into agriculture which so agitated Russian public opinion. As often happens in such controversies, neither theory is completely right nor completely wrong. By studying a particular region and generalizing the results, either one of the two theories can be easily justified. An analysis of statistical data by N. N. Sukhanov has shown that the economic character of tenancy actually varied from region to region.[40]

In the sparsely settled regions of the east and south, where semicapitalistic farming was developing among the upper strata of the peasantry, the fact of commercial land leasing could not be ignored. But, in the central part of Russia, subsistence leasing prevailed. Lack of pasture and meadows, as was pointed out earlier, frequently made leasing necessary. There was also forced "mousetrap" leasing, caused by the highly inconvenient intermingling of peasant and estate lands. A legacy of serfdom, this intermingling, in the absence of leasing, made trespassing and damage by the peasants' cattle inevitable, for which the peasants were financially responsible. Many a landlord made a profitable business by renting out such mousetraps, often exacting in exchange labor services from the peasant.

The economic status of the peasant leaseholder strongly influenced the rents charged for the land. "The less land the peasant has, the smaller his holding, the poorer he is and the more he has to pay for [leasing of] the land," wrote M. I. Tugan-Baranovskii.[41] Smaller holdings usually created a strong demand for leased land in order to enable the peasant to make ends meet, and this led to rising rents. For instance, in the Riazan district of central Russia, peasants who had 1.5 to 3 desiatinas of their own allotted land paid 11.21 rubles per desiatina of leased land; those with holdings of 3 to 5 desiatinas paid 6.49 rubles and those possessing over 5 desiatinas only 5.77 rubles. In the Orel district, rents were higher in sections with poor soil and lower in those where the soils were more productive.

Much of the leasing, especially among the poorer peasants, was on a sharecropping basis; or the landlord was compensated by work on estate fields. Among the different types of tenancy, sharecropping was the most expensive to the peasants and most susceptible to abuses. Work tenancy, too, had a great disadvantage in that the peasant was forced to work for the landlord during the most valuable period of the rather short agricultural season, often to the neglect of his own crops. The fact that peasant leases were generally for a short term was disadvantageous because the highest rents were exacted for these leases. The rents went up considerably toward the end of the nineteenth century. Thus in Poltava province, for instance, the rents for land leased by peasants for subsistence purposes were 12.6 rubles per desiatina in 1900, compared with 8.6 rubles in 1890, or nearly one half greater. Rents for agricultural land leased for commercial purposes were lower and increased less during the same period—from 6.56 rubles per desiatina to 8.68 rubles, or less than one third.

That peasant leasing of land played a major role in the prerevolutionary agricultural economy should be clear even from this sketchy account. It was a link between peasant and landlord which profoundly affected the economic position of both. Leasing was made especially profitable for the landlord by the fierce competition among the peasants for land. Conversely, the alternative, that the landlord farm on his own account, was rendered unattractive by the low prices of agricultural products which characterized the last decades of the nineteenth century. If the peasant, as said above, was often part-owner and part-tenant, the landlord too was frequently operator, rent collector, and often rack-rent collector. Thus the leasing system provided ample material for all kinds of difficulties and irritations between the peasant and the landlord. At the same time, it deprived the primarily leasing type of estate of any progressive mission as *Kulturtraeger,* a spearhead of improved farm practices, which the proponents of the estate system often claimed in its justification and which was certainly true of some of the owner-operated estates. Kaufman, one of the ablest defenders of the progressive role of the estates, held that when estate land is merely leased to the needy rural population, the system "is not only one of the sharpest and most unjust methods of exploiting the labor of others, but it also has no justification from the standpoint of agricultural technique and productivity; and far from bringing any advantage, it is definitely harmful." [42]

While avidly leasing and, to a lesser extent, purchasing estate land, the Russian peasant continued to consider himself cheated and never ceased to dream of a new division of estate land (*chernyi peredel;* literally, black [peasant] repartition). For him, as always, only those who tilled it had a rightful claim to the land. This, of course, was well known to the Russian government, and it was a veritable nightmare. Consequently, "anything that could in the least remind the peasants of a supplementary allotment of land, not only at the expense of private estates, but even of public domain, was carefully avoided [by the government] as a harmful and dangerous principle." [43]

Still the idea of a supplementary allotment cropped up again and again in vague rumors that plagued the government. To put a stop to such rumors a special circular was issued on June 10, 1879, by Minister of Interior Makov, positively denying the possibility of supplementary land allotments and pledging inviolability of private property in land. But, according to some testimony, this had a reverse effect. [44] In any event, the rumors continued. Thus the governor of Pskov province stated, in his annual report for 1900: "The peasants, while not missing an opportunity to purchase land, at the same time cling to a vague expectation of some government measure that would allot land to the newborn generation. Every decree dealing with colonization, and every step taken in connection with the Peasant Bank, is interpreted by the peasants in this sense." [45] Although it was usually assumed that the signal for a *chernyi peredel* would be given by the tsar, the rumors were sometimes couched in religious terms and were associated with the expected triumph of justice on doomsday. [46]

"The fact of widespread conviction on the part of the peasants of the inevitability of a general redistribution is only too well attested," writes Alexandra Efimenko. [47] Many instances were recorded where peasants refused land offered to them on highly advantageous terms or, conversely, accepted onerous terms in the optimistic expectation of a general redistribution. Iakushkin, the author of a well-known bibliographical work on Russian customary law and a government official in Iaroslavl province, wrote in the 1870s that the rumor of a *chernyi peredel* spread with such force among the peasants of his province that, in spite of their strong desire to acquire land, they refused to buy even when it was offered to them at very cheap prices; and it took a great deal of effort to persuade those who came to him for advice that they should purchase the land.[48] To take another example, when a landlord in one of the Ukrainian provinces gave a piece of land to the peasants as a gift, they were heard to say: "See what a clever gentleman! He does not wait for the division but gives the land away himself." [49] The sense of grievance and resentment harbored by the peasants, because of the loss upon emancipation of part of the land they had tilled as serfs, was certainly not diminished when the peasants often had to lease the very land that had been taken away from them or their fathers. "In the consciousness of the folk," wrote Manuilov, "memories are alive of how the masters were slicing off the land that was formerly used by the peasants . . . Now, however, the peasants have to lease the very same plots at excessive rentals. What fertile ground for the idea that the landlords illegally own peasant land!" [50] Another observer pointed out that, because of memories of serfdom, "the moral significance of each estate desiatina many times exceeds its economic significance" in the eyes of the peasants.[51] The general attitude of the Russian peasant toward estate land can be well characterized as a refusal to recognize the right of the landlord to his property.

4

The Mir

Of cardinal importance in coloring the Russian peasant's outlook on the land problem, as well as the government's agrarian policy, was the institution of the mir, with its communal land tenure. The mir was a survival from the era of serfdom, preserved in no small measure by the emancipation legislation for fiscal and administrative reasons, and also because the architects of the reform, motivated by practical or ideological considerations, were against disturbing the prevailing land-tenure arrangements, at least as an immediate proposition. Consequently, in those regions where hereditary tenure prevailed, principally in the Ukraine, Belorussia, and Lithuania, it was continued undisturbed. Similarly, there was no interference with the mir's repartitional system, which was the predominant type of land tenure in the rest of Russia. Thus, according to the land census of 1905, the most extensive source of information on the subject, about four fifths of the allotted land of European Russia (exclusive of Congress Poland and Finland) was held under mir repartitional tenure, including communes that never practiced repartition; the rest of the land was in hereditary possession. Mir tenure also prevailed in Asiatic Russia, except for Turkestan (Central Asia) and Transcaucasia.

Upon emancipation, the mir became an object of intense controversy which did not cease until the Revolution of 1917. No other institution of Russian rural society was so much idealized or so much disparaged. None had so many friends and so many enemies in all political camps—conservative, liberal, and radical. The prolific writings by publicists and scholars in diverse fields (jurists, historians, sociologists, economists) attest to the tremendous interest the mir excited. Certainly Russian agrarian development betweeen emancipation and the collectivization of the 1930s cannot be adequately understood without a proper evaluation of the role of the mir.

Features and Origins

What were the essential characteristics of the mir system? First, the mir was a community consisting of former serfs, or state peasants and their descendants, settled as a rule in a single village, although sometimes a village included more than one mir and, conversely, several villages were sometimes combined in a single mir. Second, the title to the land was vested in the mir and not in the individual peasant. Members of the mir had a right to the allotment, on some uniform basis, of a holding that each member cultivated separately. As a rule, at the time of emancipation only families that participated in this original allotment of land were entitled to a holding. Such is the evidence of one of the earliest investigations of the mir under the joint auspices of the Imperial Free Economic Society and the Russian Geographic Society.[1] Even former soldiers who were in service in 1861, for instance, were not entitled to a holding in a district of the Riazan province.[2] From the same volume we read: "In general, it is difficult and expensive for a new member to enter the mir because there is a shortage of land and the mir is saving it for the future generations. Similarly, to leave the mir is quite difficult." [3]

Third, a holding could not be sold or bequeathed without the consent of the mir. A corollary to the right of a holding was the duty to accept it and bear the corresponding share of the tax obligation, even when this was disadvantageous. The peasant household held the homestead and usually the kitchen-garden plot attached to it (*usadebnyi uchastok*) in hereditary possession. (These are the well-known gardens with which we shall become better acquainted when we come to deal with collective farming.) There was, as a rule, a common pasture with shepherds hired by the whole mir and sometimes common meadows and hay cutting. There was usually a common crop-rotation system because of the scattered-strip system of holdings. With these exceptions, there was no joint or cooperative farming of the mir land as a unit, as in the modern kolkhoz, but only family peasant farming. This fundamental distinction cannot be overstressed, in view of the tendency in the West to picture the kolkhoz as a lineal descendant of the mir.

Fourth, as a consequence of its collective tenure, the mir had the power to repartition the land from time to time among its constituent households. Repartition, including in some cases leased land and arrangements for common cutting of hay and pasture use, as a rule formed the extent of agricultural functions and responsibilities of the mir, as distinguished from its administrative and fiscal functions. Not the mir but the peasant household was the actual farm unit. It owned or hired draft animals and implements, performed all the farm operations, cooperating on occasion with a few other households, and disposed of its produce on a free market, if it had anything to dispose of. The peasant household was also the actual unit of land allotment and had a voice through the head of the household in the governing body of the mir, the assembly. The mir, then, dealt primarily with the household and not with the individual.

The mir also had responsibility for the assessment and payment of taxes, including redemption payments for the land, under a system of unlimited liability of all its members. This was highly important because tax arrears were responsible for most of the intervention on the part of the mir in the affairs of individual households. To ensure payment, the mir could hire out a member of the defaulting household or could remove the head of the family, appointing in his place a different member of the household.[4]

Only a few words need to be said here about the genesis of the mir, which, like many other phases of the subject, was enveloped in controversy and partisanship in prerevolutionary Russia. While logically the question of origins might appear irrelevant to the burning issues of the nineteenth century, the fact is that both friends and enemies of the mir appealed to history to buttress their respective claims. Broadly speaking, there were two schools of thought. One saw in the mir a spontaneous or natural product of folk history, an institutional form either peculiar to the Slavic world or common in the early history of many peoples. The other school viewed the mir as essentially a late development, primarily a creation of the state and the serfowner, who used it as a fiscal weapon.

How these divergent historical conceptions were woven into debate on the mir is not difficult to see. If the mir has deep historical roots in folk history, this would *prima facie* strengthen its contemporary position; precisely the reverse would be true if the mir were merely an artificial body of recent growth, grafted from above onto the peasant world. The controversy on this point began in the 1850s, when the Russian intel-

ligentsia was still largely divided into two ideological camps: the Slavophiles, who idealized the mir as the embodiment of the traditional Russian folk spirit, and the Westerners, who regarded it as a state-made
product and an obstacle to the continued development of Russia on
European lines. It was in fact a Westerner, B. N. Chicherin, who coun-
tered the Slavophiles by propounding, in 1854, the state-fiscal theory of
the origin of the mir.[5] The challenge was picked up by the Slavophile
historican I. D. Beliaev, and the debate went merrily on.

A new page was turned at the beginning of the present century, when
the discussion was joined by A. A. Kaufman. He attacked the methodology hitherto employed, particularly the exclusive reliance on documentary historical evidence, on archives such as court cases. The farther one
delved into the past, the more meager were these documents, and by their
very nature they often did not reflect the normal state of affairs. Kaufman
proposed to enlist the aid of what he called the "living history" of the
mir: the rich ethnographic material gathered by investigators in the many
regions of Asiatic Russia where primitive conditions still held sway.

These data threw much light on the evolution of communal land
tenure, demonstrating that by far the most potent cause of repartitional
practices was the growing pressure of population on land. When population was sparse and land abundant, land was quite easy to come by.
Everyone could have as much as he could cultivate. But as population
increased and land became scarcer, "the original squatter type of tenure
became more and more irksome for the majority. As a result of insistent
pressure, a gradual transition to a regulated form of tenure took place,
assuming an increasingly egalitarian character, leading to the practice of
repartition." State or administrative interference was found to be a
secondary or accidental factor which could "only accelerate the natural
evolution but could not thrust undesired or strange institutions upon
peasant life." [6] It is also thought that in the more settled, older regions of
European Russia, the repartitional mir developed through a similar
natural evolution and not primarily because of administrative or fiscal
pressure, as was presumed by so many Russian scholars, from Chicherin
in the 1850s to Paul Miliukov in the early 1900s. But the problem has still
not been definitely settled.

The Populist View

The basis on which repartitions of land were made by the mir, and their
regularity or frequency, varied from region to region and from period to
period. Not all communes repartitioned their land at regular intervals

and some did not repartition at all, although the power to do so remained. But with the growing pressure of population on land, an increasing number made repartitions. One study of data for 6,830 communes in 66 districts of European Russia indicated that, whereas during the 1880s 65 percent had not repartitioned their land to any extent, during the period 1897–1902 only 12 percent failed to do so; 59 percent repartitioned largely on the basis of the number of males in a family, 8 percent on the basis of working adults, 19 percent on the combined basis, and 2 percent on only a partial basis.[7] The equitable adjustment of the burden of taxation to changes in population and other factors was a constant preoccupation of the mir, and from this fact stemmed much of its repartitional activity.

At first, after the emancipation, the government did not interfere with repartitions, leaving the question entirely to the discretion of the majority of the mir. However, with the changing agrarian policy under Alexander III and the increased realization that frequent repartitions were harmful to agriculture, a law was enacted in 1893 which required a two-thirds majority for a decision to repartition, fixed the minimum interval between repartitions at twelve years, and subjected them to strict administrative supervision. In general, the peasant family held the land, except for the homestead and the attached kitchen garden, only until the next repartition, when the holding was likely to change in size and location. If the land was given up for one reason or another by a member, it reverted back to the mir, which had the right to redistribute it. But the member still retained his right to an allotment. In other words, the peasant had a right to a holding but not to a particular holding, and he could not dispose of it freely.

In repartitions, the democratic spirit of the mir was strikingly manifested. Although the more prosperous peasants, the kulaks, usually exercised considerable influence on mir affairs, this was as a rule less true of repartitions that touched the general interest. Such, at any rate, was the testimony of peasants, elicited by the investigation of the Free Economic and Geographic societies referred to above.[8] The very decision of the mir to repartition usually marked the victory of the poorer elements of the village in what was often a prolonged controversy for a more equitable distribution of land.

Repartitions kept alive in the peasant's mind the idea of the egalitarian distribution of land in accordance with the dictates of rough primitive justice. But why should such egalitarianism stop at the artificial boundary line that divided allotted from estate lands? And it did not stop, for the peasant, unaccustomed to legalistic niceties, saw no reason for such a segregation. Repartitional mir tenure contributed to the peasants' conception that the property rights of the landlords were less than sacrosanct. The conservatives, strangely enough, were rather slow in grasping the revolutionary implications of this fact. To them, the mir embodied the quintessence of the old paternalistic traditions of Russian life and was a substitute of a kind for the tutelage formerly exercised over the peasants by their masters. They learned from August von Haxthausen, that Prussian aristocrat-scholar whose writings put the Russian mir on the intellectual map, that the mir was a means of safeguarding Russia against the "social plague"—the growth of a modern proletariat and its concomitant, the socialist movement. The mir, therefore, was not only idealized by the Slavophiles, who came closer to representing Tory democracy than any other group in Russia, but also gained favor in official circles where it was regarded as a guardian of the existing order.

But, as so often happens in the history of social thought, the opposite side, in this case the radicals, appropriated the idea and gave it a contrary twist. The fathers of Russian socialism, Herzen, Chernyshevskii, and Bakunin, viewed the mir, stripped of its police and fiscal functions, as the germ of socialism, which under favorable conditions could mature to full collectivist stature. Chernyshevskii, one of the earliest and ablest socialist defenders of the mir, believed that the introduction of farm machinery would facilitate the development of cooperative farming in the mir, replacing small individual peasant cultivation.[9] The more scholarly among the narodniks (populists) were willing to admit that the mir was a sort of Janus, with one face turned toward socialism and the other toward individualism. What direction it would finally take depended upon the future development of Russian economic life. The narodniks were banking on the putative embryonic socialism of this primitive peasant communism. They pinned their hope on the mir and the cooperatives of artisans, the artel, for the attainment of their socialist ideal.

What made this outlook so attractive to the narodniks was the belief that the mir and the artel would enable Russia to arrive at their socialist haven, skipping or by-passing capitalism and the painful effects of the industrial revolution. Capitalism was considered an inevitable step toward socialism according to the Marxist doctrine of economic evolution, and it was widely accepted by Western socialist thinkers. However, in the overwhelmingly agrarian circumstances of nineteenth-century Russia, where industrial capitalism was in its infancy and its future prospects were considered by the narodniks rather unpromising, an acceptance of the strict Marxist theory would have relegated socialist hopes to a remote future. The mir, as an incipient form of socialism, provided a way out of this dilemma. In modern parlance, it was a method of building socialism in a predominantly agricultural country without going through the process of capitalistic industrialization. Hence the enthusiasm of the early Russian socialists for the mir, even though they recognized many of its existing defects.

Now it is noteworthy that this attitude was, to some extent, shared by Karl Marx and his friend and collaborator Friedrich Engels. While in the preface to the first edition of *Capital,* Marx directs some shafts against Alexander Herzen and his "Russian communism" (the mir), he not only omitted the abusive passages in later editions but actually took up cudgels for the mir. With their growing popularity among the Russian intelligentsia and a closer study of Russian economic and social conditions, Marx and Engels seemed to have shed some of their early antipathy toward the mir.* Marx, in fact, defended it in a letter to his friend Kugelman, refuting the view that the mir caused the poverty of the Russian peasant. This argument he likened to one that sometimes attributes poverty to the abolition of serfdom instead of to the peasants' loss of their land. "The poverty of the Russian peasantry," wrote Marx in the letter, "was caused by the same factors that caused the poverty of the French peasantry at the time of Louis XIV—the taxation system of the country and payments in favor of large landowners. As far as the communal system of land tenure is concerned, not only did it not cause the suffering of the peasants but, on the contrary, it alone helped to alleviate hardships." [10]

Engels, however, preceded Marx in the public expression of a qualified approval of the mir, in his polemic with the Russian revolutionary leader, P. N. Tkachev, a mir enthusiast. Writing in 1874, Engels pointed out that, while the mir had passed its pinnacle and was apparently on the way to dissolution, nevertheless he envisaged the possibility of its transition to a "higher [socialist] form of economy . . . by-passing the intermediate stage of bourgeois small property. But this can take place only if there should occur in Western Europe, prior to the final disappearance of the mir system, a victorious proletarian revolution, which would provide the Russian peasants with the necessary conditions for such a transition, particularly the material means which they would need for a corresponding radical

---

* Marx was favorably impressed by the fact that the first foreign translation of *Das Kapital,* in 1872, appeared in the Russian language. Earlier, however, in a letter to Kugelman on October 17, 1868, Marx talked in unflattering terms about the "kindness" showered on him by the Russians whom, as he said, he had "continuously" attacked for twenty-five years and not only in German, but also in French and English. He pointed out that Russian aristocrats, who in their youth study in German universities and in Paris, like the French aristocrats of the eighteenth century, "always are grasping for the most extreme that the West can offer . . . This does not stop the Russians from becoming scoundrels as soon as they enter government service." "The Propaganda of Karl Marx's Works in Russia in the 1870s," *Krasnaia letopis',* 1:121 (January 1933).

change in their system of farming." [11] Engels' acceptance of the mir as a road to socialism in Russia was thus conditional on its ability to withstand the corroding influence of capitalism and on the occurrence of a revolution in the West. This revolution appears to be the *sine qua non* running like a red thread through Marx's and Engels' attitude toward the mir.

In 1877, the narodnik leader and sociologist N. K. Mikhailovskii wrote an article defending Marx against criticism leveled at his theories by another publicist, N. I. Zhukovskii. But, at the same time, he questioned the applicability of the Marxist evolutionary scheme to Russia. Marx responded by drafting a letter, which was not published until ten years later in a St. Petersburg law review, when he was no longer alive. Marx repudiated any claim to authorship of a universal theory of historical evolution. He wrote: "If Russia is striving to become a capitalist nation on the pattern of Western European countries—and during the last few years she harmed herself a great deal by doing so—she will not attain this without converting a large part of her peasantry into proletarians; and after that, once she is in the capitalist fold she will be subject to inexorable laws just the same as any other nation . . . If Russia continues on the same road on which she has traveled since 1861, she will lose the best opportunity that history has afforded a nation to escape all of the troubles of capitalism." [12]

Four years later, in the only public joint statement on the subject, from an introduction written especially for the Russian translation of the *Communist Manifesto,* Marx and Engels reiterated the proposition that the mir might serve as the starting point of socialist development, if a Russian revolution should give the signal for a working-class revolution in the West.[13] Perhaps the most important pronouncement of Marx on the mir, strangely enough, did not see the light of day for over forty years. In 1923, there was published for the first time an exchange of letters, which took place in 1881, between Marx and Vera Zasulich. She voiced great perplexity over the role of the mir in the light of Marx's teaching about economic evolution. Marx replied: "The analysis presented in the *Capital* throws no light on [gives nothing for or against] the question of the vitality of the Russian mir. Special research, which I undertook on the basis of original material, convinces me that the mir is the fulcrum of social regeneration of Russia [of Russian society]. But in order that it should function as such, it would be necessary, first of all, to remove the baneful influences which oppress it from all sides and then to secure for it conditions of independent development." [14] Marx spent much time drafting this letter. "He changed and revised it many times, so that while the actual letter runs to some forty lines, the various drafts run to more than nine hundred lines." [15] This hardly bespeaks easy confidence.

When Engels returned to the subject ten years later, he was much more pessimistic about the socialist prospects of the mir; but even then he did not dismiss it entirely. He wrote in a letter to Nikolai-on: "I am afraid that we shall soon have to look upon your mir as no more than a memory of the irrecoverable past, and that in the future we shall have to do with a capitalistic Russia. If this be so, a splendid chance will unquestionably have been lost." [16] We see, then, that even the founders of Marxist socialism gave their blessing to the mir—albeit a limited one, with reservations and serious qualifications. That it was a serious concession cannot be doubted in view of Marx's earlier remark concerning the Russian communism of Herzen and in view of his well-known antipeasant bias. It is all the more intriguing because it contrasts so sharply, as we shall see later, with the attitude of Marx's Russian pupils.

Was Marx sincere in his changed attitude toward the mir—was it really induced by more thorough study, by greater familiarity with Russian conditions, as he claimed? Or did he adopt it with tongue in cheek to placate his Russian followers? There is probably some truth in both views. It is likely that Marx was sufficiently impressed by the case made by Chernyshevskii, for whom he expressed great admiration, and by other narodnik defenders of the mir, not to reject it out of hand. He was also eager to encourage the Russian revolutionaries. Despite this, Marx was obviously unwilling to give the mir unqualified support. The narodniks, however, could derive considerable satisfaction from Marx's attitude.

While the radical narodniks and their even more numerous sympathizers were attracted to the mir through socialist messianism, it appealed to others for reasons more practical than ideological. The element of economic security in the mir particularly attracted many liberal Russian economists. Thus N. A. Kablukov wrote of the mir: "It facilitates more than any other form of land tenure, except the ownership of land by the state, the retention of land in the hands of the people tilling it." [17] A. A. Manuilov pointed out that under a communal system of land tenure the impoverishment of the peasantry could result only from the operation of "natural" laws, that is, from a disparity between the land and the number of people it must support. By contrast, when the system of land tenure bestows unlimited property rights on the owner of the land, a shortage of land may be due simply to the concentration of land ownership in the hands of a few; the surplus population is thus forced into the urban and rural proletariat. "It is against the development of this type of overpopulation that the communal form of land tenure acts as a guarantee; and in this consists its greatest significance from a social and economic point of view." [18]

The same idea underlies A. A. Chuprov's view of the mir as a form of mutual insurance for peasant families against the disadvantages of rapid population increase.[19] The chemist Mendeleev, who was deeply concerned with the economic progress of Russia, argued in favor of communal tenure. He thought that under certain conditions it might lead to the development of large-scale farming and to a considerable improvement in agricultural technique. He also foresaw the possibility of using the mir for establishing auxiliary rural industries.[20] Thus, for one reason or another, the mir found favor among the most diverse elements of public opinion: socialists, Slavophiles, liberals, and conservatives.

Opposition to the Mir

The mir was not without criticism and opposition. It began during the period of preparation for emancipation, in the 1850s, and stemmed from the small group of adherents to the Manchester school of economic thought. This group opposed the mir largely on ideological grounds and battled the socialists and Slavophiles in literary reviews, which had grown like mushrooms during the period. Among the chief spokesmen of the opposition were I. V. Vernadskii, who is remembered for a lively controversy with Chernyshevskii; Chicherin, who challenged the Slavophile view of the genesis of the mir; and the economist F. R. Terner. But this opposition to the mir on the basis of individualism did not attain any marked degree of popularity or success in the 1860s and, during the following two decades, became a minor discordant note in a general chorus of approval.

The signal for a new large-scale attack on the mir was given by the cleavage in Russian socialism in the 1880s, when one wing of the heretofore solid narodnik movement embraced the orthodox Marxist faith. A spirited controversy over the economic evolution of Russia developed between the Marxists and the older, peasant-oriented current of socialism (which traced its intellectual ancestry to Herzen, Chernyshevskii, and Bakunin).

The Russian Marxists, who founded their first party in 1882, the Association for the Freedom of Labor, rejected, despite the partial support of Marx himself, the current narodnik theories on the "peculiar" development of Russia and the possibility of by-passing the capitalist stage. They held that the traditional Marxist scheme of economic and social development was as applicable to Russia as it was to Germany, where industrialization revolution was also relatively recent. Perhaps what counted most with the Russian Marxists was that the development of capitalism and the concomitant growth of an industrial proletariat promised greater success in the struggle against autocracy than had been achieved by two decades of revolutionary narodnik activity. That movement, though imbued with populist ideals, nevertheless failed to win the support of the peasant masses and reached an impasse after the assassination of Alexander II in 1881. In any event, the Marxists were convinced that Russia was destined to follow the European road of economic and social development and could not escape the capitalist "purgatory." Far from lamenting, they rejoiced in this fact, just as the Westerners had thirty years earlier.

But the peasant mir, with its egalitarian tendencies and barriers to proletarianization, was a stumbling block to the Marxist scheme, since the latter postulated a continuous concentration of property and a polarization of the population into a capitalist class and a proletariat, in town and countryside alike. The Marxists solved this difficulty by their doctrine that the mir would disintegrate under the impact of the developing money economy. The first draft of a Social Democratic program, prepared by George Plekhanov and published by the Association for the Freedom of Labor, declared: "The patriarchal communal forms of peasant land tenure are rapidly being broken down, and the mir is being converted into a means of enslaving the peasant population to the State; in many places it also serves as an instrument of exploitation of the poor members of the mir by the rich. At the same time, by directing the interest of a large number of producers toward the soil, the mir hinders their mental and political development, confining their outlook to the narrow boundaries of village traditions." Thus the orthodox Russian followers of Marx and Engels rejected the much-heralded collectivist promise of the mir. Far from seeing in it the germ of socialism, the Marxists considered it an obsolete, decaying institution of small peasant farming, which could retard but not prevent the inevitable development of capitalism. Russia, they believed, was destined "to boil in the capitalistic caldron" before she was ready for socialism. Nor were they at all impressed by the egalitarian aspects of the mir, which appealed so strongly to many Russian intellectuals. At best, they saw the mir as providing equalization of poverty; more often, though, it acted merely as a screen to conceal the process of class stratification and exploitation of the poor by the rich. The rich peasants, the Marxists claimed, were concentrating the mir land in their hands by leasing the holdings of their poor neighbors, who were unable to cultivate them either because there were not enough workers in the family or because of a lack of horses and other equipment. Peasants in such straits sometimes hired themselves out to the lessors of their own holdings or found employment in the city. Some peasants were anxious to have their holdings (which they could not legally sell) taken off their hands just in order to be free of tax obligations.

The Marxist thesis with respect to the mir was developed over a period of fifteen years, beginning with the appearance in Geneva, in 1885, of Plekhanov's *Nashi raznoglasiia* (Our Controversies). He was followed by a galaxy of Marxist writers, including Peter Struve, the Russian-American economist I. M. Hourwich, Lenin, and others.[21] Needless to say, the narodniks did not remain passive, and a lively controversy developed,[22] reminiscent of the debates between the Westerners and the Slavophiles half a century earlier, and the disputes to come about industrial growth and agricultural collectivization, in the 1920s. Even though there was a certain tolerance exhibited by the government, since the 1860s, toward purely theoretical discussion of social and economic subjects, the controversy in the 1890s was a remarkable one for a country where political activity was taboo. It is "a most singular fact that in Russia the first able writers to point out the beneficent effects of capitalism and to study its history and the part it has played in the development of the country have been the followers of Karl Marx." [23] Perhaps the secret of the official toleration of the controversy may be traced to the ambivalence of government policy at this time. One may conjecture that a defense of capitalism was not unpalatable to the administration which, under the energetic leadership of Witte, was pushing industrialization with all the means at its disposal. On the other hand, since the government was strongly committed to the mir system of land tenure, the defense of it by narodnik writers was not objectionable either, so long as references to socialism were sufficiently veiled.

A detailed review of this ideological warfare, which wrote brilliant pages into the intellectual history of Russia, would take us too far afield. It suffices to point out that actual events belied both the pessimistic diagnosis of the narodniks for the prospects of capitalism and, to a lesser extent, the jeremiads of the Marxists against the mir. Industrial capitalism was developing rapidly during the last two decades of the nineteenth century. After an interruption during the early 1900s, owing to depression and political crisis, it continued its forward march until the First World War. On the other hand, the fact that the mir was not losing its vitality is attested to by the growing number of repartitions. It was a portent that the poorer peasants were gaining an upper hand in the inner struggles of the village community. This is at least a partial refutation of a rather common criticism that the mir was completely controlled by the rich peasants by means of usurious loans and vodka. Even more remarkable was the revival of the mir after the determined onslaught by the government during the decade preceding the Revolution—after 1917 it became the mechanism for new land distributions. The more objective narodniks recognized that often a mute struggle was taking place in the mir between, in the words of the writer Zlatovratskii, "a deep, organic, almost unconscious striving for solidarity, for equality, and common interests, on the one hand, and a heavy demoralizing arbitrary power and economic oppression on the other hand." Zlatovratskii, in common with other narodniks, stressed the vitality of the mir and the stubbornness with which the peasants strove to preserve the basic customs of communal organization.[24]

But the Marxists were precluded by their anticapitalist bias from acknowledging any wholesome elements in the peasant individualism that tried to force its way through in the mir. And because of their antipeasantism and rigid adherence to the doctrine of superiority of large-scale production in agriculture (at a time when serious cracks had been made in this doctrine in the West by the Revisionists), the Russian Marxists failed to appreciate the viability of small peasant farming, particularly during the pre-tractor age. The Marxists did perform a useful service in focusing attention on the economic, or class, differentiation in the Russian village, which existed despite the mir. But they failed to explain the process adequately, particularly by neglecting the demographic factor, that is, shifts in the composition and size of the family.[25] Larger holdings, which the Marxists considered a result of the invidious process of capitalistic development in the village, were often associated with larger peasant families, and vice versa. As a rule, the larger the family, the greater the number of workers. One or two extra workers meant that more land could be taken on from the mir or leased from fellow peasants or the neighboring estate. If a large peasant family were short of horses or farm equipment, it could dispense with some of its workers, who could seek employment in the cities and, with the extra money earned, purchase the needed livestock or tools. On the consumption side, too, the larger the number of mouths to be fed, the greater the incentive to increase the holding, which was the source of food, or to work it more intensively. Thus the growth of a family and, conversely, family divisions would tend to have an effect on the size of the farm, though this influence might be modified by a number of other factors (crop fluctuations, the existence or lack of subsidiary non-agricultural occupations, and so on). In any case, the resulting economic mobility and instability of Russian peasant farming militated against the existence of a Marxist type of class stratification in the village.[26]

Leaving the Marxist critique, what about an older and much more common criticism of the mir, that it was an obstacle to agricultural progress because of its scattered-strip system of farming? During the decade preceding the Revolution, this became one of the main charges in official indictments of the mir, though both in Russia and in other countries the strip system has also been associated with hereditary individualistic systems of land tenures. A brief description of strip farming may be useful here. The cultivated land of each peasant is not concentrated in one or a few tracts, as on an American farm, but is scattered in a number of narrow noncontiguous strips, intermingled with those of other peasants. This was instituted under the repartitional type of land tenure in order to equalize, without the help of modern land-surveying methods, the holding of each peasant in terms of the quantity and quality of land and its location in relation to the peasant's homestead. Thus, soil, topography, and distance from the village were all taken into account. The less uniform the various conditions, the greater the divisibility of holdings and the more numerous the number of strips.

In the non-black-soil belt, characterized by considerable diversity of soil conditions and landscape, with an abundance of forests, marshes, and lakes, the number of strips in the peasant holdings was very large. Holdings of a few acres sometimes were divided into one hundred or more separate strips. In the black-soil area, where the landscape and soil conditions are more uniform, the divisibility of the holdings was smaller. Other factors that tended to increase the divisibility of holdings were the scattered locations of the farmland of the mir as a whole and its irregular configuration—faults that had accompanied the original allotment of peasant land during emancipation. When the cultivated area of a mir was in a number of widely scattered tracts, it was customary to allot land to each member in every tract. For the more remote the field from the village, the greater the expenditure of time in reaching it and, therefore, the less advantageous its occupancy. Distant fields were usually not manured and, in general, were cultivated less intensively than those nearer the village.

Instrumental in the creation of very small strips was the practice of partial repartition, when only some of the holdings changed in size. The tendency toward partial redistribution was stimulated by heavy taxation, which often made the larger holdings more burdensome. Consequently, when the number of workers in a family decreased, it tried to get rid of the excess land. For its part, the mir was eager to allot land and the accompanying share of the fiscal burden to each peasant who reached working age. The result was frequent redistribution of land and increased subdivision of holdings, which "is not observed where the taxation burden is smaller and where the income from the land is higher." [27]

That the strip system has many evils is not open to doubt. The narrow strips make modern machine methods of cultivation impossible. Likewise, the use of pure and improved seed by an individual farmer is difficult because, with broadcast seeding, impure seed used by neighbors often finds its way into the strips of other farmers. Uniform crop rotation for all the farmers is practically a necessity, for it is inadvisable to plant one crop in one strip and another crop in the neighboring strip, since the result is likely to be a mixture of the two crops. It is also difficult to plant and harvest crops with varying growing periods and maturity on different strips in the same field. This is compounded by the fact that the stubble after harvesting is, as a rule, used as a common pasture. Thus the strip system greatly hinders the introduction by farmers of new or improved varieties of crops or rotation systems. Among other disadvantages must be mentioned the necessity of using land for boundary lines between strips and for roads or paths, which reduces the area of cultivated land. With the shortage of land often experienced by peasants, such wasteful use cannot be overlooked. Boundary lines are a fine breeding ground for weeds.

The greater the parceling of a holding and the smaller the average strip, the greater is the labor expenditure per unit of land—because of the waste of time and increased transportation requirements involved in moving from one strip to another during fieldwork. This is illustrated by an investigation by G. A. Studenskii of seventy-two farms in Penza province in central Russia (see Table 6). In agricultural economics, the input expenditure of labor and/or capital per unit of land is considered a criterion of the intensity of farming. But the data in Table 6 suggest that the use of such a criterion without qualification would be misleading in

Table 6. Labor input in man-labor days by soil regions, on seventy-two farms of Penza province

Strips (in desiatinas)	Man-labor days	
	Non-black-soil region	Black-soil region
Under 0.2	29.1	—
0.2–0.4	28.8	22.1
0.4–0.8	20.9	21.7
0.8–1.2	—	16.6
1.2 and over	—	12.6

Source. G. A. Studenskii, "Intensity and Pseudo-Intensity in Peasant Agriculture," *Trudy Samarskogo sel'skokhoziaistvennogo instituta* (Works of the Samara Agricultural Institute), IV (1927), 15.

the case of Russian peasant farming, because of its irrational territorial organization. Certainly the term "pseudo-intensity," suggested by Studenskii, fits much better the Russian system of scattered-strip farming.

Now the strip system, as pointed out earlier, is not peculiar to mir land tenure or to Russia before collectivization. It is characteristic also of the hereditary tenure that prevailed in the western part of Russia (in the Ukraine and Belorussia), and we meet it in the peasant agriculture of many other countries, even those so modern as twentieth-century France and southern Germany, where land tenure is entirely individualistic. In fact, many students of the problem—Posnikov, Manuilov, Oganovskii, and others—have argued that, under individualistic tenure, excessive scattering and divisibility of holdings is more difficult to correct than under the mir system, with its power of land redistribution. The proponents of the mir called attention to the fact that where conditions had become generally favorable for a transition to intensive farming, as in the more industrialized north-central provinces of European Russia, there was a movement among the land communes to reduce the number of strips, to widen them, and also to shift from the traditional three-field crop cycle to more intensive cropping methods.

Population growth, however, is the crux of this matter of the effectiveness of the mir. It is possible that, with a stationary or slowly growing population, a mir system of land tenure could be compatible with technical progress without any radical transformation. The holdings need not be too small or too scattered or too frequently repartitioned. But would not a rapid growth of population have the reverse effect and make intensification and technical progress much more difficult? It is all very well to talk about the economic security provided by the mir. But what if the right to land, by increasing subdivision, should be reduced to the right to starve on a plot that is insufficient to feed a peasant family? The further question arises whether mir tenure itself was a factor in stimulating rapid population growth. Some students of Russian agrarian conditions give a positive answer, especially for the black-soil area.[28] Even Chuprov, who was more sympathetic to the mir and did not hold it primarily responsible for the rapid population growth in nineteenth-century Russia, pointed out that this form of land tenure is grounded in the principle of "reproduce and multiply." "By eliminating the strongest check against the growth of population it is capable of producing an unfavorable effect" on the whole mir.[29]

But such qualms were alien to the Marxists, no less than to the narodniks or even to conservatives, none of whom had a trace of Malthusianism in their ideology. The Marxist opposition to the mir did not disturb the government's pro-mir policy. The scattered critics from the conservative and liberal camps were also voices crying in the wilderness. A policy favoring the mir seemed to be justified, from the government's standpoint, by the apparently placid temper of the peasantry in the face of acute distress and mounting land hunger. But all this was radically altered by the revolutionary storm that broke in 1905.

5

The First Agrarian Revolution and Stolypin's Reform

Despite his heritage of rebellion, the Russian peasant remained remarkably peaceful during the last third of the nineteenth century. Disturbances on a significant scale occurred only for a relatively short period immediately following the Emancipation Manifesto—when the peasants gave vent to their disappointment with the reform, sometimes caused by lack of understanding. There were more than 1100 outbreaks of disorder in the villages during the period 1861–1863, according to official statistics.[1] In a number of incidents military force had to be used, but only a few assumed serious proportions. Considering how poorly the manifesto and the complicated legislation were explained to the illiterate peasants, who had to continue serving their masters for two more years, it is surprising that there were not more disorders.[2] The government, prepared for much worse, was easily able to cope with the situation. The wave of disturbances soon spent itself, and the peasants began to make their adjustment to the new freedom.

The placidity of the peasants was not disturbed by the strongly pro-peasant narodnik movement of the 1870s and 1880s. The revolutionary intelligentsia found just as little support among the peasant masses as did its liberal precursors a half a century earlier, the Decembrists. This lack of support was as characteristic of the earlier nonviolent phase of the narodnik movement as it was of the later, violent phase. Goaded by government persecution into terrorist tactics, the narodnik revolutionaries of the People's Will Party succeeded in 1881 in their plot to assassinate Alexander II. It was widely believed by the peasants that the assassination was engineered by the landlords, whose vileness and conspiracies, they thought, prevented the tsar from doing right by his faithful peasant subjects.[3] Turgenev symbolized this attitude in one of his prose poems: when a revolutionary, "a friend of the people," is hanged, the people are chiefly interested in obtaining a piece of the rope for good luck.

Disillusionment with the failure of their revolutionary propaganda to arouse the peasant unquestionably contributed to the disappointed intellectuals' turn to orthodox Marxism and away from populism: Marxism was banking on the class-conscious industrial proletariat rather than on the mir and the muzhik. "The rural population," wrote Plekhanov, "living at present under backward social conditions, not only is less capable of conscious political initiative than the industrial worker, but is also less receptive to the movement originated by our revolutionary intelligentsia."[4] What was merely an act of faith of the Marxists in the early 1880s became, with quickened economic development, a reality in the late 1890s. Strikes of factory workers, particularly those in the summer of 1896 in St. Petersburg, marked the beginning of the Russian labor movement; the peasant still was not heard from. Were not the Marxists and the government both right in their conviction of the docility of the peasant? Events soon proved decisively otherwise. Research by Soviet scholars in recent years indicates that the peasant during the 1890s was not entirely placid. While there were no extensive waves of disturbances, such as occurred after the emancipation and again in the twentieth century, there were many local conflicts with landlords and the authorities in which the peasants used legal and illegal methods, including violence, to defend their interests.[5]

Revolt and Reform

The early years of the present century witnessed an increased belligerency in the peasant temper. In 1902, a wave of disturbances, directed against the landlords, swept through several Ukrainian provinces. These disturbances were suppressed by the government with considerable severity, and the number of violent manifestations of unrest declined in the next two years. But this was merely a lull before the storm. In 1905, following the unsuccessful war with Japan, revolutionary disturbances, which badly shook the Russian autocracy, spread from the cities to the countryside. During the years 1905–1907 there were recorded, altogether, over 7000 instances of peasant unrest, ranging from strikes and refusal to pay taxes to arson, appropriation of estate land, and other forms of violence and destruction.[6] Geographically, this agrarian revolution was concentrated in the black-soil area of European Russia, which accounted for three fourths of the total number of such incidents. It was especially strong in the central black-soil provinces, where the agrarian crisis was most acute. Though widespread, the peasant disturbances, as in the past, were local in character and lacked effective organization and leadership.

There is no doubt that the central objective of the uprisings was estate land. It is not too great an overstatement to say that the peasants "expected miracles" through an egalitarian distribution of land, in which they saw a "magic means" for the achievement of happiness and well-being.[7] How extensive was this much-coveted area? According to the land census of 1905, close to 200 million acres were owned in European Russia by nobles, the business and professional classes, the imperial family, and the clergy. The nobles had the largest slice of this area—144 million acres in 107,300 estate properties. Of these, 9,300 had more than 2,700 acres of land each, which accounted for 72 percent of the entire estate land of the nobility. About 25 percent of the land was in 13,200 estates, varying from 270 to 2,700 acres. But most of the estates (more than 60,000) had areas of less than 270 acres each, and 22,500 of these less than 27 acres. Yet even the smaller estates were capable of arousing the peasants' envy. Nearly 12 million peasant households had 375 million acres of allotted land and 66 million acres purchased from the nobility since emancipation, or altogether, in round figures, 440 million acres. Business corporations and various institutions owned 20 million acres of land, but probably little of it was available for distribution. This was also true of the public-domain land, most of which was concentrated in regions not suitable for agriculture. So the real reserve for further distribution in 1905–06 was mostly the privately owned 200 million acres, plus a little picked up from other categories of nonpeasant land. A much larger proportion of this area than of peasant land, by the way, was in forests. This was the land coveted by the peasants, and a considerable amount of it was already leased by them. There were many cogent arguments against further division, but the peasants responded only to force, which the government did not spare in the defense of the estateowners.

The peasant revolt in 1905 made land reform a burning political issue. The All-Russian Peasant Union, with provincial member associations, came into being and tried to serve as an articulate and organized spokesman for the peasantry in the political arena. The Peasant Union was launched by a congress which met secretly in Moscow on July 31 and August 1, 1905; it was attended by 100 delegates from 22 provinces.[8] It adopted a radical program of land reform strongly influenced by the Socialist Revolutionary Party, which, together with the liberal Union of Liberation (*Soiuz Osvobozhdeniia*), had helped to organize the Peasant Union. Another congress met, this time legally, in Moscow on November 6–10, 1905. The Union followed the example of some of the radical political parties in boycotting the elections to the First Duma in 1906, demanding the convocation of a constituent assembly. At the same time, the link between the Peasant Union and the liberals was dissolved. The Union participated in the elections to the Second Duma in 1907 and succeeded in electing a number of candidates. But the government had already started to take repressive measures, with arrests and prosecution of the Union's leadership in 1906. With the revolutionary squall dying down, the Peasant Union ceased to function after 1907, until the next revolution ten years later. Although the peasant deputies in the duma were scattered among a number of parties, those in the First and Second Dumas mostly joined the large labor group (*trudovaia gruppa*), which ideologically was a parliamentary narodnik organization attached to the principles of socialization of land and egalitarian repartition, patterned on the mir. There was also a small labor group in the generally conservative Third Duma (1907–1912) and the Fourth Duma. In the latter it was led by the lawyer Alexander Kerensky, who was to win world fame in 1917.

To the various socialist parties—narodnik as well as Marxist—which had long advocated the nationalization or socialization of all land, the peasant uprising was, of course, just so much grist for their mill and they became more insistent in their radical demands. The narodniks proclaimed the formula of "all land to all the people," with possession to be limited to holdings that could be cultivated by a family without resorting to hired labor. Land in excess of such a limit, a "labor norm" that varied for different regions, was to be confiscated and placed in a national reserve for distribution among those whose existing holdings were below the norm—this, too, was patterned on the familiar model of mir repartition. Since the right of each citizen to an allotment of land was postulated, the landless were also eligible. It is hardly necessary to comment on the unrealistic character of an almost unlimited distribution of so limited a resource as land. No doubt, popular misconceptions regarding the abundance of land in Russia, which did not take into account climatic limitations and the rapidly growing population, contributed to such quixotic ideas. Apart from its utopian aspect, the narodnik program of land distribution was attuned to the aspirations of small peasant farmers who were already on the land, particularly where mir land tenure prevailed. They did not understand or care for the subtle distinctions between socialization, nationalization, and municipalization; but they understood only too well how to divide estate land. This was confirmed by the experience of 1917.

The Marxists found themselves in a more difficult position than the narodniks, who had no qualms about small-scale production. For in 1901, before the Social Democratic Party split, Lenin set forth unequivocally the orthodox Marxist position on the agrarian question: "To attempt to save the peasantry, to protect small farmers and small propertyowners from the onslaught of capitalism, would mean a useless hindrance to social development and would fool the peasants by the illusion of a possibility of prosperity under capitalism." But when the revolt broke out in 1905, he changed his tone: "The duty of the rural proletariat and its ideologue, the social democrat, is to work with the peasant bourgeoisie against all elements of the feudal system and the feudal landlords, and then work with the urban proletariat against the peasant bourgeoisie and every other bourgeoisie." A short time later he returned to the same theme: "The party of the proletariat must support the peasant uprising. It will never defend the present estate system from the revolutionary onslaught of the peasants; but, at the same time, it will always strive to develop class struggle in the village." [9]

After the peasant disturbances began, the Bolshevik wing of the Social Democratic Party resolved at its Third Congress, in May 1905, to give "support to all revolutionary actions of the peasantry, including confiscation of private estates, government, church, monastery, and crown lands." This vague pronouncement was elaborated at the Fourth Congress of the party in April 1906, which united the Bolshevik and Menshevik factions. It demanded, in addition to the confiscation of land, equal rights for peasants vis-à-vis the rest of the population, as well as a transfer of the confiscated land to the democratically elected organs of local self-government—a municipalization of land. Should this proposal fail, the party declared, there should be "division among the peasants of estate land on which small farming is actually carried on or which is necessary to round out the holdings of small farmers." However, the declaration included a strong reservation, stressing the conflicting interests of the rural proletariat and the peasant bourgeoisie; favoring the independent class organization of the agricultural proletariat; warning against the inefficacy of small-scale farming in lifting the peasant masses out of their poverty; and insisting that only socialism could do away completely with poverty and exploitation.[10]

Lenin's proposal at the 1906 congress did not differ in spirit from the agrarian plank finally adopted, except that he was opposed to municipalization as a form of nationalization and did not favor the division of estate land among the small holders. A division, he was reported to have said, though not harmful, would be a mistake since it did not take into account the future, that is, the changeover from a "bourgeois-democratic" to a full-fledged socialist revolution. It is significant that Lenin had no such misgivings in 1917, when in his climb to power he needed the peasants' support or, at least, their neutrality.

The proposed liberal solution to the agrarian question during the period 1905–1907 was probably of greater practical significance than the socialist solution, for liberalism then represented a more likely alternative to the tsarist regime. After all, even the Bolsheviks, as their draft resolution at the 1906 congress showed, did not aim beyond a democratic republic in their political demands. It is not surprising, then, that the solution proposed by the liberals differed only in degree from the radical proposals. The liberals, represented in the main by the Constitutional Democratic Party, became convinced that the coexistence of large estates and small peasant farmers—an uneasy situation since emancipation—was no longer tenable. They believed that only by distributing most of the estate land among the peasants, particularly the land leased by them, could the violent agrarian unrest that endangered the whole Russian state be allayed. The liberals, therefore, also strongly advocated distribution of estate land among those peasants who were most in need. They based their proposals not on rejection of the institution of private property, but on the legal principle of eminent domain, which permits compulsory acquisition of private property by the state, with fair compensation to the owners, when this is dictated by the public interest. The emancipation legislation of 1861 was cited as a precedent in this connection. On the economic side, the liberal attitude found support in the assumed unprogressive character of Russian estate farming outside of the western provinces. The indictment was that many a landlord found it more profitable to lease land to the peasants at high rents, or at best to employ nearby peasants to work the land with their own implements and horses, rather than to farm on his own.

Thus the consensus in liberal circles was that since Russian estate farming, for the most part, was no *Kulturtraeger,* the socioeconomic losses suffered through its disappearance would not be serious. And where important losses would occur, exceptions could be made. This is certainly a debatable economic argument, but it was the revolutionary emergency and not economic considerations that made the reform urgent in the eyes of the liberals. As Herzenstein, the principal and most persuasive spokesman on the subject for the Cadet Party in the First Duma, put it, "Now we have a conflagration and it must be extinguished. Only an increase in the [peasant] land area can extinguish it." [11]

Bills for distribution of estate land were introduced by liberals and socialists in the First and Second Dumas, in 1906 and 1907. The liberal proposals for land reform, unlike the socialist schemes for outright confiscation, involved fair compensation to owners of the estate land that was to be distributed. Such compensation was to be borne partly by the state, partly by the recipient of the new land allotments. The reform proposals also provided for exemptions and safeguards when land distribution would tend to affect production adversely, as, for instance, in cases of valuable industrial crops like sugar beets, grown primarily on estates. Land purchased by the peasants after emancipation in small plots from the landlords and held in fee simple, as distinguished from allotted land, was also to be exempt from distribution. Although there were differences of opinion among liberal reformers regarding the form of ownership of the distributed land, there was no question about the continuation of individual family farming on this land.

Moderate advocates of land reform realized that distribution of the estates was no panacea for Russia's agrarian ills, but only a first step in the solution of the problem. To conservative opponents, who claimed that division of estate land would be a palliative rather than a cure, the economist Kaufman replied that when a seriously ill patient is suffering from a high fever it is essential, first of all, to break the fever before further therapy can be administered.[12] This is precisely what the liberal proponents of land reform sought to accomplish in 1905–07. They fully recognized, as the writings and speeches of Kaufman, Herzenstein, and other experts and leaders demonstrated, that land redistribution must be accompanied by an all-out effort to increase production by raising the technological level of peasant agriculture, through education and through technical and credit assistance. The reformers may have been overoptimistic on what actually could be accomplished. Perhaps they were too strongly influenced by the example of intensive peasant agriculture in Western Europe. Possibly, with the advent of the tractor still several decades in the future, they were not sufficiently alive to the advantages of large-scale farming on the vast Russian steppes. But they rightly criticized the government for doing nothing or very little to improve peasant farming and, at the same time, advocating increased production as an alternative to land reform.

Even the government itself, when the revolutionary disturbances were at their height, toyed with the idea of land reform based on the distribution of estate properties. A bill [13] to this effect was drafted in the winter of 1905–06 by N. N. Kutler, Minister of Agriculture in Witte's cabinet.* But by the spring of 1906, the government felt that it was riding out the revolutionary storm, and even moderate proposals for land reform became unacceptable. Once it had a firm grip on the situation, the government adamantly turned its back on the division of estates. This position was made clear by the new Prime Minister, I. L. Goremykin (who replaced Witte in April 1906), in response to an address to the throne, submitted by the First Duma in May 1906. It was restated in the parliamentary speeches of other members of the administration and in a special government communiqué of June 19, 1906.[14]

The tsarist government succeeded in crushing the revolution in 1906, and the estates were saved for their owners for another decade. Herzenstein, who championed the peasants' interests in the First Duma, was slain by the rightist Black Hundreds. There were to be no land reforms of a liberal-democratic character. Similarly—and this is highly important—there was to be no genuine representative constitutional government in Russia. The experience of the first two short-lived parliaments, dissolved by the tsar, proved conclusively that such a government would be deeply committed to the kind of land reform that was anathema to tsarism. So the government, now under Stolypin, staged a coup by changing the election law on June 3, 1907, which succeeded in producing an obedient duma.

Because of the strong link between land reform and constitutionalism, it may be argued with excellent reason that Russia's failure to adopt the reform precluded the emergence of a constitutional government. This had fateful repercussions not only in Russia, but far beyond its borders. I think it is not farfetched to speculate that the history of this century would have been vastly different if, by 1914, Russia had emerged from the turbulence of the early 1900s as an agrarian and political democracy; and it could not become one without becoming the other. It might have proved much stronger in the encounter with imperial Germany, and the world might have been spared Bolshevism.

Stolypin's Legislation

The tsarist government did not stop with physical suppression of the revolution and rejection of the liberal scheme for agrarian reform. Its new head, P. A. Stolypin (July 1906–September 1911), who replaced the

* After his dismissal from the government, early in 1906, Kutler joined the Cadet Party and became one of its leading authorities on the agrarian question, replacing Herzenstein, who was murdered by rightist terrorists.

mediocre and reactionary Goremykin, realized that some alternative to the distribution of estate land was essential. Furthermore, a bulwark must be erected against another revolution in the village, and new allies must be found there. The government also became conscious of the importance of fostering technical progress in Russian agriculture. It was hoped in official circles that these objectives would be accomplished by encouraging the development of a class of independent peasant proprietors, who would be attached to the principles of private property and would act as a buffer between the estateowners and the mass of small peasant farmers. Stolypin aptly characterized this policy of agrarian individualism as a "wager" on the strong peasants at the expense of the weaker ones. To this end, his administration and that of his successor, V. N. Kokovtsev, along with the able Minister of Agriculture A. V. Krivoshein, dedicated their energies during the interlude between the 1905 Revolution and the First World War. And, since the chief obstacle to the development envisaged by Stolypin appeared to be the mir, communal land tenure had to go.

This decision was also strongly influenced by the government's disappointment in the mir after the events of 1905. Disillusion set in among the influential conservatives, who had considered the mir the essential part of that patriarchal system which was to save Russia from the "Western disease" of proletarianization and social unrest. But the mir had not prevented an agrarian revolution in 1905. In fact, some conservatives began to blame the mir for the peasant uprising, which, however, was by no means confined to the regions with communal land tenure. Another evil, now even more often attributed to the mir system, was strip farming, the fragmentation of holdings. The measures to abolish communal land tenure were technically justified on the grounds that they were required by the cancellation of land-redemption payments beginning in 1907, in accordance with a manifesto of November 3, 1905. But this was a formal reason. Actually, the government wanted to reverse its mir policy as a result of the disturbances of 1905. The dissolution of the mir and the individualization of peasant land ownership became the leading objectives of agrarian policy.

There were individuals in the ranks of the bureaucracy—such as Count Vorontsov-Dashkov, Minister of the Imperial Household and later viceroy of the Caucasus,[15] or V. I. Gurko, an influential official of the Ministry of Interior—who had long favored the abolition of the mir. The change in the government's attitude really began early in 1906, during the administration of Count Witte. The matter went so far as a bill, substantially similar to that enacted later in the year under the Stolypin administration, which was drafted in the spring of 1906. But its enactment was deferred because of the approaching convocation of the First Duma.[16] Commissions for local land organization (*zemleustroitel'nye komissii*), which were destined to become the principal instrument in carrying out Stolypin's land program, were established by a decree of March 4, 1906.

An attempt to revive the proposal against mir tenure was made during the Goremykin administration, in the days of the First Duma. Gurko, one of the architects of the new legislation, claimed: "I tried to persuade the Council of Ministers to present to the [First] Duma the project of a statute allowing the peasants freely to leave their communes, a project which had been rejected by the State Council of the Empire for formal reasons during Witte's ministry. But Goremykin took a definite stand against it. Stolypin did not utter a word in its defense, and it was again rejected."[17] After Stolypin became head of government, coincidentally with the dissolution of the First Duma, far-reaching changes in land-tenure law were put into operation, as an emergency measure, by an imperial decree of November 9, 1906. Several years later, the measure was approved by small majorities of both chambers of the Duma and became a full-fledged law on June 14, 1910.

According to the new land legislation, any member of the mir could demand that the title to his allotted holding (heretofore legally owned by the mir) be transferred to him and that the scattered strips of arable land be consolidated into one plot. Whether the holding was to be consolidated or to remain scattered, the land became the hereditary personal property in fee simple, with some restrictions, of the peasant and was not subject to further repartition. The common tenure in meadows and pastures was, as a rule, retained by those who "separated" themselves from the mir. The communes that had had no repartition since the land was allotted to them were declared dissolved without their consent (if the allotment had taken place prior to 1887), and the holdings became the personal property of those occupying them. The mir also could abandon communal land tenure by a two-thirds-majority vote. If the amount of land held by a peasant withdrawing from the mir exceeded that to which he would be legally entitled if a new repartition had taken place, he could retain the additional land by paying the mir the "redemption" price, instead of the usually much higher market price. This last provision was criticized by opponents of the legislation in and out of the duma, as giving the individual an undue advantage over the mir; but in itself it does not seem to be particularly unreasonable. A more important target of criticism was that a small minority could break up or seriously hamper the communal system of landholding by requiring a separate allotment of land, which would make general repartition extremely difficult or even impossible. The mir system was thus at the mercy of a small group, and its hostile action was being encouraged by the authorities.

Another serious break with tradition was the provision in the new legislation that, under individual tenure, the holding belonged exclusively to the head of the household. Formerly the arable land was legally allotted by the mir to the household as a whole, until the next repartition, and the land under buildings and the kitchen garden was a hereditary possession of the whole household. Now the head of the household became the owner of all the land. Thus the new individualism of the government's agrarian policy attacked, in one sweep, the communal and the household (family) property system.

Yet certain restrictions were preserved with respect to the peasants' allotted land. It could not be mortgaged to any private individual or institution and could be sold only to another peasant. Moreover, a limit was placed on the amount of such allotted land which any one peasant might purchase in a particular district. The inheritance of allotted land was still governed by local peasant custom and not by the general law on real property.

With the enactment of the new legislation and with little hope left for the division of the estates, peasants in large numbers began to take advantage of the right of withdrawal from the mir and conversion from repartitional to individual hereditary tenures. Certainly those who stood to lose from the next repartition, as well as households desiring to sell their holdings in order to migrate to Siberia or to the industrial centers, swelled the number of applicants petitioning for withdrawal. The movement for conversion from communal to hereditary tenure reached its peak in 1908, as will be seen from the following tabulation.[18]

Year	Households petitioning for conversion (thousands)	Households securing conversion titles (thousands)
1907	211.9	48.3
1908	840.1	508.3
1909	649.9	579.4
1910	341.9	342.2
1911	242.3	145.6
1912	152.4	122.3
1913	160.3	134.6
1914	120.3	97.9
1915	36.5	29.9
	2,775.6	2,008.4

In addition to the above figure of around 2 million, there were 469,800 households that secured titles because their communes never repartitioned land after the emancipation.[19] There were also, according to incomplete data, 140,000 peasant households whose tenure became hereditary because their communes exercised the right to dissolve by a two-thirds vote.[20] Adding all these categories, we obtain in round numbers 2.6 million households that legally changed their tenure from communal to hereditary during the years 1907–1915, with documented confirmation of the titles. There was also an additional large number of uncertain cases of tenure among households in nonrepartitioning communes which did not apply for confirmation of their titles. Leaving them aside and counting only the 2.6 million about which there can be no doubt, we have a number of peasant households with new hereditary tenure almost equal to the communal number recorded in the 1905 census—2.8 million out of a total of nearly 12 million households in European Russia. Assuming normal increases, it would appear that the number of peasant households with hereditary tenure by 1916 was no less than 40 percent of the total, about 15 million households, and even larger if the considerable number of cases of uncertain tenure status is added. The sharp downward trend after 1909, shown by the above tabulation, combined with results of some special investigations, tends to support the thesis of N. P. Oganovskii and others that, in the main, two groups sought conversion of tenure: those who were severing their ties with farming, at least in a particular locality, and the more prosperous peasants, who managed to hold on to more than their due share of land. The hard core of "middle" peasants was apparently little affected by the process.[21] This did not augur well for a speedy end to the mir.

That the rapid changes in land tenure, spearheaded by zealous officials, produced considerable friction in the rural population was not unwelcome to the government. The divisive effect of the new land legislation, the breaking down of the united front in the village which was hostile to both landlord and state, fitted in with what Stolypin sought to accomplish. As he himself admitted, the new legislation was not concerned with the poorer strata of the peasantry: "What is mainly necessary when we are passing a law for the whole nation is to have in mind the sensible and the strong and not the drunkards and the weak . . . [The government] has wagered not on the weak and the drunkards but on the strong and powerful . . . It is impossible, gentlemen, to enact a law having in mind exclusively the weak and the feeble." [22] It is, on the whole, an apt characterization of the new anti-mir legislation by its principal sponsor.

This method of breaking down the communal system was resented and strongly opposed in liberal and radical circles, even by those who were not generally proponents of the mir. Miliukov epitomized the liberal assessment of the Stolypin land reform as follows: "Stolypin proposed his own landlord-tainted reform in opposition to those democratic proposals which led to the dissolution of the first two Russian parliaments. The Stolypin reform tried to divert peasants from the division of the land of the nobles by the division of their own land for the benefit of the most prosperous part of the peasantry." [23] It was also argued that far too much stress was put on the system of land tenure as a factor in agricultural progress, that "it is not the mir system of land tenure which handicaps agriculture but the deficient input of capital and labor in farming which helps to preserve mir land tenure. In other words, the mir is not a cause but a symptom of the economic backwardness of peasant farming." [24] Lenin, on the other hand, did not share the sentiments common to most of the liberal and radical opposition, and welcomed the breakdown of what he called the "old medieval system of land tenure." He wrote in 1912: "The most reactionary are those Cadets from the [newspapers] *Rech'* and *Russkie vedomosti* who reproach Stolypin for the breakup [of the mir] instead of demonstrating the necessity for an even more consistent and decisive breakup." [25]

The evaluation of Stolypin's anti-mir legislation was bound to be strongly influenced by ideological and political preconceptions. Certainly the economic benefits per se are debatable. Uncontestable, however, is the fact that the mere transition from communal to private peasant ownership did not eliminate the evil of strip farming and did not lead to that physical segregation of holdings which is the essence of individualistic agriculture. The legislation of 1906 and 1910 regarding the mir was severely criticized precisely on this score—for instance, on March 24, 1910, by V. I. Sergeevich, the noted legal historian and rather conservative member of the Council of Empire. But the administration had not neglected the problem of consolidation, dealing with it not only in the original decree of 1906 but by a special law passed on May 29, 1911, aiming to encourage the process. The task was assigned to special land-organization commissions and, particularly after 1911, considerable progress was made. Thus, during the four years 1907–1910, some 321,500 consolidated holdings were formed, and in 1911–1914 the number more than doubled, to 726,148.[26] Two general types of consolidated holdings were developed: the *otrub,* in which the separate strips were consolidated into larger fields in a single tract of land, but with the peasant family continuing to live in its former dwelling in the village; and the *khutor* or segregated farm, including a farmhouse and involving a complete resettlement of the peasant household. Since the khutor type of holding meant the most complete individualization of peasant farming, it was highly favored by the tsarist government and later became an object of hostility of the Soviet government. In the official zeal to promote this type of land tenure, little regard was paid to its suitability in a particular region, such as the availability of water in the treeless steppes, the right kind of land to provide a balanced holding (especially meadows and pasture land), and adequate roads.

None of this should detract from the great value of the consolidation program in gradually eliminating the inefficient strip system. The progress made during the decade preceding the Revolution of 1917 was impressive. Consolidation of scattered-strip holdings was particularly marked, exceeding the national averages in two diverse regions: the northwest, where intensification and commercialization of peasant farming was making headway; and the south and southeast, the areas of commercial grain production. For forty-seven provinces of European Russia, new consolidated holdings of one type or another, organized with government assistance, comprised about 10 percent of the peasant holdings, with an area of over 34,000,000 acres of allotted land and over 43,000,000 acres when purchased land is included.[27] To these must be added an unknown number of old segregated holdings, mainly khutors, in the western part of Russia, which existed prior to 1906 or were organized without government assistance.[28]

Other Reforms and Changes

Perhaps no less important from the standpoint of agricultural progress was the increased attention paid by the central government and the zemstvos to agronomic assistance through the organization of new experimental stations and agricultural schools and through financial aid in acquiring modern implements and seed. Increased appropriations for these purposes constitute a good index. Such appropriations for the Ministry of Agriculture increased from 15.3 million rubles during the period 1898–1902 to 20.9 million in 1903–1907, and to 58.7 million in 1908–1912. Similar expenditures of the zemstvo, which in 1900 amounted to only around 2.3 million rubles, increased by 1912 to 13.1 million. In addition, a zemstvo loan fund established for these purposes was increased from 4.1 million rubles in 1900 to 20.5 million in 1910.[29] Also highly important was the new spirit that animated this work and the interest manifested by the peasant farmers.

Steps were also taken to improve the legal status of the peasantry. The vexatious mutual responsibility for tax payments was abolished in 1903. Some of the other legal disabilities which segregated the peasantry into a special class in the body politic were removed by a decree of October 5, 1906. Particularly important was the liberalization of passport regulations. The veto power of the mir and the head of the peasant household over the issuance of passports was abandoned, and the status of the peasants was made equal to that of the rest of the citizenry. The rural chiefs were deprived of the disciplinary power over the peasants with which they were endowed by the law of 1889 and retained it only with respect to elected peasant officials.[30] A fairly wide peasant representation in the duma was effected in 1906, in the curious expectation that the peasant deputies would play a conservative role. Precisely the opposite happened in the first two dumas, as we have seen, with respect to the land question. Peasant parliamentary representation was, therefore, seriously curtailed by a reactionary law of June 3, 1907.

Rural migration from regions of dense population to sparsely settled areas, which was officially discouraged after emancipation, was now strongly encouraged and aided by the government. The disappointment of the peasants with the abortive revolution of 1905 spurred this resettlement movement, and the possibility of selling the allotted land, prohibited prior to the Stolypin legislation, helped to pave the way. But even with the best intentions and the willingness of all concerned, large-scale migration to Asiatic Russia would hardly have been possible without the extensive railroad construction started at the end of the nineteenth century; at the beginning of this century, the Trans-Siberian railway and the Orenburg-Tashkent railway, connecting European Russia with Central Asia and Turkestan, were completed. The total number migrating into Asiatic Russia from 1896 to 1905, which included the two years of the Russo-Japanese War, amounted to less than 1.4 million. It reached nearly 2.3 million during the four years 1906–1909. During the next four years, the migratory movement declined to less than 1.2 million and became a mere trickle during the First World War.[31] The decline after 1909 may be attributed, at least in part, to the improvement that was taking place on the agrarian scene—an improvement to which the earlier large-scale resettlement had undoubtedly contributed. The role of migration in draining off surplus population will be best appreciated when it is remembered that it most affected precisely those densely populated areas and those strata of the rural population which experienced the shortage of land most acutely. The average landholding of families migrating to Asiatic Russia was only ten acres before migration, as against an average of thirty acres for all peasant holdings in European Russia, according to the census of 1905.[32]

A correlative aspect of the resettlement movement was its tremendous influence on the agricultural development of the "great open spaces" of

Asiatic Russia. Thus the crop area of western and central Siberia and northern Kazakhstan, for which continuous statistical data are available, more than doubled between 1905 and 1914, increasing from 11.5 million acres to 24 million acres.[33] Moreover, the productivity of peasant labor was higher in the new regions, with a consequent favorable effect on the whole national economy.[34]

The peasants not only were helped to acquire new land beyond the Urals, but also were avidly purchasing estate land in European Russia. After the events of 1905–06, the landlords no longer felt safe and for a price were willing to part with their land. Although they had voluntarily begun to dispose of their land soon after emancipation, the process was greatly accelerated after 1905 with the aid of the Peasant Land Bank, established by the government in 1882 and expanded in 1905–06. The additional land, however, was acquired by peasants at a stiff price. Thus the value of land purchased through the Peasant Bank, the main source of such operations, increased from an average of 71 rubles in 1895–1905 to 131 rubles in 1906–1915,[35] making purchases by poor peasants more difficult. The strong preference given by the Peasant Bank to purchases of individuals over collective purchases by the mir or associations specially formed for the purpose also tended to discourage buying by poor peasants. Another factor slowing down the acquisition of land by peasants was the insistence by the bank on segregation of holdings, preferably in the khutor form, as a prerequisite for its financing of transactions.

Transfer of the estate land to less needy peasants through voluntary purchase, arranged by the Peasant Bank, was therefore not considered a satisfactory solution by the proponents of liberal agrarian reform. "The activity of the Peasant Bank," said N. N. Kutler during the debate on the agrarian question in the Second Duma in 1907, "inevitably leads to an excessive rise in the sale price of land . . . Furthermore, the Peasant Bank does not accomplish its purpose because it transfers the land not to those who need it, but to those who could well get along without it." [36] This judgment, however, cannot be accepted without reservations. It seems quite likely that the bank's purchases of estate land tended to raise land prices higher than they otherwise would have been, especially in the years of revolutionary disturbances when the landlords were anxious to get rid of the estates. But the interest rate on loans to peasants was lower than what the bank paid on its own obligations, with the government absorbing the loss. The peasants also benefited from a long repayment period. Moreover, even if the value of the land was too high when purchased, its value was increasing with the improved economic situation.[37] In the opinion of one liberal critic of the Stolypin policy, Kaufman, the opportunity to purchase land through the bank was highly prized by the bank's peasant clients, who were remarkably prompt in meeting their obligations.[38] Both Kaufman and Oganovskii (a stronger critic of government policy) asserted that, among the buyers of land, the landless peasants and those with small holdings predominated.[39]

It is highly significant that, during the ten-year period after the revolution of 1905, the peasants acquired, mainly with the aid of the bank, over 28 million acres of land. This constituted close to 8 percent of the allotted peasant land and nearly 40 percent of the total purchased peasant land since emancipation.[40] Thus on the eve of the Revolution of 1917 the peasants, who farmed with the aid of their families and almost no hired labor, owned approximately two thirds of all land in European Russia that was not in the possession of the state. The latter owned little land that was suitable for farming. When measured by sown acreage, in which leased land was also included, the importance of peasant farming was still greater. According to the census of 1916, it accounted for nearly 90 percent of the total sown area, with regional variations from almost 100 percent in Siberia to about 75 percent in the Baltic and southwestern provinces. Even discounting the exaggeration of the 1916 data, because of the heavy wartime decline in estate agriculture, land statistics indicate that Russia was increasingly becoming a country of small peasant farming. Yet the remaining estate sector doubtless represented the strongest part, the hard core, of the formerly vast estate system.

While the Stolypin agrarian policy, on the whole, favored the better-off peasants and thereby contributed to economic stratification in the village, there were other factors that had a general uplifting effect on the Russian countryside. Among them must be mentioned the upward trend of agricultural prices during the early years of the present century, which became all the more beneficial as Russian agriculture became more commercialized. The weather also favored the Russian farmer in the years before the First World War: of the five prewar harvests, only one, that of 1911, was poor.

Good harvests and strong foreign demand made Russia, before the First World War, the leading exporter of grains in the world. Russian exports averaged close to 11 million metric tons of wheat, rye, barley, oats, and corn in 1909–1913, which accounted for 30 percent of world grain exports. Doubtless, this large export trade during a period of rising prices contributed to the general prosperity of Russian agriculture. The growth of agricultural production can be gauged from a rise in the index of crop production by 36.9 percent, on the average, in the 50 provinces of European Russia for the years 1909–1913, as compared with 1896–1900. Similarly, an average increase of 40.8 percent is indicated for the 72 provinces of the Russian Empire, which include Congress Poland and

Asiatic Russia, the latter with its rapidly increasing crop area.[41] Although it is considered by most scholars that the figures of the Central Statistical Committee, on which the index is based, considerably underestimate the basic grain yields, as well as the actual level of production, there is no definite evidence that the degree of underreporting varied enough during the period to affect the indicated increase. But the level was somewhat understated because of the noninclusion of cotton, the production of which was rising rapidly during the decade preceding the First World War. That even the proletarian and semiproletarian elements did not miss out on the new prosperity is demonstrated by the fact that the daily wage rates of hired farmworkers were between 23 to 64 percent higher in 1913 as compared with the 1901–1905 average, while the local market price of rye, the peasant's staple food, increased by only 10–16 percent.[42]

A significant index of agricultural improvement was the growing use of farm machinery, both imported and of domestic manufacture. Average imports of farm implements, mostly machinery, amounted to 20.8 million rubles in 1901–1905, 30.7 million in 1906–1910, and 54.6 million in 1911–1913. Domestic factory production of farm machinery increased from 13.3 million rubles in 1900 to 38.3 million in 1908 and 60.5 million in 1913.[43] In many regions the iron plow, a harbinger of agricultural progress, replaced the wooden plow or more primitive implements, such as the *sokha*. This was particularly true of the southern provinces of the Ukraine and North Caucasus, where, according to the census of farm implements in 1910, less than 10 percent of them were wooden plows. Here could also be found a large number of other modern farm implements. Less progress was made in the more northern provinces, but modern implements made inroads there as well.

Another favorable influence on agricultural improvement, though less tangible than those mentioned above, was the reduction of illiteracy. The miserable conditions revealed by the census of 1897, though sometimes cited as if prevailing twenty years later, were rapidly being repaired. For the age group of twenty to twenty-four years, the 1897 census had shown that in European Russia only 51 percent of the men and 22 percent of the women were literate. For the same age group according to the 1920 census, 82 percent of the men and 47 percent of the women were literate. Thus literacy had more than doubled among women and had improved by nearly two thirds among men. Another interesting fact is that while 60 percent of army recruits were illiterate in 1896, by 1913 the proportion had decreased to 27 percent.[44]

The tsarist government, which prior to the revolution of 1905 seemed to have a phobia against a literate citizenry, was forced to give way under the pressure of public opinion. The zemstvos were also taking an increasingly active part in the field of elementary education. The gains would have been even greater had it not been for the disruptions of the First World War. The achievement of universal elementary instruction, however, was not far beyond the horizon. Thus Russia before the Revolution, with all its poor educational legacy from the nineteenth century, was by no means the dark, illiterate nation of the Bolshevik propaganda stereotype. Although much remained to be done before Russia could reach the educational level of its Western neighbors, especially at the rural level, substantial progress had been achieved.

A factor still more imponderable, but probably one of the most vital in accounting for general progress, was the growth of the spirit of freedom and independence, the fruit of the revolution of 1905, which subsequent political reaction could not kill. It is true that the Russian peasant, like the Russian citizen generally, was far from being a politically free man in the Western sense. The "reign of law" was very far from perfect, though immensely stronger than it has been in the Soviet period because of the existence of an independent bar and a more independent judiciary.[45] But the legal gap dividing the peasantry from the rest of the citizenry was narrowed, and all men were less amenable to the oppression and browbeating of the police state. The greater personal freedom of the common man, and the change in intellectual climate which this spelled, meant a release of energy that benefited agriculture as it did all other phases of Russian life.

Cooperatives

One of the most promising by-products of the changed sociopolitical atmosphere, as far as Russian agriculture was concerned, was the new vigor manifested by the cooperative movement. Agricultural cooperation in Russia traced its origin to the 1860s, when the first credit cooperative was established.[46] Despite its early start and the aid of the zemstvo and the Peasant Bank, the cooperatives met with failure or indifferent success until after 1905, when great strides were made. The agricultural credit cooperative, which in Russia often combined the functions of marketing of products and bulk purchases of supplies for its members, was the most typical form of rural cooperation. On January 1, 1908, there were 3,145 credit cooperatives with nearly 1,400,000 members, or six and a half times the membership of eleven years before. By 1914, the total number of cooperatives had increased to 13,615 with an aggregate membership of 8,250,000, or nearly a sixfold increase in six years. Further growth took place during the war years, and by January 1, 1917, membership was nearly 10.5 million. That participation in the credit cooperatives was not confined merely to the kulaks, as often alleged by Soviet sources, is brought out by this finding: "On the whole, there is no doubt that the lower limit of participation in credit societies coincided with the line that separates the peasant groups which are engaged in farming for their own account from those groups which are not. All groups above that line, without exception, constitute the social milieu in which cooperative credit develops." [47]

The aid and encouragement of the zemstvo, which showed a spurt of activity in this direction in the decade before the First World War, as well as increased government credit, no doubt contributed to the vigorous development of the cooperative movement. But the causes of this new vitality must also be sought in the more active and informed attitude of the rural population, energized by the revolutionary events of the early 1900s. In fact, despite the liberalization of the legislation dealing with cooperatives, it still contained many restrictive features and there was much red tape and interference on the part of the authorities, who continued to scrutinize all forms of public activity with a jaundiced eye. This was particularly true with regard to the organization of central associations or unions of cooperative societies, generally considered a highly desirable practice. Only during the war years was government interference sufficiently relaxed to permit the increased association of cooperatives, with the result that the number of centrals rose from 11 on January 1, 1913, to 84 on July 1, 1916.

Another type of agricultural cooperative that showed rapid growth during this period was the so-called agricultural society, which combined agricultural extension work, the financing of agricultural improvements on a small scale (such as acquisition of improved seed and farm machinery), and bulk purchasing, warehousing, and marketing of farm products for members. In 1906, there were 584 such societies; by 1914 the number rose to 4,685, and by 1916 to 6,500. Nearly 95 percent of these societies were of the general-purpose type, but a few concerned themselves with special branches of agriculture: apiculture, gardening, poultry farming, and so on. Here, again, the zemstvos and the government aided the development, but it could not have taken place without a strong interest on the part of the farmers themselves.

The most spectacular success, however, was scored by dairy cooperatives in western Siberia. These groups, under the leadership of M. Balakshin, made their mark in the annals of the Russian cooperative movement and in the history of Russian foreign trade by developing a new export industry: butter. The first cooperative creamery in Siberia was organized in 1895; ten years later the number was 118. The Union of Siberian

Creamery Associations was organized in 1907. It grew from a member-ship of 65 cooperative creameries, with a total of less than 5 million pounds of butter sold in 1908, to 922 creameries with total sales of 106 million pounds in 1916. By 1918, the number of creameries exceeded 2,000.

It is worth noting that, while cooperation in the fields of credit market-ing and processing was successful, efforts to establish cooperatives in production failed. In both its successes and its failures, Russia recapit-ulated the nearly universal experience with cooperatives. The reader should remember that I am discussing voluntary democratic forms of agricultural cooperation. This needs to be emphasized because of the prevalence in Russia of nonvoluntary types of producers' associations, such as the mir, with its mainly hereditary membership, or the modern kolkhoz, which is a rigorously state-controlled institution. But the ex-perience during the period 1905–1917 demonstrates that voluntary coop-eration also sprouted well in Russian soil, once the frigid political climate had become somewhat milder. Here was a portent for the future that outweighs in importance even the solid practical achievements of the cooperative movement.

Industrialization

Less direct in its influence on agriculture than most of the other factors mentioned above, but nonetheless of cardinal importance, was the re-sumed march of industrialization, retarded during the early years of the century by business recession, war, and political disturbances. The new industrial upswing can be illustrated by a few production statistics.[48]

Commodity	1900	1909	1913
		(million poods)	
Pig iron	177.5	175.0	283.0
Coal	1,003.0	1,591.0	2,215.0
Cotton (mill consumption)	16.1	21.3	25.9
Sugar	49.0	92.6	108.4

The index of Russian industrial production in the period 1909–1913 was nearly 40 percent higher than in 1901–1905, and 73 percent higher than in 1896–1900; in 1913 the index was 58.5 and 96.0 percent above those periods.[49] These few figures suffice to indicate that Russian industry was booming during the years 1909–1913. On the eve of the First World War, Russia was definitely set on the path toward the position of a great industrial nation. And it was doing this while becoming less dependent on the state.[50] The seeds planted by Witte and Vyshnegradskii were bearing fruit. But agriculture, thanks largely to the revolution of 1905, ceased to be the Cinderella of the nation, even though the peasants' aspirations for division of estates were not fulfilled.

For the Russian farmer, industrialization meant, first of all, an expanding domestic market, particularly for the products of intensive agriculture, such as dairy and other animal products, fruits, and vegetables, which were consumed in greater quantities by the industrial population, with its relatively higher standard of living, as compared with the rural population. But even for grain, Russia's principal agricultural export, the domestic market was growing with the rising urban population. It is possible to demonstrate this fact statistically because the great bulk of marketable Russian grain was shipped by rail; railroad statistics provide a convenient breakdown between shipments to export points and those to internal markets. Internal shipments showed a steady increase, from an average of 297 million poods in 1896–1900 to 328 million in 1901–1905, 434 million in 1906–1910, and 429 million, on the average, in the three years 1911–1913. They constituted 48.4 percent of the total grain railroad shipments in 1906–1910, as against 44–45 percent during the preceding two five-year periods.[51] Thus the process of industrialization, by expanding markets and helping to make the Russian farmer more prosperous, also provided a favorable economic milieu for the agrarian individualism of the Stolypin era.

The growing industry also provided an outlet for the surplus of farm workers in the overpopulated Russian village. The number of workers in the manufacturing and mining industries increased from about 1.2 million in 1890 to 2.2 million in 1900 and 2.9 million in 1913.[52] It is true that the heavy protectionist tariff system for industry constituted a disadvantage for agriculture, with its export basis. It affected adversely both the landlords and the peasants, especially during the agricultural crisis of the 1880s and 1890s.[53] But the tariffs, even though in some cases misplaced and unnecessarily high, could no longer offset the benefits of the advance of industrialism, especially when it stimulated substantial investments of foreign capital. It also should not be overlooked that pre-revolutionary industrialization had a more balanced character and did not sacrifice the interests of the consumer, as has been the case with Soviet industrialization.

Because of the growing numbers of the proletariat, industrialization held a serious threat of revolution, which might have occurred before Stolypin's "counterrevolutionary" measures in the villages would have had time to produce their full effect. With the advantage of historical hindsight, who can seriously doubt that the villages would not have followed suit if revolution had broken out again in the cities, say, in the early summer of 1914. The date is not chimerical. A good barometer of the serious unrest prevailing in the industrial centers and especially in the capital, according to official data, was the growth in the number of strikes. They increased from 222 in 1910, with less than 50,000 workers participating, to close to 3,500 strikes during January–July 1914, with some 1.3 million workers involved. Of these, over 2,500 strikes, with more than one million workers taking part, were classified by official sources as political in character.[54] It was said, and this is symptomatic of the temper of the time, that the "Marseillaise" was heard in St. Petersburg in July 1914, not only at official receptions for the visiting French President, Raymond Poincaré, but also in working-class quarters where it had radically different overtones.

Political discontent was by no means confined to the active elements of the working class and the progressive intelligentsia. It was fanned by the reactionary anticonstitutionalist course increasingly pursued by the government, which disenchanted even the more conservative circles typified by such parliamentary leaders as Guchkov and Rodzianko, who had supported the regime during the early post-1905 period. Conservatives were, above all, scandalized by the close relations of the imperial family with the infamous Rasputin, who did so much to discredit the Romanov dynasty during the last years of its reign. Entirely apart from the international situation, therefore, the Russian political atmosphere was tense. Another revolutionary explosion, although not necessarily inevitable, was nevertheless possible. In fact, something can be said for the view that the war with Germany, which for a time stopped all oppositionist activities, actually postponed the revolution.

Yet it is possible that if the First World War had not occurred when it did, or had ended quickly, Russia could have avoided a revolution. Political concessions might have been made by the regime and, combined with an improvement in the economic situation through agricultural reform, might have made Russia immune to another revolutionary outburst. This is certainly an arguable proposition. But peace was not destined to last in Europe. After an interval of less than a decade, Russia with most of Europe stumbled into another war, more disastrous and prolonged. This added to the stockpile of inflammable material and eventually provided the spark that touched off the revolutionary conflagration in 1917.

6

World War I and the Revolution of 1917

When the catastrophe of world war became a reality, Russian agriculture was undeniably stronger than it had been ten years earlier, on the eve of the Russo-Japanese War, even though the peasants' land hunger was only partly assuaged. If agriculture and, indeed, the whole economy of Russia did achieve a considerable measure of progress during the interlude between the revolution of 1905 and the First World War, the same cannot be asserted regarding political developments—this was the Achilles heel of the nation. But the Russia of 1914 was no longer the Russia of Pleve and Pobedonostsev.

Although the domestic political situation was tense, the beginning of the war in August 1914 seemed to banish for a time the revolutionary specter on a wave of patriotic fervor. This is the consensus of contemporaries, in which the writer can join as a witness. But all of this soon changed. The war, instead of coming to a speedy and victorious end as originally expected, dragged on endlessly, exacting terrible sacrifices and bringing many reverses and few victories. It revealed poor preparation for what had obviously been an imminent danger for at least a decade, with one international crisis following another. This was, of course, true in some degree for all the belligerents. In Russia, however, the war demonstrated the utter inability of the tsarist regime to make the necessary political and administrative adjustments, as Great Britain had done under Lloyd George and France under Clemenceau. Quite the contrary: the regime manifested increasing irrationality, with the growing influence of Rasputin and the hysterical empress. This is probably best symbolized by the notorious leap-frog game of changing ministers in which, at the end, the most reactionary, discredited, and incompetent bureaucrats came to the top. As a result, the gulf between the government and the people steadily widened. Anger and frustration extended even to the moderate pro-war section of the public, which in the duma was represented by the newly formed Progressive Bloc, a coalition of all parties except the extreme right and the extreme left. Its sentiments were expressed in the famous duma speech by Miliukov in November 1916 (sometimes called the prologue to the revolution) in which the accusations against the government were punctuated by the query, "Is it treason or is it stupidity?" Four months later, following disturbances in the capital in which the shortage of bread was the final catalyst, the regime toppled.

Agriculture and the War

The villages dutifully and patiently responded to the demand for men and horses and other government war measures. The peasantry bore the brunt of the war by having to provide millions of soldiers, who, poorly equipped, were led recklessly to slaughter by incompetent military leaders. Yet there was no military collapse until the summer of 1917. The enemy's penetration into Russia was nowhere near so deep as during the Second World War or the Napoleonic War in 1812. During the last prerevolutionary summer of 1916, the Russian army even took the offensive, achieving a limited success. From 1914 to 1916 more than 13 million men were drafted into the armed forces, and in 1917 half a million more were added. It is estimated that "altogether up to 40 percent of the able-bodied population of the villages were called to the colors." [1]

The mobilization of men and horses, large though it was, at first had relatively little effect on peasant farming. Agriculture had long suffered from underemployment, a surplus of underoccupied workers which included many women and adolescents. Peasant labor could indeed be used more intensively, as the occasion required; in many regions too, particularly in the non-black-soil area, peasants were only partly occupied in farming. But the pinch was increasingly felt as more and more millions were thrown into the vortex of martial struggle. The depressing atmosphere in one village in Samara (now Kuibyshev) in the summer of 1917 was thus described by the traveling correspondent of the *Manchester Guardian*, M. Philips Price:

> A feeling of depression lay everywhere. It is true that a red flag, flying from the roof of the windmill on the outskirts of the village, was a joyful sign of the great deliverance last March. But on entering the house of my host, an old peasant, I soon felt that the gloom which had temporarily been lifted by the Revolution from the rural hearth was settling down again upon the inmates under the prospects of another winter's war. Of the four sons of the house one was alive. He was cross-eyed and half-witted, and so not fit for service. The three daughters of the house had all been married; not one of their husbands was alive now.[2]

During the early phases of the war, the villages saw some prosperity which came in on the crest of wartime inflation. But the inevitable concomitants of inflationary pressure, high prices and scarcity of goods, soon brought home to the peasants the declining purchasing power of the ruble.

In contrast to peasant agriculture, estate farming began to experience trouble early in the war. The difficulty of replacing mobilized workers was compounded by the lessened need of the peasant population to seek outside employment, because of increased wartime income, and by a heavier demand on the peasants to devote more time to their holdings. The extensive use of prisoners of war and, on a more limited scale, refugees from occupied territories made up for no more than half of the workers lost by the estates.[3] As a result of the shortage of labor and of draft power and other inputs needed in agriculture, such as fertilizer, the crop area and the output of estates drastically declined. Estate grain acreage (exclusive of enemy-occupied territory) decreased by 20 percent between 1914 and 1916. Even the increase in peasant production, indicated by statistics, could not offset the detrimental effect of a sudden sharp contraction of estate output on supplies for the market (commercial production).[4] For, because of inflation, peasant consumption and stockpiling increased probably even more than they usually do with larger production.

The seriousness of this declining estate production becomes patent when we remember that the estates accounted for more than a fifth of the peacetime commercial production of the four principal grains. Already in 1915, despite a good harvest, marketable production of grains had decreased by one third as compared with the previous year.[5] The adverse effect of this decline was partly offset by the cessation of grain exports (the Black Sea and Baltic ports had been blocked). Since the First World War was fought on the fringes of the Russian Empire, hardly touching the rich surplus-producing granary of the country, German occupation of part of Russia's territory was a minor influence on production. But the situation was aggravated by wartime shifts of population and its excessive concentration in the western part of the country, where grain deficits were the rule. This resulted in a serious dislocation of normal distribution and transportation channels, accentuated by inefficient management. Here was the beginning of the perennial "bread problem," which led to the riots in March 1917 and was to plague the country for decades. But on the eve of the Revolution of 1917, it was a problem primarily for the government and the cities, not for the village.

The Democratic Revolution

Outwardly all was quiet on the agrarian front during the war years. Even when revolution broke out in the cities, the countryside remained at first so calm that the agrarian question, which had played such a crucial role in Russian politics before the war, was not even mentioned in the first public appeals and declarations issued by the new Provisional Government.[6] There was, as several writers have suggested, an inevitable time lag in the reaction of the villages to the ferment in the cities, owing to the slow pace at which news had to travel in that pre-radio age. This lag was accentuated by the wartime mobilization, stripping the village of its most active elements. Still, the rural calm was deceptive. Soon after the overthrow of the tsar, the peasantry began to make itself heard. Disturbing reports of peasant unrest and direct action against the landlords arrived at the capital. The new liberal Minister of Agriculture, A. I. Shingarev, was preoccupied with food-supply difficulties and was fearful that agitation over agrarian reform might interfere with spring sowings. He was reported as wanting to guarantee producers against losing the fruits of their harvest.[7] Accordingly, on March 9, 1917, the Provisional Government responded to reports of peasant disturbances in Kazan province by ordering them suppressed and the instigators prosecuted.

But the people who knew the villages best were well aware that a revolt could be forestalled only by convincing the peasants that a comprehensive agrarian reform was in the offing. The council of the Moscow Agricultural Society urged the government to announce that it would immediately begin active preparation for such a reform "in the interest of the working peasants"; at the same time, the peasants should be cautioned against any "destructive action directed at the estates as being clearly contrary to the national interest, particularly in wartime." There were others, such as the influential populist and future Minister of Food A. V. Peshekhonov, who urged the government to make haste in settling these problems. "If these questions are not solved immediately, anarchy will result and, as a consequence, the kind of agrarian order for which all the democratic parties are striving will not emerge." [8]

On March 17 the Provisional Government issued its first appeal to the peasant population. It stated that the land question must be solved not by force but by legislation to be passed by the people's representatives. Such legislation would require extensive preparation involving the gathering of considerable data. "The government considers it an imperative duty to complete promptly the preparatory work on the agrarian question so as to present all the materials and information to the people's representatives." More than a month passed before the Provisional Government announced, on April 21, its decision to set up land committees. The Main Land Committee, headed by a well-known economist and populist sympathizer, A. S. Posnikov, had a cumbersome organizational structure and was heavily slanted in its makeup toward political moderation. It was charged with the task of drafting the agrarian-reform legislation. The local land committees also had some vague administrative functions. In a new appeal to the population, issued when the committees were announced, the government again called upon the peasants to refrain from arbitrary action, "to wait peacefully . . . for the Constituent Assembly, which will find a just solution to the land question and will establish a new agrarian order." The appeal also sought to reassure peasants in the armed forces that "in their absence and without their participation no decision will be made regarding the land question." [9]

The government's pronouncements indicate that it had chosen a Fabian course of action in the matter of agrarian reform. It stuck to this course until the end of its short life, even in the face of rapidly developing revolutionary emergencies and despite repeated warnings and proddings from its Socialist Revolutionary Minister of Agriculture, Victor Chernov, and from the land committees. Only a few palliative measures were adopted by the Provisional Government in the summer of 1917—such as the prohibition of private land sales (this was urgently needed to break up growing land speculation). Also the Stolypin land-tenure laws were suspended. With these exceptions all significant action was deferred, according to the standard formula, until the convocation of the Constituent Assembly, which was supposed to settle everything. The calling of this body was first delayed by the Provisional Government until the autumn, then September 17, 1917, was set as the date. Then on August 9 the elections were postponed until November 12 and the opening until November 28. In a more normal period such delays might not be objectionable, but these were anything but normal times. The Provisional Government and democracy were both swept away by the Bolsheviks before the elections could be held. Meanwhile, twenty-four commissions and subcommissions under the Ministry of Agriculture had been working "ceaselessly" to prepare a detailed plan of land reform and organization.[10] This work was interrupted by the October Revolution, and a draft of the new agrarian legislation was never completed.[11] When it is recalled how much work had already been done in this field by various government commissions and agencies, by the zemstvos, by political parties and individual scholars, and by the dumas, it seems strange that so much additional toil and time would be needed to prepare such a measure in 1917. One is reminded of the wise dictum of Walter Bagehot, that generalizations must not be postponed until all the facts are gathered. Substitute "laws" for "generalizations" and the dictum is applicable to the situation just described. Even if long preparations were desirable in a less critical period, there was no justification for a delay in an emergency.

A much earlier deadline for agrarian reform could have been set if it had been given high priority. Why was the sense of urgency about the agrarian problem, so characteristic of the liberal and radical parties when they were in opposition under tsarism, absent when they attained power in 1917? This is one of those fateful questions of the Russian Revolution about which we will probably never cease to wonder and speculate. The Socialist Revolutionary Party, which with its massive peasant support became the main pillar of the Provisional Government, has been particularly criticized in retrospect for the delay in agrarian reform.[12] But it is essential to keep in mind the central fact that Russia's revolution occurred in the midst of a great war. It is true that the ardor with which the war was supported by the coalition parties diminished as one moves along the political spectrum from right to left. By the same token, the attachment to the slogan, "peace without annexation and reparation," was strongest among the rightist groups. But what weighed most heavily in favor of reform postponement with the right wing (the Cadet Party), and probably a considerable part of the center, was the fear that land reform would disrupt the prosecution of the war and worsen the precarious food situation. It cannot be said that this apprehension was unjustified. On the contrary, there was a "clear and present danger" that a drastic redistribution of land, carried out during the war, would have a detrimental effect on production, especially commercial production, and thus further strain the food-supply situation. Equally important was the possible adverse effect of land redistribution on the morale of soldiers at the front. It was feared that, no matter what the government assurances might be, the soldiers would suspect that in a general redistribution their interests would be overlooked or disregarded.

Postponement of the agrarian reform until the end of the war seemed the path of wisdom. To this was added the hope of political moderates that, with the passage of time, the strong passions aroused by the revolution would subside and that it would be possible to adopt agrarian legislation less radical in tenor and less disturbing to the national economy. All this would have been very well were it not for the dangerous state of the peasants' mood, the mounting agrarian unrest and tension in the summer of 1917, cleverly exploited by Bolshevik propagandists. The Provisional Government failed almost to the very end to take seriously or, at any rate, to do anything decisive about this danger until it got out of control. There can be no certainty but it is possible that a land reform, less disturbing to agriculture than a peasant revolt, might have been effected if the Provisional Government had acted early and energetically enough.

Peasant unrest was manifested in the immediate demand for land, voiced in the congresses of peasant deputies in May and in direct action by the impatient and irate peasants, who would brook no delay in what they considered the payoff of the revolution. They were afraid that the landlords would meanwhile skim off the cream of their estates. The peasant attitude is typified by a conversation overheard in a village in Smolensk province: "Well, Nicholas was overthrown without the Constituent Assembly; why can't the nobles be driven from the face of the earth without it?" [13] As in 1905, jacqueries, pillage, seizure of land and other property of the landlords, strikes, and, at the very least, nonpayment of rents became common in the summer and early autumn of 1917. The well-publicized fact that numerous commissions organized by the government were toiling hard over new agrarian legislation had no effect on the disturbed peasant masses. Lenin's demagogic exploitation of the peasant movement for Bolshevik purposes made the situation worse, but it was common for the democratic parties at the time to underestimate the Bolshevik threat. Thus the dilemma in which the Provisional Government was caught was not merely that of external war as against agrarian reform, but also of agrarian reform as against internal war.

A struggle was taking place within the cabinet between Prime Minister Lvov, the proponent of the status quo, and Minister of Agriculture Chernov, who vigorously advocated immediate land reform. Prince Lvov's invocations to local authorities to use force in re-establishing law and order in the countryside were mostly empty words. The weak government lacked the power needed for such purposes. Attempts to use military force, resulting for the most part in peasants pitted against their more rebellious brothers, ended largely in fraternization between armed and unarmed peasants. Furthermore, the local land committees, close to the villages, were as a rule unsympathetic to what seemed to them the stand-pat attitude of the government. On occasion they even came into open conflict with the central authorities, which sometimes led to arrests. The Main Land Committee also became alarmed about the gravity of the situation and on August 3, 1917, addressed through its chairman, Posnikov, an appeal to the Provisional Government for a speedy enactment of land reform.

Prince Lvov finally left the government in disgust; but the new Kerensky cabinet did not follow the course advocated by Chernov and the land committees. Considering any further participation in the cabinet futile, Chernov resigned shortly after the departure of Lvov. But as an influential leader of the then powerful Socialist Revolutionary Party and a gifted publicist, Chernov continued his campaign for immediate agrarian reform. His successor as Minister of Agriculture, S. L. Maslov, who was appointed to this post early in October 1917, also pressed for immediate reform, though on more moderate lines. On October 20 a conference of ministers under the chairmanship of Maslov began considering his proposed draft for agrarian legislation. Its key feature was the setting up of a provisional reserve of land for leasing to poor peasants, pending the settlement of the land question by the Constituent Assembly.[14] This reserve was to consist of (1) private estate land that had been leased for no less than three of the previous five years; (2) all state and crown land; (3) private estate land that had been cultivated during the previous five years entirely with the aid of peasant draft power and implements; (4) land taken away from its owners or leaseholders because of a threatened serious decline in value or its remaining unseeded; (5) land for which leases had expired; (6) land voluntarily transferred to the reserve. Finally, even estate land cultivated by the owner with his own draft power and implements could be expropriated, provided: it was found by the land committee that a severe shortage of land existed among peasants in the community; surplus manpower to cultivate the land on the basis of non-capitalist family farming was available; and productivity of land transferred to peasants would not be greatly impaired. An adequate holding had to be left to the estate owner for the needs of his household, employees, and livestock. Rent was to be charged for the leased land from which local and national taxes were to be deducted and the remainder paid to the owner. The land reserve was to be administered by the local land committees, which were to be authorized to reduce excessive rents and otherwise to protect the interests of the peasants.

This law, which the Kerensky government was discussing during the last days of its life, might have satisfied the peasants in June; but it was too late and too little in October. It fell far short of the demands of the dominant socialist parties for nationalization or socialization of all estate land without compensation to the owners. The Socialist Revolutionary Party was bitterly taunted for its proposed draft by Lenin.[15]

Right after the Revolution, in March 1917, there were reported for the whole of Russia only 49 cases of peasants who took direct action against the estates. But in April the number of cases jumped to 378 and in May to 678, affecting 174 and 236 districts respectively. In June, with 988 cases in 280 districts, the agrarian unrest reached its first peak. It declined during the harvest period in July and August, with 957 and 760 cases respectively. The tide rose again in the last two months before the Bolshevik coup, in September to 803 and in October to 1169 cases.[16] There could be no question that the young Russian democracy was being confronted with a sweeping peasant revolt that gained in violence with the passage of time and was no less formidable because of its unorganized character. At first the peasants were engaged largely in tactics of "disorganization," making existence for the estateowners and managers unbearable through a succession of petty acts of interference, noncooperation, and sabotage. Although acts of violence also occurred at this stage, they were sporadic as compared with the later months when arson, pillage, forcible seizure of property, and even murder of estate owners and their agents assumed wide proportions. Here is one such episode from the province of Tambov in central Russia:

> At the meeting the peasants split into two groups. One proposed to take the estates from the nobles in an orderly way and divide up all the property proportionately among the population, but to preserve the gentry's buildings for cultural purposes. The other group proposed to burn down all the estates . . . "By orderliness," they said, "we shall never drive the nobles from the estates." . . . During the night of September 7–8 a sea of conflagrations swept over the estates of our country. On the morning of September 8 along the road to the village crowds of people were straggling with stolen property: some with wheat, others with a bed, cattle, or a broken armchair.[17]

There was an incident in Chernigov province in northern Ukraine. On the estate of the former Marshal of Nobility Sudienko, "the stock, equipment, furniture, etc., were divided by the peasants, each taking whatever he could. The land was divided among the peasants, and all the buildings burned down. In the mansion house there were many historical treasures and an enormous collection of books, which the peasants tore up to roll cigarettes." [18]

In their violent attacks on the estates the peasants did not spare, as a rule, the good landlords, those who were known to be kind and helpful to their village neighbors. For instance, the estate of a well-known philanthropist, S. S. Ushakov, in the Kozlovsk district of Tambov province did not escape pillage despite the fact that Ushakov had built an excellent school and was generous with financial assistance to peasants in need. Yet his neighbors joined the mob from other villages in staging the jacquerie. "All furniture was removed from the manor and immediately divided up among the new owners. After that, the manor was set on fire from all sides. The fire spread to other buildings, and within an hour there remained only the pitiful ruins of a large, progressive estate. Even the apiary was destroyed by the mob." Peasant violence often spread out in a chain reaction; during the night of September 11, 1917, for example, thirteen estates in the Kozlovsk district were destroyed and during the next day four more.[19]

The Provisional Government, as pointed out earlier, had no reliable force to cope with the violence, no Cossacks and dragoons as the tsarist government had in 1905. When, for instance, a detachment of soldiers was dispatched to quell the disturbances in the Kozlovsk district, they sided with the rebellious peasants: "On arriving at the scene of the jacquerie, the soldiers usually fired in the air and then hastened to join in the pillage." [20]

Such was the climate of rural Russia during the last two months of the Kerensky government. This was a ferocious, primitive, and contagious peasant war—Pushkin's image of "Russian mutiny, terrible and senseless." In 1917, as in 1905, the worst violence occurred in the black-soil area; the rural sections of the more industrialized non-black-soil region escaped much of the havoc. If any lingering doubt remained as to the urgency and intransigence of the peasants' demand for division of the estates, it should have been dispelled by these events of the autumn of 1917. But this does not mean that the peasants were influenced by such slogans as the demand for abolition of private property and socialization of land. To the peasant rank and file, socialization had at best a purely pragmatic value as a convenient formula for land seizure—it conjured up not the statist giant kolkhoz of the future, but the familiar world of the mir with its egalitarian distribution of land and family farming. And as an immediate proposition this was true even of the Socialist Revolutionary ideologists who had proclaimed socialization at the Congress of Soviets of Peasant Deputies in May and June.

We have already seen how negative and tardy was the response of the Provisional Government to this emergency. It is time now to look at the responses from the other side of the political fence. Little need be said about the right opposition, represented mainly by the Union of Landowners that was organized after the February Revolution. An attempt to attract the upper strata of the peasantry failed. The alliance that Stolypin tried to promote among these elements had not materialized, since the more prosperous peasants preferred to be a part of a united village front or, at best, to remain neutral.[21] The union, therefore, remained composed of the same landowners who had staunchly opposed a moderate agrarian reform ten years earlier. It had not changed its standpat attitude and saw in Minister of Agriculture Chernov its principal enemy. One of the leaders of this group coined a slogan playing on the words *chernyi* (black) and Chernov: a *chernyi peredel* (total peasant land redistribution) would be preferable to a Chernov *peredel* (a Chernov type of land reform). History was soon to write an epitaph for this approach.

Lenin and the Agrarian Revolution

At the other political extreme was Bolshevism and its undisputed master, Lenin. In the early 1890s, after a brief sojourn in the narodnik camp, Lenin embraced Marxist orthodoxy without ifs or buts. For him there did not exist the qualifications and concessions previously made by Marx and Engels to the Russian narodniks. Lenin also went a step further than the founders of Russian Marxism, Plekhanov and Axelrod. He believed that the Russian village was well along the road of capitalist evolution, with its landmarks of class division and class struggle, leading to the eventual extinction of small peasant farming.[22]

Despite significant tactical deviations, there is no evidence that Lenin ever changed his view. Thus in 1917, before the Bolshevik coup, in addressing a congress of peasant representatives he reiterated this thesis, which in his mind had acquired added significance as a result of the destruction caused by the First World War: "If we continue as in the past with small peasant holdings, even though as free citizens and on free land, we are, nevertheless, threatened by inevitable ruin because the collapse is approaching with every day, with every hour." [23] Lenin never doubted that the victory of the peasants over the landowners would result in a new struggle rather than in harmony. He envisaged two stages in the agrarian revolution: a "democratic" stage, in which the socialists would support the peasants' demand for land; and a "socialist" stage, in which a class struggle on the classical Marxist pattern would take place in the village. For Lenin an alliance with the peasantry as a whole against the landowners was bound to be a temporary marriage of convenience, ending in hostility and divorce. The course of events shows how prophetic was this appraisal.

This theoretical antagonism was early tempered by pragmatic political considerations.[24] Lenin was quick to perceive the opportunity for an alliance of revolutionary workers and peasants in the struggle against Russian absolutism. His strategy in the summer and autumn of 1917 was consistent with the course he had charted during the revolution of 1905. It may be characterized as mollifying the peasants in a bid to gain immediate political power for the Bolsheviks, relegating notions of class struggle and the "doom" of small peasant farming to the next stage. Already in April 1917, in a proposed party platform, Lenin was advocating immediate nationalization of land, with its actual disposition left to the local soviets of peasant deputies. The peasants were advised not to wait for the Constituent Assembly and to proceed immediately with the confiscation of estate land. However, the estates should not be divided but run as model farms by the soviets of agricultural workers' deputies. In this we can detect Lenin's doctrine of class division among the peasants, as in his advocacy of soviets of poor ("semiproletarian") peasants and separate factions within the broader soviets of peasant deputies. "Without this, all the sweet *petit bourgeois* phrases of the narodniks about the peasantry as a whole will only serve as a cover for a defrauding of the poor masses by the prosperous peasants, who represent merely one of the varieties of capitalists." [25]

As the summer passed and the peasants became more rebellious, Lenin increasingly stressed a tactical rapprochement with the peasantry. "We are not doctrinaires. Our teaching is not dogma, but a guide to action," he wrote. "The peasants want to retain small farming, distribute the land on an equal basis and periodically equalize the holding. Let them. Just because of this, no sensible socialist will break with the poor peasants . . . The transfer of political power to the proletariat—this is the essential thing." [26]

This was actually the course followed by the Bolsheviks upon seizing the reins of government. One of their first acts was the promulgation of the celebrated decree "Concerning the Land" on November 8 (October 26), 1917 (henceforth referred to as the Land Decree). According to Miliutin, the first Commissar of Agriculture, though he and Larin had prepared the original draft of the Land Decree, the final formulation belonged to Lenin.[27] It provided for the immediate abolition of the property rights of landlords, with no compensation, and the confiscation of all estates, which were to be administered by the local land committees and the district soviets of peasant deputies, pending the final solution of the land problem. In addition, the decree embodied a summary of instructions (*nakazy*) from peasants to their representatives in a congress of peasant soviets held in the summer of 1917, which had been dominated by the Socialist Revolutionaries. The main points of the document were: private property in land was to be abolished, with consequent prohibition of the selling, leasing, and mortgaging of land; the land was to become the possession of all the people, to be used by those who tilled it; all land was to be turned into a general national reserve administered by the local self-governing bodies, with the exception of special land such as orchards and nurseries (these were to become national or communal property). From this reserve every citizen who wished to engage in farming was entitled to an allotment, but only if he cultivated the land himself and employed no hired labor. The allotments were to be equalized on the basis of a labor or consumption standard or norm, with periodic redistribution depending on the growth of population and increased productivity. The form of land tenure was to depend entirely on the peasants themselves.

Lenin forestalled the taunts that the Bolsheviks had virtually taken over the agrarian program of their opponents, the Socialist Revolutionaries, by declaring, in the speech introducing the Land Decree, that the question of authorship of the new law was immaterial. The essential thing was the aspirations of the peasants themselves, which every democratic government had to respect. The peasants should have firm assurance that there would be no more landlords in the village and that they would be able to order their lives in their own way. "We must follow life itself; we must give complete carte blanche to the peasants to proceed with the agrarian revolution along their own lines." [28] It is not surprising that, shortly after the seizure of power, the Bolsheviks formed a new coalition with a group of Left Socialist Revolutionaries. One of their representatives, A. Kolegaev, received the portfolio of Commissar of Agriculture. The legislation resulting from this coalition was a new comprehensive agrarian law, "Decree Concerning the Socialization of Land," proclaimed by the Soviet government on February 6/19, 1918, only a few months after the issue of the first Land Decree.

This law was essentially a reiteration of the socialization program of the first decree. But it is true that a mandate was also given to the government to facilitate the development of collective farming at the expense of individualistic farming, "for the purpose of transition to a socialist economy" (article 11d). Preferential treatment in land allotment was to be given to various types of collective and cooperative farming (articles 22 and 35). The socialization law appears to justify, on the face of it, the characterization that it had a "double soul," individualist and socialist.[29]

Yet its collectivist aspect is not organically related to the main purpose, that of securing equitable distribution of land among individual small peasant-farmers. With this end in view, the socialization law included an elaborate scheme for a nationwide distribution of land. This objective was envisaged as a gradual long-range process, and it had no effect on the actual distribution of land.

The real legal basis for distribution was "a temporary instruction for transitional measures to carry out the law for socialization of land," published on January 30, 1918.[30] The "instruction" first of all ordered the ejection from their estates of all landlords and their managers and agents. It further instructed the land departments of the local soviets to take charge of the confiscated properties and to divide the land temporarily on an egalitarian basis among the local population. The actual division of land was thus to be implemented on the local level, without reference to the complicated plans for national distribution. The local authorities, in turn, often shifted the task to the peasants themselves, who carried it out with little official direction or control. They used the time-honored distribution methods of the Russian mir. The following is a more or less typical account of the process in one district in central Russia: "The distribution of land took place under the conditions of local self-determination and was guided only by the experience of the repartitional land commune. The peasants themselves, literally, distributed the confiscated land between small administrative units [the volosts] in the district, between villages in the volost and individual households in a village. They distributed equally, arithmetically, as well as they knew how, in accordance with such suggestions as they could derive from the old repartitional communal experience." [31]

This use of the mir during the first stage of the agrarian revolution confirmed the worst fears of its conservative critics. But even in the Ukraine, where hereditary land tenure prevailed, the process of revolutionary land distribution was not very different, as shown by the following statement from a report of the Commissariat of Agriculture for the Ukraine: "In the absence of any statistical data for planning and also in view of the limitation of technical resources, the land authorities had to distribute the [confiscated] estate land for spring sowing without assistance from surveyors, entrusting this process to the population itself through the volost land departments and commissions. In many places, however, the distribution of the land took place spontaneously; it was carried out by the population itself without the participation of the land authorities." [32]

The peasant revolution, even after it was legalized by the new regime into a land reform, remained essentially a grass-roots affair, conducted with little reference to government legislation, which in any event was couched in generalities. Sometimes district authorities even enacted their own legislation; the Syzran district of Simbirsk province, for instance, passed a separate socialization law.[33] The situation was frankly summed up by Minister of Agriculture Sereda, at the All-Russian Conference on Party Work in the Village: "The process of fragmentation, the process of partition of land, occurred to a considerable extent spontaneously . . . frequently we found arable land without any hay land, the proper relationship between different kinds of land use disturbed, and implements destroyed." [34]

The peasants divided among themselves not only the estate land, but whatever other property they could lay their hands on. "Everything was divided, including the piano . . . Large buildings which could not be divided were left without frames, doors, and stoves." [35] This description from one province epitomizes the general situation. Yet there were also peasant communities that were reluctant to proceed with land division without the sanction of a constituent assembly. The reluctance was due not to any lack of desire for additional land, but to a feeling of insecurity over possibly invalid acquisitions.[36] The foreboding was prophetic, since in a little over a decade the right to possess land, in the traditional sense understood by the Russian peasants, was lost under collectivization.

The agrarian revolution of 1917, which may be rightly called a peasant revolution, destroyed beyond possibility of revival the Russian estate system and the landlord class. W. H. Chamberlin has written this epitaph: "Pitiless the Russian agrarian revolution was; but from the peasants' standpoint, it was by no means senseless. The flowering of aristocratic landlord culture had cost them too dearly in toil and sweat. And the very fierceness and brutality which marked their upsurge are in some measure an indictment of the social and economic system which they swept away. It had built no adequate protective dikes; it had not given the peasantry enough education, enough sense of a stake in the land, enough feeling for property to insure itself against a violent collapse." [37] Obviously this is only one facet of the picture, since it fails to take into account the progress made between 1905 and 1914 or the full effect of the revolution on the peasants' welfare, let alone its influence on the nonagricultural sector. The revolution did not stop, as a radical agrarian reform would have stopped, with the driving out of the landlords and the division of their property. Nor, as a rule, did the larger peasant holdings, the individually owned land that had been purchased privately by peasants from the estates before 1917, escape the revolutionary melting pot. This caused particular anguish and bitterness in the villages, which showed a solid front in the liquidation of estate land. As one peasant who lost his purchased land expressed it: "By God, I never thought that peasants would rob each other. And I, the sinner, joined in robbing the princes [estates] and thought the end had come for the gentlefolk, and the peasants would have full reign. And now it [expropriation] even reaches us." [38] Peasants who sold their holdings at home and purchased distant estate lands were ejected from their new places of settlement and sent back to claim land in their native villages.[39] Larger peasant holdings and even some middle-sized holdings suffered not only from the loss of privately owned land, but also from attacks directed against them by the so-called Committees of Poor Peasants, organized at the government's behest in the middle of 1918. Frequent land subdivisions by the mir, which had been vigorously reactivated by the revolution and imbued with the egalitarian spirit of *poravnenie* (equalization) of landholdings, was another potent leveling influence. Yet considerable inequalities persisted between regions.

It has already been pointed out that the process of land distribution was confined to local administrative districts. There was no transfer or resettlement of population to achieve a better national distribution of land resources. Rarely did the area of land distribution extend beyond the boundaries of the uezd (roughly equivalent to a county in the United States). As a rule, the actual arena of distribution was the smaller unit of the volost (township). Even there the land of a particular estate was generally distributed among the peasants of the village with which it had historic ties dating to serfdom. The fact that peasants of another village purchased or leased such land, and badly needed it, or that there was little or no confiscated land nearby was usually not taken into consideration. Their more fortunate neighbors felt entitled to the land of the estate of their former master, even if their landholding was above the average for the area. This extreme parochialism in the revolutionary land distribution gave rise to numerous disputes between the villages, sometimes accompanied by violence.[40]

By the end of 1918, the peasant revolution had accomplished its main objectives. The landlords were driven out, and the estate land and larger peasant farms were subdivided. The official label of "temporary" attached to the revolutionary distribution of land was correct in the perspective of history. But the new land arrangements basically continued for more than a decade, until they in turn were swept away by collectivization. What, if anything, did the Russian peasants gain from the revolutionary upheaval in 1917? Let me recapitulate the distribution of land on the eve of the Revolution (see Table 7). Large estate farming, including the estates of the imperial family, accounted in prerevolutionary European Russia for 31 percent of the land, public domain for 7 percent, and small holdings for the remaining 62 percent. Thus, despite heavy purchases of estate land

Table 7. Distribution of land in European Russia, 1916

Type of property	Desiatinas (millions)	Acres (millions)	Percent
Large private estates [a]	75.0	202.5	28.3
Imperial estates	6.5	17.6	2.5
Peasant land [b]	165.2	446.0	62.4
Public domain [c]	18.0	48.6	6.8
Total	264.7	714.7	100.0

[a] Properties over 50 desiatinas (135 acres).

[b] The allotted land and land in small holdings purchased from estates, estimated at 26.4 million desiatinas (71.3 million acres).

[c] Land outside the five northern provinces where it is mostly under forests and is of little agricultural significance.

Source. A. N. Chelintsev, "Estate Farming before the Revolution," in *Zapiski instituta izucheniia Rossii* (Prague, 1925), I, 10.

by peasants (more than 70 million acres after emancipation), over a third of the total land in European Russia suitable for agriculture was still in large farms and public domain. If all this land had been transferred to the peasants, they would have increased their total holdings in European Russia by close to 270 million acres, or by 60 percent. Only a small proportion of the confiscated land remained in the hands of the state and was used for the organization of state farms and as a land reserve, so that the peasants in European Russia gained an additional area that was more than half of what they owned prior to the Revolution.[41]

For the country as a whole, the gain was proportionately less because the Asian territory, with the exception of Transcaucasia and Turkestan, was overwhelmingly a section of small peasant farming; there were no estates to distribute. The total "privately owned" land area in 1913 in Siberia, the Soviet Far East, and Kazakhstan amounted to less than 4 million acres.[42] Yet a much larger land gain by the peasants is implied by Soviet statistics, which give a figure of 531 million for peasant holdings and 376 million for private estates and holdings of the imperial family and church—or a total of 907 million acres.[43] No indication is given whether public-domain land is included in these figures, but it is further stated that the peasants obtained more than 375 million acres of new land that was "formerly in the hands of estate owners, bourgeoisie, imperial family, monasteries and churches, and also part of the public domain." Actually a considerable area of the latter, perhaps over 100 million acres, must have been included in the figure of 375 million. Much of the public domain was in forests or was marginal and submarginal as far as agricultural use is concerned. Some of the public land that was suitable for farming was, in any event, part of the colonization reserve assigned for allotment to peasant farmers whose migration from the overpopulated regions of European Russia had been encouraged by the old regime. Such additional land was in no sense an acquistion resulting from the Revolution. It remains true, however, that an enormous area, exceeding 250 million acres, was transferred to peasant hands. Only a small proportion, about 3–4 percent of the agricultural land in European Russia, was retained for state and collective farming.[44] Small individual peasant agriculture became supreme over the whole vast territory of Russia.

The average gains of individual peasant farmers, when compared to the aggregate figures, appear much less impressive. "The enormous area of land divided up among the millions of peasants produced insignificant results. A special survey by the Central Department of Land Investigation indicated that the increase of the per capita area [of the agricultural population] was measured in insignificant quantities of tenths or even hundredths of desiatinas. In a large majority of provinces this increase did not exceed half a desiatina; only in a few did it reach a full desiatina." [45] The situation was aggravated by the fact that the number of claimants to land was swelled by an influx of returnees from the cities—peasants who migrated during the years before the revolution and were driven back to the villages by lack of food and jobs in industry. It was estimated on the basis of censuses of 1917 and 1920 that the migration from the towns to the country reached the huge figure of 8 million.[46]

Another qualification to recall is that a considerable proportion of the newly acquired land had been leased and actually farmed by the peasants long before the Revolution. Therefore, the net increase in the area available for actual peasant exploitation was less than indicated by the figures of revolutionary distribution of land. With land leased from estates estimated to be close to 70 million acres, and with much of the public-domain land suitable for agriculture also leased to the peasants, the additional area available for peasant use after the revolution was roughly 150 million acres. But—and this is highly important—the revolution freed the peasantry from the payment of onerous rents for the leased land, which were estimated by A. L. Vainshtein for the year 1912 at 289 million rubles for the fifty provinces of European Russia and nearly 270 million for the postrevolutionary Russian territory.[47] These rental payments are often lumped with installment payments on the purchase price of private land to show how large the peasants' total payments for land were before the revolution. In making comparisons with the postrevolutionary period, however, it should be borne in mind that peasants who had bought additional land were usually deprived of their purchased acres; other peasants who received the land benefited from the remission of payments. But even when these two outlays (rents and purchase installments) are combined, their total is much less than the figure of 700 million gold rubles cited by an official Soviet source.[48] Thus Vainshtein, in a careful analysis, estimated total payments by peasants for leasing and buying land in 1912 in European Russia at 376 million gold rubles, or half the figure cited above. This constitutes less than 6 percent of the income of the peasant population, estimated at 6,700 million gold rubles.[49] Against the gains resulting from the removal of rental and purchase payments for land must be set off the loss of earnings by peasants from work on the estates. There were other even more important offsetting factors, arising from government policy, to be discussed in the next chapter.

So far I have dealt with the peasantry en masse. But even though it was bound by certain uniform interests, characteristics, and traditions, particularly by an appetite for estate land, it was not an economically homogeneous whole. Rather, as a result of the interplay of demographic and economic factors, peasant society had a stratified, differentiated economic structure. This stratification was manifested in the variability of peasant landholdings as well as in variations in the supply of different forms of capital, family composition, and so on. How was this structure affected by the Revolution?

Landholding is the most important element. Table 8 shows the distri-

Table 8. Distribution of peasant households in Soviet Russia by sown area

Desiatinas	Acres	1917 Number of households	1917 Percent	1919 Number of households	1919 Percent	Percent 1919 is of 1917
Without sowings		49,087	11.49	30,415	6.57	62.0
Up to 2	Up to 5.4	122,643	28.70	198,647	42.87	162.0
2–4	5.5–10.8	123,590	28.92	135,966	29.34	110.0
4–6	10.9–16.2	62,601	14.65	57,301	12.37	91.5
6–10	16.3–27.0	47,678	11.16	33,814	7.30	70.9
10–16	27.1–43.2	16,432	3.84	6,393	1.38	38.9
16–25	43.3–67.5	4,178	0.98	756	0.16	18.1
Over 25	67.6 and over	1,082	0.26	98	0.01	9.1
	Total	427,291	100.0	463,390	100.0	108.4

Source. Compiled from official Soviet sources by A. Peshekhonov, "Dynamics of the Peasant Economy," in *Zapiski instituta izucheniia Rossii*, II, 17.

bution of peasant holdings in 1917 and 1919, that is, before and after the peasant revolution. But let me point out, too, that the total number of peasant households had increased by 8.4 percent in the course of two years. Such a growth was "exceptionally high—in peacetime it fluctuated usually around 1 percent and did not exceed 2 percent." [50] The sharp increase has been attributed partly to the return to the village of peasant workers from the cities and, to a greater extent, to the increased division of peasant households. Such divisions took place in order to escape both excessive government requisitioning of foodstuffs and *raskulachivanie,* or forced splitting of farm units, a procedure that threatened larger holdings more than the smaller ones.[51] The great increase in the number of households during so short a period signalizes the growth of smaller, weaker farm units at the expense of the larger, stronger ones. The data in Table 8 bear this out. There was, first of all, a considerable reduction in the number of households at the bottom of the scale, those which had no sowings at all and in the past had to hire out their labor or seek employment in the cities. Second, the decline of these proletarian elements was accompanied by a sharp increase in the number of the smallest holdings, those of up to 5.4 acres. A much smaller increase took place in middle-sized holdings of between 5.5 and 11 acres. Finally, a decrease occurred at the other end of the scale, in holdings of larger size. The greater the size, the higher proportionately was the decrease in numbers. Essentially the same pattern emerges from data of land distribution in different provinces

Table 9. Distribution of peasant holdings in small districts by sown area in Balashov uezd, Saratov province (lower Volga region)

Desiatinas	Acres	Samoilovsk volost		Ust-Shchedrinsk volost	
		1917	1920	1917	1920
Without sowings		23.3%	20.8%	6.1%	4.0%
Up to 2	Up to 5.4	9.5	36.7	11.8	5.2
2.1–4	5.5–10.8	17.1	28.7	15.4	33.6
4.1–6	10.9–16.2	14.6	9.7	18.1	25.2
6.1–10	16.3–27.0	18.8	3.9	22.2	28.2
10.1–16	27.1–43.2	11.6	0.2	14.5	3.7
16.1–25	43.3–67.5	4.1	—	8.6	0.1
Over 25	67.6 and over	1.0	—	3.3	—
Total		100.0	100.0	100.0	100.0

Source. *Materialy po istorii agrarnoi revoliutsii v Rossii* (Materials for the History of the Agrarian Revolution in Russia), ed. L. Kritsman (Moscow, 1929), II, 325–326.

Table 10. Distribution of peasant holdings in small districts by sown area in Romenskii uezd, Poltava province (Ukraine)

Desiatinas	Acres	Bobritsk volost		Khustiansk volost	
		1917	1920	1917	1920
Without sowings		8.2%	4.6%	5.3%	1.2%
Up to 2	Up to 5.4	39.9	28.4	14.0	11.2
2.1–4	5.5–10.8	16.6	37.2	15.5	38.6
4.1–6	10.9–16.2	11.1	19.5	18.7	31.1
6.1–10	16.3–27.0	14.2	9.3	24.7	16.6
10.1–16	27.1–43.2	6.0	1.0	15.8	1.2
16.1–25	43.3–67.5	2.8	—	4.9	0.1
Over 25	67.6 and over	1.2	—	1.1	—
Total		100.0	100.0	100.0	100.0

Source. *Materialy po istorii agrarnoi revoliutsii v Rossii*, II, 49–52.

and in volosts, though in some cases the number of the smallest holdings of less than 5.5 acres dropped (see Tables 9 and 10). It is possible that the picture is to some extent distorted by the underestimation of middle-sized and large holdings.[52] Yet this cannot alter the basic fact that the post-revolutionary economic structure of Russian peasant farming had become much more level—the landholding extremes were flattened out.

In examining statistics for livestock—the principal form of capital in peasant farming—we again encounter a similar improvement at the bottom and a decline at the top (see Tables 11 and 12). The number of holdings without horses or cows decreased, and those having only one horse or one or two cows increased. At the other end, the number of holdings with more than one horse or more than two cows decreased. Note that the decrease in the number of holdings without horses took place despite the fact that the total number of horses enumerated by the sample censuses also decreased from 448,313 in 1917 to 432,300 in 1919, or by 3.6 percent. This means that there were fewer horses in relation to a larger number of farm holdings. It is true that the total number of cows during this period increased by 25,587—from 497,489 to 523,076. But this was still less than the rise of 36,099 in the number of holdings. Normally it would have resulted in the rise of the number of holdings without cows. We know that the opposite occurred and that the reduction in the number of holdings without cows was accompanied also by a sharp decrease of holdings with many cows. Livestock as well as land became more evenly distributed, though regional inequalities persisted. It is important to note

Table 11. Number of cows per peasant holding

| | 1917 | | 1919 | | |
Number of cows	Number of holdings	Percent	Number of holdings	Percent	Percent 1919 is of 1917
None	77,767	18.2	73,766	15.9	94.9
1	242,187	56.7	282,303	61.0	116.6
2	80,909	18.9	87,690	18.9	108.4
3 and more	26,428	6.2	19,631	4.2	74.3
Total	427,291	100.0	463,390	100.0	108.4

Source. Compiled from official sources in Peshekhonov, "Dynamics of the Peasant Economy," *Zapiski instituta izucheniia Rossii,* II, 19.

Table 12. Number of horses per peasant holding

| | 1917 | | 1919 | | |
Number of horses	Number of holdings	Percent	Number of holdings	Percent	Percent 1919 is of 1917
None	122,826	28.75	116,138	25.06	94.6
1	203,469	47.62	278,714	60.15	137.0
2	75,072	17.57	56,973	12.30	75.9
3	16,990	3.98	8,356	1.80	49.2
4	5,304	1.24	2,224	0.48	41.9
5 and over	3,630	0.84	985	0.21	27.1
Total	427,291	100.00	463,390	100.00	108.4

Source. Peshekhonov, "Dynamics of the Peasant Economy," *Zapiski instituta izucheniia Rossii,* II, 18.

that, though the Revolution resulted in a leveling of Russian agriculture, it was essentially a leveling downward.

Thus the agrarian revolution in its immediate effects benefited the average peasant (the middle peasant or *seredniak,* in Soviet terminology) as well as many of those below the average (the poor peasant or *bednota*). But it also hurt a minority who were above the average, the economically stronger and usually better farmers, who were indiscriminately dubbed kulaks. A prophecy made years before the revolution by that staunch supporter of a moderate land reform, Kaufman, was fulfilled: "How will the agrarian reform be ultimately accomplished—particularly, will it be based on the principles advocated by the Party of Peoples' Liberty [Cadet] —who can tell? One thing can be said with certainty; the longer it is delayed by the bureaucracy, which is not willing to part with its autocratic rule, the more strongly will it [the bureaucracy] resort to repressive measures to fight that which can only be combated by political and social reforms—the more radical will the land reform be." [53]

The radicalism of the peasant revolution was bound to accentuate its adverse effects on the national economy, certainly in the short run. The extreme fragmentation of farming, the sudden disappearance of larger properties, even of larger peasant properties, which are normally characterized by higher yields and commercialization of crops, the growing self-sufficiency of small peasant agriculture, that is, the tendency to consume on the farm more of what was produced, and the revival of the scattered-strip system—all impaired the efficiency of Russian agriculture at a time when it was already weakened by four years of war and revolution. As one Russian authority put it: "Peasant individual farming, having become en masse smaller and more uniform, assimilated all the negative features of petty agriculture, consisting in low productivity of labor, implements, and livestock. This is shown by a decrease of more than a fifth in the sown acreage per draft horse between 1916 and 1921. The same would be true if it were possible to estimate precisely the amount of work per male or female worker. As a result of the reduction of sown area, labor productivity became lower. The land and means of production, diffused over a larger number of farm units, were utilized less rationally." [54]

Of utmost importance from the standpoint of the national economy was the fact that extreme farm subdivision increased the propensity toward self-sufficiency, characteristic of very small farming under the Russian conditions of extensive cultivation. Thus the ascendancy of small peasant farming was bound to weaken the link with the market at a time when the cities already were faced with a serious food shortage. But the economic policy of the government, which I shall discuss next, bears an even heavier responsibility for the widespread deterioration in food supply and distribution. Still, politically, the revolutionary distribution of land, carried out in this non-Marxist fashion, paid off: by temporarily appeasing the peasant masses it helped to consolidate the Communist regime in Russia. The harmonious relationship between the Bolsheviks and the peasants did not last long. As Lenin had prophesied, a new struggle soon began in the villages.

Part Two. The Peasant under Communism

7

War Communism

The years from mid-1918 to the spring of 1921, known as the period of War Communism, were characterized by a civil war between the Red forces and the loyalist White; by a sharp conflict between the new Soviet regime and the peasants; by a severe decline in agriculture and a general economic decay and disorganization, connected to the effort of the regime to communize the national economy. Hunger and general distress were the end results. It is not the object of this study to treat War Communism as a whole, but only its agrarian facets. The key factor is the conflict between the regime and the peasants, beginning on the heels of a successful revolution that terminated the peasants' age-old struggle with the landlords.

The Food Shortage and the Soviets

The immediate cause of the friction was the extremely critical state of the food supply. It will be recalled that the food situation in the cities had become progressively worse as the First World War dragged on. The shortage of bread in Petrograd served as a prologue to the revolution in

March 1917. To cope with the grain crisis, the Provisional Government took a radical step; it established a state grain monopoly on March 25, 1917. All grain in excess of that needed by producers for their own consumption or for seed was to be delivered to the state. The government lacked real authority to carry out the stringent monopoly law, since it would have involved coercion of producers, and it remained a dead letter.[1]

The crisis grew more serious with the general economic dislocations following the October Revolution. The estates, the main suppliers of commercial grain, no longer existed. The peasants who possessed grain had no incentive to deliver it to the government at low fixed prices under inflationary conditions—currency was rapidly depreciating and the supply of high-priced manufactured goods was dwindling. It is only necessary to look at the astronomical increase in the issue of paper money to visualize a galloping inflation that practically led to the abandonment of a money economy (see Table 13). Between November 1917 and mid-1921, the quantity of paper money in circulation increased more than one hundred times, and prices increased even faster, with a consequent catastrophic depreciation of the ruble (reflected in the third column of Table 13). Looking at the other component of inflation—the goods supply—we also find a dire situation. The gross output of the manufacturing and mining industries in 1920–21 was less than one sixth of the prewar output (1912).[2] Only about 18 percent of the manufactured textile goods purchased by the rural population before World War I was supplied in 1920.[3] This goes to show how abnormal conditions were for the exchange be-

Table 13. Money in circulation, 1914–1921

Date	Money in circulation (million rubles)	Real value (money in circulation deflated by the price index)
July 1, 1914	1,603	—
March 1, 1917	11,786	—
Nov. 1, 1917	22,446	2,200.6
Jan. 1, 1918	27,312	1,315.6
Jan. 1, 1919	60,764	370.5
Jan. 1, 1920	225,014	93.0
Jan. 1, 1921	1,168,596	69.6
July 1, 1921	2,346,139	29.1

Source: L. N. Iurovskii, *Na putiakh k denezhnoi reforme* (On the Road to Monetary Reform; Moscow, 1924), pp. 19–21.

tween town and country on which the flow of foodstuffs normally depended.

The food situation was further aggravated in 1918 by the loss of some of the principal surplus-producing grain regions in the south and east, a result of foreign occupation (German occupation of the Ukraine) and the civil war. In Lenin's words, the "bony hand of hunger" gripped the Soviet state.[4] How to break this grip, particularly to feed the city workers—the mainstay of the young regime—became one of the principal preoccupations of Lenin and his colleagues during the first four years of their rule.[5] Although they attributed the food crisis to the evil machinations of the bourgeoisie, the Communist rulers understood that, in the words of Commissar of Food Supply, A. D. Tsiurupa, "only by satisfying the demands of the village, by supplying it with necessities, could the hidden grain supply be brought out. All other measures are mere palliatives." [6]

A goods-exchange scheme proposed by Tsiurupa was adopted in a government decree of April 2, 1918. Actually, "a distribution of an insignificant quantity of goods was carried out which did not cover even 20 percent of the requisitioned products. The distribution was based on per capita norms and not in accord with the quantity of grain delivered. Goods were allocated to those who produced least and delivered even less." [7] It was expected that the peasants who had no grain to deliver would bring pressure to bear on those who had. In the words of another Commissar of Food, this was "the class principle lying at the root of Soviet food policy." [8] But the "class principle" worked two ways. Peasants with some surplus grain had no wish to deliver it to the government, and they lost interest in production beyond the needs of the family. Thus was peasant self-sufficiency still further increased and so was, ipso facto, the plight of the cities and that very industrial proletariat in whose name and interest the Bolshevik regime was ostensibly operating. The catastrophic decline in grain supply to the cities can be seen from the fact that, whereas in November–April 1918 the monthly deliveries of grain averaged 3,730 carloads, they declined by May 1918 to 1,622, during June to 1,086, and during July and August to 707 and 784 respectively.[9]

The government decided in May 1918 to adopt drastic measures to extract grain from the peasants. On May 14 there was published a decree "concerning special authority vested in the People's Commissariat of Food Supplies for the struggle against the rural bourgeoisie dealing and speculating in grain." [10] The title of this measure—which became known as the decree of "food dictatorship"—foreshadowed the general line taken in the ensuing campaign. According to official theory, it was a struggle with kulaks, who were accused of holding out grain from the hungry masses of poor peasants and city workers in the expectation of higher prices. On this indictment was based the justification for forceful extraction of grain. The decree of May 14 confirmed the principle of grain monopoly and fixed prices, and required all those who possessed grain to declare within a week any surplus above the established norms for seed and personal-consumption requirements. Severe penalties were provided for failure to comply with the law. The regime, unable to nationalize all 18 million peasant holdings, undertook instead to nationalize their output, leaving the peasants the barest minimum of food and sometimes not even that.[11]

To aid the government in the grain requisition, the poorer peasants were enlisted. A decree of June 11, 1918, called for the organization of village and volost committees of the poor (*komitety bednoty,* or *kombedy,* the abbreviated title by which they became known), which were also put in charge of distributing whatever supplies were allocated to the village.[12] The more complicated agricultural implements were also to be transferred to the volost kombedy for the purpose of organizing collective cultivation and harvest of crops by poor peasants. These peasants were to be given a share of the requisitioned grain at no cost or at discount prices, depending on the speed with which the requisitioning was accomplished. Thus incentives were offered for the speedy collection of grain. The kombedy were not slow in launching an offensive in which not only grain but land, implements, livestock, and supplies of various farm products were expropriated and distributed among the poor peasants. The expropriated peasants offered resistance which, with the presence in the villages of demobilized soldiers who often retained their arms, resulted in many pitched battles between the two camps. Military detachments were actually formed in conjunction with a number of kombedy.[13]

This campaign succeeded in splitting the peasantry into warring factions and unleashed the class struggle that Lenin had said would follow the ejection of the landlords. The "struggle for bread," as the campaign came to be known, is usually represented in Soviet literature as a drive against the kulaks. But that the middle peasants were also a target for hostilities was acknowledged even by the Soviet leadership. Lenin and Tsiurupa warned local authorities, in a sharp telegram on August 17, 1918, that local reports frequently indicated that the interests of the middle peasants were being violated by the kombedy. "The slogan of organizing the poor has been incorrectly interpreted in many localities in the sense that the poor must be set off against the whole remaining peasant population—against the known kulaks and the rich (*bogatei*), as well as against the middle strata of peasantry which only yesterday went hungry and began to breathe freely only under the Soviet regime . . .

The kombedy must be revolutionary organs of the whole peasantry, opposed to the former landlords, kulaks, merchants, and priests, and not merely organs of the rural proletariat set off against the whole remaining rural population." [14]

Lenin asserted with regard to the kombedy period that "our village . . . itself experienced an 'October' revolution." [15] Yet the kombedy, for all the early official enthusiasm they aroused, were short-lived. An exception was the Ukraine, where they were organized only in 1920 and continued until 1929.[16] The kombedy were dissolved by the action of the Sixth All-Union Soviet Congress in November 1918.[17] They were merged with the local soviets, which were purged of "bourgeois" elements through new elections. The explanation for their demise usually given in Soviet literature is that the kombedy often arrogated or interfered with the functions of the rural soviets, with a consequent overlapping of authority, confusion, and waste of personnel. This explanation is true as far as it goes—but it does not go far enough. A serious drawback from the Soviet standpoint was the fact that the kombedy often retained much of the requisitioned grain for their own needs, leaving little for the cities.[18] The kombedy, therefore, were not a very efficient instrument for the acquisition of grain and, at the same time, aroused the violent antagonism of the rest of the peasantry, not only the kulaks.

The Soviet government still had no intention of giving up the use of force in grain procurements. In fact, it found a more effective instrument in special workers' food detachments (prodovol'stvennye otriady), which came on the scene when the kombedy did. Detachments of workers and sailors began to be dispatched to the grain-producing regions by November 1917, in accordance with a decree of the Military-Revolutionary Committee of November 5, 1917.[19] The employment of these food commandos was haphazard, but on August 6, 1918, a decree of the Council of People's Commissars (Sovnarkom) was published, calling for the participation of workers' organizations in grain procurement; [20] this led to the mushroom growth of these groups. The decree authorized unions, factory committees, and local soviets to form food detachments, consisting of workers and the poorest peasants, "to travel to grain regions for the purpose of acquiring at fixed prices or requisitioning grain from the kulaks." Half of the procured grain was to be delivered to the organization responsible for sending the detachment, and the other half was to be turned over to the Commissariat of Food Supply.

Regulations issued on August 20, 1918, set forth in greater detail the staffing and functions of these detachments.[21] Each group was to consist of no less than 75 workers, with two to three machine guns. On reaching their destination, the food detachments were instructed to organize kombedy and, with the latter, to disarm the population. Some of the weapons were to be left with the kombedy for the organization of a militia. Then the detachment was to take an inventory of the grain supplies in the area, preliminary to the requisition of the surpluses. Part of the requisitioned grain was to be turned over to the peasants who did not have enough grain to last until the next harvest.

The drive to organize food detachments resulted in the creation of a veritable army, numbering from 20,000 to 45,000 at various times between 1918 and 1920. Beginning in February 1919 the task of organizing the food detachments in different regions was concentrated in the Military Food Bureau of the All-Russian Council of Trade Unions.[22] The requisition levy was also regularized by the decree of January 11, 1919, setting up quotas for different districts which were supposed to be allocated ultimately among the various peasant households. However, the very unsatisfactory state of crop statistics at the time—the tendency of some local authorities to underestimate production in order to reduce the levy—militated against fair distribution, even if this were desired by the government. Actually the operations of the food detachments often encroached on vitally needed supplies for the local population and led to, or intensified, starvation in whole provinces.[23] That the food detachments were considered a success, even indispensable, is indicated by the report of the Food Commissariat for 1918–19, which stated that "only in those localities where food detachments operated was it possible to find and procure surplus grain." [24]

The same report stressed the continued use of force in acquiring grain from the peasants. This is precisely the course followed by the Communist rulers, who tried to alleviate hunger among the politically favored sectors of the population with the help of a rationing system favoring industrial workers. But starvation was the result in the villages, and even the cities were not fully taken care of and had to depend for more than half of their grain supply on the now illicit and high-priced free market.[25] The device was called *meshochnichestvo* (from the word *meshochnik,* "bagman") because thousands upon thousands of people invaded the countryside, despite repressive government measures, to buy a bag of flour or grain for personal consumption or resale. A dual system of an inefficient black market and inadequate rationing had replaced the prerevolutionary grain trade.

The forced extraction of grain by the Bolsheviks was accompanied by growing deterioration in Russian agriculture. The best indicator of this is the continuous reduction of the crop area. During World War I, between 1914 and 1917, the crop area for the country as a whole declined relatively little, by 7 or 8.5 percent (according to different estimates using 1913 or 1914 as the base year).[26] It is true that there was a considerable regional variation in crop-acreage trends, with large declines in some important regions and stable or increased acreages in others—and estate agriculture proved especially vulnerable. Commercial production sharply declined even during this period, and there were food-procurement difficulties accentuated by government price policies, transportation bottlenecks, and other distribution defects. A large general reduction of acreage, with a corresponding decline of total production, made the food situation in 1918–1921 much grimmer than it had been in 1917 before the October Revolution. The crop area by 1921 was roughly one fifth below the prerevolutionary period for comparable territory.[27] The decline was expecially severe in the more valuable cash crops, such as wheat, sugar beets, flax, and cotton. But the acreage under rye, the principal bread grain for peasants, decreased but little, and the acres under potatoes and sunflower seed (again consumed chiefly on the farms) increased. The livestock population also declined significantly during the period. Particularly ominous was the reduction of 17 percent in the number of horses. Cattle numbers also decreased by 16 percent (1921 figures, compared with the census data of 1916).[28]

Two factors were principally responsible for the serious agricultural decline: the civil war between the Reds and the Whites, and the Communist requisition policy, which left no incentives for the peasants to produce beyond their own needs and often deprived them even of the necessities of life. Of the two factors, the government's policy was more detrimental:

The regions most affected by the civil war show smaller declines than regions in which the civil war terminated early and which were under the complete control of the Soviet government for a longer period. In the Ukraine, where civil war was especially severe and continued up to 1921, the crop area in 1921 was 96.4 percent of what it had been in 1916. In Siberia, another area where civil war lasted a long time, the crop area in 1921 was 98.2 percent of the area in 1916. But in the grain surplus area of European Russia, always occupied by the Soviet government, the crop area in 1921 stood more than 25 percent below the area of 1916. In the territory of White Russia, another region early under Soviet control, the crop area had fallen in 1921 to 78.6 percent of the area of 1916, and in the grain-deficiency area of Russia to 85.5 percent. Thus, in the regions where Soviet control was complete, the crop area declined between 1916 and 1921 more than in regions where civil war raged longer. The disorder created by the civil war affected peasant agricultural activity less than the strict communist policy of the period of war communism in regions controlled by the Soviet government.[29]

The harmful effect of the requisition system under War Communism was subsequently admitted by the Bolsheviks. As one Soviet textbook puts it: "Receiving nothing in exchange for the grain levy, the peasant began to reduce the sown area; crop yields per acre and livestock numbers declined . . . The peasant, as a small producer, must be personally interested in the increased productivity of agriculture. Such a personal interest could not have existed during the period of War Communism with its grain levy." [30]

Collectivization: The First Round

Lenin probably realized this truth about economic incentives even as he was becoming engrossed in the divisive tactics of fanning class struggle in the villages. His non-Marxist concern over the middle peasant points to this. But it was only after four years of misery for the people of Russia that the principle of economic incentives was put into operation. In the meantime another solution, much more in harmony with Marxist ideology, was sought for the agricultural and food crisis. By the summer of 1918, as Lenin said, "painful hunger forced us toward a purely Communistic task." [31] But now the Bolsheviks were also free to pursue an ideologically independent, uninhibited course. For a final break had occurred with their allies, the Socialist Revolutionaries of the left, who were vehemently opposed to the kombedy and the class struggle in the village, and who until the summer of 1918 dominated Soviet agrarian policy. Now Lenin and his colleagues began to stress the inadequacy of the SR program of egalitarian land distribution. On November 8, 1918, Lenin stated:

> We Bolsheviks were opposed to the law of socialization of land, but we signed it because we did not want to go counter to the will of the majority of peasants . . . We did not want to foist upon the peasantry an idea which is strange to it, the futility of the egalitarian division of land. We considered that it would be better if the laboring peasant masses realized through their own experience [in their own hide] that egalitarian division is nonsense. Only then could we have asked them about the way out of that ruinous condition, of that kulak dominance which took place on the basis of land division. The division was a good thing only at the beginning. It should have signalized that land had been taken away from the landlords, that it was being transferred to the peasants. But this is not sufficient. The way out is only in collective cultivation of land. You [the SRs] were not con-

scious of this, but life itself is bringing you to this view. Communes, cooperative cultivation, associations of peasants—here is the salvation from the disadvantages of small farming; here is the means of raising the level and improving farming, of economical utilization of resources and of combating the kulaks, parasitism, and human exploitation.[32]

Thus class struggle in the village was to be followed by the introduction of socialism in the traditional Marxian sense, replacing the distributive collectivism of the mir. Here was, in Lenin's view, the key to the mastery of the crisis, a way to raise agricultural productivity. "Of course," said Lenin in the same speech, "it will not be possible to make a transition everywhere at once to collective farming. The kulaks will resist in every way, and the [other] peasants themselves are frequently stubbornly opposed to the application of communal principles in agriculture. But the more the peasantry is persuaded by example, by its own experience, of the superiority of communes, the more successful will the movement become." He objected to merely theorizing about the superiority of collective agriculture or about the use of force as distinguished from persuasion by practical deeds. From this commitment to gradualism, Lenin permitted himself only a momentary flight of fancy, when he declared in 1919 that if the peasants were given 100,000 tractors they would plump for communism. But he immediately corrected himself by saying that, under prevailing conditions, this was mere "fantasy." [33] He could also remind the public that communes and other types of collective farming had already been singled out as the goal in the socialization law of February 19, 1918, in which the Communists were more or less passive partners of the Left SRs. This was largely peripheral to the main purpose of the socialization law, however, and Lenin was correct only in the formal sense.

An impetus to collective farming came from the fact that some demobilized soldiers, on return to their villages, found their farms so disorganized that they banded together and founded communes, the first in the nation. They appealed to the government for aid, and on April 27, 1918, the first loan was granted to an agricultural collective by the Commissariat of Agriculture.[34] It is noteworthy that the first type of collective farm established in Soviet Russia and supported by the state was of a completely communistic type, in which production and, to a large extent, consumption were socialized (common kitchens, dining rooms, and such). On May 30, 1918, a special bureau to deal with the organization of agricultural communes was created, and during the following year and a half considerable activity was manifested by the government in this sphere.

On July 21 a model charter for an agricultural commune was approved by the Commissariat of Agriculture. The following principles were formulated in article 3: "Everything belongs to all, and no one in the commune can call anything his own except for articles of personal consumption; everyone in the commune works according to his capacity and is remunerated according to his needs, depending on the economic condition of the commune; work is carried on collectively; the surplus of products, after covering all the requirements of the communes, are delivered for collective use through the local food organs of the Soviet government in exchange for commodities needed by the commune; a commune cannot use hired labor." These basic principles and other details were reiterated or amplified in further instructions from the Commissariat of Agriculture for drawing up charters for communes, issued on August 3, 1918.[35]

Here was the officially prescribed pattern for a full-fledged, completely egalitarian commune. No individual incentives were to be provided for producers, and surpluses above need (a very vague concept) were to be taken over by the state. And all this was to happen not to a small group of idealists, to people imbued with special religious fervor, or to those who had grown up in a communist society, but to large masses of ordinary workers and peasants accustomed to a noncommunist socioeconomic order. By all rational economic tests, this *was* a fantasy—but not for the Bolsheviks, who declared that communes were to be established to maximize foodstuff production "by raising the productivity of agriculture, by increasing the sown area, and by the fullest and most effective utilization of farm implements and other equipment." [36]

During this honeymoon period, the Bolshevik leadership could not predict its later stock objection to this type of collective farming—that the commune is too consumption-minded at a time when expansion of production is particularly urgent; that the commune concerns itself predominantly with the interests of its membership, disregarding those of the state. At this early time, the Soviet state actively supported the communes by financial subsidization and in other ways. On July 3, 1918, the Sovnarkom appropriated 10 million rubles (presumably gold) for "measures for the development of agricultural communes." Again one month later, 50 million rubles were budgeted for loans to local authorities for financing agricultural departments and the organization of communes. On November 2, 1918, a further appropriation was made by the Sovnarkom for grants and loans to communes and other types of collective farms. Two conditions were set for such loans: (a) farming methods and measures for improvement required by government authorities should be followed; and (b) loans should be repaid in kind (in agricultural products). Communes were also to be given priority in allotment of land in single, consolidated tracts and in securing the farmsteads, implements, and livestock of the estates.[37]

The new orientation toward collectivism received its fullest legal expression in another comprehensive land law, promulgated on February 14, 1919, about a year after the enactment of the socialization law. The title of the new law clearly indicates its purpose: "Concerning Socialist Land Organization and Measures for Transition to Socialist Agriculture." [38] Here was no vague expression, so characteristic of former land legislation, that the land belongs to all the people. Such a formulation had been intended to distinguish the socialization of land from nationalization. The new law established in unmistakable terms the principle of state ownership of land. It further declared, in article 3, that all forms of individualistic farming "must be looked upon as dying out" and that the transition to cooperative farming was necessary to establish a unified system of socialist agriculture. Large soviet (state) farms, communes, cooperative cultivation of soil, and other types of collective farming were deemed the best means to this end. They were to have priority in the allocation of land and the technical assistance and surveying needed for proper territorial farm organization (*zemleustroistvo*). The highest priority was to be given to state farms, followed by communes and other types of collective farming. Small peasant family farming took last place on this scale. The fundamental aim of the new law was clear: to replace small-scale peasant farming by state or cooperative types, from which a full-fledged socialist organization of agriculture would finally emerge.

The number of communes increased rapidly at first—from 975 at the end of 1918 to 1,961 at the end of 1919—and slowed down during 1920, when only 156 communes were added. A number of communes were quite short-lived, in some cases existing only for a few months.[39] Some were cryptocommunes—and this applied to other types of collective farming—adopting the collective form as camouflage for tabooed types of individualistic farming, such as the khutor.[40] The communes were rapidly outpaced by another type of collective, the artel. This was the prototype of the modern kolkhoz, which is not as fully socialized as the commune. Only land and other means of production are socialized in an artel; consumption remains entirely a function of the individual household, and distribution is based on the members' labor contribution. At the end of 1918 there were only 604 artels; by the end of 1919 they had increased to 3,606, exceeding by 84 percent the number of communes. On May 19, 1919, a model charter for an agricultural artel was approved by the Commissariat of Agriculture, pointing to the growing importance of the form.[41] At the end of 1920 the number of artels was two and a half times greater than a year earlier. Data for 1920 are given in the following tabulation.[42]

	Communes	Artels	Other collectives	Total
Number of farms	2,117	8,581	946	11,644
Agricultural land (acres)	496,000	2,027,000	131,000	2,654,000
Population	82,528	487,831	55,477	625,836

It will be observed that, despite the rapid tempo of development, only about 625,000 out of the 100 million rural population had joined collective farms of one kind or another before 1921. Further evidence of the minor importance of collective farming is provided by the census of 1920, according to which it accounted for less than 1 percent of the total sown area. Although the census data are quite incomplete, they are sufficiently representative of the position of collective farming in the Russian agricultural scheme at that time. Notwithstanding their relative insignificance, there is evidence that collectives aroused considerable hostility among the peasants, especially the communes and less so the artel. This hostility went so far that, as reported from Gomel province, there were violent attacks on the communes and massacres of their members.[43] In some instances this attitude was due, as Lenin acknowledged, to the efforts of overzealous local authorities in forcing peasants into such farms.[44] But the preferential treatment by the Soviet state and the presence in considerable numbers of town or nonlocal people in the membership of the collectives were probably other contributory causes. The peasants objected especially strongly to the use of allotted land for such purposes.[45] It is probably no accident that the collectives, particularly the communes, were predominantly organized not on the allotted peasant land, but on other (prerevolutionary) categories of land, as shown by the figures following.[46]

Category of land	Communes	Artels
Peasant (allotted)	10%	31%
Privately owned (estate)	74	48
Church	12	10
Public domain	4	11
	100%	100%

Peasant hostility to the commune was claimed to have been overcome in some instances when commune members won respect as efficient farmers, and particularly when they proved helpful to their neighbors.[47] In spite of the favors granted by the government, the communes often found themselves in a difficult position because of shortages of draft power, seed, and implements and lack of technical knowledge. A shortage of horses in the commune was a serious handicap. Here lies a very important difference between collectivization in 1918–1921 and in the 1930s, in that the latter was linked with mechanization. But the collectives of 1918–1921 were more genuinely voluntary than the kolkhozes organized after the 1930s. In the meantime the official attitude was becoming less optimistic. A high Soviet official declared that "the productive effect of collective and state farms was not far from zero." [48] Lenin himself showed traces of disappointment with the communes at the First Congress of Agricultural Communes and Artels in December 1919.[49] Another Soviet official summed it all up by stating that "banking on collectivization for the purpose of drawing the peasantry into a socialist economy or for technical improvement of peasant farming must be abandoned." [50]

I have discussed the collective farms proper, the kolkhozes—producers' cooperatives—which were formed by pooling the holdings of formerly independent peasant farmers or by organizing communes on former estate land. Another type of agricultural collective was the state farm, the sovkhoz, constituting a system of government-owned estates or plantations, managed and staffed by hired workers as were the nationalized factories. Thus the two parallel institutional forms of collectivization were born during the period of War Communism. Both were children of a marriage of exigency. The food crisis and the conflict it engendered with the peasantry suggested to the Bolsheviks the desirability of organizing large factory-like farms, which would make the food supply of the cities less dependent on the productive efforts and marketing decisions of the peasants.[51] Such a scheme appealed to the Soviet leadership not only for pragmatic reasons but also because it harmonized with the ideological climate of the period, with its emphasis on communization and nationalization. Thus former private estates, or what was left of them after the peasants were through, were to be used to organize "factories producing grain, meat, milk, fodder, etc., which would free the socialist order economically from dependence on the small property owner and, at the same time, would provide a better organization of production and distribution." [52] It was also hoped that the sovkhozes would serve as model farms, demonstrating improved farm methods to the peasants. The high hopes aroused by the sovkhoz idea in official circles were voiced by Commissar of Agriculture Sereda, who stated in December 1918 that the sovkhozes and communes were a principal factor in the socialist reconstruction of the whole of agriculture.[53]

Apart from ideological considerations or larger questions of policy, there was an immediate practical problem posed by the need of processing industries to obtain raw materials, for which they had depended on private estates. For example, the sugar industry needed sugar beets. Here again the establishment of state farms pointed to a solution, and the first to be organzied were the 218 sugar-beet farms created in accordance with a Sovnarkom decree of July 13, 1918.[54] A decree of July 19, 1918, led to the organization of 111 state stud farms and other purebred livestock farms.[55]

On October 1, 1918, the Sovnarkom issued a decree on the direct transfer to the control of the Commissariat of Agriculture of estates with valuable crops, livestock, and processing facilities for agricultural products, as well as large estates that generally employed progressive farm methods.[56] The further division of estates was prohibited. This decree can be considered the first general charter for state farms. The new land law of February 13, 1919, followed it up by devoting two large sections to state farms. A further stimulus to state farming was given by the Sovnarkom decree of February 15, 1919, permitting the allocation of unused land to factories, trade unions, and various government agencies and institutions, including the city soviets, for the purpose of growing food for their staffs.[57] It was, of course, in the interests of both management and employees to mitigate the severe food shortage through the organization of such attached (*pripisnye*) or "captive" sovkhozes. The following figures indicate the growth of state farms.[58]

Year	Number of sovkhozes
1918	3,101
1919	3,547
1920	4,292
1921	4,391

The reality of the performance during this period differed greatly from the original concept behind the sovkhoz. Though the sovkhozes were growing in numbers, in 1921 they had a sown area of only a little over 500,000 acres. Actually not much was left of the private estates for the sovkhozes to take over. The best land, livestock, and implements had already been distributed. As a rule, only parts of the former private estates were used for organizing state farms.[59] Managerial skill was also lacking, since the former estate managers had been removed or had fled during the Revolution. The sovkhozes, therefore, were greatly handicapped from the start, and the government was in no position to help: "On the whole, the sovkhozes were in a very difficult situation and were not able to fulfill the role in the process of collectivization which was assigned to them by the state." [60] The official hopes that the sovkhozes would become large grain, meat, and milk "factories," and models for progressive farming, were dwindling by the end of 1920.[61] By 1920–21, collective and state farming, the socialist sector of agriculture, as it later came to be known, was still a tiny island in the ocean of small peasant agriculture, which it could influence but little.

"To hope to be able to reconstruct the village via a gradual strengthening of the sovkhozes and kindred voluntary collectives means to follow a utopian course. *Socialism is to be built only by the transformation of the whole economy, of all its units, simultaneously;* and not by multiplying cooperative factories—oases in a bourgeois desert." [62] The italicized part of this quotation gives the gist of the new direction of Soviet agrarian policy taken at the end of 1920, in the words of its principal architect N. (V. V.) Osinskii. Despite a more realistic outlook regarding the sovkhozes, communes, and other collectives, the Soviet government was not yet ready to give up collectivization as a short-range objective. And given the ideological predispositions of the Soviet leadership, the difficult food and agricultural situation was bound to militate against any easy yielding to a noncollectivist alternative. In fact, the idea for a new mode of collectivization originated in the Commissariat of Food Supply, which was headed by Osinskii. A Soviet legal authority defined it as "a compulsory state regulation of peasant farming . . . a compulsory organized intervention with peasant production and its compulsory mass organization." [63] Osinskii developed this thesis of state control as follows: "The principal factor of the socialist reconstruction of agriculture is a compulsory regulation of agricultural production as a whole—regulation which will penetrate deeper and deeper and will develop into a state organization of production." [64] Another Soviet official explained that peasants are state workers, working on state land, and therefore must follow the plans and directives of the government with respect to the size of the area and the kind of crops to be seeded.[65] Parenthetically, this sounds curiously like an echo of the "state peasants" of the serfdom era. We shall encounter again from time to time such throwbacks to the past.

The goal of the new policy, then, was to bring the peasants en masse into a state-controlled agricultural economy. This certainly was a more formidable effort at the mass collectivization of peasant agriculture than the organization of the early communes and sovkhozes. It was to begin with relatively simple regulatory measures and be extended gradually, ending with thoroughgoing collectivism. In embarking on the new program the Soviet leaders realized that "in order to revive the village [agriculture], it is necessary to supply it with a normal quantity of the products of urban industry; but the city in turn must be supplied with a definite quantity of raw materials and food. How does one escape from this vicious circle?" The answer was to force the peasants to work harder and better, thus increasing agricultural production; for it was held that efficient farming was "the primary duty of the peasant." [66] With Lenin's backing, the proposed policy was approved by the Eighth All-Russian Congress of Soviets in December 1920. He was ambivalent, though, saying to the congress: "The peasants are not socialists. And to build our social-ist plans as if they were socialists means to build on sand; it means not to have understood our problems; it means not to have learned during three years to correlate our programs and carry through our undertakings in accordance with that impoverished and wretched reality in which we live." Although Lenin still stressed persuasion of peasants, he approved Osinskii's strong-arm methods: "Certainly no comrade could be found now who would doubt the need for special highly energetic measures of aid, not only of encouragement but of compulsion, in order to expand agricultural production . . . In a country of small peasant farming our main and basic objective is to be able to pass on to state coercion in order to raise the level of peasant agriculture, beginning with measures most necessary, urgent, simple, and clearly understood by every peasant." [67]

If Lenin was cogitating at the time of the Eighth Congress about an alternative noncollectivist solution to the agricultural crisis, one that he adopted only two and a half months later, he gave no evidence of it. But other Soviet leaders vehemently rejected it. According to Osinskii, to replace requisitions by taxation and to permit the peasant to dispose freely of the rest of his produce, including sale on the market, meant, in the absence of a sufficient supply of goods for exchange, the ruin of the whole Soviet food policy. Government procurements would become impossible "if parallel with them there should develop a free trade in grain. Then all products will flow into this channel. Just open this door a little and immediately the grain will disappear; and whoever opens it is leading toward a crash of our food policy and the destruction of our national economy." [68] It is well to remember this prophecy in view of what was to transpire shortly.

The law approved by the Eighth Congress on December 28, 1920, set forth the general principles of the policy of state regulation, which was elaborated upon by a series of supplementary decrees and regulations issued early in 1921.[69] The main features of the new agricultural scheme were as follows. (1) A national plan was set up for the sowing of acres to various crops. These targets were to be distributed among different provinces, smaller administrative divisions, villages, and ultimately the millions of peasant households, so that each household would have as-signed to it an acreage allotment. Such sowings were compulsory and aimed to eliminate the dangerous decline of sown areas. A provision, however, was made for a certain portion of the acreage to be sown by the peasants at their own discretion. (2) Measures were prescribed for safeguarding the essential seed supply by requiring farmers to store their seed in public warehouses or by periodic inspection of the seed stored on the farm, for which the peasant was held responsible. (3) The shortage of draft power and implements on peasant farms was also to be alleviated, either through state assistance or through the "compulsory mutual assistance" of neighbors. The latter were to be repaid through labor services. (4) Not only were acreage goals and allotments set, but compulsory rules were laid down for improving farm practices in order to raise the low crop yields per acre. (5) To help carry out these various measures, special "committees for expansion of sowings and improved cultivation of soil" were to be created for each province, smaller administrative division, and village.

Although there was criticism of the details of the new agrarian legislation at the congress, especially of the new sowing committees, basic opposition to the compulsory state scheme was voiced only by the Mensheviks, who were then still admitted to the Soviet congresses. A resolution introduced by David Dallin in the name of the Menshevik delegation declared: "Agricultural production in Russia is carried on by 15 million small peasant farms, principally using family labor and not susceptible to systematization and control. The organization of this type of production by means of state compulsion not only cannot yield fruitful results, but will also lead to still further decline in the productivity of these farms and to a colossal growth of bureaucracy." [70] The Mensheviks proposed another program for dealing with the agricultural crisis. Its main planks were: replacement of requisitions by taxation; the free marketing by peasants of their surpluses and the consequent legalization of private trade; the securing of existing peasant tenure on estate and public-domain land occupied during the revolution; abolition of the kombedy; retention by the state of only the best, economically profitable sovkhozes and lease of the others to the peasants, with preference given to collective forms of exploitation; freedom for the peasants to create their own cooperative political, cultural, and other organizations.[71] These proposals were received with abuse and derision at the congress, and the Mensheviks were dubbed the "ideologues of the kulaks." Only a few months later, however much of what they proposed, except the last feature, was put into operation by Lenin.

No sooner was the new Soviet program developed, early in 1921, than it was relegated to limbo by an abrupt about-face in agricultural policy; the new turn sounded the death knell of War Communism and, for the time being, of the associated ideas of collectivized and planned agriculture. Nonetheless, in addition to its historical interest, the agrarian legislation of 1920–21 is instructive as the prototype of much that was done by the Soviet state less than a decade later.

8

The New Economic Policy

In the spring of 1921 the growing agricultural crisis of underproduction was still the dominant national problem. It had been aggravated by drought in many regions in 1920. The resulting decline in yield per acre came on top of a serious drop in the grain acreage itself, referred to earlier. The combined effect of these reductions brought the 1920 harvest of the seven principal grains, according to the data of the State Planning Commission (Gosplan), 21 percent below 1919 and 39 percent below 1909–1913.[1] At the same time, the number of rationed people whom the government had to feed increased from 12 million in 1918–19 to 23 million in 1919–20 and to 35 million in 1920–21.[2] Government grain procurements in 1920 were considerably larger despite a poor harvest. (See Table 14.) In part this reflected the expansion of the territory under Soviet control, which was extended now to important surplus-producing regions. Yet because the Soviet apparatus was still weak in the grain regions of Siberia and the North Caucasus, where transportation difficulties were also considerable, large collections had to continue, according to Lenin, "in provinces with the poorest crops, and, because of this, the crisis of peasant agriculture became much sharper."[3] If additional

Table 14. Government procurements of all food and forage grains, 1916–17 to 1927–28

Year	Quantity (thousand metric tons)
1916–17	8,323
1918–19	1,768
1919–20	3,480
1920–21	6,012
1921–22	3,814
1922–23	5,916
1923–24	6,842
1924–25	5,248
1925–26	8,913
1926–27	11,616
1927–28	10,993

Source. *Statisticheskii spravochnik SSSR za 1928 g.*, pp. 702–703.

evidence is needed of the gravity of the situation, it can be found in the fact that on January 22, 1921, the already scanty bread ration was cut by one third in the capital and the large cities—and this when other food-stuffs were even scarcer. Not to be overlooked, too, is the acute fuel shortage, which greatly hampered grain transportation by railroad from the producing to the consuming regions. The truth of the matter is that the agricultural crisis was organically related to the growing paralysis of the whole economic system, as the latter was being increasingly communized.

The National Crisis

How can the catastrophic dimensions of this situation be visualized today? If we turn to the American national experience in search of analogies, the only example of something approaching an economic catastrophe, at least in the twentieth century, is the Great Depression of the 1930s. Paul Samuelson writes: "If you ask an economic historian just what the Great Depression really meant, his single best answer would be: from a 1929 NNP [national net product, or national income] of 95.8 billion dollars there was a drop to a 1933 NNP of 48.8 billion dollars. This halving of the money value of the flow of goods and services in the

American economy caused hardship, bank failures, riots and political turmoil." [4] But real national income in the United States (the money value of the national income deflated by the price index) decreased not by half but by a little over a third. For Soviet Russia there are no such accurate figures of national income in that period. But estimates by the best authority in the field indicate a decrease of per capita real national income between 1913 and 1921 of more than 60 percent, and between 1916–17 and 1921 of 55 percent.[5]

In Russia it was not lack of money income accompanied by plentiful supplies of goods, as in the United States, but an acute shortage of physical supplies, the necessities of life. Certainly, the Russian people suffered immeasurably greater privation during this period, which climaxed six years of war and revolution, than did the American people during one of their most severe crises. "The country as a whole," wrote Chamberlin of Soviet Russia as it was in the winter of 1920–21, "was cold, hungry, disease-ridden, exhausted and embittered; and this was true as regards the majority of the industrial workers and a good many of the rank-and-file Communists." [6]

Even in the face of this, the Soviet leadership clung desperately to a collectivist solution to the agricultural crisis and to the policies of War Communism generally, with the emphasis on strict regimentation. One highly important difference in the grim Soviet picture was that the country was at long last at peace. Yet, as Chamberlin said: "The masses began to demand more and more insistently an improvement in living conditions, which were intolerably bad. The peasants, whose stocks of surplus grain were much smaller because of the poor harvest of 1920, became increasingly resentful of requisitions. Distrust and antagonism grew between the nonparty workers and the Communists and between the rank-and-file Communists and those who were in higher posts." [7]

There is corroborative testimony from Soviet sources of the growing peasant hostility to requisitions, as in the following words of a leading executive of the Food Commissariat: "The peasantry formerly tolerated the grain levy and the lack of supplies of goods in the name of the victory over White Guard generals who were backed by the landlords. Now, with the liquidation of all [military] fronts, the peasantry patently showed that its patience was exhausted." [8] It is also well to recall that the rising fiscal burden on the peasantry in 1920–21, according to the lowest possible estimates, was no less than double that before World War I, including purchase and rental payments for land.[9] Discontent was rampant not only among peasants but also among factory workers and even in the ranks of Communists. But the peasants in many parts of the country went much further in their opposition to the regime, subjecting it "to the most effective criticism—the criticism of armed rebellion." [10] Thus bands of the insurgent peasant anarchist chieftain, N. I. Makhno, who took a prominent part in the civil war, sometimes fighting with the Reds against the Whites but more often fighting against both, were still roving in the Ukraine in the winter and spring of 1921. A serious peasant revolt broke out in western Siberia in the winter of 1921, interrupting communication and shipments of grain on the Trans-Siberian railroad.

The most formidable peasant uprising centered in east-central Russia, in the province of Tambov and the adjoining districts, which also had been the scene of agrarian revolts in 1905 and 1917. This insurrection is associated with the name of its leader, A. S. Antonov, a former political exile who called himself a Socialist Revolutionary. The movement is esti-mated to have been at its height in the winter and early spring of 1921, with 20,000 armed insurgents. The principal cause of the uprising was the grain requisitions and many a Soviet agent engaged in such opera-tions was murdered by the insurgents. Although some traces of Socialist Revolutionary slogans and demands were used, "in the main 'Anto-novism,' as the Tambov movement was sometimes called, like all the peasant insurrections of the Russian civil war, was elemental and destruc-tive. It was the spontaneous outburst of a tormented population that knew that Soviet conditions were intolerable, but had little constructive idea of what to set up instead." [11] This and other uprisings, while highly symptomatic of peasant discontent, were probably not seriously dan-gerous to the regime, since they were geographically scattered and the Red Army was now free to concentrate on the suppression of what the Bolsheviks called banditry. And this was accomplished in the most ruth-less manner—such as the destroying of the homes of insurgent peasants and the shooting of hostages and those who harbored rebels. But no matter how thoroughly the peasants' opposition was crushed, this could only lower their morale and efficiency as producers, and did not overcome the agricultural crisis.

Curiously enough, it was not on agricultural policy that the top Com-munist hierarchy was focusing its attention as it prepared for the con-vening of the Tenth Party Congress in March 1921. Rather, the Com-munist leaders were preoccupied with the role of trade unions in Soviet society.[12] In this fierce controversy Trotsky, the advocate of ironclad regimentation, set himself against the more moderate position of Lenin, and both were staunchly opposed to the syndicalist Workers' Opposition, led by A. G. Shliapnikov and Alexandra Kollontai. Even though agrarian policy was shunted to a back seat in the Communist political arena, Lenin apparently kept a sharp eye on the situation. It is impossible to say when he first changed his mind, but there is evidence that by early

February 1921 he was veering toward abandonment of the requisition system and the substitution of a less burdensome and definite tax in kind, with some freedom for the peasants to market what was left of their output after settling with the state.[13] These proposals obviously involved a shift from the use of forcible collections to increased reliance on economic incentives. A discussion of the question of taxes versus requisitions was started in *Pravda,* but it did not attract much attention as compared with the more spectacular issues agitating the party.[14] Still it provided Lenin with a good alibi when he was later reproached for springing a surprise with his tax proposal. The first public intimation of an impending change in agricultural policy was contained in Lenin's speech at the plenum of the Moscow soviet, delivered on February 28, 1921.[15] He thought that the idea of a tax suggested by some peasants made sense and promised that the question would be brought up at the approaching party congress.

The Tenth Congress met on March 8, 1921, in a tense atmosphere, for at this time a rebellion broke out at the naval base in Kronstadt, following labor unrest and strikes in Petrograd.[16] Since 1917 the sailors of Kronstadt, though in many ways unruly, had been the bulwark of Bolshevism, "the pride of the revolution." Despite Soviet propaganda, which tried to link it with broader counterrevolutionary movements, the Kronstadt uprising was actually a rebellion within the Communist house. So it was a severe shock to the party. Some of the demands of the Kronstadt revolutionaries reflected peasant discontent, and this contributed to the creation of a favorable climate at the congress for revising the agrarian policy of War Communism.

Lenin was ready with his proposals, which had already been approved by the Central Committee of the party. He said in his report to the congress on the opening day: "We must understand that, faced by a crisis in peasant farming, we cannot exist otherwise than by appealing to peasant agriculture for help to the city and the village . . . The most important thing for us is to give the peasant a certain amount of freedom of local trading and to replace the levy by a tax, so that the small farmer can better plan his production." A full week passed before the congress turned again to the agricultural problem and heard Lenin's report on the agricultural tax, on March 15, 1921: "Only an agreement with the peasantry can save the socialist revolution in Russia until a revolution occurs in other countries . . . We must say in a straightforward fashion that the peasantry is dissatisfied with the type of relationship we have established with them; that they don't want this kind of relationship and will no longer stand for it . . . We must satisfy economically the middle peasant and permit free trading; otherwise it is impossible, economically impossible, for the proletariat to retain power in Russia while the tempo of the international revolution is slowing down . . . We exist under such conditions of impoverishment, ruin, and exhaustion of the principal productive forces, the peasants and the workers, that everything for the time being must be subordinated to this basic consideration—to increase production by all means." [17]

Lenin's characterization of the policy under War Communism was further elaborated in a pamphlet he wrote on the food tax shortly after the Tenth Congress, an excerpt from which is relevant here:

> "War Communism" consisted in this—that we took from peasants all surpluses and sometimes not only the surpluses but a portion of the food needed by the peasant for his own consumption; we took these to feed the army and the workers. We took mainly on credit, for paper money. Otherwise we could not have won a victory over the landlords and capitalists in a ruined country of small peasant farmers . . . "War Communism" was forced by war and devastation. It was not and could not have been a policy suitable to the economic objectives of the proletariat. It was a temporary measure. A correct policy for a proletariat exercising its dictatorship in a country of small peasant farmers is the exchange of grain for industrial products needed by the peasants.[18]

Lenin could cite in this connection a pamphlet he had written in the spring of 1918, in which he advocated such a policy of exchange between nationalized industry and peasant agriculture. He could also attribute, with a considerable measure of truth, the hated requisition system of War Communism to the food difficulties resulting from the civil war. That War Communism had its own ideological momentum in the Bolshevik philosophy, Lenin seemed to ignore. When one of his lieutenants, Miliutin, spoke of Soviet agrarian policy as a "harmonious system," Lenin took him to task. "That harmonious system which was created was dictated by military and not by economic needs, considerations, and conditions." [19] It may be legitimately asked why the system of War Communism was not terminated immediately when the war came to an end, in the autumn of 1920, instead of being intensified, with Lenin's blessing, at the Eighth Party Congress in December 1920. In any case, the reasons behind War Communism were undoubtedly mixed.

The truth of the matter is that Lenin at the end of the Russian civil war, like Alexander II at the end of the Crimean War, saw the handwriting on the wall. Both realized the inevitability of a drastic change in agrarian policy, if the nation was to be nursed back to health. They had the courage to make a highly unpalatable decision, which is the essence of statesmanship. Lenin admitted that there were many errors and exaggerations in Soviet economic policy during 1918–1921: "We went too far along the road of nationalization of trade and industry, along the road of suppressing local trade. Was this a mistake? Undoubtedly." He then urged the need for "a stimulus, an incentive, to the peasant from an economic standpoint. It is necessary to say to the small farmer, 'you are the farmer, go on producing and the state will impose merely a minimum tax.' " [20] The appeal to economic incentives in dealing with farmers has since become almost a perennial slogan of Soviet agrarian policy, but, except during critical periods, it remains largely a slogan.

While advocating the urgently needed breathing spell for an exhausted nation, Lenin frankly acknowledged that this involved a partial retreat from socialism to capitalism. He left no doubt that he meant the retreat to be temporary; the march toward socialism would be resumed when food and fuel supplies had made possible the recovery and development of large-scale industry. Lenin was followed at this session of the congress by Food Commissar Tsiurupa, who, though agreeing on the basic principles of the reform, nevertheless warned in strong terms about the difficult transition to the new system. He also spoke against the proposed repeal of restrictions on cooperatives, for which a larger function was envisaged by Lenin. A short debate took place, in which but four speakers participated before it was cut off, and only one of them, M. I. Frumkin, opposed any important facet of the reform. Lenin made some closing remarks, and his resolution embodying the proposed economic policy was voted on and passed.

The basic features of the reform were: abolition of requisitions to procure grain and other agricultural products; the replacement of the levy by a progressive tax in kind, with clear indication of the taxpayer's obligation in advance of the sowing season and with deductions or exemptions as a reward for efficient farming. The new tax—and this is very important—was to be lower than the requisitions and was to cover only the minimum requirements of the army and the nonagricultural population. Moreover, it was to be reduced as industrial and transportation recovery enabled the state to obtain an increased amount of farm products in exchange for the products of nationalized industry. A highly important corollary of the introduction of a definite tax was to permit the farmer to dispose of the remainder of his produce as he saw fit, including voluntary exchange for goods offered by state industry as well as a certain freedom of private trading on a local scale. New legislation was to be framed to implement these principles.[21] It was the permission of limited private trading to peasants, involving a breach of the state monopoly on distribution of grain and other important agricultural products, which aroused the ire of Frumkin—both on the practical grounds that it would seriously interfere with the state collection of necessary supplies and on the ideological grounds that it was a retreat from socialism. He proposed an alternative resolution at the Tenth Congress, eliminating the free trading in farm products, but it was voted down.[22]

The principles of the tax measure approved by the congress were embodied in legislation by a decree on March 21, 1921.[23] Thus, without fanfare, a historic decision was taken that ushered in a significant change not only in agricultural policy but in all of Russian economic life. War Communism was laid to rest, and the New Economic Policy (NEP) was born. Although the ultimate objectives of Communism remained intact, complete collectivization of the economy was postponed for nearly a decade. Just as in the autumn of 1917 Lenin stole the thunder from the Socialist Revolutionaries by adopting their un-Marxist agrarian platform, so in March 1921 he took over the Menshevik agrarian program that had been presented at the Eighth Congress of Soviets in December 1920.

Only the bare foundation of the NEP was delineated by Lenin at the Tenth Congress in March 1921. It took some time before the blueprint was fully developed and its implications realized at home and abroad. Perhaps it was Lloyd George, with that "sixth sense" attributed to him by Keynes,[24] who came closest to grasping the immediate significance of the policy. Defending the recently concluded trade agreement between the British and Soviet governments, he said in the House of Commons on March 22, 1921: "There is a change in Russia itself; there is a change from the wild extravagant Communism of a year or two years ago, or even a few months ago . . . It would be a very good thing to circulate Lenin's speeches as an antidote to the propaganda of the Labour Party in this country . . . He thought he could run his country on some theories of Karl Marx. What does he find? Starvation, famine and his railways completely out of repair. You cannot patch up locomotives with Karl Marx doctrines." [25]

The Development of the NEP

The new policy that passed so easily at the Tenth Congress aroused considerable misgivings and uncertainty in the party and government apparatus. It became necessary to call a special party conference in May 1921, two months after the Tenth Congress, to reaffirm the NEP, which was by that time broadened in scope.[26] Lenin repeated his stand: "Our basic objective is the recovery of large-scale industry; without raising the level of peasant agriculture, we shall not be able to solve the food problem." He held that since it was impossible to achieve the first without the second, a temporary expansion of capitalism during the transitional period was necessary. This was not dangerous because political power, large industry, and transportation—what came to be known as the "commanding heights"—were still concentrated in the hands of the proletariat or, more correctly, the Communist Party. But Lenin did not envisage the period as a short one. He approved the slogan coined by Osinskii, which found good reception at the conference, that all doubt must be removed, that the new economic policy "is absolutely accepted by the party as a policy to be carried out seriously and for a lengthy period of time." [27]

The new agricultural tax had a profound effect on the whole economy. It was the opening wedge for the re-establishment of a money economy and the payment for all goods and commercial services supplied by the state. It ushered in a revival of private trade and small industry. An end was put to inflation; the currency was stabilized and a gold standard adopted in 1924. The new agricultural-tax law, reinforced by subsequent legislation, marked a radical departure from the previous Soviet agrarian legislation in that it largely restored independent small farming. As we have seen, previous Soviet legislation had interfered in one form or another with agriculture by requiring continuous readjustment for the purpose of equalization of holdings (the socialization law of January 1918), by pushing reorganization along collectivist lines (the law of February 1919), or by directly intruding into the process of farming (the legislation of December 1920). Although much of this remained a dead letter, the intent was unmistakable. The agricultural-tax decree, on the other hand, was premised on the economic independence of small peasant family agriculture in land utilization and farm management, as well as in the disposal of output. As stated above, this was Lenin's conception of the best way to expand agricultural production during the transition from capitalism to socialism. Originally there was one other legal obligation on peasant farming, namely, to lay in a supply of seed for sowing, in accordance with the December 1920 legislation on the state regulation of agriculture. But this requirement was repealed by a decree on January 30, 1922. [28]

This new economic freedom needed appropriate legislation to give it legal force, particularly to secure, once and for all, the possession of land seized during the revolution and its maximal use. Actually steps in this direction antedated the NEP. An important straw in the wind was a decree of April 30, 1920, which prohibited frequent redistribution of land as detrimental to productivity and intensive cultivation. Accordingly, permission from local land authorities was required for repartition, and it could not be done until after three crop-rotation cycles (that is, nine years for the widely used three-field rotation). History was seemingly repeating itself, for there is a strong resemblance here to what the tsarist government had tried to do nearly three decades earlier. There was also a series of decrees beginning with one of May 27, 1920, which permitted an increase in the local norm of land allotment for intensive agriculture, provided no hired labor was used.[29] Of far wider significance was the decree of March 23, 1921, issued after the new tax law was passed, which legalized the then-existing distribution of seized estate and public-domain land. Such land could not be retaken by the state either for the purpose of equalizing farmholdings or for the organization of collective farms. An exception was made for land formerly used for special purposes, such as orchards, experiment stations, and the like. But even this land could not be taken away from the peasants without allotting them other land in return.[30] Any socialization or collectivization of agriculture was to assume a voluntary, cooperative form, which could be encouraged financially by the state but not forced on the peasants.

The culmination of the NEP land legislation was the comprehensive land code of the RSFSR, adopted on October 30, 1922.[31] Its basic principles were announced in the Law of Toilers' Land Tenure (*zakon o trudovom zemlepol'zovanii*) of May 22, 1922.[32] Similar codes patterned on that for the RSFSR were adopted by the other republics and, while there were some local variations, these did not affect the basic principles. There was no federal land law, just as there was no federal ministry of agriculture, until near the end of the NEP.

The Land Code reaffirmed the principle of nationalization of land, but for the time being this was largely academic (except for the prohibition of the sale of land). The code also legalized in article 141 existing titles to land the peasants were occupying on May 22, 1922, provided it was cultivated primarily by family labor (*trudovoe khoziaistvo*). Exceptions were made for a few areas such as the Crimea and some regions in the Caucasus and Central Asia, where revolutionary distribution of land did not take place or had been interrupted by the civil war. For these regions the problem of land tenure was settled by special legislation. To further assure the stability of land tenure, article 142 prohibited future redistribution of land by state action, the purpose being to equalize holdings between different villages and volosts as sanctioned by previous agrarian legislation.

One important feature of the code was that it allowed peasants freedom of choice among the different types of land tenure so long as each type was within the framework of family farming. It was formulated as the right to land, or the right to land to be cultivated by one's own labor *(trudovoe pol'zovanie)*. It could be exercised by the peasant as a member of a land community *(zemel'noe obshchestvo* or the mir), accepting, by the same token, the land arrangements adopted by the community; or it could be exercised individually, with no membership in a land community (article 10). All types of tenure were permissible: communal-repartitional, collective, individual-hereditary, or in homesteads *(khutor)*, segregated tracts of land *(otrub)*, and scattered strip holdings (articles 12 and 90). The code thus assumed almost complete neutrality in the matter of land tenure, if it were "toil" tenure. This overturned not only all the previous Soviet legislation, but also all the tsarist legislation after 1861, which had thrown its support first to the mir and later to individualistic forms of tenure.

The peasant's tenure in his holding was in perpetuity and terminated only in cases strictly specified by law, such as dissolution of the household, cessation of farming by the whole household, migration, conviction for certain crimes, absence of the farmer for no less than six years without reliable information concerning his whereabouts, and voluntary renunciation of the holding by all members of the household (article 18). The procedure required to activate the last provision, which aimed at the protection of the peasant household, was spelled out in a separate article (19). The code, in fact, made the peasant household *(dvor)* the unit of land allotment (article 67) and restored the institution of common household (family) property, which had been converted by the Stolypin legislation into the personal property of the head of the household.

Further security and a free hand in farming were given to the peasants by articles 23–26. Article 23 provided compensation for any land taken by the state for public purposes and for losses suffered thereby. Article 24 allowed the peasant to use any farm practices and cropping patterns he chose in cultivating his holding and to erect and use any structures on his land he desired, except those that might interfere with the interests of the neighbors. Article 25 reiterated that all structures, crops, and other property on the land were the absolute personal property of the peasant household. Finally, article 26 prescribed the procedure for obtaining redress for violations of the farmer's land rights. Changes from communal tenure to individual, segregated, or enclosed holdings—the crucial point of the Stolypin legislation—were freely permitted during general land repartitions, either to single peasant households or to groups of households (article 135). It can be said that for the first time since the early 1890s, when the intention was to buttress the mir, the government had adopted a neutral attitude in the matter of land tenure. But it was neutrality with reservations, and a short-lived one at that.

Although the code went pretty far in making the farmer the master of his land, it did not go the whole distance; some serious limitations remained. Land that was legal state property could not be sold, bartered, mortgaged, donated, or bequeathed. On the death of a member of the household (whether or not he was the head), the land and other common property were to continue in the possession of the household, except that under repartitional tenure the landholding could be decreased. There were also restrictions in the code on the leasing of land and the employment of hired labor, in order to check any capitalistic development. Only farms that temporarily became economically weak because of a shortage of labor, draft power, or implements were permitted to lease land for a period not exceeding one full crop-rotation cycle or, in the absence of regular crop rotation, not exceeding three years (articles 28 and 29). Hired labor was "auxiliary," that is, used to assist the peasant household only if at the same time all of its able-bodied members also worked on the farm (articles 39 and 40). This requirement can be traced back to the fundamental proposition of the code that tenure must be based on the actual working of the land. Only a temporary deviation from this rule was allowed in leasing land, when necessitated by special circumstances, and even then the lessee had to work it himself.

The various restrictions of the code which were irksome and frequently evaded, bear traces of the previous socialization trend. Permission for limited leasing of land and the use of hired labor represented a decisive break with the traditions of early Soviet agrarian legislation. The land code of 1922 was called "the Magna Carta of the Soviet farmer." [33] Significant as it was at the time, it proved to be an exceedingly transitory Magna Carta. In 1917 Lenin had given the peasants carte blanche to seize estate land, but the Bolsheviks soon began to expropriate the output, and conflict ensued. The code of 1922 may be viewed as the climax of the move initiated by Lenin in March 1921 to make peace with the peasants. It permitted them to become not only the masters of the land but also of its products, on the condition that they pay a definite tax and maximize output. The peasant revolution was at last to bear fruit. In this first round of his struggle with the Communist government, the peasant emerged victorious.

Unfortunately, the ordeals of the peasant population did not end with the replacement of War Communism by the NEP. The Russian climate not only exercised a veto on the expansion of production, but was responsible for further retrogressions. For the second successive year, a vast area of the country, centering on the Volga region, was stricken by a devastating drought that led to terrible famine. A vivid account of the tragedy is given by H. H. Fisher in his excellent history of the famine. "Men noticed the sign of its coming early in 1920 . . . The spring and early summer of 1921 fulfilled the dark omens of the autumn months, and the certainty of a colossal crop failure brought panic to the Volga lands . . . Early in the summer great numbers of peasants were already without food and all up and down the Volga and as far east as the Urals they were beginning to mix grain with ground straw, weeds, and bark. Those who were without food and those who were in sight of the end of their resources, in panic joined the swelling multitudes of refugees in flight from the scorched lands." [34] Later it became known that, in addition to the great area in the central and eastern parts of the country, a considerable region in the southern Ukraine bordering on the Black Sea was also afflicted by drought and famine. Thus most of the surplus-producing agricultural area of Russia was, so to speak, out of commission.

While generally there was considerable disagreement over crop figures between the two top Soviet statistical agencies—the Central Statistical Administration and Gosplan—both agreed within one percentage point that production of the seven principal grains (wheat, rye, oats, barley, corn, buckwheat, and millet) was in 1921 less than half of the average for 1909–1913 (43–44 percent). Even if the large exports abroad were deducted from the 1909–1913 grain figure as well as the quantities shipped to the Polish and Baltic regions no longer part of Russia after the Revolution, still the remainder was more than double that of the 1921 production.[35] In other words, only a little over a half of the grain supply available for domestic needs during 1909–1913 was theoretically available in 1921. I say "theoretically available" because the breakdown of transportation and dislocations in the distribution apparatus made the movement of grain to famine-stricken areas extremely difficult. Although attention was centered on grain as the crucial crop, other food crops and hay were also badly damaged by the drought. The production of oilseeds, for instance, was down by one third.

The situation was greatly aggravated by requisitions, which left the peasants with no grain reserves. The Soviet government, of course, knew about this. Lenin often referred to the poor 1920 crop in the spring of 1921, when he advocated the shift to the NEP. But he was slow in admitting the dangerous situation, despite forecasts published as early as December 1920 of the unfavorable weather outlook for 1921.[36] Ironically enough, Lenin was following in the footsteps of the tsarist government, which he had so vehemently denounced twenty years earlier for concealing famine conditions from the people.

Not until the opening of the Third All-Russian Food Conference, on June 16, 1921, did Lenin sound the alarm of a crop failure, which "draws for us a picture of terrific danger . . . The population in a number of provinces will find itself in a hopeless situation, in a situation of unheard-of difficulty." [37] The alarm was taken up by the Soviet press, and on June 26 *Pravda* reported that about 25 million people were stricken by famine. The Soviet government now became quite concerned with the problem of famine relief.[38] But where could it obtain the necessary quantities of food? The only possibility was help from abroad and that meant at the time primarily the United States. The American Relief Association (ARA), headed by Herbert Hoover, had been engaged for some time in large-scale relief activities in Europe. It offered its services to the Soviet government in 1920, but the latter attached conditions to acceptance which would have nullified the cardinal principle of the ARA operation—independent distribution of food supplies with no strings attached.

The worsening of the Russian food situation in the summer of 1921 made the Communist leaders more tractable. On July 11 an appeal, purported to be unofficial, was issued for foreign food aid, signed by Patriarch Tikhon of the Orthodox Church and Maxim Gorky. Herbert Hoover responded, and negotiations began on August 10, 1921, in Riga between representatives of the ARA and Maxim Litvinov. These negotiations were not easy. The Americans had to insist on the independence of the ARA in the control of relief operations, for experience proved that to be essential for success and for political neutrality.[39] This was unpalatable to the Russians, whose representative, Litvinov, reiterated that "food is a weapon." Finally, on August 20, a satisfactory agreement was concluded, and in a few days there began perhaps the most remarkable human salvage operation in history. It was remarkable not only because of the magnitude of the task, but also because of the deep ideological and political gulf that separated the United States from Communist Russia. Even though the Soviet government was not diplomatically recognized by the United States, the ARA was able to secure congressional appropriations, without which the scale of relief would have been greatly reduced.

The difficulties and obstacles strewn about by the Soviet authorities were not easily overcome. But despite frequent crises, the ARA succeeded in completing its task after almost two years of relief work. At the peak of its operations, it fed more than 10 million adults and children daily and distributed medical supplies to more than 4000 institutions.[40] The tribute paid to the ARA by the Soviet government is the best testimony to the important contribution made by the United States in putting the Russian economy back on its feet. Kalinin wrote of the "great role played by foreign organizations, particularly by the ARA." [41] A generous tribute was paid to ARA by the Soviet government at the close of operations in July 1923. In an official resolution, the Council of People's Commissars declared: "Due to the enormous and entirely disinterested efforts of the A.R.A., millions of people of all ages were saved from death, and entire districts and even cities were saved from the horrible catastrophe which threatened them . . . The people inhabiting the Union of Soviet Socialist Republics will never forget the help given them by the American people, through the A.R.A., seeing in it a pledge of the future friendship of the two nations." [42] The same theme was reiterated by a number of Soviet officials during the festivities preceding the departure of the ARA mission.

That the American aid was well remembered by the Russian people, the writer can testify from personal experience. In the course of travels in Siberia in 1935, I had to deal with a Soviet official who was not particularly friendly when I first met him. But he thawed out later and confided that as an adolescent he owed his life to the ARA. There were, no doubt, many other grateful Russians. They may have rued the fact that, because of the barriers erected by their government, United States aid was not called for and could not even have been volunteered during a subsequent terrible famine.

But if the ARA could not be easily forgotten in the early 1930s, its image could be completely distorted in the now familiar manner, until it bore no relation to facts as they were set forth earlier by the Soviet leadership itself. This is precisely what was done during the cold war. The second edition of the Large Soviet Encyclopedia, published in 1950, discarded the objective account of American relief given in the first edition (1926) and speaks of the "espionage-sabotage activities and the support of counterrevolutionary elements" by the ARA. It cites as a source of further information an article in a purportedly scholarly historical magazine, with the suggestive title: "Anti-Soviet activities of the ARA in Soviet Russia in 1921–1922." [43] It is worthwhile, therefore, to keep the record straight on this almost forgotten episode in Soviet-American relations.

The Recovery

The crop failure and famine of this period resulted in the further deterioration of Russian agriculture. Shortages of seed and animal feed led to another serious drop in acreage and livestock, including draft animals, which reached their low watermark in 1922 (see Tables 15 and 16). But already in that year the yields per acre showed a substantial increase due to markedly better weather conditions, exceeding even the 1909–1913 average. The year 1922, therefore, may be regarded as a turning point on the road to agricultural recovery. It had to be stimulated by new policies. The restrictions embodied in the land code of 1922 on the leasing of land and the use of hired labor, though an important step forward

Table 15. Total sown area and total grain area of the USSR, 1913 and 1921–1929

Year	Total sown area (million acres)	Total grain area (million acres)
1913	288.4	253.8
1921	223.1	197.2
1922	192.0	163.6
1923	226.6	194.2
1924	242.4	204.8
1925	257.7	215.7
1926	272.6	231.5
1927	277.7	234.0
1928	279.2	227.8
1929	291.6	237.2

Sources. For 1913, *Kontrol'nye tsifry, 1928–29*, p. 408; for 1921–1929, *Sotsialisticheskoe stroitel'stvo 1934*, pp. 4–5.

compared to previous prohibitions, were found to be too rigid. They hindered agricultural expansion and led to a considerable amount of evasion. Also, the arbitrary administrative practices of War Communism died slowly in the villages, and the behavior of the rural Communist officials still provoked a great deal of discontent among peasants. A. I. Rykov, who succeeded Lenin as the chairman of the Sovnarkom, characterized the situation in the countryside in the spring of 1925 as follows: "Administrative abuses instead of enforcement of Soviet law; illegal taxation of the local population; lack of faith on the part of the peasantry in the possibility for free exchange of goods; absence of genuine elections to rural soviets; and numerous attacks on the peasant correspondents of the Soviet press." [44]

To remedy these unsatisfactory conditions and to stimulate agricultural productivity, the post-Lenin leadership decided early in 1925 on a further liberalization of policy in regard to individual peasant farming. At this time the outstanding Bolshevik theoretician Nikolai Bukharin openly proclaimed the advantage to the state of "enriched" peasants and voiced the unorthodox view that even so "alien" an element in a socialist body as the kulaks might eventually be assimilated with the help of the cooperative movement. He said: "Our policy with respect to the village must develop in the direction of narrowing and partially removing restrictions hindering the growth of prosperous and kulak farmers." [45] Not

Table 16. Livestock numbers (million head), 1916 and 1921–1938 (June–July)[a]

Year	Cows	Cattle (incl. cows)	Hogs	Sheep and goats	Horses
1916	26.0	60.6	20.9	121.2	35.8
1921	27.2	50.8	19.4	110.9	29.6
1922	24.8	45.8	12.1	91.1	24.1
1923	26.1	52.9	12.9	95.3	24.6
1924	27.1	59.0	22.2	109.9	25.7
1925	28.6	62.1	21.8	122.9	27.1
1926	29.7	65.5	21.6	132.5	29.2
1927	29.9	68.0	23.2	139.7	31.6
1928	30.7	70.5	26.2	146.7	33.5
1929	30.4	67.1	20.4	147.0	34.6
1930	26.7	52.5	13.6	108.8	30.2
1931	24.4	47.9	14.4	77.7	26.2
1932	21.0	40.7	11.6	52.1	19.6
1933	19.6	38.4	12.1	50.2	16.6
1934	19.5	42.4	17.4	51.9	15.7
1935	20.1	49.2	22.5	61.1	15.9
1936	22.1	56.7	30.5	73.7	16.6
1937	23.3	57.0	22.8	81.3	16.7
1938	25.2	63.2	30.6	102.5	17.5

[a] Pre–World War II boundaries.
Source. *Zhivotnovodstvo, 1916–1938*, p. 4.

only Bukharin, who later joined the Right Opposition, but even Kamenev, one of the future leaders of the Left Opposition, staunchly defended the progressive, strong, individual farmer. "We would have been mad," said Kamenev, "if we considered a kulak to be that peasant who utilizes conditions created by the Soviet state to increase his prosperity and to raise the level of his farming. We would be cutting down the branch on which we sit." [46] This liberalized attitude was reflected in the decisions of the Fourteenth Party Conference and the Third Soviet Congress in April and May of 1925, which were also approved by the Fourteenth Party Congress in December of that year.

By far the most important practical step taken by the leadership was the relaxation of restrictions on leasing land and hiring labor. The legal leasing period was extended from one to two rotation cycles for a sequence of six or more crops, or twelve years in case of a smaller number of crops or the absence of regular rotation. By a decree of April 18, 1925, hired labor used to supplement that of the peasant family was exempted from the jurisdiction of the general labor code and was subject to special rules that were more elastic in such matters as the length of the working day and employment of young persons.[47] Much attention was also given to the problem of curbing the irritating methods of Communist officials in the village. With this end in view, it was decided to democratize and popularize the village soviets. A similar policy of checking arbitrary administrative interference was to be pursued with respect to the rural cooperative movement.

The agricultural tax, now a money tax, was reduced and, to make it more certain and equitable, a number of improvements were ordered in its administration. A large share of the receipts from this tax was to be allocated to the rural district soviets. Considerable emphasis was laid on increasing the efficiency of peasant agriculture, particularly on consolidating the scattered fields, a task that, in the case of poor peasants, was to be performed at the expense of the state. These and various other measures served to round out and deepen the NEP in the countryside and to eliminate the administrative survivals of War Communism.

Thus it appears that the post-Lenin leadership was placing a strong wager on individual peasant farming. But since they discarded a frontal collectivist attack on agriculture, the Communist rulers had to discover some alternative road to socialism. This came to be a sort of "boring from within" by means of the revived cooperative movement, which was given the new important mission of carrying socialism to the village. This was, in fact, an ideological legacy that Lenin left to his party. About a year before his death, he wrote two short but significant articles on cooperation in which he developed the thesis that, with political power and ownership of the means of production in the hands of the proletarian state, cooperation becomes exceedingly important as a method of transition to the new order, a method that is "simple, easy, and accessible to the peasant." [48] This was an appealing idea. It was used by Bukharin and became the leitmotif of numerous Soviet pronouncements and much of the writing on the agricultural problem in the middle twenties.

The Soviet encouragement of cooperatives was, therefore, motivated primarily by the desire to inculcate the communal spirit and habits of socialized production and distribution among the population, not to better the economic condition of members, which is the mainspring of cooperative movements in the non-Soviet world as it was in prerevolutionary Russia. But although it is true that in the Soviet Union "the dominating purpose of the cooperatives is to aid in the construction of a socialistic society based upon the plans and principles of the Russian Communist Party,"[49] still the help rendered by cooperatives to small peasant agriculture during the NEP should not be overlooked. The number of various types of cooperatives is shown in Table 17.

Table 17. Number of cooperatives and membership

	Oct. 1, 1926		Oct. 1, 1927	
Type	Number of cooperatives	Number of members	Number of cooperatives	Number of members
Rural consumers	26,265	6,965,319	26,272	9,151,580
Reclamation	5,776	695,653	6,109	773,950
Farm machinery	8,871	122,438	14,775	223,594
Livestock	2,396	128,495	3,217	157,192
Seed	1,032	28,670	1,673	64,273
Other producers' cooperatives	1,403	33,532	2,448	49,811
Credit	12,330	4,978,522	11,284	6,120,360
Marketing and processing	15,577	1,636,787	12,440	2,187,789
Total	73,650	14,589,416 [a]	78,218	18,728,549 [a]

[a] Membership in different types of cooperatives overlapped.

Source. *Statisticheskii spravochnik SSSR za 1928 g.*, pp. 786–787, 792–793.

The rural consumers' cooperatives, the most numerous of all, became a thoroughly controlled trade arm of the state, utilized especially to distribute scarce commodities. Many of these cooperatives probably could not have stood on their own feet and, were it not for the Soviet campaign against private retail trade, would not have been essential to the needs of the peasantry. Likewise, collective farms, which again began to be favored by the government in the mid-twenties after a lapse during the early NEP, were by nature antithetical to individual peasant farming. But such diverse types of cooperatives as marketing, processing, credit, seed, machinery, and others dealing with some specialized aspect of agriculture not only did not compete with or supplant family peasant farming, as collective farms did, but actually supplemented and reinforced it where the farmers themselves deemed it necessary. As a matter of fact, when peasant agriculture became collectivized, these cooperatives were liquidated. While they existed, many of them contributed to the recovery and progress of small peasant agriculture.

What about the dynamics of agricultural recovery? Here we again face the difficulty caused by the controversial character of Soviet statistical data, especially crop statistics. There can be no question about the upward trend in acreage and production after 1922. But the precise nature of the increase was in dispute at the time between the Central Statistical Office, which was primarily responsible for the collection of such statistics, and Gosplan, which had to use them in its planning activities. Gosplan considered the estimates supplied too low because of underreporting by the peasants, to avoid taxation. The Central Statistical Office had tried to adjust the primary data on crop areas and yields in order to allow for the farmers' understatement, but this was not considered sufficient by Gosplan, which employed the balance method of testing crop-production figures.[50] Under prodding from Gosplan, the official estimates for the early 1920s were raised. These official figures were considered comparable with pre–World War I crop data only when the latter were also raised by 9 percent for acreage, 9 percent for yields, and 19 percent for production in order to correct for underestimation. After the 1930s, the upward correction of the pre–World War I figures was for some reason dropped by Soviet statisticians, thus distorting the comparative extent of recovery and expansion during the Soviet period. Whether the statistics should have been raised as high as they were is a moot question. What is not debatable is that only increased figures for 1913 must be used for comparisons with statistics for these later years.

Acreage data constitute the best indicator of agricultural recovery as well as decline. In examining the figures for the total sown area and for its principal component—grains—we find a rapid increase during the years 1923–1926 and a much smaller upward movement and even a decline during the next three years. This is shown by the following tabulation.

Year	All sown area	Grains
1913	100.0%	100.0%
1922	66.6	64.5
1923	78.6	76.5
1924	84.0	80.7
1925	89.4	85.0
1926	94.5	91.2
1927	96.3	92.2
1928	96.8	89.8
1929	101.1	93.5

Year	All sown area	Grains
1923	18.1%	18.7%
1924	7.0	5.5
1925	6.3	5.3
1926	5.8	7.3
1927	1.9	1.1
1928	0.5	−2.6
1929	4.4	4.1

Not until the end of the decade, when the NEP also came to an end, did the total sown area slightly exceed the prewar (1913) area, while the grain acreage was still 6.5 percent below. The situation was aggravated by unfavorable weather during the winter of 1927–28, when a good deal of the fall-sown (winter) grain was damaged and not fully resown in the spring of 1928. There were regional variations in the degree of recovery. It was greater in the western and central grain-deficient regions than in the eastern and southeastern surplus-producing regions. But in Siberia the prewar level was considerably exceeded.[51]

Obviously a higher rate of growth after 1926, especially in grain acreage, not only would have speeded the recovery but would have resulted in the further expansion of production, similar to that which took place in Russia before World War I. The need for increased agricultural output was even greater than before World War I because of the growth of population (from an estimated 138.2 million on January 1, 1914, to nearly 154 million on January 1, 1929) and the disappearance of the large commercial estates, so important in feeding the cities and for exports. Further, because of the nature of small peasant agriculture, even more production would have been necessary to provide such supplies than in the days of estate farming. The slowing down of the tempo of recovery in the later twenties, however, should not obscure the substantial progress achieved by peasant agriculture after the bleak years of War Communism and famine. If we compare the years 1927 and 1928 not with 1913, but with the low point of 1922, we find that gross agricultural production increased around 40 percent, the total sown area 45 percent, the grain area 39–43 percent, and that the wheat acreage more than doubled.[52] The proportion of the higher-yield winter wheat was increasing at the expense of lower-yield spring wheat and rye in the Ukraine and North Caucasus. While grains, primarily bread grains, still greatly dominated the Russian crop pattern, there was some progress toward diversification. As the tabulation below indicates, the proportion of the total acreage under crops other than grains increased from 10 percent in 1913 to nearly 16 percent in 1927.[53]

Crop	1913	1922	1927
All grains	89.9%	85.2%	84.3%
Wheat only	(30.1)	(18.5)	(27.8)
Flax	1.3	1.3	1.4
Sunflowers	0.9	2.8	2.5
Hemp	0.6	0.6	0.8
Sugar beets	0.6	0.2	0.6
Cotton	0.7	0.07	0.7
Potatoes	2.9	5.0	4.9
Other	3.1	4.8	4.8
All crops	100.0	100.0	100.0

Not only was the great decline in animal husbandry overcome but, by 1926, livestock numbers, with the exception of horses, exceeded the 1916 level. The upward trend continued in 1927 and 1928. The 1920s also saw significant progress in Russian agricultural science, continuing the prerevolutionary tradition and maintaining contact with Western science under the leadership of such outstanding scientists as Vavilov, Glinka, Tulaikov, Prasolov, and Prianishnikov. This was also true of agricultural economics and statistics under the leadership of Kondrat'ev, Chaianov, Groman, and Studenskii. As the peasants became masters of their land, their farm techniques began to show some signs of improvement: there was increasing use of summer fallow (*par*) in such semiarid regions as the steppe Ukraine, use of better varieties of seed and animals, and the like.[54]

The peasants even made a modest beginning in the use of tractors and, either individually or cooperatively, owned nearly 11,000 of the 24,500 tractors on farms as of October 1, 1927. However, shortage of draft power remained a serious handicap. The number of work horses in 1928 was still 12 percent below 1916, while the number of peasant households increased by more than 40 percent. Many of these small holdings lacked draft animals. In 1926, according to a sample census, in such an important region as the North Caucasus 40 percent of the peasant households were without work animals, while in the Ukraine the number was 45 percent. These peasants were often faced with the alternative of hiring implements and livestock from their more well-to-do neighbors or of leasing land and, perhaps, hiring out their labor.[55]

Where the recovery of Russian agriculture lagged most seriously was in commercial production, that is, in the part of the farm output shipped outside of the village, on which exports depended as well as the food supply of the cities and the rural grain-deficit areas. In 1926–27 and 1927–28 gross agricultural production as estimated by Gosplan exceeded by 5–6 percent that of 1909–1913. But by 1927–28 commercial production was still one third below that of 1913.[56] Commercial grain production was less than half of the amount in 1913. This fact was most disconcerting to the government, which was embarking on an ambitious industrialization program requiring a large supply of cheap foodstuffs and agricultural raw materials for export and domestic consumption. By 1926–27 agricultural exports, which before the war constituted the backbone of Russia's active balance of trade, had hardly reached one fourth of their 1913 volume.[57] The situation was particularly unfavorable with respect to grain exports, despite favorable harvests in 1925 and 1926. During the five years before World War I, Russian exports of the principal cereals—wheat, rye, barley, oats, and corn—averaged nearly 11 million tons; but in 1925–26 and 1926–27 they amounted to only 1.9 and 2.5 million tons respectively.

Analysis of the causes of the lagging commercial production reveals the drawbacks that accompanied the victory of the small peasant cultivator and the serious flaws in the government's economic policy—a combination proving fatal to the NEP. To begin with, the disappearance of the estates, as might be expected, had an adverse effect on commercial production. Despite the previously described inroads of peasant agriculture on estate farming, the estates played a significant part in commercial agriculture before the war, especially in such important export crops as wheat. Because of better land and improved techniques, the estates yields were higher than those of peasant holdings, and obviously a much larger proportion of this output was sold on the market since the peasants had to produce essentially for their own consumption. For instance, in the case of wheat, it was estimated that during the years 1909–1913 the peasants in twenty-three surplus-producing provinces of European Russia brought a little over half of their wheat production to the market, compared with approximately 80 percent supplied by estates.[58] As a result, the large farms with only 14 percent of the gross wheat production accounted for 20 percent, or 70 million bushels, of the commercial wheat supply of these provinces, which was equivalent to more than 40 percent of all Russian wheat exports during this period. Even when the estateowners leased most of their land to the peasants, the latter had to sell more produce on the market in order to pay cash rents or, in the case of sharecropping, give the landlord a larger supply for sale. In the 1920s this factor no longer operated to bolster production for the market. Thus the disappearance of the estates, especially since it was effected in one stroke, was bound to leave a gap in commercial agricultural production.

Not only were the estates broken up, but the peasant holdings themselves decreased in size and increased in number. In 1916, it was estimated that there were less than 18 million peasant households in the territory of the USSR; by 1925 there were nearly 24 million, and during the next three years they increased by another 1,600,000.[59] The size of the peasant farm unit can be better visualized by a comparison of the average acreage sown per farm in the USSR and in the United States. In the leading Russian wheat-producing regions, it varied from 13 to 35 acres, according to the sample census of 1927; [60] in the most important wheat-growing states of the United States, the range was from 140 to 270 acres per farm, according to the census of 1925. There is abundant evidence that under Russian conditions the smaller farm unit placed a smaller proportion of its output on the market.[61] Incentives to stimulate production for the market were, therefore, especially important. These could not be developed in the Soviet Union, however, because agriculture was adversely affected by an unfavorable relation between the prices of agricultural products and those of industrial products. In the Soviet literature these sets of prices were often likened to the two blades of a scissors and the disparity between them to the opening and closing of the blades. Henceforth I shall use the term "scissors" to denote the discrepancy between agricultural and industrial prices, which had become a serious obstacle to increased agricultural production.

What was the economic environment in which a scissors crisis could develop? First, the large-scale manufacturing and mining industries, with some insignificant exceptions, remained nationalized during the NEP. In 1928–29 state industry, together with state-controlled cooperative enterprises, was responsible for more than two thirds of all commercial industrial output.[62] On this nationalized industry the peasants had to depend for such products as kerosene, matches, sugar, and most of their textiles. Second, state enterprises and state cooperatives accounted for close to 90 percent of the volume of retail trade in 1928–29.[63] Finally, the marketing of agricultural products, particularly grain, had also become increasingly concentrated in the hands of state organizations, operating under a unified national plan. At the same time, private trading was edged out by various forms of economic and administrative discrimination and pressure. Here are a few examples of the growing role of government procuring operations in the total marketing of farm products—or commercial production, as the Russians call it—which excludes intravillage trade. For wheat, the share of government procurements in total marketing increased from 64.1 percent in 1925–26 to 85.9 percent in 1926–27 and was only slightly less (84.9 percent) in 1927–28. For rye, a less commercialized grain, the figures for the same years were 49.1, 64.5, and 67.5 percent. For meat, the proportion of government procurements in total marketing also rose from 16.5 percent in 1925–26 to 23.4 percent in 1926–27 and 45.8 percent in 1927–28.[64] The same trend toward etatization of trade was also manifested with respect to most other farm products.

The government took over these industrial and marketing operations while their efficiency was low and the production and marketing costs high, which contributed to the high prices of monopolistic industry. Thus millions of small individual peasant producers were pitted against an increasingly centralized, essentially monopolistic, and politically directed high-cost apparatus, with an authoritatively determined price system. This provided an ideal setting for the scissors phenomenon. But it was clinched by the government's policy of rapid and lopsided industrialization and the channeling of capital for this purpose.

Some of the statistics characterizing the scissors are presented in Tables 18 and 19. It will be noted that during three of the four years shown,

Table 18. Index of prices paid to farmers for all sales and government procurements (average 1910–11, 1912–13, 1913–14=100)

Commodity	1925–26 [a]		1926–27 [a]		1927–28 [a]		1928–29 [a]	
	All sales	Procure-ments	All sales	Procure-ments	All sales	Procure-ments	All sales	Procure-ments
Grains	161.1	151.8	124.6	118.7	134.6	129.1	190.4	154.4
Oilseeds	107.8	98.8	108.8	101.2	124.4	118.0	137.3	128.8
Flax fiber	134.7	134.7	128.6	128.6	146.0	146.0	178.0	177.9
Cotton	129.4	129.4	129.4	129.4	129.4	129.4	129.4	129.4
Sugar beets	133.3	133.3	126.7	126.7	133.3	133.3	133.3	133.3
Potatoes	183.3		170.8		208.3		270.8	
Butter	153.0	135.5	169.3	164.3	172.5	169.0	209.5	197.6
Eggs	191.7	179.1	195.2	188.9	208.7	192.2	243.3	220.7
Meat	166.7	165.9	176.9	172.7	176.9	167.5	184.1	172.5
Wool	227.1	153.2	278.7	175.7	268.6	177.3	251.4	177.3
All agricul-tural com-modities	158.8	146.3	149.3	133.9	156.4	141.4	183.3	157.3

[a] Year beginning October 1.

Source. *Kontrol'nye tsifry, 1929–30,* pp. 579–580.

Table 19. Index of retail industrial prices, 1925–26 to 1928–29 (1913=100)

Year beginning October 1	Socialist sector	Private trade	All trade
1925–26	210.2	242.4	220.5
1926–27	198.9	242.3	210.0
1927–28	188.3	241.6	198.4
1928–29	191.3	268.7	202.7

Source. *Ekonomicheskoe obozrenie,* 1929, no. 11, p. 180.

prices paid to farmers for their products were from about 50 to 60 percent above the pre–World War I level for all sales, including those in the higher-price private market, and 34 to 46 percent for government-procured products; the retail prices the farmers had to pay for industrial goods were double or more than double. Even in 1928–29, when agricultural prices increased, they were still only 57 to 83 percent above the pre–World War I level, while industrial prices were more than double. According to special indices of the farmers' purchasing power, a pood (36 pounds) of wheat in the important export regions of the southern Ukraine and northern Caucasus could buy in October 1926 only about 50 percent of the manufactured goods which it bought in 1913, and in October 1927 a little over 60 percent.[65] In one village in the former Samara province of the Volga region, peasants questioned by Soviet investigators pointed out that before the war a pood of sugar cost 6 rubles and a pood of wheat 1 ruble; in 1927 the prices were 12 rubles and 0.8 rubles.[66] Similar figures are available for other manufactured goods.

The situation became particularly adverse for grains. The grain price index, which in 1925–26 was higher than the index of all agricultural prices, was considerably lower during the following two years. For grains, therefore, the scissors increased during 1926–27 and 1927–28. Consequently, when the peasants needed cash, they preferred to sell other products or to sell grain on the limited private market at higher prices than those paid by the government. That the low grain prices had an unfavorable effect on acreage expansion was admitted in Soviet sources.[67] The drop in grain prices was due to the reduction of the procuring prices decreed by the government, whose purchases greatly outweighed private sales by the peasants. Note also that for grain, as for a number of other farm products, government-fixed prices were lower than the prices on the limited private market, which were determined by the interrelation of supply and demand. For instance, the average procurement prices for wheat during 1925–26, 1926–27, and 1928–29 were 129, 104, and 209 kopecks per pood; the private market prices were 147, 128, and 137 kopecks.[68] Thus there existed a dual price system: low government prices alongside higher private-market prices. Although prices of such nongrain crops as sugar beets and cotton were also low, this was compensated for by certain advantages enjoyed by producers, such as a reduction in the agricultural tax for sugar-beet growers and aid to cotton growers in the maintenance of irrigation systems and in the supply of commercial fertilizer and grain at favorable prices.[69] There were also regional variations in scissors. For instance, the ratio of the price indices of farm products sold and manufactured goods purchased by farmers in October 1927 varied in different regions from 57 to 86 percent.[70]

In terms of an unfavorable relation between agricultural and industrial prices, the scissors has also been a familiar problem in capitalist countries, especially during depressions and recessions. This is the consequence of industry's superior strategic market position and its more effective control of output and prices. But as the prominent Soviet oppositionist economist Preobrazhenskii admitted, compared with monopoly capitalism, "the concentration of the whole of a country's large-scale industry in the hands of a single trust, that is, in the hands of a workers' state, increases to an extraordinary extent the possibility of carrying out a price policy on the basis of a monopoly, which is merely another form of taxation of the private economic sector." [71] In other words, the scissors was not merely a sign of economic maladjustment, but became an instrument of taxation of agriculture or forced savings. The importance of this was enhanced by the fact that the egalitarian distribution of income after the Revolution greatly impeded the process of capital formation. At the same time, the outright repudiation by the Soviet regime of the prerevolutionary foreign debt and subsequent policies militated against long-term investments of foreign capital, which had played so seminal a role in prerevolutionary industrialization.

The Soviet price scissors had another important peculiarity. It was accompanied by the so-called goods famine, the physical shortage of manufactured goods and their poor quality as compared with prewar Russian standards. This chronic goods shortage, one of the most serious problems in Soviet economic life, was not fully reflected in the prices fixed by the government. As a result, the peasants were often unable to buy manufactured goods or had to pay exceedingly high prices in the private market. They had no incentive to produce for the market and even curtailed production. Thus the scissors accentuated that tendency toward self-sufficiency to which the small size of the farm unit made post-revolutionary Russian agriculture so susceptible. It was the only weapon available to the farmer for economic defense against the industry-oriented collectivist state. The fact that the peasant relied predominantly on himself and not on hired labor, which would require cash for wages, facilitated this elasticity in self-sufficiency and the resistance to the government squeeze. But there were limitations on the use of such a weapon. The most obvious was the need of cash for taxes and certain other outlays, such as compulsory insurance payments and dues to cooperatives, the aggregate of which increased from 275 million rubles in 1925–26 to 713 million in 1928–29 (a rise of 160 percent).* Of greater importance was the fact that self-sufficient small family agriculture was incompatible with a socialist regime bent on ambitious industrialization.

* Despite the sharp increase, cash outlays of peasants in 1928–29 for taxes, insurance, and cooperative dues were less than before the Revolution (direct taxes, insurance, and payment of rents or purchase price for land). The ratio of such outlays to the income of the agricultural population was 8.1 percent in 1912 for the fifty provinces of European Russia for which such estimates are available (less for the whole of the USSR) and 4.4 percent in 1928–29. Indirect taxes, reflected in prices of commodities and not requiring independent cash outlays, were not included in these calculations. See for 1928–29, *Kontrol'nye tsifry 1929–30,* pp. 470, 480; for 1912, Vainshtein, *Oblozhenie i platezhi krest'ianstva,* p. 148.

9

Decline of the NEP and a New Offensive

The relatively liberal attitude of the Soviet government toward individual peasant farming, which reached its zenith in 1925, was virtually repudiated by the end of 1927. This repudiation was preceded by a bitter controversy within the Bolshevik Party in which the fundamental tenets of Soviet economic and agrarian policy were put to the acid test. The basic question of principle and policy underneath this controversy, apart from its numerous factional or personal aspects, was the future of socialism and the tempo of industrialization in the Soviet Union, which involved the interrelation of socialized industry, peasant agriculture, and the economic stratification of the peasantry. Although this question has many ramifications, the present discussion must be limited to those aspects pertaining to the government's agricultural policy.

Early Concern with Stratification

The mixed economic system of the NEP was a rather unstable dichotomy of socialist and capitalist elements. This dualism did not greatly matter in the early years of the NEP, when the urgent need was for a breathing spell and the recovery of production after the catastrophic decline of the revolutionary years. But as the critical period passed, new difficulties appeared and new misgivings developed within the Bolshevik Party. These characteristically coincided with the fading of the prospects for world revolution, which Lenin hoped would aid his cause in Russia.

It was feared in Communist circles that capitalism would grow more rapidly to encircle the socialist elements in the Russian economy. In agriculture especially, the restored economic stratification of the peasantry after the great leveling of the Revolution caused much apprehension among the Communists. The party showed a great deal of concern over the kulak danger—the growth of a class of relatively prosperous peasants who, because they possessed livestock, implements, and other forms of capital, were in a position to exploit the peasants who had land but no means to cultivate it.

The resumption of this stratification was generally admitted, but its extent and particularly its tendencies were the subjects of acrimonious debate. The Left Opposition, which by 1926 included such prominent leaders as Trotsky, Kamenev, and Zinoviev, in accordance with classical Marxian dogma, emphasized polarization, the development of extreme groups in the peasantry: the kulaks and the poor peasants. But how small the number of kulak farms was is indicated by the fact that, in so important an agricultural region as the North Caucasus, the number of peasant holdings with four or more draft animals amounted, in 1926, to only 4.8 percent of the total; in the Crimea it was 6.9 percent; in all other European regions of the USSR the proportion was less, and in the central black-soil area only a fraction of a percent. Holdings with a sown area of 10 desiatinas (27 acres) or over accounted in only a very few regions for 10 percent or more of the total number of holdings and constituted a much smaller proportion in most regions.[1] Although even the most prosperous peasants were very small producers, especially when judged by Western standards, the kulak specter loomed large in the eyes of the Left Opposition, which accepted as gospel Lenin's teaching that "small-scale production gives birth to capitalism and the bourgeoisie constantly, daily, hourly, elementally, and in vast proportions."[2] The influence of the kulaks on the rest of the peasantry was considered out of all proportion to their small numbers.

On the opposite side, there was a group in the party, represented by equally prominent leaders such as Bukharin and Rykov, which minimized the kulak danger and which, as already noted in the discussion of the 1925 legislation, welcomed the increasing prosperity of the peasants. Allied with this right wing was a brain trust of academic and professional economists and statisticians, such as Kondrat'ev and Groman. Kondrat'ev saw some virtue in stratification because it led to accelerated economic development in the country.[3] It was thought by the Right Opposition that the development of a prosperous stratum of peasants would yield the twofold economic advantage of larger commercial production and increased propensity to save, with a resulting improvement in the productive capacity of agriculture. For not only industry but agriculture badly needed capital for replacement and technological improvement after the years of war and revolution.

During 1925 and 1926 the party leadership, which was dominated more and more by Stalin after Lenin's death, tried to steer a middle course between the Scylla of the left and the Charybdis of the right, though leaning much more to the right. It did not deny the existence of the kulak danger but minimized its seriousness, pointing to the general economic leveling upward of the whole peasantry, including the poor and particularly the middle peasants. The latter constituted a new non-Marxist category in the official Bolshevik terminology introduced by Lenin who, even during War Communism, repeatedly stressed the importance of keeping on good terms with them. However, the "middle peasant" came into vogue with the NEP and the goal of *smychka* (rapprochement between the peasants and the workers' state). With the commanding heights of economic life—industry, transportation, credit, and foreign trade—in the control of the socialist state, it was claimed by the leadership that the process of stratification in the village would not take the same form as in the capitalist countries. There it supposedly led to the erosion of the middle group and the creation of the two extremes—the proletariat at the bottom and the capitalist at the top. Under Soviet conditions, it was held that the poor peasants had "an increasing opportunity to move into the middle groups of peasantry."[4] The middle peasant was, in Lenin's words, the "central figure" of agriculture and, according to the official doctrine prevailing under the NEP, was destined to remain in this role for a long time to come. The idea of some Communists that economic stratification in the village called for a rekindling of the class struggle was characterized by Stalin in 1925 as "empty chatter."[5]

The most serious bone of contention in the intraparty debates was the problem of industrialization, which of course closely affected agricultural policy. There was no disagreement in the Bolshevik Party about the necessity of industrialization. In fact, there were objective economic premises—agrarian overpopulation and the country's vast resources—calling for an active industrial policy, no matter who the rulers of Russia were; it had been pursued by the tsarist government as well. Agrarian overpopulation was accentuated by the movement of people out of the cities during the Revolution and the breakdown of industry and trade, which had provided much temporary employment to the peasants. Industrialization, it was believed, would not only relieve the village of surplus labor but, by expanding the urban market, would also tend to stimulate the intensification of Russian farming and thus increase the opportunity for the application of labor in agriculture. This policy was also dictated by military motives and, above all, by the basic belief of Marxism that modern technology is the base and the factory worker the spearhead of socialism. According to Lenin, each new factory was "a new stronghold" of the working class, strengthening its position in the national economy.

There was considerable disagreement among the Bolsheviks with respect to the tempo of industrialization, however. Marx's tenet of the close link between socialism and industrialism was, of course, common ground for all Russian Marxists, whose sensitivity to the question was heightened by the long struggle with the populists over the problem of industrial development, discussed in an earlier chapter. The Left Opposition advocated the utmost speed in industrialization in order to strengthen the socialist elements in the national economy and to overcome the disparity between industry and agriculture. It was, in no small measure, because the progress of industrialization was considered inadequate that the opposition manifested such jumpiness with respect to the kulaks.[6] That the necessary capital resources for such industrial development would have to come largely from agriculture was recognized, since foreign capital was now unavailable. Consequently, the Left Opposition was in favor of higher taxation of the more prosperous peasants and of relatively high prices for industrial products, which would make possible a larger accumulation of capital in industry. "First, the accumulation of capital and, on this basis, the lowering of production costs and then the reduction of prices," wrote Preobrazhenskii.[7]

In giving precedence to capital accumulation over reduction of industrial prices, Preobrazhenskii was voicing the general concern of the Left Opposition over the financing of industrial development. He stressed the danger of arbitrarily lowering prices without paying due regard to the necessities of capital accumulation. "We must," he insisted in answering his critics, "proceed not from lower prices to savings, but from savings to lower prices." [8] He also pointed to the political impossibility in the USSR of wage reduction as a means of lowering industrial costs. It was in order to provide a theoretical framework for solving the problem of capital for socialist industrialization that Preobrazhenskii developed his highly controversial theory of "original socialist accumulation." [9] He drew a parallel between the process of capital formation required for socialist industrialization in an underdeveloped peasant country like Russia and its counterpart during the era of early capitalism, as portrayed by Marx in the celebrated bristling chapter on original (primitive) capitalist accumulation in his *Capital.* By analogy with original capitalist accumulation, the sources of capital which could be tapped outside of the socialist sector of large industry, primarily peasant agriculture, were likened to colonies. By the exploitation of such colonial areas through methods of "socialist protectionism" and monopolistic trading, the terms of exchange could be turned to the advantage of the "metropolis"—in this case, socialist industry.

This process would promote a diversion of resources from agriculture to socialist industry. To put it another way, in the absence of important external sources of capital, such as foreign borrowing, agriculture must be largely relied upon for initial capital formation for industrialization, in the form of price scissors or higher taxes, or both. This condition would prevail until socialist industry was mature and its productivity high enough to meet its own capital requirements. Preobrazhenskii's use of such terms as "exploitation" and "colony" made his doctrine particularly vulnerable to attack, by Bukharin and others, for its alleged undermining of the party line of *smychka.* In replying to his critics, Preobrazhenskii maintained that this was not a specific policy recommendation but a theoretical model of Russian economic development during the transitional period between capitalism and socialism.[10] Actually it was both.

On the crucial question of taxing agriculture and the rest of the private economic sector for purposes of industrial development, Preobrazhenskii's position was that the objective should be high taxation, higher than under capitalism, but on an assumed greatly increased income. And with approval he quoted Bukharin, his principal opponent, who declared that "capital accumulation in a socialist industry with a large proportion of peasant farming is a function of savings in the peasant economy." [11] It is only fair to point out that Preobrazhenskii did not make a fetish, an end in itself, of his doctrine of original socialist accumulation, as Stalin did of the emphasis on heavy industry. Preobrazhenskii, like the oppositionists in general, remained essentially consumer-minded; the increase of capital investment was for the purpose of augmenting, in the not too distant future, the supply of consumer goods and to improve the standard of living. It was also commonly held in the party, as Preobrazhenskii's reference to Bukharin's position indicated, that industrialization depended to a considerable extent on the diversion of material resources from agriculture to industry. As the stormy polemics demonstrated, there was a serious difference of opinion on what the contribution of agriculture to industrial development should be.

The Left Opposition believed that the peasants could bear a heavier burden and were against humoring, let alone appeasing, them, especially in carrying out the economic program of the government. When the plans for the procurement and export of grain miscarried in 1925, Kamenev, at the Fourteenth Party Congress, complained bitterly that "the peasantry is tying our hands in the matter of expansion and reconstruction of our industry." [12] The Left Opposition could also argue convincingly, as Preobrazhenskii did, that a reduction of industrial prices under conditions of a goods shortage, without other deflationary measures or rationing, would lead to the enrichment of the private trader, the "Nepman"—through his hands a considerable quantity of commodities in short supply would filter for sale at much higher prices.[13]

On the other hand, the party leadership and an overwhelming majority of the economists and statisticians were apprehensive of the threat that this course held for *smychka,* the declared keystone of the NEP. It would actually be an attempt to cure the price scissors by a stronger dose of scissors, and the Kremlin believed that the immediate adverse effect on the peasants' production would worsen the illness for which this strong medicine was prescribed. The leadership was less optimistic about the economic "squeezability" of the peasants and apprehensive that they would "strike" and withdraw from the market if the supply of manufactured goods were inadequate: "The peasant's desire to trade with the town is fairly elastic and becomes very elastic as soon as the terms of exchange are pressed appreciably against him. Hence the town can only press its advantage against the village at the expense of diminishing fairly sharply the volume of trade between them. Conversely, to the extent that peasant demand (in terms of effort) for the products of industry is elastic, every improvement in the terms of exchange offered to him by the town will encourage him to extend his efforts in producing for the market and will considerably increase the volume of trade between village and town." [14] This, of course, presupposes reliance essentially on economic means and not on coercion, from which even Stalin was shrinking in the mid-twenties, when the gruesome memories of War Communism were still vivid. An additional argument of the ruling group was the danger of high monopolistic industrial prices, leading to stagnation and "parasitic decay" while the industrial trusts smugly enjoyed their high profits. This view, stressed by Bukharin, found official expression in a resolution of the Central Committee passed in February 1927.[15]

Rejection of the proposals of the Left Opposition was made emphatic at the Fifteenth Party Conference in the autumn of 1926, which declared in its resolutions: "The way of viewing the peasantry merely as an object of taxation, in order to extract more resources from peasant agriculture by means of excessive taxes and high factory prices, must inevitably arrest the development of productive forces in the village, decrease the marketability of agricultural products, and threaten a breakdown of the alliance between the working class and the peasantry—thus endangering the task of building socialism." [16] Yet the bitter intraparty struggle and the clamor of the opposition about the kulak danger did begin to have its effect on the agrarian policy of the Soviet government. A much narrower interpretation of the electoral law in 1926, which deprived many prosperous peasants of suffrage, more frequent official pronouncements against the kulaks, and a general drive against private trade were harbingers of the approaching change. The relatively favorable attitude of the government toward individual peasant farming was waning by the end of 1927, only a year after it had been reaffirmed at the Fifteenth Conference.

A major modification in official policy was first announced in October 1927, in the proposals of the governing party organs prepared for the approaching Fifteenth Congress. These proposals called for the resumption of a "more decisive offensive against the kulaks" and for a number of new measures "limiting the development of capitalism in the village and leading peasant farming in the direction of socialism." [17] The new course of agrarian policy was approved by the Fifteenth Congress in December 1927. This was the same congress which excommunicated Trotsky and his followers and brought Stalin a step closer to unrivaled domination of the party. A certain resemblance, therefore, between the official party resolutions quoted above and the platform of the Left Opposition adopted in September 1927 is very curious. The opposition stated: "The growth of private proprietorship in the country must be offset by a more rapid development of collective farming. It is necessary systematically and from year to year to subsidize the efforts of the poor peasants to organize in collectives . . . The task of the party in relation to the growing kulak class ought to consist in the complete limitation of their efforts at exploitation." [18] Paradoxically, then, the Left Opposition were beginning to have an effect on agrarian policy just as it was being read out of the party. Public attention at the time both within and outside the country was riveted on the spectacular ousting and exile of Trotsky. But the Fifteenth Party Congress will be remembered in history chiefly as marking the onset of what W. H. Chamberlain has called "the Iron Age of Soviet Russia" and Leonard Schapiro, "a new social revolution." From now on, agriculture was to share the stage with industrialization.

Legal Discrimination against the Kulaks

Each previous period of Soviet agrarian policy had its characteristic legal expression in some basic land legislation. The new policy approved at the Fifteenth Party Congress at the end of 1927 also resulted in fundamental land legislation, promulgated on December 15, 1928.[19] The salient feature of the new law was the frankly discriminatory treatment of the kulaks—a term not even employed in the code of 1922. The definition of the term remained loose, encouraging arbitrariness on the part of officialdom. The preferential status given to collectives and the poorer peasants in all matters again made for instability in land tenure. The new law was also characterized by a more restrictive attitude toward the leasing of land and the employment of hired labor, reversing the tendencies of 1925–26. The organization of the more individualized segregated farms, *otrub* or *khutor,* was discouraged or entirely prohibited when it was deemed as leading to the kulak type of farming. The control of the mir over its members was strengthened while it, in turn, was subjected to greater supervision by the political village soviets. To deprive them of their influence in the mir, the kulaks were divested of voting rights. The law of December 15, 1928, is primarily interesting as a historical landmark, indicating the long distance traveled by the official policymakers from the objectives of only a few years back, when the strengthening of individual peasant farming had been the acknowledged aim. Soon this law would be forgotten in the sweeping tide of wholesale collectivization and the "liquidation of the kulaks as a class."

Not only land policy but also the instrument of taxation was increasingly used to combat peasant individualism. The "single agricultural tax," which was the only direct tax levied by the central government in the village, was revised in accordance with the instructions of the Fifteenth Congress to yield 25 percent more revenue in 1928–29. Since the intention was to place this increased burden primarily on the upper strata of the peasantry, the progression of the tax was made even steeper. This was not all. The use of an additional so-called individual method of assessment was permitted in the case of the kulaks, ostensibly to prevent evasion but actually, because of its arbitrariness, to serve as an important weapon in the anti-kulak struggle. The Soviet leaders later admitted that individual assessment was often greatly abused and applied indiscriminately not only to the kulaks but to the middle peasants; this is not surprising in view of the elusive line of demarcation between the two.[20]

It is uncertain how far and how fast the shift inaugurated in the autumn of 1927 would have proceeded had it not been for the fact that, shortly after the new anti-individualistic slant was announced, the country found itself in the throes of a serious grain crisis. Procurements of grain by the government from the smaller 1927 crop, which was at first overestimated, were running dangerously below those of the preceding year; at the same time, the responsibilities of the state for the supply of the towns and deficit rural regions increased with the growing restriction of private grain trade. The low grain prices had come home to roost. Ideological and political motives which had dominated the decisions of the Kremlin in the autumn of 1927 were soon reinforced by the threat of famine. So the government resorted to force, as it had ten years earlier. Accompanied by outcries against the "kulak speculators" in the controlled press, the Bolsheviks proceeded during the early months of 1928 to extract grain from the recalcitrant peasants by the tactics made familiar during War Communism.

The peasants reciprocated in kind, and a tug of war developed. Early in 1928, the abandonment of the NEP, as far as its application in the village was concerned, seemed to be fairly complete. It is true that in the spring of that year, when the immediate grain difficulties were over, the coercive measures were officially characterized as temporary or "extraordinary." The Kremlin even condemned what were now declared to be aberrations or perversions of the party line in dealing with the peasants.[21] In spite of these declarations, the grain front became, for a number of years after 1928, the principal theater of war between the peasants and the government. As the later purged Commissar of Agriculture Chernov put it, "grain procurements form the principal arena for the struggle of the kulaks against the socialist reconstruction of the country." [22]

The grain situation did not improve in 1928 and 1929. The nub of the difficulty was the deterioration of the wheat and rye supply. Bread-grain production declined for three years in succession (see Table 20). Govern-

Table 20. Combined area and production of wheat and rye, 1925–1929

Calendar year	Wheat and rye		Wheat and rye	
	Million acres	Percent	Million quintals	Percent
1925	132.7	100.0	435.3	100.0
1926	143.1	107.8	481.0	110.6
1927	144.8	109.1	457.2	105.0
1928	129.5	97.6	412.7	94.8
1929	135.2	101.9	392.4	90.1

Source. *Sotsialisticheskoe stroitel'stvo, 1934*, pp. 176–177.

Table 21. Grain procurements, 1925–26 to 1929–30 (1000 metric tons)

Year beginning July 1	Wheat and rye procurements[a]	Total grain procurements[a]
1925–26	5,579	8,397
1926–27	8,428	10,806
1927–28	8,034	10,115
1928–29	6,389	9,735
1929–30 (first half)	7,505	13,854

[a] Excludes so-called decentralized procurements undertaken for local needs.

Source. *Ekonomicheskoe obozrenie,* December 1927, p. 179; January 1929, p. 192; March 1930, p. 191.

ment procurements of bread grains decreased only by 4.7 percent in 1927–28, compared with the preceding year, but by more than 20 percent in 1928–29 (see Table 21). The situation was not helped by the fact that the decline in production and procurements took place as the population was increasing at an annual rate of 3.4 to 3.5 million. Moreover, this coincided with Stalin's decision to step up industrialization and with a worsening of the international situation when Great Britain broke off diplomatic relations (resumed in 1929 after the electoral victory of the British Labour Party).

For the unsatisfactory grain situation both weather and government policy must take the blame. Extensive winter killing of fall grains reduced production for the 1928 harvest. Drought during the growing season in some regions further depressed the yields. But unfavorable weather conditions, as Soviet sources acknowledged, were not the whole story.[23] As a result of the new policies regarding the kulaks' land, taxation, and the use of force in extracting grain in the winter of 1927–28, the individual peasant farmer found himself in a cul-de-sac. There was no incentive or possibility for growing along individualistic lines, for one then would be classified as a kulak. The more prosperous peasants, who were particularly subject to the various pressures, were reducing their acreage.[24] Even if the middle and poor peasants did tend to increase their sowings, as was claimed, the fact that the economically strong farmers, who ordinarily produced surplus grain for the market, were curtailing production was bound to aggravate the grain-supply difficulties.

The re-emergence of the grain crisis stirred up a new controversy within the Politburo—this time between Stalin and his recent allies,

Bukharin and others of the right, who were dubbed "Right Deviationists." The debates, which followed closely on the heels of the Trotsky controversy, took place behind the scenes. Since Bukharin, unlike Trotsky, was not first exiled abroad and then assassinated, but liquidated with his adherents inside his native country, what is known about the controversy is mostly what Stalin deemed it desirable to divulge; we have little of the opposition's rebuttal.

During the early phases of the controversy, in the spring and summer of 1928, the official pronouncements on agrarian policy were somewhat ambivalent. On the one hand, there was a strong reaffirmation of the NEP, coupled with an increase in grain prices and the censure of coercive methods of grain procurement and arbitrariness in tax assessment; on the other, there was an emphasis on a continuing offensive against the kulaks. There was also a new accent on the technological backwardness of small peasant grain farming and the need for its transformation into large collective farming. An important practical measure was revived—the idea of grain factories, large mechanized state farms that would diminish the dependence of the state on the peasants. As far as industrialization was concerned, a fast rate of growth and the priority of heavy industry began to be stressed. This by itself presaged a tough agrarian policy.

No one was more explicit about the plans for industrialization than Stalin. He said in May 1928:

> To diminish the speed of development of industry would mean weakening the working class . . . On the contrary, we must maintain the present rate of development of industry and, at the first opportunity, still more accelerate it, in order to pour cheap goods into the rural districts and to obtain from them the maximum amount of grain . . . and in order to industrialize agriculture and to increase its marketable surplus . . . Perhaps it would be wise, as a measure of greater "caution," to retard the development of heavy industry, with the object of making light industry, which produces chiefly for the peasant market, the basis of our industry. By no means. That would be suicidal. It would mean undermining our whole industry, including light industry. It would mean abandoning the slogan of the industrialization of our country and transforming it into an appendage of the capitalist system of production.[25]

How this superindustrialization, from which Stalin never swerved during the next twenty-five years of his rule, affected the peasantry was bluntly stated in a speech on July 9, 1928, at a session of the Central Committee of the party, published many years later.

[The peasantry] not only pays the state the usual taxes, direct and indirect; it also *overpays* in the relatively high prices for manufactured goods . . . and it is more or less *underpaid* in the prices for agricultural produce . . . This is an additional tax levied on the peasantry for the sake of promoting industry, which caters to the whole country, the peasantry included. It is something in the nature of a "tribute," of a supertax, which we are compelled to levy for the time being in order to preserve and accelerate our present rate of industrial development, in order to ensure the industrialization of the whole country, in order to further raise the standard of living of the rural population and then to abolish altogether this additional tax, this "scissors" between town and country. It is an unpalatable business, there is no denying. But we would not be Bolsheviks if we slurred over it and closed our eyes to the fact that, unfortunately, our industry and our country cannot *at present* dispense with this additional tax on the peasantry.[26]

Except for the absence of "colony" and "exploitation," this passage sounds like an echo of Preobrazhenskii's terminology. Stalin's use of the phrase "something in the nature of a tribute" provoked Bukharin's criticism of "military-feudal" exploitation of the peasantry.[27] Bukharin, in the only extensive piece of economic analysis he was able to publish after the start of his controversy with Stalin, also warned against too high a rate of capital investment and too rapid industrialization. This would put too great a strain on the economy and was inconsistent with the more cautious course approved at the Fifteenth Party Congress.[28] Stalin, in his speech on "The Industrialization of the Country and the Right Deviation" of November 19, 1928, staunchly defended the rapid tempo of industrialization as necessary to catch up with and overtake the advanced capitalist countries.[29]

On the purely agrarian side, the Right Opposition, judging from what Stalin disclosed, was alarmed over the grain crisis, which it attributed to the degradation or retrogression of Russian agriculture.[30] It was opposed to the use of the notorious "emergency" (coercive) measures to extract grain, because they destroyed the peasants' incentives to produce. Thus it proposed the importation of grain as a substitute in an emergency situation. To expand agricultural production, particularly of grain, the Right Opposition advocated a resumption of the relatively liberal policy toward peasant farming. Although it paid obeisance to the kulak danger and to the resolutions of the Fifteenth Congress, it apparently did not take them too seriously. As far as the organization of new state farms was concerned, the Right Opposition displayed a cautious, conservative attitude and advised, in the words of one of its spokesmen, Frumkin, against employing "shock or supershock tactics."

Stalin favored a diametrically opposite policy. Although adhering in his public statements to the prevailing party-line distinction between kulak and middle peasant and admitting that the latter was often hit by anti-kulak measures, he nevertheless emphasized the kulak danger. He approved the use of coercion in grain procurements, though he too went on record as being against "excesses." Stalin, of course, was also anxious to overcome the crisis of grain underproduction. But unlike the Right Opposition, he banked more on agricultural collectivization and much less on unleashing the future productive potentialities of individual peasant agriculture.

It may be taken for granted that grain-procurement difficulties strengthened Stalin's commitment to collectivization, just as they apparently diluted any immediate interest that the Right Opposition may have had in collective farming. While the controversy continued, however, Stalin formally hewed to the gradualist course laid down at the Fifteenth Congress. On April 1929 he still stressed the supplementary role of collective and state farms in agricultural production, assuming that for some time to come the leading place would belong to the middle and poor peasants. He wrote in the summer of 1928, criticizing a letter of Frumkin's of June 15, 1928: "At the present stage, the principal stress must still be laid on raising the level of individual small, and middle-peasant farming. But . . . this task alone is no longer enough . . . The time has come when this task must be practically supplemented by two new tasks—the development of collective farms and the development of state farms." Speaking on July 13, 1928, on the "Results of the July Plenum," Stalin said: "There are people who think that individual peasant farming has exhausted its potentialities and that there is no point in supporting it. That is not true, comrades. These people have nothing in common with the line of our party. There are people, on the other hand, who think that individual peasant farming is the be-all and end-all of agriculture. This is also not true." [31]

As the Right Opposition was losing its battle in the spring of 1929, the First Five-Year Plan was adopted at the Sixteenth Party Conference, projecting "a sweeping growth of the socialist sector" of the national economy.[32] But even this plan set up as a goal for 1932 a sown area on collective and state farms of 40 to 46 million acres, as against 298 to 303 million acres in individual holdings. This may be compared with the less than 6 million acres of sown area in collective and state farms in 1927. For 1932–33, the plan also specified that collective and state farms were to account for 13–15 percent of gross agricultural production and 23–25 percent of commercial production, as against less than 2 percent of gross and 4 percent of commercial production in 1927–28.[33] Despite the projected increase in agricultural collectivization, individual peasant farming was still to dominate the Russian agrarian scene at least until the end of the First Five-Year Plan period. But by the autumn of 1929, when Bukharin and his Right Opposition were thoroughly defeated, Stalin felt free to embark on a more thoroughgoing collectivization program.[34]

10

Collectivization and the Ordeal of the Peasants

Just as the first great events in Soviet history—the October Revolution, War Communism, and the NEP—are inextricably linked with Lenin's name, so is total collectivization of agriculture bound up with Stalin's. It is well, therefore, to begin this chapter with a blueprint of Stalin's revolutionary collectivization program.

Stalin on Collectivization

Underlying Stalin's program, which he adumbrated in January 1928 and developed in greater detail in two speeches made in November and December 1929, is the Marxist thesis of the superiority of large-scale production in agriculture, as in industry, without qualifications or limitations.[1] He recognized that large-scale farming could develop on either capitalist or collectivist lines and considered the promotion of the latter one of the chief tasks of the Soviet state. Stalin believed that even if certain forms of large-scale farming, such as grain factories, did not take root in capitalist countries, they would thrive under Soviet conditions. For with government ownership of land, they would not have to pay rent and could be operated with a minimum profit, or even without profit, and would enjoy special credit and tax privileges unknown under capitalism.[2] This, in bold relief, is the doctrine sanctioning huge farm units and large physical output regardless of economic limitations; it led the Russians to many a costly mistake, not the least among them those connected with the large grain factories of the Stalin era.

Another basic assumption Stalin first set forth in his statement in January 1928, and repeated in December 1929, was the impossibility of building socialism on two different foundations—large socialized industry and small-peasant agriculture.

> Can the Soviet system persist for long on these heterogeneous foundations? No, it cannot . . . We must realize that we can no longer make progress on the basis of a small, individual peasant economy, that what we need in agriculture are large farms capable of employing machines and producing the maximum marketable surpluses. There are two ways of creating large farms in agriculture: the *capitalist* way—through the wholesale ruin of the peasants and the organization of big capitalist estates exploiting labor; and the *socialist* way— through the union of the small peasant farms into large collective farms, without ruining the peasants and without exploitation of labor. Our Party has chosen the socialist way of creating large farms in agriculture.

The logical conclusion was to speed up agricultural collectivization. The earlier failure of collective farming was disregarded. Naturally Stalin thought that the effectiveness of the large farms would be greatly augmented with the introduction of new machine techniques and tractor farming. "The great importance of collective farms lies precisely in that they represent the principal base for the employment of machinery and tractors in agriculture, that they constitute the principal base for remolding the peasant, for changing his mentality in the spirit of socialism." Stalin considered it unnecessary to wait until it would be possible to supply agriculture adequately with modern machinery. He believed that simple peasant implements and animal draft power in larger units could lead to greatly increased production. It would particularly facilitate a considerable expansion of crop acreage, to which Stalin attributed the utmost importance. He was aware that there were contradictory individualist and socialist elements in the psychological make-up of the kolkhoz peasants, and it was a mistake to think they had already been converted to socialism. He considered it a long-range task, which could be accelerated by the mechanization of farming. But at the December 1929 conference of Marxist agricultural specialists, Stalin criticized the tendency of some Communists—doubtless having in mind the economist Larin—to belittle the socialist character of the kolkhoz and its importance as "a lever for socialist transformation of the countryside." [3]

What of the peasants' allergy to collectivization? What about the proverbial attachment to their own land? The answer that Lenin had given, and Stalin endorsed, was that 100,000 tractors would convince them. In 1929 the tractors were no longer such a fantasy as they had seemed in 1918, but there were still not enough of them to sway the peasants. Stalin had another line of argument—that land nationalization facilitated the transition to collective farming in the USSR, for the Russian peasant farmer thereby lost the attachment for his land which was characteristic of his counterpart under capitalism. To make his argument stronger by contrast, Stalin quoted a famous passage from Engels' *The Peasant Question in France and Germany*: "We are decidedly on the side of the small peasant; we shall do everything at all permissible to make his lot more bearable, to facilitate his transition to the cooperative should he decide to do so, and even to make it possible for him to remain *on his litlte plot of land for a protracted length of time* to think the matter over, should he still be unable to bring himself to this decision." [4]

This kind of "circumspection" was necessary in the West, according to Stalin, but not in the Soviet Union where private ownership of land was absent. Now, as indicated earlier, there are grounds for holding that communal tenure, with its redistributions of land and the absence of firm property rights in a particular plot, did diminish the stability of land tenure in Russia. The revolutionary upheaval did even more in this direction. But Stalin's argument about the effect of the Soviet land nationalization is largely sophistry. For this process, while curtailing the peasant's freedom to dispose of his land legally, in no wise interfered with his possession and management of the holding. De jure it was owned by the state; de facto it belonged to the peasant, who was assured of his occupancy by the 1922 legislation. As events were shortly to prove, it was a gross distortion for Stalin to say: "There is no private ownership of land in our country. And precisely because there is no private ownership of land in our country, our peasants do not display that slavish attachment to a plot of land which is seen in the West. And this circumstance cannot but facilitate the change from small-peasant farming to collective farming." [5]

Only the middle and poor peasants were to find a new haven in the collectives. What about the kulaks? Stalin thought that with the spread of collectivization it would be possible to replace the kulaks' output with that of the collective and state farms. Therefore the kulaks, no longer needed, could be dismissed without a qualm. "That is why we have recently passed from the policy of *restricting* the exploiting tendencies of the kulaks to the policy of *eliminating the kulaks as a class* . . . It is now ridiculous and foolish to discourse at length on de-kulakization. When the head is off, one does not mourn for the hair." This was the first authoritative announcement of the liquidation of the kulaks as a class, the *raskulachivanie* (de-kulakization), as an immediate aim of the intensified drive on the agrarian front: it brought spoliation, economic ruin, and physical annihilation to millions of Russian peasants. It is not surprising that, at the same time, the NEP was also given short shrift by Stalin. "If we adhere to the NEP it is because it serves the cause of socialism. When it ceases to serve the cause of socialism, we shall get rid of it. Lenin said that NEP had been introduced in earnest and for a long time. But he never said it had been introduced for all time." [6]

Such was the Stalinist theory of total collectivization as it had crystallized by the end of 1929. It was bolstered by the combined effect of Soviet strength and weakness. The strength lay in the extent of recovery achieved during the NEP, through nationalized industry, and the weakness lay in the inadequate commercial grain production of individualistic agriculture. How tempting it must have been for one who knew so little about the complexities of farming as Stalin, but who read and believed Marx and Lenin, to attempt a straight Marxist solution in order to launch a new era of industrial expansion, with its requirement of a firm agricultural base. Or to put it in another way, the Soviet state needed cheap grain, and needed it on terms of trade between agriculture and industry which were favorable to the latter. The effort to achieve this objective brought the regime into a head-on collision with the peasants, of whom the Communists could say, in the words of the poet: "The love was without joy, the parting will be without sorrow." And in the background was their Marxist-Leninist heritage, beckoning them to follow the straight collectivist path, with alluring promises of increased farm productivity, larger output, and effective control or subjugation of the farmer. The result of all these factors would be easier acquisition of the grain and other food supplies needed by the state.

In terms of tactics this meant a shift further away from gradualism, which Stalin was still professing as late as the Sixteenth Party Conference in April 1929. But it did not automatically call for hasty, wholesale collectivization, brutally carried out. Why did he do it? Why did he not adhere to the gradual yet quite rapid collectivization course laid down in the First Five-Year Plan adopted under his leadership in the spring of 1929? Stalin's plunge can probably be explained first by an eagerness to obtain grain in a hurry and, second, his own "dizziness from success" (the favorite phrase he used to criticize others): his complete victory in the intraparty fight and the routing of the Left and Right Oppositions; success in extracting grain from the peasants during the second half of 1929; and success in corralling the mass of the peasantry into kolkhozes. These represent, to use an analogy, the visible part of the iceberg to which political decision making may be likened. The invisible part is usually much harder to uncover even in an open society with its many available sources of information. It is much more difficult in the case of Stalin who, with his suspiciousness, secretiveness, and deviousness, was the very personification of the iron curtain drawn at its tightest over the Kremlin.

The Offensive Begins

The intensified Communist offensive in the countryside was already in full swing when Stalin made public his plans for total collectivization. As usual, it began on the grain front, with the procuring campaign of 1929–30. Not only high targets were set up but utmost speed was demanded by the government, which wanted to obtain the great bulk of the grain during the first half of the campaign, that is, by January 1930.[7] The whole Soviet apparatus—government, party, trade union, and cooperative—was mobilized for the campaign. Just as during the days of War Communism, groups of factory workers, Komsomol (Communist youth) workers, and party activists were sent in large numbers to the countryside on the procurement mission.

A new weapon was forged for procurement of grain in the contract system, which formerly was used only for industrial crops like cotton. Theoretically the system provides for an arrangement whereby peasants or groups of peasants were to contract with the government, prior to the sowing season, to sell most of their crop in exchange for a money advance and preference in the distribution of agricultural machinery, seed, and so forth. Actually the system had developed by the autumn of 1929 into a lever for compelling the peasants, particularly the upper strata, to part with their grain. This was clearly intended by a Sovnarkom resolution dated October 7, 1929, which said: "In order to facilitate the fight against the kulaks and to overcome their resistance to the socialist reconstruction of agriculture, all members of village [land] communities and producers' associations are to be considered bound by the decision of the majority of their middle and poor peasants who favor the conclusion of contract agreements."[8] In other words, the upper layer of the peasantry, which usually had the surplus grain, was denied any voice in the matter of its disposal. Even before this official action, the poorer peasants were used to force their more prosperous neighbors to disgorge their grain by means of the contract system.[9] By the same token, the class struggle in the village was supposed to be fanned and a wedge driven between the different levels of the peasantry just as in the days of the kombedy of War Communism.

The 1929 procurement campaign developed very much on the lines of the sequestration drives of War Communism. Quotas were assigned to each administrative district and village which had to be fulfilled and overfulfilled. "Every conceivable pressure was brought to bear upon the peasants in order to force them to give up the planned amount of grain. The pretense that the peasant could sell his grain wherever he liked was given up." [10] Those who ventured to bring grain for sale on the private market frequently ended with confiscation of their supply. Again, as under War Communism, in a number of districts minimum quantities of grain for the peasants' own use were set up and the rest was to be turned over to the state. In the Tver region (now Kalinin), the minimum grain left for the peasants was claimed to have been even less than under War Communism.

To estimate prospective yields, on which the quotas were then based, inspection of peasant granaries and even the crops standing in the fields was resorted to by the authorities. Calvin Hoover, who was in the USSR in 1929–30, heard from German colonists, fleeing from the excesses of the anti-kulak drive in Siberia, that a preharvest estimate of the crop by one agricultural expert sent to their village was held to be too low and he was imprisoned. His estimate was more than doubled by a second inspector, with the result that the peasants found it impossible to deliver the quota from their own supplies. In some cases they tried to meet the exaction by purchasing grain on the private market at ten or twelve times the official procurement price. Those peasants who were not able or willing to do so "were severely fined and, in many cases their animals, houses and even furniture were sold in order to pay the fine." [11] Here we have a repetition, only on a larger scale and more ruthless, of the forced sales of peasant property for tax arrears practiced during the second half of the nineteenth century in tsarist Russia. Similar harsh measures to procure grain were adopted in other regions. A vivid picture is painted by the celebrated Smolensk documents.* In this region, failure to deliver

---

* A number of documents from the party archives in the city of Smolensk, the administrative seat of the western oblast between 1929 and 1937, were captured by the German army in 1941, shipped to Germany, and fell into American hands at the end of the war. This unique collection of largely secret Soviet material, dealing with the administration of one region (and not available for any other region), was digested and analyzed by Merle Fainsod in *Smolensk under Soviet Rule* (Cambridge, Mass., 1958). The documents shed much light on collectivization practices.

the quotas within two to five days was punishable by a fivefold fine for the first offense and by a year's imprisonment or forced labor for a second offense. Even more severe penalties of two years in prison, or forced labor with deportation, and seizure of all or part of the property were provided for the same offense if committed by a group with "collective premeditation" to resist Soviet orders.[12]

In practice, more summary techniques were used with peasants who failed to deliver their assigned quota and who were considered recalcitrant kulaks. The officials and party or village activists "simply raided the household and confiscated any grain 'surpluses' which could be located on the premises." The ruthlessness of the procuring procedure even caused on a number of occasions a cleavage between the local officials and the Communist emissaries from the cities. According to the Smolensk documents, one emissary accused a party official of being too lenient because he insisted that enough grain be left to the kulaks for seed and for feeding the children. The emissary said: "When you are attacking, there is no place for mercy; don't think of the kulak's hungry children; in the class struggle philanthropy is evil." [13]

Although not all the emissaries were this belligerent, many of them complained of the softness and passivity of local officials and village Communists, who were making such statements as: "Why such pressure on the kulak? We will turn him and the whole population against us. This will be fatal for NEP . . . We are constantly taking and taking . . . until there will be no more to take in the village . . . Why are you constantly yelling about the kulak? We have no kulaks here. There is no food here, and the state norms of purchases are rising." One report lamented that even some of the emissaries became lax after spending time in the countryside: "They slowly fall into a system of more restrained tactics; they hesitate to squeeze everything from peasant households; they grow pacifist." [14]

As for the peasants, the Smolensk documents reveal that they showed a remarkable solidarity in resisting the grain exactions. The cleavage between the kulaks and the middle and poor peasants certainly proved much less sharp than postulated by Communist theory. With a sound instinct which told them what to expect, some of the poorer peasants were reported as saying: "Now they are confiscating bread from the kulaks; tomorrow they will turn against the middle and poor peasants." To the peasants, Communist grain collectors generally were seen as thieves, bandits, or parasites. Indeed, instances were reported where villagers actually shielded and defended their richer neighbors, asserting that "the whole village is equal; quotas should be equally distributed." Some of the emissaries admitted that, when pressed by their superiors, they would seize grain from everyone indiscriminately and not only from the kulaks, justifying their actions by that well-known Bolshevik excuse: "When wood is chopped, chips must fly." [15]

The peasants, for their part did not submit without resistance. It took various forms—from hiding grain to bribery and even to violent attacks on officials and activists involved in the confiscation. The peasant reprisals mounted as the ruthlessness of the government drive gathered momentum. The prosecutor (procurator) of the western oblast reported an increase of terroristic acts from thirty-four during July–August 1929 to twenty-five during September alone and to forty-seven in October. Even the Soviet prosecutor did not attribute all such cases to the kulaks but implicated a considerable number of middle and poor peasants who, he alleged, were "closely allied with the kulak elements by 'family and economic ties' and still manifested a 'petty bourgeois ideology'." [16] Here is a grudging official recognition of the peasants' solidarity. If the stern measures described above were not successful in breaking the solidarity of the village, and in fact often accomplished the very opposite, they were successful in the rapid procurement of a large quantity of grain. During the first six months of the campaign (up to January 1930), 28 percent more grain was procured than during the whole previous record year of 1926–27. What made it even more of a feat was the fact that the 1929 procurements were extracted from a smaller crop, since the 1929 total grain crop was 6.6 percent below that of 1926. This was the opening wedge of a terrible famine which was soon to sweep the Russian countryside.

How was collectivization affected by these events? While collective farming made considerable strides in 1928 and the first part of 1929, it was still a small island in the ocean of individual peasant agriculture. The number of kolkhozes increased from less than 15,000 in the summer of 1927 to more than 57,000 in the summer of 1929. The number of peasant households included in the collectives rose during this period from less than 1 percent to 3.9 percent of the total and the sown area from 0.7 percent to 3.6 percent of the total. Most of the increase occurred between the summer of 1928 and 1929, when the new government drive developed (see Table 22). Even when state-farm acreage is added, the proportion of the socialist sector in the total sown area was only 5.5 percent in 1929. But collective and state farming in the Soviet agrarian scheme was no longer in the position of a poor relation.

The success of the 1929 grain-procurement campaign had a strong catalytic effect on the tempo of collectivization. It intoxicated Stalin and the Communist leadership and, by the same token, crushed the peasants' spirit, which no longer could be bolstered by memories of the failure of War Communism. Even some of the upper strata of the peasantry began

Table 22. Course of Collectivization, 1918–1938 [a]

Year	Collective farms (thousands)	Households in collectives (thousands)	Percentage of peasant households collectivized
1918	1.6	16.4	0.1
1919	6.2	81.3	.3
1920	10.5	131.0	.5
1921	16.0	227.9	.9
1922	14.0	217.0	.9
1923	16.0	228.0	.9
1924	16.3	211.7	.9
1925	21.9	293.5	1.2
1926	17.9	247.0	1.0
1927	14.8	194.7	.8
1928	33.3	416.7	1.7
1929	57.0	1,007.7	3.9
1930	85.9	5,998.1	23.6
1931	211.1	13,033.2	52.7
1932	211.1	14,918.7	61.5
1933	224.6	15,258.5	65.6
1934	233.3	15,717.2	71.4
1935	245.4	17,334.9	83.2
1936	244.2	18,448.4	90.5
1937	243.7	18,499.6	93.0
1938	242.4	18,847.6	93.5

[a] Prewar boundaries.

Source. I. V. Sautin, ed., *Kolkhozy vo vtoroi Stalinskoi Piatiletke* (Collective Farms in the Second Stalin Five Year Plan; Moscow, 1939), p. 1.

to think of the kolkhoz as the only safe refuge against de-kulakization. To the middle and poor peasants it became crystal clear that there was no future in individual farming, that success and growth would only land one in the kulak category with all its dire consequences. For all the vaunted Communist propaganda about aiding the poor and middle peasants, they realized that this was a fiction as far as the individual farmer was concerned. If any further evidence were needed, there was the case of the tractors, proclaimed since Lenin's day the great engine of agricultural progress. By a decree of December 21, 1928, the sale of tractors even to small associations of peasants, let alone to an individual farmer, was permitted only in exceptional cases, which in reality meant never.[17]

Under such conditions it became easier for the Communist authorities to push collectivization along with their grain-procurement drive.

Liquidation of the Kulaks

In his article on the twelfth anniversary of the October Revolution, entitled "The Year of the Great Turning Point," Stalin delineated the basic change on the agrarian front: "In the development of our agriculture from small and backward individual farming to large and progressive collective farming . . . the new and decisive aspect of the present kolkhoz movement is that peasants join the collectives not in separate groups, as formerly, but in whole villages, counties, raions, and even districts. What does this mean? It means that the middle peasants are flocking into kolkhozes." A resolution of the Central Committee of the party dated November 17, 1929, echoed Stalin's line about the turning point (*perelom*) in the attitude of the peasant masses toward kolkhozes.[18] At the same time, it called for a still further intensification of the drive against the kulaks and a continuing advance in the "socialist reconstruction of the village." At the same session, the Central Committee took an important organizational step by providing for the creation of a federal Commissariat of Agriculture. This was officially sanctioned by a decree of December 7, 1929.[19] Prior to that time only such constituent republics as the RSFSR and the Ukraine had commissariats of agriculture.

All of this foreshadowed the next and final stage—that of wholesale collectivization and extermination of the kulaks. The two objectives were closely linked by Stalin and, now that the grain-procuring campaign was over, the party was ready for the two-pronged attack. To assist in dekulakization and collectivization, an army of more than 30,000 city workers was mobilized.[20] A decree of December 29, 1929, provided for their compensation, re-employment rights, and certain privileges, such as priorities in the allocation of housing, in the admission of their children to schools, and in the award of scholarships.[21]

Already at the November 1929 party Plenum there were voices warning against the forced pace of collectivization, against kolkhozes that existed on paper only. Thus S. V. Kossior, the Ukrainian party head who later perished in Stalin's purges, stated: "We had complete collectivization of tens of villages, and then it appeared that all this is blown up and artifically created. The population does not participate, does not know anything about it." Another member of the Central Committee, N. A. Kubiak, pointed out that even where collectivization developed on a healthy and voluntary basis, "we were not able to deal with it properly from an organizational and economic standpoint." The party secretary of the Lower Volga region, B. P. Sheboldaev, asked: "Are we prepared for the collectivization movement which we now have in some regions and evidently will have soon throughout the country? I think that at present we are not prepared." [22] A letter from a party worker read at the plenum complained about the methods used by local authorities in the collectivization drive, which included such a slogan as "whoever does not join a kolkhoz is an enemy of the Soviet regime." Another malpractice was the organization of a kolkhoz by a decision of the village assembly; those villagers who did not wish to join were told to file a statement giving their reasons for not joining. Extravagant promises of tractors, machinery, and credits were made: "Everything will be given—join the kolkhoz." The author of the letter pointed out that in this manner 60 or 70 percent of the collectivization was formally achieved. But the kolkhozes were unstable and weak. "Thus there is a wide gap between the quantitative growth and the qualitative organization of the large farms." The letter also called attention to the large sale of cattle and oxen (presumably to avoid collectivization) and, in general, to a difficult situation in the district. Stalin's comment on this was: "What, you want to organize everything beforehand?" [23]

Generally, Stalin at this stage and during the three following crucial months remained impervious to the warnings of some of his party comrades regarding the runaway, disorganized, and inflated character of the collectivization movement; this encouraged party workers to continue along the same lines. He certainly manifested little, if any, concern over the widespread use of force in the villages. This is indicated by his correspondence with the writer Mikhail Sholokhov, disclosed thirty years later by Khrushchev in his speech of March 8, 1963.[24] Sholokhov complained to Stalin in a letter dated April 16, 1933, about the outrages committed by Communist officials in exacting grain from peasants in the writers' native Don region, and he asked for a thorough investigation "to ferret out not only those who used on peasants the disgusting 'methods' of torture, beatings and abuse, but also those who inspire such actions." Stalin, in reply, thanked Sholokhov for writing and uncovering "a weak spot in our Party-Soviet work, uncovering how sometimes our workers, wishing to curb the enemy, inadvertently hurt friends to a point of sadism." But he did not agree with Sholokhov and reproached him for looking at only one side of the matter, whereas in politics it is necessary to see the other side as well: "The respected grain farmers of your region (and not of your region alone) were sabotaging and not averse to leaving the workers and the Red Army without bread. The fact that the sabotage was quiet and externally inoffensive (bloodless)—does not change the situation that the respected grain farmers essentially were carrying on a 'quiet' war against the Soviet regime . . . Of course, these circumstances can in no way justify the outrages which you insist were perpetrated, and the guilty ones must be properly punished. But it is as clear as day that the respected grain farmers are not such innocent people as may appear from a distance."

Such was Stalin's private reaction to charges of abuses. His public reaction was quite different. The Sholokhov-Stalin exchanges and similar material on collectivization were revealed for the first time at the Twenty-Second Party Congress in October 1961, and they represent a kind of mild revisionism in the Soviet literature on the subject.[25] They confirm what Western students have known generally about Stalin's role and the horrors of collectivization, still euphemistically called "errors" and "excesses" in the Soviet Union. Being a product of de-Stalinization, they do not spare Stalin but attribute to him, squarely and properly, the central responsibility for the outrages committed—the blame is not shifted to the lower Communist echelons, as was formerly done. Among the new disclosures was that on December 5, 1929, a special commission of the Politburo had been established, chaired by the Commissar of Agriculture, Ia. A. Iakovlev, to draft legislation for collectivization. It is claimed that Stalin used the results of the commission's work for his de-kulakization speech at the Conference of Marxist Agrarian Specialists.[26] The commission concentrated on drafting a master decree. The key question before it was the tempo of collectivization in different regions, some of which were considered better prepared for it than others. In general, the commission held that collectivization should be completed, with the exception of some Asian and northern regions, during a five-year period. Priority was recommended for the southern and central regions. The first slated to be completely collectivized were the Lower Volga and the Crimea, by the fall of 1930, followed by the North Caucasus, the Middle Volga, and the Tatar Republic in the spring of 1931, with the steppe regions of the Ukraine, the central black-soil region, and the Urals in the fall of 1931. Collectivization of the more northern and eastern regions was to follow during the next two to three years.

Another important question, the organizational form of the kolkhozes, claimed the attention of the commission, since there was a considerable diversity of opinion and practice on this point. Thus in the Lower Volga the basic form was the artel. In Siberia the party leadership promoted communes and *toz* (cooperatives for joint cultivation of land), while in the Urals communes were emphasized. Confusion also developed as to precisely what property was to be collectivized. The commission recommended the artel, in which only the principal means of production are collectivized but not the peasant household economy. The commission also recommended legalized confiscation of all the property of the kulaks and deportation of "those kulak elements who actively resist the new order of socialist agriculture." An exception was to be made for kulaks who were willing to work conscientiously in the kolkhozes without voting rights, so that their labor could be used in collective farming as their property was being confiscated. When the Politburo discussed the proposed draft of the decree on December 25, 1929, Stalin raised objections and the draft was sent back to the commission. Stalin favored even greater speeding up of collectivization in the leading grain-producing regions and the exclusion of the provision limiting collectivization of peasant livestock and simple implements, as well as a number of provisions dealing with the organizational structure of the kolkhozes. And Stalin's word was law. The final draft of the decree also excluded two other proposed articles. One had prohibited the classifying of districts with weak kolkhoz movements as completely collectivized, thus confronting the peasants with a fait accompli. The second article had set up as a yardstick for measuring the success of collectivization not only the number of peasant households joining kolkhozes, but also the extent to which a raion expanded its acreage and production. Although it appears that Stalin favored the acceleration and extension of collectivization, as opposed to the majority of the commission, the two sides were really not so far apart, except possibly in the important matter of the peasants' retention of some livestock.

The modified draft was adopted on January 5, 1930, as the decree "Concerning the Tempo of Collectivization and Aid of the State in the Organization of Kolkhozes." [27] The decree stated that, instead of the collectivization of 20 percent of sown area contemplated for 1932 by the Five-Year Plan, it would be possible to collectivize a large majority of the peasant holdings. Collectivization of such important grain regions as the Lower and Middle Volga and the North Caucasus could be completed, in the main, by the autumn of 1930 or, in any event, by the spring of 1931. Collectivization of other grain regions (presumably surplus regions) could be completed during the autumn of 1931 or in the spring of 1932. These dates should be borne in mind in view of what actually happened. The decree confirmed the "inadmissibility" of kulaks to the kolkhozes and held that the artel was the acceptable kolkhoz type, not the toz or the commune. The drafting of a model charter for the artel was accordingly ordered. Local party organizations were urged to "head and shape" the collectivization movement, which was represented as "spontaneously developing from below." This meant, in plain language, that party and state authorities must take the initiative and exercise close supervision over collectivization if the desired results were to be achieved. The decree cautioned against any retardation in collectivization because of a lack of tractors or modern machinery. At the same time, it warned against collectivization by fiat, against playing a "collectivization game," that is, collectivization merely on paper. The term "voluntary" is not explicitly used in the decree, though it does try to give the fallacious impression that collectivization was a spontaneous movement.

On February 1, 1930, another decree was issued, even more sweeping than that of January 5.[28] It revoked the law permitting the renting of land by individual farmers and the employment of hired labor in regions of collectivization. The authorities of the different regions and autonomous republics were empowered to use "all necessary measures for the struggle with the kulaks," up to full confiscation of property and deportation. The confiscated property of the kulaks was to be transferred to the kolkhozes, except what was necessary to repay the obligations to the state.

This was bristling and ominous enough. Yet it fails to convey the sense of the terrible ordeal through which the peasantry had to pass. It does not tell us of the utter confusion, misery, and destruction that constituted "primitive" rural collectivization. By comparison, the horrors described in Marx's celebrated chapter on original capital accumulation in *Capital,* or the horrors of the British industrial revolution portrayed by humanitarian historians and writers, pale into insignificance. And bleak as was the lot of the Russian peasants under serfdom in the eighteenth and nineteenth centuries, it is debatable whether it offers any parallel to the total uprooting of peasants under collectivization. Even Stalin, that "man of steel" who spawned collectivization and spoke so blandly about the extermination of the kulaks, confessed to Winston Churchill during his wartime visit to Moscow that the terrible strain of the struggle with the peasantry exceeded that of the war.[29]

No doubt when other Soviet archives like Smolensk's are opened to scholars, they will yield numerous additional details on collectivization, and it will be possible to trace more confidently the regional variations that are inevitable in so large a country. But new material will probably not essentially change the grim story of collectivization as it is known from sources available today—though it may help some writer, say a future Kliuchevskii or Tolstoy, to paint the picture on a broader canvas.

I shall now try to reconstruct, in their stark reality, the features of the final stage of the collectivization campaign that began in 1930. Clearly, the determination of the Stalin administration was to uproot from the village the upper-level minority in order to dragoon or induce more easily the often recalcitrant majority of peasants to join the kolkhozes. By the same token, the kolkhozes were to be the beneficiaries of the confiscated property of the liquidated households. Generally the liquidation consisted in the total confiscation or expropriation of the peasant household and its farming. This included land, implements and livestock, houses and other farm structures, household goods, food supplies, and personal belongings including clothing.[30] This was a repetition on a grand scale of the liquidation of the landlords during the 1917 Revolution. Peasants labeled kulaks who had not disposed of their property beforehand were deported from their districts, usually to faraway areas, or at best were resettled on poor land within the district. At worst they were shot, especially if they offered resistance. Calvin Hoover met deported kulaks from Tambov, in central Russia, working on the Turkestan-Siberian railroad near the Chinese frontier. He saw "as late as May 1930 . . . a train of box cars filled with kulaks and their families who were being deported from the Urals to Tashkent in Central Asia." John Scott encountered deported kulaks during the construction of the Magnitogorsk steel mill in the 1930s.[31]

Some kulaks, sensing their impending doom, were "liquidating" themselves. A report of the secret police (OGPU) found among the Smolensk documents states: "A wave of suicides was sweeping the richer households; kulaks were killing their wives and children and then taking their own lives. In order to prevent complete property confiscation, many kulaks and their wives were entering into fictitious divorces, in the hope that at least some property and the lives of wives and children would be spared." [32]

A unique account of the de-kulakization operation in the district of Velikie Luki has been reconstructed from the Smolensk documents.[33] The decision by the district party committee to deport the kulaks and confiscate their property was made on January 28, 1930, and the completion date was set for March 1. To manage the operation in the district and in each raion, there was designated a special troika, consisting of the first secretary of the party committee, the chairman of the Soviet executive committee, and the head of the OGPU. Twenty-six people were also dispatched to the raions to assist the local authorities. Detailed instructions ordered all raion troikas to make a complete inventory of kulak property within a two-week period. The owners were to be warned against unauthorized sale of the property on penalty of immediate confiscation. Kulak households were divided into three groups. The first group, considered most dangerous by the authorities and described as the "counterrevolutionary kulak *aktiv*," was to be arrested. It is significant that meetings of poor peasants and agricultural workers could make recommendations through raion troikas for additions to the "list." The second group consisted of less dangerous kulaks, who were to be deported to remote regions. The third group was comprised of households that were to be removed from areas designated for complete collectivization and resettled on marginal land within the district. They were to retain "an indispensable minimum of work implements" in order to be able to cultivate their newly allotted land, and were to be held strictly responsible for the fulfillment of the delivery quotas. They were also required to perform special compulsory labor services in forestry, road construction, and similar operations: in other words, the resettled kulaks would be pariahs.

The de-kulakization instruction to the raion authorities "unconditionally prohibited" the deportation and resettlement of poor and middle peasants under the guise of kulaks. It was explained that "this warning is issued because in many cases [government] emissaries de-kulakize and arrest poor peasants on the ground that the latter are ideologically kulaks." Despite this admonition, deviations from the official directives were taking place on a sweeping scale in the Velikie Luki district—in fact, over the length and breadth of the whole country. Middle and poor peasants and even members of the village intelligentsia "were being arrested and persecuted by anybody—by raion emissaries, village soviet members, kolkhoz chairmen, and anyone in any way connected with collectivization." Most pathetic was the de-kulakization of peasants who, as reported by the OGPU, were hired hands before the Revolution and who managed to own by 1930 an extra horse or a cow.[34] Hoover relates a similar story heard from a peasant family: "The cow had a calf. We kept it until it became a cow. We had one horse and after saving a long while we bought another. We had always been considered seredniki [middle peasants], but now we are called kulaki, and all our things have been written down on a list and we are held responsible for them until they can be sold. They have not taken the two cows and two horses yet because the kolkhoz does not have enough forage for them. But we are told that in the spring we will be turned out of our home and everything taken away from us."[35]

The process of confiscation often turned into looting on a grand scale, which did not benefit the kolkhozes but the individual expropriators. According to an OGPU report of February 28, 1930, in many villages

"certain members of the workers' brigades and officials of lower echelons of the Party-soviet apparatus" deprived members of kulak and middle peasant households of their clothing and warm underwear (directly from the body), "confiscated" head-wear from children's heads, and removed shoes from people's feet. The perpetrators divided the "confiscated" goods among themselves; the food they found was eaten on the spot; the alcohol they uncovered was consumed immediately, resulting in drunken orgies. In one case a worker tore a warm blouse off a woman's back, put it on himself with the words, "You wore it long enough, now I will wear it." The slogan of many of the dekulakization brigades was: "drink, eat—it's all ours." [36]

The Soviet press stressed the active participation of poor and middle peasants in de-kulakization.[37] Yet "Many poor and middle peasants considered dekulakization unjust and harmful, refused to vote approval of deportation and expropriation measures, hid kulak property, and warned their kulak friends of pending searches and requisitions. In many cases poor and middle peasants were reported as collecting signatures to petitions testifying to the loyalty and good character of kulaks, millers, and other well-to-do elements. The high-handed tactics of indiscriminate and arbitrary confiscation and deportation turned many poor and middle peasants into bitter opponents of the regime." A top-secret report of the OGPU on the popular attitude toward deportations of kulaks assembled in the city of Roslavl indicates considerable manifestation of sympathy with these unfortunates. "Groups of women watching the departure of the deported commented: 'It is in vain that these poor families are so mistreated . . . they have been suffering for the last two years . . . everything was in any case taken away from them through taxes . . . this is horrifying . . . children are taken together with adults . . . with only what is on their backs . . . It is impossible to comprehend why all this is happening to the people.'" The same report quotes a bookkeeper as saying: "I saw cattle trains readied for the kulaks who are obviously to be taken to Karelia . . . the best and hardest workers of the land are being taken away (with the misfits and lazybones staying behind)." Another bookkeeper was quoted to the effect that the Communists "were themselves propagandizing: 'Go to the countryside, build up cultured farms, raise good cattle, etc.'—the peasants did just that. They acquired this and that, and now they are dekulakized for having two cows and horses and for having stopped eating filth. Are these kulaks? What kind of kulaks can they be—they who have just begun to enjoy their own piece of bread. The real kulaks are sitting and looking on." [38]
Occasionally kulaks even found protection and a helping hand among the lower echelons of officials and party members. But, taking their cue from Stalin, not the slightest expression of sympathy or pity was voiced by the top Soviet hierarchy during the winter of 1930. Thus Kalinin,

the "all-Russian peasant elder" *(vserossiiskii starosta)* of Soviet propaganda, who was looked upon as a kind of a people's representative in Communist ruling circles, epitomized this attitude:

> The policy of de-kulakization is, at the present moment, indispensable as a kind of prophylactic measure, as an anticapitalistic vaccination. However cruel it may appear, this measure is absolutely indispensable, because it guarantees the healthy growth of the collective-farm organism in the future, and it insures us against numerous expenditures and against an enormous dissipation of human lives in the future . . . Of course the measure is very cruel to the individual person. Still, de-kulakization is indispensable because it is being dictated by such decisive political conditions as the interest of many millions of the toiling masses.[39]

Somewhat apologetically, Kalinin here echoes Stalin's hard line; but there were some qualms in the provincial bureaucracy. The Smolensk party chief, Rumiantsev, in a circular letter to district party secretaries dated February 20, 1930, censured the persistent errors and lawless actions in de-kulakization, despite "exhaustive" and precise instructions from the oblast authorities. Among the abuses stressed by Rumiantsev was "the dekulakization of middle peasants and the mass inclusion of such peasants in kulak lists based only on 'vicious rumor' and 'possible provocation.' " Ten days later, on March 2, 1930, a top-secret circular by the oblast committee followed Rumiantsev's letter, reprimanding the district committees for "brutal abuses committed by raion and village officials against the dekulakized." [40]

By this time, denunciations had reached the public level, following the publication of Stalin's encyclical "Dizziness from Success." A decree of the Central Committee issued on March 15, 1930, instituted a reexamination of the list of those de-kulakized and deprived of suffrage. It ordered the correction of any errors committed with respect to middle peasants, former Red partisans, members of the families of rural teachers and of personnel in military service who were loyal to the regime.[41] How large the proportion of people erroneously or unjustly de-kulakized was, even by tough Soviet standards, can be seen from the results of the reexamination in one raion, documented in the Smolensk archives. Out of 121 de-kulakized households, 44 cases were reversed and 8 were referred to the OGPU for further investigation and were likewise reversed. Thus 43 percent of these families were liquidated by mistake.

But de-kulakization and mass deportations had not stopped by the spring of 1930. An elaborate operation was carried out in the Roslavl district in the spring of 1931. Late in March, 437 families, totaling 2202 persons, were gathered in the assembly points of Roslavl, preparatory to deportation. The turning point came with the issue of a secret decree, dated May 8, 1933, and signed by Stalin and Molotov, which ordered that mass deportation and indiscriminate arrests "be immediately stopped . . . Deportation may be permitted only on a partial and individual basis and only with regard to those households whose heads are carrying on an active struggle against collective farms and are organizing resistance to sowing and state purchasing of grain." [42] The decree prohibited all arrests by unauthorized persons and frowned upon pretrial imprisonment for "insignificant crimes." It also set up maximum deportation quotas for a number of regions which could not be exceeded; that for the Western oblast, for instance, was 500 households.

The Stalin-Molotov decree was followed on May 25, 1933, by a secret circular of the party's Central Control Commission and the Commissariat of Workers' and Peasants' Inspection, reiterating and confirming, as is the custom in Soviet official documents, some of the main points made by the decree and instructing local organs to watch over its implementation.[43] These steps were significant primarily for the future. For although the Stalin-Molotov decree ordered a review of the cases of those imprisoned in various detention centers, it envisaged that a number of the detained kulaks would be promptly deported to OGPU camps and labor settlements.

How large was this uprooted population? According to an authoritative Soviet source, 240,757 kulak families were deported in 1930–1932, or about one fourth of all kulak households. This would mean about a million people. But large as the figure is, it does not tell the whole story. It was admitted that many middle and even some poor families were caught in the *raskulachivanie* net. This is corroborated by the statement in the same source that, in some raions, as many as 15 percent of peasant households were liquidated.[44] Presumably they were not included in the above figure. There is other statistical evidence on the kulaks. According to Vice-Commissar of Agriculture A. Gaister, the kulak population declined between 1928 and 1931 from 5.4 million to 1.6 million.[45] A Soviet statistical publication gives the number of kulaks in 1928 as 5,618,000, and on January 1, 1934, as 149,000.[46] These figures suggest that, in the course of a few years, as many as five and a half million people—a number exceeding the population of Denmark—were economically or physically exterminated. De-kulakization, like other Stalin purges, provided a source of very cheap labor for Soviet industrialization in unattractive areas. But the liquidated kulaks represented the elite of the Russian farming class, which was deeply attached to the soil and on which leadership in agricultural improvement must depend, as in every country. The elimination of these hard-working peasants and the squandering of their property was bound to affect agricultural production unfavorably, and this entirely apart from any humanitarian considerations (which are legitimate concerns in this presumably civilized world).

Incidentally, among the liquidated or fleeing peasants there was a large majority of foreign settlers, drawn to Russia mostly from Germany after the reign of Catherine the Great. They were unquestionably among the best farmers in Russia. But Stalin was so obsessed with the Marxist dogma of the superiority of large-scale farming, especially with what machinery could do, that he was completely oblivious to the human factor, to what the loss of millions of the most efficient farmers meant for Russian agriculture. It would be conceivable for a dictator like Stalin to be aware of this loss, and deliberately disregard it for ideological reasons, but I find no such awareness in his writings. An indirect corroboration of this is supplied by Khrushchev's secret speech at the Twentieth Party Congress in 1956, stressing Stalin's lack of knowledge of conditions in the Russian countryside and his failure to learn at first hand about the agricultural situation. One can only speculate whether quite so strict a ban would have been imposed on admission of kulaks into the kolkhozes if the Kremlin had realized what their elimination would mean for agriculture. At any rate, total de-kulakization, which a humanitarian historian must brand as genocide and an agriculturalist must classify as a serious brake on progress, became an accomplished fact in the early 1930s. It only need be added that the de-Stalinization operation under Khrushchev did not bring an ex post facto repudiation of de-kulakization, save for an attempt to minimize its effects.[47]

Mass Collectivization

De-kulakization was intended to serve as a catalyst for the mass collectivization of the remaining peasantry. In January and especially in February 1930, collectivization assumed landslide proportions. Whereas on July 1, 1929, less than 4 percent of all peasant households were in kolkhozes, by February 1, 1930, 32.5 percent had joined and by March 1, 1930, the proportion increased to 56 percent. The number of collective farms increased from 57,000 in July 1929 to 87,600 on February 1, 1930, and to 110,300 on March 1, 1930.[48] In some regions the speed of collectivization exceeded the national scale. In one raion of the Moscow district, the proportion of peasant households in kolkhozes increased from 9 percent on January 1, 1930, to 24 percent on February 1 and to

78 percent during the second half of February.[49] The central black-soil region reported 82 percent of its peasant holdings collectivized by March 1930. Incidentally, neither the black-soil region nor the Moscow region was supposed to be in the first group of collectivized regions.

The Soviet press and official statements gave the impression during the collectivization drive in January and February 1930 that the mass of the peasantry was willingly, if not spontaneously, joining the kolkhozes; in Molotov's words, "the middle peasant turned toward socialism." It is true that a cautionary note crept into Molotov's speech made on February 25, 1930, to the enlarged presidium of the executive committee of the Communist International. He warned "against infringement of the voluntary principle when bringing peasants into the collective farms and against bureaucratic methods of collectivization . . . and the chase after exaggerated speeds of collectivization."[50] The last point had been stressed even more emphatically two months earlier by another high Soviet official, S. I. Syrtsov, who stated: "Nothing should delay the growth of the collective-farm movement. But it is necessary to fight against a peculiar kind of sporting contest for a mere quantitative growth of the collective farms . . . At the present time we should stress the qualitative aspects of collectivization. The important thing is not that one region should keep up with another in point of quantity . . . We need no Potemkin collective farm villages."[51] Yet such dissonant notes were drowned in the official chorus of enthusiasm and self-congratulation over the miracle of mass collectivization. An official investigation conducted by vice-chairman of the Sovnarkom of the RSFSR, Ryskulov, of the collectivization of the Lower Volga region failed to bring forth any complaints of force being used to drag peasants into the kolkhozes, although 70 percent of the peasant households were collectivized at the beginning of the year. He reported that "in connection with the scarcity of directing staffs for the collective-farm movement, some of the local comrades quite incorrectly concluded that we must not develop the collective-farm movement at such a rapid pace."[52]

But were the middle and poor peasants really willing to join the kolkhozes? What about the "voluntary principle" of peasant collectivization about which Lenin seemed to be so solicitous and to which Molotov alluded in his speech on February 25, 1930? It should be clear that, with the threat of de-kulakization hanging over peasants who had not joined the kolkhozes, the concept of voluntarism in collectivization had to become meaningless. Those peasants who were not labeled kulaks had no choice, and willingness to join was a non sequitur. The pill was slightly sugar-coated by the government through the transfer of liquidated kulak property to kolkhozes (or by the opportunity to loot it) and by dangling promises to supply more tractors and to provide very shortly a more abundant life for the kolkhozniks. But this little bit of sugar was insignificant compared to the big stick wielded by the government. Still, even under such conditions there was surprisingly stubborn opposition on the part of many peasants and a strong resistance to collectivization. An illuminating description of the methods used to force the peasants into kolkhozes, which may be considered fairly typical, was given by a village Communist to an American writer:

> When we were told of collectivization . . . I liked the idea. So did a few others in our village, men like me, who had worked in the city and served in the Red Army. The rest of the village was dead set against it and wouldn't even listen to me. So my friends and I decided to start our own little cooperative farm, and we pooled our few implements and land. You know our peasants. It's no use talking to them about plans and figures; you have to show them results to convince them. We knew that if we could show them that we earned higher profits than before, they would like it and do as we did.
>
> Well, we got going. Then, one day, an order comes from the Klin [a county seat in Moscow province] party committee that we had to get 100 more families into our little collective. We managed to pull in about a dozen. And, believe me, this was not easy. It needed a lot of coaxing and wheedling. But no coaxing could get us even one more family. I went to Klin and explained the situation to the party committee. I begged them to let us go ahead as we started and I promised them, if they did, to have the whole village in the collective by next year. They wouldn't listen to me. They had orders from Moscow, long sheets saying how many collectives with how many members they had to show on their records. That was all. They told me that I was sabotaging collectivization and that unless I did as I was told I would be thrown out of the party and disgraced forever. Well, I knew that I couldn't get our people in, unless I did what I heard others were doing, in other words, forced them. When I had first heard of people doing that, I thought I would rather die than do it myself. I was sure that my way was the right way. And here I was with no other choice. I called a village meeting and I told the people that they had to join the collectives, that these were Moscow's orders, and if they didn't, they would be exiled and their property taken away from them. They all signed the paper that same night, every one of them. Don't ask me how I felt and how they felt. And the same night they started to do what the other villages of the USSR were doing when forced into collectives—to kill their livestock. They

had heard that the government would take away their cattle as soon as they became members of a collective.

I took the new membership list to the committee at Klin, and this time they were very pleased with me. When I told them of the slaughter of cattle and that the peasants felt as though they were being sent to jail, they weren't interested. They had the list and could forward it to Moscow; that was all they cared about. I couldn't blame them, they were under orders as well as I was.[53]

The Smolensk archives contain several letters written by peasants to the farm newspaper, *Nasha derevnia,* mostly unpublished, which confirm the hostility to kolkhozes and the coercion used by the Communist authorities to herd the peasants in.[54] Information from other regions, reported in the Soviet press after the grand collectivization offensive, fully corroborates the picture of intimidation, deceit, and coercion used in driving the peasants into the kolkhozes. Some of these reports go beyond general declarations and cite specific cases of abuse. *Pravda* on March 15, 1930, reported several. In certain districts the Komsomol "took the chickens away from the inhabitants and compelled the bedniaks to join the collective farms and to surrender their only cow and pig." In another region an official "intimidated the peasants 'who refused to enter the collective farms,' by handing them a paper and saying to them 'if you won't go into the collective farms, sign this.' The peasants, fearing legal prosecution, entered the collectives." Another official

threatened the peasants with a gun and shouted "every one of you will go into the collective farms." In another region a bazaar was closed "before the very eyes of the regional executive committee and without opposition from the regional committee of the party" . . . In a certain region "there was a practice of summoning to the regional executive committee those peasants who had not joined the collective farms in order to make to them the appropriate administrative suggestions; there were individual cases of imprisonment of those not desiring to join the collective farms, and at many meetings discussing collectivization, threats were made to deprive of their land those bedniaks and seredniaks who remained outside of the collective farms, or to banish them into the swamp of the woodcocks." . . . In [other] regions, collectivization [organizers] brought about collectivization by "handing out right and left impossible promises of an unlimited supply of tractors, machinery, etc." . . . [One organizer] announced at a meeting of peasants that "all farmers not joining the collective farms will be evicted. Foodstuffs will be concentrated in warehouses and there each collective farmer will be given a pound of bread a day."

Pravda on March 14, 1930, cited telephone orders stating that "by February 10 the whole raion must be collectivized to the extent of 100 percent." On March 12 *Pravda* reported that in one village "a bedniak woman was forced into a collective farm at the point of a revolver and, in another place, bedniaks and seredniaks who refused to join collective farms were exiled beyond the 'boundaries of the okrug.'" *Izvestiia* on March 25, 1930, stated that in one village the chief of the fire brigade "made an inventory of the property owned by the peasants under the pretext of submitting information to the organs of the State Insurance Department. The next morning the whole village was declared collectivized and the inventoried property was socialized."

That much of the collectivization during January–February 1930 was on paper only must be obvious from the examples cited above. Peasant agriculture was disorganized, but no really viable collective farm units were yet created. A further weakness, later officially recognized, was the tendency toward gigantomania—the setting up of huge unwieldy kolkhozes. This went hand in hand with the establishment of communes, which were supposed to be relegated to the final stage of the collectivization process. A good example is a case in the Ural region where, within a period of ten days, five thousand families, most of whom even then belonged to various artels and tozes, were forced into a commune that already had four thousand families.[55]

The resentment of the peasantry toward browbeating and maltreatment created serious unrest. One manifestation was the widespread slaughter of livestock, which was not confined, as Bolshevik propaganda asserted, only to the kulaks. Middle and poor peasants entering kolkhozes behaved similarly: they tried to become members minus animals. Even the bedniak in Sholokhov's novel *Broken Earth,* a man in favor of the kolkhoz, slaughtered his only cow and feasted on the meat, with rather unpleasant consequences. The situation had all the earmarks of a veritable "flight from the livestock." This early alarmed the Kremlin, which on January 16, 1930, had issued a decree "On Measures of Combating Predatory Slaughter of Livestock."[56] The decree attributed the wholesale slaughter of livestock to machinations of the kulaks and in the first article prescribed various punitive measures against them, which were hardly necessary in view of the de-kulakization campaign then going on. But the second article approved the decision of the All-Union Council of Collective Farms, forbidding admission and requiring expulsion from kolkhozes of those peasants who sold or slaughtered their livestock before joining. But all indications are that the decree had no effect on the critical livestock situation.

Peasant unrest also assumed more violent manifestations. The Bolshevik terror was met by peasant terror. Its obvious target was the city workers, the "twenty-five-thousanders" who were sent to help with dekulakization and collectivization, and other party and government officials involved in the campaign. Hoover reported a case where four workers from a Moscow factory were sent to the countryside only to be promptly murdered by infuriated peasants. "The most appalling stories of torture and mutilation of these workers by the peasants were spread by word of mouth, for the government rarely permitted news of these peasant assassinations to appear in the press." [57] Nor were kolkhozniks and kolkhozes immune from violent attacks. A procurator's report in the Smolensk archives, dated September 30, 1929, relates the following incident:

> On September 2, of this year, in the village of Lialichi, Klintsy okrug, a mob of 200 people made an open attack on the kolkhozniks who were going out to work the fields. This attack consisted of the dispersal of the kolkhozniks from the field, the destruction of their equipment, clothes, etc. They chased after the leaders of the kolkhoz, but the latter succeeded in saving themselves by fleeing. The majority of the attackers were women, who were armed with staves, pitchforks, spades, axes, etc. On the night of September 3rd a threshing floor with all the harvest, belonging to a member of the kolkhoz, was destroyed by fire. [58]

Arson, the "red cock" (*krasnyi petukh*), was a frequently employed weapon against kolkhozes just as it was in the past against the estates.

More than the numerous cases of violence by individuals or small groups, there were also mass uprisings of peasants which were never publicized by the Bolsheviks. While many of these flared up in areas inhabited by national minorities in the Caucausus and Turkestan, they were not confined to these areas. For instance, the province of Riazan in central Russia, close to Moscow, was also a scene of peasant insurrection. Disaffection was reported to have spread even among the troops sent to put down the peasant revolts. [59] The ties of the army to the village could not be ignored. This applied to the rank and file, as well as to the officer corps, of which a very large proportion were reported to have been sons of kulaks. [60]

The sharp discontent and peasant mutinies (though these are claimed to have been organized by kulaks) were recognized in the Soviet historical literature.[61] No less ominous, from the government's standpoint, was the danger that the peasant unrest held for the success of the spring sowing campaign, on which the national food supply depended. The situation in the early spring of 1930 was in many respects reminiscent of that in the spring of 1921, when Lenin sounded the strategic retreat from War Communism. And Stalin followed in the footsteps of the master by now ordering a strategic retreat from total collectivization. Far from restraining the maddening tempo of collectivization during January–February 1930, Stalin urged it on. This was not because of any lack of information. Stalin, as well as Molotov and Kaganovich, received regular reports every seven to ten days on the situation in the villages and therefore were well informed on what took place. For instance, a report of January 24, 1930, indicated that peasants were leaving the kolkhozes in droves in the Chapaevsk raion of the Samara (Kuibyshev) district.[62] On February 9, replying to questions raised by students of the Sverdlovsk Communist University, Stalin, while opposing de-kulakization in regions of incomplete collectivization that was undertaken independently, "without collectivization," urged them "to work harder for collectivization in the areas where it is incomplete." [63]

Certainly there was no discouragement here of all-out collectivization. Suddenly, on March 2, 1930, Stalin issued a veritable blast at the "excesses" of collectivization by publishing an article in *Pravda,* "Dizziness from Success." [64] The central theme of this disquisition is not that Stalin and the top leadership were "dizzy" and permitted abuses. The blame for all the errors was placed entirely on the lower echelon of officials and party workers, on the little man—and this despite the fact that for months the "comrades" had been badgered from above to proceed with total collectivization.[65] They were accused of pushing collectivization too far and too fast, not taking into account the diversity of regional conditions and extending collective farming into regions unready for it—such as northern European Russia and Central Asia. Here, incidentally, was a marked difference between Stalin and Lenin, who used to say "we made mistakes" and did not shift responsibility to henchmen.

Stalin also condemned the violation of the voluntary principle, in the use of force in collectivization. He mentioned a number of areas in Central Asia where the peasants, unwilling to join the kolkhozes, were threatened with the use of armed force and with deprivation of vital irrigation water and of manufactured goods. Ignoring the officially recommended artel type of collective in favor of a full-fledged commune was another sin denounced by Stalin. His article was followed by similar criticisms in a decree issued by the Central Committee on "The Fight against Distortions of the Party Line in the Collective-Farm Movement." [66] Another and more comprehensive article by Stalin on the same subject, "A Reply to Collective-Farm Comrades," appeared on April 3, 1930.[67] The Soviet press, taking its cue from the dictator, was now full of various abuses reported in connection with collectivization. That Stalin did not fool all his comrades all the time is shown by an interesting letter addressed to him by a factory worker, after the appearance of "Dizziness from Success." "Is one who was not able to avoid succumbing to the noise and clamor raised about the questions of collectivization and leadership in kolkhozes guilty? All of us, the lower echelons and the press, missed the basic question of leadership in kolkhozes, while Comrade Stalin probably slept soundly at that time, and did not hear or see our mistakes. Therefore you also must be corrected. And now Comrade Stalin shifts all responsibility to the local officials, while protecting himself and the top echelon." [68]

In the meantime, what was happening in the villages? Let us first hear again from the kolkhoz organizer who was compelled to force peasants into kolkhozes:

Then last March the papers and radio were full of Stalin's article "Dizziness from Success." He laced into us for forcing peasants to join the collectives. We village Communists had gone too far, Stalin scolded. That was exactly what I had said right from the beginning. But our local authorities wouldn't listen because they had orders from Moscow and were afraid to disobey them. Everybody in the village now laughed at me. I wanted to go away and never return. But the committee wouldn't let me go. "No," they said, "you carry on but do it right this time." As if they didn't know that I had been right all along and that I was made to pay for other people's mistakes. They made me spit into my own face. And here we are now, the same twelve families working together as we had started only with our livestock gone, our minds confused, and the villagers laughing into my face. The other night at a meeting when I told them about new taxation, they made fun of me and asked: "How do we know that you are not going to blunder again this time?" [69]

Although the new party line obviously caused much confusion in the spring of 1930, the dominant factor on the rural scene was decollectivization—the mass withdrawal of peasants from the kolkhozes. From more than a half of all peasant households officially reported in kolkhozes on March 1, the proportion decreased by the summer of 1930 to less than a fourth of the total. This was, undoubtedly, a major retreat by Stalin in his war on the peasantry. Yet, to look at the other side of the picture, despite all the confusion and disorganization, a sixfold increase in the number of peasant holdings in kolkhozes and a ninefold increase in the collective sown area occurred during a single year (between the summers of 1929 and 1930). Moreover, the retreat was truly strategic in the sense that it was temporary, merely a prelude to a new attack.

The collectivization campaign was resumed in the autumn of 1930. The Sixth Congress of Soviets, which met shortly afterward, posed this question to the peasants who had not entered the kolkhozes, "Are you for or against the kolkhozes?" [70] Neutralism was not to be tolerated. Only those middle and poor peasants who supported the collective movement and helped to fight the kulaks were henceforth to be considered allies of the Soviet state. That many peasants remained hostile to the kolkhozes is revealed by the grumbling reported by the first secretary of the Roslavl Party Committee: "We shall not enter the kolkhoz until we slaughter our last cow. How stupid it was to call oneself a poor peasant— now we are expected to be the first to enter the kolkhoz . . . the kolkhozniks do nothing. Food is rotting. We will all starve to death in the kolkhoz." [71]

But all this did not matter; the collectivization steamroller pushed relentlessly forward. During January, February, and the first ten days of March 1931, 2.8 million households joined kolkhozes.[72] By March 10 of that year, 9.4 million peasant households, or 37 percent of the total, already were reported as being in kolkhozes. In the principal grain regions (the Middle and Lower Volga, the steppe zone of the Ukraine, the Crimea and North Caucasus), the number of peasant households collectivized reached 74 percent on that date.[73] But even in the grain-deficit Smolensk area, where collectivization was expected to be at a much slower tempo, the Roslavl raion had 64.8 percent of households in kolkhozes by April 21, 1931.[74] By the middle of 1931, the number of kolkhozes exceeded 200,000, compared with less than 90,000 a year earlier, and it included again more than half of all the peasant households, with close to 60 percent of the total sown area. (See Table 22.)

On August 2, 1931, the Central Committee issued a decree, "Concerning the Tempo of Further Collectivization and the Problems of Strengthening the Kolkhozes." [75] The decree established a new criterion: the complete collectivization of a region. It required no less than a 68–70 percent inclusion of middle and poor peasant families in kolkhozes, accompanied by not less than a 75–80 percent collectivization of the sown area. Accordingly, such regions as the Middle and Lower Volga, North Caucasus (exclusive of some national minorities areas), the steppe Ukraine, the Crimea, and Moldavia were declared as basically having completed the collectivization process and were required to focus on the organizational strengthening of the kolkhozes. Other central and eastern grain regions of the country, as well as the cotton regions of Central Asia and Transcaucasia and the sugar-beet regions of the Ukraine and Central Russia, were to complete collectivization by 1932. The target for all other regions was set for 1932–33. The local authorities were cautioned by the decree against an "unwholesome chase after inflated percentages of collectivization." But in the course of the next year (1931–32) another sizable expansion of the collective sector, both in number of households and in sown area, took place. Collective farming, it appeared, had gained a foothold in Russian agriculture as a result of the Communist drive.

So far I have dealt only with what may be termed the external aspects of collectivization, in which considerable success was achieved by the Soviet leadership. But from the standpoint of internal organization and functioning and production results, the picture was anything but bright. Behind the official facade of its rapid progress, the new collective agriculture was beset by grave problems. Of overriding importance during the early collectivization period, since it involved the physical survival of millions, was once more the "bony hand of hunger." For mass collectivization brought in its train a food crisis, which by 1932–33 turned into a disastrous famine.

Ironically enough, the Sixth Congress of Soviets declared in March 1931 that, thanks to the agrarian policy of the party, "we have overcome the grain crisis . . . we have conquered the famine." [76] As events soon proved, nothing could be further from reality. The official grain-production figures did not seem to herald so acute a food crisis, assuming a normal increase of population. Both in 1930 and 1931 an increase in grain area was reported and, though it declined in 1932, it was higher than in any year prior to 1930 (see Table 23). Weather conditions were also favorable to crops in 1930, and a high yield per acre was reported which, together with an increased acreage, resulted in a bumper crop. The situation was less favorable in 1931, when crops in a number of southeastern regions were adversely affected by a drought, with consequent low yields per acre and small production. Yield and production were only slightly higher in 1932. As far as grain supplies were concerned, the relatively low production should have been partly offset by the carry-over from the 1930 crop and the reduction in the quantity of grain needed for forage because of the drastic decline in livestock during collectivization.

But, as has been correctly pointed out, there is a serious question of the reliability of crop statistics in 1930–1932. [77] This period witnessed so

Table 23. Selected statistics of grains, 1925–1932 [a]

Year	Sown acreage (million acres)	Yield per acre (metric tons)	Production	Government [b] procurement (million metric tons)	Exports [c]
Average 1925–29	229.3	0.79	73.3	11.7	1.2
Annual					
1929	237.2	0.75	71.7	16.1	1.0
1930	251.5	0.85	83.5	22.1	5.4
1931	258.0	0.67	69.5	22.8	4.4
1932	246.4	0.70	69.9	18.5	1.4

[a] All bread and feed grains, including grain legumes.

[b] Government procurements from the crop harvested during the year.

[c] Five principal grains (wheat, rye, barley, oats, corn) exported during the crop years beginning July 1.

Sources. Acreage, yields, and production: *Sotsialisticheskoe stroitel'stvo, 1934*, p. 203. Government procurements: 1925–1927, from *Statisticheskii spravochnik SSSR, 1928*, p. 703; 1928–1932, from *Sel'skoe khoziaistvo SSSR. 1935*, p. 215.

much confusion, conflict, and inefficiency in the countryside, as well as the strong propaganda effort to paint an optimistic picture of the results of collectivization, that crop statistics could hardly have remained uninfluenced. The wholesale purge of the Soviet statistical apparatus in 1930–31, including such authorities as Kondratiev, Groman, and Studenskii, also does not inspire confidence in the official statistics of that period. How much of the officially reported increased acreage in 1930 and 1931 actually had produced grain, and how much had grown weeds or was sown only on paper, will probably never be known.

If, as we must strongly presume, grain crops were officially overestimated, even a moderate reduction of 5 to 10 percent in 1932 would have seriously worsened the supply situation. Yet even a greater downward adjustment may be necessary in order to arrive at the true figures of barn crops. If there are any doubts with respect to the volume of production, there certainly are none about the intensified government procurements, which reached a peak during the 1931 crop year. Even after declining in 1932, procurements were still substantially higher than in any year prior to 1930. There is also no question about the ruthlessness with which the government exacted this grain or the tightness with which it held on to it. Instead of feeding the villages, the government preferred to increase grain exports in 1930 and 1931. On a smaller scale, exports were continued even in 1932, when famine already stalked the country-side.

The famine resulted from high government exactions and low grain production, which was caused partly by the weather but mostly by the inefficiency of the new collective farms and the passive resistance of the bullied peasantry. It climaxed in a catastrophe in the winter and spring of 1932–33, and this despite the boast of the Congress of Soviets in March 1931 that the famine was conquered. W. H. Chamberlin, who made a firsthand investigation, stated: "On the basis of talks with peasants and figures supplied not by peasants, who were often prone to exaggeration, but by local Soviet officials and collective-farm presidents, whose interest was rather to minimize what had taken place, I have no hesitation in saying that the southern and southeastern section of European Russia during the first six months of 1933 experienced a major famine, far more destructive than the local famines which occurred, mostly on the Volga, in exceptionally bad drought years under Tsarism, second in the number of its victims probably only to the famine of 1921–1922." [78] Chamberlin's grim account is corroborated by Otto Schiller, then German agricultural attaché in the USSR: "Entire villages were emptied, where the crisis raged at its worst. In numerous houses the windows had been replaced by wooden planks. They spoke an eloquent language." [79] While famine conditions were apparently at their worst in the southern and southeastern regions of European Russia and Kazakhstan, other regions also experienced considerable food stringencies, undernourishment, and hardship. Among these was the Smolensk area, in which a number of secret official reports stressed the critical food situation.[80]

Chamberlin is right in placing the responsibility for the 1932–33 famine squarely on the Soviet government. No appeal for foreign aid was made, as in 1921, and the veil of secrecy was drawn over the famine areas, access to which was denied to foreign correspondents. Actually, as Chamberlin notes, the government could have greatly relieved the situation by using its own resources, by reneging on exactions in the stricken areas, by discontinuing grain exports, and by diverting some of its foreign exchange to the importation of foodstuffs. The attitude toward famine relief was epitomized by a provincial official: "To have imported grain would have been injurious to our prestige. To have let the peasants keep their grain would have encouraged them to go on producing little." [81]

It is impossible to quantify the vast amount of human suffering, the blood, sweat, and tears, of those who survived collectivization. But the number of lives lost during the collectivization period has been estimated by competent statisticians at the staggering figure of five million. The famine accounted for most of these deaths.[82] Thus the collectivization of Russian peasant agriculture began with the horrors of mass deportation and ended with the ordeal of mass famine.

11

Collectivized Agriculture in the Prewar Period

During the period of a little over twenty years which elapsed between mass collectivization and the death of its principal architect, agrarian policy passed through several stages of development; these alternated between toughness and a somewhat softer line while all the time adhering to fundamental collectivist tenets. Let us begin with a general review of these different stages.

The Early Years

"In the beginning there was chaos": such can be said of the situation in the kolkhozes during and immediately following the initial period of mass collectivization, which lasted roughly until 1933. Not that chaotic conditions were ever fully overcome in collective agriculture, but the confusion was strongest in these formative years. The nub of the difficulty was that, though it proved possible to achieve a breakthrough in collectivization by forcing the farmers into the kolkhozes, it was another matter to make them work anywhere near as efficiently as when they farmed their own little strips, let alone to achieve the great upsurge of production that the Kremlin expected from such an operation. Commissar of Agriculture Iakovlev summed up the situation in September 1931, when he likened the new farm units to houses in the process of construction: externally they seem to be ready, but on going inside one notices that they lack floors and ceilings.[1] This apparently came as a surprise to the Soviet leaders. Molotov complained in January 1933 that, once the peasant cedes his horse to the kolkhoz, he ceases to consider it as his own and fails to take proper care of it.[2] Another Bolshevik official lamented the fact that the peasants who, under an individualistic system, considered it a sin and a crime to steal, "do not give a hang" for collective property, and theft had become a common phenomenon.[3]

On the other hand, even Soviet publications severely criticized from time to time the highhanded attitude assumed by certain government and party officials toward the property of kolkhozes, and this, to say the least, could hardly inspire respect for collective property on the part of the peasants. To take a relatively mild example, one district agricultural office received money to purchase horses from a group of collectives, but distributed the purchased horses among other collectives and administrative institutions which did not pay for them. "This one fact, selected from hundreds of similar facts in other districts, shows the 'careless attitude' of many agricultural officials toward the money of the kolkhozes." [4] There were also numerous complaints about the poor working discipline in the kolkhozes. Commissar Iakovlev stated at the Sixth Congress of Soviets in March 1931 that even at the peak periods of farm work, when every worker counts, only one third to two thirds of the labor force in collectives was actually working in the fields.

But poor peasant morale was linked with lack of incentives or sheer physical exhaustion and starvation. And there is abundant evidence in Soviet literature that peasant lethargy was matched by glaring mismanagement of collectives resulting from the ignorance, inefficiency, drunkenness, and cupidity of many of the newly installed managers and from bureaucratic regimentation. The difficulties were compounded by the unceasing pressure of the state for grain and other farm products, leaving little for distribution among peasants. The production situation was aggravated by a severe shortage of draft power, that long-standing problem of Russian agriculture. Even during the NEP, over 30 percent of peasant households in the principal grain regions, according to a sample census of 1927, lacked draft animals.[5] It was this condition, among other things, that collectivization was supposed to have remedied. But with the slaughter of livestock by the peasants during the collectivization campaign, and indifferent or poor care of the animals in the kolkhozes as well as a shortage of feed, the number of horses declined steadily during the years of collectivization; in 1932 it was 43 percent below that of 1929. This reduction was only partly offset by the increase in the number of tractors. Late sowings, abundant growth of weeds, and delayed and inefficient harvesting, with ensuing large crop losses, were an inevitable consequence of the conditions prevailing during the early 1930s.

One other point cannot be stated too often: with the large number of the best farmers driven off the land or exterminated, the result of de-kulakization, the qualitative depletion of human resources was bound to impair the productive capacity of Russian agriculture, at least temporarily. It meant, among other things, that the Kremlin had to rely on nonfarmers, often little versed in agricultural matters, or on mediocre farmers for leadership in the kolkhozes. The livestock sector showed even a greater deterioration than crop production did. Besides horses, other types of livestock were also drastically reduced through slaughter, poor care, lack of adequate shelter, and especially shortage of feed.

The tragic consequences for rank-and-file kolkhozniks, recorded by the secret police, are revealed by the following samples preserved in the Smolensk archive:

> I will have grain for five months, and the rest of the time I will have to sit without grain; and how I'll live this year I can't imagine. Such a situation in regard to grain exists not only with me, but also with many other kolkhozniks . . . This year it will be very bad to live in the kolkhoz; by spring there will be no grain for the majority of the kolkhozniks, and if in the future we sow according to such plans, we will perish from hunger. If the leaders would not give us plans, but would sow according to our plans, from experience, then things would be better; we have sown a great deal, but there is no grain and will be none. Even the grass under the rye and flax, of which there was a great deal, the board of the kolkhoz does not permit us to cut for our cows, and they themselves do not cut it. And it will turn out that the kolkhoznik will have nothing with which to feed his cow . . . The Ukraine is hungry . . . and we in the kolkhoz also have no bread, and we will not have it, because they do not permit us to sow what we need and they give us more flax [to sow]. The working of the land is poor; they plow once and usually not on time. The working force in the village is resettling in the cities, in industrial centers, because in the kolkhoz it is not profitable to work. We work all year, and you don't know what you'll get.[6]

Soviet leaders acknowledged serious shortcomings in the functioning of the new kolkhozes, but they did this only after indulging in a Madison Avenue glorification of the brilliant successes of collectivization. A scapegoat for the difficulties was again found, surprisingly enough, in the "kulak influence," despite the prior de-kulakization. Thus Kaganovich stated at a Ukrainian party conference on July 8, 1932: "In sowing and especially in harvesting in a number of kolkhozes the *quality* of farm work was *poor,* resulting in enormous losses in the out-turn of the harvest . . . Basically we liquidated the kulak. However, it would be incorrect to say that the kulak influence has already disappeared. It still exists. Kulak influences strengthened petit-bourgeois habits, which found their expression in a number of kolkhozes in poor work and large harvest losses, in low productivity of labor, in the slaughter of cows, and in the neglect of horses." [7] The alleged kulak influence was adduced by Soviet leadership as an important reason for not leaving things alone (*samotek*) in the kolkhozes and for "guiding" them through the party-state apparatus, a euphemism for strong-fisted regimentation. Particularly in connection with grain procurements, the apparatus was exhorted to play this active role, which resulted in the terrible famine described in the preceding chapter.

The use of force was thus continued, though it was usually camouflaged in the published official speeches and decrees. But occasionally the draconian measures of the regime were revealed in all their stark reality. Such was the ill-famed decree of August 7, 1932, concerning the protection of public (socialist) property, which provided the death penalty for the theft of kolkhoz property, including crops in the fields. In extenuating circumstances the death penalty could be reduced to imprisonment of not less than ten years. Furthermore, no amnesty was to be applied for such offenses. Any threat or use of violence against the kolkhozes or kolkhozniks on the part of the kulaks and "other antisocial elements" was punishable by five to ten years' imprisonment in a concentration camp. The monstrous severity of the sentences meted out under this law (which had no analogy in pre-Soviet legislation) even for "theft" of ears of grain remaining in the fields after harvest, or for stealing a few kilograms of vegetables by the mother of a large family, was made plain by Vyshinskii.[8] No doubt the food shortage of the early thirties led to theft from the fields by the so-called barbers, who would cut off the ears of grain. This required an elaborate system of protection of the fields, a task for which children were recruited in numerous cases.

A decree of January 30, 1933, extended the application of the law of August 7, 1932, to frauds in connection with accounting in the kolkhozes and to the acts of "wrecking," which of course are broadly interpreted in the Soviet Union.[9] The same decree introduced a rule that a member of the kolkhoz who refused to perform a task without a good reason would be subject to a fine by the executive board of the kolkhoz and, in case of a repeated refusal, might be expelled. Another stern measure was the decree of January 28, 1933, dealing with the organization of spring sowing in the North Caucasus, where serious difficulties had developed in the collectivization of Cossack farmers and of various national minorities.[10] It was also one of the worst famine-stricken areas of the USSR. The decree, of course, does not mention this grim fact, but concerns itself with the execution of the spring sowing plan and various farm operations pertaining to it. Among these were the assembling of an adequate seed supply, timely sowing, and weed control, which became a very vexing problem because of poor cultivation. To combat weeds, the North Caucasus authorities were empowered to mobilize the services of the local population. The decree declared that "without firm labor discipline, spring sowing cannot be carried out" and that "absenteeism and a negligent attitude toward field work on the part of some kolkhozniks must be punished without mercy, including expulsion from kolkhozes." Local officials were also warned by the decree that "any leniency shown to the enemies of the people sabotaging the sowing campaign will be viewed as assistance to the kulak and the counterrevolutionary wrecker." The savage law of August 7 on protection of public property was to be applied "without leniency" to the theft of seed from barns and drills and to any act of sabotage in connection with field work—this could cover a multitude of sins, many of them imaginary.

This catalog of repressions is not complete without recalling once more the famine of 1932–33. The fact that the government did not try to avert it and undertook no relief measures lends strong weight to the view of Chamberlin and others that the famine became a punitive measure, aiming to starve the peasants into complete submission and to keep them from future resistance to the regime. Only one exception to this policy was made, and then in a matter in which the government had a direct interest: the shortage of seed in the Ukraine and North Caucasus, which threatened the planting of crops in 1933 and, consequently, government procurements. Seed loans in this region were granted by a decree of February 25, 1933, which stated that unfavorable weather conditions had resulted in a partial loss of the harvest and the inability of collectives and state farms to lay in the needed seed supply.[11] The loans were to be repaid in kind in the fall of 1933, "without interest" but with a 10 percent charge for administrative and transportation expenses. That there was a severe shortage of food is not mentioned in the decree, since the government had no intention of offering any relief to the starving people, even on a loan basis. Before concluding, it is worth noting that the harsh behavior of the Soviet regime during the famine of 1932–33 had no precedent in the early Soviet period under Lenin (the famine of 1921–22) or in the frequent famines under the tsars, when some relief, though often delayed and inadequate, was usually given.

Stalin encouraged the use of coercion by his insistence on the continuous and thoroughgoing regimentation of collectives. In a significant speech on "The Work in the Village" in January 1933, he pointed out that some Bolsheviks did not realize that the achieving of collectivization should increase the responsibility of the party and the government for the condition of agriculture. While individual farming prevailed, the party could confine its intervention to separate acts of assistance and advice, since the individual peasant farmer would have to attend to such affairs as sowing and harvesting, if he did not want to starve. With the transition to collective farming, this responsibility would rest not so much on the individual member as on the management of the kolkhoz. Moreover, since the kolkhoz is a large farm unit, it could not be managed without a plan; hence a plan must be supplied. All of this required, Stalin said, systematic intervention and assistance on the part of the Soviet government.[12]

In accord with this policy, there were created in the winter of 1933 the so-called political departments, the machine-tractor stations and state farms, staffed by trusted party members. The political departments (*politotdely*) were entrusted with sweeping powers and wide functions. They were to serve, in the words of the decree of the Central Committee of January 11, 1933, as "a party eye and control in all branches of the work and life of the machine-tractor stations and state farms and of the kolkhozes served by the machine-tractor stations."[13]

One of the primary functions of the politotdel was to secure the observance of what Stalin called the first commandment—the fulfillment by the kolkhozes of all obligations to the state. The political departments were to combat all forms of sabotage and theft of collective property and to secure the proper enforcement of the Soviet penal laws. They were also to check up on the dependability of the members of the collectives and party and government local officials, many of whom were purged. In 1933, over 18,000 party members were mobilized to work in the political departments, and of these 58 percent were factory workers.[14] That the politotdels used their wide powers quite fully is attested by the reports of those who staffed them.[15] Created as emergency organizations to combat the crisis in the village, the politotdels were combined, at the end of 1934, with the general rural organs of the party, also reorganized at the time.

The reaction of the peasants after three years of mass collectivization is illustrated by the following item, selected at random but nonetheless typical. A group of peasants, writing to a newspaper to point out that their particular kolkhoz was considered the best in the district, had this to say: "Not everything, however, is well in the kolkhoz. We heard from people and know from the papers that the collective farmers should be the bosses of their kolkhoz, should know what is taking place and why, and that the executive board must report to the membership. But there is nothing like this in our kolkhoz. We are through with the harvest; but we don't know how much we earned during the season. The executive board tells us nothing and doesn't ask us about anything. For more than four months we had no meeting." [16] If this was the situation in the best kolkhozes, what about the others?

Strengthening the Kolkhozes

Although the government under Stalin was ready to use force without stint against the peasants, it realized that this was not enough to make collective agriculture work. Some incentives, a little of the traditional carrot, had to be offered to the peasants who received so many blows from the Communist stick. The government was also aware of the need to strengthen the management of collectives and to stabilize their legal status. The increased official attention given to these matters characterizes the next stage in the development of collectivism, the period officially designated as that of the strengthening or bolstering of the kolkhozes, which extended roughly from 1934 to 1939. But the groundwork for this phase was laid in 1932–33. The first legislative step in this direction was allowing peasants legally to resume private trade under certain conditions. A decree dated May 6, 1932, provided that after the somewhat reduced goals of grain procurements in 1932 were fulfilled, and the seed supply for next spring's sowing laid in, the kolkhozes and their members were free to sell their surplus grain on the private market. Local authorities were called upon to facilitate the trade, but at the same time they were to "eradicate the private trader, the middleman-speculator." [17] Kolkhoz trade in other farm products (dairy, meat, vegetables) was also legalized and became much more important than grain trade.

A decree of May 20, 1932, implementing previous legislation, sanctioned the principle of free competitive prices, determined by the interaction of supply and demand in the private market for agricultural products. It also exempted kolkhoz trade from taxation.[18] The decree confirmed the ban on the middleman, which was even more strongly reiterated in a special edict of August 22, 1932, "Concerning the Struggle against Speculation." This set a penalty against private traders (speculators) of five to ten years in a concentration camp, without opportunity for amnesty. The legal proscription of the middleman, of course, further restricted the scope and effectiveness of such kolkhoz trade as could develop following the heavy exactions of the state. Yet to sell farm products in this limited market at free competitive prices, which were several times higher than the fixed, artificially low government prices, often meant a difference between starvation and subsistence for those kolkhozniks who could avail themselves of the opportunity. By the same token, private trade has now come to play a significant role in the food supply not only of kolkhozniks but of the urban Soviet population, despite the de jure elimination of the middleman.

It was all very well to legalize private kolkhoz trade. But in 1932 it must have seemed hypocritical to the starving peasants who were confronted by indiscriminate government commandeering of foodstuffs. By the end of the year even the Soviet government became convinced (though the experience of War Communism could have taught the lesson much earlier) that a regularization of the procurement system was essential if any economic incentives were to be provided. So a reform was initiated by a decree of January 19, 1933, implemented by other legislation and regulations,[19] with respect to grains. In the course of a year it was extended to potatoes, sunflower seed, meat, dairy products, and wool. Since the procuring system will be discussed at length in a later section, it suffices to say here that the heart of the reform was the setting in each district, in advance of the harvest, of firm delivery quotas at fixed prices. Repeated levies, which had been commonly practiced and aroused intense hostility among peasants, were strictly (but in practice not very successfully) prohibited. The compulsory deliveries had the legal status of taxes, though low fixed prices were paid by the government.

The reform of 1933 introduced the principle of certainty, an attribute of any good tax system. The peasants were assured that whatever they produced in excess of the tax they could legally call their own, and they were not to be left to the mercy of the tax collector. This should have stimulated production in the kolkhozes, even though the original tax rates were high. In the leading regions they often amounted to more than a third of the 1928–1932 average yields. A major loophole also developed in the new system because of the growing volume of payments in kind for work performed by the machine-tractor stations, which were not fixed but varied with officially determined and usually inflated yields per hectare. The planned acreage targets were also too high in a number of cases. Yet, despite the various flaws, the new procuring system was an improvement over the unbridled exactions preceding it. The burden on the peasants was further reduced by a government decree of February 27, 1934, canceling all arrears on grain deliveries in 1933 and extending the period during which seed loans were to be repaid to three years.[20]

The reform of the procurement system in 1933 bears some resemblance to the NEP, which was also ushered in by the replacement of the unlimited requisitions of War Communism with a tax in kind and the legal restoration of a free market. But it was a very attenuated NEP, since the private trader was now taboo. A more positive use of economic incentives was the payment of premium prices for the sale to the state of farm products above the plan quotas. Such premiums, expressed as percentages of the standard fixed procuring price, were steeply graduated on a basis of the increase in quantity delivered. In some cases they reached as high as 400 percent of the standard price. The system of differential prices was introduced first in the case of commercial crops (sugar beets, cotton) and in 1936 was extended to wheat. In line with increased attention to economic incentives were the steps taken by the government to assure the distribution of grain among kolkhozniks. Regulations were issued which limited the obligatory withholding of grain for distribution in kolkhozes only to what was necessary to provide seed and fodder and prohibited local authorities from requiring the establishment of other reserves. But kolkhozes could set up such reserves by a majority vote of the general assembly, provided two thirds of the membership was present at the meeting.[21] In this same area there was government assistance to the kolkhozniks who did not own cows to acquire calves on credit.[22] Priority was to be given in this matter to the best, "shock," kolkhozniks.

There was another problem to be solved: the instability of kolkhoz landholdings. This was a weakness characteristic of Russian peasant farming under repartitional tenure before collectivization, and it was aggravated during the early postrevolutionary period, with its frequent repartitions. Collectivization was supposed to cure this evil, but the principle of stability was often violated by the transfer of kolkhoz land to state farms and other institutions, arbitrary changes by local authorities of kolkhoz boundaries, and changes of the land area when members left the kolkhozes. Obviously there could be no incentive to take proper care of the land as long as its possession was so uncertain. A decree of September 3, 1932, sought to introduce stability into land arrangements by ordering that the existing kolkhoz boundaries remain fixed and by prohibiting land redistribution between kolkhozes. Local authorities were enjoined against arbitrary changes of kolkhoz land area without authorization by newly established commissions, which were given jurisdiction over all land controversies. Finally, peasants who chose to leave a kolkhoz were not to be allotted any of its land, but only free state land if available. If a reduction of the area was authorized, the kolkhoz had to be compensated for any prior improvement made on the land.

Legal safeguards were now set up against the worst abuses of the peasants by local bureaucrats. In this category was the secret circular letter of Stalin and Molotov, on May 8, 1933, calling for a halt to the repressive measures in the countryside.[23] But there was a wide gap between a law on the statute book and its observance or implementation. Violation of the law was often tacitly encouraged by the ambivalent attitude of the regime or by the setting of tasks or targets that could not be fulfilled by normal, legal means. A case in point is the illegal, repeated grain levies, the so-called counterplan (*vstrechnyi plan*), from which the kolkhozes suffered so much. Local authorities responsible for the fulfillment of quotas continued to press those kolkhozes with grain, to make up for the shortages of other farms, though sometimes even grain for seed was not spared. No amount of legislation or exhortation could change this practice, as long as the basic policy of the Kremlin remained unaltered.

The Model Charter of 1935

The relatively more liberal policy toward collectives was reflected in the revised model charter promulgated in February 1935. A similar constitutional charter had been adopted in March 1930, during the early stage of mass collectivization, when the government was promoting the artel over the rival commune and toz types. The model was based on the socialization of land and other means of production and the distribution of income according to the labor contributed by members. The household economy of the peasants was continued on an individual basis, including the small garden plots and the ownership of a few animals. By 1935 it was felt that amendments were needed, though with no alteration in the basic principles of the charter. The new draft was prepared jointly by the agricultural section of the Central Committee and the Ministry of Agriculture, and was submitted to a specially convoked Second Congress of Shock Collective Farmers (February 11–17, 1935) which represented approximately 1500 of the best kolkhozes. Stalin and other leaders also took part in the congress. Here the draft was discussed by delegates during a general debate and then was sent for detailed examination to a commission consisting of 167 delegates, including Stalin, Molotov, and Kaganovich. Stalin, it was reported, took an active part in the deliberations of the commission, which made a number of changes in the draft. On February 17, 1935, the amended charter was adopted by the congress and on the same day was approved by the Council of People's Commissars and the Central Committee, which imparted to it the status of a basic law of collective farming.[24] This was reaffirmed by the Soviet Constitution of 1936. What gave the charter prestige was the personal interest and participation of Stalin in its drafting. It served as a pattern for the charters that each kolkhoz was to adopt individually, with minor variations, to suit differing local conditions.

The charter was especially concerned with two problems: the instability of kolkhoz land and the status of small personal farming. That the decree of September 2, 1932, was unsuccessful in solving the problem of instability of land tenure is clear from the evidence adduced by high officials at the congress.[25] To remedy this situation and to provide an incentive for the collectivized peasantry to work its land better, the government decided upon a stronger course of action. The charter declared that the kolkhozes were to hold the land they occupied, which legally was national property, "in perpetuity, that is, forever." This curious reiteration was added on Stalin's initiative, in order to strengthen the text,[26] and was confirmed by the 1936 Constitution. It was further decreed that a title deed was to be issued to each kolkhoz after the land had been surveyed and the best arrangement from the standpoint of land utilization had been adopted. After the completion of surveying operations and issuing of the deed, the area of each kolkhoz could not be reduced. It could be increased at the expense of state land or holdings of individual peasant farmers who decided to enter the kolkhoz.

Although these provisions were actively implemented by the issuance of numerous title deeds to the kolkhozes, they were practically nullified by wholesale mergers of collectives or their conversion into state farms, which took place in the 1950s. Thus the 1935 land-tenure measure proved to be of no lasting significance. The opposite is true of the individual farming of the kolkhozniks, which continues to be a burning issue: it involves the national food supply, the ability of the peasants to make a living, and the question of competition between household farming and the collectivized farm economy, to which in theory it was supposed to be merely ancillary. Allotment of small plots to kolkhozniks and individual possession of a small number of animals had been sanctioned in general terms by the old charter of 1930. But as Iakovlev, the government rapporteur at the 1935 congress, pointed out, there were actually many kolkhozes where the peasants had no plots of their own. Conversely, in other kolkhozes, the amount of land held privately was excessive.* As for the possession of livestock by kolkhozniks, the fact

---

* What the government considered excessive was brought out by examples given by Iakovlev. The first was that of a kolkhoz in Kursk province, which had 76 hectares in collective sowings and 51 hectares in private plots. The number of peasant households in the kolkhoz was not given, but the proportion of privately held land seems high. In another kolkhoz in the same province 42 households had 62 hectares in private

that the government found it necessary to adopt special measures to supply them with cattle tells the story.

In 1935, Stalin took the side of the kolkhozniks when he gave his blessing to personal farming as against the extreme restrictionist tendencies manifested in some sections of the party. He made his attitude clear during the discussions of the drafting commission:

> If you do not have in the artel an abundance of products, and you cannot give to the kolkhozniks and their families all that they need, the kolkhoz cannot undertake to satisfy both the collective and the personal needs. Then it is better to be straightforward and to say that a certain part of the work is collective and a certain part personal. It is better to admit, in a straightforward, open, and honest manner, that the collectivized peasant household must have its own personal farming, on a small scale but personal. It is better to take the position that there is artel farming, collective, large, and of decisive importance, necessary to meet collective needs, and there is, side by side with it, small personal farming necessary to meet the personal needs of the kolkhozniks . . . The combination of the personal interests of the kolkhozniks with the collective interests of the kolkhozes—here is the key to the strengthening of the kolkhozes.[27]

The objective of the new charter, then, was to put on a firm footing and equalize on a regional basis the private sector in the kolkhozes while keeping it subsidiary to the collective sector. The size of the plots of the kolkhozniks, exclusive of area under buildings, was fixed by the 1935 charter at a quarter to a half hectare (0.6 to 1.2 acres) and in some cases at one hectare (2.5 acres), depending upon regional conditions.

With regard to personal ownership of livestock, the kolkhozes were divided into four regional groups, with varying numbers of animals permitted each peasant family, depending upon the importance of livestock in the agriculture of the region. In the first group, in which such major crops as grain, cotton, sugar beets, and flax predominated, the minimum of privately owned livestock was allowed. And in the fourth and last group, in which nomadic animal husbandry still prevailed, the maximum of privately owned livestock was permitted. Here was the most important concession made by the government to peasant individualism,

---

plots, or about 1.5 hectares per household. Iakovlev mentions the existence of private plots of 2 to 3 hectares in other regions. (*Vtoroi vsesoiuznyi s"ezd kolkhoznikov-udarnikov*, p. 13.) These were probably exceptional cases, since the total area under private plots at the end of 1934 was small. In no region did it reach 10 percent of the collective area and in most regions was much smaller. *Sel'skoe khoziaistvo SSSR. Ezhegodnik, 1935* (Agriculture of the USSR. Yearbook, 1935; Moscow, 1936), pp. 232–233.

made not only to propitiate the peasantry but also to remedy the sorry plight of animal husbandry under the collective regimen. While the provisions regarding personal ownership of livestock in the charters of 1935 and 1930 applied specifically to artels, extension of such rights to members of the few remaining communes had been legalized in 1933.[28] Further legislation enacted in 1934 permitted the communes, including those converting to the artel form, to transfer to private ownership up to one third of the communal livestock, to be paid for at low state procurement prices in three annual installments.[29] Such changes helped to obliterate the distinction between communes and artels and paved the way for the conversion of the extant communes. This was in accordance with Stalin's policy, laid down in 1930, which ruled out the egalitarian commune because of its tendency to concern itself with producing for its own consumption.

Both the 1935 and 1930 charters made the kolkhozniks, with some exceptions, the residual claimants to kolkhoz income, after state claims and production requirements were satisfied. The charters adhered to the principle of distribution of income to kolkhozniks on the basis of skill, amount of work performed, or output. Although it has undergone certain modifications over the years, this differentiated system, with its built-in economic inequality, has become basic to the artel form. An exception was made in the early days in the regulation, approved by the Sovnarkom on April 13, 1930, permitting an allocation of 5 percent of kolkhoz income for distribution in accordance with the amount of property contributed by members. But the next year the proportion was reduced to 3 percent, and soon even this small concession to individualism was dropped and found no place in the 1935 charter.[30] There is no indication that this provision was used widely during its shortlived existence. More common, apparently, judging from strictures in the Soviet press of the 1930s, were lapses from the differentiated system of payment in the direction of a straight daily wage, which the regime strongly disapproved.

The 1935 charter reaffirmed the democratic, self-governing, voluntary character of the collectives, whose managers were elected by the membership. But the farms were enjoined to function in accordance with government plans, prepared in Moscow, which were becoming more detailed and often difficult or impossible to fulfill. In the effort to enforce these unrealistic goals, local party and government authorities virtually nullified what self-governing and autonomous features there were, and subjected the kolkhoz to extensive regimentation in violation of the charter. This was compounded by the bureaucratic habit of meddling and a lack of effective institutional restraints. What Voltaire said of the Holy Roman Empire, that it was neither holy nor Roman nor an empire, could be paraphrased with respect to the kolkhoz: it was neither democratic nor self-governing nor a voluntary cooperative.

The Kolkhoz and Socialist Industry: Economic Performance

I have called attention to a comparison between the agrarian policy of the mid-thirties and that of the NEP. But the agrarian "liberalism" of the mid-thirties had a much narrower scope than the NEP's and also proved to be of more limited duration. There was of course nothing like a decollectivization that could be considered equivalent to the abandonment of War Communism in 1921. The application of economic incentives, the essence of liberalization, was also seriously restricted. The Soviet state still gave little to the peasant and was able to take much from him. The shortages, high prices, and poor quality of consumer goods continued. The unsatisfactory consumer-goods situation paralleled Stalin's policy of speedy industrialization during the first two five-year plans. That it bore fruit in a rapid albeit lopsided industrial development is the consensus of Western specialists, even though almost all regard the official Soviet index of industrial production during the 1930s as greatly overstated.[31] Yet because of the priority given by Stalin in allocating resources to heavy industry—producer goods and armaments—it greatly outpaced light industry and its consumer goods. This is brought out by Tables 24–26, in which the official index of Soviet industrial pro-

Table 24. Official Soviet index of gross industrial output (1928=100)

Year	All goods	Producer goods	Consumer goods
1928	100	100	100
1932	202	274	156
1937	445	654	311
1940	645	1,003	414
1945	592	1,125	246
1948	760	1,303	409
1950	1,118	2,055	511
1952	1,452	2,688	654
1955	2,067	3,906	899
1958	2,774	5,375	1,149

Source. *Narodnoe khoziaistvo, 1959*, p. 141. Territorial coverage corresponds to the boundaries of the respective years.

Table 25. Index of Soviet industrial output (1928=100)[a]

Year	All goods	Producers and military goods	Consumer goods
1928	100	100	100
1937	274	426	171
1940	294	452	183
1948	294	536	128
1950	434	781	197
1955	715	1,290	323
1956	773	1,400	344

[a] Soviet definition of industry, which includes mining, power generation, logging, and fishing. Territorial coverage corresponding to the boundaries of the respective years.

Source. D. B. Shimkin and F. A. Leedy, "Soviet Industrial Growth," *Automotive Industry*, January 1, 1958, p. 51.

Table 26. Index of Soviet industrial output (1927–28=100)

Year	All industrial products	Machinery	Other producer goods	Consumer goods	Foods	Nonfoods
1927–28	100.0	100.0	100.0	100.0	100.0	100.0
1932	153.5	286.8	192.1	109.4	104.9	113.6
1937	248.7	601.5	310.7	164.1	156.8	171.1
1940	262.7	504.4	334.1	181.0	163.7	197.0
1945	135.1	200.0	201.4	74.0	74.0	74.1
1950	369.0	1,470.6	467.3	184.2	149.9	215.5
1952	438.7	1,473.5	567.8	234.4	185.9	279.1
1955	583.4	2,002.9	748.1	313.6	234.9	385.6
1958	746.5	2,720.6	966.4	378.8	281.7	467.7

Source. Adapted from "An Index of Soviet Industrial Output" by Norman M. Kaplan and Richard H. Moorsteen, *American Economic Review*, 50: 296 (June 1960).

duction is given together with indexes computed by Western specialists. The large increase in the output of consumer goods shown by all indexes is due in considerable measure to commercialization, that is, to a substitution of factory products for domestic processes, incidental to the rapid growth of the urban industrial population (bread baked in commercial bakeries instead of home-made bread, for instance). Thus the reported increase did not wholly represent a net gain, particularly since the assortment and quality of goods often deteriorated with commercialization during the "deficit" years, when the consumer was the forgotten man in the USSR. An increase of roughly 15 percent in population between 1928 and 1940 also must not be overlooked.

A further significant fact is that in government-controlled distribution, especially of scarce commodities, the urban population was given the highest priority and the village received the tail end of a thin supply of manufactured goods. In 1935 rural districts accounted for 9,429 million rubles of the trade in nonfood, that is, manufactured commodities of state and cooperative retail stores, or a little over half of the urban

Table 27. Government procurements of principal agricultural products and their share of production [a]

Commodity	Average 1928–32		Average 1933–37		Average 1938–40	
	Quan-tity	Percent of production	Quan-tity	Percent of production	Quan-tity	Percent of production
All grains (million metric tons)	18.2	24.7	27.5	37.7	32.8	41.2
Sugar beets (million metric tons)	9.0	91.8	14.2	97.3	15.6	98.7
Potatoes (million metric tons)	4.3	9.4	6.3	12.7	6.0	12.5
Flax fiber (thousand metric tons)	224.0	51.6	277.0	75.9	245.0	76.6
Sunflower seed (thousand metric tons)	909.0	49.6	848.0	66.6	1,238.0	61.0

[a] Includes all types of procurements from collective, state, and individual farms, as well as payments in kind for services of machine-tractor stations. Procurements, especially since 1933, were supposed to be in standard units, taking account of variations of quality below or above a certain prescribed standard. It is not believed, however, that the deviation from the physical quantities distorted the trend in procurements or their relation to production.

Source. *Sel'skoe khoziaistvo SSSR, 1960*, pp. 198–200.

volume of 17,815 million rubles in such trade.[32] Granted that rural people (about 70 percent of the total population) made some purchases in the cities, the great unevenness in the distribution of manufactured goods is still patent. At the same time, the Soviet state, through the use of its taxation and price-fixing powers and control over collective agriculture, was able to exact increased quantities of farm products both in absolute tonnage and relative to the size of crops (see Table 27). In the most important case, grains, average procurements during the last three years before World War II were three times as large as those of the last precollectivization year, 1928.

While quantities of farm products procured grew by leaps and bounds in the 1930s, the prices paid for them by the government increased but little and were far below the cost of production. In fact, the increase seems ridiculously small in view of the galloping inflation with which the Soviet Union was afflicted. This was doubtless the reason for the extreme reticence of the government to publish price data, which were abundant in the 1920s. Publication of price indexes was completely abandoned in the 1930s. Table 28 shows that procuring prices of different grains increased from only 5.5 to nearly 28 percent between 1928–29 and 1937. Consumer-goods prices in state and cooperative stores increased sevenfold and in the collective-farm market more than sevenfold. The rise of consumer-goods prices continued, and by 1940 prices in state and cooperative stores were ten times as high as in 1928 and on the kolkhoz market nearly eighteen times as high.[33] But there was no further increase in grain-procurement prices. The price situation for a few technical crops, notably cotton, the output of which the government was anxious to expand rapidly, was more favorable, particularly since the producers

Table 28. Grain procurement prices, 1928–29 and 1937

	1928–29	1937	Percent 1937 is of 1928–29
	(rubles per metric ton)		
Wheat	77.52	90.30	116.5
Rye	53.89	67.40	125.1
Oats	44.06	56.30	127.8
Barley	59.14	62.40	105.5

Sources. *Ekonomicheskoe obozrenie*, September 1929, pp. 178–179; I. V. Sautin, ed., *Proizvoditel'nost' i ispol'zovanie truda v kolkhozakh vo vtoroi piatiletke* (Productivity and Labor Utilization in Kolkhozes in the Second Five Year Plan; Moscow, 1939), pp. 129–130.

were also supplied with deficit consumer goods and grain at lower concession prices.

But compulsory government procurements, with their low fixed prices, do not exhaust the marketing of farm products in the USSR. There is the kolkhoz market with its much higher prices. Although the volume of grain sold on this market was small, it was larger for sunflower seed and quite substantial for potatoes, vegetables, meat, and milk. The estimated 1938–1940 share of the kolkhoz market in total marketings of different farm products is shown in the following tabulation.[34]

Commodity	*Percent*
Grain	5.6
Potatoes	19.1
Vegetables	55.8
Sunflower seed	14.0
Milk and dairy products in terms of milk	37.8
Meat	45.0
Eggs	46.3

The kolkhoz market, therefore, exercised an upward pull on average prices realized by farmers from all marketings, including even grain prices, where the effect was the least. This is illustrated by the percentage relationship of estimated prices realized by peasants from all marketings in 1937 and 1928.[35]

Grain	321
Sugar beet	361
Seed cotton	585
Flax fiber	219
Potatoes	581
Milk	773
Meat and livestock	954
Eggs	985

Clearly the plight of collective farmers would have been even worse were it not for the kolkhoz market. But though compulsory deliveries were a universal burden, many kolkhozniks and kolkhozes, especially in areas far from the cities, could not avail themselves of the opportunity of selling on the collective-farm market, even if they had a disposable surplus, because transportation facilities were inadequate or lacking. With the middleman banned, the kolkhoznik (or the kolkhoz, when trading as an institution) had to be his own retail distributor, no matter how small the quantity marketed. The consequent increase in the real cost of production should not be overlooked when the higher prices in the kolkhoz market are compared with those in state retail stores. Thus the kolkhoz market was only partly successful in counterbalancing the confiscatory effect of the compulsory procuring system.

Besides the low prices for compulsory deliveries, the kolkhozes had to pay an increasing proportion of their output in kind for the work of the machine-tractor stations (MTS). The ratio of payments in kind to MTS to the total grain crop of the kolkhozes increased from 13.9 percent in 1937 to 16 percent in 1938 and 19.2 percent in 1939.[36] Prior to collectivization, peasant farmers relied on animal draft power, produced and maintained on the farm, not in the factory as with tractors and their fuel supply. All this would have mattered less if production had greatly increased upon collectivization, as was optimistically expected by the Communist regime. If the pie were larger, both the state and the peasant could have had larger slices. Such expectations failed to materialize. This fact was for a long time obfuscated by the distortions of official Soviet statistics, a problem that must be briefly discussed in order to obtain a clear picture of the production situation.

It is not the first time in this study that we have encountered difficulties with Soviet crop statistics. But previously they arose because of the inadequacy or unreliability of the primary data, attributed to the tendency of the peasant farmers to understate crops in order to avoid taxation. Those crop figures therefore need correction, though the question of extent is a debatable one. The situation changes radically for the 1930s. Beginning with the 1933 harvest, a statistical practice was adopted by the government which deliberately over-reported crop figures. It consisted in the publication exclusively of what were termed "biological" yields, that is, estimates of crops standing in the field ("on the root") before the harvest. To put it another way, mere forecasts based on the "condition" of crops before harvest were substituted for estimates of actually harvested crops. The rationale for this procedure, set forth by Osinskii,[37] was a good argument against its adoption: that figures of crops harvested and stored in the barn do not take into account the huge losses caused by delayed and inefficient harvesting and by theft. Crop statistics, according to Osinskii, could be used as a weapon in the struggle of the Soviet state against such abnormalities. Since stolen grain and other crops form a part of total consumption, they should also be counted in with the crops stored in the kolkhoz barn. But to deliberately include in statistics of production those unharvested crops involved in the large crop losses, and to call such inflated figures actual production, can be considered normal only by the standards of an Alice in Wonderland world.

When this estimating procedure was first propounded by Osinskii, he made a distinction between purely biological yields, which he considered a theoretical concept of a crop excluding harvest losses, and what he called a normal economic crop, which would exclude only the unavoidable losses bound to occur in harvesting. Osinskii considered that a deduction of up to 10 percent for such unavoidable losses was permissible. But actual crop losses were much larger—20 to 30 percent was not uncommon—and they were obviously only partially accounted for by Osinskii's deductions. No mention was made even of these modest deductions in later Soviet sources. In fact, an official directive issued on July 21, 1939, for estimating a number of nongrain crops such as cotton, flax, sunflower seed, sugar beets, and potatoes, prescribed that "actual yields per hectare" must include unharvested crops left in the field or lost during shipment.[38] A Soviet reference book on social-economic statistics defines crop yields as "the actual yield of crops per hectare, at the time of maturity, estimated before the beginning of a timely harvest of such crops." [39] In 1942 even the use of the threshing data during the harvest was prohibited because they "under-report the actual yields." [40]

The opportunities that such a crop-estimating system opened up for the manipulation of statistics can be readily imagined; and it was manipulation upward, as far as the Kremlin was concerned. Certainly the fact that under-reporting was considered the only crime, as if the opposite difficulty never existed, did not help to restrain local officials.[41] The mechanics of this long-suspected upward manipulation was revealed in 1962 by Khrushchev, who pointed out that biological yields or, as he put it, the crop-condition forecasts (*vidovaia urozhainost'*) were overestimated. He explained that such figures were determined by special functionaries, the inter-regional inspectors, who tried to fit their estimates to the procurement targets. "If the crop-condition figure was lower than the planned targets of [kolkhoz] payments in kind, it would be raised by the inter-regional inspectors and adjusted to correspond to the target figure. Besides, in arriving at national figures, supplementary corrections were made in the data supplied by the inter-regional inspectors—and always upward. Consequently, determination of crop-condition figures was based not on actual crop conditions, but was fitted to the target quantity of grain that was to be obtained through payments in kind. Thus crop-condition figures exceeded the actual outturn of grain not only because of possible harvest losses, but also because of arbitrary corrections." [42]

The inflation of crop figures which thus took place after 1933 no doubt helped the government to parade the "great success" of collectivization and, by the same token, to justify the heavy exactions from agriculture. An important direct incentive for over-reporting yields was the use of biological yields as a base for determining payments in kind to the MTS for the operations they performed in collectives. Payments varied according to the crop yields per hectare on a progressive scale; the higher the official yield, the larger the payment for a specific operation like plowing, seeding, or cultivation. Thus the fiscal interest of the state was bound up with propaganda motives to make over-reporting of crop yields profitable.

For many years only Western specialists skilled in statistical detective work were in a position to criticize publicly these padded statistics.[43] Any criticism by Russian specialists was forbidden after an abrupt change in the statistical climate, culminating in a mass purge of economists and statisticians in the early 1930s. It liquidated or temporarily "refrigerated" most of the best statistical and economic talent in the country, including such men as Kondratiev, Groman, Bazarov, Chaianov, and Studenskii. Also the best economic journals, such as *Ekonomicheskoe obozrenie* (Economic Review), *Statisticheskoe obozrenie* (Statistical Review), and *Biulleten' kon"iunkturnogo instituta* (The Bulletin of the Institute of Economic Conditions), were discontinued in 1930. (Officially the first two were merged in May 1930 with *Planovoe khoziaistvo*, Planned Economy.) The purge brought to an end what had been a veritable renaissance of Russian statistics during the NEP. And probably in no sector was the situation worse than in crop statistics, where it was not merely a matter of concealment and blackout, as in price and monetary statistics, but of actual distortion through deliberate over-reporting.

As this blackout was imposed on the publication of barn-crop figures, the government was, of course, well aware through required collective-farm reports of the actual quantities of harvested crops. It took twenty years and the exit of Stalin before the biological-yield gimmick was repudiated. Malenkov declared in his speech before the Supreme Soviet in August 1953 that "it should not be forgotten that our country, our collective farms, prosper with a crop gathered in the barn and not with a crop standing in the field." [44] Khrushchev followed in the same vein a month later, in his first long agricultural report to the Central Committee.[45] Another six years passed before the Kremlin finally disclosed the barn-crop figures of the 1930s. The total grain barn crop was on the average 23 percent below the originally published biological figures for 1933–1937.[46]

On the basis of these newly disclosed barn figures, grain production in 1933–1937, a period that included the bumper harvest of 1937, averaged slightly below that of 1928. An increase on the average of 9 percent over

255

1928 took place during the last three years before the Second World War, in 1938–1940. Production of cotton, sugar beets, and potatoes increased in the 1930s, the first two substantially; but production of flax fiber and sunflower seed declined. Livestock numbers, though starting to recover in 1934–35 from the catastrophes of early collectivization, were in 1938 still below 1928, with the exception of hogs. Hog numbers in 1938 increased spectacularly following the abundant harvests of the previous years. In other years they too were below the 1928 figure. In turning from individual products or sectors to the aggregate agricultural output, even the Soviet index indicates that it was lower in 1929–1939 than in 1928, with the exception of 1937.[47]

An index of gross agricultural output calculated by Johnson and Kahan from Soviet official data, using 1926–27 price weights (presumably used in the Soviet index), also shows a smaller total production in every year from 1931 to 1938, except for 1937. Similar results are indicated by their index of net agricultural output, except for a slightly higher 1938 figure.[48] Yet the smaller output did not diminish the appetite of the state, which demanded a larger slice. It is true that the remainder was now to be divided among fewer peasant mouths, for one highly important consequence of the demographic catastrophe caused by the famine, the heavy migration to the cities and the forced-labor exile system, was the decline of farm population both in absolute numbers and in relation to total population. But this was not sufficient to overcome the negative effect of low production and the large state exactions on the average per capita farm income. This subject, touching as it did on Stalin's first commandment, was among the unmentionables in Soviet public discussions during this era. Yet even the Kremlin became concerned when, following the excellent 1937 crop, it found that many kolkhozes were still distributing little cash to their members and some none at all. The blame was placed in a government decree of April 19, 1938, on excessive and ineffective capital investment and heavy administrative expenses.[49] Actually, Soviet agriculture suffered from chronic underinvestment; but undoubtedly some kolkhozes did resort to excessive investment in relation to their resources, and more often to unnecessary or ineffective investment. How such expenditures were encouraged by superiors, I myself witnessed during a visit in 1935 when I heard a supervisory official suggest to the chairman of a kolkhoz that, since another collective in the vicinity had a flour mill, it would be well for his farm to have one also. The chairman retorted, "Must every collective have a separate flour mill?"

But the low cash disbursements to the kolkozniks, about which the Kremlin voiced concern in 1938, was only a part and not the most important part of a larger problem. This was the low total farm income, in which payments in kind, mainly grain, predominated. Although there are Soviet data for the 1930s for distribution of several components of farm income, notably grain and cash, figures of average total income per kolkhoz household were published only for 1932 and 1937 as 2,132 rubles and 5,843 rubles respectively.[50] The difficulty with these figures is two-fold: they are inflated because income in kind is valued in the high kolkhoz market prices of 1937 instead of as average realized prices secured by the farms, which averages the low government procurement prices with the high kolkhoz market prices; the figures include not only earnings from agriculture but those off the farm. Even these inflated figures amount to only 834.71 rubles of 1928 purchasing power per household, or 362.92 rubles per able-bodied kolkhoznik.[51] Assuming between 270 and 280 man-days worked on the average by a kolkhoznik, we obtain 1.30–1.34 rubles earned per man-day. This is a little less than the earnings of a peasant in 1928, estimated by Naum Jasny at 1.35 rubles per man-day from agriculture alone.[52] The fact that 1937 was an exceptionally good harvest year while 1928 was about average, and the existence of an infla-tionary price bias in the 1937 figure with the inclusion of nonagricultural earnings, cannot be overlooked. The Soviets obviously wanted to dress up the average kolkhoznik's income, and that is why the best harvest year was selected—why the high kolkhoz market prices were used and off-farm earnings added for good measure. But all these decorations did not make the 1937 income figure shine. More reliable estimates have been made by Western scholars.

An estimate of total Soviet net farm income for 1937, that is, the in-come of households from agriculture, was made by Abram Bergson as part of a painstaking estimate of national income and gross national product.[53] These estimates were further refined subsequently, putting the net farm income in 1937 at 56 billion rubles at current prices. A corresponding figure for 1928 in prices of that year was 10.84 billion rubles.[54] Assuming a sevenfold increase in retail prices and living costs between 1928 and 1937 (calculated by averaging price indexes—see Table 29), the 1937 net farm income in rubles of 1928 purchasing power would have amounted to 8 billion, or 26 percent below 1928. However, with an estimated 18 percent decrease in farm population, from 112.4 million in 1928 to 92.2 million in 1937, the per capita farm income in 1937, in terms of 1928 purchasing power, was 10 percent less than in 1928.[55] But 1937, as we know, was the best harvest year during the interwar period, and 1928 was a year of average or below-average crops. In a poor harvest year such as 1936 or 1938, per capita farm income was considerably

Table 29. Index numbers of retail prices, 1928–1954 (1937=100)

| Year | Official prices | | Kolkhoz market prices | Average prices, all retail markets | |
	1937 weights	Given-year weights		1937 weights	Given-year weights
1928	—	—	—	16.8	11.5
1937	100	100	100	100	100
1940	132	126	200	138	132
1948	333	300	350	335	305
1952	216	198	208	215	199
1954	180	170	214	183	173

Source. Janet G. Chapman, *Real Wages in Soviet Russia since 1928* (Santa Monica, 1963), p. 355.

lower. Thus Jasny, who used a different estimating procedure, considered that in 1938 the per capita income of the kolkhoz and of individual peasants was 30 percent or more below that of 1928.[56]

Estimated earnings of kolkhozniks in 1937 are given by Bergson at 52.7 billion rubles, divided as follows: money payments to kolkhozniks on a labor-day basis, salaries of kolkhoz executives, and premiums, 7.3 billion rubles; income in kind at farm prices, 25.2 billion; and earnings from outside work, 6.7 billion. To earn this amount the kolkhozniks worked an estimated 32.8 million man-years, of which some 22.5 were devoted to work in kolkhozes, 8.0 to private holdings, and 2.3 off the farm.[57] If we eliminate off farm work and earnings, we obtain 30.5 million man-years of work for which kolkhozniks earned an estimated 46 billion rubles, or 1,508 rubles per man-year. Assuming 280 man-days per man-year, this would result in earnings of 5.39 rubles per man-day in 1937. With an approximately sevenfold increase in prices between 1928 and 1937, this sum would amount to 0.77 of a ruble in terms of 1928 purchasing power. This may be compared with 1.35 rubles per man-day earned by farmers in 1928.[58] Bergson's figures include both earnings of kolkhozniks from collectives and net receipts from their private holdings. Another estimate by Jasny of kolkhozniks' receipts per man-day in 1937 from collectives alone, including theft, was 0.65 (64.7 kopecks) in 1926–27 rubles. But these low figures, to repeat, were earned during an excellent harvest year. For 1938, a poor year, Jasny's corresponding figure is only 0.45 rubles (44.8 kopecks).[59] Even in a good year like 1935, not a bumper harvest, grain distributed per kolkhoz household was only a little over half of that distributed in 1937 and cash was nearly one third less.[60] The meager earnings from collectives underscore the vital importance of private holdings for the livelihood of the kolkhozniks.

Conclusions drawn from farm-income estimates, which under Soviet conditions are bound to be, at best, rough approximations, can be tested only to a very limited extent by actual statistical surveys of income and outlay, for such data were also subjected to the statistical blackout of the 1930s. What little statistical information of this nature is available confirms the deterioration of the standard of living of the rural population as indicated by national income estimates. Thus a Soviet source reported in 1937 the purchase of manufactured goods for personal consumption per surveyed peasant family in 28 oblasts as 659.2 rubles, of which 135.5 rubles was for foodstuffs. With slightly over four persons per average family, this would amount to a little more than 160 rubles per capita, or about 23 rubles in terms of 1928 prices. (Jasny cites a figure of 20 rubles.) In 1927–28, the per capita expenditures of the rural population for manufactured goods amounted to 30.52 rubles, or nearly one third higher.[61] Moreover, as Jasny points out, a much larger proportion of these purchases in 1937 was for processed foodstuffs (mainly bread), formerly produced on the farm.

While there was considerable variation in individual earnings between kolkhozes, enough has been said here to drive home the point that the rose of "prosperous" living on the collective farms could not be plucked from the thistle of the low level of real incomes. This made a mockery of Stalin's dictum at the Seventeenth Party Congress in 1934: "It would have been useless to have abolished capitalism in October 1917, and go on building socialism for a number of years, if it could not achieve an abundant life for the people. Socialism does not mean poverty and privation but the abolition of poverty and privation and the development of a prosperous and cultured life for all members of society." [62] Moreover, there was a general failure to provide adequate economic incentives to expand production, though there were some partial successes. And the consequence of this failure was that it made kolkhozniks less effective and willing workers than they otherwise might have been and, in turn, materially contributed to the low level of farm output and income.

To be sure, labor discipline in kolkhozes improved in the later thirties as compared with the early days of collectivization, if the figures on rising number of workdays mean anything. From 118 workdays per able-bodied worker and 257 per kolkhoz household in 1932, the figures rose to 194 and 438 in 1937.[63] There were, as we have seen, other important causes of lagging farm output, such as underinvestment and faulty investment in agriculture, inefficient farm management and practices, bureaucratic ineptitude, and planning rigidity. Even so, the inadequacy of labor input, particularly when compared with that under independent family farming, cannot be gainsaid. This is not because of the actual shortage of hands in the then still overpopulated Russian village. Rather, the reasons can be found in the stories in the Soviet press of kolkhoz foremen having to awaken sleeping peasants during the peak season in the summer, of their tardiness, of having to soldier them on the job, and other aspects of poor working discipline.

Official recognition of the lack of incentives because of low earnings is found in the aforementioned decree of April 19, 1938. It pointed out that kolkhozniks were often driven to look for work outside the kolkhozes, resulting in a labor shortage. To make matters worse, some kolkhozes confronted by such labor bottlenecks resorted to the use of hired labor recruited outside the kolkhoz, paid wages higher than the kolkhozniks, and thus further depleted the resources available for payment to kolkhoz members. For example, out of 1,629 kolkhozes in the Stalingrad oblast studied in 1937, 820, or more than half, hired additional manpower for fieldwork; 556 collectives used hired labor in construction, and 459 in auxiliary enterprises. Altogether, hired labor in the kolkhozes of the Stalingrad oblast in 1937 worked 1,336,000 man-days, of which 679,000 were in fieldwork.[64] It is not surprising that kolkhozniks were either lured into the cities by higher wages or, if they remained in the village, applied their energies to the little plots and livestock in their own possession. This made private farming a serious competitor of the collective-farm economy for the labor input of the peasants, and it was soon to provoke a hostile government reaction.

Whereas kolkhozniks predominated in the farm labor force and population, there was another small but important category of workers, those on state farms and the machine-tractor stations, who fared better economically. In 1937 more than 40.7 million worked in kolkhozes. The average annual number of workers on state farms reached 1,970,000, and over 1.3 million in the MTS.[65] These employees were paid wages and, unlike the kolkhozniks, were not merely residual claimants to the income of their enterprises. Many of them were skilled and represented the new farm aristocracy of mechanizers (tractor drivers, combine operators, machinists, and chauffeurs) who were generally better paid, some much better than the rank-and-file kolkhoznik. The difference in economic status between kolkhozniks and the MTS and state-farm workers reminds one of the distinction between private serfs and state peasants during serfdom, except that today all work for the Communist state. The expense of the large administrative structure of the collective-farm system, not encountered in self-managing private farming, depressed the share of the income that went to the workers engaged directly in production. In 1937 the MTS and machinery repair shops employed 32,592 agronomic personnel, 40,026 engineering and other technical personnel, and 95,832 tractor brigadiers.[66] At the end of 1937, in addition to 236,528 chairmen-managers, the kolkhozes employed 147,861 deputy managers; 181,483 supervisors of livestock sections; 68,335 livestock brigadiers; 5,643 animal-husbandry specialists; 46,832 veterinary assistants; 16,113 agronomists and crop specialists; 528,602 field brigadiers; and 248,390 bookkeepers,[67] as well as a large number of guards. Since most of these categories were also better paid than ordinary production workers, the share of the income available for distribution was further reduced.

Legality and the Great Purge

Soviet agrarian policy in the mid-thirties met with no greater success in the political than in the economic sphere. Terror in the village had diminished, but then there was less need for it as collectivization became an accomplished fact. As indicated before, legality was a fiction as far as the self-government of the kolkhozes was concerned. The elected kolkhoz chairmen, like the elected village officials under the tsarist regime, were creatures of the regime. This does not mean that they or, for that matter, local government officials did not at times side with the peasants. The frequent accusations of "anti-state tendencies" hurled at these functionaries, because of underfulfillment of targets for grain procurements, would suggest that there were some embers beneath all that Soviet smoke. But there was great risk in favoring the peasant. The mere suspicion of anti-state tendencies carried the speedy retribution of summary removal or worse for the suspected official.

What played havoc in the late thirties in the sphere of legality was the Great Purge, which paradoxically came in the wake of the new Constitution of 1936; that document set forth various safeguards of individual rights in the best up-to-date liberal fashion. The purge, which was initiated by Stalin and which affected all branches of national life, still baffles us in its gigantic proportions. For the nearest historical parallel, one must go back nearly four centuries, to the reign of Ivan the Terrible and his struggle with the boyars. I shall not go into the general causes of this upheaval, which would lead into areas of social psychology and psychopathology, but shall deal briefly only with the concrete effects of the purge on agriculture. It made its impact in the first instance on the various echelons of the party and government bureaucracy, and the agricultural segment was no exception.

261

The purge resulted in an extensive liquidation, from top to bottom, of the administrative and technical personnel that piloted the ship of collectivized agriculture. Nor is "from top to bottom" merely a figure of speech. It is true that the Commissariat of Agriculture had become accustomed to the loss of its high officials, who were often accused of "wrecking" activities, even prior to the all-out purge. In the early thirties, two assistant commissars, Wolf and Konar, were shot without a public trial and a third, Markevich, the originator of the MTS, was liquidated in an unspecified manner. But in 1937 the victim was the Commissar of Agriculture himself, M. A. Chernov, who was dismissed from his post, tried with N. I. Bukharin, A. I. Rykov, and other leading Soviet Communists early in 1938, convicted, and shot. His successor, R. I. Eikhe, who fulminated, as did Chernov, against wreckers in the commissariat, silently disappeared from the public view shortly after his appointment. This fact was officially confirmed by the routine announcement of the appointment of another commissar a few months later. (Eikhe, incidentally, was among the purged Communists who were politically rehabilitated in the 1960s.) The assistants of the commissar and other high functionaries of the Commissariat of Agriculture were also for the most part removed and subsequently referred to in the press as "Trotskyist-Bukharinist wreckers" and "enemies of the people"—on their shoulders was placed most of the blame for the inefficiency, waste, and mistakes in the management of Soviet agriculture. The same condition prevailed in the Commissariat of State Grain and Livestock Farms, where commissars followed one another in rapid succession.

Still another highly placed victim of the purge was the head of the Agricultural Department of the Central Committee and former Commissar of Agriculture, Ia. A. Iakovlev. The fate that befell high officials epitomizes the situation throughout the ranks of the agricultural administration, not only in Moscow but also in the provinces. For instance, according to *Sotsialisticheskoe zemledelie* in September 26, 1938, as many as three thousand new directors of MTS were appointed in 1938, which meant something like a 50 percent replacement in less than a year. How many of the ousted directors were themselves recent appointees, who had succeeded earlier victims of the purge, it is impossible to say. There is no doubt that the tenure of the new officials was often very short, as exemplified by a case cited in the same newspaper of a MTS director in the Volga region who was appointed in January 1938 and dismissed four months later. Many unfilled vacancies were reported in the managerial staff of state farms, MTS, and other branches of the agricultural administration.

The sweeping change that took place in the ranks of Soviet officialdom may perhaps be better visualized if compared with the rapid turnover of government personnel in the United States, before Civil Service, whenever a new administration came into power—except that the consequences for many of the "outs" in the Soviet Union were often more painful, going beyond temporary unemployment, and the tenure of the "ins" was frequently a very brief one indeed. An even better analogy would be the hypothetical case of a sudden wholesale change of the executive, administrative, and technical personnel of a big business corporation—say United States Steel or General Motors. For it must be remembered that the tendency was more and more for Soviet agriculture to be operated as one big state concern, with detailed uniform plans laid down from above.

It is obvious that the wholesale and frequent replacement of officials who must make important managerial decisions cannot but engender a great deal of instability, confusion, and demoralization, and result in a loss of much valuable experience. In Russian agricultural administration, errors of management are magnified and are bound to lead to heavy losses because of the large scale of farm operations and the often difficult climatic conditions, where speed of sowing and harvesting is of the essence. The numerous difficulties experienced in the sowing and harvesting campaigns in the late thirties, and the resulting heavy crop losses, must be attributed in no small measure to the disorganization caused by the Great Purge.

It is true that the purge weeded out some incompetent, corrupt, and inefficient officials, devotees of red tape and arbitrariness who were the frequent butt of criticism in the Soviet press. Yet it was not only the incompetent official who was eliminated; the purge blindly punished the innocent along with the guilty. A typical example is that of Comrade Gavrilov, who was the director of an MTS in the Omsk province of Siberia. His superiors considered him one of the best directors and his station was one of the most efficient in the province. A regional party committee, however, expelled Gavrilov from the party as an enemy of the people and, as is invariably the case, he was ousted from his post. Numerous instances of this nature occurred, according to the official *Sotsialisticheskoe zemledelie.*

This appears only natural when it is remembered that a purge like this is bound to produce an atmosphere of mass hysteria and panic of which the unscrupulous take advantage to vent their private grudges, advance their selfish interests, or save ("insure," as the Russians put it) their own skins. Furthermore, many of the difficulties for which officials are held responsible are due not merely to personal incompetence or lack of integrity but also to the unrealistic, conflicting, and ill-balanced character of the official plans. The Soviet press and Commissars of Agriculture Eikhe, Chernov, and Iakovlev cited in their speeches numerous examples of such faulty planning with respect to the introduction of new systems of crop rotation, improvement of seed supply, and similar matters.[68] Of course, in accordance with the standard formula, defective planning was also attributed to sabotage, although plans were usually passed upon by the highest Soviet authorities.

Kolkhoz officers and even rank-and-file kolkhozniks did not escape the purge that wrought so much devastation among officials. There was bound to be strong general temptation to take advantage of the shibboleths of "mass sabotage," "wrecking," and "counterrevolutionary activities," in order to discover scapegoats for all sorts of mistakes and difficulties. A good illustration of this was provided during the 1937 harvesting campaign in the Saratov region. It appeared that difficulties were experienced in harvesting the grain by combines because they were poorly repaired and there was a shortage of spare parts.[69] As a newspaper report put it, "The army of combines stopped as soon as it encountered the tall grain." Local authorities immediately attributed the harvesting difficulties to mass sabotage rather than to inefficient organization. The conduct of officials during inspection visits was described as follows by a member of the executive board of a kolkhoz: "They scold the chairman of the collective or the party organizer because a great deal of grain is accumulated in the threshing yard; make accusations of anti-state tendencies and sabotage, and then depart. They scold and make any accusation that comes to their heads but do not size up the situation and indicate concretely what must be done." This criticism of the authorities was repudiated by *Izvestiia* a few days later as "politically erroneous" and representing "an enemy sortie"; the writer Mikhail Suvinskii, was dismissed from the staff of the paper.[70]

It is easy to see that, in such an atmosphere, abuses were likely to flourish in the kolkhozes as well. The Kremlin itself revealed this in the spring of 1938, when it spoke in a voice of thunder about the iniquitous treatment suffered by the peasants at the hands of local officials. It was officially disclosed that wholesale expulsion of peasants from kolkhozes had taken place. In the province of Sverdlovsk, 2,262 families were expelled during the second half of 1937; in Novosibirsk province during the same period, 5,705 families were expelled; and in the North Caucasus (Ordzhonikidze), 6,000 in 1937 and early 1938.[71] And so the story goes from region to region, with a monotonous uniformity attesting to the widespread character of the abuses. The model charter of 1935 provided that a member could be expelled only as a last resort and by decision of a general meeting of the kolkhoz at which two thirds of the membership were present. Violations of this, and other provisions of the charter, began at the very outset. But in the 1937 expulsion epidemic, the charter was entirely forgotten.

In the spring of 1938 even the Kremlin became alarmed. It decreed that "a predominant majority of expulsions from the collectives were entirely unjustified and took place without any serious cause and for the least important reason," even though the consequence of such an action was "to doom one to starvation." [72] Again, as so often before (notably during the forced collectivization drive in the spring of 1930), Stalin blamed the local soviet and party officials, who not only did not stop excesses on the part of kolkhoz managers but frequently encouraged the illegal expulsion of peasants "under the guise of purging collectives from socially foreign and hostile class elements." This was a familiar, stereotyped formula and is, therefore, not very illuminating. The intriguing question remains as to whether the rural purge followed some specific pattern. What end, if any, did the purge serve?

Some peasants were expelled for "religious convictions and a long beard," [73] which suggests that nonconformity was one of the objectives of the purge in the countryside. There were also reported many instances of expulsion because peasants had stood up for their legal rights and privileges.[74] One of the examples cited was that of a peasant named Golyshev who actively fought against violations of the charter of his kolkhoz and was expelled for "breaking down discipline." What his fellow peasants thought of him can be seen from the fact that, when he was later readmitted to the kolkhoz, they elected him chairman. Economic reasons were clearly discernible in another important category— the widespread expulsions of the families of kolkhozniks who found employment in state industries. Since such treatment was highly embarrassing to the government, which was anxious to recruit labor for its various undertakings, it was strongly condemned. The motive behind these expulsions seems to have been the reduction of the number of claimants to the income of the kolkhoz. It is not unreasonable to assume that the same motive, perhaps disguised, operated in other expulsions.

The Kremlin now became concerned about the disruptive consequences of the purge on the managerial and supervisory apparatus. A decree pointing to the unsatisfactory preparation for the 1938 spring sowing campaign lamented the fact that "at the height of the preparation for sowing, a considerable number of machine-tractor stations and repair shops and local agricultural administrations remained without supervisory personnel." [75] There was added uneasiness about the detrimental effect on peasant morale and production caused by the miscarriage of what purported to be a moderately liberal agrarian policy. To redress this, three decrees were issued simultaneously on April 19, 1938, and published in the press on April 20. The first of these, already referred to, sought to remedy the unsatisfactory distribution of cash income in the kolkhozes. The heart of this decree was the categorical requirement that not less than 60 to 70 percent of the cash income be distributed among kolkhoz members. A corollary provision limited to 10 percent the allocation of kolkhoz cash income to investment (indivisible fund) instead of the former requirement of 10 to 20 percent, which was frequently exceeded. In this manner it was proposed to alleviate the situation whereby little or no cash income was allocated for distribution by kolkhozes among their members. A later decree, similarly motivated, published on October 23, 1938, ordered the liquidation of industrial ventures organized by kolkhozes that did not relate to agriculture and caused heavy losses that diminished cash disbursements among kolkhozniks.

It will be noted that no attempt was made by the regime to come to grips with the fundamental cause of low kolkhoz incomes—the low prices paid for the large compulsory acquisitions of farm products. The object of the second decree was to stamp out the competition of what little was left of the individual peasant sector. It criticized the management of the kolkhozes for hiring outside peasants and paying them more than the kolkhozniks. Local authorities were also rebuked for allegedly permitting tax evasion by outside peasants who, incidentally, were taxed much more heavily than the kolkhozniks. Yet the lot of this surviving band of free peasants may still have seemed tempting to a kolkhoznik, in spite of the pressure of heavy taxation and economic discrimination to which individual farmers were subjected. This temptation had to be removed. Accordingly a new high tax was imposed on horses owned by individual farmers. It was claimed that they used the horses not for their own farm work (they had but little land) but for "speculation and profit," or to perform work for others.[76] This new pressure was probably responsible for the fact that individual farmers, who early in 1938 constituted only about 7 percent of the total number of peasant households, began to flock to the kolkhozes.

The third decree was directed against the arbitrary expulsion of peasants from kolkhozes and prohibited expulsions of the families of kolkhozniks who worked in state industries. In general, ousting of kolkhozniks was to be resorted to only as an extreme measure after all other corrective measures had failed. The provision of the collective charter, that a member may be expelled only by a general meeting at which two thirds of all members are present, was reiterated. Even this action was not to be final until approved by the raion executive committee, and in the meantime the kolkhoznik was to retain all his rights and privileges. For violation of these rules, the officers of the collective and local government and party officials were liable to criminal prosecution. Local authorities were admonished to pay careful attention to any appeal of kolkhozniks against expulsion. A few days later, still another decree ordered a speedy consideration by raion executive committees, together with raion committees of the party, of the appeals of all the peasants who had been expelled from kolkhozes.[77]

The Screw Turns Again

Soon after these 1938 decrees, the liberal period of the agrarian policy of the mid-thirties—the "Stalinist concern for the collectivized peasantry," as it was officially designated—came to a close.[78] For several months the Soviet press continued to expose and to attack various violations of the new provisions, also claiming a considerable measure of improvement in the situation. But suddenly this policy was reversed in its most important particular. A new decree issued on December 4, 1938, abandoned the requirement of the distribution of not less than 60-70 percent of kolkhoz income among members, which was really the constructive reform enacted in April.[79] At the same time, the limit for capital expenditures was increased from a maximum of 10 percent to 12–15 percent in grain regions and 15–20 percent in regions where industrial crops or livestock farming predominated. Thus kolkhozniks reverted completely to their former status as residual claimants to the income of the collective.

No reason for this reversal of policy was given, beyond the statement in a preamble to the decree that it was issued in response to petitions of local authorities and kolkhozes. There was no inkling of the impending change in the Soviet press prior to the publication of the decree on December 5, 1938. *Pravda* as late as December 3, 1938, carried a leading editorial, "To Observe Strictly the Charter of the Kolkhoz," in which it condemned the disregard of individual rights and interests in the distribution of kolkhoz income. But, then, quick shifts of much greater importance have not been unusual in Soviet agrarian policy. One only need recall the transition from War Communism to the NEP in the spring of 1921 and the sudden halt in the rural collectivization campaign in the spring of 1930, to cite the most notable examples.

It is characteristic of government policy that propitiating gestures to the peasants alternate with a tightening of the reins. The course of the 1935–1938 appeasement provides still another illustration of this historical pattern. Events soon bore out what could have been only adumbrated in December 1938, that Soviet agrarian policy was hardening again. This became evident when in the spring of 1939 the Eighteenth Party Congress assembled, five years after the preceding one. The official keynote sounded on behalf of the Politburo by V. M. Molotov and A. A. Andreev was that of apprehension over the growth of "acre and a cow" farming in the kolkhozes. "Is it a normal situation," asked Molotov, "when there are many kolkhozniks—kolkhozniks in name only—who do not earn a single 'labor day' in a year, or earn some 20 or 30 'labor days' for show only, so to speak? Are they real kolkhozniks and should they be accorded all the privileges that are bestowed on collective farms and farmers?" [80] Andreev also complained that "in some places the personal farming of the kolkhozniks began to outgrow the collectivized economy and became the basic part; while collective farming, on the contrary, became secondary . . . The income from personal farming, from vegetable gardens, orchards, milk, meat, etc., in some collective farms began to exceed the earnings based on 'labor days.' This could not but have an adverse effect on the working discipline in kolkhozes." Andreev concluded his speech on an ominous note, that it was essential "to liquidate the useless practice (not needed by anyone) of nonintervention into the internal life of kolkhozes and replace it by constant care and help to the collective farmers . . . It must be realized that kolkhozes need serious guidance and wish this guidance from us."

It was not necessary to wait very long for the implementation of the new hard line. On May 27, 1939, an important decree was issued by the Kremlin with the symptomatic title "Concerning Measures for Safeguarding the Socialized Land of Kolkhozes against Squandering." [81] It castigated the illegal expansion of personal farming in violation of article 2 of the model charter and called for a halt to such farming within the bounds set by the charter. With this end in view, the decree ordered a new land survey in the kolkhozes during the summer of 1939, confiscating all land used by peasants in excess of the prescribed legal limits, which varied between 0.6 and 1.25 and, more rarely, 2.5 acres per household. Plots allotted to those who had not worked continuously in the kolkhozes were also to be forfeited. The common fields of the kolkhoz were to be segregated from the personal plots of kolkhozniks, and in no circumstances was the common area to be reduced again without the government's permission. Where, as a result of this, a shortage of land available for allotment for kitchen gardens developed, migration to sparsely settled regions was recommended. Kolkhozniks who had homesteads outside of the village, as was sometimes the case in the Ukraine, Belorussia, and other western regions, were to be speedily moved into the villages, where they would be easier to control. The holdings of arable land of individual farmers were limited to the following: in irrigated cotton regions, to one tenth of a hectare; in nonirrigated cotton and also in sugar-beet and truck-gardening regions, to a half hectare; and in all others, to one hectare. The tax on the earnings of kolkhozniks from private sources was considerably increased.

The farmsteads of individual farmers (including land occupied by farm buildings and kitchen gardens) were limited by the decree to one tenth of a hectare in irrigated regions and to two tenths of a hectare in nonirrigated regions. All individually held land in excess of these limits was to be turned over to kolkhozes mainly for use as private plots for kolkhozniks. Similar use was to be made of plots of pseudo-kolkhozniks, who did not work or worked but little in the kolkhozes. One can only speculate on how far the renewed interest in the settlement of the eastern regions was related to the international situation. Yet the decree of May 27 was actually concerned less with the small area of privately cultivated land than with the diffusion of labor input. For the first time since collectivization, the requirement of an annual minimum amount of work to be performed by men and women in kolkhozes was introduced. Kolkhozniks falling short of the minimum were to be expelled from the kolkhoz and lose their household plots. Kolkhozniks who were employed in other state enterprises retained their household plots only on the condition that the able-bodied members of their families fulfilled the required minimum of collective-farm work.

Following the new curbs directed at private land and labor inputs, the Kremlin turned to the vital economic center of the kolkhoz household sector—livestock. The recovery of livestock numbers between the low point of 1933–34 and 1938 was impressive, even though the 1928 level was not reached (see Table 16, Chapter Eight). But this recovery would have been impossible were it not for the private sector, which played an even greater role than disclosed by the statistics of livestock numbers because of the dependence of kolkhoz herds on the purchase of young animals from kolkhozniks. How important the private livestock sector was in 1938 is shown by the share of different kinds of farms in the total livestock population.[82]

	Cattle	Sheep and goats	Hogs	Horses
State farms, other state and cooperative enterprises	7.3%	10.5%	11.0%	12.5%
Kolkhoz (collective sector)	29.0	34.2	24.4	76.8
Kolkhozniks (personal livestock)	49.3	46.2	49.8	4.7
Workers and other population	11.4	5.4	12.5	3.1
Individual farmers	3.0	3.7	2.3	2.9
Total	100.0%	100.0%	100.0%	100.0%

The private sector, in which the kolkhozniks predominated, accounted for more than 60 percent of all cattle, 65 percent of hogs, and 55 percent of sheep and goats. The socialist livestock sector, though growing, took a back seat as animal husbandry rapidly recovered from the ravages of the collectivization campaign. The proportion between the private and socialist sector in total livestock between 1933–34 and 1938 changed little, or to the advantage of the former. The private sector accounted on January 1, 1934, for 62 percent of all cattle, and on January 1, 1938, for 64 percent. The figures for cows were 75 percent for both years, for hogs 45 and 65 percent, and for sheep 51 and 50 percent.[83] Little interest was shown in collectivized (communal) livestock not only by kolkhozniks, who seldom obtained dairy or other animal products in payment for their labor, but also by management.[84] The reason for this was that communal livestock required a great deal of care and effort. There was a shortage of shelter space, and a considerable amount of labor was needed to provide the communal livestock with feed. The great shortage of horses made the carting of coarse feedstuffs difficult; and poor feeding of the communal livestock, especially in the spring when feed supplies were at a low ebb, reduced production of milk and meat and, by the same token, made compulsory delivery of animal products more burdensome. In order to meet the required quantity of meat by weight, the kolkhoz had to deliver poorly fed, low-weight young animals, requiring many more heads of cattle and hogs. As a consequence, the goals for the growth of communal livestock were not fulfilled.[85]

A factor that seriously militated against communal livestock was the low prices paid by the government for the delivered products. For instance, kolkhozes were receiving 5 kopecks per liter of milk, while the retail price in Moscow in the late 1930s was 1.6 to 2.10 rubles per liter.[86] At the same time, communal livestock required a large amount of labor in terms of kolkhoz workdays, with the result that the payment per workday was bound to be low. Thus the kolkhozes had no incentive to develop communal livestock and shied away from it. At best they depended upon the acquisition of young stock for communal herds from the kolkhozniks. This was the situation when in 1939 the government swerved toward a more determined collectivist policy. By a decree of July 8, 1939, each kolkhoz was required to have a specified minimum number of communal cattle and either hogs or sheep.[87] The specified minimum depended on the total acreage of the kolkhoz and varied from region to region. According to the customary Soviet practice in such cases, the country was divided into several zones. For example, in the Ukraine a kolkhoz with an area up to 500 acres was to have no fewer than ten cows and six sows, if communal hog raising were adopted; in a kolkhoz with more than 500 acres but less than 1,250 acres, no fewer than twenty cows and ten sows. In Moscow province, all kolkhozes with more than 375 acres had to have no fewer than eight cows, and so forth. The kolkhozes were expected to acquire at least 60 percent of the specified minimum by the end of 1940, and all of it not later than the end of 1942.

The decree of July 8, 1939, also instituted a basic change in the system of government meat procurements. Instead of being required to deliver specified quantities of meat per head of collective livestock, the kolkhozes were obliged to deliver specified quantities of meat per hectare of kolkhoz land, again differentiated by zones. Thus in the Ukraine, which was in the first and highest zone, the rate of deliveries was 4.5 kilograms of meat (live weight) per hectare, whereas in the Kazakh Republic, which was in the eighth, lowest zone, the rate was only one half of a kilogram. All kolkhozes in a district were supposed to have the same rates of deliveries; but deviation of 30 percent upward or downward could be authorized so long as the average approved rate for the district was maintained. By basing meat deliveries on the land area of a kolkhoz, the Kremlin sought to reinforce its command to increase rapidly the collective livestock sector by making its build-up essential in order to meet the delivery obligations. A little sweetening was added: kolkhozes establishing the full complement of communal livestock herds with a specified minimum of animals were entitled to a reduction of 10 percent in meat deliveries. The decree also recommended payment of bonuses to managers, specialists, and workers for overfulfillment of planned goals and for extra quota sales to the government, as well as premiums in terms of extra workdays to supplement the relatively low state purchase prices paid to kolkhozniks for calves.

The decree did not stop at measures fostering the collective sector, but also discriminated against the private sector through the familiar method of heavy taxation. Whereas kolkhozes were supposed to deliver from 0.5 to 4.5 kilograms of meat per hectare, kolkhozniks who seldom had more than one hectare, and for the most part less, had to deliver from 32 to 45 kilograms per household, depending upon the zone. The rates of deliveries for the handful of remaining individual farmers were even steeper, double those imposed on kolkhozniks and ranging from 64 to 90 kilograms. Workers and employees of state enterprises living in rural areas were subject to the same rates as kolkhozniks, provided their livestock did not exceed the limits prescribed for the latter; otherwise, the higher rates imposed on individual farmers were to be applied.

Thus, by high, ingeniously framed taxes in kind, the government aimed not only to increase meat procurements but indirectly to stimulate the socialist livestock sector at the expense of the private sector. The socialist sector did increase, but it was more than offset by the decrease in the private sector, with a resulting decline in total livestock numbers (tabulation in million head).[88]

	Cows		Cattle and cows		Hogs		Sheep	
	1939	1940	1939	1940	1939	1940	1939	1940
Kolkhoz, state farms, other state enterprises	5.7	6.2	18.8	20.9	9.1	9.7	32.6	37.9
Private sector	18.3	16.6	34.7	26.9	16.1	12.8	37.3	28.7
Total	24.0	22.8	53.5	47.8	25.2	22.5	69.9	66.6

A new slump in livestock numbers, on the way up after the mid-thirties, took place on the eve of World War II, as the Kremlin stepped up its drive to collectivize animal husbandry.

A new method of meat procurements was introduced by the decree of July 8, 1939, and was the initial step in the reorganization and stiffening of the whole system of compulsory deliveries.[89] No longer were they levied on the number of livestock on the sown acreage specified by the government plan, but on each hectare of either the total land or the arable land of a kolkhoz. This applied not only to crops (with the exception of such commercial crops as cotton, for which the contract method of procurements was continued) but to animal products. The changed basis of procurements opened an easy legal way to enlarge the quantities of farm products extracted from the kolkhozes to meet current consumption needs as well as to build up large emergency stocks. The exactions were further increased for the more successful kolkhozes by repeated levies. Local authorities continued to resort to this device, despite its strict prohibition under the new law, whenever shortfalls would develop in the fulfillment of the planned targets.

The foregoing review of the outstanding 1939–40 agrarian legislation leaves no doubt that, in the last two years before the German invasion, government controls over the countryside were increased. What were the reasons for the tighter squeeze? Was it linked to the growing international tension of the late thirties and the clearing of the decks for the approaching armed conflict? Was it, perhaps, sparked by the very recovery of Soviet agriculture from the wounds inflicted at the start of collectivization, making it safe now for Stalin to plug the remaining loopholes in the edifice of agrarian collectivism? Did Stalin's total victory over his opposition, signalized by the end of the Great Purge in 1939, contribute to the increased toughness of agrarian policy? It is impossible to give a precise answer to these questions without knowing what was taking place inside the Kremlin. But it is fair to assume that probably all the reasons mentioned here, and perhaps others unknown to us, played a part in the redirection of agrarian policy.

12

Collectivized Agriculture and the War

As the screw was being tightened on the peasant in 1939–1941, the Hitler-Stalin Pact was concluded on August 23, 1939. But on June 21, 1941, at the beginning of the harvest, Hitler struck at the Soviet Union. For the third time in a quarter of a century, the country was in the throes of a severe agricultural and food crisis.

The War Crisis

The central fact in the Soviet agricultural and food situation during the Second World War was the rapid loss of productive cropland and human and material resources. At the same time, the demand for food went up. A comparison with World War I may help to drive the point home. After two years of hostilities, including the disastrous retreat of the Russian army in the summer of 1915, about 10 percent of the prewar crop area was in territory overrun by the enemy. The famous Russian breadbasket was hardly touched by that war except on its southwestern fringes. The picture was very different during the Second World War.

A territory comprising 47 percent of the prewar crop area and 45 percent of the livestock in terms of cattle was overrun by the enemy.[1] This included highly productive land in such fertile regions as the Ukraine, the Crimea, most of the central black-soil area, and the Don–North Caucasus. Since yields were higher in these regions than in the rest of the country, the loss of output was even greater than acreage figures indicate.

This area normally shipped wheat and other grains, oilseeds, and sugar for export and to the consuming or deficit zones of the USSR: the northern European regions, with their inferior soils, where the largest Russian cities, Moscow and Leningrad, and a number of industrial centers were located. The marketing of these surpluses was also aided by relatively better transportation facilities in the occupied zone, which accounted for 55 percent of the Russian railroad network.[2] During the years 1932–1934 the Ukraine, the North Caucasus, and the central black-soil areas, which were invaded in 1941–42, shipped out on the average 3 million metric tons of grain and flour.[3] The next and the last prewar year for which similar data are available is the very good crop year of 1937, when the Ukraine and North Caucasus alone shipped a total of more than 5 million tons.[4] Some of this grain went into such regions as Belorussia and Smolensk, which were also invaded. But most of it was destined for the uninvaded territory, which was deprived of these supplies during the war. Agricultural expansion in the eastern regions (the Urals, western Siberia, and Kazakhstan) prior to and during the Second World War no doubt helped fill the gap though eastern grain yields were low.[5] The share of the Ukraine in total grain production decreased from 25 percent in 1913 to 23 percent in 1940, and of the North Caucasus from 12.6 to 10.6 percent; the Urals increased its share from 8.4 to 9.7 percent, Siberia from 7 to 11.7 percent, and Kazakhstan from 2.8 to 3.4 percent.[6] But population had also increased in the east, and it increased still more during the Second World War. The population of the uninvaded zone, swelled by the evacuees and the army, was not lower than 130 million, or 67 percent of the prewar population of the USSR.[7]

Not only the land input but farm implements, labor, and draft power were greatly curtailed during the war. Here again a comparison with the First World War is instructive. It is estimated that "up to 40 percent of the able-bodied male population of the villages were called to the colors." [8] This drain of manpower was offset by a considerable surplus or underemployment of labor in peasant agriculture, though estate agriculture suffered from a labor shortage, with a detrimental effect on commercial production. During World War II a much higher proportion of the rural population was mobilized.[9] In addition, some kolkhozniks found employment in war industry, which was augmented in the uninvaded area by the evacuation of many factories from the war zone. This was particularly true of Siberia and the Urals. The Siberian industrial center of Omsk, for instance, attracted more than 65,000 new factory workers, mostly from kolkhozes.[10] As a consequence of war mobilization and a shift to industrial employment, agricultural manpower sharply declined. The number of able-bodied males in the kolkhozes of the un-invaded zone on January 1, 1945, was less than a third of that on January 1, 1941, while the number of women decreased by 9 percent (see Table 30). The number of women actually participating in collective-farm work in the uninvaded zone first increased from about 8.5 million in 1940 to 9.2 million in 1942, and then dropped by a million to a little over 8.2 million by 1944. The number of participating male workers decreased from 7.8 million in 1940 to 2.6 million in 1944. The number of adolescents also increased from 2.3 million in 1940 to over 3.8 million in 1942, and declined during the next two years to 3.4 million.[11] The aged and incapacitated workers in kolkhozes showed a small rise, from 2,125,000 in 1940 to 2,344,000 in 1944. These three categories—women, adolescents, and the aged—had to bear the brunt of the farmwork.

The role of women, who on the eve of the war accounted for more than half of the able-bodied kolkhoz labor force in the uninvaded zone, was particularly significant. The proportion of women in kolkhozes rose to nearly 80 percent by January 1, 1944, and declined to 76 percent on January 1, 1945, as the number of men began to increase. But the effort of women, adolescents, and the aged was not equivalent to that of the men they replaced; and it is estimated that, when the necessary adjustments were made, the agricultural labor force actually decreased during

Table 30. Available labor force in kolkhozes of the uninvaded zone, January 1, 1941–1945 (*in thousands*)

	1941	1942	1943	1944	1945
Able-bodied adults					
Men	8,657.3	5,890.3	3,605.0	2,340.8	2,769.7
Women	9,531.9	9,532.9	9,590.7	9,094.0	8,661.2
Total	18,189.2	15,423.2	13,195.7	11,434.8	11,430.9
Adolescents					
(aged 12 to 16)	3,818.8	3,779.4	4,035.0	3,820.9	3,524.5
Aged and sick	2,360.0	2,369.0	2,378.8	2,387.9	2,390.5
Total	24,368.0	21,571.6	19,609.5	17,643.6	17,345.9

Source. *Istoricheskii arkhiv*, 1929, no. 6, p. 29.

the war by one fourth.[12] Women also replaced men to a considerable extent among the greatly reduced skilled cadres of the machine-tractor stations. The following tabulation shows the proportion of women among the different categories of workers of both sexes.[13]

	1940	1942
Tractor drivers	4%	45%
Combine operators	6	43
Chauffeurs	5	36
Brigadiers (foremen)	1	10

Of the 2 million workers trained for such jobs during the war, 1.5 million were women.[14] They toiled longer and harder than before the war. The average number of workdays per able-bodied kolkhoznik increased from 250 in 1940 to 275 in 1944.[15] The sown area per able-bodied kolkhoznik increased from 8.2 acres in 1940 to 10.8 in 1942.[16] The acreage load was especially heavy in the Urals and Siberia, where the wartime reduction of manpower exceeded that for the uninvaded zone as a whole, amounting to 45 percent and 37 percent respectively between 1941 and 1944. In these eastern regions the acreage per able-bodied kolkhoznik was twice as high as in most of the European regions of the USSR.[17]

The manpower shortage was aggravated by the reduction of draft power and usable implements. At the beginning of the war, the tractor was already the dominant form of draft power, but the supply decreased. A large number of powerful "caterpillar" tractors were requisitioned for army needs. It was planned to take 22,000 tractors from the war zone, but only a little over half this number were actually evacuated. With the destruction or conversion of factories to war production, the new supply of tractors, combines, and other implements, as well as spare parts, was reduced to a trickle. During 1942 and 1943 only 900 new tractors were received by the MTS.[18] There was already a dwindling supply of equipment before the war,[19] and it was virtually cut off after the hostilities began. "Because of the shortage of fuel, spare parts, cessation of the supply of new machinery and lower qualification of the operators of mechanical equipment, mechanization of agriculture naturally declined, the productivity of tractors and machinery decreased." This was true of the MTS as well as the state farms. In the former, the average annual amount of work per 15-horsepower tractor in terms of plowing equivalent decreased from 411 hectares in 1940 to 216 hectares in 1943. On state farms the corresponding figures were 322 and 209 hectares. The reduced number of tractors and machinery, coupled with their decreased productivity, resulted in a 60 percent decline in the volume of all mechanized collective-farm operations between 1940 and 1943. Yet 52 percent of the spring plowing, 46 percent of the fall plowing, and 45 percent of the plowing of summer fallow was mechanized in kolkhozes even during the most difficult year, 1943.[20]

What about that old ally of the Russian peasant, the horse? Although the number of horses was slowly increasing after the catastrophic drop of the early 1930s, it was down to 21 million at the beginning of 1941 compared to 36 million in 1928 and 38 million in 1916.[21] Another setback occurred during the war, when many horses were mobilized for the army. Their number in the uninvaded zone decreased by one third between 1940 and 1943. But the share of horses in the total supply of farm draft power differed from region to region. In 1940 it constituted 28 percent in the Volga region, 43 percent in Siberia, 47 percent in the Urals, and 60 percent in central Russia.[22] Horses, therefore, were of greater help in the central than in the more mechanized eastern regions. But generally they were utilized to a greater degree and more intensively than before the war, though feed shortage often militated against their maximum effectiveness. Not only horses but cows were widely used for fieldwork, despite their being poorly adapted for draft purposes and the unfavorable effect it had on milk production. Financial incentives were even offered for the use of the kolkhozniks' privately owned cows for work in kolkhozes.[23] Yet the use of cows and horses could only partly fill the gap. Human power, usually woman power, also had to be resorted to for pulling implements or cultivating with spades. This is perhaps the most eloquent testimony to the extreme shortage of draft power experienced during the war.

Other inputs, such as mineral fertilizer, were also in very short supply. In 1940 kolkhozes received 2,505,000 tons of mineral fertilizer and in 1942 only 98,000 tons.[24] This had a deleterious effect on the yields of important industrial crops, especially cotton. Serious shortages of seed also developed, especially following the poor crop in 1942, and led to a reduction in seeding rates with unfavorable repercussions on yields, or to replacement of more valuable crops by less valuable ones (millet for wheat, say). All in all, the war period was one of extreme difficulty and hardship for Soviet agriculture, even in the uninvaded territory; it taxed the mettle and ingenuity of the peasants, especially the peasant women. Certainly the optimism with which many Soviet writers, beginning with Voznesenskii, treated the critical agricultural situation was too glib and deserved the reproaches heaped upon it by Arutiunian.[25]

The response of government policy to the agricultural crisis was, first of all, an expansion of the sown area in the uninvaded zone. This actually began on the eve of the war, when a decree of January 4, 1939, requiring the planting of a larger acreage to winter grains in the eastern regions, where spring crops predominated.[26] The expansion, which began in the fall of 1939, continued during the following two autumns. The seeded area in the kolkhozes increased by 3.7 million hectares, mainly because of increased fall sowings.[27] This was a considerable achievement, but it was largely nullified by poor farm techniques and bad weather. There was much winterkill and some of the sown area remained unharvested. For example, the unharvested grain area in 1942 in the eastern regions amounted to 617,500 hectares.[28] A distinction must be made, therefore, between sown and actually harvested area. While the harvested acreage increased in some regions, it declined in others and changed but little for the uninvaded zone as a whole in 1941 and 1942 (see Table 31). By 1943 the reduction of harvested acreage became general. An exception were the grain-deficit republics of Central Asia and Transcaucasia, where valuable industrial and specialty crops were replaced by grain.

While the government concentrated on expansion of acreage, yields went down; already in 1942 grain production was nearly 40 percent below 1940, despite a slightly higher harvested acreage. A further decline in yields took place in 1943, on top of reduced acreage, bringing production down to less than half that of 1940 (Table 31). Responsibility for this is shared by a combination of related causes: deficient inputs spread thinly over a wider area, deterioration of farm techniques and management (the level of which in the still new kolkhoz system was low to begin with), extension of farming into marginal areas, and adverse weather conditions. An additional factor in pushing grain yields downward, as Arutiunian points out, was the excessive expansion of winter crops and millet.[29] It is true that winter-grain varieties when grown in suitable climatic conditions have higher yields than spring-sown varieties. Also, winter crops relieve the workload during spring as well as during the harvest, because they mature earlier and provide a good insurance against the failure of spring crops. But the climate of Siberia, the Urals, and Kazakhstan, their severe and prolonged winters, was anything but favorable to winter crops; and even spring crops do not find the climate of this semiarid zone hospitable. As for the relief of the spring workload, this was partly offset by the diversion of scarce resources to winter crops; these resources might have been used to prepare the land ahead of time for spring sowing. As for millet, two features—modest seed requirements and a short growing season—made it an attractive crop in wartime. But much labor was required for cultivation to keep it clear of weeds, and labor was a scarce commodity. The result was generally low yield and no crop at all in part of the expanded area.

The precarious character of the Soviet wartime grain supply is obvi-

Table 31. Harvested grain area and production in kolkhozes of
the uninvaded zone, 1941–1943, as percent of 1940

Region	1941	1942	1943
North and northwest			
Area	94.7	91.8	85.3
Production	69.6	66.3	53.9
Central non-black soil			
Area	100.8	94.4	100.8
Production	83.9	77.2	67.1
Central black soil			
Area	89.4	93.3	70.4
Production	91.9	57.3	31.9
Volga			
Area	93.7	91.6	69.7
Production	84.3	40.3	29.1
Urals and West Siberia			
Area	96.8	97.3	78.7
Production	100.5	59.4	38.3
East Siberia and Far East			
Area	106.1	109.9	87.9
Production	65.3	57.9	33.3
Kazakhstan			
Area	110.4	117.9	99.7
Production	167.2	98.0	55.8
Central Asia and Transcaucasia			
Area	102.6	114.3	126.1
Production	98.3	100.6	94.6
Total			
Area	98.7	100.4	86.7
Production	97.4	61.1	46.0

Source. Iu. V. Arutiunian, *Sovetskoe krest'ianstvo v gody velikoi
otechestvennoi voiny* (Soviet Peasantry during the Years of the Great
Patriotic War; Moscow, 1963), p. 165.

ous, especially when it is related to the increased number of people to
be fed—at least 130 million in the uninvaded zone, compared to 105
million before the war, or nearly one fourth more.[30] A considerable dose
of optimism was injected into the treatment of the wartime grain problem, not only by the publicity given to temporary and often illusory
expansion of acreage but also by the legend of considerable grain stocks
piled up in the government granaries. Although the legend was fostered

by the government,[31] no actual figures were released until many years after the war; and when finally published, they proved to be much lower than originally supposed. (At the time I, in common with Naum Jasny and other Western observers, was skeptical about the existence of exceedingly large grain stocks in the USSR.[32]) "The reserves and stocks of rye, wheat, oats, flour, and groats reached 6,162,000 tons by January 1, 1941. The accumulation of state reserves and mobilization stocks made it possible to provide four to six months' food and forage supplies for the army in wartime." [33] Assuming that in terms of grain these stocks amounted to about 8 million tons, this would have constituted one fourth of the average annual procurement and about 10 percent of the average production for 1938–1940.[34] Some of these stocks, perhaps even the largest part, might have been stored in the occupied zone and so were lost to the Russians. Note that only modest claims are made by official Soviet historians for the role of stocks in the wartime food supply. A final cautionary note: Soviet scholars and specialists who wrote about agriculture during the war, prior to the revision in the 1950s of the inflated grain-production figures based on biological yields, tended to take a more optimistic view of the grain situation than those writing during the late fifties and sixties.

The wartime pattern observed in the case of grain—expansion of the sown area eastward, at least during the first two war years, accompanied by low yields—was characteristic of a number of other crops. Some of these, such as sugar beets, were introduced into regions where they had never been grown before. In 1942 sugar beets were grown for the first time in twenty-two provinces and republics, and in 1943 the number increased to thirty-two.[35] The area under sugar beets, which dwindled from more than 1.1 million hectares in 1940 to 94,500 hectares in 1941, increased to more than 260,000 hectares in 1942 and 1943. But the yields were very low, declining in 1943 to less than a fourth of the prewar level. In addition to shortages of mineral fertilizer and labor, a factor contributing to the low yields of new crops was the lack of technical knowledge on the part of farmers. Sugar beets provide yet another illustration of the detrimental effect on yields when crops are extended into climatically unsuitable areas. In the case of sugar beets, such a region was the Uzbek Republic, where a sizable expansion of acreage took place during the war. But the abundance of sunshine, high temperatures, and dry air adversely affected the crop, lowering its sugar content.[36]

Although the government generally strove for an expansion of crop acreage and the introduction of new crops in the uninvaded zone, an exception was made for cotton. It was a long-established crop, grown under irrigation in the Central Asiatic and Transcaucasian republics. In the 1930s, with that disregard for climatic limitations characteristic of Soviet agricultural policy, a considerable extension of cotton growing into the southern European part of the country was decreed. But the yields in these new unirrigated regions were very low, so that while it accounted for about one fourth of the total cotton area, production was only about 10 percent of the total.[37] When this region was invaded by the Germans, the loss was much less than the acreage figures alone would indicate, and cannot be compared to the sugar-beet losses. The irrigated cotton acreage, which accounted for 90 percent of the output, was entirely in the uninvaded zone. But it was reduced to make room for grain and other food crops—the reverse of the shift that took place in the 1930s when the policy was to replace grain by cotton. The area under irrigated cotton decreased from 1,496,000 hectares in 1941 to 1,100,000 hectares in 1943. But because of the scarcity of mineral fertilizer, which was used rather generously for cotton, and the serious labor shortage accentuated by decreased economic incentives to cotton growers, the yields of this highly labor-intensive crop went down nearly 60 percent between 1941 and 1943. Decreased economic incentives resulted from a halving of the amount of grain sold by the government at concession prices to farmers against deliveries of cotton. Also low out-turn eliminated bonuses paid for higher cotton yields. Under the combined impact of reduced acreage and yields, production declined by more than two thirds, from 2.3 million tons of unginned cotton in 1941 to 700,000 tons in 1943.[38]

The war marked a substantial expansion in the growing of potatoes and vegetables. This was a process in which not only the socialist sector but the whole population participated. The increased growing of potatoes and other vegetables was general throughout the country, but it mushroomed in the vicinity of the industrial centers, especially in the new cities in the east.[39] The expansion of these crops was aided by two developments: the organization or transfer of state farms to various enterprises and institutions, including the Red Army in the front zone, in order to help feed their personnel; and government encouragement of widespread gardening by the population. This spurt of gardening activity boosted the private sector, which accounted before the war for more than half of the area under potatoes and other vegetables. But in kolkhozes the trend was also upward. From 1,353,000 hectares in the uninvaded zone in 1941, which was less than half of the national prewar potato area, it increased to 1,799,000 in 1943 and 2,482,000 in 1944.[40] (The increase in 1944 may have been magnified by the inclusion of liberated territory.) As with other crops, production did not keep pace with the area expansion because of a decline in yields. Still the kolkhoz potato production increased between 1941 and 1944 from 7.4 million metric tons to more than 11.9 million, and the output of vegetables, though hampered by the shortage of seed, rose from 1.9 million tons to more than 3.3 million.[41] The expanded production of potatoes and vegetables during the war was a great boon to the nation, especially when it is considered that an acre of potatoes normally yields one and a half times as many calories as an acre of grain.

Livestock in the uninvaded zone suffered from inferior care, epidemics, and deterioration of the feed supply. Fewer concentrates were available; the supply of feed grains, oats, and barley declined. Supplies of other concentrates (potatoes, oilcake, millfeed) were also curtailed or cut off because of increased human consumption or shortage of transportation. Though concentrates, in peacetime, were used less for animal feeding in the USSR than in the West, still a reduction in their supply and greater reliance on less nutritious feeds was bound adversely to affect livestock productivity.[42] The shortage of concentrates most severely affected hogs—whose numbers in kolkhozes were down by nearly a half in 1943, compared with 1941. Cattle and particularly sheep, the latter depending little on concentrates, were hurt less. Their herds also benefited from the evacuation of livestock from the war zone. More than half a million cattle out of a total of 7.5 million in the kolkhozes of the war zone, and about 1.7 million sheep and goats out of a total of 9 million, were evacuated in the face of enormous difficulties.[43]

An even higher proportion of the smaller sovkhoz herd was saved, but hogs were slaughtered rather than evacuated. The evacuated livestock was largely used for meat deliveries to the government, enabling kolkhozes and sovkhozes in the uninvaded zone to preserve more of their own stock. Kolkhoz herds were also augmented by contract purchases of young stock from kolkhozniks. In 1942 purchases from kolkhozniks amounted to 2.5 million cattle (or approximately 15 to 20 percent of the kolkhoz herd), 200,000 hogs, and 1.7 million sheep and goats. In 1943 2 million cattle, 1.5 million sheep and goats, and 100,000 hogs were similarly acquired. State farm purchases were much more modest—60,000 cattle in 1942 and 85,000 in 1943.[44] Strict rules regarding slaughter promulgated during the war exerted pressure on farm management to keep livestock numbers up.[45] These factors—gains from evacuation, contract purchases from kolkhozniks, and the pressure on farm managers to maintain herds—more than outweighed the increased mortality of animals, especially young stock, and the decreased fertility of cows used for fieldwork. The number of cattle, sheep, and goats in the socialist sector actually increased in the uninvaded zone between 1940 and 1943. But this was more than offset by the decline of livestock owned by the kolkhozniks, with consequent overall reduction of livestock numbers.

This is shown by the following percentage figures of livestock numbers in 1943 as compared with 1940.[46]

	State farms and other enterprises	Kolkhozes	Kolkhozniks	Total
Cattle (including cows)	111%	107%	73%	89%
Cows only	102	94	96	95
Sheep and goats	102	123	61	92
Hogs	71	72	40	55
Horses	80	66	—	66

War and the Struggle for Bread

As agricultural production was declining in the uninvaded zone, the demand was growing for foodstuffs for the army and the swollen population in the industrial centers. The old "struggle for bread" was no doubt softened somewhat by patriotic sentiments, which the farmers shared with the rest of the population. However much it was furthered by Soviet propaganda or Hitler's aggressions, patriotism alone was not enough. In the face of declining output, considerable effort and much pressure had to be exerted by the authorities to extract the necessary quantities of grain and other foodstuffs. The prices paid were so low that Arutiunian characterizes them as "frequently symbolic," with the peasantry giving over the main part of its output "practically free." [47] Whatever its state of war preparedness in other respects, for this operation the Stalin regime was well prepared. The institutional framework, the apparatus of government coercion, required only minor adjustments to be placed on a war footing. They were, in fact, not far from it as Russian agriculture had begun to emerge from the state of internal warfare caused by collectivization before being plunged into the crisis of a world war.

The mechanism of heavy exactions of farm products and the methods used to legitimize them already existed. The escalation of procurement quotas began on the eve of the war, with a change in the basis for their calculations from the sown area to the whole arable land of a kolkhoz, including potential cropland not cultivated. This provision, aiming at the parallel objectives of high quotas and acreage expansion, remained operative during the war when the area actually cultivated declined. It was a weapon for extracting as much grain as possible and hit most painfully those kolkhozes in eastern regions with large land holdings which they were unable to cultivate. Then there was the old gimmick of using inflated biological yields as a basis for calculating payments in kind for the work done by the MTS. What aggravated this form of exaction was the gap between biological and actual yields, which became much greater during the war as productivity went down. This made the MTS services much more costly. At the same time, the government, without raising the nominal rates of payment, obtained more produce per unit of MTS work, expressed in hectares of plowing equivalent. Kazakhstan serves as a good example. The biological yields during the years 1940–1943 in centners per hectare were respectively 6.4, 10.9, 9.1, and 5.6; the actual yields were 4.8, 7.2, 3.9, and 2.6. In 1940 the gap between the two series was 33 percent; by 1941 it rose to 51 percent and exceeded 100 percent in 1942 and 1943.[48] Efforts were even made at the height of the agricultural crisis to prevent the gathering of any statistical information on production and distribution of crops save the biological yields, lest the farmers use it as a reason for requesting a reduction of quotas. Preparation of grain balances based on actual production and utilization data were forbidden. But this ostrich-like attitude did not prevail completely. The representative of the Commissariat of Procurements in the Altai region, where grain balances were condemned, still considered it necessary to gather more detailed information, and so did a number of officials in other regions.[49]

The use of biological yields could only partly offset the downward pull on payments in kind by the reduced volume of MTS work. Compulsory deliveries also decreased, and the government, desperate to obtain more grain, resorted to supplementary procurements in the guise of contributions to the "defense fund" and the "Red Army Fund." The latter particularly, as Table 32 shows, helped to reduce the wide gap opened by the decline in the traditional sources of grain procurements. Yet a sharp reduction of 25 to 50 percent in total procurements of grain, oilseeds, cotton, milk, and eggs in the uninvaded zone between 1940 and 1943 could not be avoided. A smaller reduction of about 10 percent took place in the procurement of potatoes, while meat and vegetables even increased. Yet it is significant that in kolkhozes the reduction in grain procurements was smaller than that in production, 50.8 percent and 55 percent per hectare between 1940 and 1943. On state farms the reduction per hectare was greater than in the kolkhozes both in production and in procurements, 57.6 and 63.8 percent respectively.[50] The greater decrease in the output of mechanized state farms is not surprising, for in wartime such farms were almost inevitably relatively vulnerable to shortages of labor, fuel, and machinery. That had also been the experience of the estates during World War I. But it is puzzling that procurements decreased more than production on the state farms.

Table 32. Distribution of all grains and legumes in kolkhozes, 1940–1945 (in thousand centners)

Distribution	1940	1941	1942	1943	1944	1945
Compulsory deliveries	142,511.0	71,530.2	53,703.8	46,775.9	107,745.6	95,958.1
Payment in kind to MTS	148,988.0	70,519.0	43,602.1	24,090.2	46,473.4	34,081.3
Red Army fund	—	—	10,431.7	14,432.4	17,424.8	11,204.2
Defense fund	—	575.0	1,003.8	873.4	1,722.6	581.3
Return of state seed and fodder funds	24,315.4	8,979.7	4,474.7	3,750.7	13,502.7	13,856.1
Commercial sales to the state	13,301.6	1,691.1	608.5	3,994.8	1,604.3	1,112.1
Total deliveries to the state	329,116.0	153,295.0	113,824.6	93,917.4	188,474.4	156,793.1
Sold on kolkhoz market	3,819.9	1,972.7	2,187.3	1,340.8	1,640.6	1,636.3
Designated for sale but not sold	5,083.6	5,578.9	745.6	587.8	913.9	564.2
Seed, including reserves	134,429.9	73,034.8	59,625.5	55,252.3	82,254.9	80,405.7
Animal feed, including reserves	108,844.7	39,597.1	19,596.7	12,181.6	17,548.5	16,124.8
Food reserve	9,648.3	3,597.9	1,781.6	1,116.6	1,817.3	1,387.8
Welfare supplies [a]	5,750.5	3,288.7	1,951.8	1,467.5	2,439.5	2,004.1
Waste	19,301.3	15,324.1	14,911.3	13,488.9	18,759.9	19,112.2
Distributed on the basis of workdays	101,512.3	43,515.7	22,402.0	29,470.8	42,068.0	37,871.1
Total	717,506.5	339,204.9	237,026.4	208,773.7	355,917.0	315,899.3

[a] For the support of invalids, orphans, and the like.

Source. Arutiunian, *Sovetskoe krest'ianstvo v gody velikoi otechestvennoi voiny*, p. 437.

There is indirect evidence of the effectiveness of the squeeze on the kolkhoz peasants. The volume of procurements obtained from kolkhozes during the war was partly at the expense of reduced earnings for the kolkhozniks. The amount of grain and potatoes per workday, the chief ingredients allocated for distribution among farmers, was almost half of those distributed in 1940.[51] Actually it was even less; as Table 32 shows, the grain distributed was considerably smaller than the amount allocated for this purpose. It was necessary for a kolkhoznik to work much harder to approximate prewar earnings, and this is especially true of family earnings since there were fewer working family members. It was argued that the produce distributed to kolkhozniks was worth much more than before the war, because the prices of foodstuffs on the private market had risen fantastically. But it was small compensation to the many who had little if anything to sell, or for whom access to the market was difficult. Even more important was the deleterious effect of the severe inflation and the great scarcity of manufactured goods in the exchange between village and town. Black-market barter thrived between the peasants and town people, who exchanged food for clothing and other household goods.

A few figures will show the reorientation of Soviet industry during the war. In 1940, on the eve of the war, heavy industry, which was geared primarily to war needs, accounted for 61.2 percent of the gross industrial output; the consumer-good industry accounted for 38.8 percent. In 1945, the next year for which information is available, and a year when some reconversion to a peacetime basis was already taking place, the respective proportions were 74.9 and 25.1 percent. While the output of the heavy industry in 1944 was 36 percent above 1940 and in 1945 was 12 percent above 1940, the output of the consumer-goods industry in 1944 and 1945 was 46 and 41 percent below 1940.[52] It should not be overlooked that the consumer-goods industry during the war was also largely oriented to meeting war needs.[53]

Not only did the kolkhoznik's share suffer from the pressure of procurements: the seed supply too was often not spared, even though this adversely affected production. It is hardly surprising that the kolkhozes resisted the procurement steamroller. It is more surprising that the resistance was not greater and that it was confined to various forms of deception. The government in turn continued or intensified its customary repressive tactics, such as searches for grain and arrests by the NKVD, removal from office of kolkhoz managers, prosecutions, and long-term imprisonments. Another practice reported in 1943 from a raion in south Kazakhstan was that peasants "who did not possess grain were forced to sell their houses, household goods, and livestock" [54]—an old method of extracting taxes from peasants. As usual, excesses committed by officials were from time to time criticized publicly by higher-ranking function- aries, with no evidence of tangible results.

The government experienced less difficulty with the procurement of livestock products. In so important a region as Kazakhstan, for instance, wartime livestock procurements from kolkhozes and sovkhozes greatly exceeded prewar amounts. But the socialist sector, while accounting for the bulk of marketable grain, was less important in livestock marketings, which were dominated by individual producers. Procurement of livestock products from the scattered small producers was bound to be a harder task than grain collection from a relatively small number of large state farms. It was aggravated by the fact that livestock prices on the private market exceeded procurement prices more than a hundred times, and that manufactured goods, which could be offered in exchange to farmers, were very scarce. Partly because of these difficulties and partly because animal products were much less important in the Russian diet than grain, less coercion was used in extracting livestock products from the individual producers. The lag of the individual sector is illustrated by the case of milk. While total procurements (all categories of farms) de- clined in 1942 by 53.5 percent as compared with 1941, the reduction for the individual sector was 73.3 percent.[55] One other observation with respect to procurements in wartime was the large staff used at a time of a serious manpower shortage. In the Altai province alone, procurement agencies had 18,000 employees, or approximately four for each collective and state farm. In addition, special agents and party workers were de- tailed during the season to push the procurement campaign, while the regular and security police took part in guarding the grain.[56]

In spite of all these difficulties, the Soviet regime was still able to obtain considerable quantities of food during the war. Although the collective system could not stem the serious decline in acreage, livestock numbers, and agricultural production, it again proved to be an asset to the regime in the compulsory acquisition of farm products. It was much easier for the government to collect grain and other products from 200,000 collective and state farms, geared to very high levies in kind, than to deal with politically influential landlords and millions of independent small producers, as during World War I. The Kremlin showed no inclination to relax the firm grip that collectivization had established over agricul- ture. This did not preclude a more liberal attitude toward small house- hold farming. The liberalization was most pronounced in the strong encouragement and aid given by the Stalin administration to the grow- ing of food by citydwellers, similar to the "victory gardens" in the United States during the war. In the Soviet Union it was called individual and collective kitchen gardening (*ogorodnichestvo*). For this purpose, unused land around cities (including unused land of neighboring kolkhozes) was allotted to various enterprises and institutions and through them distributed in small plots for individual and group cultivation. A decree of November 4, 1942, provided that the land thus allotted was to be retained for a period of five to seven years as long as the workers continued to be employed by the same establishments.[57]

Another decree issued on February 19, 1944, declared that the government, "attaching great significance to the further development of individual and collective kitchen gardening," adopted a number of further measures.[58] The most important of these was the decision to expand the acreage in gardens by no less than 20 percent and to supply the gardeners with seed and simple tools through "timely" sales. Symptomatic of the importance attributed to this type of individual farming was the allocation of 1,500 tons of the very scarce mineral fertilizer. The decree of February 19 also provided that in each oblast a high official, a deputy chairman of the oblast executive committee, assume local leadership of the garden project. The national direction of this activity was centered in a special committee of the Central Council of Trade Unions, established early in 1943.[59] An editorial in *Izvestiia* epitomized the new significance of the kitchen gardens: "From an amateur occupation of a small group of persons in the recent past, it became, during war years, a movement of millions—a potent source of improvement in the supply [of food] for the working people." [60] The area devoted to kitchen gardens in 1944 amounted to more than 1.4 million hectares (nearly 3.5 million acres), or 83 percent more than in 1942. The number of city workers engaged in such gardening reached 16.5 million in 1944, two and a half times as many as in 1942 and 40 percent more than in 1943. The garden plots yielded close to 10 million metric tons of potatoes, vegetables, and other crops in 1944.[61] This is a significant quantity when it is considered that the total production of potatoes and vegetables before the war probably was less than 60 million tons.[62]

The other aspect of the relaxed attitude toward the private sector was the expansion of the private farming of kolkhozniks, though there was no formal change in official policy. With a difficult food situation confronting them, the authorities looked the other way when a kolkhoznik family cultivated a little more land, which might have otherwise remained unused, and thus brought in a little more produce to sell on the kolkhoz market. Perhaps a certain weakening of the party-state bureaucratic apparatus owing to the war mobilization and a desire, if not to appease, at least not to add to the peasants' resentment in wartime may have contributed to the more lenient official attitude.

The government also sought to strengthen the collective system's capability to deal with the war emergency. To be sure, the main pattern of agricultural organization already existed. It was only necessary to fill in details, to dust off some old weapons. Among these were the re-established political sections (politotdels) of the MTS and state farms.[63] Legislation was adopted to cope with the labor shortage, high turnover, and absenteeism. A year before the war, a decree was issued (June 26, 1940) which increased the working hours and days in state enterprises, strictly regulated job changes from one enterprise to another, and provided for criminal prosecution and penalties for the unauthorized leaving of jobs and absenteeism. This law was applicable also to the permanent employees of the MTS and state farms. On July 17, 1940, a supplementary decree was issued which brought under the purview of the law, with some exceptions because of the seasonal character of the work, tractor drivers in the MTS, brigadiers of tractor brigades, and their assistants.[64]

As far as kolkhozniks were concerned, the compulsory annual minimum of workdays, established by the law of May 27, 1939, was amended in two important respects. The minimum was considerably increased, from 60–80 workdays in the three zones into which the country was divided for this purpose, to 100–120–150 workdays respectively. The new minimum was also subdivided on a seasonal basis. The sanctions for its nonfulfillment continued to be expulsion from the kolkhoz and loss of private plots. These were supplemented by criminal prosecution, with a penalty on conviction of up to six months' "corrective labor" in the kolkhoz and a deduction of 25 percent in earnings (workdays credited). Kolkhoz managers and brigadiers who failed to initiate prosecution of kolkhozniks who did not meet the minimum were themselves liable to prosecution.[65] It was one of the important functions of the politotdels of the MTS to supervise the implementation of this legislation. Actually the number of convictions was small; only 3 percent of the kolkhozniks did not fulfill the minimum in 1944.[66] Expulsion from a kolkhoz was a more common penalty, varying according to zone. In the zone with the lowest minimum, 15.2 percent of the kolkhozniks who did not meet it were expelled; the figure is 5 percent in the intermediate zone and 3.4 percent in the zone with the highest minimum. This suggests that the minimum in the last two zones was too high and therefore enforced less strictly. The nonfulfillment of the higher wartime labor minimum was less than before the war: 18.3 percent in 1940 and 12.8 percent in 1944 for women, and 6.2 and 5.7 percent for men. The average number of workdays per able-bodied kolkhoznik rose steadily during the war—from 312 in 1940 to 344 in 1944 for males, and from 193 to 252 for women.[67] This represented an increase of 10.3 percent for men and 30.6 percent for women. Though a comparison with the prewar figures is not precise because of various changes in the calculation of workdays during the war, an upward trend can hardly be doubted. How much the coercive character of the minimum workday legislation was responsible for the intensification of the labor input, and how much was due to other factors, it is impossible to tell. But it is clear that the workday minimum was a potent influence.

The differential system of payment by results was also continuously emphasized as a means of stimulating increased efforts. An elaborate bonus scheme, based on rising productivity goals, was introduced on the eve of the war and was extended after hostilities began by a series of decrees, which applied not only to kolkhozes but also to the MTS and state farms.[68] The advantage of the bonus was that, at a time of severe depreciation of currency, it was paid mostly in kind, even on state farms where workers were previously paid in cash. The number of kolkhozes that adopted the bonus scheme increased from 19.4 percent in 1942 and 19.8 percent in 1943 to 44.1 percent in 1945.[69] The fault of the system was that the performance goals on which the bonuses were based were set far too high, depriving most farmers of extra payments. Even when farmers were legally entitled to such payments, these were sometimes withheld, in part or in full. At any rate, the bonus scheme, as described by Commissar of Agriculture Andreev in 1945, was at best spotty in its operation.[70]

While generally striving to intensify the labor input in agriculture and to draw into the farm labor force a much larger proportion of peasant women, adolescents, aged, and invalids, the government also addressed itself to the problem of relieving the labor shortage during the critical seasonal peaks, especially during the harvest. A decree was issued on April 17, 1942, which provided for mobilization of nonfarm population not employed in factories or transportation, including schoolchildren and college students.[71] Subject to mobilization were men from the ages of fourteen to fifty-five and women from fourteen to fifty. They were paid on the same basis as other farmworkers and in addition retained 50 percent of their regular wages; the students retained their stipends. The kolkhoz, sovkhoz, or MTS reimbursed these workers for travel expenses.

Large numbers were mobilized for farmwork: 4 million during the first year, 1942, and 2.8 million and 3.3 million during the subsequent two years for the harvest alone.[72] In 1944 the majority, 56 percent, were highschool students, followed by rural nonfarm people, city workers, and nonworking people and college students. The performance of this additional labor force presents a mixed picture. Lack of training and low physical endurance, especially of the adolescents, impaired productivity.

Although the Commissariat of Agriculture issued an order for such training in November 1941, a critical newspaper review five months later showed that precious little was accomplished along these lines,[73] which is hardly surprising considering the trying war conditions. Inefficient organization also decreased the productiveness of this labor. There were delays in the release of mobilized workers from their former jobs, premature recall of the workers, inadequate provision of food and housing, and faulty labor management. In a kolkhoz in Kuibyshev oblast, for instance, thirty mobilized workers were turned away because not enough bread had been baked that day. Similar shortages were reported in other kolkhozes in the region. Inadequate supervision led to some soldiering on the job.[74]

Poor recording of the work done often diminished the already low earnings of the mobilized workers, especially adolescents; and since they were paid at the end of the year, the city people sometimes did not want to make a trip to the farms to claim their small share.[75] A rough indication of the contribution of the mobilized outsiders is provided by the number of workdays credited to them: 4 percent of the total number in 1942, 12 percent in 1943, and 2.8 percent in 1944.[76] This contribution was substantial in 1943 but much less in 1944, when the territory under Soviet control expanded. One advantage of the outside labor force was its availability for straight crop-production work during the most strenuous peak periods. The value of the outside help on farms varied from region to region. In the Ivanovsk oblast of the central industrial region, 11.1 percent of the total replacement of kolkhozniks (in terms of workdays) was supplied by outside help in 1943, as against 72.8 percent derived from more intensive labor input and 16.1 percent from an increased number of working kolkhoz women, adolescents, and aged. In another industrial province, Sverdlovsk in the Urals, the proportion was 25.1, 63.7, and 11.2 percent respectively.[77] The measurement is necessarily rough since it involves a comparison of workdays during the war with the prewar period; but it confirms the subordinate, though regionally variable, importance of the mobilized outside help. With these changes—which, to repeat, did not involve the modification of basic principles of policy or organization—Russian agriculture was expected to maximize food production. Still, the strenuous, often heroic, effort of the Russian peasants, depleted in ranks and stripped of much of their fertile land and other means of production, was not enough. America had to come to the rescue.

And through lend-lease assistance it did so on a large scale. Considerable quantities of fats and oils, dairy products, sugar, and other commodities were added to the Soviet food supply. Because of their concentrated character and high caloric value, the dietary importance of lend-lease food is inadequately conveyed by mere figures of tonnage (see Table 33). The importance of the contribution was substantial, although after the war the Russians tried to minimize it. With this help the Soviet government was able to feed, after a fashion, the large Red Army and workers in defense plants. But a very tight food situation prevailed for the great mass of the civilian population. Rationing of food, especially bread, was introduced in the cities shortly after the outbreak of the war. It differentiated between various categories of consumers on the basis of their contribution to the war effort or their standing in the party hierarchy. The prewar prices of the rationed products were retained. An important aspect of food distribution was the growth of canteen feeding (*obshchestvennoe pitanie*), which relieved more women workers of part of their domestic responsibilities.[78]

Apart from the privileged top level of the party-government bureaucracy, which depended on unpublicized, "closed" distribution centers, the highest rations were reserved for the workers in the heavy war industries, particularly those engaged in hard physical labor (such as miners); children up to twelve years of age and pregnant women and breast-feeding mothers were also entitled to special rations. In general, as a United States official document stated, "Russian rations limit civilians to a woefully inadequate diet." [79] What was worse, rations, except for bread, often were not fully met or inferior products were substituted. A case was cited of a Moscow family of four that had three working members and so was in a high rationing category. Even this family, better off than the more typical family with a large number of nonworking members, "cannot get along on its rations, so it buys in the open market, where collective farmers sell their own produce after having sold a given proportion to the government at a fixed price. In the market bread costs not 1 ruble a kilo but 140 to 150 rubles, sugar not 5½ rubles but 800 rubles a kilo, cereals not 6 to 20 but 150 rubles and butter not 50 but 1,000. In the open market potatoes cost 60 to 70 rubles a kilo, and this family buys potatoes whenever it can afford them, and cabbage, which is a great must in a Russian's diet. This family finds that its rationed food lasts fourteen to twenty days, depending upon how much of the rationed food it has been able to obtain, for sometimes there is a shortage." [80] Many families fared worse. But some improvement in the low dietary level is indicated toward the end of the war, as an increased number of people were obtaining rations of higher categories.[81] The magnitude of the task that confronted the Soviet government is underlined by the size of the rationed civilian population, which by the end of the war reached 76.8 million. This exceeded the prewar urban population of 60.6 million and was nearly double that of the rationed population in 1934, when it amounted to 40.3 million.[82]

The Nazi Occupation

Enough has been said to show the gravity of the food problem and the policies adopted to cope with it. But what of the section of the country under German occupation, which lasted a few months in some of the central and southeastern regions, and up to three years in a large part of the Ukraine and Belorussia? Since German agricultural policy in the occupied areas has been exhaustively treated,[83] I shall confine myself here to a few highlights. At the root of the Nazi policy in Russia and, indeed, one of the objectives of the war itself was the assumption that Russian agricultural resources under German control could assure Ger-

Table 33. United States shipments of agricultural products and foodstuffs to the Soviet Union under lend-lease, 1941–1946, and UNRRA, 1945–46

Item	Unit	Lend-lease	UNRRA[a]
Meat and meat products	1,000 lbs.	2,152,881	264,889
Gelatin, edible	1,000 lbs.	6	—
Fats and oils, edible and inedible	1,000 lbs.	1,884,506	53,760
Essential oils	1,000 lbs.	78	—
Milk, processed	1,000 lbs.	218,769	89,856
Cheese	1,000 lbs.	69,814	12,063
Eggs and egg products, dried	1,000 lbs.	242,458	[b]
Fish, salted, pickled, and canned	1,000 lbs.	290	4,375
Grains and grain products			
Wheat, including flour and semolina	1,000 bu.	25,047	—
Rye	1,000 bu.	10	—
Barley	1,000 bu.	474	—
Oats, including oatmeal	1,000 bu.	3,725	—
Corn, including hominy, grits, cornstarch, and flour	1,000 bu.	132	9
Buckwheat	1,000 bu.	6	—
Rice, milled, including rough rice and flour	1,000 lbs.	135,808	3,983
Grain cereals and other products	1,000 lbs.	17,612	301
Soy flour	1,000 lbs.	52,453	400
Pulses	1,000 lbs.	567,186	30,415
Vegetables and vegetable products	1,000 lbs.	53,970	33,159

Table 33. *Continued*

Item	Unit	Lend-lease	UNRRA[a]
Fruit and fruit preparations			
Fresh or frozen fruit	1,000 lbs.	254	—
Canned fruit	1,000 lbs.	129	[b]
Dried and evaporated fruit	1,000 lbs.	4,728	—
Fruit preparations	1,000 lbs.	25	27,707
Fruit juices	1,000 gals.	369	992
Nuts and nut preparations	1,000 lbs.	5,604	7,884
Soybeans and other oil seeds	1,000 lbs.	1,768	213
Grass and field seeds, including clover	1,000 lbs.	19,692	11,705
Vegetable seeds	1,000 lbs.	13,230	7,105
Feeds	long tons	26	—
Hops	1,000 lbs.	40	—
Sugar, refined	1,000 lbs.	1,035,265	2
Table beverages (coffee, tea, cocoa)	1,000 lbs.	2,829	118
Chocolate	1,000 lbs.	30	—
Candy	1,000 lbs.	939	1,468
Spices and imitations	1,000 lbs.	607	24
Glucose	1,000 lbs.	35	60
Salt	1,000 lbs.	4,550	—
Yeast	1,000 lbs.	450	—
Fish oil (medicinal), vitamins	1,000 lbs.	3,026	82
Vinegar	1,000 gals.	129	—

[a] United Nations Relief and Rehabilitation Administration figures have not been published since December 1946. However, shipments had begun to fall off at that time, and the period covered contains the bulk of the shipments. Shipments of foreign merchandise not included.

[b] Less than 500 pounds.

Source. Compiled from U.S. Department of Commerce publications and from records of U.S. Office of Foreign Agricultural Relations.

many self-sufficiency in the matter of food supply. A parallel premise of Nazi policy was the *Untermensch* concept of the inferiority of the Russian and other Slavic and non-Slavic people of the Soviet Union. They were to be mere hewers of wood and drawers of water for the *Herrenvolk*. This naturally led to an emphasis on the exploitation of agricultural and human resources by dictate rather than through the cooperation of the conquered peoples.

Such were Nazi Germany's general objectives—the immediate wartime end was to extract as much food as possible for the German army and the

Fatherland. This led to what seems a paradoxical decision by the Nazis: despite all their professed hostility to Bolshevism, they chose to retain the kolkhoz system rather than to propitiate the peasantry by its dissolution. Thus a German economic policy directive issued on May 23, 1941, one month before the invasion, spoke of the agricultural "battle of production" expected in the invaded territory. It declared that a prerequisite for the collection of surpluses "is the retention of large-scale farm enterprises . . . In view of the mentality of the Russians, an increase in production is possible only by decree from above . . . Subdivision into several million family farms renders any influence upon production illusory. *Any attempt at dissolution of the large-scale enterprises must, therefore, be fought with the most drastic means.*"[84]

In July 1941 Goering declared that, in order "to avoid, as far as possible, halts in production and interruptions in the delivery of agricultural products, the present kolkhoz system . . . will have to be maintained." To the fear of the disruptive effects of decollectivization on production, on procurements, and on German control in the countryside was added the pro-kolkhoz stand of the prospective German colonizers. They were mainly from the ranks of Himmler's elite guards (the SS), who looked forward to being awarded estates in the east. This would-be landed aristocracy and its patron saw only complications arising from the division of the large farms before they could take possesion of them.[85]

Yet in the ranks of German officialdom, particularly in the foreign office, there was considerable anti-kolkhoz sentiment. They were anxious, for political reasons, to capitalize on the antagonism of the Ukrainian and Russian peasants toward the collective system and to enlist their collaboration.[86] With mounting evidence of the hostility of the native population to the collectives, the anti-kolkhoz stand also gained adherents in high army circles. A controversy developed and the result was a compromise, embodied in the so-called New Agrarian Order, an edict signed on February 15, 1942, and published on February 26 together with a proclamation by the Minister of Soviet Occupied Territories, Alfred Rosenberg.[87] The edict provided for a gradual and limited transition from collective to individual farming. All Soviet law on collective farming was declared null and void, and the kolkhozes were to be replaced by communal farms (*Gemeinwirtschaft*). The principal differences between the kolkhoz and the communal farm were: no restriction on individual ownership of livestock by members of communal farms (of no great practical significance during the period of wartime requisitions); and permission to enlarge the household garden plots to an extent that would not interfere with the work of farmers within each communal farm. Such plots were to become the private property of the farmers and exempt from taxation.

The communal farms, like the kolkhozes, were subject to compulsory delivery quotas. The farm managers were to be responsible for the timely fulfillment of the quotas. The edict also confirmed the ownership by the German administration of the MTS and state farms. Thus far, the insitutional structure prescribed by the New Agrarian Order did not deviate much from the Soviet model. But the reform provided for a kind of hybrid between collective and individual farming by the conversion of the communal farms into farmers' cooperatives, with special permission in each case from the German authorities. This was to be coincidental with allotment of strip holdings to the individual farmers. Under such a system plowing and seeding were to be done jointly, in accordance with a common crop plan for the cooperative. But further care and harvesting of the crops was to be left to individual farmers on permanent plots in each field. The third type of land tenure provided by the edict of February 15 was the allotment of consolidated tracts of land to deserving farmers who collaborated with the German authorities, a repetition of one of Stolypin's experiments; this dispensed with the common cultivation stage. An adequate supply of draft power and implements was requisite for such a complete transition to individual farming, again out of the question in wartime. The whole procedure appears very complex and unrealistic.

The results of this agrarian "reform" were meager. It is true that all kolkhozes were renamed communal farms; but their transformation into farming cooperatives proceeded at a slow pace. Approximately two thousand kolkhozes were converted into cooperatives in the Ukraine during the occupation.[88] This was less than 10 percent of the total number of kolkhozes. But a number of large kolkhozes were split into smaller units, usually ten households, which continued to be operated as collective farms. There the process of dissolution stopped. Outside of the Ukraine, in the northern and central occupied regions, the process of decollectivization proceeded more speedily, skipping the intermediate stage of farming cooperatives. These regions are characterized by a heterogeneous terrain, criss-crossed by forests, bushland, marshes, and lakes, which is much less favorable to large farm units than are the level southern steppes. As a deficit area it was, unlike the Ukrainian breadbasket, of no great agricultural significance to the Nazis, and the question of land tenure was left to the discretion of the local German authorities and the army command. Another occupied area where the dissolution of kolkhozes was pushed for political reasons was the North Caucasus, particularly the mountainous regions, inhabited by non-Russian tribes. It is also true that the prohibition of unauthorized division of land by the 1942 edict was not always observed in villages remote from cities and railroads, where German control was light.[89]

By the summer of 1943, even the top Nazi leadership had discovered that the dictum of Arthur Young, "the magic of property turns sand into gold," could apply also to Russia. A proclamation issued by Rosenberg on June 3, 1943, promised full property rights in land to the Russian peasantry.[90] But it was too late. The tide had already turned against the Nazis, and the occupation was soon to end. The pro-kolkhoz stand of the Nazis was one ingredient in a policy which also included merciless requisitions of foodstuffs and livestock, deportation for forced labor in Germany, and inhuman treatment of the native population. What emerges clearly is that the preservation by the Nazis of the institutional matrix of collective farming played right into Communist hands. It not only aroused or increased the resentment of the peasants against the occupiers, but also made it easier for the Soviet government to restore the status quo ante.

Here an analogy with the Napoleonic war of 1812 comes to mind. Napoleon, it will be recalled, did not touch serfdom and it continued unabated for the next fifty years. Whether Napoleon and Hitler would have been more successful in their invasions if they tried to satisfy the aspirations of the Russian peasant and evoke his cooperation, whether, in fact, the peasant response would have been greatly different, is one of those speculations that defies an answer. Perhaps only Napoleon had an alternative; Hitler did not because of his hatred and contempt for the *Untermensch.*

A large area of the invaded zone was laid waste by the fighting and by the scorched-earth practices of the retreating forces. Thus one American war correspondent reported: "Although the country around Kharkov is among the richest agricultural countries of the Ukraine, the town was left by the Germans in a state of economic chaos, and organization for at least the initial period of food-supply services into Kharkov by army authorities is essential." [91] Another correspondent wrote on a visit to the Ukrainian front: "The Ukraine, once the 'breadbasket' of Russia, is a semi-wilderness. Almost 50 percent of its rich black earth lies fallow. One of Russia's most mechanized agricultural areas before the war, the Ukraine, now has been reduced to the most primitive methods of cultivation. Women and children wander barefoot over the parched earth, foraging for food. The scars of war are everywhere. Villages are masses of rubble. Wrecks of trucks, tanks and guns litter the landscape. During a trip lasting several days I could count on the fingers of my hand the number of intact farmhouses seen in the area, where rivers once flowed peacefully through rich cherry and apple orchards and sunflower and wheat farms immortalized in Russian literature." [92]

Not all of the invaded zone was subjected to so severe a physical devastation, but much of it was. Tremendous losses were inflicted on livestock and farm machinery in the occupied zone. It was claimed that 7 million horses out of 12 million, 17 million cattle out of 31 million, 20 million hogs, 27 million sheep and goats, and 110 million poultry were slaughtered or taken to Germany. There were destroyed or damaged 111,800 tractors out of 191,700; 44,800 combines out of 63,500; and 10,500 trucks out of 16,100.[93] Numerous MTS and state-farm buildings, including repair shops and research facilities, were ruined. Crop acreages and yields drastically declined. Such was the somber agricultural scene in the large area that suffered the bitter experience of Nazi invasion.

And what of the invaders? As stated, the control of Russian agricultural resources as a means of securing Germany's food supply was a highly important goal of Nazi policy. To exploit the food potentialities of the occupied territory, following the devastation caused by fighting and burning, considerable investment by Germany was necessary in agricultural reconstruction. The main item was farm machinery. Up to March 31, 1944, almost 15,000 carloads of farm machinery were shipped from Germany to occupied Russia, including 7,146 tractors and 20,110 wood-gas generators to convert Soviet tractors to the use of wood as fuel. A variety of farm implements, as well as pesticides, breeding stock, and machinery for the damaged food-processing industry, were shipped from Germany.[94] But the occupation regime did not last long enough, especially in the fertile areas of the Ukraine and the North Caucasus, for the reconstruction process to bear much fruit. On the other hand, the Russians were denied any benefits from it because of the destruction left behind by the Germans in their turn.

With the exception of oilseeds, Germany itself obtained relatively little food from occupied Russia. Between midyear 1941 and 1944, some 684,000 tons of oilseeds, or 220,000 tons in terms of vegetable oil, were shipped to the Reich from occupied Soviet territory. Konrad Brandt points out that "this contribution to the German fat balance was undoubtedly the most valuable achievement in respect to the German food economy. Yet per annum it meant only slightly more than 70,000 tons of fat vis-à-vis a peacetime requirement of 2 million tons in the Reich." Net imports of 1.2 million tons of grain in almost three years was not a very significant addition to the German grain supply, when the total annual German grain crop during the war amounted to 23 to 24 million tons. Other food shipments were insignificant. Yet such highly competent authorities as Brandt and his associates conclude that "the fact that Germany could pass through World War II without a food catastrophe was due in part to the utilization of the agricultural resources of the occupied Soviet territories. The most important credit item on the food ledger of the Soviet territories was the major part of the food supplies for the German eastern army of 4 to 6 million men. Considering the high rations of the Wehrmacht, the food for these millions of priority consumers represented an item of such size in the German food-balance sheet that its supply from domestic Reich sources would promptly have created a major calamity." [95] Thus the occupiers, able to live off the invaded country, helped their own domestic economy and fared much better than their Napoleonic precursors.

13

Postwar Recovery

With two exceptions, every major war in which Russia was engaged during the nineteenth and early twentieth centuries brought in its train a significant modification in agrarian structure, usually involving concessions to the peasantry. Thus the Crimean campaign of 1854–55 was followed by the abolition of serfdom, and the Russo-Japanese War of 1904–05 by serious agrarian disturbances and the Stolypin laws that radically altered land tenure. The first war with Germany led to the agrarian revolution of 1917 and the liquidation of landlordism. The civil war following the Bolshevik revolution ended with the NEP. But World War II, like the Napoleonic struggle, ended without much change in the agrarian order. The status quo ante bellum was to be restored in its entirety. As soon as the Germans were driven out, all organizational deviations from the standard Soviet pattern were promptly redressed.

In the annexed Baltic, former Polish and Rumanian territories reconquered from the Germans, forced collectivization of peasant agriculture was pushed through, spurred on by mass deportations of peasants who were considered hostile. The Communist "land reform" enacted at the beginning of the Soviet occupation, which took place in 1939 and 1940, was a prelude to collectivization in these regions. It provided for limitation in the size of farms (most of which were already moderate or small) and distribution of the "excess" land among landless peasants and smallholders. Some of the divided farms were too small to be economically viable, but this suited the Communists, since it made collectivization more plausible. The speed of the collectivization process, once underway, may be illustrated by the experience of Lithuania, which at the beginning of 1948 had only about 20 kolkhozes; the peasants were reluctant to join. However, following a big deportation operation in May, the number of kolkhozes increased to 250 in July, according to *Izvestiia* on July 22, 1948. Three years later it was officially reported that 92 percent of the Lithuanian peasants had joined collective farms.[1] Yet the Russians were not able to completely eradicate that symbol of peasant individualism, the separate farmstead (khutor), which was especially prominent in the Baltic states and which had long been a thorn in the Communist side.

Along with the extension of collectivization into the newly acquired colonial empire, there was a crackdown on the expanded private sector closer to home. This was one of the principal aims of the decree of September 19, 1946, the first significant postwar agricultural legislation, entitled "Measures for the Liquidation of Violations of the Kolkhoz Charter."[2] It stated that the previous decree of May 27, 1939, dealing with the safeguarding of kolkhoz land against illegal use, had been "forgotten" by officials and that "squandering" of kolkhoz land had again assumed massive proportions. That it was also "forgotten" during the war by the central government was not mentioned. The September 1946 decree specified the following instances of squandering: increases in the kolkhozniks' kitchen-garden plots and use of kolkhoz land for establishing farms by various institutions and enterprises as well as for the kitchen gardens of city workers (which the Soviet government had been so anxious to foster during the war).

This decree ordered the strict enforcement of the law of May 27, 1939, requiring that the narrow limits imposed by the kolkhoz charter on the size of kolkhozniks' garden plots be strictly observed. A survey of land use in each kolkhoz was to be completed by November 15, 1946, and the prescribed documentation and registration of land in kolkhozes was to be restored. All land found to be held illegally by individuals or institutions was to be returned to the kolkhozes. The fact that they might not be in a position to use the land productively was immaterial. In fact, the September 1946 decree repealed a provision of a wartime law of April 7, 1942, which permitted republics and provincial authorities to authorize industrial enterprises and army contingents to farm temporarily unused land of the kolkhozes, "with their consent," when there was no free municipal or state land available for growing food. All land thus used was to be returned. The September 1946 decree also aimed to stop the increased misappropriation of other kolkhoz property.

With conversion to a peacetime basis, the private household sector was once more destined for curtailment; the campaign for strict limitation in the size of private plots, initiated in May 1939, was resumed. Altogether about 14.5 million acres of land were returned to kolkhozes, or more than twice as much as during the similar campaign in 1939–40.[3] With a considerable portion of this land near cities, it was of some significance, even though the area was small in relation to total sown acreage. The land recovered from kolkhozniks was a small proportion of the area returned. According to preliminary data reported by Minister of Agriculture Andreev to the February 1947 session of the Central Committee, published in the Moscow press on March 7, 1947, only 1.3 million out of nearly 12 million acres of land returned was recovered from kolkhozniks. However, it was not this small area of land that concerned the Kremlin, but rather the fear of its divisive effect on collective agriculture.

The September 1946 decree also addressed itself to the problem of tightening up the administrative control over farming. For this purpose a new high-ranking agency was created, with wide powers, the Council of Kolkhoz Affairs. Almost nothing has appeared in Soviet published sources about the functioning of this agency during its relatively short lifetime. It was quietly abolished in 1953, shortly after Stalin's death.[4] The September 1946 decree made it clear that the central target of Soviet postwar agrarian policy was the full restoration of the prewar pattern of collective agriculture. This was confirmed a few months later by another lengthy decree passed by the Central Committee, following the comprehensive report by Andreev in February 1947.[5]

Slow Agricultural Recovery

Although it was easy for the Kremlin to order a return in terms of organization, the recovery of agricultural production was another matter. In 1945, which may be considered a transitional year between war and peace, the total sown area was nearly one fourth below that of 1940. The acreages of some valuable crops had declined even more; wheat, 38 percent; sugar beets, 30 percent; cotton, 41 percent; and flax fiber, 52 percent. The decline was less sharp for some food crops of mass consumption, such as rye, millet, and buckwheat; and the acreage had increased for potatoes and vegetables, which the whole population was encouraged to grow in wartime. (See Tables 34 and 35.) Crop yields also declined; and

Table 34. Acreage under crops in farms of all categories in selected years (million acres)

Crop	1940	1945	1950	1953	1956	1959	1960
Winter wheat	35.3	22.2	30.8	44.0	31.9	43.0	29.9
Spring wheat	64.2	39.3	64.2	75.4	121.3	112.6	119.3
All wheat	99.5	61.5	95.0	119.4	153.2	155.6	149.2
Winter rye	57.1	50.2	58.3	50.2	45.5	42.2	n.a.
Winter barley	2.0	—	1.1	1.0	1.6	3.4	n.a.
Spring barley	25.9	10.4	20.1	22.7	27.7	20.4	n.a.
All barley	27.9	10.4	21.2	23.7	29.3	23.8	n.a.
Oats	50.0	35.6	40.0	37.8	37.3	35.4	n.a.
Corn for grain	9.0	10.4	11.9	8.6	23.0	21.5	27.7
Millet	14.8	14.6	9.4	10.1	15.8	6.7	n.a.
Buckwheat	4.9	4.4	7.4	6.4	6.7	3.3	n.a.
Rice	.4	.5	.3	.3	.4	.2	n.a.
Legumes	5.9	3.7	4.9	4.0	3.2	2.6	n.a.
Other grain	3.5	19.5	5.8	3.2	2.6	4.4	n.a.
Total grain	273.0	210.8	254.2	263.7	317.0	295.7	300.7
Sugar beet (factory)	3.0	2.1	3.2	3.9	5.0	6.8	7.5
Cotton	5.1	3.0	5.7	4.6	5.1	5.3	5.4
Flax (fiber)	5.2	2.5	4.7	3.1	4.7	4.0	4.0
Flax (seed)	.9	.5	.9	1.1	1.2	.6	n.a.
Sunflower	8.7	7.2	8.9	9.6	11.1	9.6	10.4
Hemp	1.5	.7	1.4	1.3	1.5	.9	n.a.
Tobacco	.2	.2	.3	.3	.3	.2	n.a.
Makhorka	.3	.3	.3	.3	.2	.1	n.a.
Potatoes	19.0	20.5	21.1	20.5	22.7	23.6	22.5
Vegetables	3.7	4.4	3.2	4.0	—	3.6	n.a.
Corn for green feed and silage	—	—	—	—	36.1	33.9	42.0
Other fodder crops	44.7	25.2	51.2	70.9	67.0	96.1	98.8
Other crops	6.4	3.8	6.4	5.1	9.2	4.7	n.a.
Total sown area	371.7	281.2	361.5	388.4	481.1	485.1	501.6

Source. *Sel'skoe khoziaistvo SSSR, 1960*, p. 133, and *SSSR v tsifrakh 1960*, pp. 176–179.

Table 35. Index of acreage under crops in farms of all categories in selected years (1940=100)

Crop	1945	1950	1953	1956	1959	1960
Winter wheat	62.9	87.2	124.6	90.4	121.8	84.7
Spring wheat	61.2	100.0	117.4	188.9	175.4	185.8
All wheat	61.8	95.5	120.0	154.0	156.4	149.9
Winter rye	87.9	102.1	87.9	79.7	73.9	n.a.
Winter barley	—	55.0	50.0	80.0	170.0	n.a.
Spring barley	40.2	77.6	87.6	106.9	78.8	n.a.
All barley	37.3	76.0	84.9	105.0	85.3	n.a.
Oats	71.2	80.0	75.6	74.6	70.8	n.a.
Corn for grain	115.6	132.2	95.6	255.6	238.9	307.8
Millet	98.6	63.5	68.2	106.8	45.3	n.a.
Buckwheat	89.8	151.0	130.6	136.7	67.3	n.a.
Rice	125.0	75.0	75.0	100.7	50.0	n.a.
Legumes	62.7	83.1	67.8	54.2	44.1	n.a.
Other grain	557.1	165.7	91.4	74.3	125.7	n.a.
Total grain	77.2	93.1	96.6	116.1	108.3	110.1
Sugar beet (factory)	70.0	106.7	130.0	166.7	226.7	250.0
Cotton	58.8	111.8	90.2	100.0	103.9	105.9
Flax (fiber)	48.1	90.4	59.6	90.4	76.9	76.9
Flax (seed)	55.6	100.0	122.2	133.3	66.7	n.a.
Sunflower	82.8	102.3	110.3	127.6	110.3	119.5
Hemp	46.7	93.3	86.7	100.0	60.0	n.a.
Tobacco	100.0	150.0	150.0	150.0	100.0	n.a.
Makhorka	100.0	100.0	100.0	66.7	33.3	n.a.
Potatoes	107.9	111.1	107.9	119.5	124.2	118.4
Vegetables	118.9	86.5	108.1	—	97.3	n.a.
Corn for green feed and silage	—	—	—	—	—	n.a.
Other fodder crops	56.4	114.5	158.6	149.9	215.0	221.0
Other crops	59.4	100.0	79.7	143.8	73.4	n.a.
Total sown area	75.7	97.3	104.5	129.4	130.5	134.9

Source. *Sel'skoe khoziaistvo SSSR, 1960*, p. 133, and *SSSR v tsifrakh 1960*, pp. 176–179.

under the combined downward pull of these two factors, production dropped sharply, as shown by the following tabulation (in million metric tons).[6]

	1940	1945
Wheat	31.7	13.4
All grains	95.5	47.3
Potatoes	75.9	58.3
Vegetables	13.7	10.3
Sugar beets	18.0	5.5
Oilseeds	3.22	1.0
Flax fiber	0.349	0.15
Unginned (seed) cotton	2.24	1.16

Total grain production in 1945 was less than half of the 1940 figure and the output of oilseeds and sugar beets, less than a third. Even potatoes, despite the increase in acreage, showed a decline of nearly a fourth. Livestock numbers also sharply declined, nullifying the laborious advance made after the collectivization catastrophe. The reduction was especially drastic in hog numbers—more than two thirds less at the beginning of 1945 than in 1941. The number of cows decreased by more than a fifth and the number of sheep by more than a fourth. (See Tables 36 and 37.) Total agricultural production declined between 1940 and 1945 by 40 percent, crop output by 43 percent, and livestock output by 36 percent, according to Soviet estimates.[7]

There was also great deterioration in the capital-technical base of Soviet agriculture: tractors, farm implements, trucks, and buildings. Between the end of 1940 and 1945, the number of tractors decreased from

Table 36. Livestock numbers (*million head*)

Year (January 1)	Cows	All cattle	Hogs	Sheep	Goats	Horses
1941	27.8	54.5	27.5	79.9	11.7	21.0
1945	21.6	44.2	8.8	57.9	12.3	9.9
1946	22.9	47.6	10.6	58.5	11.5	10.7
1950	24.6	58.1	22.2	77.6	16.0	12.7
1952	24.9	58.8	27.1	90.5	17.1	14.7
1953	24.3	56.6	28.5	94.3	15.6	15.3

Source. *Zhivotnovodstvo SSSR, 1959,* p. 23.

Table 37. Index of livestock numbers, specified years (1941 = 100)

Year (January 1)	Cows	All cattle	Hogs	Sheep	Goats	Horses
1945	77.7	81.1	32.0	72.5	105.1	47.1
1946	82.4	87.3	38.5	73.2	98.3	51.0
1950	88.5	106.6	80.7	97.1	136.8	60.5
1952	89.6	107.9	98.5	113.3	146.2	70.0
1953	87.4	103.9	103.6	118.0	133.3	72.9

Source. *Zhivotnovodstvo SSSR, 1959*, p. 23.

531,000 to 397,000; combines from 182,000 to 148,000; and trucks from 228,000 to 62,000.[8] In percentages, the reduction was 25 percent for tractors, 19 percent for combines, and 78 percent for trucks. Many of the tractors were worn out and actually unfit for use. The draft-power situation was further aggravated by the fact that the number of horses, already 42 percent smaller at the end of 1940 than in 1928, had decreased again by more than a half by the end of the war. Combined draft power—tractor and animal—went down from 40.1 million horsepower at the end of 1940 to 22.6 million at the end of 1945.[9] The 1946 figure is, no doubt, overstated in view of the operational unfitness of many tractors recorded in the inventory. The situation was more or less similar for other farm implements. Production of mineral fertilizers dropped from the prewar peak of 772,900 metric tons in 1939 to 253,100 tons in 1945, with adverse effects on yields of such intensive crops as cotton, sugar beets, and flax.[10] Reduction of livestock numbers led also to a seriously diminished supply of manure, which was the chief cause of low yields in the central and northern regions.

That massive capital investment was required to speed up agricultural recovery needs no elaborate demonstration. Furthermore, there was no longer an abundance of labor in the countryside which could be substituted for capital. The war, in this respect, served as a real watershed between two eras. True, the extreme labor shortage of the war years passed, but huge war losses, coupled with growing manpower requirements of industry, curtailed the supply of farm labor. No longer could the regime rely so heavily on a massive input of labor from the overpopulated Russian village to achieve its production goals, as it had in the 1930s. But only after the end of the Stalin era did this begin to be fully understood by the leadership. To Stalin the most urgent objective at the end of the war, as in the 1930s, was the reconstruction and continued rapid growth of heavy industry. Consequently, the postwar Five-Year Plan, 1946–1950, gave to this task, and to the reconstruction of the railway network, the highest priority and the lion's share of capital investment.[11]

Stalin's emphasis on that hoary doctrine of "capitalist encirclement" of the USSR in his only significant postwar speech (February 1946) revealed his continued adherence to superindustrialization—this despite the radical change in the international balance of power. Russia's former adversaries were now either prostrate or greatly weakened, and the country was to become one of the two great powers of the world, validating De Toqueville's prophecy of a hundred years earlier about the ascendancy of America and Russia on the world scene. Stalin was still unmoved by the yearning of the Soviet masses for a better life after so many years of hardship and privation. And again agriculture had to play second fiddle to industrialization, with underproduction the inexorable outcome.

During 1946–1950 investment in agriculture by the government amounted to 2,673 million rubles, and by the government and kolkhozes together, to 5,788 million. These totals may be compared with 15,084 million invested in heavy industry and 4,945 million in transportation. The consumer-good industry was allocated only 2,080 million rubles of state investment.[12] This disparity illustrates the secondary role of agriculture in Stalin's scheme of things. The upshot was a very slow increase in technical equipment in agriculture, especially when compared with the United States, as the following figures show (in thousands).[13]

	USSR		United States	
	End of 1940	End of 1950	End of 1940	End of 1950
Tractors	531	595	1,665	3,678
Combines	182	211	225	810
Trucks	228	283	1,095	2,310

On this basis there were more than 600 acres of sown land per tractor in the Soviet Union in 1950, compared with less than 100 acres in the United States. The relationship was even more unfavorable to the Soviet Union because the 1950 official figure on tractors appears overstated, since a considerable proportion was of prewar vintage and of doubtful operating fitness. With about 300,000 new tractors manufactured during the years 1946–1950,[14] the real working inventory probably had not exceeded 400,000 and may not have even reached that figure. Perhaps there were more tractors than essential in the United States, but the Russians clearly had too few. The tractor situation, which may be considered the keystone of farm technological progress, indicates the slow rate of development of Soviet agriculture during the postwar reconstruction period.

Passing on to the human factor, I have already pointed out that labor abundance was a casualty of the war. What is worse, there was no improvement but rather a deterioration in the incentives for peasants to work hard and efficiently. The appeal to patriotic sentiments, which no doubt had some influence during the war, especially after the vicious abuses by the Nazis in occupied regions became known, were no longer effective in peacetime. And it did not help matters that the peasants were disappointed in their hopes for concessions on the part of the regime. That economic incentives were grossly inadequate during this period was stressed time and again after Stalin's death by his successors. Prices paid by government for compulsory grain deliveries increased insignificantly, and prices of potatoes and meat even decreased from prewar levels. The situation was more favorable to the producers of milk and industrial crops (see Table 38). As a Soviet economist writing in 1958 put it: "The procurement prices for a number of important products which existed prior to 1953 were low. They did not cover production costs of kolkhozes and did not secure the minimum conditions necessary for the development of the collective economy." [15] In the same year another Soviet economist said: "Because low procurement prices for a number of the most important products did not recoup the labor and material expenditures of kolkhozes, and consequently did not secure the minimal conditions for the development of the collective economy, serious and

Table 38. Average procurement prices (rubles per metric ton)

	1937	1950	Percent 1950 is of 1937
Grain [a]	88	91	103.4
Potatoes	53	40	75.5
Meat (live weight)	950	700	73.7
Milk (including milk products converted to milk equivalent)	240	300	125.0
Sugar beets	44	110	250.0
Cotton, unginned	1,570	3,600	229.3
Flax fiber	1,050	4,423	421.2

[a] Estimated.

Source. Nancy Nimitz, "Soviet Agriculture and Costs," in *Comparisons of the United States and Soviet Economies* (U.S. Congress, Joint Economic Committee; Washington, D.C., 1959); based, with minor adjustments, on J. Karcz, *Soviet Agricultural Marketing and Prices* (RAND Corporation, Santa Monica, July 2, 1957).

prolonged retardation occurred in a number of branches of agricultural production." [16]

Another facet of the postwar procurement situation was the elimination of higher prices paid by the government for purchases of grain above the delivery quotas. Such payments were sharply curtailed for a number of other products as well. There were other onerous features in the procurement system. One was that higher quotas for meat and milk deliveries per hectare were set up for districts and kolkhozes which managed to develop husbandry, even though natural conditions did not differ from those in other districts and kolkhozes failing to do so. As a consequence, kolkhozes achieving high livestock production were penalized, contrary to the original underlying principle of the quota system based on land area.[17] The above, of course, was not the Soviet evaluation of the procurement system while Stalin was alive. But it became standard under his successors, especially after Khrushchev's secret speech in February 1956.

Data are lacking for determining the precise relationship between the prices paid by farmers for products bought and the prices they received for products sold. But we do know that, while procurement prices of important farm products were kept at a very low level, other prices soared during the wartime and postwar inflation. The index of retail prices (including foodstuffs) in state and cooperative stores in the last quarter of 1947, prior to a deflationary currency reform, was more than five and a half times higher than in 1937; in 1950 they were still nearly four times as high as in 1937.[18] The index of retail prices of manufactured consumer goods in state stores in Moscow in 1948 was about three times higher than in 1937; in 1952, after several successive reductions, it was still more than double.[19] These pronounced upward movements, which may be considered indicative of national price-level changes, point unmistakably to a wider spread between the two blades of the scissors, to a further worsening of the terms of trade between agriculture and industry.

One important exception favorable to agriculture was the skyrocketing of prices in the collective-farm market. During the last quarter of 1947, collective-farm market prices were 16.5 times higher than in 1937; in 1948 they were nearly six times and, in 1950, four times higher.[20] The physical volume of sales on the collective market (excluding intravillage trade) increased 63 percent between 1940 and 1950, according to Soviet estimates.[21] Receipts by kolkhozes, kolkhozniks, and other smallholders from such trade greatly exceeded government payments for the products. In 1952, the year for which the data on both items are available, government payments amounted to about 27 billion rubles, and collective-farm sales to 53.7 billion rubles.[22] Because of the collective market sales, the average realized prices were higher than procurement prices. But the collective-farm market trade puts a premium on location. It favors those kolkhozes near the cities and, conversely, discriminates against the more remote kolkhozes to which the cities are not easily accessible without time-consuming trips. This applies especially to kolkhozniks who are not permitted individually to own horses and trucks. (Both kolkhozes as institutions and kolkhozniks as individuals can trade on the private market.) The number of kolkhozes and kolkhozniks who in those lean years had little or nothing to sell on the private market must have been large. Thus the benefits of trading on the private market were spread much more unevenly among producers than were the disadvantages of the procurement system.

At any rate, the impact on the collective sector of the large government procurements at very low prices produced the familiar vicious circle, characteristic of Soviet agriculture. It reduced the capacity of kolkhozes to pay their members adequately which, in turn, depressed their incentive to work in kolkhoz fields and barns and impelled them to concentrate on their own household farming. This had a further adverse effect on collective production and the ability of the kolkhozes to remunerate labor—and so it went on, in spiral-like fashion. "The work of most kolkhozniks," said Khrushchev of this period many years later, "practically was not compensated. For instance, cash distributed per workday in 1952 was 1 kopeck in the Kaluga and Tula provinces; 2 kopecks in the Riazan and Lipetzk provinces; 3 kopecks in Briansk and Pskov provinces; and 4 kopecks in the Kostroma and Kursk provinces. Many kolkhozes for years had not distributed a single kopeck." [23] While payments in kind predominated in the earnings of kolkhozniks, no systematic data were published for the postwar Stalin period. But Khrushchev gave the earnings of kolkhozniks, in kind and in cash, for the one year, 1952. They averaged only 1,827 rubles per kolkhoznik per year.[24] This may be compared with an average wage of all hired workers ("workers and employees") officially reported for 1950, at 7,668 rubles and, with fringe benefits, at 9,888 rubles.[25] It should be noted that 1952 was a good harvest year; earnings were doubtless lower during poor harvests. There were considerable deviations from the average as a result of differing economic and natural conditions, apart from variations in the amount of time worked and the occupation of the worker. A farm survey in the Moscow province revealed variations in the average kolkhoznik's yearly earnings in 1952 from 338 rubles in the lowest group to 1,798 rubles in the highest group.[26] Under such conditions the kolkhozniks had to rely heavily on their household plots and livestock, the collective-farm market, and non-farm earnings wherever possible, to make ends meet. Yet the income of kolkhozniks from their personal farming was subject to burdensome taxation. This was officially admitted when the post-Stalin agricultural tax reform was announced.[27]

To complete this account, still another item must be added to the debit side of the ledger: the sharp deflationary effect of the currency reform of December 1947. The reform, directed against wartime inflation, called in and exchanged all outstanding ruble notes at a ratio of 10 old to 1 new ruble. But savings-bank deposits and bonds were exchanged at a more favorable rate than cash holdings. This discriminated mainly against those peasants who had accumulated rubles from sales at high prices on the collective-farm market during the war, money they were not able to spend because of the lack of manufactured goods.

Stalin's Production Program

Granted, then, that the Stalin administration had in practice neglected, with the exception of some industrial crops, economic incentives as a spur to agricultural production; granted that it was primarily concerned with heavy industry. Does this also mean that it was not interested in expanding agricultural production? Such is the impression given by Khrushchev's strong indictment of Stalin's leadership in agricultural affairs in his de-Stalinization speech:

> All those who interested themselves even a little in the national situation saw the difficult situation in agriculture, but Stalin never even noted it. Did we tell Stalin about this? Yes, we told him, but he did not support us. Why? Because Stalin never traveled anywhere, did not meet city and *kolkhoz* workers; he did not know the actual situation in the province.
>
> He knew the country and agriculture only from films. And these films had been dressed up and beautified the existing situation in agriculture. Many films so pictured *kolkhoz* life that the tables were bending from the weight of turkeys and geese. Evidently, Stalin thought that it was actually so.
>
> Vladimir Il'ich Lenin looked at life differently; he was always close to the people; he used to receive peasant delegates and often spoke at factory gatherings; he used to visit villages and talk with the peasants . . .
>
> And when he was once told during a discussion that our situation on the land was a difficult one and that the situation of cattle breeding and meat production was especially bad, a commission was formed

which was charged with the preparation of a resolution called "Means toward further development of animal breeding in *kolkhozes* and *sovkhozes*." We worked out this project.

Of course, our proposals of that time did not contain all possibilities, but we did chart ways in which animal breeding on *kolkhozes* and *sovkhozes* would be raised. We had proposed then to raise the prices of such products in order to create material incentives for the *kolkhoz*, MTS and *sovkhoz* workers in the development of cattle breeding. But our project was not accepted and in February 1953 was laid aside entirely.

What is more, while reviewing this project Stalin proposed that the taxes paid by the *kolkhozes* and by the *kolkhoz* workers should be raised by 40 billion rubles; according to him the peasants are well off and the *kolkhoz* worker would need to sell only one more chicken to pay his tax in full.

Imagine what this meant. Certainly, 40 billion rubles is a sum which the *kolkhoz* workers did not realize for all the products which they sold to the Government. In 1952, for instance, the *kolkhozes* and the *kolkhoz* workers received 26,280 million rubles for all their products delivered and sold to the Government . . . the proposal was not based on an actual assessment of the situation but on the fantastic ideas of a person divorced from reality.[28]

Thus Khrushchev accuses Stalin of a highly unrealistic attitude toward the agricultural problem, born of ignorance and combined with stubbornness, high-handedness, and arbitrariness. Khrushchev did not say, however, that these qualities had characterized much of Stalin's agricultural policy since the beginning of mass collectivization, though he probably was right that Stalin's actions during his last years showed an increased irrationality. Yet Stalin also had a positive program for the expansion of agricultural production after the war. It had two facets. One was the supposedly new "agrotechnique," or improved farm practices in accordance with what was considered the last word in agricultural science. This was incorporated into the grandiose "Stalin Plan for Transforming Nature," approved on October 20, 1948.[29] Beneficial effects on crop yields in the vast subhumid area, with its frequent droughts, were expected from the adoption of the scheme. It harmonized with the goal of the postwar five-year plan to increase production primarily through higher yields. The other facet of the program was the enlargement of the kolkhozes into supercollectives through widespread mergers, aiming thereby to increase their efficiency.

The agrotechnique part of Stalin's program was associated with the names of the two men from whom it received its theoretical inspiration: V. R. Williams and T. D. Lysenko. Williams (1863–1939), the son of an American engineer who came to Russia as a builder of railways, became a soil scientist and a professor at the Timiriazev Agricultural Academy in Moscow. He had long been a critic of the dominant Russian school of soil science, whose brilliant achievements had made it world famous. Williams' own scholarly reputation in the profession was not high. One American soil scientist wrote that "he was not a systematic experimenter and in his voluminous writings one can hardly find data based on his work." [30] After the Revolution Williams joined the Communist Party and his authority soared, especially after collectivization. In the 1930s he was one of the chief pillars of the official agricultural science.

The nub of Williams' agrotechnical recommendation was the incorporation of a sod or grass crop in rotation, which in itself was nothing new. The planting of a grass crop, principally clover, had come into use in the peasant farming of the northwestern and north central districts of Russia at the beginning of the present century. Grass, mostly clover, was grown to augment the forage supply for livestock, which was essential for farming in these regions, since crops could not be grown on the poor soils without the use of manure. Moreover, clover is an important source of nitrogen both directly by the ability to fix it from the air and indirectly by enriching the manure of the animals to which it is fed. The value of clover is enhanced when there is a shortage or lack of mineral fertilizer, as was the case in Russia and in Western Europe in the early nineteenth century. The introduction of grasses, it will be recalled, was an achievement of zemstvo agronomy, of which it was justly proud. The novel feature of Williams' proposal was his emphasis on the universal adoption of grass in rotation as a crop to improve soil structure. He insisted that, in order to have the best effect on the soil, the sod crop must consist of a mixture of legumes and perennial grasses, and this principle was incorporated as a must in the official program under the name of grass rotation (*travopol'nyi sevooborot*).

The use of a mixture of grass and legumes in the cropping system conforms to practices recommended in the United States: "Grass and legumes in rotation improve the structure of the soil by making it more granular and thus increasing its ability to absorb water. Residues from grass and legumes that are returned to the soil as green manure increase organic matter and nitrogen in the soil." [31] But the universal applicability of Williams' rotation scheme, particularly in the subhumid regions, is another story. It was not supported by so outstanding an agronomic authority as D. N. Prianishnikov, who had long been concerned about the low yields of crops in Russia. He advocated various forms of crop rotation, with or without grasses, as well as other means of raising productivity. Prianishnikov stressed the increased use of mineral fertilizers and organic matter, barn and green manure, which Williams did not consider important.[32] This had been, as Prianishnikov pointed out, the road to high yields in Western Europe after the middle of the last century.[33] In 1951 I wrote of the Williams scheme: "It seems questionable, in the light of the practice in the United States, that grass should be introduced into rotation in regions where moisture is a limiting factor, as had been prescribed by the Soviet government. It was stated, for instance, by an American authority [C. E. Leighty] that in dry land regions, 'sod crops, an integral part of rotation practice in humid and sub-humid areas, are unsuitable for short rotations, because of the dry condition in which they leave the soil, and their value in deferred rotations is still to be determined.' " [34]

To the Soviet leadership the Williams program was very attractive, since it had the imprimatur of a bona fide scientist and did not involve a large additional expenditure of resources, as the more extensive input of fertilizer certainly would have. And so the Kremlin plumped for Williams' approach. The acreage under grasses increased between 1940 and 1953 by over 20 million acres, or more than 50 percent, and its share in total crop acreage went from 10 to 14.8 percent. But grain acreage declined during the period by 9.5 million acres, and the yields of grain and grasses remained low. This perpetuated the problem of underproduction, which Stalin passed on to his successors to wrestle with. But one of Williams' dogmas was challenged during Stalin's lifetime, by none other than Lysenko. It became evident to the Kremlin that Williams' negative attitude toward the growing of winter (fall-sown) grains clashed with the government's objective of expanding grain production, to which the high-yielding winter wheat and rye varieties could contribute substantially. In so important a wheat region as the Ukraine, winter varieties were being replaced by the lower-yielding spring wheat. When this incredible error was recognized, Williams' doctrine had to be repudiated, though without completely discrediting his authority. This was the mission that Lysenko undertook to perform by his article in *Pravda*, July 15, 1950.[35]

Lysenko was at the zenith of his power in 1950, when he was exposing Williams' errors. Shortly before this, with Stalin's blessing, he became the virtual dictator of Soviet biological and agricultural science. After suffering a temporary setback upon Stalin's death, Lysenko continued to wield considerable influence under Khrushchev's patronage, though without the monolithic power of the earlier days. It was the downfall of Khrushchev which at last brought about the eclipse of Lysenko and Lysenkoism. I am reserving for a later chapter a more detailed tracing of the negative role of Lysenkoism in agricultural development. Suffice it to say here that its detrimental effect on scientific research, on which agricultural progress and increased productivity so greatly depends, was substantial. Certainly during the late Stalin period an alliance with genuine agrobiological sciences was spurned by the regime, enticed by the Lysenkoist pie-in-the-sky promises of rapid increases in production.

It is natural that, in the quest for increased farm output, Stalin's postwar program should have attempted to grapple with that old affliction of Russian agriculture, the drought.[36] As a matter of fact, a severe drought occurred during the first postwar year, 1946; coming as it did in the wake of wartime devastation, its impact was particularly painful. A planned economic system can ill afford the disruptive influence of excessive crop fluctuations. The problem of how best to combat drought, therefore, challenged the Soviet regime almost since its inception; one only need recall the terrible drought of 1920–21. In attacking this problem, a number of soil-moisture conservation practices had long been advocated by Russian specialists. Prominent among these were (1) summer fallow (*par*), that is, plowing the land, preferably after the harvest in the fall, and keeping it unseeded for a year and free of weeds; (2) plowing the land in the fall in preparation for seeding during the following spring (*ziab*); (3) snow retention in the fields; (4) planting tree shelterbelts as a means of protecting crops in the treeless steppes. As a matter of fact, afforestation is a method of conservation in which the Russians have done considerable pioneering work, under the leadership of the great soil scientist Dokuchaev, who established in the 1890s the first experimental station for the study of tree shelterbelts. These shelterbelts are supposed to perform a double function. In the first place, they help to retain snow on the ground, which acts as a protective cover for winter grain, improves the moisture-retaining capacity of the soil, and is itself a highly important source of moisture. Second, shelterbelts diminish wind erosion and evaporation, thus helping to improve growing conditions for crops.

Following a severe drought in 1938, a systematic program for combating droughts was inaugurated by a decree of October 26, 1938.[37] It focused on the use of various moisture-conservation practices, local irrigation, and better adaptation of the cropping system to the climate of the subhumid regions. The implementation of this scheme was interrupted by the war and Nazi invasion. But when peace was restored, the threads were picked up again and, almost exactly a decade after the prewar drought program had been announced, the above-mentioned "Stalin Plan for Transforming Nature" was announced. The outstanding feature in its agrotechnique section was the accent on reforestation, to protect the crops in the steppe and wooded steppe regions.

The 1948 reforestation program was to extend over a fifteen-year period and was divided into several projects: the planting of national forests on watershed divides and on river banks such as the Volga and Don; the planting of tree shelterbelts for the protection of crops on collective and state farms, on banks of ravines and gullies, and around ponds and reservoirs; and afforestation and stabilizing of shifting sands on public-domain land. Then, in addition to a network of national forests, the planting of trees on 10.4 million acres of kolkhoz land was called for. Of this total, nearly 9 million acres were to be planted by the kolkhozes at their own expense, paying the MTS for such aid as they might give. The Ministry of Forestry, later merged with the Ministry of Agriculture, was to be responsible for the afforestation of the remaining 1.4 million acres, mostly ravines and gullies but kolkhoz labor was also to be used. State farms were to plant trees on an area of 1.45 million acres. Kolkhozes and state farms were required by the October 1948 decree to restore in 1949–50 all damaged shelterbelts planted during earlier years. The Ministry of Forestry was charged with the afforestation of 800,000 acres of sandy land in the steppe and semidesert regions.[38] The October decree went into great detail in specifying ways and means of implementing the shelterbelt program, including the creation of 270 special MTS to handle the mechanized operations. The decree laid down the rule that the official agricultural plan for a district, kolkhoz, or state farm was not to be considered fulfilled unless the required operations connected with afforestation were carried out on schedule.

Tree shelterbelts in principle had gained wide acceptance in the Soviet Union. However, specialists abroad are by no means convinced of their effectiveness in protecting crops, particularly in view of the cost involved. The cost includes not only the direct expense of preparing the soil, planting, and subsequent care of the trees (which required a great deal of manual labor owing to inadequate mechanization), but also the loss of crops that could have been grown on the land used in afforestation. Incidentally, the cost was born primarily by the kolkhozes themselves. The viability of the trees, if they grew at all, was low, especially in the steppe proper, as distinguished from the wooded steppe. But it is precisely in the steppe regions that crops need protection most. Tree shelterbelts had other disadvantages,[39] not entered in the official ledger, which made their usefulness less certain than might appear from the Soviet literature.

A complicating factor was the foray of Lysenko, whose cocksureness by now knew no bounds, into the field of afforestation. He advocated a new "nest" method of planting trees, which was of course promptly adopted, as were so many other "discoveries" of the Kremlin's favorite authority. But the method simply did not work; the plantings refused to grow. This time professional foresters, particularly the distinguished scientist V. N. Sukhachev, cried out that "the emperor wore no clothes." Sukhachev, in his controversy with Lysenko—which was the first public challenge to Lysenko's authority—took advantage of one of Stalin's sudden about-faces when unexpectedly, in a discussion on linguistics, the dictator opposed doctrinal or factional monopoly in science and pretended to be a protagonist of freedom in scientific discussion. Using this new approach as a shield, Sukhachev partly won, in the teeth of bitter opposition from Lysenko and his cohorts. As a consequence, new instructions for planting tree shelterbelts, embodying a compromise solution, were adopted in 1952.[40]

Apart from this controversy, the official line was that the full success of the program was marred only by the poor maintenance of the shelterbelts. "Tree shelterbelts, if they are maintained in good condition, exert an influence toward higher yields already in the early stage of growth," stated one of the officials directing the program.[41] There were also complaints about the poor planning of the shelterbelt projects, which "often were not coordinated with the production capabilities of kolkhozes, state farms, and forest farms, as a result of which the planting of tree shelterbelts took place with gross violation of the agrotechnique, without taking into account the [environmental] conditions for the growth of trees, and without providing for necessary maintenance. As a consequence, the viability of the planted trees in many regions proved to be unsatisfactory."[42] More than 6.4 million acres of tree shelterbelts were planted during the three and a half years after the start of the program,[43] but in 1955 the area in kolkhozes and sovkhozes amounted to only 1.7 million acres. This modest figure plainly indicates that the large program was a fiasco. Yet on a much lower level gradual progress was made, as shown by an increase of tree shelterbelts to 2,022,000 in 1958, the last year for which statistics were published.[44] The tree shelterbelts present a familiar landscape to a traveler in the countryside of the southeastern part of European Russia. But the very fact that no statistics have been published for a number of years, and that the subject has hardly been mentioned by Soviet leaders, points to a minor role for the device in the protection of crops from drought.

A radical though costly remedy for drought is irrigation. For a long time irrigated agriculture in the Soviet Union was largely confined to the desert regions of Central Asia, where it had existed since time immemorial, and to the arid southeastern regions of Transcaucasia. Of the 15 million acres of irrigated land in 1938, 68 percent was in the Central Asian republics, including Kazakhstan, and 17.5 percent in Transcaucasia.[45] The technical level of the irrigation network was low. A considerable proportion of the irrigated land was unusable because of salinity or swampiness. Cotton has been the most important crop grown under irrigation; in fact, cotton and irrigation are practically synonymous in the Soviet Union. Repeated droughts in the European part of the country, from which the middle and lower Volga Basin suffered most acutely, brought to the fore in the early 1930s the idea of resorting to irrigation in this region. It was embodied in a government decree issued in May 1932, which called for the irrigation within the next five years of between 10 and 11 million acres in the Volga Basin, to be devoted to wheat production.[46] Two years later Stalin, touching on the same subject in his report to the Seventeenth Party Congress, stated that "as far as the irrigation of the Trans-Volga area is concerned—and this is the principal thing from the standpoint of combating the drought—this matter should not be delayed too long." [47] He pointed out that the delay was due to "certain factors in the international situation," which took away large resources for other purposes. The tense international atmosphere, culminating in World War II, continued to block for nearly two decades the implementation of this costly project.

The first postwar five-year plan called for an expansion of the irrigated acreage by only a little more than 1.6 million acres. But there was a great deal to be done to repair the existing irrigation network and to rehabilitate the land. A new era in Soviet irrigation dawned in 1950. By a swift succession of government decrees in August and September of that year, a series of projects were announced for hydroelectric power development and irrigation in the middle and lower Volga regions, the North Caucasus, southern Ukraine, northern Crimea, and Turkmenistan.[48] These "Great Construction Projects of Communism," as they were acclaimed by the Soviet press, were scheduled for completion between 1955 and 1957. They were to provide water to irrigate nearly 15 million acres in the above-mentioned semiarid and arid regions. The irrigation projects were to be supplemented by water conservation programs, which consisted of the building of wells, ponds, and basins to take advantage of seasonal precipitation and various means of utilizing the seepage from irrigation systems and the overflow from all types of reservoirs; these were expected to maintain pasture and to support the growth of wild hay.

This new scheme of water development impresses one not only by its huge dimensions but also by a significant geographical departure: the extension of irrigation into the European part of the country. Of the 14,950,000 acres slated for irrigation, 11,250,000 were in the European regions. Though cotton was high on the list of the crops to be grown on the irrigated land, a considerable acreage would have been devoted to wheat. No doubt irrigation would have increased and stabilized yields.

In these dry regions, application of fertilizer to raise yields becomes feasible under irrigation. Such disadvantages as the tendency of irrigated wheat to "lodging" could be overcome by the introduction of new varieties.*

Some features of Stalin's water-development programs were criticized during the Khrushchev era, on technical and economic grounds.[49] In any event, after Stalin's departure, the implementation of the irrigation scheme was abandoned by his successors, who had different notions about the method of expanding agricultural production. For a decade the question of large-scale irrigation outside the traditional cotton-growing regions was dormant, until the catastrophic drought of 1963 revived it.

While the postwar Stalin administration centered its attention on the extensive dry area, it neglected the agricultural problem in the humid northern and north central European regions. The chief agricultural drawback of this nonblack-soil zone, as its name implies, is its relatively infertile, podzolic soils, which need lime to neutralize acidity, drainage, and, particularly, fertilizer. Its dependence on manure and consequently on livestock, which in turn requires hay and other fodder, makes diversified farming essential in this area. But it possesses an important climatic advantage over many of the other more fertile areas, since it does not suffer from frequent droughts. It is the consensus of Russian agronomic authorities that, under proper conditions of liming, fertilization, and drainage, fairly high and stable yields of a number of crops can be achieved in the nonblack-soil zone. The fact that Moscow and Leningrad and a number of other important industrial centers are located in this zone, providing an easily accessible outlet for farm products, should make intensive farming economical. This is the pattern of agriculture in the neighboring industrial countries of Western Europe, where infertile soils do not preclude high yields. In the mid 1930s the government, influenced largely by strategic considerations, had pushed agricultural expansion, particularly grain production, in this traditional grain-deficit area, in order to increase its self-sufficiency in food supply. But after the war no special attention was paid to the region, which suffered much devastation.

During the first five years after World War II, there were no significant organizational or institutional changes in collective agriculture, while it was being restored to its prewar status. But in 1950 a far-reaching change was inaugurated. It was the wholesale merger and enlargement of the

---

* Lodging takes place when the stalks of grain grow tall and are then blown over by the wind, rain, or hail. Irrigation causes the grain to grow taller and the heads to be larger, thereby making lodging more probable. The new varieties were to have shorter, stronger stalks.

kolkhozes, which in one year were reduced in number by more than half. This movement toward giant supercollective farms, which began during the last years of the Stalin era under the direction of Khrushchev, continued unabated during the latter's regime. I shall discuss the subject in greater detail at a later stage. Here I want only to call attention to the elements of disorganization and instability which the rapid mass mergers produced in the countryside. It is curious that Stalin himself did not comment publicly on the mergers—not even in his "last testament," the much-publicized *Economic Problems of Socialism in the USSR*.[50] So important a development as a merger campaign was inconceivable without Stalin's approval. But apparently he did not want to take public responsibility for it—perhaps remembering the collectivization drive of the 1930s—and thus kept open a road to retreat in case of failure; then the blame could be shifted elsewhere, in the characteristic Stalinist manner.

But to return to Stalin's last testament: it spells out his conception of the future of collectivism and is nothing less than the eventual amalgamation of all sectors into one all-embracing production and marketing system. Under such conditions, market exchange and the "money economy" would disappear. Until then, it must remain "a necessary and very useful element in the system of our national economy." But the continued existence of the two sectors, the kolkhoz–sovkhoz and market exchange, would increasingly hinder, according to *Economic Problems of Socialism,* productive development "by blocking the all-embracing state planning of the national economy and particularly of agriculture."

Stalin is, at first, vague about the method for consolidating the two sectors, except that he disapproves of the outright confiscation of kolkhoz property. At the end of his essay, Stalin becomes more concrete and more ominous. He proposes the elimination of private kolkhoz trade and the substitution of direct exchange—a sort of barter system between the kolkhoz and nationalized industry. In Stalin's own words, "it is essential . . . gradually to raise kolkhoz property to the level of all-national property, and also gradually to replace market exchange by a barter system, in order that the central government or some other socioeconomic authority can encompass the whole product of social production in the interests of society." As an example of what he had in mind, he points to a partial development of such an exchange in the existing method of "contracts" between the state and collective farms producing such industrial crops as cotton, sugar beets, and flax. In these cases the state undertakes to supply the kolkhozes delivering their specified quotas with certain essentials. This system, *otovarivanie,* Stalin would eventually extend to the whole kolkhoz sector. He does not elaborate his proposal, but simply asserts that the expanded state-kolkhoz barter, by shrinking the private market, would facilitate the transition from the present stage of socialism to communism and would make possible "the inclusion of the basic property of the kolkhozes—their production—into the general orbit of overall national planning." Stalin cautions that the new barter system "will require an enormous increase in the volume of goods supplied by the cities to the villages, and therefore it will have to be introduced without undue haste as urban [industrial] output is accumulated. But it must be introduced steadfastly, without wavering, reducing step by step the sphere of market exchange and expanding the sphere of barter."

Stalin was doubtless aware that the course he advocated would deal a serious blow to the personal farming of the kolkhozniks by eliminating the private market. But he was as silent on this subject as on the merger of the kolkhozes, which was also accompanied by some reduction in the kolkhozniks' private plots. It is easy to see that the merger movement blended in well with Stalin's new barter proposal; both converged on the road toward a more complete etatization of agriculture. From the standpoint of such a goal, Stalin's opposition to the transfer of the MTS to the kolkhozes, as proposed by some economists, also seems consistent. In an appendix to *Economic Problems of Socialism* Stalin replied critically to A. V. Sanina and V. G. Venzher, who proposed to sell the MTS in order to shift the "burden" of investment from the state to the kolkhozes. They considered the kolkhozes capable of bearing such a burden, but this contention was denied by Stalin. It is impossible to know from the scant quotations given by Stalin whether the two economists mentioned had in mind the new situation created by the kolkhoz merger.

Such was the blueprint for etatization charted by Stalin five months before his death. But his successors could not implement it even if they wished to, for they had to grapple with the serious problem of agricultural underproduction. Still the official tone during the last months of Stalin's life was one of undiluted optimism as far as agriculture was concerned. In his 1956 anti-Stalin speech Khrushchev maintained that this was not the mood of Stalin's entourage, which had voiced its apprehension to no avail. But publicly, during Stalin's lifetime, the Soviet hierarchy kept on repeating the optimistic slogans. In such a vein was Malenkov's evaluation of the agricultural situation at the Nineteenth Party Congress, in October 1952, where he spoke as Stalin's alter ego. He said: "As a result of the measures adopted by the party and the government, the difficulties created by the war and by the severe drought of 1946 were successfully overcome; prewar output levels in agriculture were regained and exceeded in a short space of time . . . The grain problem, which in the past was regarded as our most acute and gravest problem, has thus been solved definitely and finally. (Loud and prolonged applause.)" [51]

For the statistical bolstering of such claims, Malenkov relied on exaggerated crop figures. Suffice it to say that when the revised figure of the 1952 total (barn) crop was published several years after Stalin's death it was 30 percent below that given by Malenkov. Even this much deflated figure of 91.8 million metric tons represented the largest grain harvest since the prewar period. But it was a result of favorable weather conditions, which are rarely repeated two years in succession in the Soviet Union. Just as one swallow does not make a summer, so one good crop year is not a test of a successful solution to the crucial grain problem. Moreover, even the outstanding 1952 crop was below the good prewar 1940 crop, and far below the goal of the 1946–1950 plan of 127 million tons. It is difficult to believe that this was not known to Stalin, Malenkov, and Khrushchev, who could not have been deluded by the biological-yield smoke screen. There must have been available to them unpublished figures of the actually harvested crop. How the method of biological yields worked to overreport crops, made plain by Khrushchev in a document prepared in 1953–54 and not published until 1962, we saw in an earlier chapter. The estimates were made by special officials (interregional inspectors) with an eye to the government's procurement targets. Especially important among these were the increasing payments in kind for the work of the MTS, which were supposed to vary with the officially determined yield figures of the kolkhozes. If the biological yields appeared too low to meet the targets, they were simply corrected upwards by the estimating officials. Further corrections, and always upward, were introduced on a national scale. "Thus estimates based on crop conditions [biological yields] exceeded the actual yields not only by the amount of harvesting losses but also through arbitrary corrections." [52]

The lag in agriculture is underscored by a contrast with the progress in industry. Whereas industrial production in 1952 was 67 percent above that in 1940, according to realistic estimates by Western specialists, and two and a half times above prewar levels, according to an inflated official index, agricultural output during the good harvest year was just barely above the prewar level.[53] If there was some ground for optimism in 1952, it had vanished by 1953. The grain harvest declined to 82.5 million tons, or about the level of 1950–51. A decline in cattle numbers below those of the preceding three years, despite a good harvest, signalized the highly unsatisfactory livestock situation in 1953. Livestock numbers generally at the beginning of 1953 were below those of the precollectivization period (1928), and cattle numbers were even below those of 1916, when Russia was in the throes of World War I. The goals for livestock numbers set by the Stalin regime for 1951 were nowhere near achievement. The situation was aggravated by a decrease in the proportion of cows in the cattle herd, from a half or more before the Second World War to 43 percent in 1953, with a consequent detrimental effect on dairy production.

A glaring example of this deterioration was the decreased production of butter in Siberia as compared to the period before the First World War, when that area was the principal butter exporting region of Russia. Siberian butter production in 1952 was only 65,000 metric tons as compared with 75,000 in 1913,[54] and this despite the large increase in population and the vaunted agricultural development of Siberia under the Communists. In comparison with the United States, with a population of about a fifth that of the USSR, the latter had 37 million, or 40 percent, fewer cattle and 26 million, or nearly 50 percent, fewer hogs at the beginning of 1953. Only with respect to sheep, of which the United States had 32 million, was the USSR much ahead. To complete the dismal picture, it is essential to add to the low production indicators the causally related apathy of the peasantry, widely noted by foreign observers and recorded in post-Stalin Russia in belles-lettres, and the paralyzing effect of the Stalinist terror on administrative, technical, and scientific personnel. For, as Merle Fainsod puts it, "Under Stalin terror literally became a system of power. The concentration camp was its symbol, and the secret police its instrument." [55]

The many weak spots of Soviet agriculture in the early 1950s still do not add up to the kind of a crisis that occurred during the collectivization drive of the 1930s or in the period of War Communism and famine of the early 1920s. However, the chronic weakness of agriculture acted as a serious brake on the long-promised improvement in standard of living. Stalin was so firmly entrenched, nonetheless, that he did not need to be disturbed by the pace of the advance, contrary as it was to the rising expectations of the people after an exhausting but victorious war. There is a considerable body of evidence that toward the end Stalin was preoccupied with preparations for a new large-scale purge, heralded by the infamous Doctors' Plot; improvement of the lot of the common man, especially the peasant, cannot be on the agenda of a reign of terror. Whether by human design, as some think, or fate, the country was spared this ordeal when on March 5, 1953, the dictator joined his ancestors.

*Part Three. Collectivized Agriculture
under Khrushchev*

14

Khrushchev: The Agrarian Leader and Reformer

When Stalin died in March 1953, a new era of "collective leadership" was officially proclaimed to replace the "cult of personality," a euphemism for the Stalinist tyranny. But the rapid rise of Khrushchev in the power structure largely nullified any collective leadership on the national scene. As far as agriculture is concerned, the first post-Stalin decade must be associated from the very outset with Nikita Khrushchev. He had made agriculture his particular province while serving as Stalin's lieutenant, and later his name became virtually synonymous in the public mind with Russian agriculture.

Khrushchev was well aware of the nature of Stalin's legacy to agriculture, and he recognized the urgency of the rising expectations of the Russian people and the need to pay the long-overdue promissory note for an improved standard of living. The slow pace Stalin could afford in this matter would not do for his less powerful successors: *Quod licet Jovi, non licet bovi* (what is proper for Jupiter is not proper for the ox). So Khrushchev committed the Kremlin to a serious qualitative improvement in the food situation by publicly promising, on a number of occasions, more abundant and better food. He said that you cannot make a soup from stoppages in the food supply,[1] and held out the prospect that by the early 1960s Russia would even catch up with the United States in the per capita production of meat and milk. In the meantime, the national food needs were growing as the population increased. It is true that demographic catastrophes—resulting from revolution, collectivization, famine, and war—and its large land area spared Russia the kind of Malthusian pressure of population on food supply which afflicted so many countries of Asia and Africa. To paraphrase Sir Dennis Robertson, the "devil of Malthus" was still chained as far as the USSR was concerned.[2]

The postwar period witnessed the resumption of a rapid growth of population, which by the end of 1954 slightly exceeded prewar (1940) levels and, at the end of Khrushchev's regime, was about 18 percent higher. More serious, from the government's standpoint, was the pronounced upward trend of the urban population, which by the beginning of 1953 was already 27 percent above 1940 and nearly double ten years later. Of course, the food supply for the cities was always the focus of the government's concern, and swift urbanization did not make the problem any easier. The logic of events dictated a rapid upsurge in agricultural production; and this Khrushchev and his colleagues publicly acknowledged as a primary task. They also recognized the need for major changes in agricultural policy to bring it about.

Although Khrushchev no doubt was responsible for charting the new agrarian course, it fell to Georgii Malenkov and Minister of Finance A. G. Zverev to announce the beginning of the post-Stalin reforms. Though it must have been in the air, there was no public statement of the impending change during the first five months after Stalin's death— unless one considers as a hint the phrase in the announcement of the liquidation of Lavrentii Beria (who was originally regarded as one of the big three among Stalin's heirs) that he "obstructed in every way a number of urgent decisions regarding agriculture."[3] Whether this was true or not may never be known, since the Beria entourage was pretty thoroughly decimated in the best Stalinist fashion. Then without forewarning, at a session of the Supreme Soviet in August 1953, Minister of Finance Zverev outlined, during his presentation of the annual budget, proposed changes in the agricultural tax levied on kolkhozniks.[4] It was to be drastically reduced in amount, with the arrears for former years canceled and the character of the tax simplified. As in 1921, the new agricultural tax sprung suddenly on the country was a harbinger of further reforms. It was next Malenkov's turn to unfold the new agrarian program.[5] His analysis of the agricultural situation in August 1953 was much less optimistic than his remarks at the Nineteenth Party Congress eight months earlier.

To be sure, Malenkov still recited the old shibboleths about the successes of collective agriculture. The country was, according to him, "secure in its grain supply." There was a large increase in the government procurements of cotton, sugar beets, meat, and milk, though he did not disclose the production figures for the last two commodities or for grains. Now, for the first time since its introduction twenty years earlier, there came a public attack on the biological-yield method of crop estimating. Malenkov stated: "In order to strengthen the campaign against crop losses and to increase the actual output of grain and other crops, it is necessary to end such a faulty practice as the evaluation of the work of kolkhozes with respect to production of grain and other crops by their pre-harvest condition, and instead to base it on the actual output. It should not be forgotten that our kolkhozes can be well off only from a crop stored in the barn and not a crop on the root."

Thus, by repudiating biological yields, Malenkov sustained the Western critics of the crop-estimating methods of the Stalin era. Ipso facto, he implicitly acknowledged the exaggerated character of many of the Soviet production claims, though it took another five years before this was explicitly confirmed. By dwelling not only on "achievements" (*dostizheniia*) but also on the seamy side of the agricultural situation, with more than the customary Soviet obeisance to "criticism and self-criticism," Malenkov in effect dispelled the official Stalinist myth of a rapidly progressing socialist agriculture:

> The successes of agriculture are significant. They are the undisputed achievements of our kolkhozes, our machine-tractor stations, our state farms, our social order. Yet it would be a serious error not to see the backwardness of a number of important branches of agriculture, not to note that the current level of agricultural production does not correspond to the increased technical equipment and potentialities of the kolkhoz system. We still have a number of kolkhozes and even whole regions where agriculture is in a neglected condition; in many regions of the country, collective and state farms have low yields of grains and other crops and large harvest losses; because of the weak development of the socialized farm economy, some kolkhozes still have inadequate income in kind and in cash and distribute little cash, grain, and other products to kolkhozniks. It must be acknowledged that the situation is unfavorable with respect to the development of animal husbandry and, as a result, that we are still far from adequately supplying the growing needs of the population for meat, milk, eggs, and other animal products.[6]

Malenkov further noted the lag in production of potatoes and vegetables, which adversely affected the food supply both directly and indirectly by reducing the available supply of animal feed. He also admitted the deterioration of the personal farming of the kolkhozniks "because of short-comings in our taxation policy," which was reflected in the reduction of the peasants' income and the decline in privately owned livestock, par-ticularly cows. This was a very significant admission in view of what we know about the role played by this type of farming in the peasants' economic life and in the food supply of the cities.

The essence of the agricultural problem was formulated by Malenkov as underproduction and the low morale of the farmers. It was the same old problem; the only novelty was its frank admission by the Soviet government. Malenkov asserted that "the urgent task is to sharply in-crease during the next two to three years the supply of foodstuffs and industrial goods to the population." Even more important, Malenkov put his finger gently on one of the greatest hindrances to improvement in the standard of living and in agriculture: the Soviet emphasis on heavy industry. He reviewed the development of industrial production and the flow of capital investment and pointed out the disparities be-tween the status of heavy industry and that of light industry and agri-culture. While reiterating the Stalinist dogma that high priority for heavy industry had been essential to the building of a socialist society, Malenkov also admitted that the "attained volume of production of consumer goods cannot satisfy us." Formerly it had been impossible to develop the light and foodstuffs industries at the same rate of growth as heavy industry. "Now," said Malenkov, "on the basis of successes reached by heavy industry, we have all the prerequisites for organizing a sharp upswing in production of consumer goods . . . At present we can and consequently should, in the interest of securing a more rapid rise in the material and cultural living levels of the population, force as rapidly as possible the growth of light industry."

Thus Malenkov, speaking for the post-Stalin administration, recog-nized the dilemma: superindustrialization versus improved standard of living. The time had come to redress the imbalance in the Soviet economy and to change the allocation of resources in favor of the consumer, that is, of the masses of workers and peasants. This message was spelled out in much greater detail by Khrushchev a month later at the plenum of the Central Committee, in a report made on September 7, 1953, and pub-lished on September 15. With this document the role of Khrushchev as the architect of post-Stalin agrarian policy was established.

Krushchev's Personal Approach to Agriculture

What were the qualities and characteristics Khrushchev brought to the task of directing Soviet agriculture? It may be fairly said that Russia was never ruled, in modern times at any rate, by one so steeped and interested in agriculture as Nikita Sergeevich Khrushchev. To begin with his background, it is significant that Khrushchev was the only man of peasant origin among the Soviet leaders. He was born in 1894 in the village of Kalinovka, Kursk province, in central Russia, and was brought up as a typical peasant boy, doing chores and working as a shepherd on the nearby estate. At the age of fifteen Khrushchev went to work in the industrial and mining Donetzk (Donbas) region, to which apparently his family had moved. Although there is little factual information on the early period of Khrushchev's life, his was no doubt the hard lot of the Russian peasant and industrial worker, as he later indicated. Certainly it was a much less comfortable life than that of the other country boy in the top Soviet echelon, Leon Trotsky, the son of a prosperous capitalist farmer, who studied at a good secondary school at an age when Khrushchev was already earning his living.[7] The same is true of Lenin and even of Djugashvili-Stalin who, though a poor cobbler's son, still managed to enter a theological seminary.

The Kalinovka experience stood Khrushchev in good stead later when he had to deal with agricultural problems, since it provided him with the kind of insight into the life and psychology of the peasant which only an insider could have. Khrushchev knew how to talk to peasants and certainly retained their rough wit. Probably his early agrarian background also accounted for his scorn of what he called the *barskii* (genteel) attitude displayed by some Communists in responsible positions, who looked down upon agriculture as a kind of a second-rate occupation, unworthy of educated, intelligent people. "Such people do not understand the simple truth that without the advance of agriculture the problems of building communism cannot be successfully solved. Communist society cannot be built without an abundance of grain, meat, milk, butter, vegetables, and other agricultural products." [8]

It was a theme that Khrushchev never tired of reiterating. This attitude probably had something to do with the effort to move agricultural specialists from the cities, where they tended to settle, to the villages, where they would be closer to the agricultural problems and more helpful to farmers. He was quick to observe during his visit to the United States that American farm specialists were not averse to manual work on farms when necessary, in contrast to the squeamishness of their counterparts in Russia. Khrushchev himself tried to remain in touch with the grass roots, never missing an opportunity to visit farms and experiment stations during his frequent travels in the USSR as well as abroad. In fact, a number of the trips, including the one in the late summer of 1964, shortly before his downfall, were undertaken primarily for agricultural purposes, to see for himself how things were. During such inspection visits Khrushchev was no passive observer. He asked searching questions, did not hesitate to give advice gleaned from observing farms in different regions and countries, criticized, harangued, praised—all in the interest of increasing yields and reducing costs.

For example, during a visit to a state farm in the Rostov province in August 1964 where he met with officials and specialists, Khrushchev interrupted the manager, who was praising two relatively new, high-yielding varieties of wheat (Mironovka 808 and Bezostaia or Beardless 1), with a little lecture of his own on their advantages. He said that his native Kalinovka obtained even higher yields of one of the varieties with the application of fertilizer, which was not used on the Rostov farm. Khrushchev recommended that experiments with proper controls be set up on the Rostov farm to learn the effect of fertilizer in raising yields of these varieties. He admonished that "before applying fertilizer, it is necessary to have a chemical analysis of the soil to determine what elements are lacking in the soil in order to apply the proper kind of fertilizer." [9] Then Khrushchev said to the manager: "You spoke only about yields of Mironovka 808. To what extent is this wheat resistant to lodging?" On learning that there was some lodging, Khrushchev began to extol the other variety, Beardless 1, for its resistance to lodging under all sorts of difficult conditions. Khrushchev insisted that the disadvantages of a plant variety must be brought out as well as its good qualities. He also called attention to a superior variety developed by a plant breeder in Odessa which might be highly productive on the Rostov farm. Khrushchev discussed a number of other technical questions at this meeting, including the pros and cons of implements for clearing the fields quickly of straw after the harvest.

Khrushchev possessed a shrewd knowledge of the ways of Soviet bureaucracy, of its propensity to accept Potemkin villages and other forms of falsification. He called a spade a spade. This may be illustrated by the following incident. During the Rostov visit he complained that people who lack a knowledge of agriculture were appointed to positions in the local administrative apparatus, where their function was to instruct farmers how to increase production. When someone in the audience commented that all such functionaries in that district were specialists, Khrushchev retorted, "It is probably because of my arrival that the nonspecialists were removed and the specialists brought in."

Khrushchev's trips often began or ended with a regional conference attended by local government and party officials dealing with agricultural matters, farm specialists, scientists, farm managers, and a sprinkling of outstanding farmers. The peripatetic Khrushchev would usually deliver a lengthy major address and actively participate in the subsequent deliberations as a persistent questioner and critic. The regional conferences had their national counterparts in special plenums of the Central Committee, several of which were considerably expanded by the inclusion of agricultural personnel. Here too Khrushchev dominated the proceedings. Published stenographic reports contain, in addition to the usual propaganda, much useful and critical material on the functioning of Soviet agriculture, to a great extent penetrating the guarded secrets of the Stalin era; * and so do the eight volumes of Khrushchev's speeches, reports, memoranda, and comments devoted to agricultural matters, which testify to his preoccupation with the subject. Thus Khrushchev could not be accused of a lack of interest or firsthand knowledge of agriculture—the charge he leveled against Stalin in his 1956 speech. Foreign visitors who had an opportunity to hear Khrushchev discuss agriculture could not fail to be impressed by the wide range of his technical knowledge. I vividly remember the enthusiasm he displayed when, during a visit of U.S. Secretary of Agriculture Orville Freeman and his party, in the summer of 1963, Khrushchev referred to a report of a German farmer on his success in producing meat with an unusually small quantity of feed. This was not a small technical detail; it had an important bearing on the crucial livestock problem. The point is that Khrushchev appeared to be well versed in all the intricacies of the subject.

Khrushchev's zeal for technological progress and innovation was largely instrumental in dispelling much of the scientific isolationism and xenophobia so marked under Stalin. While praising the achievements of Russian science, Khrushchev realized and admitted that the Soviet Union had much to learn from the West and from some of the other Communist countries. His feelings on the international scope of science and technology were most forcefully stated in his last published document on the directives for the new five-year plan. In the introduction of the latest scientific and technological achievements, he said: "It is impossible to tolerate autarky. Autarky is harmful in economics; it is especially dangerous for the development of science and technology. No country, not even the most developed, will be able to advance rapidly if it is not capable of effectively utilizing the achievements of the world's scientific-technical thought. Our research and designing organizations should not lock themselves up within their walls; they should not invent what has

---

* To give one illustration, the disclosure by Khrushchev in his 1958 plenum speech of comparative data on labor productivity for Soviet and American farms, which were highly unfavorable to the former, could hardly have happened under Stalin. But Khrushchev was not above peddling information that he knew was wrong or misleading. The outstanding example is, again, the use of inflated grain-production figures.

already been invented, but utilize widely their own as well as foreign scientific achievements and progressive production experience." [10]

The contact between the Soviet Union and the international scientific community, all but stifled under Stalin, was re-established under Khrushchev with the reciprocal exchange of numerous scientific and technical delegations. As far as agriculture was concerned, Khrushchev advocated borrowing and adapting a number of foreign practices and techniques. Though he hoped to "bury" the United States, he greatly admired American farm technology and productivity and sought to emulate them. In fact, Khrushchev went too far in some cases, notably in the expansion of corn growing. In any event, he insisted during a visit to a Czechoslovak poultry farm not long before his downfall: "We must adopt all that is best in our own and in foreign science and experience." [11] Observing that he might be criticized for praising the achievements of capitalist countries, Khrushchev stated: "I am not afraid of such criticism. We must study the best achievements, the best foreign practices, and adopt them, in order to attain higher productivity of labor." Khrushchev was himself eager to learn the best in foreign agriculture by visiting farms during his trips abroad, by contacts with foreign specialists, such as the American Roswell Garst, and probably by considerable reading. He was no less eager to share this knowledge with his countrymen, to whom an increasing stream of foreign agricultural information was made available through the press and technical literature.

Another characteristic of Khrushchev was his cost consciousness, his insistence that "it is impossible to carry on farming without a thorough analysis of the cost of commodities produced and without control by means of the ruble." [12] The word *podshchitat'*, to calculate, to figure out, was a favorite in Khrushchev's lexicon. This cost-profitability consciousness was a far cry from the Stalin days when even calculations of the cost of producing commodities in kolkhozes were considered superfluous. Khrushchev understood that without the help of economic calculus, without balancing returns and costs, a new spirit of rationality and efficiency could not be instilled into the management of Soviet agriculture, heretofore preoccupied largely with physical targets. A result of this concern was progress in economic science and the increased influence of economists. Though Soviet economic science did not overcome all of its many serious shortcomings and handicaps during the Khrushchev era, owing to the continued dominance of Marxist-Leninist dogma, still the period had the earmarks of a renascence in economic analysis and research, of a ferment in economic discussion very unlike the sterility of the Stalin days. [13]

This was also true of statistics. Only a trickle of data was published during Stalin's postwar days, and then irregularly and often in fragmentary form. As far as published agricultural statistics were concerned, there are still many lacunae in the Khrushchev era. Some important data, like those on household budgets, on the earnings of kolkhozniks, and on utilization of farm commodities, were withheld. Grain-production statistics said to represent barn yields were later revealed not to be true barn figures but were records of the grain issuing from the bunker of a combine (bunker weight), which thus contained moisture and trash. It is difficult to believe that Khrushchev was not aware of this repetition of the history of biological yields, against which he fulminated so much. And it was Khrushchev who castigated the falsification of reports and accounts by lower echelons of the bureaucratic apparatus—he had a law enacted in May 1961, making it a criminal offense. But after all the criticisms are in, it is impossible not to recognize the difference, on the statistical front, between the Stalin era, when not a single statistical yearbook was published after the prewar years, and the Khrushchev period with its resumption of the publication of statistical information.

Shortcomings in Khrushchev's Approach

The new emphasis by Khrushchev on economics reflected a very significant shift in basic principle from the Stalinist reliance on force—on a command economy in its extreme form—to a reliance on economic incentives. This distinction, which is central in the whole modus operandi of directing agricultural production, Khrushchev understood well in theory; but there were many lapses in practice. What has been said so far about Khrushchev's personality points to a bold, dynamic, realistic, if flamboyant, leader, one who knew the score and knew what makes the Russian peasant tick. Khrushchev, no doubt, was a charismatic leader. But there were other traits, such as impulsiveness, impatience, lack of scientific education, Marxian dogmatism, cocksureness, overoptimism and a willingness to gamble for large stakes, which often marred his realistic outlook and pragmatic approach. These traits were responsible for plunges into ventures which seem dubious, risky, or ill prepared. The rapid expansion of acreage in the low-yielding virgin lands of the dry eastern zone, the pushing of corn throughout the vast country regardless of differences in climatic and soil conditions and the degree of preparedness in terms of techniques, proper seed varieties, fertilizers, implements, and the like, the concomitant drive against grasses and oats, the campaign to catch up with the United States in per capita production of livestock products, the merger and enlargement of farms—these are cases in point of major questionable schemes espoused by Khrushchev. The aims, increased and more efficient production, were worthwhile per se. The fault lay in the means adopted or the manner in which they were pursued.

I have dwelt on Khrushchev's intense interest in technical aspects of agriculture, certainly a commendable quality. But his self-confidence led him to believe that he could judge all the different recommendations and practices, even though lacking in systematic scientific training. This resulted in serious policy errors in promoting or prohibiting certain crops and farm practices. Khrushchev, strangely enough, exhibited the same disregard that Stalin did for the regional variability of natural and economic conditions in decision making and planning. I have called this strange because on a number of occasions Khrushchev criticized that kind of wholesale, stereotyped approach. In fact, early in his administration (April 1955), he sponsored a law on the decentralization of agricultural planning which aimed precisely at the adaptation of production to the varying conditions of different regions and farms. This law remained a dead letter. Nearly a decade later, toward the end of his regime, Khrushchev was again instrumental in the enactment of even stronger legislation, which was left to his successors to implement.

These pitfalls were compounded by the lack of independent expert criticism which would dare to dispute basic premises of policy decisions made by Khrushchev. Unless public discussion is invited by the Kremlin, as in the case of the industrial reform associated with Libermanism, criticism is usually confined to the execution of details. We know that privately agricultural experts submitted some basic criticisms to Khrushchev, such as the memorandum of the scientists who objected to reducing the area under grasses in Lithuania. But publicly this could be divulged only by Khrushchev, who did it in order to ridicule the authors of the memorandum.[14] There was no public discussion of so momentous a step as the expansion in the virgin lands, though some experts must have had objections or reservations. Later Khrushchev himself disclosed the existence of considerable opposition to the project at the top party level, charging Molotov with this "crime." The emphasis on corn, too, was immune to public criticism until the 1963 crop failure compelled a reappraisal.

In connection with his well-publicized wish to catch up with the United States in the production of milk and meat by the early 1960s, Khrushchev did seek the advice of some unnamed economists, which he scornfully rejected as too conservative: they considered that 1975 would be a better target date, and even that might be overoptimistic.[15] In such a climate, among the lower and middle echelons of officials and experts there was a conformist climb-on-the-bandwagon psychology. Once the policy was adopted, the only concern voiced was related to implementation. And so official pressure would be brought on farm managers throughout the country, from the northern forest regions of Vologda and Kirov to the dry steppes of the south and east, to plant corn, or peas, or sugar beets, or not to plant grasses and oats, regardless of whether the crops were suitable or not.

Khrushchev was well aware of this bandwagon psychology and its deplorable results. Speaking at the December 1958 plenum about a geographical shift in wheat and corn planting, he warned: "If we adopt the method of administrative pressure, some kolkhozes and sovkhozes will restructure the planting pattern in such a way that they will have neither wheat nor corn. A rational creative approach is needed in this matter. Corn areas should be increased only in those regions which have mastered corn growing and actually will be able to obtain a good harvest. If, however, a general directive should be given—grow more corn—then we may ruin grain production. Of course, kolkhozes will plant corn; but not all of them will cultivate it. There will be no crop to harvest, and this will cause a loss to agriculture." [16] But Khrushchev did not always use such sensible language or live up to his precepts.

Nor was Khrushchev, though much better informed on agricultural matters than Stalin, immune to the blandishments of a pie-in-the-sky approach; this probably goes far to explain his support of Lysenko. It is all the more puzzling since at the beginning of his regime Khrushchev apparently was cool to Lysenko, though he never attacked him personally but only some of his disciples. Although Lysenko had to give up his prestigious post as president of the Lenin Academy of Agricultural Sciences, he later regained Khrushchev's favor and was reappointed to the presidency in 1961. He held this post for a short time and was replaced by his close collaborator, Mikhail Olshanskii. Khrushchev was probably not interested in and did not understand the theoretical aspects of the controversy between Lysenkoism and its opponents. He obviously did not believe the criticisms of Lysenko's deleterious influence on the progress of agricultural science, which appeared even in Soviet scientific publications. What must have impressed Khrushchev, a practical man, was Lysenko's supposed contribution, as a practical farm expert, to increased production. Lysenko's tempting promises of quick results, based on shortcuts, no doubt contributed to Khrushchev's naive faith in the man and his pseudo-science. Lysenko's peasant origin probably helped to strengthen the empathy and to establish rapport with Khrushchev for whom, after all, academically trained scientists and other intellectuals "lived on the other side of the tracks." But there was a significant change. Although Lysenko wielded great influence under Khrushchev, he ceased to be the dictator of agrobiology that he was under Stalin, when he enjoyed a tight monopoly in dogma and used terrorist methods to suppress his opponents. Yet by encouraging Lysenkoism, even on a moderate scale, Khrushchev hurt the very cause he espoused—improved agricultural productivity was achieved in the West largely on the scientific basis that Lysenko scorned and repudiated.

Another serious limitation in Khrushchev's pragmatic outlook was his unswerving devotion to collectivist dogma. How much of Karl Marx he read is uncertain, but he accepted without ifs or buts the Marxist-Leninist-Stalinist line on collective agriculture and the superiority of large-scale production. Despite Khrushchev's virulent denunciations in other matters, Stalin's decisive role in collectivization drew only a mild rebuke, and that for passing on the responsibility for shortcomings and errors to others.* The Stalinist collectivization drive with all its iniquities and horrors was not questioned, let alone condemned. Indeed, how could he question the Stalinist collectivization model when he himself was the proponent of supercollectivization through the indiscriminate mass merger and enlargement of kolkhozes? Perhaps the strength of Khrushchev's attachment to the principles of agricultural collectivization is best revealed by a sermon he delivered to peasants during a visit to Poland in the summer of 1959. He strongly recommended the path of agrarian collectivism—and this in a country where the Communist regime a few years earlier had to permit a mass decollectivization in the wake of de-Stalinization.[17]

Like Stalin and Lenin, Khrushchev made concessions to the private sector when the situation clearly demanded it, but only on a temporary emergency basis and only when the collectivist structure would not be impaired. Khrushchev was explicit about this in his September 1953 report, and his subsequent restrictive course with respect to the private sector confirmed the fundamental position. It follows that any significant move for agricultural improvement and reform had to be within the collectivist orbit, which limited the available alternatives. But within

---

* In criticizing Mao Tse Tung's "great leap forward" at a Soviet-Polish friendship rally in Moscow on April 15, 1964, Khrushchev had this to say: "The Chinese leadership accused the local party organs of causing the failure of these adventurist plans by distorting the directives of Peking. Such methods, of declining all responsibility, are well familiar to us. The same thing happened in the Soviet Union in 1930 when after excesses were committed in collectivization, Stalin published the letter on 'Dizziness from Success,' in which he shifted the whole responsibility to local party organs. Then our country was under extreme strain. In some regions mutinies had already started among peasants. This period was well described by M. A. Sholokhov in his book *Broken Soil*. Under the conditions existing at that time, when there was the beginning of a famine in the country, dizziness from success was out of the question." *Pravda*, April 16, 1964.

this orbit Khrushchev recognized no sacred cows and did not hesitate to make radical changes. In fact, he was criticized by his successors for making too many and too frequent changes, particularly in the organization of the agricultural party-state apparatus. Perhaps the best example of Khrushchev's break with tradition was the liquidation of the MTS, whose pivotal role in collective agriculture he himself had once enhanced. There was no question of decollectivization under Khrushchev, just as there was none under Stalin in the mid-1930s, despite some temporary concessions to the private sector during both periods. There was no Khrushchev NEP, in sharp contrast with the situation in Poland and Yugoslavia where major decollectivization took place in the mid-1950s. The whole thrust of Khrushchev's agrarian policy was to strengthen and develop collectivist agriculture.

Khrushchev's Policies

Khrushchev as a leader represents a curious amalgam of sound and unsound views, dogmatism and pragmatism, realism and extremism, orthodoxy and heterodoxy. The complexity and ambivalence of his personality are reflected in his agricultural reforms, though a combination of other factors beyond his control—political, economic, technological, and natural—also played a part in the results. The more important reforms will be discussed in the following chapters, and at this stage I shall confine myself to a general blueprint.

As in the mid-1930s under Stalin, the roster of Khrushchev's reforms began with a temporary liberalization of the restrictive policies against the private sector in collectivized agriculture. I say "temporary" advisedly, since it did not take very long for the attitude of the government to change. The liberalization dovetailed with the general effort of the Khrushchev regime to improve economic incentives for the kolkhozes through increased agricultural prices, changes in taxation and credit, reorganization of the procurement system for farm products, some adjustment in the distribution of kolkhoz income, and the introduction of a social-security program on a national scale. Investment of capital and the physical inputs represented by it (tractors, other machinery, buildings) were increased. Measures were taken to provide specialists, managerial personnel, and skilled workers.

On the organizational and institutional side, the size of the farm unit was continuously enlarged and the number of kolkhozes was drastically reduced through mergers. Accelerated etatization of collective farming took place by the conversion of kolkhozes into sovkhozes, but the state-owned MTS were abolished and their farm machinery purchased by kolkhozes or transferred to sovkhozes. There was also a succession of changes in the administrative party-state apparatus, aiming at a more effective control of farm operations. Decentralization of the rigid agricultural planning from Moscow was attempted. Special programs were developed to expand the output of specific commodities and regions, which involved a restructuring of the traditional crop pattern. The two most famous programs of this nature were the bringing under cultivation and planting, mostly to wheat, the eastern virgin lands and the rapid extension of corn areas throughout the country.

Despite this impressive list of reforms, the unsatisfactory performance of agriculture presumably played a large part in Khrushchev's ouster, judging from the subsequent campaign of vilification directed against him by his successors. This does not mean that agricultural difficulties were the only bone of contention in the struggle that led to Khrushchev's downfall, though official silence has been maintained with regard to most of the other issues in dispute. Certainly the Chinese-Soviet quarrel, in which Khrushchev showed great intransigence, was one highly important area of difficulty. Another may have been the question of rapprochement with West Germany, which Khrushchev was apparently promoting toward the end of his regime. Other thorny questions were the setting of goals and allocation of resources for different sectors of the national economy in the new plan that was to follow that for 1959–1965, and the future course of de-Stalinization, with which Khrushchev was so strongly identified. Still another issue was the downgrading of the party apparatus by splitting it into agricultural and industrial sectors. There were also old scores to be settled in the power struggle with Khrushchev, and the Cuban missile fiasco. Which of these issues really tipped the scale against Khrushchev is one of the Kremlin's well-guarded secrets. But the pluralistic theory suggested here need not detract from the major role of agriculture in his downfall.

A number of euphemistic epithets have been applied to Khrushchev and his work after he became an "unperson"—such phrases as subjective approach, not adhering to objective economic laws, voluntarism, unscientific, arbitrary, know-it-all, amateurish interference, and so forth. They are not very meaningful, except as a kind of an official litmus paper to detect lingering traces of Khrushchevism. But a proliferation of articles in the Soviet daily press and scholarly journals have presented serious criticisms of Khrushchev policies and programs, which will be dealt with in the next three chapters. Of considerable importance in this connection are the proceedings of the plenum of the Central Committee in March

1965, devoted entirely to agriculture and specifically to the debunking of Khrushchev and the approval of a new agricultural program presented by Brezhnev.[18]

What emerges from all this as the central charge against Khrushchev is that, despite his dynamic policy, agricultural production in the early 1960s was stagnant, in the face of rising demand and the optimistic goals he himself had approved. This had a detrimental effect on the whole national economy. Measures adopted on Khrushchev's initiative either were not able to overcome the stagnation or actually contributed to it. It is also generally agreed that during the early years of Khrushchev's agricultural stewardship, 1953–1958, a rapid growth of agricultural production took place, variously measured at 40 to 50 percent (see Table 39). A major contribution to this growth came from the rapid expansion of planted area, which increased during the period by 24 percent, largely as a consequence of Khrushchev's virgin-lands campaign. Greater economic incentives to farmers and increased inputs of resources also helped to stimulate production, and several years of favorable weather were a highly important factor in boosting output. A significant indicator of improvement in the feed situation and care of animals was the fact that livestock numbers, which were at a low ebb in 1953, showed a large gain. Between the end of 1953 and 1958 cattle numbers increased by about 27 percent and were above the precollectivization level; hogs increased by 46 percent, sheep by 30 percent.

After 1958 the situation changed. Even the Soviet index of gross agricultural production, which includes the inflated bunker-weight grain figures, showed an increase of only 7 percent in 1962 over 1958, and less during the previous three years. The United States Department of Agriculture index of net output (which tries to eliminate the inflation of grain figures and excludes feed crops used to produce the livestock component of the total agricultural output) was only slightly above 1958 in 1961 and 1962, and 6 to 5 percent less during the previous two years. Both indexes, and especially the American one, showed a downward dip in 1963—and this in the face of the 1959–1965 plan for a 70 percent increase in agricultural output. The production situation was even less favorable on a per capita basis as the population increased by more than 8 percent between the end of 1953 and 1958. Although the deterioration may be partly explained by less favorable weather conditions, climaxing in the disastrous crop failure of 1963, agricultural policy and its administration under Khrushchev must assume the rest of the blame. For there was delay or retrogression in the application of some important measures, such as those related to economic incentives and investments, and other

Table 39. Indexes of Soviet agricultural output, 1953–1965

Year	Gross-production index	Net-production index
	1953=100	
1953	100	100
1954	106	104
1955	116	117
1956	132	131
1957	137	126
1958	150	142
1959	151	134
1960	154	136
1961	159	144
1962	161	144
1963	149	135
1964	170	158
1965	171	145
	1958=100	
1958	100	100
1959	100	94
1960	103	95
1961	106	101
1962	107	101
1963	99	95
1964	113	111
1965	114	102

Sources. Official gross production index from *SSSR v tsifrakh, 1965*, p. 70; net production index based on U.S. Department of Agriculture estimates of calendar year crop and livestock product output weighted in terms of 1957–59 average West European producer or wholesale prices. Deductions are made for the value of crops used to produce livestock output.

programs were poorly implemented or downright counterproductive. The combined effect of these developments on production was depressing and in poor years accentuated the adverse effects of weather.

The influence of weather on crops was minimized by Khrushchev and official Soviet statements until the 1963 fiasco. The primary responsibility for the state of the harvest on a particular farm was placed on management. Somehow managers were supposed to overcome the difficulties caused by the inadequate inputs of various factors of production and unfavorable weather conditions. But in 1963 Khrushchev did blame the weather for the catastrophic situation, which forced the government to import nearly 12 million tons of wheat at a cost of about 800 million dollars and led also to some restrictions on bread consumption, a deterioration in its quality, and the slaughter of livestock, especially hogs. That a leading wheat-producing country, traditionally a large exporter and an insignificant importer, should suddenly have to scramble to buy all the wheat it could from its competitors (with one of whom, the United States, it had declared itself to be in an agricultural race) probably symbolized to the Soviet public and the Kremlin, more than anything else, the failure of Khrushchev's agricultural stewardship. It must have been a traumatic, humiliating experience for him.* Even though Khrushchev's successors did not blame him publicly for the imports, it is reasonable to assume that the question came up during the secret discussions in the Presidium and the Central Committee. That very poor weather was not just an alibi I can confirm from my travels in the agricultural regions of the USSR in the summer of 1963. But had a higher level of grain yields and production been secured during the previous years when weather conditions were more propitious, stocks could have been accumulated which would have obviated such large imports. Even a small addition to the yield over a large area would have spelled a significant increase in output. To obtain an equivalent of 12 million tons of wheat imported from abroad, it would have been necessary to raise the yield by less than two centners per hectare, or less than 3 bushels per acre, over a period of several years.

The size of Soviet grain stocks has always been a deep secret; but if the published production figures were not grossly overestimated, there should have been ample stocks available by 1963 on the basis of a reasonable analysis of bread-grain utilization. The fact that imports were necessary undercuts the credibility of the official grain statistics.[19] It is difficult to believe that Khrushchev was not kept informed of this situation, but it is equally difficult to reconcile his awareness of the low stocks with the sanctioning of the high level of wheat exports up through 1963, even though most of them were destined for other Communist countries (see Table 40). Khrushchev could also point with pride to the remarkable recovery that took place during 1964, this time largely thanks to the good weather in Khrushchev's favorite virgin-land bailiwick, which performed so poorly during the preceding two years. Khrushchev heeded the warn-

* Only two years earlier Khrushchev boasted at the Twenty-second Party Congress, "The Soviet Union will occupy in the near future a position on the international grain market which will make the Messrs. Imperialists aware how our agriculture is growing. (Stormy applause.)" *Izvestiia,* October 19, 1961.

Table 40. Annual average exports of specified grains and flour, 1904–1964 (1,000 metric tons)

Year	Wheat, including flour [a]	Rye, including flour	Oats	Barley	Corn	Total grain and flour
Annual average [b]						
1904–08	3,408	983	1,054	2,487	516	8,448
1909–13	4,507	876	1,027	3,752	721	10,883
1923–27	560	439	28	328	147	1,502
1928–32	1,153	452	158	556	119	2,438
1933–37	628	137	84	323	28	1,200
1955–59	3,865	534	171	593	212	5,375
1960–64	4,549	807	59	612	629	6,657
Annual						
1960	5,672	683	42	324	122	6,843
1961	5,115	1,088	180	1,007	406	7,796
1962	5,079	1,300	25	467	1,256	8,127
1963	4,451	815	22	594	723	6,605
1964	2,430	150	28	666	639	3,913

[a] All flour exports from 1955 through 1964 included under wheat at an 80 percent extraction rate.

[b] For 1904–1937, year beginning July 1; for 1955–1964, year beginning January 1.

Sources. 1904–1937, Lazar Volin, *A Survey of Soviet Russian Agriculture,* Agriculture Monograph No. 5 (U.S. Department of Agriculture, Washington, D.C., 1951), p. 179; 1955–64, Ministerstvo vneshnei torgovli SSSR, *Vneshniaia torgovlia SSSR za 1959–1963 gody* (Foreign Trade of the USSR for 1959–1963; Moscow, 1965), pp. 50–53, 122–127, and Ministerstvo vneshnei torgovli SSSR, *Vneshniaia torgovlia SSSR za 1964 god* (Foreign Trade of the USSR in 1964; Moscow, 1965), pp. 33–34.

ing of the 1963 harvest and the resulting imports. Now he pinned his hopes on the increased application of mineral fertilizer in regions where it would be most effective and on the expansion of irrigation to raise yields and diminish their fluctuation. To build up grain reserves and to increase economic incentives for farmers, Khrushchev was apparently determined to make readjustments in the allocation of resources. But the sands of time were running out.

It is tempting to look for historical analogies to the Khrushchev phase of Soviet agrarian policy, remembering, of course, the imperfect resemblance of all analogies. The closest example is the quasi-NEP that took place in the middle 1930s under Stalin, following the collectivization catastrophe. Then, too, there was no decollectivization but considerable emphasis on economic incentives, the self-government of collective farms, the small private farming of collective farmers, and so on. Going back further into history, it seems to me that there is also some resemblance between the Khrushchev era and the Stolypin period, unlike as the two men were, one a Communist Party leader and the other a tsarist prime minister who endeavored to save the throne. Khrushchev, like Stolypin, tried to make significant adjustments in the agrarian order without tampering with the basic principles on which that order was grounded. Both the admirers and critics of Stolypin might concede today that he would have been more successful in his main objective, the forestalling of another agrarian revolution, if he had not stopped short in his "wager on the strong," if he had assuaged the peasants' land hunger by moderate land reform in 1905–06, by some compulsory distribution of estate land with fair compensation to the owners. Similarly, Khrushchev's brand of agrarian reformism would have produced greater results, as far as production and food supply were concerned, and certainly as far as peasant morale and contentment were concerned, if the iron grip of collectivism had been relaxed, leading to more liberal policies with respect to capital investment in agriculture, supply of consumer goods, and managerial decision making on the farms.

15

Capital Investment and Land

A key feature of Khrushchev's agrarian policy was the beginning of a significant infusion of capital into agriculture, even though the gap vis-à-vis heavy industry remained wide. It is a well-known fact that the input of capital and other production requisites, such as mineral fertilizer and other chemicals, has marked the agricultural development in advanced countries. At the same time, labor and, in the United States, land inputs have decreased as productivity increases. In the Soviet Union, agriculture not only had low priority in capital allocation during the Stalin era, but it was systematically drained of capital through low farm prices and incomes. However, some capital investment incidental to collectivization and the parallel effort to modernize what Theodore Schultz calls traditional agriculture could not be avoided even under Stalin.[1] Thus the mass slaughter of horses during the collectivization campaign made urgent their replacement by tractors and other machinery. In the early 1930s, the Soviet government invested in the importation of tractors and combines and in the development of a domestic farm-machinery industry. The desire of the government to achieve self-sufficiency in the matter of cotton supply and to increase the output of other industrial crops led to the expansion of irrigation systems and of the fertilizer industry. The creation of the kolkhozes, sovkhozes, and MTS necessitated the construction of shelters for communal livestock, farm buildings, repair shops, offices and other facilities. All these required capital expenditures.

In addition to augmenting this supply of capital, it was necessary to invest in human capital—in the training of managerial and technical personnel and the new skilled workers needed in mechanized farming. The abundant, if not very efficient, rural labor supply before World War II tended to diminish the importance of material capital input. But after the war, the labor supply dwindled and the role of capital was enhanced. This was compounded by Khrushchev's massive programs for agricultural expansion and intensification. Thus the plowing up of some 90 million acres of new land in four years had to lead to a considerable increase in the number of tractors, in new housing for many additional workers, and in new storage and other facilities. Increased livestock production involved construction of additional shelters for animals. So it was with other projects. The shift to more intensive farming required more or special kinds of machinery, more fertilizer, improved varieties of seed, and more irrigation. An overall increase in capital input was inevitable.

Capital for investment in Soviet agriculture comes from two sources: (a) budget appropriations by the government, savings that state enterprises are permitted to retain, and long-term loans by the state banks to the kolkhozes; (b) investments by individual kolkhozes from their incomes through allocations to the "indivisible fund." Soviet statistics further distinguish between two categories of agricultural investment, the "productive" and "unproductive." Productive investment, which is by far the largest and most significant, consists of expenditures for construction and equipment directly related to production. These include farm implements (tractors, combines, trucks), storage facilities, barns, irrigation, electrification, and the planting of orchards and vineyards. Unproductive investment includes expenditures for housing, schools, children's nurseries, hospitals and cultural centers (clubs) on the state and collective farms. Unproductive investment is customarily about 10 to 15 percent of the total investment in agriculture.

Tables 41–43 show an upward trend in gross agricultural capital investment in both the productive and the unproductive components. Though there may be some question about the accuracy of the figures, this does not affect the validity of the trend. Total agricultural investment by the state farms and kolkhozes during the last two years of Stalin's rule was already 75–84 percent above the average for the preced-

347

Table 41. Gross investment in agriculture and in the whole economy, 1929–65, in comparable prices[a]

Year	Agricultural investment (million rubles)			Investment in the whole economy (million rubles)[b]	Ratio of agricultural to all investment (percent)
	Produc- tive	Unproduc- tive	Total		
Annual average					
1929–32 [c]	281	32	313	1,652	18.9
1933–37	424	45	469	3,233	14.5
1938–41 [d]	402	222	624	4,691	13.3
1941–45 [e]	345	55	400	3,564	11.2
1946–50	1,077	81	1,158	7,605	15.2
1951–55	2,454	324	2,778	14,783	18.8
1956–60	4,646	789	5,435	27,484	19.8
Annual					
1951	1,861	162	2,023	11,767	17.2
1952	1,933	207	2,140	13,214	16.2
1953	1,910	243	2,153	13,913	15.5
1954	2,762	455	3,217	16,445	19.6
1955	3,804	561	4,365	18,575	23.5
1956	4,024	630	4,654	21,387	21.8
1957	4,203	683	4,886	23,780	20.5
1958	4,741	785	5,526	27,358	20.2
1959	5,071	950	6,021	30,933	19.5
1960	5,192	1,035	6,227	33,961	18.3
1961	5,723	1,159	6,882	35,871	19.2
1962	6,415	1,096	7,454	38,100	19.7
1963	n.a.	n.a.	8,213	40,400	20.3
1964	n.a.	n.a.	9,695	44,300	21.9
1965 [f]	n.a.	n.a.	10,000	46,600	23.2

[a] Includes state and kolkhoz investment in agriculture. Not adjusted for capital consumption. Excludes cost of acquisition of livestock, state reforestation, and repairs and overhauling of equipment and buildings.

[b] Excludes the cost of *private* construction of homes and apartments which averaged about 1.1 billion rubles during 1951–55 and 2.4 billion during 1956–60.

[c] Includes the last quarter of 1928; the First 5-Year Plan period.

[d] January 1, 1938, to July 1, 1941; 3½ years of the Third 5-Year Plan period interrupted by the Russo-German war.

[e] July 1, 1941, to January 1, 1946.

[f] The series was adjusted downward slightly in the *SSSR v tsifrakh, 1965.*

Sources. *Narodnoe khoziaistvo, 1962*, p. 434; *SSSR v tsifrakh, 1963*, p. 136; *Kapital'noe stroitel'stvo*, pp. 152–153 and 155; *Narodnoe khoziaistvo, 1964*, pp. 511 and 517; *SSSR v tsifrakh v 1965 g.*, pp. 105 and 111.

Table 42. Gross state investment in agriculture and all state investment, 1929–65, in comparable prices [a]

Year	Agricultural investment (million rubles)			All investment (million rubles)	Ratio of agricultural to all investment (percent)
	Productive	Unproductive	Total		
Annual average					
1929–32	213	30	243	1,580	15.4
1933–37	240	33	273	3,034	9.0
1938–41	225	27	252	4,315	5.8
1941–45	66	4	70	3,233	2.2
1946–50	502	33	535	6,975	7.7
1951–55	1,281	164	1,445	13,437	10.8
1956–60	2,246	424	2,670	24,683	10.8
Annual					
1951	1,025	88	1,113	10,846	10.3
1952	971	96	1,067	12,141	8.7
1953	881	104	985	12,735	7.7
1954	1,536	256	1,792	15,010	11.9
1955	1,992	273	2,265	16,455	13.8
1956	2,118	291	2,409	19,123	12.6
1957	2,343	360	2,703	21,576	12.5
1958	2,279	404	2,683	24,515	10.9
1959	2,021	474	2,495	27,407	9.1
1960	2,471	590	3,061	30,795	9.9
1961	2,984	743	3,727	32,747	11.4
1962	3,386	794	4,180	34,808	12.0
1963	3,904	893	4,797	37,010	13.0
1964	4,819	967	5,786	40,374	14.3
1965 [b]	5,200	1,100	6,300	42,100	15.0

[a] Exclusive of the cost of acquisition of livestock and reforestation.

[b] The series was reduced slightly in the 1965 source.

Sources. *Kapital'noe stroitel'stvo*, pp. 39–40, 155; *Narodnoe khoziaistvo*, 1962, p. 436; *SSSR v tsifrakh, 1963*, p. 136; *Narodnoe khoziaistvo, 1964*, pp. 511–517; and *SSSR v tsifrakh, 1965*, pp. 105–114.

ing five year period, 1946–1950. The upward trend became even more pronounced in 1954 and 1955 with the beginning of the virgin-land program, when increases in investment reached nearly 50 percent and over 35 percent respectively. After 1955 the annual increase in total agricultural investment slowed down, averaging less than 10 percent.

Table 43. Gross investment by kolkhozes, 1951–65, in comparable prices (million rubles)[a]

Year	Productive investment	Unproductive investment	Total investment
1951	836	74	910
1952	962	111	1,073
1953	1,029	139	1,168
1954	1,226	199	1,425
1955	1,812	288	2,100
1956	1,906	339	2,245
1957	1,860	323	2,183
1958	2,462	381	2,843
1959	3,050	476	3,526
1960	2,721	445	3,166
1961	2,739	416	3,155
1962	3,000	274	3,274
1963	3,158	258	3,416
1964	3,523	386	3,909
1965	3,806	512	4,318

[a] Exclusive of the cost of acquisition of livestock and 1,800 million rubles spent on machinery and equipment acquired from MTS in 1958 and 1959.

Sources: *Kapital'noe stroitel'stvo*, p. 155; *Narodnoe khoziaistvo, 1962*, p. 436; *Narodnoe khoziaistvo, 1964*, p. 517; *SSSR v tsifrakh, 1965*, pp. 112–113; and *Strana Sovetov*, p. 206.

State and Kolkhoz Investment

State investment alone decreased in 1958 and 1959, but the upward trend resumed in the 1960s as agricultural difficulties mounted. The share going to agriculture in all state investment increased significantly in 1954–1957, declined in 1958–1960, and increased again continuously in 1961–1965. Larger state investment in agriculture after the mid-1950s was, to a considerable extent, a function of rapid growth in the state-farm sector, which expanded on the new lands and absorbed a considerable number of kolkhozes. The share of these farms in state agricultural investments increased from 25 percent or less in the early 1950s to 64 percent in 1964. (See Table 44.) This does not include government subsidies for state-farm operations. Not only did the total investment in state farms grow after the early 1950s, but so did the investment per acre of the larger sown

Table 44. Gross investment in state farms, 1951–1964, in comparable prices (million rubles)

Year	Productive	Unproductive	Total	Ratio to all state investment in agriculture (percent)
1951	238	41	279	25
1952	196	47	243	23
1953	198	44	242	25
1954	370	110	480	27
1955	581	152	733	32
1956	624	147	771	32
1957	774	165	939	35
1958	883	191	1,074	40
1959	1,132	295	1,427	57
1960	1,475	409	1,884	61
1961	1,850	492	2,342	63
1962	2,139	583	2,722	65
1963	2,267	698	2,965	62
1964	2,867	814	3,681	64

Sources. *Kapital'noe stroitel'stvo*, p. 167; *Narodnoe khoziaistvo, 1964*, p. 518.

area. Between 1953 and 1964 the state-farm sown area increased from 37 million acres to 216 million, and the investment per acre (productive and unproductive) rose from 6.5 rubles to 17 rubles. The massive shift of state investment to sovkhozes coincided with the disbanding of the state-owned MTS in 1958, placing the responsibility for acquiring and maintaining farm machinery on kolkhozes.

Although the mechanics of investment in kolkhozes differs from that in state farms, it was also trending upward after 1954. (See Table 43.) Because the kolkhoz sector was shrinking, the trend is best illustrated in Table 45, relating investment to the collective sown area and to the number of households, both of which declined principally as a result of the conversion of many kolkhozes into sovkhozes. Note that between 1958 and 1962 there was no increase in unproductive investment per acre and per household, but productive investment continued to grow. During the Stalin era considerably more was invested per acre in the relatively small state-farm sector than in the kolkhoz sector. But in the 1960s this investment gap was eliminated, according to Soviet statistics. A considerable part of the increase in kolkhoz investment after 1958 was used for the purchase of new machinery formerly supplied by the state, through the

Table 45. Gross investment in kolkhozes per acre of sown area and per household (*rubles*)

	1953	1958	1962	1964
Investment per acre of sown area				
Productive	3.2	7.6	10.5	n.a.
Unproductive	0.4	1.1	1.1	n.a.
Total	3.6	8.7	11.6	14.3
Investment per household				
Productive	52	131	181	n.a.
Unproductive	7	19	18	n.a.
Total	59	150	200	246

Sources. *Kapital'noe stroitel'stvo*, pp. 152 and 155; *Narodnoe khoziaistvo, 1962*, pp. 330 and 436; *ibid., 1964*, pp. 390 and 517.

operations of the MTS. The state was presumably reimbursed for such capital expenditures through a share of the payments by kolkhozes for MTS services. This suggests that part of the kolkhoz payments to the MTS can be looked upon as a form of concealed investment, which should be added to reported investments in order to make a comparison with the period after 1958 fully valid. The kolkhozes also had to pay 1.8 billion rubles to the state for the tractors and other machinery transferred to them upon the liquidation of MTS, and these are not included in the investment figures.

Theoretically, kolkhoz investments are made by the decision of the membership to appropriate a certain proportion of income to the indivisible fund, but in practice this is decided by the kolkhoz management, subject to a review by supervising authorities. Since the income of kolkhozes from which investments are made depends so much on prices paid by the government for farm products, the state indirectly influences the level of kolkhoz investment. More directly, the government sets up general goals in terms of the proportion of cash income which kolkhozes must strive to allocate to the indivisible fund. This question has had a checkered legislative history. The first kolkhoz charter, that of 1930, provided for allocation of 10 to 30 percent of the *total* income of a collective. The model charter of 1935 changed this to 10–20 percent of the cash income. The decree of April 19, 1938, which was directed against financial malpractices, including excessive and wasteful capital expenditures, limited the allocation to 10 percent and further required that no less than

60–70 percent of the cash income be distributed among kolkhozniks on the basis of workdays. But only a few months later the edict of December 4, 1938, abolished the 60–70 percent requirement and increased the allocation to 12–15 percent in grain regions and 15–20 percent in regions where industrial crops and livestock predominated.[2] In 1952 a required allocation of no less than 15 and no more than 20 percent was adopted.[3] In 1958 a further rise in the proportion set aside for the indivisible fund was "recommended" in connection with the liquidation of the MTS.[4] At the December 1958 plenum, Khrushchev urged the channeling of increased resources into indivisible funds, for to the latter he attributed a highly important role in the eventual etatization of the kolkhozes.[5] An appropriate resolution was adopted by the plenum.

In 1962 Khrushchev had to beat a retreat from his strongly expansionist investment policy because it reduced the funds available for distribution among the kolkhozniks, thus weakening their incentive to work. And so he had to admit at the March 1962 plenum that in some kolkhozes, at any rate, the investments were excessive.[6] The conflict between investment and economic incentives was an old one, exacerbated by the small size of the pie to be divided up. It explains the zigzag policy of the government, which pushes kolkhoz investment upward until it encroaches too much on the wage fund, with adverse repercussions on production when it must be pulled back.

The proportion of cash income allocated for capital purposes varied only slightly during the years 1952–1957, between 17.3 and 17.7 percent. But in 1958 it jumped to 23 percent and in 1959 to 24.3 percent.[7] In the subsequent years the absolute amount of capital allocation continued to increase with the growth of kolkhoz income, but its share decreased; in 1964 it was 20.2 percent.[8] In some regions the proportion allocated to the indivisible fund was higher than the national average, lower in others. In the Ukraine it was close to 19 percent in 1953–1957 instead of less than 18 percent for the country as a whole; in the Altai province of western Siberia it was around 28 percent in 1958 and 1959.[9] In addition to allocating a share of the cash income for capital purposes, all proceeds from the sale of capital assets, as well as capital formation by kolkhozes from their own resources, as in construction of farm buildings with kolkhoz labor, are credited to the indivisible fund, for which a special account is maintained at the State Bank.

As a partial offset to the excessive investment targets and administrative pressure, government long-term loans are provided to kolkhozes at low interest rates, 0.75 percent per year;[10] these are in a sense a subsidy. The rapid growth of such loans is shown by the following tabulation.[11]

Year	Million rubles
1952	264.0
1953	282.3
1954	n.a.
1955	442.5
1956	n.a.
1957	n.a.
1958	431.6
1959	530.7
1960	621.2
1961	781.9
1962	849.3
1963	939.8
1964	1,251.2

Compared with previous years, loans increased more in 1961–1964 than these figures indicate because the financing of some operations, such as the purchase of fertilizer, was transferred from long-term to short-term credit. Also the continuing shrinkage of the collective area must be taken into account, so that loans per acre show an even greater rise than the above figures do. In 1964 loans accounted for about a third of all kolkhoz capital investment and are expected to increase to about a half in 1966–1970.[12] Interest charges were reduced in the early 1960s, and the terms of the loans were liberalized.[13] At the March 1965 plenum, 1,450 million rubles in the outstanding loans of some of the weaker kolkhozes were canceled, and so was the remaining indebtedness to the state of 180 million rubles for the machinery and other equipment acquired by kolkhozes from the defunct MTS.[14] The amount of the loans canceled in 1965 exceeded the total made in 1964. The greater use of state credit and cancellation of a considerable proportion of the indebtedness helped to lighten the effect of increasing investment on kolkhoz income; and by the same token, it increased the funds available for distribution among the kolkhozniks.

The bulk of the loans were made for construction of livestock shelters, including installation of mechanical equipment, and for the purchase of farm machinery. In 1964 these two items accounted for about 33 and 39 percent respectively of the total loans. About 7 percent was for electrification and radio installation; 4 percent for the purchase of livestock; 4 percent for reclamation, irrigation, and afforestation; and the remaining 13 percent for miscellaneous purposes.[15] There is considerable variation in the use of long-term credit between different regions and kolkhozes. Thus with the national average in 1964 of 1,000 rubles per 100 hectares of arable land, it was 3,200 in the Georgian Republic; 2,530 in Latvia;

2,120 in Turkmen Republic; 2,280 in Kostroma province; 1,100 in Lipetzk province; and 990 rubles in Gorkii province.[16] These and other data suggest that the volume of long-term credit is larger in regions of more intensive agriculture; but this may not be the whole story. Evidence indicates that long-term credit plays an important role in capital investment of the economically weaker kolkhozes. Thus six kolkhozes in different parts of the country, which allocated in 1963 only from 2.4 to 7.1 percent of their cash incomes to the indivisible fund, totaling 109,963 rubles, were granted 718,184 rubles in loans, or 6.5 times more.[17]

A serious drawback of the Soviet long-term credit system has been the required uniformity of the repayment period for broad categories of loans. Thus all types of construction loans must be repaid in twenty years, with repayment beginning during the sixth year; for tractors and combines, the corresponding periods are eight and three years respectively. Such regulations do not take into account the ability of some kolkhozes to repay more rapidly than others. A more differentiated and flexible approach to repayment, which would be tailored to the economic capability of the kolkhozes, to the amortization schedule, and other relevant factors, has been advocated in the pages of Soviet economic journals.[18] Short-term loans to kolkhozes for capital purposes are also made by the State Bank to tide over temporary shortages of funds.

Adequacy and Effectiveness of Investment

Although investment in agriculture grew markedly during the Khrushchev era and contributed to greater production, it is not suggested, and is not claimed by the Russians, that the capital input was adequate in the light of Soviet requirements. Far too small a proportion of agricultural investment was devoted to electrification, only 4.4 percent in 1964. Considering the extensive dry zone of the country, not enough was invested in irrigation, 10 percent on the average in 1959–1963; but the proportion rose to 13 percent in 1964. As for machinery, according to Khrushchev, agriculture needed nearly 2.7 million tractors to perform farm operations during optimum periods, whereas only 1,329,000 were on farms at the end of 1962, or less than half of the required number.[19] The situation was even less satisfactory with respect to other types of machinery.

To demonstrate the inadequacy of capital equipment in Soviet agriculture, Minister of Finance Garbuzov resorted to a comparison with American agriculture at the March 1965 plenum.[20] The capital stock per average yearly farm worker, according to Garbuzov, was equivalent to

10,000 rubles in 1963 in the United States and was only 2,000 rubles in the Soviet Union. The United States had almost four times as many tractors per 1,000 hectares (2,500 acres) of arable land as the USSR; the number of combines per 1,000 hectares of small grains was 3.7 times greater in the United States than in the USSR. The United States had three times as many motor trucks on farms and used more chemical fertilizer, pesticides, and herbicides. Garbuzov made the usual caveat about the lack of full comparability of such data, since "the advantages of large socialist agriculture make it possible better to utilize farm implements." Although the point is not without some validity, it ignores inefficiencies in the use of machinery, which largely offset the putative theoretical advantages of socialized agriculture. Even so, Garbuzov admitted Russia's great lag in capital equipment. Nonetheless, the volume of metal allocated for the manufacturing of tractors and other machinery reportedly was 20 to 40 percent less during the first years of the Seven-Year Plan (1959–1965) as compared with 1957, and some farm-implement factories shifted to the production of other machinery.[21]

Much has been said and written in the USSR about the gap existing between the so-called progressive kolkhozes and the backward ones. The management of the more efficient farms is applauded by the press and officials, while the management of the retarded farms is criticized and told to "pull up" (*podtianut'sia*) to the level of the others. What is often overlooked in such pronouncements is the role played by the supply of capital and the quality of land, though various Soviet studies do trace a close correlation between differences in capital investment and the economic performance of kolkhozes.[22] It was estimated that the more efficient kolkhozes in 1962 had 2.45 times greater capital investment per 100 hectares of arable land than the average for all kolkhozes. The advanced farms also applied 3 times more mineral fertilizer and 2.2 times more organic matter per hectare than the average for all kolkhozes; the payment of labor was 2 to 2.5 times higher and the output per 100 hectares was 2.6 times higher.[23]

One interesting illustration of this issue is the kolkhoz of Kalinovka, Khrushchev's native village, which he held up on several occasions as a model farm thanks to its efficient management. The capital investment per 100 hectares in Kalinovka was more than 4 times larger than the average for the whole Kursk province where the village is located. Significantly, the share of the state in capital formation in Kalinovka was 78.8 percent and, for all kolkhozes of the province, 44.8 percent. Nearly 7 times as much mineral fertilizer was used in Kalinovka than the average for Kursk province, and production per 100 hectares was 5.6 times greater.[24]

Adequacy of investment is measured not only by its quantitative growth but also by its effective utilization. This question has received much attention from Soviet economists, who have devoted considerable effort to the concept of the economic effectiveness of investment and to the methods of evaluating it.[25] But, for ideological reasons, they have not been able to employ fully the yardstick of interest charges as an integral part of production costs and to use the tools of marginal economic analysis to determine the profitability of capital investment. To put it another way, Soviet economists were caught between Marxist ideology and economic rationality, "between the absence of a value attached to capital as such, and the necessity for Soviet planners to husband their very scarce capital resources." [26] Some Soviet economists attempted to bring interest into the picture through the back door. Thus V. S. Nemchinov advocated the addition of a percentage charge on the value of capital assets of an enterprise, including fixed and working capital (*osnovnye i oborotnye fondy*) to the production costs. Such charges must be regarded, according to him, as "an objective method of planning the profitability of an enterprise."It would permit "the liquidation of the costlessness [*besplatnost'*] of the fixed capital investment and at the same time will make for a more economical utilization of capital." [27]

No matter what the approach may be to the problem of assessing the effectiveness of capital investment, it presupposes first of all a reasonably efficient physical operation of a particular capital good, whether it be a tractor or a livestock shelter. The opposite has often been the case in Soviet agriculture. Perhaps the most concrete example of this is the familiar scene of tractors standing idle during the busy agricultural season because of breakdowns, lack of spare parts, inadequate repair facilities, and inexperienced operators. A few other common examples of wasted capital are: the leaving of farm machinery in the open all year round, prey to the elements; the deterioration of valuable mineral fertilizer by having it stand for a long time on railroad sidings unclaimed and unprotected; and the failure to use productively a substantial proportion of an irrigated area that represented a costly initial investment.

A second presupposition underlying any concept of capital effectiveness is that of the general suitability of a particular capital instrument to its expected use. But again this is often violated in the USSR by excessive standardization of equipment, its faulty distribution, and the failure to draw distinctions between the requirements of divergent farming regions; thus a farm might receive a machine it cannot use and fail to get one it needs. In the same category are the elaborate livestock shelters that were often constructed during the 1950s without mechanized facilities. These "cow palaces" came in for considerable criticism, capped by Khrushchev's condemnation of fancy pigsties in a speech in Tselinograd in November 1961.[28] Generally, insofar as investment involves construction, the agricultural sector was afflicted by the same ills as the other sectors of the economy. These were the shortage of building materials and a tendency to fan out in too many directions, to start numerous projects without being able to complete them within a reasonable time.[29] The result was a disproportionately large volume of incomplete construction and tied-up capital. Also the tendency to use overaged or obsolescent equipment hampered efficient utilization, requiring frequent repairs, always an expensive and difficult operation under Soviet conditions.* The rather haphazard fashion in which capital investment was often made by the individual kolkhozes, without proper planning and coordination of the different elements of a program, has not helped matters.[30] These drawbacks must be regarded as a serious burden on the process of capital investment in Soviet agriculture. Or, to put it another way, though there was a considerable increase in capital during the Khrushchev era, much of it was dissipated because of inefficient utilization.

The stress on the role of capital in the technology of modern agricultural production, particularly in intensive agriculture, should not obscure the importance of other elements, such as economic incentives, progressive farm practices, efficient management, and an experienced and knowledgeable labor force. These may be significantly enhanced by an adequate supply of capital. For instance, the proper timing of farm operations like sowing and harvesting, so crucial in the Soviet Union with its short season, is aided by the availability of a large number of tractors and combines. But even an abundance of tractors would not help if management

---

* The reluctance to retire obsolete and worn-out equipment under conditions of capital scarcity is understandable and may be justifiable up to a certain point, as has been argued by some Soviet economists (A. Notkin, *Ocherki teorii sotsialisticheskogo vosproizvodstva;* Essays in the Theory of Socialist Reproduction; Moscow, 1948, pp. 94–95). But as Alexander Erlich comments apropos this argument: "The gains secured by accretion of large quantities of modern equipment would be partly offset by the cumulative wear and tear of the older parts of capital stock. Moreover, the claims put forward by these inferior kinds of equipment for cooperating productive factors, some of them particularly scarce and not easily augmentable for reasons of slow gestation process, natural limitations, or bulky indivisibilities involved in their production, would reduce correspondingly the amounts of these factors available for purposes of construction and operation of the new productive plant. In other words, while the volume of capital in operation at any given moment of time would be larger, the increase in efficiency per unit of resources invested in enlargement and modernization of capital stock would be slower, the degree of strain and friction higher, and the flexibility in response to unforeseen changes smaller than under a more resolute scrapping policy." Alexander Erlich, "Comments," in Abram Bergson, ed., *Soviet Economic Growth* (Evanston, Ill., 1953), pp. 95–96.

is not alert and efficient, if the labor force lacks know-how, and if research that is supposed to develop new technology is stifled or misdirected. Finally, as J. K. Galbraith points out: "The best considered forms of agricultural investment or the most sophisticated techniques of agricultural extension are worthless if the cultivator knows out of the experience of the ages that none of the gains will accrue to him." [31] But after all is said and done, expanded agricultural production must depend largely on the increased application and more efficient utilization of additional capital inputs, since, as the years go by, inputs of land and labor are likely to be smaller.[32]

Land, Climate, and Soil

Although modern agriculture requires large capital investment and sophisticated implements, farming can be conducted with very little capital and with primitive implements. It cannot, of course, be carried on without land, and here the Soviet Union, it would seem, scores heavily. A glance at the map reveals a huge land mass of 8.6 million square miles, or nearly three times larger than the continental United States; but much of this vast area is unsuitable agriculturally for climatic reasons: it is either too cold or too dry. Thus agriculture is confined largely to a heartland represented by the so-called fertile triangle. The base of this triangle stretches, roughly, from Leningrad on the Baltic Sea in the north, along the western frontier to the Black Sea in the south, with the apex located at Krasnoiarsk on the River Enisei in central Siberia. To the north is the forest zone and beyond are the tundra wastes; along the southern and eastern borders are high mountain chains; and in the southeastern part are large deserts.

But even in this area, which comprises more than 500 million acres under crops, there are serious climatic limitations on agriculture. Much of it is characterized by "a cool continental semiarid climate similar to that of the spring wheat region of the Prairie Provinces of Canada and the Dakotas of the United States." [33] Moisture deficiency is the most serious drawback in a large part of this agricultural area. The boundary of the moisture-deficiency zone, which includes much of the southern and eastern part of the country, may be indicated on a map by a line of 16 inches of annual precipitation. Areas with precipitation below this figure are considered as being in the subhumid or dry zones. The rainfall is not only light but irregular from year to year during the growing season, and is often accompanied by high summer temperatures, high evaporation, scorching winds, and dust storms. Thus spring and early summer droughts frequently occur, affecting most adversely such early spring cereals as wheat. Late crops such as corn, sunflowers, and sugar beets, which can utilize rains during the later part of the season, fare better. The disastrous effect of summer drought is aggravated when the preceding fall is dry and there is little or no snow during the winter, or when alternate freezing and thawing occur. Under such conditions fall-sown crops—winter wheat and, to a lesser extent, the more hardy rye—suffer most.*

Another serious climatic handicap is Russia's short growing season, a function of the northern location of the country. How far north the Soviet Union is located can be best visualized when it is pointed out that Yalta, at the southern tip of the Crimea, is approximately in the same latitude as Rochester, Minnesota; and Odessa, on the Black Sea, is in the same latitude as Duluth, Minnesota. The short growing season, coupled with severe, prolonged winters over much of the agricultural area, limits the choice of crops and varieties, as exemplified by the case of winter and spring wheat. It necessitates the concentration of farm operations over a short period, increasing thereby the seasonal load and accentuating the problem of idleness or underemployment of the farm labor force during a large part of the year. However, the cold temperature in the more northern regions is to some extent compensated for by longer daylight during the growing season which, together with the use of such hardy crops as barley and rye, makes possible the extension of agriculture in such conditions.

We can say, then, that the crucial disadvantage of the continental Russian climate is the reverse relation between the territorial distribution of heat and moisture.[34] As the amount of heat increases, from north to south and west to east, moisture tends to diminish; the most heat is accompanied by the least moisture in the deserts of Soviet Central Asia, where only oasis agriculture with irrigation is possible. Exceptions are the

---

* Rye, a bread grain second in importance in the Soviet Union only to wheat, is sown in the fall or late summer and harvested the following summer. Wheat is seeded both in the fall and in the spring, but the varieties, the geographic area of cultivation, and the magnitude of yields per acre differ. The high-yielding winter wheat, accounting for 27–28 percent of the total wheat acreage, is grown in the southern and central regions of the Soviet Union, chiefly in the Ukraine and North Caucasus. Spring wheat is grown mainly in the eastern part of the country, where severe winters make the cultivation of winter varieties hazardous or impossible. While the yields of spring wheat are light, the quality of the grain, particularly its protein content, is high, though deterioration has been reported in recent years (Iu. Chernichenko, "Russian Wheat," *Novyi mir*, November 1965, p. 194). Not reported separately among spring-wheat varieties is the durum or macaroni wheat (also called hard wheat in Russia), which was introduced from Russia into the United States at the end of the nineteenth century.

subtropical region of the eastern (Caucasian) coast of the Black Sea, with its high moisture and temperature, and the Kuban region of the North Caucasus and parts of the central Ukraine, where a more advantageous combination of climatic elements prevails. Since expansion of acreage has been the principal reason for the growth of agricultural production, it is important to note that in the twentieth century, up through the Khrushchev era, the expansion has been predominantly eastward into regions with less favorable climatic conditions, where land was available to be brought under the plow. Because of the severe climate in these regions, the Soviet farmer has to wage a stiffer battle with nature than his American and West European counterparts.

Experience and new practices have made it possible to overcome or compensate for some of these climatic disadvantages. The highly productive Kholmogory breed of dairy cattle, in north European Russia, is one such adaptation. Other examples are summer fallow, stubble mulching, and similar conservation methods, which make farming less hazardous in the dry regions. In this respect, the record of both the Stalin and the Khrushchev administrations, as already indicated, was not a good one. The actions taken resembled the throwing of a gauntlet to challenge the weather, rather than attempts at sensible adaptaion. Only toward the end of the Khrushchev regime can a significant change be perceived.

Soil resources in the Soviet Union are more favorable to agriculture than climate is. This is largely because of the existence of a considerable area of fertile black soil (*chernozem*) and its close relatives. These soils are characteristic of the steppes of the central and southern European part of the USSR, and they extend in a narrow belt into southwestern Siberia and northern Kazakhstan. Chernozem soils occupy less than 10 percent of the total area of the country, but they comprise a large part of the crop acreage and have been the natural foundation on which Russian agriculture has developed in the nineteenth and first half of the twentieth centuries. The gray podzolic and marshy peat soils, comprising a large area to the north of the black-soil region, are much less fertile. Yet their agricultural significance should not be minimized, for they are in the humid zone where drought seldom occurs. With the proper use of fertilizer and with liming and the drainage of wet sections, a considerable part of the European USSR, especially the western region with its relatively milder climate, is fit for agricultural production, particularly the growing of rye, flax fiber, potatoes, various root crops, and hay. Dairy farming is also well adapted to parts of this area. Frequent cool and wet weather during the crop season are hazardous for crops other than forage on the podzolic and peat soils, as drought is the hazard for the crops on the black soils. But if the plans of the post-Khrushchev regime are carried out, the nonblack-soil area will become agriculturally more important in the future than it has been in the past.

The last frontier of agricultural expansion seemed to be reached during the Khrushchev era, with the plowing up of 110 million acres of virgin land in the eastern regions. A significant addition to sown area could be made through new irrigation systems, mainly in the southeast, or through reclamation in the humid western and north-central parts of the country (the nonblack-soil area), involving such operations as drainage, clearing of brushland, and the like. But no major expansion of acreage has been mentioned since 1963. During his conference with U.S. Secretary of Agriculture Freeman in the summer of 1963, Khrushchev stated the possibility of a reduction of acreage in the virgin-land region after yields had improved; and, in fact, the crop acreage there was reduced in 1964 and 1965.

Fertilizer

Beginning in 1961, and more emphatically after 1963, Khrushchev heralded the end of the long, extensive period of agricultural expansion and the shift to intensification and the improvement of crop yields. But such terms as "intensification" and "improvement of yields" were often bandied about in Soviet speeches and official statements with no real substantive basis and probably with little expectation of tangible results. Still, Khrushchev showed that he meant business when in 1963 he initiated a program of greatly increased production through the use of mineral fertilizer, making it the principal weapon in his intensification crusade. The yield-raising properties of fertilizer have been well established throughout the world, and data from experiment stations and the more progressive farms indicate its value for the Soviet Union as well.[35] Contrary to a widely held view, no less than half of the arable land of the USSR is characterized by a relatively low supply of basic plant nutrients, particularly nitrogen; with the intensification of agricultural production, the need for applying organic and mineral fertilizer increases.[36] But until the mid-1960s, mineral fertilizer was used extensively only for a small number of the most valuable crops, such as cotton and tea, where it resulted in a significant increase of yields.[37] (Cotton yields more than doubled in comparison to the 1930s.)

The large-scale use of mineral fertilizer is a relatively recent phenomenon in Russia. For a long time fertilization meant the use of manure, which was particularly important in the northern and central belts of poor podzolic soils. Manure was obtained through feeding livestock hay from natural meadowland and chaff from the threshing floor. Mixed farming was therefore essential for crop production in this zone. In the more fertile black and chestnut-soil regions of the south, and in the more arid regions of the southeast, manure was used for fuel and not as fertilizer. The situation is changing in this zone too, where continuing and more intensive crop production requires more plant nutrients. To quote P. M. Zemskii, "In all regions with divergent natural and economic conditions, the use of manure is one of the main factors in obtaining high crop yields." [38] This assessment of the value of manure runs throughout the writings of Russian agronomists, and it does not conflict with the importance attached to mineral fertilizer. The academician D. N. Prianishnikov, who more than anyone else promoted the cause of mineral fertilizer in the USSR, had this to say: "It is necessary to end decisively the underestimation of the tremendous significance of manure as the most important basic link in a correct system of fertilization. It is necessary to understand that *without a radical change in the extent to which our fields are supplied with manure, there is no use thinking about creating a normal relationship between the incoming and outgoing sides of the balance of nitrogen* and other plant nutrients in our agriculture, of increasing systematically fertility and of raising the yields to a proper level." [39]

In addition to the direct beneficial effects, the usefulness of manure consists in its ability to return to the soil a considerable proportion of the plant nutrients removed by feed crops. This process is enhanced when nitrogen-fixing legumes are also grown. Although in the United States an abundant supply of cheap mineral fertilizer of superior quality had largely replaced manure by the mid-twentieth century, this is not true of Western Europe, despite a sharp upward trend in fertilizer use. In western Germany, for instance, before World War II, 63 percent of all the nitrogen used, 40 percent of the phosphoric oxide, and 56 percent of the potash were derived from manure, the rest from mineral fertilizer. The proportion from manure declined considerably after the war, but was still substantial. In 1961–62 it amounted to 45 percent, 30 percent, and 44 percent for the three ingredients.[40] The supplanting of manure is farther off in the USSR, where the amount of mineral fertilizer used in the early 1960s was only about 40 percent of the amount used in the United States. The low yields in the humid nonblack-soil zone were mainly attributed to decreased manuring, which was caused by the reduction of livestock numbers and feed, the use of more straw for bedding, shortages of hauling facilities and mechanical equipment, and inefficient kolkhoz management.[41] Prianishnikov was of the opinion that far too much mineral fertilizer, and too little manure, was used in the cotton-growing regions of Central Asia.[42]

Table 46. Soviet production of mineral fertilizer, 1913 and 1928–1965 (1,000 metric tons)

		Standard units or gross weight				
Year	Nitrogen	Phosphoric oxide	Potash	Ground phosphate	Total[a]	Plant nutrients, total[a,b]
1913[c]	13.8	67.3	—	7.9	89.0	16.9
[d]	13.8	47.1	—	7.9	68.8	13.1
1928	11.2	111.5	—	12.7	135.4	25.6
1929	16.6	145.1	—	46.5	208.2	39.3
1930	19.4	302.9	—	181.3	503.6	95.0
1931	27.5	361.4	—	312.1	701.0	132.5
1932	55.6	478.7	1.9	384.6	920.8	174.8
1933	110.9	545.0	45.8	332.0	1,033.7	206.8
1934	226.0	691.9	196.0	284.3	1,398.2	311.2
1935	374.5	1,125.8	291.6	530.9	2,322.8	509.5
1936	552.8	1,256.6	406.6	623.0	2,839.0	635.8
1937	761.6	1,472.7	355.8	649.9	3,240.0	703.0
1938	828.2	1,595.7	357.9	631.5	3,413.3	737.1
1939	958.9	1,637.9	383.2	582.2	3,562.2	772.9
1940	971.8	1,351.9	532.3	381.7	3,237.7	746.0
1945	746.8	233.6	130.7	10.1	1,121.2	253.1
1946	896.4	560.9	203.5	50.6	1,711.4	383.0
1947	1,126.3	798.8	357.1	75.6	2,357.8	543.3
1948	1,356.2	1,411.1	465.7	238.0	3,471.0	780.8
1949	1,689.7	1,930.2	594.1	375.3	4,589.3	1,025.7
1950	1,913.0	2,350.5	750.4	483.2	5,497.1	1,235.7
1951	2,084.7	2,472.1	820.4	553.6	5,930.8	1,336.2
1952	2,243.0	2,654.8	904.7	598.8	6,401.3	1,446.4
1953	2,365.2	2,918.7	1,048.4	145.1	6,977.9	1,589.4
1954	2,668.9	2,350.3	1,294.6	766.4	8,082.4	1,858.0
1955	3,009.7	3,833.7	1,898.3	924.0	9,668.6	2,299.4
1956	3,455.7	4,435.2	2,094.2	951.4	10,939.0	2,590.0
1957	3,769.7	4,573.4	2,309.8	1,119.1	11,775.7	2,801.8
1958	4,124.2	4,650.6	2,412.6	1,227.8	12,419.4	2,952.4
1959	4,408.3	4,722.7	2,474.4	1,303.1	12,915.6	3,064.5
1960	4,892.3	4,878.1	2,605.9	1,472.5	13,866.6	3,280.5
1961	5,664.2	5,047.0	2,753.1	1,758.6	15,322.0	3,593.3
1962	6,904.7	5,161.0	3,198.1	1,874.2	17,258.2	4,077.9
1963	8,574.6	5,860.4	3,364.8	1,997.4	19,935.1	4,646.5
1964	10,222.0	7,522.0	4,553.0	3,155.0	25,562.0	6,009.0
1965	13,217.0	8,550.0	5,691.0	3,690.0	31,300.0	7,400.0

[a] Since 1954, includes boric and boric magnesium preparations.

[b] Standard units of gross weight converted to plant nutrients content on the basis of 20.5 percent of N for nitrates, 41.6 percent K_2O for potash, 18.7 percent P_2O_5 for phosphoric oxide, 19.2 percent P_2O_5 for ground phosphate, and 9 percent H_3BO_3 for boric magnesium preparations.

[c] Present boundaries of the USSR.

[d] Boundaries as of September 17, 1939, excluding annexed territories.

Source. *Promyshlennost' SSSR, 1964*, p. 142; *Narodnoe khoziaistvo, 1964*, p. 176; *SSSR v tsifrakh, 1965*, p. 56; *Narodnoe khoziaistvo, 1965*, p. 188.

The use of mineral fertilizer can increase the supply of manure by raising the yield and production of feed crops, especially legumes, and the supply of straw. But there is one practice of associating manure and other organic fertilizers with mineral fertilizer and lime which proved fallacious. When Lysenko extended his sphere of activity to soil science, he began to advocate using mineral fertilizer, manure and other organic matter, and lime in preparing compost, but with considerably reduced quantities of the ingredients than when one applied them separately.[43] Western specialists saw no special advantage in this compost system— only extra work and expense. Sharp criticisms of the practice were published after Khrushchev's downfall.[44] On economic and technical grounds, it would seem reasonable to expect the USSR to follow the Western European model of a supplementary combination of mineral fertilizer and farm manure and other organic materials, rather than the American model of preponderant reliance on mineral fertilizer. But there are technological fashions which almost every Soviet farm manager strives to follow, and mineral fertilizer has currently become the "rage."

Before World War I, Russia relied predominantly on imports of mineral fertilizer. Domestic production was insignificant and confined to phosphates. As Table 46 indicates, the development of a domestic fertilizer industry dates to the 1930s. By 1939 the Soviet Union produced an equivalent of 773,000 tons of plant nutrients, or 3,562,000 tons in standard units (the Soviet measure). Thus the USSR had become one of the half dozen ranking fertilizer-manufacturing countries of the world. In spite of this advance, there was serious opposition from the influential V. R. Williams, whose panacea was the use of perennial grasses to improve the soil structure. On this point he locked swords with D. N. Prianishnikov, the principal exponent of mineral fertilizer. The resolutions of the Eighteenth Party Congress on the Third Five-Year Plan (1938–1942) do not mention chemical fertilizer, but do speak of grasses in rotation.[45] In any event, a serious setback occurred during the war, though the drastic decline in production was made good by 1948 and an uninterrupted upward trend ensued. The trend slowed down in 1959–60, particularly in view of the high goal of 35 million tons set for 1965 by the seven-year plan. After 1961 production gained momentum and made especially rapid strides in 1964 and 1965, though the goal of 35 tons was not quite reached.

Not all of the annual output of mineral fertilizer was available to domestic agriculture. In 1964 less than 22 million tons were delivered to agriculture out of the 25.6 million tons manufactured, much of the remainder going for export (see Table 47). More serious was the reduced effectiveness of the available mineral fertilizer because of poor quality, excessive filler, and inefficient transportation, storage, and application.

Table 47. Delivery of mineral fertilizer to Soviet agriculture (1,000 tons)

	1950	1958	1960	1962	1963	1964
	Standard units					
Nitrogen	1,497	3,348	3,749	5,218	6,634	8,584
Available phosphoric oxide	2,366	4,391	4,403	4,562	5,184	6,865
Phosphate rock	472	1,095	1,392	1,764	1,852	2,972
Potash	1,015	1,786	1,842	1,985	2,166	3,416
Total	5,350	10,620	11,386	13,529	15,836	21,961
	Plant nutrients					
Nitrogen	307	686	769	1,070	1,360	1,759
Available phosphoric oxide	442	821	823	853	969	1,284
Phosphate meal	90	208	265	335	352	565
Potash	422	743	766	826	901	1,421
Total	1,261	2,458	2,623	3,084	3,582	5,040

Source. *Narodnoe khoziaistvo, 1963*, p. 300; *1964*, p. 338.

To these must be added a lack of proper knowledge of soil conditions and plant-nutrient requirements on specific farms, a situation stressed in Soviet sources.

The press also voiced numerous complaints about the common malpractice of dumping fertilizer on railroad sidings and leaving it there in the open to deteriorate until the kolkhoz or sovkhoz to which it was consigned was ready to claim it. No great power of imagination is required to visualize the damage resulting from such "storage," and the facilities were no better on the farms themselves. Khrushchev spoke of it sarcastically as providing ice hills in the winter down which children could slide. It was not always inefficient management or lack of interest that was responsible for the failure to haul fertilizer from the railway points. There were shortages of shipping facilities, particularly during the seasonal peak; the roads in the Russian countryside were often impassable; and financial difficulties could lead to apathy among the farm managers.

The large proportion of heavy filler in Soviet mineral fertilizer inflates transportation costs. It was calculated that in 1963, out of the total railroad transportation bill for mineral fertilizer of 361 million rubles, 277 million, or more than three fourths, was attributable to the filler. The regional distribution of different kinds of fertilizer has also been faulty. Phosphates and potash were delivered to the humid regions with podzolic soils, but there was an "entirely inadequate" amount of nitrogen, in spite of the fact that nitrogen is the limiting fertility factor in this zone.[46] Although it is well established that the effectiveness of fertilizer depends on the general level of farm technology, this is often disregarded on the farms. Increased application of fertilizer is viewed by some farm managers as a means of covering up and offsetting inferior practices.[47] The words of the chemist Mendeleev, who was also a fertilizer enthusiast, are often quoted: "I am against those who preach by word of mouth and in print that fertilizer is everything and that, by using large quantities, one can till the soil any which way."

There have been, in addition, serious defects in the fertilizer price structure. The prices of mineral fertilizer to the farmers were too high and so were manufacturing costs, making factory production unprofitable. For 1965 it was estimated that the prices of mineral fertilizers were, on the whole, 50 percent higher in the USSR than in the United States and Europe, and they are not compensated for by extra-product returns. The unsatisfactory physical form of the fertilizer manufactured in the USSR increases the cost. The price of ammonium nitrate, for instance, is 62.8 rubles a ton. Because it comes in large caked lumps instead of powdered or granulated form, there is an additional cost for preparing it for application of about 20 rubles per ton. With a further minimum cost of 20 rubles for applying it to the soil, the total expenditure would come to about 100 rubles per ton. The extra grain produced would at best not exceed 2.5 tons, which also costs on the average 100 rubles.[48] Thus no economic gain would result from the application of fertilizer. This difficulty is compounded by the fact that prices fixed for chemical fertilizers do not cover the cost in a number of cases; the worst case is potash and, among the nitrogenous fertilizers, urea.[49] This does not stimulate the much needed improvement of quality. Probably the manufacturing costs are too high, and the whole pricing system needs to be rationalized. Another anomaly is that fertilizers of different makes, containing the same plant nutrients, are differently priced. Thus a ton of nitrogen contained in ammonium nitrate costs 141.5 rubles, and that in sodium nitrate, 417 rubles; a ton of phosphoric acid in superphosphate costs 85 rubles, and that in ammoniated superphosphate, 200 rubles; a ton of potassium oxide in potash salt costs 17.5 rubles, and that in potassium sulphate, 67.3 rubles.[50]

Such a large disparity in prices, determined administratively and supplemented by the allocation of limited supplies, is bound to make for considerable inequalities in the cost of fertilizer (in terms of plant nutrients) to different farms. This is accentuated by the fact that the farms have to bear the cost of transportation from the factories. As a result of variations in transportation expenditures, in 1964 a ton of superphosphate cost 16.96 rubles in Moscow province, 19.73 rubles or 16.3 percent more in Krasnodar province, and 34.58 rubles in the Far Eastern Maritime province. The ratio of transportation cost to factory price varied from 4.1 percent for Moscow province, to 21.3 percent for Krasnodar, and 113.5 percent for the Maritime province. For potash the variation in cost was even sharper.[51] Also the extra hauling cost for the many farms remote from railroads adds to the inequities and disincentives in the use of fertilizer.

In the humid podzolic regions, where the use of fertilizer holds the greatest promise, liming to neutralize the excessive acidity of soils is essential to an effective use of fertilizer. Much has been written about this.[52] But of the more than 50 million acres of arable land reported in need of liming in 1963, less than 3 million were thus treated. Only 2.8 million tons of lime were used for soil improvement in the USSR in 1962, compared with 26 million tons applied in the United States.[53]

The volume of criticism about fertilizer use swelled during the months immediately preceding the December 1963 plenum of the Central Committee called by Khrushchev to deal with a whole spectrum of problems of the chemical industry, particularly fertilizer production. The criticisms continued at the plenum and long after it. Among this literature a public letter addressed to the Central Committee by a group of scientists is noteworthy. It stated that in the "use of fertilizer there are serious shortcomings. Agriculture is not provided with warehouses for storage and with equipment for applying fertilizer. Most of it is supplied to the farms in bulk, without bagging . . . This leads to tremendous losses of fertilizer and deterioration of its quality." As a consequence, "the country is not obtaining from the use of fertilizer even one half the benefit it could have with good organization." [54] The authors of the letter believed that, with improved quality and better utilization of fertilizer, less of it would be needed to achieve the high 1970 agricultural goals. Incidentally, they also considered the estimated requirements for 1970 of 9.4 million tons of mineral feedstuffs for livestock grossly excessive—a figure exceeding several times world consumption. To attain better utilization of fertilizer, the scientists recommended more investment in such areas as machinery and storage and transportation facilities, even if it meant some reduction on the manufacturing end.

The Soviet Union was well beyond the take-off stage by 1965 in production and use of mineral fertilizer. But, even so, the 1963 target for 1970, 80 million tons, would have required a quadrupling of production in the course of seven years. Actually the goal for 1965 was reduced after Khrushchev's downfall from 35 million tons to 33.5 million tons,[55] and output was even less: 31.3 million tons. The plan for 1966–1970 reduced the 1970 production goal to 62–65 million tons and set the delivery target to agriculture at 55 million tons, or double the quantity delivered in 1965.[56] Of great importance is the planned allocation of about 40 percent of the fertilizer to grain crops; until the mid-sixties it was used in insignificant quantities for this purpose.[57] It was reported that 7 million tons were to be applied to grain crops harvested in 1964.[58] In terms of increasing yields, an additional 10 to 12 million tons of mineral fertilizer applied by 1970 may result, on a conservative estimate, in 15 to 24 million more tons of grain.

The trimming of the fertilizer program by Khrushchev's successors made it more realistic, and the muting of publicity should not detract from its significance as a promising instrument of agricultural expansion. Despite flaws and operational difficulties, the fertilizer program differs from other Soviet crash projects in that it is in the mainstream Western tradition of economic progress. By relying on fertilizer as a key to higher yields and greater intensity, the Soviet Union is traveling the well-trod path that Western Europe took in the nineteenth century and the United States and Japan in the twentieth. What is also significant is the program's recognition of limitations on the effectiveness of fertilizer in the different zones of the country. Khrushchev insisted at the 1963 plenum that the limited supply of mineral fertilizer should not be distributed on the principle of a little bit to everyone, but allocated in significant quantities to areas where it would be most effective in increasing production. The rule since then has been clearly spelled out and is today especially appropriate in the framework of the development of the nonblack-soil area. The creation of a national agrochemical service, with a network of field laboratories for soil analysis and experimental studies, should eventually help in the proper distribution and application of fertilizer. In the short run there is still a problem of training and staffing these agencies.

Although mineral fertilizer, in conjunction with the proper use of manure, constitutes the heart of the new fertilizer program, there has also been much stress on the use of peat. It is a material used to a much greater extent for soil improvement in the Soviet Union than in the United States, since peat deposits are extensive and other fertilizers are in short supply. The amount of peat applied on collective farms increased at a rapid rate, from 11 million tons in 1953 to 48 million in 1958 and to 71 million in 1959.[59] The 1965 goal for production of peat for agricultural use was set at 130 million tons, in addition to 20 million tons for animal litter.[60] In the United States peats are used primarily because they "improve the water-holding ability of most soils and give better physical structure to fine soils." [61] In addition to these qualities, peat is valued in the Soviet Union also for its contribution to plant nutrients, low though it may be. The significance of the latter function may diminish as the supply of mineral fertilizer increases.

Pesticides

Scientific and industrial developments in the nineteenth century provided agriculture with highly important chemical means of plant protection against insects, diseases, pests, and weeds. It is true that damage has been caused to wildlife by the indiscriminate and often ignorant use of toxic substances, but this only underscores the need for following safer methods of using these chemicals—their contribution to the high level of production in modern agriculture cannot be gainsaid. In the Soviet Union much has been written about the heavy losses from diseases, insects, and especially weed infestation. Such losses were corroborated by one visiting team of U.S. Department of Agriculture crop specialists, who found that potato fields were generally infected with viruses; in some, 70 percent or more of the plants were infected.[62]

The Soviet government has shown a growing awareness of the importance of pesticides. Their production more than quadrupled between 1958 and 1965, when it reached 103,000 tons of active substance, compared with 125,000 tons set as a goal by Khrushchev.[63] This was only 28 percent of the estimated 367,000 tons produced for agricultural purposes in the United States in 1962, but it was possible for the first time to apply herbicides over a large area (12 million acres in 1964) in the virgin-land region. Khrushchev's 1970 goal of 450,000 tons was probably lowered by his successors, as were other chemical targets; but no figure was given in the directives for the five-year plan or in Kosygin's report on it at the Twenty-third Party Congress. Nonetheless, the use of agricultural chemicals may be expected to increase.

Irrigation

Water is the major limiting factor in agricultural production over a large part of the world. The vital role that irrigation played in many ancient civilizations and the dependence on it of modern agriculture are well-established facts. With irrigation, high and stable production is possible in arid regions; without it, a meager, fluctuating output is usually the result. Irrigation and mineral fertilizers go together in these dry regions, because minerals in the soil can be absorbed by plants only when they are in solution. Thus fertilizer without water is ineffective, or worse—it may have a negative effect.

Cotton is an excellent example. It cannot be grown in Central Asia or Turkestan, its principal region, without irrigation, despite favorable temperature conditions. The yields were light, averaging 13 centners of unginned cotton per hectare before World War I, but they reached 19–21 centners with heavy applications of mineral fertilizer. In the Central Asian cotton-growing regions, irrigation is of ancient origin and existed long before the Russian conquest of the area in the mid-nineteenth century. During Russian rule there was an extension and modernization of the irrigation network and the introduction of American cotton varieties to replace the inferior native cotton. For a long time, however, irrigation was confined to Central Asia and Transcaucasia.

The idea of irrigation as a means of combating recurrent droughts in the semiarid zone of European Russia is of more recent origin. During the Stalin era, it was twice embodied in specific programs. In the spring of 1932, following a serious drought the year before, the government decreed the irrigation over five years of 10 to 11 million acres in the Volga basin, to be devoted to wheat.[64] This region had been the scene of frequent droughts. Touching on the same subject in his report to the Seventeenth Party Congress in January 1934, Stalin said: "As far as the irrigation of the Trans-Volga area is concerned—and this is the principal method of combating the drought—this matter should not be delayed too long." [65] He pointed out that the delay was due to "certain factors in the international situation," which diverted large resources for other purposes, but he saw no reason for postponing this task longer. Here Stalin was or pretended to be optimistic. It was a year after Hitler gained power, and the international situation was growing worse. Industrialization and armaments continued to drain the nation's resources; and even though droughts occurred every other year (1934, 1936, and 1938), the expensive irrigation cure was not applied.

Another ambitious irrigation program in the basins of the Volga, Don, Dnieper, and other rivers was announced toward the end of Stalin's rule, but it was shelved by Khrushchev, who opted for the cheaper virgin-land project. Several years later, at the January 1961 plenum, Khrushchev evinced much interest in irrigation. He acknowledged the error in planning an extensive development of hydroelectric power by not having linked it with agricultural irrigation. Priority should have been given to Central Asia instead of Siberia. At the Twenty-second Party Congress in October 1961, Khrushchev declared: "Now that we have a powerful industry, the time has come to execute a wide program of irrigation in order to create a stable base of agricultural production which would guarantee against any eventuality." [66] He proposed that the irrigated area be increased from 22–23 million acres to 70 million by 1980.

The tremendously large goal set for twenty years off was no doubt pleasant for Soviet planners to contemplate, but it made no dent in the immediate problem. It took the traumatic experience of 1963 to focus Khrushchev's interest on irrigation as a major remedy for agricultural ills. He was particularly concerned with irrigation as a means of creating a stable reserve, which would serve as the core of the grain supply each year, independent of the vagaries of weather. For this purpose the irrigated area devoted to grain was to be increased by better utilization of the existing planted area and by extension of planted area in the course of a few years. According to Khrushchev's calculation, 6.4 million acres of the old area were to yield 15.6 million tons of grain; and 6.9 million new acres, 17.4 million tons. With an added 2 million tons to be obtained from the second crop, the total is 35 million tons.[67] Corn and rice—the latter formerly imported in large quantities from Communist China—were to be the main grains grown, followed by wheat, peas, and other grains and legumes. This indeed would have been a substantial reserve, equal to more than half of the government's record grain procurements in 1964. However, Khrushchev's estimate was predicated not only on a large and costly enlargement of the irrigated area, but on an unrealistic increase of yields. Thus in 1962 the average yield of irrigated small grain was 11.8 centners per hectare (17.5 bushels per acre) and of corn 18.2 centners per hectare (29 bushels per acre); Khrushchev's 1970 targets were 40 and 80 centners respectively.[68]

In pursuance of this program and also to increase the acreage under cotton and other industrial crops, E. E. Alekseevskii, the official in charge of the irrigation program, stated at the February 1964 plenum that about 1.9 million acres had to be added to the irrigated area in 1964–65, with an annual addition of about 2.5 million acres during the subsequent five years, totaling 12.5 million acres. This figure was cut by Brezhnev at the March 1965 plenum to about 7.4 million acres, which would exceed by 30 percent the 5.7 million acres added to the irrigated area during the preceding twenty years.[69] Much of the planned increase in irrigated area was in the traditional cotton and rice regions. The 1970 target for irrigated grain was also cut from about 35 million tons specified by Khrushchev to 11.5–13 million tons. This would be four times larger than the less than 3 million tons reportedly harvested in 1964.[70] Among grain crops much stress has been laid by the irrigation program of the 1960s on rice, in order to eliminate the reliance on imports. Rice is also not very demanding on the soil and grows on heavy and saline soils that are not suitable for other crops.

The growth of irrigation in the USSR has not been hampered by a lack of water, which in most years is sufficient to irrigate a much larger area. Rather its considerable capital investment and maintenance cost has restricted expansion. Khrushchev gave a figure of 2,600 rubles as the capital cost of irrigating a hectare of land, or over 1,000 rubles per acre. On this basis, the total investment in irrigating 7.4 million acres would amount to over 7.4 billion rubles, or 2.2 billion more than the record total state investment in agriculture for productive purposes during 1965.

The limitation arising from high capital need has been accentuated by gross inefficiency in the utilization of the irrigated area. This takes several forms. Perhaps the most puzzling is the failure to irrigate a large area already equipped for irrigation. Thus in 1963, of the 23.5 million acres of land with an irrigation network, about 2.5 million acres were never actually irrigated, and close to 1.3 million acres were in meadows and pastures; hardly an effective use of irrigated land. More than 400,000 of the 2.5 million acres were never irrigated because the irrigation network and water-pumping equipment were in disrepair. As Alekseevskii pointed out, each year a large amount of money was used for new irrigation construction, and it would have been cheaper to use some of the funds to repair existing facilities.[71]

An important reason for underutilization of irrigated land is its salinity and swampiness, caused by poor drainage and by faulty irrigation construction and operation. The prevailing gray soils of the irrigated Central Asian regions are rich in alkalies, and salinized soils are easily formed if irrigation is defective. Even on slightly salinized soils, cotton yields can decrease by 10 to 12 percent or more, and it was estimated that an area of up to 7.5 million acres was affected in various degrees by salinization.[72] Because of the accumulation of salt, an area of 294,000 acres was lost to agriculture, and it largely offset the addition of the new irrigated area of 383,000 acres.[73] For a long time this danger was underestimated.[74] But increasing emphasis has been given to salinity control in the 1960s. Brezhnev, in his speech at the March 1965 plenum, underscored the crucial significance of the drainage system: "It is necessary to categorically forbid the construction of an irrigation network without simultaneous construction of a drainage system. This must be a real engineering project, built in accordance with modern hydrological technology. Otherwise we cannot retain very much longer the fertility of irrigated land." [75] This is a big order, especially when it is considered that much also has to be done to improve and extend the drainage system that services the existing irrigation network.

It has been pointed out by American irrigation specialists that in the USSR "irrigation system water losses are high. More than half of the water diverted is lost to deep percolation and excessive runoff. This is estimated to amount to 25 billion cubic meters of water." According to a Soviet estimate, this represented a loss to the national economy of a billion rubles, assuming the lowest cost of 3.5 kopecks a cubic meter for water.[76] Low yields on irrigated land, its use for uneconomic crops, and inefficient labor practices and management were some of the other deficiencies highlighted by Soviet sources. Irrigation shares with other branches of Soviet economy the existence of bottlenecks in the supply of construction materials and machinery. Nor has it escaped the glaring gap between modern technology, used in the construction of main canals and reservoirs, and primitive methods of irrigating crops by hand.[77] Brezhnev and Kosygin seem to be more strongly committed to irrigation development than their predecessors were. But the existing potentialities for agricultural irrigation have still been only lightly exploited.

Another problem is the need for providing watering facilities for livestock on the extensive pasturelands in the eastern steppes. Lack of water hinders the effective utilization of much of this land, which could contribute materially to the feed supply. This important issue was mentioned by Khrushchev in his discussion with Freeman; but Brezhnev did not refer to the subject at the March 1965 plenum. The question is bound to claim further attention from the government. While agriculture in the southeast of the USSR suffers from a shortage of water, the reverse is true of the northwestern corner of the country, where there is a considerable area of marshy land or land with excessive moisture. Such land can be turned into productive acreage by proper reclamation and drainage. Some land overgrown with brush can also be reclaimed for agricultural purposes. It has been planned to step up reclamation during 1966–1970 with a target of 15 million acres, compared to the 7.5 million acres reclaimed during the preceding twenty years. This drive is in line with the effort to expand agriculture in the humid nonblack-soil zone.

Land Conservation

The existence of a considerable degree of soil erosion has been amply documented in published Soviet sources. According to one authority, about 75 million acres of land in European Russia are subject to water erosion. Deterioration on 25 to 27.5 million acres resulted in the diminution of their productivity by 70 to 80 percent. It was estimated that annually 535 million tons of soil is washed away, causing a loss of more than 1.2 million tons of nitrogen, more than 590,000 tons of phosphates, and approximately 12 million tons of potash in a form potentially assimilable by crops.[78] A rapid increase in the number of ravines and shallow rivers are among the consequences of this process.

Wind erosion also causes great damage in the dry regions, especially where soils are light and have lost their structure as a result of frequent cultivation. In Kazakhstan there are more than 30 million acres of this kind of land, or about 40 percent of the arable area.[79] The plowing up of millions of acres of level grassland in this region intensified or started the process of wind erosion. But other regions in Siberia, the Volga area, the North Caucasus, and the Ukraine also have much land subject to erosion. The damage caused by wind consists in the destruction of crops as well.[80] Especially injurious are the frequent dust storms. In the spring of 1960, for instance, dust storms in ten provinces of the Ukraine, in several provinces of the North Caucasus, and in the Lower Volga and Don basins damaged 8.6 million acres of crops.[81] The figure was even higher according to Minister of Agriculture Volovchenko: 15 million acres in the Ukraine alone, with winter crops especially hard hit.[82] There is also a considerable area in the southern Ukraine, the North Caucasus, Volga basin, parts of the Urals, and North Kazakhstan which is subject to both water and wind erosion.[83]

The danger of soil erosion has become increasingly recognized by the government. In 1962 the Collegium of the Ministry of Agriculture of the USSR made recommendations regarding erosion control for different zones of the country. Research and educational institutions were upbraided for neglecting this field, and the criticism was repeated by Volovchenko at a large conference, held at the Lenin Academy of Agricultural Sciences in July 1963, devoted to the soil-erosion problem.[84] Although there is a growing interest in the problem and probably a better understanding of its various facets, soil conservation in the USSR is still in an embryonic stage.

A number of faults in the utilization of farmland were also pointed out by Volovchenko at the February 1964 plenum.[85] Each year about 3 million acres of tillable land is taken out of cultivation and permitted to revert to sod. This is a way of letting the land rest and restoring its fertility after continuous cropping under primitive, extensive farming. But it is not appropriate to modern agriculture, which must rely on other methods of restoring soil fertility. Some land is permitted to become swampy or overgrown with brush and is thus lost to agriculture. Each year up to 1,250,000 acres, including 500,000 acres of arable land, is transferred to various nonagricultural uses. Volovchenko cited examples of valuable agricultural land squandered, as in the transfer of 460 acres of irrigated land to a cement factory in the Kirgiz Republic. Among the remedial measures suggested by Volovchenko was a cadastral survey of land, modeled on the one in East Germany, where all land is evaluated on a percentile scale that reflects a number of indicators. It can be said that many of the difficulties encountered because of the misuse of land stem from the failure to charge or impute rent, which would exert automatic pressure for a more effective allocation and utilization of land resources.[86]

16

Incentives and Procurements

Probably no problem of collective agriculture has attracted so much attention as that of economic incentives. In theory the party has recognized, with ample support from Lenin's writings, the importance of economic incentives from the early days of collectivization. Because of this, the communes and other forms of egalitarianism in the distribution of income were banned. In practice, however, economic incentives were in the foreground only in critical periods, receding when the emergency had passed. Still it is an interesting fact that even Communists recognized their efficacy, at least theoretically. Thus an editorial in the principal Soviet agricultural newspaper declared: "Practical experience has shown that where the principle of material interest is consistently adhered to, there exists, as a rule, good working discipline; technology and land are used very productively; and the output is greater and cheaper." [1]

The efficacy of economic incentives in many underdeveloped countries has been doubted on the ground that habits of leisure and certain forms of conspicuous consumption take priority over an increase in work effort or productive thrift.[2] But the idea of the effectiveness of economic incentives in Russian peasant agriculture is evidenced in contemporary literature by the works of such writers as Dorosh in his "Village Diary," Panferov in "Volga," Abramov in "One Day in the New Life," and others who attempted to sketch a more or less realistic picture of Russian rural life. If the general principles underlying economic incentives in Soviet agriculture are not in doubt, however, their adequacy and form have been very much questioned, particularly during the post-Stalin era when the futility of reliance on sheer coercion, or terror, became apparent even to the Kremlin.

A distinction must be made in this matter between the two sectors of socialist agriculture, the sovkhozes and the kolkhozes. In the sovkhozes, financed through the state budget, wages were determined as in other areas of state employment of hired workers. They did not depend upon the income and financial status of a particular farm. Conversely, kolkhozniks were not paid wages; they shared in the fluctuating income of the kolkhoz of which they happened to be members. But, and this cannot be overemphasized, this was essentially a residual claim—like that of a common stockholder in a business corporation—which was settled after state taxes were paid, as well as after the current production expenses of the kolkhoz and its annual capital-investment requirements were met. Between the last three items and the residual share available for distribution among kolkhozniks, there was an inverse relationship. The smaller the current expenses, the capital investment, and the share of the state in the annual income of a particular kolkhoz, the larger the proportion going to kolkhozniks.

I discussed above the upward trend in kolkhoz capital investment, which was strongly encouraged by the state. I pointed out the possible adverse effect of such a trend on kolkhozniks' earnings, especially when combined with wasteful capital-utilization practices that diminish the fruitfulness of investments by raising the level of the future income-producing capacity of the kolkhozes. Excessive production expenditures also affected adversely the residual available for distribution to kolkhozniks. But it is generally agreed that the greatest stumbling block to higher economic incentives has been the exactions of the state, the system of compulsory deliveries or procurements of farm products. Since they constitute the predominant outlet for marketable production, procurements are central in the kolkhoz income structure, particularly in cash income, and thus determine the amount available for distribution among the kolkhozniks. This therefore became the logical area of reform for Khrushchev and his successors.

Basic Procurement Practices

The system, it will be remembered, hit the kolkhozes from two directions: high delivery quotas per unit of land and fixed low prices for the products delivered. A differentiation of the quotas between the stronger and weaker kolkhozes within a district was introduced in 1947 in the wake of the war, replacing the uniform rates for a district as a whole, set by the procuring reform of 1939–40. Although this was helpful to the weaker kolkhozes, it often had the undesirable effect of imposing an excessive burden upon the more efficient kolkhozes. As Khrushchev sarcastically remarked in his September 1953 report, "no sooner does a kolkhoz rise above the level of its neighbor than the procuring agencies proceed to trim it, just as a gardener trims bushes in the garden with his shears." The practice of saddling the more efficient kolkhozes with high delivery quotas often took the illegal but familiar form of repeated levies. These were usually imposed by the authorities in order to avoid the dire consequences of nonfulfillment of the high goals set by the procuring plan for a whole district or province, goals to which the weak kolkhozes could not make an adequate contribution. Thus, in practice, the kolkhozes had no certainty with respect to their obligation to the state, and it hampered their planning. The state, in effect, appropriated the "efficiency wages" of kolkhoz labor and management as well as the differential rent and quasi-rent arising from better land, more advantageous location, and superior capital endowment. Here we have a serious disincentive to kolkhozes to rise above the level of mediocrity. But it was the syndrome of high quotas and low prices that made the picture so dismal at the end of the Stalin era.

Procurement prices for nonindustrial crops changed little after the 1930s, in sharp contrast to prices and wages. Moreover, the extra-quota purchases of the government at higher prices dwindled after the prewar period, thus depressing the average price paid by the state for farm products. Only for a limited number of industrial crops, such as sugar beets, cotton, and citrus fruit, were prices raised after the war in order to encourage the expanded production desired by the regime. Under Khrushchev the government reduced the quotas, considerably increased prices, and revived extra-quota purchases at still higher prices. The reform began in September 1953 with animal products, potatoes, and vegetables and was extended successively to other farm products. The first procuring-price increases ordered in September 1953 were as follows: livestock and poultry products, more than 5.5 times; milk and butter, doubled; potatoes, 2.5 times; and other vegetables on the average of 25 to 40 percent. Extra-quota prices were raised on the average of 30 percent for meat and 50 percent for milk.

Further price increases followed during the next four years, supplementing some of the actions taken in 1953 and extending the process to other commodities until almost all agricultural products were covered. The complicated procurement system, with its variegated pattern and multiple prices, was retained intact during the period 1953–1957. There were four principal types of procurements.

First there were the compulsory delivery quotas (*obiazatel'nye postacki*) of crops per hectare of arable land and of livestock products per hectare of total farmland. The prices paid for these by the government were the lowest.

Second there were extra-quota purchases by the government at much higher prices. Even after the compulsory delivery prices were raised and the gap between them and the extra-quota prices greatly diminished, the latter were still two or three times higher.[3] Extra-quota purchases, which became very small during the postwar period, had grown increasingly at the expense of compulsory deliveries, particularly of livestock products, during the early post-Stalin period. The share of extra-quota purchases in total procurements of meat and milk was more than 40 percent in 1957 compared with about 20 percent in 1940; and the share of compulsory deliveries was correspondingly 18–22 percent and 56 percent of the total.[4] For grains, the share of extra-quota purchases increased from 5.2 percent in 1953 to 23.9 percent in 1956.[5]

While extra-quota purchases were generally increasing after 1953, their share in total procurements varied from kolkhoz to kolkhoz and district to district, with a consequent variation in the average realized price— that is, the average of compulsory deliveries and extra-quota deliveries was associated with a high average price, and vice versa.[6] Obviously, the stronger kolkhozes, which were able to sell to the state in excess of the quotas, profited from this arrangement.

Third, the contract method of procurement was used for industrial crops. These were crops like cotton and sugar beets, serving as raw materials for light industry. Even in the Stalin era the government had employed price and other incentives, such as cash advances and distribution among the growers at concession prices of certain needed products like grain, textiles, oil cake, and sugar. As far as prices were concerned, a characteristic feature of the contract system was the payment of large premiums above the basic price for deliveries in excess of quotas set by the plan.[7]

As a consequence, the premium price and not the basic price played the dominant role in the price structure of contracted crops. Thus it came about that the state paid different prices to different kolkhozes for the same product, depending upon the extent of deliveries above the plan. It was a repetition, only in an exaggerated form, of the extra-quota situation. Khrushchev, in his report dealing with the price reform at the June 1958 meeting of the Central Committee, illustrated this situation by several examples. One cotton-growing kolkhoz realized an average price of 369 rubles per centner as a result of premium payments, while another kolkhoz in the same district which delivered merely the planned quantity received only 297 rubles per centner. Similarly with flax fiber and other industrial crops: the basic procuring price paid for flax fiber was 5,562 rubles per ton and premiums amounted to 8,931 rubles.[8] The multiplicity of prices under the contracting method, as under the extra-quota method, favored a relatively small number of economically strong kolkhozes. For instance, in 1954, 38 percent of all flax-growing kolkhozes sold to the state 45 percent of the total quantity procured and obtained 85 percent of the premiums paid.[9]

Although in 1956 the procuring prices of cotton and sugar beets were increased and premiums were scaled down, the stronger ("advanced") kolkhozes still were far ahead in the average prices they received. This is shown by a sample survey of 27 cotton-growing kolkhozes in Tashkent province in 1936.[10] The kolkhozes were divided into three groups: eight advanced, nine average, and ten relatively backward. The average price received for cotton in the three groups was 398, 331, and 285 rubles per centner; the payment per workday to kolkhozniks was 27, 17, and 14 rubles respectively, of which 21, 12, and 11 rubles were paid in cash. It is clear that a peculiar economic stratification of kolkhozes was engendered by the multiple price structure.

Finally, payments in kind to the MTS for servicing kolkhozes accounted for an increasingly large proportion of procurements, especially grains. An important change in the method of calculating payments in kind took place in 1953. Variable rates charged for the same type of field work, depending upon the inflated official yields for a whole district, were discontinued and replaced by flat rates which were less burdensome to kolkhozes.

The economic stratification of kolkhozes created by the multiple price structure became a source of concern to the government because of the plight of the weaker kolkhozes. In discussing cotton farming, Khrushchev said that the weaker kolkhozes were treated "as if they were being penalized, compared with the advanced kolkhozes. This, of course, failed to stimulate them." [11] The fact that the low income earned by such kolkhozes resulted in small payments to kolkhozniks, offering insufficient incentives to work, and prevented adequate capital investment only perpetuated the weakness of these farms. The multiple price structure was not related to production costs and made rational economic calculation and planning difficult. Cumbersomeness and high costs were the other weaknesses of the procurement system. Finally, the liquidation of MTS in 1958 meant that an essential link in the procuring chain disappeared. The situation was ripe for a comprehensive reform.

Khrushchev's Procurement Reforms

The reform began by a decree of July 4, 1957, which abolished compulsory deliveries from holdings of kolkhozniks and other smallholders, beginning on January 1, 1958.[12] This was officially motivated by the fact that the share of the individual sector in total procurements had sharply declined with the reduction in the quotas of kolkhozniks and with the growth of the socialist sector. The meat procurements of the private sector declined from 23 percent in 1952 to 10.2 percent of the total in 1957, and milk procurements from 31 percent to 7.1 percent. Consequently, there was no longer the same urgency for the state to collect small quantities from millions of smallholders. It was relatively more economical to let the products reach the consumer through the kolkhoz market or voluntary sales to state and cooperative trading organizations. On June 18, 1958, a complete reorganization of the procuring system was decreed by the Central Committee, following Khrushchev's report on the subject. The details were filled in by a decree of the Council of Ministers on June 30, 1958.[13] The term "procurement" (*zagotovki*) itself, which had such a long currency, was jettisoned in favor of "purchases" (*zakupki*), though the compulsory principle remained. The different types of procuring operations—compulsory deliveries, extra-quota purchases, contracting—were combined into one system, with a single price for each commodity within a region.

The purchase quotas were to be established for a period of five to seven years, subject to an annual review which could raise the quota if the harvest warranted this. (No provision, however, was made for the lowering of the quotas.) Extra-quota prices and premiums were abolished. Payments to the remaining MTS and to the RTS (technical repair stations) which replaced them were to be in cash and not in kind. Procurement prices became more widely differentiated geographically, to take account of variations in production costs. Although the principle of price stability was proclaimed and prices were set for a period of several years, the necessity of variation to meet large fluctuations of supply was also recognized. An annual review was therefore provided to make adjustments in prices. The principle of quotas per unit of land was retained. The new purchase prices set by the government on June 30, 1958, were based on calculations of the average cost of production in collective and state farms over a period of four to five years in different regions of the country. The price was either fixed close to the old extra-quota purchase price or exceeded it. Thus the new grain price was 7.5 percent below the former extra-quota price but nearly three times above the compulsory delivery price; cattle prices were more than 50 percent above, sheep 36 percent above, and hogs 8 to 12 percent above the old extra-quota prices.[14]

Geographical differentiation of farm prices, reflecting varying regional conditions of production, became more pronounced in 1958. For wheat, for instance, there were eleven price groups, with prices ranging from 65 to 85 rubles per centner; for rye, thirteen groups with prices varying from 54 to 85 rubles; for barley, fourteen groups with prices ranging from 45 to 75 rubles.[15] Seasonal and quality differentiation of crop and livestock prices was also introduced. A premium was paid for sunflower-seed varieties of high oil content, for hybrid corn seed, and for high-grade seed of small grains; but these premiums were on the basis of quality and not, as before, merely on the basis of quantity delivered. Also there were deductions from the price for a failure to meet certain prescribed quality standards for farm products, in terms of moisture content, admixture of other crops like rye in wheat, and dockage. Kolkhozes were made responsible for the transportation of government-purchased products to delivery points only within a radius of 25 kilometers. They were to be reimbursed for shipment over longer distances. The lightening of the burden imposed on kolkhozes by transportation of deliveries to the state will be appreciated when the practical lack of all-weather roads in rural Russia and the shortage of trucks and other means of transportation are considered.

One of the features of the old contracting system which was retained, but on a more limited scale, was that of supplying growers of certain industrial crops with grain, some food products, and manufactured goods. But only sugar for beet growers and oil cake for cotton and oil-seed growers were to be supplied at concession prices. Another feature of the contracting system taken over by the June 1958 reform was of far greater importance. It was the payment of advances to kolkhozes of 25 percent of the value of government purchases prior to delivery, except for meat, poultry, eggs, and wool, for which advances were limited to 20 percent. None was paid for milk. This was to help kolkhozes financially to tide over the seasonal slack before deliveries began on a large scale. Such financial aid was all the more necessary since the cash expenses of the kolkhozes increased after they took over the functions of MTS, and consequently had to purchase fuel, lubricants, and spare parts and pay for the repair of farm implements. The growing practice of monthly cash payments to the kolkhozniks also made a continuous flow of cash receipts advantageous.

It will be noted from Table 48 that the average price paid by the government for all farm products trebled between 1952 and 1959. Prices of all crops doubled, but the very low grain prices on the average in-

Table 48. Indexes of average state purchase prices for agricultural products (1952=1.00)

Commodities	1952	1953	1954	1955	1956	1957	1958	1959	1960	1961	1962
All crops	1.00	1.32	1.71	1.69	2.07	2.09	2.03	2.06	—	—	—
Grains	1.00	2.36	7.39	5.53	6.34	6.17	6.95	7.14	7.17	7.77	8.43
Wheat	1.00	2.45	7.52	5.24	6.47	6.03	6.21	6.56	—	—	—
Rye	1.00	1.69	7.30	6.68	6.25	6.22	10.47	11.14	—	—	—
Oats	1.00	1.19	6.17	5.61	5.50	6.42	7.83	8.62	—	—	—
Barley	1.00	1.52	6.01	5.92	4.58	5.98	8.88	9.26	—	—	—
Corn	1.00	2.07	5.64	6.85	5.72	7.38	8.19	10.08	—	—	—
Other crops											
Cotton, unginned	1.00	1.05	1.02	0.96	1.14	1.15	1.06	1.07	—	—	—
Flax fiber	1.00	1.39	1.66	2.15	2.13	2.16	2.39	2.18	—	—	—
Sugar beets	1.00	1.44	1.11	1.30	2.29	2.43	2.19	2.17	—	—	—
Tobacco	1.00	0.96	1.03	1.00	1.51	1.66	1.62	1.62	—	—	—
Sunflower seed	1.00	5.28	6.26	9.87	9.28	9.47	7.74	7.83	7.68	8.12	8.48
Flax seed	1.00	1.29	2.17	2.52	2.73	4.10	3.30	3.33	3.38	3.42	3.40
Potatoes	1.00	3.16	3.69	3.68	8.14	8.59	7.89	8.36	—	—	—
Livestock products											
Livestock	1.00	3.85	5.79	5.85	6.65	7.86	11.75	12.39	12.43	12.58	15.23
Milk	1.00	2.02	2.89	3.03	3.34	3.62	4.04	4.04	4.05	4.04	4.34
Eggs	1.00	1.26	1.35	1.52	1.55	1.69	2.97	2.99	3.01	3.03	3.39
Wool	1.00	1.07	1.46	1.58	2.46	2.85	3.52	3.55	3.44	3.42	3.46
All commodities	1.00	1.54	2.07	2.09	2.51	2.66	2.96	3.00	2.99	3.04	3.32

Sources. Sel'skoe khoziaistvo SSSR, 1960, p. 117; S. G. Stoliarov, "Statistics of Prices," Tsenoobrazovanie na predmety potrebleniia (Pricing of Consumers Goods), Sh. Ia. Turetskii, ed. (Moscow, 1964), p. 115.

creased sevenfold (and much more for some grains); prices of industrial crops were only 50 percent higher in 1959 than in 1952. Among the latter group, cotton prices hardly increased at all. It will be recalled that the prices of some industrial crops were already substantially raised during the Stalin regime, and so did not need as large a boost later. Finally, the prices of animal products were raised on the average 5.6 times, and the prices of meat animals to a much greater extent. The varying rates of price increases, then, were designed to level off the disparities in the movement of different commodity-price groups and to bring them into a better relation with production costs.

Several flaws crept into the operation of the new price system. One of the basic principles of the 1958 legislation was that of price fluctuation in response to significant crop variation caused by weather. But this became a one-way street—the sliding scale was only allowed to work downward. The generally good weather and crops in 1958 led to a reduction of procuring prices; but they were not restored during the subsequent years of unfavorable weather. It was also expected, according to Minister of Agriculture Matskevich, that prices of industrial inputs, which kolkhozes had to purchase upon the liquidation of the MTS, would remain stable; instead, prices of tractors, spare parts, and trucks were raised.[16] Thus after the bountiful year of 1958 kolkhoz incomes did not increase as much as they would have if prices of farm products had not been kept down and those of industrial inputs raised. Economic incentives to the kolkhozniks could have increased more, or at least not decreased. Yet by 1959 the wide gap between procurement and retail prices in the state sector narrowed substantially. This was particularly true of grain. In 1952 the procurement price of wheat was only 19 percent above 1929, while retail state prices were more than ten times higher.[17] In 1959 the procurement price of wheat was calculated as 7.8 times above that of 1928, and retail prices in state stores 8.9 times higher.[18] The terms of trade between the town and the countryside became considerably less unfavorable.

Determination of Farm Costs of Production

To put the procurement system on a sound, objective basis, to prevent arbitrariness and other abuses in setting prices, and to make it an effective instrument of economic incentives, the cost of production became the basic criterion in fixing prices. Here the Khrushchev administration followed the well-established economic principle on the governing effect of costs on prices. Whereas in a free market economy the influence of costs on prices is exerted indirectly through variations in supply, in an authoritarian price system a more direct relationship between prices and costs is assumed. The subject was a new one in the USSR in the 1950s— new in that it was virtually ignored during the Stalin era, though it was quite familiar previously.

Farm-cost studies, which were being made in the 1920s, ceased after mass collectivization.[19] L. N. Litoshenko, who disappeared in the purge of economists and statisticians in the early 1930s, was particularly associated with these studies.[20] Subsequently some Soviet economists denied the validity of the cost concept in kolkhozes because kolkhozniks were not paid wages. The opposition to farm-cost investigations was in line with the exclusive reliance of the Stalin regime on multiple physical indicators and its disregard of economic value indicators in assessing the performance of kolkhozes and other segments of the system. As a Soviet critic of this practice put it: "Agricultural economists overrated the significance of the physical forms of accountability [*raschet*] for the kolkhoz economy, and underrated the significance of commercial-money [*tovarno-denezhnye*] relationships." [21]

When in the mid-1950s cost investigations in the kolkhozes were resumed, two fundamental questions were posed: what items are to be included in the cost of production, and what costs are to be considered as governing in the price-fixing process? In a capitalist economy, all payments by a business firm or a farmer for the factors of production used— land, labor (including management), and capital—are included. Not so in Soviet collective agriculture. Land rent and interest on capital, in accordance with Marxist theory, are not counted in the cost of production. A further difficulty arose with respect to labor costs, one that generated considerable controversy among Soviet economists. The calculation was complicated by the use of an arbitrary unit, the workday, and by payments to kolkhozniks partly in kind and partly in cash. What is more important, the remuneration of collective farm labor was residual and uncertain until 1966, depending on the total income of each kolkhoz, which varied widely from farm to farm, and on its obligations that had higher priority. Under such conditions there was a wide heterogeneity in the remuneration of labor from kolkhoz to kolkhoz. Bear in mind, also, that a kolkhoznik, unlike a hired worker, cannot pull up stakes and move to a kolkhoz that pays its members better. Thus there is no immediate equalizing influence of competition. But experience indicates that farms with low remuneration are likely to suffer, in the long run, an erosion of the labor force through migration to cities or through the preoccupation of the kolkhozniks with their private plots and animals.

One school of Soviet economists favored using actual payments to kolkhozniks for calculating labor costs. Another school felt that this method lacked a common interkolkhoz denominator or standard and, therefore, was not appropriate to calculate cost figures used in price fixing.[22] Even the second school conceded that actual payments in kolkhozes should be used for intrakolkhoz calculations. But it found a common frame of reference in wage rates on state farms which, it reasoned, should be very close to remuneration for similar work in the kolkhozes and could be used for measuring labor costs. Actually such imputed labor costs deviate from the actual costs in kolkhozes, in turn causing deviations in the calculated total production costs per unit, as shown in Table 49. It was an indisputable fact that the remuneration of workers in many kolkhozes was too low and that cost figures based on such data distorted the true picture. This was the chief cause of concern for the economists insisting on sovkhoz wage rates as a basis for labor calculations.

Why, for example, should one kolkhoz be considered as making a larger profit than another if it resulted not from increased productivity of labor, but merely from lower rates of payment to its workers? This condition could not occur if sovkhoz wage rates were used for comparison. As a supporting argument it was pointed out that Lenin, in his studies

Table 49. Average cost of production of specified farm commodities in the USSR, 1962 and 1964 (rubles per metric ton)

Commodity	1962		1964	
	I [a]	II [a]	I [a]	II[a]
Grain, exclusive of corn	44	37	48	44
Unginned cotton	247	224	281	281
Sugar beets	19	16	18	17
Sunflower seed	33	30	31	30
Potatoes	48	38	40	35
Cattle [b]	1,014	834	988	927
Hogs [b]	1,347	1,146	1,326	1,250
Sheep [b]	571	512	637	609
Milk	156	129	162	151
Wool	2,748	2,504	3,050	2,939

[a] Labor component of production cost calculated on the basis of:
I = Sovkhoz wage rates, and II = actual payments to kolkhozniks.
[b] Liveweight gain.
Source. *Narodnoe khoziaistvo, 1962,* pp. 338–339; *1964,* pp. 394–397.

of peasant farming, also deducted from income not the actual living expenditures of a small peasant farmer, but those of an average farmer, in order to determine the profitability of different holdings.[23] The opponents of the sovkhoz method retorted that economic reality in the kolkhozes must be thoroughly examined in all of its aspects. If it is found that the payment for labor is too low and does not provide adequate economic stimuli, then remedies should be sought for that situation as well as for other flaws and abnormalities in the cost structure. But this school saw no virtue in the employment of what it considered artificial elements in cost calculation.[24] Although this view does have merit, it is also true that the use of sovkhoz wage rates has considerable justification for comparative purposes. It is, among other things, useful in bringing to the surface the inequities in the remuneration for the same work done by kolkhozniks and sovkhoz workers. Thus Table 49 indicates that the disparity between wage rates in sovkhozes and labor payments in kolkhozes increased between 1962 and 1964 in favor of sovkhoz workers.

The sovkhoz-wage school dominated when cost studies were resumed in the 1950s, and only figures of this kind were published. The actual-payment school apparently won in the ensuing controversy, but not without a compromise. Farm-cost figures based on the two methods were published in the 1962 and 1964 statistical yearbooks.[25] This appears to be a sound procedure until the disparity in payment in kolkhozes and sovkhozes is eliminated in accordance with the May 1966 legislation on guaranteed wages of kolkhozniks. Then the dichotomy in cost calculations will become superfluous.

At first a complicating element in the technique of cost determination was the MTS operations, which were included in kolkhoz production costs. The problem no longer existed after the liquidation of the MTS, which was one of the important reasons for the 1958 changes in the procurement system. A price problem that cannot be considered as solved is that of average versus marginal costs arising from the high variability of land with regard to quality and location. Are prices to cover the highest production costs of the supply required or, as it is often stated, should they cover the costs on the marginal land that must be brought under cultivation to ensure the needed supply? Or should prices merely cover the average cost of production in a certain geographical area? This again has been a matter of controversy among Soviet economists. Some favor the marginalist solution and rely on taxation to appropriate for the state part of the resulting surplus or rent on farms operating under supramarginal conditions; others consider this process characteristic only of a capitalist economy and incompatible with a socialist system. They believe that a differentiation of prices based on the most advantageous regional specialization of production could be achieved, and this would avoid the marginal-cost problem.[26] They criticize the price zones for grain established in 1958 as far too large. One zone, for instance, included an area extending from Kaliningrad (Koenigsberg) to Sverdlovsk in the Urals, and included twenty provinces and six autonomous republics.[27] But that a realistic and effective scheme of regional price differentiation can be worked out is exceedingly doubtful. This school visualizes the problem as essentially that of correct price regionalization. But it seems clear that any reliance on average costs in price making, however regionalized, will not eliminate the problem of the high-cost producers who are placed in a disadvantageous position. This is precisely what happened with the zonal price differences, based on average costs, introduced in 1958.

A Soviet study disclosed that for the kolkhozes of the RSFSR the ratio between the lowest and highest zonal grain prices established in 1958 was 1:1.7, whereas a similar ratio between farm costs (calculated for 1956–1959) was 1:5.[28] In other words, the highest grain prices were 70 percent above the lowest, but the highest production cost was 400 percent above the lowest. Note that labor costs were estimated at standard wage rates prevailing on state farms and were not the labor costs actually incurred. This study showed the situation to be even more unfavorable for animal products, and only industrial crops were in a more favorable category. The analysis demonstrates that the regional differentiation of prices paid by the government for farm products has not corresponded with the cost differences between regions and between kolkhozes within a region. The 1958 price reform did not achieve one of its main objectives—relief for the weaker kolkhozes. But with all its faults, the procurement system developed under Khrushchev at least became tied to some concept of cost, and was superior to the utterly arbitrary price fixing under Stalin.

Problems with the New Procurement Practices

The much touted new system soon evoked new disillusionment in the Kremlin. In part this was due to the inefficiency and waste of a multiplicity of procurement agencies operating without proper coordination. The procuring organs were also criticized for faulty grading, usually downgrading, of the delivered products. Since such downgrading resulted in lower realized prices, it amounted to cheating the kolkhozes. Khrushchev also became dissatisfied because the procuring system concentrated on the limited business of acquiring farm products and did not concern itself with the broader production functions of the kolkhozes—it did not press for the expansion of agricultural production. He said in January 1961, at a session of the Central Committee of the Communist Party of the Ukraine: "A procurement system, to put it briefly, must contribute to the increased production of farm products. Now it does not do this . . . It is necessary to reconstruct the procurement system from the ground up. The procurement agent is an organizer of production and not a middleman or merchant, as in the past." [29]

Khrushchev's irritation can be better understood when it is considered against the background of stagnation in agriculture, which could not help undermining the ambitious growth goals of the plan for 1959–1965. Coincidentally, the liquidation of the MTS and the decentralization of the agricultural administrative apparatus left a gap in the state mechanism for controlling collective agriculture. And the Kremlin was not ready to put its trust solely in economic levers of control—the price mechanism. Hence Khrushchev's mention above of the concept of "organizer of production," a euphemism for the tighter control of the kolkhozes by the procurement apparatus. This step required further organizational changes, which were brought about by a decree issued early in 1961.[30] The decree resurrected the contracting method of procurements, applying it not only to collectives but also to state farms. The contracts were couched in terms of agreements between the state and the kolkhozes, and theoretically there was scope for negotiation between kolkhoz management and government officials, such as is practiced informally for the planned targets of Soviet industrial enterprises.[31] But actually the contracts were orders for delivery of certain quantities of farm products. Concluded for a period of two to five years, they were subject to an annual review that could introduce changes. This was a loophole that could nullify the long-term character of such transactions.

Contracts were made with several procuring agencies or processing plants (meat, milk) which specialized in the procurement of various products. For example, the Pobeda kolkhoz in Rostov province made five such contracts in 1961.[32] No one principle determined the amount to be sold to the state; considered instead was the total productive capacity of each kolkhoz vis-à-vis the regional procuring targets. This was the function of a new coordinating apparatus established by a separate decree of February 26, 1961. It created a high-level agency—the State Committee on Procurements of the Council of Ministers which, like its one-time predecessor the Ministry of Procurements, became the central directing and supervising organ of the system. It had a new local arm, the Regional State Procurement Inspection. The procurement inspectors were endowed with wide powers of supervision and the planning of procuring activities in the district, including the very important power to stop or limit cash advances to farms which did not live up to their obligations. But the 3,173 inspection units, which employed 12,566 inspectors in 1961,[33] were short-lived, victims of Khrushchev's penchant for reorganization. They were absorbed the following year in the new territorial kolkhoz-sovkhoz production administrations.

The tightening of the procurement machinery, signaled first by the creation of the inspectorates and then of the territorial administrations, was probably related to the greatly increased procurement goals. This was done despite the disclosure by the Soviet press and by Khrushchev himself that the pressure to report fulfillment or overfulfillment of targets had led to machinations and outright falsification by the farm management, often in league with the local authorities. A fairly common practice was the purchase by a kolkhoz of milk and other products at high prices in order to meet its obligation to the government, which paid lower prices. The kolkhoz, though incurring a loss, misrepresented these deliveries as coming from its own production. Even a more flagrant abuse was *pripiski,* the padding of statistical reports on production and procurements in order to meet the targets. The old practice of reporting the fulfillment of delivery targets and then turning to the government for seed and fodder also persisted.[34] Khrushchev cited the case of the RSFSR, which in 1959 needed 22 percent of its delivered grain quota to be returned to farms for such purposes. Other republics, according to him, were accustomed to turn to the state for seed and fodder, "and often it is done after the raions and oblasts of the republic report the fulfillment of the planned grain deliveries and laying in of a seed supply." Government regulations stipulated that seed supplies on farms must be laid in before making the planned deliveries to the state, and the best seed was to be used for this purpose. The government decided in 1956 that only those districts, provinces, and republics which provided fully for their seed requirements would be considered as having fulfilled their delivery targets. It was further decreed that officials who forced kolkhozes and state farms to deliver seed grain were to be prosecuted.

Khrushchev admitted that government regulations regarding seed supplies were "grossly violated" by officials who, "aiming to be first in reporting the fulfillment of their obligations . . . clean out all grain from the granaries and not only take away fodder grain, but do not even leave enough for seed; after reporting, they turn to the state and ask for fodder and seed." [35] Khrushchev correctly observed that depriving a farm of seed is tantamount to undermining agriculture, since planting with any kind of seed brought in from the outside, instead of the seed best adapted to local conditions, spells low yields. However, in the same speech he also denounced those officials and managers who tried to secure lower, presumably more realistic delivery targets, thus in effect continuing the tendency toward exaggerated goals. Brezhnev, when he came into power, also complained about these malpractices in procurements, at the May 1965 plenum. He mentioned the same appeals to the government for seed after the farms' completion of procurements, and indicated that the procurement plans were so unrealistically high that they had been met only three times over a whole decade—in 1964, 1958, and 1956.[36]

Perhaps the strongest condemnation of the reformed procurement system came from one of the most intelligent and objective Soviet agricultural economists, V. G. Venzher. He stated that, without providing adequate resources for the achievement of the production goals, the authorities

> insist on compulsory deliveries of a maximum of products, often without considering the farm needs for seed, feed, and even food . . . Moreover, it may be frequently observed that fulfillment and overfulfillment of obligations for the procurement of one kind of commodity radically undermines the possibility for kolkhozes to deliver another product or even all others. Thus the drive for a maximum procurement of grain leads to the withdrawal of a considerable quantity of feed, and this hampers the future procurement of various livestock products—meat, milk, and others. It simmers down to this, that the procurement agencies themselves forget during the peak procurement season for one product, particularly grain, about the other products to be procured . . . Preterm fulfillment and overfulfillment of contractual obligations to the state for procurement of products is permissible only if the overfulfillment does not result in losses of other commodities. It is a hundred times better, more valuable, and more useful to fulfill the obligation for the procurement of a certain product within the specified time than to fulfill it more quickly to the detriment of the procurement of other commodities.[37]

Haste in procurements often resulted in the diversion of manpower and draft power from other farm operations, such as harvesting (where delays are really harmful). Another consequence is an overtaxing of storage capacity, which creates costly delays in the actual delivery of crops like grain; it sometimes spells disaster for perishable fruit and vegetables. The ultimate responsibility for the acceleration of procurements from the farms lies with the government and its local organs. The motives for this pressure were the relatively low stocks on hand, coupled with the fear that if produce, particularly grain, was not removed but stored on the farm, much of it would disappear. Only toward the very end of his career did Khrushchev advocate the preliminary storage of procured grain on the farms. In a speech in Tselinograd in August 1964, he referred to the difficulties and heavy expenses involved in moving grain in the virgin-land region—many of the sovkhozes there were far removed from railroads, where elevators and warehouses are usually located. Khrushchev proposed centrally located granaries on the large farms: "We must abandon the entirely erroneous prejudice that sovkhozes cannot be trusted with the storing of grain. This bias originated with Stalin who demanded that grain, under any conditions, be shipped straight from the combine to the elevator. He thought that otherwise the grain would be pilfered and the state would not receive the needed quantity."[38]

Khrushchev, eleven years after Stalin's death, called such a notion "foolishness" and expressed confidence in the integrity of the sovkhoz and kolkhoz cadres. He pointed out the great economies that would result from the adoption of his proposal to organize on the farms facilities for the cleaning and preliminary storage of grain, with its gradual shipment to the elevators when this would not interfere with other operations.[39] In Tselinograd Khrushchev addressed himself primarily to the sovkhozes, but in another comment a few days earlier he had explicitly mentioned the kolkhozes as well.[40] After Khrushchev's removal, this sensible proposal was consigned to limbo, along with many other of his pet projects. An important deterrent may have been the cost and difficulty of constructing adequate grain storage on the farms. Off-farm storage also posed many problems, particularly in the virgin lands where construction, especially of elevators, lagged and where the special need to dry grain because of high moisture content creates a serious problem.[41] In general, facilities for off-farm grain storage of all kinds are considerably less in the Soviet Union than in the United States, approximately 88 million tons and 149 million tons respectively at the beginning of 1963.[42] Of the Soviet storage capacity, 12.8 percent was in elevators and 47.1 in mechanized warehouses. In the United States most of these facilities were mechanized.

Procurements also suffered from faulty planning and bureaucratic inefficiency. Reports frequently appeared in the Soviet press that state and cooperative trading agencies were unable or unwilling to accept the delivery of perishable crops from kolkhozes and sovkhozes. The kolkhoz managements in such cases had to find new outlets—usually a difficult task—or feed the crops to livestock or let them go to waste. At the same time, the city population yearned for larger supplies of fresh vegetables and potatoes, as was reported from Krasnoiarsk.[43] Great delays and lack of proper facilities have also characterized the transportation of perish-able crops, which led one party official from Astrakhan to complain: "Sometimes it is easier to grow good tomatoes than to deliver them where people are waiting for them." [44] In one of his last discussions dealing with agriculture, Khrushchev confirmed the difficulties experienced by farms in marketing vegetables and potatoes. As a remedy he suggested the opening of special stores in the cities by those kolkhozes and sov-khozes which marketed large quantities of these products. Such direct marketing, bypassing the state system, was to be linked with the process-ing of vegetables on the farms. There has certainly been an increased interest in the latter on the part of policy makers after Khrushchev, but not in the improvement of marketing.

A step forward was taken at the time of the 1958 procurement reform in doing away with the concept of territorial universality in favor of regional specialization. At the December 1958 plenum Khrushchev advo-cated the principle of concentrating procurements in low-cost areas. The expansion of grain production in 1956–1958 in the eastern virgin lands made it possible to apply this principle and to dispense with or greatly reduce grain procurements in the grain-deficit regions, where the kol-khozes often substituted an equivalent in animal products for compulsory grain deliveries. More of the locally grown grain was to be used as animal feed. But in 1961 Khrushchev expressed disappointment with the produc-tion results in these regions, and grain procurements were resumed.

Although the trend of procurement prices in the 1950s was upward, Khrushchev's ultimate goal was to lower agricultural prices, contingent on increased farm efficiency and a decline in production costs. A lower cost of living was one of the directives laid down in the basic legislation—the decree of the Central Committee of June 18, 1958. Khrushchev again raised this question a year and a half later, in a speech at a session of the Central Committee in December 1959, devoted to a review of the agri-cultural situation.[45] In some of the kolkhozes growing industrial crops, mainly in Central Asia and the Caucasus, the payments to kolkhozniks exceeded the average worker's wages. Khrushchev was strongly opposed to such a disparity and demanded a downward adjustment of prices of the crops in question. He returned to the subject in January 1961, in a speech at a meeting of the Central Committee of the Ukrainian party. Alluding to the probable yearning for higher prices on the part of some agriculturalists, Khrushchev stated: "We must realize, comrades, that the state cannot further increase the prices for the produce of kolkhozes." He believed that increased productivity and reduction of costs should be the aim. "Workers in factories are increasing the productivity of labor and periodically revising production tasks. They are concerned about lowering the costs of production so that the state can sell you tractors and other machinery cheaper. And is it not important for the [industrial] worker that agricultural products—meat, milk, butter—be cheaper? But under what conditions is it possible to lower the retail prices of agricultural products? On the condition that kolkhozes will provide a large output at low cost. Then the state will be able to reduce the procuring prices and the retail prices of agricultural products. This is our way. (Applause.)" [46]

But it did not work out this way. Khrushchev's administration had to make two further concessions to the kolkhozes later in 1961. First, the government's money advances to kolkhozes on procurements of farm products were raised to 30 percent of the amount due, instead of the old rates of 25 percent for crops and 20 percent for animal products. The advances were payable in two or three installments instead of, as before, in a lump sum. Procurement advances were of great importance in meeting the current expenses of kolkhozes, including advanced or regular payments to kolkhozniks. In 1958 procurement advances covered 19.8 percent of the current expenditures of all kolkhozes, compared with 9.4 percent of bank loans and 70.8 percent of the kolkhozes' own working capital. In 1963 the proportion of procurement advances increased to 39.3 percent, bank loans decreased to 8.6 percent, and kolkhoz working capital also decreased to 52.1 percent.[47] Second, the Soviet government assumed the full cost of shipping procured products from the farm to delivery points; formerly kolkhozes had been responsible for shipment of a distance up to 25 kilometers. It was claimed that relief from paying shipping costs would result in considerable savings to the kolkhozes.[48]

Further Price Increases in 1962–63

Despite his aversion to a further increase in prices, Khrushchev was not able to avoid it during the last years of his regime. The most far-reaching of these increases was for livestock products. The cause of the renewed concern with this situation was the stagnation of livestock production, contrary to all plans and expectations, after a significant rise in the 1950s. Livestock numbers, it is true, were continuously increasing. Between the beginning of 1959 and 1962 cattle numbers for all categories of farms increased by 7.1 percent, hogs 20.5 percent, and sheep 2.4 percent; but meat production declined from the 1959 peak of 8.9 million tons to 8.7 million in 1961, according to official statistics. Although the number of cows increased during the period by 4.5 percent, milk production was only 1.5 percent higher. The decline of privately owned herds as a result of the less liberal government policy, together with the inefficiency and high cost of production in the greatly expanded socialist sector, explain the unsatisfactory supply situation. Although cattle numbers in the socialist sector increased between 1959 and 1961 by 25 percent, hogs by 29 percent, and sheep by 3.6 percent, meat production was only 2 percent higher. While the number of cows in the socialist sector increased by 25 percent between 1959 and 1961, milk production was 8.6 percent higher.[49] The slowly rising pace of the supply of livestock products in the face of increased demand, caused by the growth of population and of purchasing power, frequently created shortages.

The form of the announcement of livestock price increases was in itself significant. On June 1, 1962, an appeal to the people was made jointly by the Central Committee and the Council of Ministers, and was spelled out in greater detail by an accompanying decree from the latter. This was a double-edged action affecting not only procurement prices paid by the state, but also retail prices charged to consumers by state stores. Beginning on June 1, 1962, average increases in procurement prices were set at 35 percent for livestock and poultry, 10 percent for butter, and 5 percent for cream. Also, the seasonal lowering of procurement prices for whole milk in the summer was abandoned, and the higher winter prices were continued. The same prices were paid to kolkhozniks and others who owned livestock individually and sold their produce voluntarily to the state. (They were not subject to compulsory deliveries.) But sovkhozes and other state enterprises were paid 10 percent less than kolkhozes. Retail prices for meat and meat products in state stores were raised on an average of 30 percent, and butter 25 percent. Increases for different kinds of meat were: 30 percent on the average for beef, 34 percent for lamb and mutton, 19 percent for pork, and 31 percent for sausage products. At the same time, the retail price of sugar was reduced by 5 percent, and rayon goods 20 percent. These reductions, unfortunately, did not go far enough in offsetting the considerably increased cost to consumers.

As might have been expected, the action of the government fanned discontent among the consuming public, to the point of rioting in some cities. Khrushchev had promised repeatedly since 1957 that per capita production of livestock products would catch up by the early 1960s with that of the United States; but instead consumers were bedeviled by shortages and drastically increased prices. The awkward situation was recognized by the government's June appeal, which examined and rejected various alternatives to price increases, such as channeling resources from the defense budget or from investment in industry and housing. The appeal finally pointed out that, even if the government could have found additional funds to increase the prices paid to farms by raising the price of vodka, tobacco, and some other commodities, it still would not have been possible to leave retail prices at their former level. With a shortage of meat, this would have created opportunities for speculation and would have made the uninterrupted supply of livestock products to the cities more difficult. Apparently an immediate restriction of the demand for meat, as well as an increase in supplies over a longer period of time, was in the Kremlin's mind. The appeal stressed the high cost of production of livestock products on the farms, which exceeded the old procurement prices, with consequent losses to many kolkhozes.

The average procurement price of beef in 1960, before the new increase, was only 65 percent of the average cost of production; for pork the price-cost relationship was 67 percent; mutton 98 percent; wool 143 percent; eggs 65 percent; and milk 86 percent. With the exception of wool, the picture is one of general unprofitableness of livestock production, especially compared with such products as cotton and small grains, for which procurement prices were on the average 64 and 55 percent above the cost of production. These are average figures for the country as a whole, and there are considerable regional deviations. In the North Caucasus, for example, with an average procurement price of 56.1 rubles per centner of beef, 57.5 percent of the kolkhozes had a production cost exceeding 70 rubles. For pork the average procurement price was 66.5 rubles per centner, but more than two thirds of the kolkhozes had production costs above 80 rubles per centner.[50] Other regional data tell the same bleak story; and the more the kolkhozes concentrated on livestock production, the greater the losses, except in the small number of farms where increased output was accompanied by rising productivity and lower costs. In most kolkhozes, however, whatever profits were made on other products and the reduction of the elastic residual payments to kolkhozniks were used to cover losses incurred in livestock production and to provide the necessary new capital. To bridge the gap between costs and livestock prices, the government raised the latter. But as indicated by a second appeal of the Central Committee and the Council of Ministers, this time only to farmers, the price-cost gap still remained in a number of kolkhozes, and the Khrushchev administration stressed the need for reducing costs.[51] (Three years later, livestock prices were again increased, but more about this later.)

By 1962, the average prices paid by the government for farm products were 3.3 times greater than in 1952; grain, 8.4 times greater; industrial crops, 43 percent greater; meat, more than 4.3 times greater. (See Table 48.) With a further increase of procurement prices for cotton, sugar beets, and potatoes in 1963, the story of ten years of rising farm prices under Khrushchev comes to an end. What about the significance of procure-

Table 50. Kolkhoz money income by sources in current prices, 1952–1965 [a]

Source of income	1952	1953	1954	1955	1956	1957	1958	1959	1960	1961	1962	1963	1964	1965
						In billions of rubles								
Delivery and sale to the state														
Crops	1.92	2.24	n.a.	3.72	5.07	4.59	6.70	6.19	6.20	6.85	7.30	7.80	9.80	
Livestock products	0.53	1.00	n.a.	1.76	2.40	2.82	4.20	5.23	4.70	4.67	5.80	5.90	5.50	
Total	2.45	3.24	n.a.	5.48	7.47	7.41	10.90	11.42	10.90	11.52	13.10	13.70	15.30	
Kolkhoz trade														
Crops	0.94	0.68	n.a.	0.84	0.72	0.76	0.90	0.92	1.00	0.81	0.90	0.80	1.10	
Livestock products	0.52	0.68	n.a.	0.73	0.67	0.60	0.60	0.53	0.50	0.38	0.40	0.40	0.50	
Total	1.46	1.36	n.a.	1.57	1.39	1.36	1.50	1.45	1.50	1.19	1.30	1.20	1.60	
Other sources	0.37	0.36	n.a.	0.51	0.60	0.75	0.80	0.81	1.00	0.86	0.90	1.10	1.00	
Grand total	4.28	4.96	6.33	7.56	9.46	9.52	13.20	13.68	13.40	13.57	15.30	16.00	17.90	20.00
Income per kolkhoz household (in rubles)	215.4	251.8	321.3	382.1	476.3	505.3	701.5	741.7	780.7	830.2	940	996	1,127	1,294

[a] Actual money receipts only. Income of kolkhozes converted into state farms during a particular year are not included. The smaller number of kolkhozes remaining in 1965 had a money income as follows in billion rubles: 1958, 10.8; 1963, 15.4; 1964, 17.5; and 1965, 20.0.

Sources. *Narodnoe khoziaistvo, 1956*; *Sel'skoe khoziaistvo, 1960*; *SSSR v tsifrakh, 1965*.

ments in the financial economy of the kolkhozes? First, as Table 50 shows, there was a substantial growth of kolkhoz earnings from procurements during the Khrushchev period, as compared to the lean Stalin years. While the rates of the growth varied from year to year, the essential point is that from a very low figure of less than 2.5 billion rubles in 1952, procurements, including all acquisitions by state and cooperative agencies, increased to over 15 billion rubles in 1964, or more than six times. One would be tempted to speak of a spectacular growth, if it had not started from such a low base. Roughly over a half of the increase must be attributed to higher procurement prices and the rest to increased volume. Second, procurements constituted an increasingly dominant component of kolkhoz cash income, rising from 57 percent in 1952 to more than 85 percent in 1964. Third, it follows that the growing earnings from procurements resulted in substantial boosting of kolkhoz cash income. Of the 13.7 billion ruble increase in cash income between 1952 and 1964, procurements accounted for 12.85 billion. Cash earnings from kolkhoz trade and other sources increased but little during this period—from 1.82 billion rubles to 2 billion—and their share of total kolkhoz cash was much smaller. In the total state payments for farm products acquired from all sources except sovkhozes, kolkhozes also predominate (see Table 51). But voluntary sales by the private sector (kolkhozniks and others) accounted in the early 1960s for about one fifth to one fourth of the total state payments for farm products. This must be added to the array of facts attesting to the continued importance of the private sector, which will be further discussed in Chapter 18.

Changes in Procurement Practices after Khrushchev

A new chapter in the story of procurements was unfolded by Khrushchev's successors at the March 1965 plenum. The principal innovation was the setting of firm procurement quotas for a period of years instead of annually, and often with long delays. This applied to the national target as well as to allocations among republics, administrative divisions, and individual kolkhozes and sovkhozes. A high premium was established by the government for extra-quota purchases which, if it is consistently adhered to, would end the practice of additional deliveries at regular procurement prices after they fulfill their obligations. This is an old evil, frequently condemned but with little practical effect. The new shield of certainty this reform provided should facilitate and strengthen decision making by farm managements, especially in the planning of land use and production. In accordance with the new program, procurement quotas

Table 51. Payments by the state for procured or purchased farm products from kolkhozes, kolkhozniks and others, 1952 to 1964 *(million rubles)*[a]

Year	Payment to kolkhozes	Payments to kolkhozniks and others [b]	Total payments
1952	2,450	680	3,130
1953	3,240	900	4,140
1954			
1955	5,480	920	6,400
1956	7,470	1,380	8,850
1957	7,410	2,300	9,710
1958	10,900	2,509	13,409
1959	11,420	3,070	14,490
1960	10,900	3,255	14,155
1961	11,520	2,980	14,500
1962	13,100	3,980	17,080
1963	13,700	4,746	18,446
1964	15,300	3,666	18,966

[a] State farms excluded.
[b] Calculated.
Sources. *Sel'skoe khoziaistvo, 1960,* p. 118; *Narodnoe Khoziaistvo, 1958,* and volumes of the same annual for 1959 to 1965.

for grain and a large number of other products were fixed for each of the six years from 1965 through 1970. For grain, the original 1965 procurement goal of 65 million tons was reduced to 55.7 million; and this also became the annual target for the remainder of the decade.*

In addition to fixing multi-year targets, the post-Khrushchev administration, like its predecessor, resorted to price increases. The procurement price of wheat for kolkhozes was raised in 1965 by an average of approximately 12 percent, and of rye 23 percent, with considerable regional variation. Thus prices of these two grains in the infertile nonblack-soil area, where costs of production are high, were increased on the average by 53 percent.[52] The same prices were fixed for wheat as for rye (the much more typical crop in this area), both before and after the increase.

* The 1965 total grain procurement target was subsequently further reduced to 53.1 million tons, compared to 68.3 million tons reportedly procured in 1964, and 49.4 million on the average during 1959–63. "Grain Procurements in 1965," *Zakupki sel'skokhoziaistvennykh produktov,* 7:1 (July 1965). Even the reduced 1965 target was not fulfilled, *Pravda,* February 3, 1965.

In the mainly wheat-growing Ukraine (exclusive of the less fertile northern wooded area, which is included in the nonblack-soil area) and in Moldavia, the price of wheat was increased from 67 rubles to 76 rubles per ton, or 13 percent; and rye, from 64 rubles also to 76, or nearly 19 percent. Here the price relationship, which is contrary to that prevailing in Western rye-growing countries like France and West Germany, indicates that rye production was strongly encouraged after its considerable decline during the Khrushchev period. In Kazakhstan, another principal wheat region, the price of rye was increased from 71 rubles to 80 rubles per ton, or 12.7 percent. For extra-quota purchases of wheat and rye, a premium of 50 percent above the basic price was set.

Prices of buckwheat, rice, and higher grades of millet, the production of which the government is anxious to expand, were also sharply increased. The price of buckwheat was raised from 200 rubles to 300 rubles, and of rice from 220 to 300 rubles.[53] With the strained Sino-Soviet relations, the Soviet government started to aim at self-sufficiency in rice and was willing to pay a high price for it. While in the United States a ton of rice in the early 1960s was worth roughly 1.7 tons of wheat at farm prices, in the Soviet Union it was worth 3.75 tons. The emphasis in the 1965 price reform was on food grains, reflecting no doubt the traumatic effects of the 1963 and 1965 crop failures. The prices of feed barley and oats were raised by 20 to 100 percent, but only in the nonblack-soil area where acreage expansion became the order of the day.[54] By contrast, nothing was done for Khrushchev's favorite crop, corn, which after a meteoric rise went down precipitously, following its patron. On the basis of the average prices for large areas, increased regional differentiation was introduced in 1965, and it should help to diminish the spread between prices and costs. Thus for the RSFSR, thirteen price zones were established for grain instead of the former eight.[55] But the Soviet policy makers appear to be overoptimistic on this score. Although the more glaring disparities in the price-cost structure may be eliminated, the problem of the marginal producer will still remain.

Of the nongrain crops, prices of cotton, sugar beets, and potatoes had already been increased during the last years of Khrushchev's regime. In 1965, to stimulate production further, the price of sunflower seed purchased by the state in excess of the quantity delivered during 1962–1964 was doubled. Also for each centner of this excess quantity, a kolkhoz could purchase from the state up to 4 kilograms of sunflower-seed oil at half of the retail price.[56] The price paid to sovkhozes for the delivery of sunflower seed was raised to the level of that paid to kolkhozes. Remember, however, that procurement prices do not play the same incentive role in sovkhozes as in kolkhozes.

For livestock products, too, a procurement schedule for each of the years from 1965 to 1970 was set up but, unlike grains, it is on an ascending scale (see Table 52). Yet the new 1965 targets were drastically reduced compared to the original plan under Khrushchev. Likewise, the new 1970 targets are below the goals set by the Khrushchev regime; for meat

Table 52. Procurements of livestock products, 1953–65 actual and 1966–70 planned

Year	Livestock and poultry (million tons of live weight)	Milk (million tons)	Eggs (billions)	Wool (thousand tons of standard weight)
1953	3.6	10.6	2.6	197
1954	4.0	11.3	2.7	190
1955	4.2	13.5	2.9	230
1956	4.4	17.3	3.3	246
1957	5.1	20.5	4.3	281
1958	5.7	22.1	4.5	315
1959	7.5	25.0	5.7	354
1960	7.9	26.3	6.5	358
1961	7.3	27.5	7.4	369
1962	8.6	29.2	8.5	374
1963	9.3	28.5	8.7	380
1964	8.3	31.4	8.3	353
1965	9.3	38.7	10.5	369
1966	8.93	34.62	10.0	361
1967	9.46	36.235	10.84	373
1968	10.02	38.39	11.92	387
1969	10.68	40.8	13.51	407
1970 [a]	11.4	43.4	15.0	430
1970 [b]	18.0	60.0	n.a.	n.a.
Averages				
1953–57	4.3	14.6	3.2	229
1958–62	7.4	26.0	6.5	354
1963–65	9.0	32.9	9.2	367
1966–70 [a]	10.1	38.69	12.2	392

[a] Planned in 1965 after Khrushchev.

[b] Planned under Khrushchev.

Sources. Figures for 1953–64 from *Narodnoe khoziaistvo, 1964*, p. 366; for 1964 from *SSSR v tsifrakh, 1965*, pp. 86–87; for 1965–70 from Brezhnev's speech at the March 1965 plenum, *Pravda,* March 27, 1965; for 1970 from Khrushchev's speech at the February 1964 plenum, *Sel'skaia zhizn',* February 15, 1964.

they went down by 37 percent, and for milk by 28 percent. Despite a substantial reduction, the new livestock quotas were rather steep, providing for more than a 30 percent increase in meat and milk procurements between 1965 and 1970, 60 percent in eggs, and 24 percent in wool. These increases in livestock procurements were considerably greater, especially for meat, than those which occurred between 1959 and 1964—11 percent for meat, 26 percent for milk, 46 percent for eggs, and a slight decline for wool.

Accompanying higher procurement quotas for livestock products were rising prices. Procurement prices were raised a number of times under Khrushchev, the last time in 1962. Yet the Brezhnev-Kosygin regime deemed the prices of livestock products still insufficient to make production profitable, and further price increases were decreed. First, the procurement price of milk was raised on an average of 22 percent beginning with January 1, 1965. The butterfat-content standard, on the basis of which milk procurements are priced, was lowered, making it more advantageous for the farms. At the same time, prices of skimmed milk sold to farmers for livestock feeding were reduced from 30 rubles per ton to 10 rubles.[57] After May 1, 1965, increments were also added to livestock procurement prices, varying regionally in accordance with the profitability of the livestock industry. The term "increment" (*nadbavka*) was used deliberately to indicate the temporary character of the measure.[58] No such additional payments were set for government purchases of privately owned livestock.

The government thus served notice that under certain undefined conditions it might later reduce livestock prices. In the meantime, considerably higher prices were paid to the farms. The increment to the procurement price of cattle is, on an average for the country as a whole, 36 percent, hogs 32 percent, and sheep 33 percent.[59] But there were considerable regional variations; in the RSFSR and the Ukraine the increment for cattle was 35 percent and for hogs 33 percent; but for Belorussia it was 55 and 40 percent respectively, and for Kazakhstan 20 and 30 percent. For sheep and goats the increment was only 10 percent in the kolkhozes of Kazakhstan and none in the sovkhozes; but in the Baltic republics it was 70 and 60 percent and, in the mountainous regions, 100 percent.[60] Further regional differentiation of livestock price increases within the republics was left to local authorities, who must maintain the average set for each republic.[61] The 1965 price increases were not accompanied by higher retail prices in state stores, as happened in 1962. Even with the retail prices substantially raised, it was claimed that the government incurred losses in the procurement, processing, and sale of meat. With a further increase in meat procurement prices in 1965, still higher losses were expected.

The possible reduction of the temporarily increased livestock prices hinges on the ability of the kolkhozes and sovkhozes to reduce production costs. Whether the Russians will be more successful in reducing livestock costs in the future than they have been in the past is uncertain. But increased incentives to farm workers, made possible by higher prices, should benefit the livestock industry and, in fact, had already contributed to its considerable recovery in 1965, after the losses suffered over the two preceding years. A reduction of compulsory grain procurements and of planned improvement in yields of crops, pasture, and hayland would also help to augment the feed supply shortages which contributed to high livestock costs. With the continuous price escalation, procurements in the mid-1960s cannot be equated with the exactions of the Stalin era. Procurement prices of grains and livestock exceeded or were near world prices after the increases in 1965, particularly when the high premiums are taken into account.[62] Instead of serving as a mechanism to pump wealth from the agricultural into the nonagricultural sector, procurements are becoming a source of growing kolkhoz revenue and could be used for economic incentives to the workers.

As stated by an official of the Soviet Ministry of Finance: "For many years there took place a certain redistribution of the national income created in agriculture, in favor of industry and other branches of the economy. At present, in order to develop the productive forces of agriculture, its share of the national income should be increased. A considerable proportion of the additional revenue obtained by kolkhozes as a result of raising procurement prices . . . will be channeled into increased payment for the kolkhozniks' labor, which will help to enhance their material interest and their labor input." [63] The beneficial effects of the new quota system were seen as hinging on two fundamental conditions: first, the setting of quotas for different farms would be equitable and arranged so that their internal needs were taken care of and surpluses disposed of at higher extra-quota prices; second, quotas and prices actually remaining firm and not being changed arbitrarily, as happened so often in the past. Of course one must not forget the weather, which influences procurements no matter what the system. It would be difficult for kolkhozes to comply with the scheduled quotas in case of a poor harvest, even with higher prices, and a reduction of procurements would spell a loss of revenue. What is worse, it could lead to the resumption of the kind of pressuring to fulfill the procurement goals which the authorities sought to avoid by raising prices. A much larger unresolved issue is involved here: can Soviet agrarian collectivism be successfully reoriented to rely principally on economic stimuli, or must it resort again to coercion?

17

Income and Consumer Goods

Now that the two major items in kolkhoz income, capital investment and procurements, have been discussed, we may turn to the heart of the incentive problem: the remuneration of kolkhozniks. Only those kolkhozniks who actually work in the kolkhoz share in the residual portion of kolkhoz income allocated for labor payments. For convenience I shall call this the wage fund. There is no interest payment or any other compensation for property contributed by individual members. The payment varies with the skill and volume of the work done; the greater the skill required and the greater the quantity and quality of work, the greater the earnings, and vice versa of course, within the limits set by the wage fund. This inequality in remuneration was deliberately imposed on the kolkhozes by the Kremlin, which prized it for its incentive qualities. The system was frequently favorably contrasted in official pronouncements with methods in which payment is not related specifically to the quantity of work performed, such as a straight daily wage. All such egalitarian methods are lumped together under the term *uravnilovka*, a contemptuous reference meaning the kind of pseudo-equality rejected by the government.

Actually, the early kolkhozes, which had greater freedom with regard to internal arrangements, usually adopted the more egalitarian methods of income distribution that were familiar to peasants from the days of the mir. This is brought out in the following tabulation, based on surveys made in 1922–1925, which shows the percent of the total number of kolkhozes in which income was distributed on one or another egalitarian basis.[1]

Region	Year	Equal per capita shares (I)	Equal per worker shares (II)	Combination of I and II
Don	1922	31.2%	29.2%	10.1%
Odessa	1923	34.0	17.0	49.0
Kiev	1924	38.2	23.4	24.2
Viatka	1925	50.0	22.7	27.3

During the early phase of mass collectivization, egalitarian methods of distribution were favored by many new kolkhozes, a number of which even adopted the commune form. But the government soon put its foot down. Payment by the day, or on some other time basis, was also ruled out.

Norms and Workdays

The preferred arrangements for compensating the farmers resemble, in a way, the piecework system in factories, though much more complicated and cumbersome. The first step is the setting of daily tasks or norms of performance in the various farm operations, such as plowing, sowing, cultivation, and harvesting. Standard or sample norms were developed by the government in 1933 for thirty-five important farm operations, as a pattern for the guidance of kolkhozes in establishing their own norms.[2] Kolkhozes either adopted the published norms without change or lowered them. This aroused frequent complaints of obsolescence. As time went on, many norms were considered far too low in the light of the possibilities for increased productivity. Revision was undertaken in a number of regions in 1940 and 1941, but many operations were not included. There were also defects in the evaluation stage, and setbacks that cropped up during and after the war were censured by the February 1947 decree.[3] To ensure that the norms would keep pace with technological progress, a decree of April 19, 1948, ordered a review within a month of kolkhoz labor norms, "taking into account special features of farm operations in kolkhozes and the degree of labor productivity achieved by the better [advanced] kolkhoz workers." [4] The same decree also required an annual review of work norms in each kolkhoz. Those that were too low, as measured by the general level of labor productivity, were to be raised.

A new set of norms, including a much larger number of operations, was also issued as a supplement to the decree. As before, the kolkhoz management remained responsible for the adoption of appropriate norms corresponding to the conditions prevailing on each farm. Yet criticism continued because poor coordination and other defects resulted in low norms and in easier accomplishment of some tasks than of others. An investigation made in 1958 by the All-Union Research Institute of Agricultural Economics in kolkhozes of two districts of Central Russia showed that 85 percent of the norms used in crop and vegetable production, involving hand labor and horse power, "did not exceed the minimum level of the obsolete and very low standard norms of 1948." [5] In another district an investigation in 1955–1957 disclosed that, of 370 norms used in kolkhozes, 163 (44 percent) were below the lower limit of the 1948 norms. In many cases the norms used constituted only 30–50 percent of the standard.[6]

That individual kolkhozniks should favor lower work norms is not surprising. One Soviet authority blamed "the backward psychology of some kolkhozniks striving to increase their earnings not by raising their productivity but by the use of lower norms." [7] That this oversimplifies the situation is evidenced by another authority, who stated that it is most often the norms in crop production that undergo upward revision, less often those in livestock production and hardly ever those in various services and administrative work; this increases or creates disparities in paying workers in different branches of farming.[8] The higher the norm is pushed, the greater the daily task and the less the compensation relative to the volume of work, assuming there is no change in payment rates—hence the resistance to changes in norms by a very considerable number of kolkhozniks. The strong drive by the regime after the late fifties for increased productivity led to an emphasis on higher norms, on "progressive and technically well grounded" norms.[9] By these are meant tasks set with the aid of time and motion studies of farm operations, accompanied by experimentation in what is known in the United States as "scientific management" (or the Taylor system). Although condemning this as an instrument of exploitation of workers under capitalism, the Soviet regime favors the method and stresses the superiority of such scientific norms over "subjective," rule-of-thumb work norms. But probably the latter will be replaced only slowly by the more sophisticated models, if for no other reason than a shortage of the trained personnel needed for such an operation.

The next problem after setting up the norms or tasks is their valuation or rating for purposes of payment in kind and in cash. Money could have been used as a yardstick. Instead an intermediate unit, the workday (*trudoden'*), was adopted, with each task rated in terms of workdays. The workday should not be confused with a man-day of labor; the latter may be worth more or less than one workday, depending on the kind of work performed. There is a difference in the relation of man-days and work-days between men, women, and adolescent workers, as shown in the tabulation below, based on a survey in 1937 in seven regions.[10]

	No. of persons working	Man-days worked	Workdays earned
Men	40.0%	57.5%	60.1%
Women	45.4	38.0	36.4
Adolescents	14.6	4.5	3.5
	100.0%	100.0%	100.0%

Although the proportion of women in the kolkhoz labor force exceeded that of men, they were not able, because of the burden of household duties, to devote as much time to collective work. Also, because they were engaged in less skilled occupations, they earned fewer workdays per unit of time worked. The latter is also true of adolescents.

For purposes of valuation in workdays, all farm operations were divided into several categories on the basis of difficulty, importance, and skill required. Tasks requiring the least skill and effort, such as that of a guard, messenger, or charwoman, were rated as less than one workday; a skilled tractor driver or combine operator, classified in the highest labor category, was entitled to several workdays for the performance of the daily norms. The decree of the Commissariat of Agriculture of February 28, 1933, set up seven categories, with a valuation ranging from one half of a workday to two workdays for the performance of a daily task. The decree of April 19, 1948, increased the number of categories from seven to nine, with the lower limit remaining at a half workday and the upper limit extended to two and a half. This classification was to apply to all kolkhozes. Additional workdays were to be credited to workers who exceeded their norms, while nonfulfillment or poor quality of work theoretically involved a reduction in the number of workdays credited to a kolkhoznik. An important appurtenance of the kolkhoznik became the record book in which his earned workdays were supposed to be entered.

The third and last phase of this complicated process is the determination of the worth of a workday in terms of products and cash. To this end, all the workdays earned by kolkhozniks during a year are added together and this figure is divided into the amount of cash and products set aside for distribution, thus establishing the value of one workday in a particular kolkhoz. Let us suppose, for example, that in a particular kolkhoz one workday is worth 4 kilograms of grain and 1 ruble in cash, and that a member of a kolkhoz is credited with 200 workdays for the year. His annual earnings will be 800 kilograms of grain (4 × 200) and 200 rubles (1 × 200). The value of a workday under this arrangement can be fully established only at the end of the year, when the results of the harvest and its disposal are known. The distribution to the kolkhozniks usually was similarly timed.

Until the late 1950s the workday was solidly rooted in the Soviet scheme of things, but certain criticisms were leveled against it. One was the tendency toward overvaluation of simple and light types of farm work, mostly service operations; and the undervaluation of the heavier, more difficult field operations requiring greater skill, such as plowing or seeding.[11] Considerable confusion also prevailed, according to an investigation made in 1947, in the way in which tasks were rated in terms of workdays. Sometimes the same kind of work, such as carting manure, was rated in three different ways in the same kolkhoz. Conversely, widely different operations were rated the same number of workdays.[12] The publication of the nine-step classification of farm operations in terms of workdays in April 1948, which was mandatory for all kolkhozes, sought to eliminate such defects. But it brought upon the workday system the opposite criticism, that of excessive rigidity. This led to resistance against the upward revision of norms, since the workdays earned were not changed. The decree of March 6, 1956, modified the provisions of the collective-farm charter and allowed kolkhozes to set up their own work norms and workday valuations.

Another charge was that the workday method was not related directly to output. For instance, two brigades, working presumably under identical conditions on two plots of land, obtained varying yields. The higher yield might be associated with the expenditure of a smaller number of workdays, or vice versa. As a result, the workers in the brigade with higher yields could earn less than those in the brigade with lower yields. This has been characterized by Soviet spokesmen as rewarding inferior work and penalizing the more efficient workers. Yet the underlying assumption, that two apparently similar plots of land in a kolkhoz planted to the same crop will produce identical yields if worked equally well, is often unjustified. Yields depend not only on human effort, but also on weather and other natural and technical conditions, which may vary over a farm as large as the usual kolkhoz. It is not easy to segregate these various factors; high or low yields may be obtained regardless of labor input. In such cases, tying the remuneration to the output of a specific crop, rather than to the labor effort measured in workdays, may unfairly reward or penalize workers.[13]

Particularly after World War II, the Soviet government was bent on linking the workday more closely with variations in output. A procedure was elaborated by the above-cited decree of April 19, 1948, which credited, in accordance with a complicated formula, a certain proportion of supplementary workdays to a brigade or smaller unit (*zveno*) to be distributed among the workers as a bonus for production in excess of the planned goals. Similarly, workdays were supposed to be deducted for failure to reach the goals, except in the event of an officially verified natural adversity.

In addition to rewards for larger output through supplementary workdays, the value of the workday itself was enhanced by special bonuses. A government decree of December 31, 1940, first applied to the Ukraine and later extended to other regions, provided that kolkhoz brigades exceeding planned goals for crops and livestock products were to receive a certain proportion of the surpluses in kind or an equivalent in cash. For instance, for grain it was to be one fourth of the amount harvested in excess of the plan; for sunflower seed, soybeans, rapeseed, and flaxwood, one third; for milk, 15 percent; and for sugar beets and cotton, an extra 50 percent of the average official delivery price for each centner produced above the plan. These bonus payments were distributed to individuals on the basis of the number of workdays earned and were in addition to the payments described earlier. And there was a third type of bonus, one depending on the timeliness of the worker's effort. To encourage the full participation of kolkhozniks in the early stages or peak periods of farm work, the number of workdays ordinarily credited for the completion of a daily norm was increased. For example, double the number of workdays could be awarded for tending sugar beets between August 1 and 25.

Bonus schemes based on planned output goals were very often nullified by the setting of unrealistic production goals, beyond the reach of even the most efficient farmer. In many kolkhozes during the 1950s the goals were held in abeyance or replaced by the more simple bonus arrangements, based on exceeding the output of the previous year or for some average period.[14] Meanwhile the proliferation of the bonus schemes contributed to the complexity and cumbersomeness of the payment system and the bookkeeping in kolkhozes. Also the bonus system, where practiced, accentuated the segregation of farm operations into "profitable" and "unprofitable" ones, with corresponding attractiveness of participation in this or that operation. If, for example, the value of a workday is higher in flax and sugar-beet growing than in grain production, it becomes difficult for management to get and keep labor for grain production.[15]

The trouble with the whole system of labor payment was epitomized by one of the characters in a topical 1956 novel: "We have loaded the system of organization and remuneration of kolkhoz labor with so many patches that the system itself is as hidden as the original cloth from which a peasant's coat was made is sometimes concealed by the patches used to repair it. For this group of crops—special regulations, a special calculation; for that—such-and-such a privilege; there a bonus; here a premium. But where is the basic payment for the ordinary workday? Sometimes a kolkhoznik receives more in bonuses than in [basic] payments for workdays. It is necessary to tear away all the patches and to see whether anything has remained of the coat itself. Or perhaps it is necessary to remake the whole coat." [16] But before trying to overhaul the badly functioning workday system as a whole, the post-Stalin regime addressed itself to one of its most irksome aspects: the uncertainty and irregularity of payment.

That this was resented by the kolkhozniks is evidenced by the reported reply of a chairman of one prosperous kolkhoz to the question why young people were leaving his farm, particularly since they did not even move to a city but merely went to work in a factory five kilometers away. "Because," he said, "there they receive a regular wage (*zarplata*) . . . Kolkhozniks receive money only once a year, in the fall, but young men need it every day. As a result, even a small regular wage seems more attractive than a large workday payment." [17] The first method of regularizing the kolkhoznik's income was to activate an old device, that of advance payments prior to the final, end-of-year settlement. Such advances during the Stalin era were limited in scope. Kolkhozes had been permitted to use for advance payments and for "internal needs," during the harvest and prior to the completion of government procurement goals, a quantity of grain not exceeding 15 percent of that already delivered to the state, 5 percent of sunflower seed and rice, and 10 percent of potatoes.[18] Advances made at harvest time, though, did not help to spread the flow of income throughout the year. Cash advances were paid several times a year to the growers of cotton and some other industrial crops, but most peasants did not benefit from them.

One of the first post-Stalin agricultural measures was to widen the use of advances, which the increase in procurement prices now made feasible. The September 1953 decree "recommended" that kolkhozes, at the discretion of the general assembly of the membership, use 25 percent of the money receipts from compulsory deliveries and extra-quota sale of livestock products for paying quarterly advances to koklhozniks. Of this total, 60 percent was to be distributed as advances on the basis of all workdays earned by a kolkhoznik during the quarter, and the remaining 40 percent on the basis of workdays earned in animal husbandry and feed production. The decree contained identical provisions with respect to potatoes and vegetables, except that monthly rather than quarterly advances were recommended. Regulations of a similar nature were promulgated regarding some other crops. The resolutions of the Twentieth Communist Party Congress in February 1956, and a subsequent decree issued by the Central Committee and the Council of Ministers, further generalized the system of advances.[19] In the words of the latter decree, "payment of monthly advances to kolkhozniks is an important incentive for increased labor productivity in kolkhozes; it enhances the importance of the workday and increases the interest of the kolkhozniks in the development of the collective economy." The decree recommended that kolkhozes, "by the decision of the General Assembly," pay the kolkhozniks throughout the year monthly advances on their earnings. They were to use for this purpose not less than 25 percent of the actual cash receipts obtained from all sectors of collective-farm production and 50 percent of the money received by the kolkhoz as advances from the state for the required compulsory deliveries and extra-quota sales of agricultural products. In turn, the decree ordered advance payments by government agencies and cooperative organizations for required deliveries from collective farms.

The implementation of these measures for advance payments has been spotty. Many kolkhozes introduced advances, but they often had difficulty in providing adequate funds for regular payment throughout the year, particularly when farming was not sufficiently diversified and depended on a few crops. An example was cited of a typical cotton-growing kolkhoz in the Turkmen Republic, which had 260,000 rubles of expenditures during the first nine months of the year and receipts of only 135,000 rubles, including advances from government procuring agencies and credits from the State Bank.[20] The economist who reported this case advocated an expansion of credit and increases of advances made by the procuring agencies.

A study by T. I. Zaslavskaia found a relationship between the advances paid and the stability of the kolkhozniks' earnings. Using the variability in their incomes during 1954–1963 as a criterion, she divided the different regions of the country into three groups. She found that in 1961 the proportion of advances paid to the total wage fund constituted 62 percent in the most stable group and 54 percent in the other two groups.[21] In some cases the kolkhoz management itself was reported as indifferent to the introduction of advances and even used funds so designated for other purposes.[22] Yet the consensus is that, where it was possible to keep up such payments, the effect was beneficial. A raion party secretary from Smolensk province made this report regarding a weak kolkhoz that had introduced advances: "The attitude of the people towards work changed beyond any recognition. If it was necessary formerly for the brigadiers to persuade kolkhozniks individually to go to work in the fields or barn-yards, now they have another worry—how to provide work for people." [23]

The Guaranteed Wage

Whatever its defects, the workday remained the ideologically undisputed base of the kolkhoz wage structure until 1958. But in that crucial year in Soviet agrarian policy—1958 also witnessed the liquidation of the MTS and a significant procurement-price reform—a new development took place in the payment system. As usual the keynote was sounded by Khrushchev, whose interest in the subject stemmed from his concern to increase farm labor productivity. He remarked at the December 1958 plenum: "A workday does not stand for any concrete quantity of labor or time. In one kolkhoz 1.5 workdays are credited for the fulfillment of a norm and in another for the same norm, the same work, a kolkhoznik is credited with 3 workdays. Under such conditions a workday cannot be considered a correct objective measurement of the labor expenses of production. Shouldn't there be a shift to more progressive forms of evaluation of labor's contribution?" [24]

The initiative of kolkhozes should not be limited in this respect, according to Khrushchev. His words, of course, were echoed in the resolutions of the plenum, which gave official blessing to experimentation by the kolkhozes. The culminating stage in the process is the scrapping of the workday, together with payments in kind, and the replacing of the mixed payment system by a guaranteed monthly money wage. Under a straight cash wage, the valuation of different work tasks are made not in workdays but directly in money terms. What has become more common than a complete monetization of labor payments is an intermediate method, which retains the workday and sets a guaranteed money value on it, paid partly in cash monthly and partly in kind following the harvest of different crops. Nonetheless cash predominates in payments under this intermediate system. It formed 58.4 percent of the total wage fund in 1959–60, 60.6 percent in 1961–62, and 67.8 percent in 1963–64. Conversely, in kolkhozes with a straight cash wage, the proportion deducted for purchases of farm products was considerable, 23 to 25 percent during 1959–1964.[25]

The new money wage was to meet the need for regularity and greater certainty in payments, and to bring about a simplification of the remuneration system in the kolkhozes. By the beginning of 1961, 7,500 kolkhozes had reportedly adopted the money-wage system.[26] But the number had increased only to about 8,000, or approximately a fifth of all kolkhozes, by the summer of 1962.[27] Actually, despite many generous claims made for kolkhoz money wages in the rapidly growing Soviet literature dealing with the subject, the path was strewn with many pitfalls and led to some dissent. The pitfalls are similar to those in advance payments: difficulties in planning and accumulating the funds required for regular monthly payments. Sometimes a stumbling block in reverse resulted from the very success of the money wage to generate an increased demand by kolkhozniks for work which the management was not able to meet, especially during the fall and winter months.[28] The remedy here is the more even flow of kolkhoz income through diversification of farming (though this is already carried out too far on some farms), increases in the processing of agricultural products on the farms and in some non-agricultural activities such as production of building materials, and, most important, the buildup of reserves. That such changes cannot be accomplished easily and quickly by many kolkhozes without substantial assistance by the state did not disturb most protagonists of the money wage, who advocated its prompt and universal adoption. Many of them considered that money wages per se act as an economic stimulus. It was pointed out by critics of this view that money wages can have an incentive effect only when they are regular and sufficiently high. "With a low level of distributed income, the money form of payment to labor gives nothing by itself." [29] Monetization of kolkhoznik income and the guaranteed level and regular frequency of its payment logically are two separate principles, but historically they became linked.

That the above criticisms are valid has been corroborated by the numerous fiascos which occurred when kolkhozes shifted to a guaranteed wage before the financial conditions for such a move were adequate. The result was usually a return to the old workday system. Note that the line of criticism was not opposed to a money wage in principle: the point was that it be introduced under proper conditions. There is another current of opposition to the money wage which is more fundamental in character. Its most articulate representative is K. Orlovskii, the chairman of one of the outstanding kolkhozes (Rassvet) in Belorussia. His farm tried the new method, but found it wanting and returned to the mixed workday system with bimonthly money advances. It was, according to Orlovskii, better adapted to the seasonal character of agricultural production and to the mores of the peasantry. He claimed that kolkhozniks are accustomed and prefer to receive the needed grain and other products directly from the kolkhoz rather than to purchase them from the kolkhoz with their wages.[30] In this connection the problem of pricing the commodities thus bought by kolkhozniks also vexed the management.

There has been conflicting evidence on the attitude of the peasants toward payments in kind, and it probably differs from kolkhoz to kolkhoz, depending upon economic and financial position. Thus a publication designed for party propagandists reports objections to these payments from members of an apparently above-average kolkhoz: "Payments in kind create for them many difficulties. It is necessary to store the grain, vegetables, and other products, to travel to the market to sell them because the personal needs of the predominant majority of kolkhoz families are more than covered by the harvest from their kitchen garden plots. Therefore it was decided at the beginning of the new year to introduce, as an experiment, payments [entirely] in cash." [31] It is well to recall also that a money wage is paid to workers on state farms, to which many kolkhozes were converted. There has been no indication of dissatisfaction on the part of kolkhozniks who became regular wage earners. What should be clearly borne in mind is that a guaranteed wage need not be a straight money wage, even if it is expressed in pecuniary terms. Tractor drivers, for instance, who worked in the MTS before 1958, were paid by the kolkhozes, on the basis of workdays, a guaranteed minimum of grain. Orlovskii also affirmed the value of regular or guaranteed cash advances. Like the other critics he insisted on the importance of a wage to provide adequate incentives to the workers, whatever its form. The situation on this score did not improve rapidly enough during the years 1959–1963. This was probably the most serious roadblock to a guaranteed wage in the kolkhozes, though the other difficulties mentioned above were also operating. Such a wage remained the official goal, as set forth by the Communist Party platform adopted in October 1961. But its implementation was left to Khrushchev's successors.

It must have been obvious to Soviet policy planners that a guaranteed wage could not be substantially and rapidly extended to the kolkhozes without raising their economic level—or without specific assistance by the government in the form of subsidies or credit. It was probably because of this that a guaranteed wage was absent from the original agricultural-relief program presented by Brezhnev at the March 1965 plenum. He confined himself to a noncommittal suggestion that the various agencies concerned prepare proposals for improvement of the system of payment in agriculture, and "to think over (*produmat'*) the question of creating reserves of cash and products for a guaranteed payment for the labor of kolkhozniks." [32] P. E. Shelest, the first secretary of the Ukrainian Communist Party, who at the plenum warmly supported the principle of the guaranteed wage, discussed the additional cost of such a measure, which may explain the lukewarm attitude of Brezhnev. For earnings of kolkhozniks to reach the level of a sovkhoz worker's wage would have required, in the Ukraine alone in 1962–1964, additional payments to them of 750 million rubles as well as the distribution of 6.4–7.5 million tons more grain.[33]

At the Twenty-third Party Congress a year later, both Brezhnev and Kosygin endorsed the principle of a guaranteed monthly wage in the kolkhozes, but made it clear that its implementation would be gradual. Brezhnev said: "It is proposed gradually to solve a large problem during the new five-year [plan] period—to introduce a monthly guaranteed payment for the labor of kolkhozniks to conform to the wage level and work tasks of sovkhoz workers doing similar kinds of work." Kosygin stated: "The work tasks, the organization, and the payment for labor in kolkhozes will increasingly approach the level and forms developed in sovkhozes. It is contemplated to introduce gradually everywhere a monthly guaranteed payment for the labor of kolkhozniks." [34] These guarded statements of the leaders, coupled with their known distaste for crash programs, pointed to an unhurried, cautious implementation. It was also thought that such an important organizational change would be first discussed at the kolkhoz congress which was to convene later in the year to approve a revised charter for collective farms. But, as so often happens in the USSR, the government had a surprise in store. Shortly after the Twenty-third Congress, a highly important decree was issued by the Central Committee and the Council of Ministers entitled, "Concerning the Raising of the Material Interest of Kolkhozniks in Socialized Production." [35] The decree recommended that kolkhozes introduce, without any exceptions, beginning on July 1, 1966, guaranteed payment for the labor of kolkhozniks in cash and in kind, based on work tasks and wage rates adopted for similar operations in sovkhozes and with adjustments in work tasks as required by "concrete conditions." Cash was to be paid to kolkhozniks not less than once a month and payments in kind were to be made when products became available. The crucial provision of the decree was the requirement that funds for the payment of labor have first priority in the distribution of income: if this is adhered to, it will radically change the status of the kolkhoznik from a residual recipient of kolkhoz income to a first claimant.

This provision, which puts teeth into the guaranteed wage, was bolstered by the requirement of allocating cash and products in the production-financial plans of kolkhozes for such payments, which could not be used for any other purpose. A parallel recommendation was the creation of a special reserve to which a certain proportion of grain and other crops are allocated. From this reserve, kolkhozniks could be supplied with products, including feedstuffs for their private livestock, which would be charged to their payments in kind. Bonus payments to kolkhozniks in excess of the guaranteed wage, based either on the quantity and quality of output obtained or on the gross income, were also recommended. Although their high priority in the distribution of kolkhoz income gave a new dimension to guaranteed payments, many kolkhozes were still faced with serious financial hurdles before the scheme could be made operational. The government extended financial assistance by instructing the State Bank to provide, with the approval of raion authorities, up to five years' credit to kolkhozes lacking funds for a guaranteed-wage scheme, with repayment of the loans beginning during the third year. Since long-term credit for 1966 had already been allocated to kolkhozes when the decree was published, its redistribution was authorized wherever necessary to support a guaranteed wage. This reduced the amount of state investment available for other purposes. It tends to confirm the impression that the decision to issue the May 1966 decree was made in a hurry.

The speed of the reform was not explained, and in the absence of significant clues, it is possible only to speculate whether the decree was an outcome of a factional dispute in the Politburo or whether it was hastened by favorable crop prospects in May 1966 or by some other unknown circumstance. The consequences of the reform may be truly epochal in transforming the kolkhoznik from a residual claimant to uncertain income, to a position approaching that of a state-farm worker of similar qualifications, as stated by Kosygin at the Twenty-third Congress. A word of caution here. The goal is not immediate equality in the incomes of kolkhozniks and sovkhoz workers, but the tendency is toward equalization. As long as the sovkhozes have a higher proportion of better-paid skilled workers, and more man-days are worked per year, their average earnings will be higher than the kolkhozes'. But this may become progressively less true with the closer approximation of the two averages. The cardinal question is, will the government stick to the program and will it be effectively implemented? How well, for instance, will the State Bank perform its important function of financing the transition to the new system? Time alone can give answers to such questions, but it is important to bear in mind that prior liberalization experiments in collective agriculture have not worked too well.

Levels of Income

The fulfillment of the central aim of a guaranteed wage, the improvement of the material condition of kolkhozniks and their incentives to produce, will depend, as I said before, not only on the regularity of

Table 53. Average quantity of grain distributed to kolkhozniks during specified years according to two different sources (kilograms)

Year	Per workday		Per household	
	1 [a]	2 [b]	1 [a]	2 [b]
1932	2.3	2.2	600	570
1933	—	2.9	—	930
1934	—	2.8	—	990
1935	2.4	2.8	910	1,010
1936	1.6	—	629	—
1937	4.0	—	1,740	—

[a] The whole territory of the USSR.

[b] Exclusive of Krasnoiarsk province, Far East, Iakutsk, Kirgiz, Turkmen, and Tadjik republics.

Sources. For 1: 1932, 1935, and 1937—I. V. Sautin, ed., *Kolkhozy vo vtoroi Stalinskoi piatiletke,* p. 110; D. Rud, *Raspredelenie dokhodov v kolkhozakh,* p. 22. For 2: N. Khmelevskii, "Incomes of Kolkhozniks in 1935," *Plan,* 21:29 (1936).

payments but also on their size. What, then, is the income of kolkhoz workers and households from collective farming, and what are the government's future goals? This is a subject on which systematic statistical information was scarce for many years. The multiple workday system of payments in kind and in cash also complicates matters. In the 1930s, data were published for several years on the distribution of the principal item of kolkhoznik earnings: grain (shown in Table 53) and, to a lesser extent, cash and some other minor items. Cash payments were often so miserably small that they were even blasted by the Stalin administration itself, in the decree of April 19, 1938, which stated that some kolkhozes did not pay their members a single kopeck.[36] As for grain, the data evidenced considerable improvement during the period 1933–1935, compared with the famine year 1932, which reflected better harvests as well as a greater work effort by the peasants. There was a steady increase in the average number of workdays per household, from 257 in 1932 to 378 in 1935, to 393 in 1936 and to 438 in 1937.[37] The pinch was still felt in a poor crop year like 1936, when distribution per workday declined by more than 30 percent compared with the good 1935 crop. But it was followed by a record increase in 1937, a bumper year. In 1938 and 1939 a smaller proportion of the grain crop was distributed to the kolkhozniks (see Table 54). Since the crops during those two years were also substantially below 1937, considerably less grain was acquired by the kolkhoz

Table 54. Percentage distribution of grain crops in kolkhozes, 1937–1939

Item	1937	1938	1939
Deliveries to the state			
Compulsory procurements	12.2	15.0	14.3
Payments in kind to MTS	13.9	16.0	19.2
Return of seed loans	1.5	2.0	4.0
Total	27.6	33.0	37.5
Kolkhoz requirements and reserves			
For seed	16.3	18.6	18.2
For feed	12.7	13.6	13.9
For aiding those in need	1.1	.8	.8
For other expenditures	1.6	2.0	2.7
Total	31.7	35.0	35.6
Sales to the state and in free market	4.8	5.1 [a]	4.0
Distribution to kolkhozniks on the			
basis of workdays	35.9	26.9	22.9
Grand total	100.0	100.0	100.0

[a] A statement was made that 1.9 percent designated for sale was unsold at "beginning of the year," presumably of 1939.

Sources. For 1937, *Sotsialisticheskoe sel'skoe khoziaistvo, 1940*, nos. 11–12, p. 30; for 1938, *ibid., 1939*, no. 12, p. 63; for 1939, *Izvestiia*, March 29, 1941.

peasantry.* The good harvest in 1940 produced some improvement, but the war catastrophe swept away whatever progress was made in agricultural production and income.

For many years after the Second World War, data on payments to kolkhozniks were fragmentary or not too meaningful. There was a virtual blackout on the subject in postwar statistical yearbooks and handbooks. Even purportedly scholarly works specifically devoted to the subject, like that of Zaslavskaia cited above, managed to avoid absolute figures and confined themselves to percentages.[38] Fortunately another Soviet scholar, V. G. Venzher, in an illuminating little book, gave figures on total payments to kolkhoz labor from 1958 to 1963. These, in conjunction with similar data given by Khrushchev for 1952 and 1957, make it possible to present a fairly good picture of the dynamics of kolkhozniks' remuneration (see Table 55).

* Kolkhozniks did not rely entirely on kolkhozes for their grain supply but also used their private garden plots for this purpose. In 1935, for instance, an additional 18 kilograms of grain per household came from this source. Khmelevskii, *Plan*, 21:31 (1936).

Table 55. Annual average payment per worker and per household in kolkhozes, 1952, 1957–63

Year	Total payments (billion rubles)	Annual average employment (million persons)	Payment per worker [a] (rubles)	Number of households (million)	Payment per household [a] (rubles)
1952	4.75	25.8 [b]	184	19.9	239
1957	8.38	25.3	331	18.9	443
1958	7.8	25.1	311	18.8	415
1959	7.7	24.1	320	18.5	416
1960	7.2	21.7	332	17.1	421
1961	7.7	20.3	379	16.4	470
1962	8.4	19.8	424	16.3	515
1963	8.3	19.2	432	16.1	515

[a] Calculated.

[b] Estimated by raising the available 1953 figure of employment (25.5 million) by 1 percent, representing the higher number of households in 1952 compared with 1953.

Sources. Total payments, from V. G. Venzher, *Kolkhoznyi stroi na sovremennom etape* (The Collective Farm System at the Present Stage; Moscow, 1966), p. 80. Employment, number of households, from *Sel'skoe khoziaistvo SSSR, 1960; Narodnoe khoziaistvo, 1956,* and volumes of the same annual for 1962 and 1964.

The very low level of total payments in 1952, the terminal year of the Stalin epoch, caused no surprise. What makes the figures more ominous is that 1952 was the best crop year since the war, and payments were no doubt even lower during the previous years of smaller crops. Under the influence of the Khrushchev reforms and a 9 percent decrease in the number of workers, payment per worker increased 83 percent by 1957. But in 1958, a year of bumper crops, the average payments dropped 9 percent. They were about the same in 1959 and slightly higher in 1960, but still below 1957. The fact that the average figures for these years include a number of higher paid former MTS workers, absorbed by the kolkhozes, shows that the payment situation was even less favorable for the rank-and-file kolkhozniks. One partial remedy was the transfer of a large number of kolkhozniks and MTS workers to the newly organized or converted sovkhozes, which removed them from the kolkhoz payroll. The average number of workers in the MTS and their successors, the RTS, decreased from 2.6 million in 1957 to 200,000 in 1960; the average on state farms increased from 3.7 to 6.3 million (see Table 56). Most of this increase came from the villages and would have swelled the number

Table 56. Employment in socialized agriculture, selected years (million persons)

	1940	1953	1964
Annual average employment, including persons not directly involved in crop and livestock production	31.3	29.4	27.3 [a]
Kolkhozes [b]	29.0	25.6	19.2 [c]
Sovkhozes and other state enterprises	1.8	2.6	8.1
MTS and RTS	0.5	1.2	— [d]
Annual average employment of persons directly involved in crop and livestock production	27.8	26.2	25.2
Kolkhozes [b]	25.8	22.9	17.7
Sovkhozes and other state enterprises	1.6	2.3	7.5
MTS and RTS	0.4	1.0	— [d]

[a] Addition of members of households engaged in small private farming results in a figure of 31 million.

[b] Annual averages of all kolkhozniks including adolescents and aged who worked during a month, irrespective of the amount of time employed. Adjustment was made for conversion of kolkhozes to sovkhozes during each year.

[c] Includes persons employed in fishery kolkhozes. The total number of kolkhozniks employed, excluding those working in fishery kolkhozes, in 1964 was 19,001,000.

[d] MTS abolished in 1958 and RTS in 1961; most of the workers transferred to kolkhozes and sovkhozes.

Sources. *Sel'skoe khoziaistvo SSSR, 1960*, p. 450; *Narodnoe khoziaistvo, 1964*, p. 419.

of claimants to kolkhoz income if the shift had not occurred. A striking indicator of regional variation in the deterioration of the kolkhoznik's income was the decline of cash distributed per man-day in a number of republics in 1960, as compared with 1957: for the Ukraine it was a decline of 18 percent; the Uzbek Republic, 17 percent; Georgia, 14 percent; Belorussia, 11 percent; and Moldavia, 29 percent. At the same time, it was claimed that the productivity of kolkhoz labor increased by 10 percent in the Ukraine, 11 percent in the Uzbek Republic, 15 percent in Georgia and Moldavia, and 22 percent in Belorussia.[39]

In the light of these figures, it is not surprising that a considerable share of kolkhoznik income continued to be derived from personal farming and private trade, that is, from an essentially individualistic economy. A special sample survey that included 17 kolkhozes in 1957 and 24 kolkhozes in 1958 disclosed that 40.4 percent and 38 percent, respectively, of the total income of able-bodied kolkhozniks was traceable to this source. The proportion varied among the different farms surveyed. In 4 kolkhozes in 1957 and 5 in 1958 this proportion rose above 50 percent, and in 5 kolkhozes in 1957 and 4 in 1958 it was below 25 percent.[40] A shift in government policy with respect to the remuneration of kolkhozniks became evident during this period, and it must bear the responsibility for the deterioration.

By May 1957 Khrushchev was beginning to stress the channeling of kolkhoz funds into the public sector, into expenditures for public welfare and village (municipal) improvement rather than into increased individual incomes for the kolkhozniks. He had this to say: "Now there should no longer be a contest as to which [kolkhoz] will distribute more per workday. Of course, the kolkhozniks must, first of all, be provided with food and clothing. But it is necessary also to think about the culture of the people." He took the same line at the December 1958 plenum. A year later, at the December 1959 plenum, Khrushchev and some other party chieftains made a frontal attack on the large distribution per workday in kolkhozes that grew high-value crops like cotton and fruit. Claiming that in some districts earnings of kolkhozniks considerably exceeded even those of industrial workers, Khrushchev laid down the principle that "remuneration of a kolkhoznik for his labor, as a rule, must not outstrip the level of a worker's wages in the same district or province," and procuring prices must be regulated accordingly by the government.[41] The wage of a sovkhoz worker was to be the specific guide that the earnings of a kolkhoznik working under similar conditions must not exceed.

Yet at the same December 1959 plenum at which Khrushchev blasted large payments to kolkhozniks, N. V. Podgornyi (then first secretary of the Communist Party of the Ukraine) lamented that "despite the growing of kolkhoz income and allocations to indivisible funds, the remuneration of kolkhozniks in the course of the last three years remained at the same level." [42] The reduction of procurement prices in 1958, the heavy expense of purchasing and maintaining machinery from the liquidated MTS, and the rising prices of new machinery and spare parts, all of which adversely affected kolkhoz revenue, were in line with this essentially negative policy of the government in the matter of economic incentives. The official preference for public-welfare expenditures over increased payments to kolkhozniks produced some extravagances, which Khrushchev later ridiculed. One of these was the establishment of schools of music in the kolkhozes. "Is it not too early to be occupied with this?" he asked. "Who busies himself with such matters? More often some famous singer 'pushes' the question of establishing a school of music in a village where he was born. And he wants to create such a school not by financing it himself but by using the money of others, state money. But if such an artist is asked to sing in his native village, he will not do this gratis." [43]

But a trend favoring larger payments to kolkhozniks re-emerged as the government became increasingly concerned with agricultural stagnation. Khrushchev acknowledged, notably at the March 1962 plenum, the error of excessive emphasis on public funds at the expense of kolkhoznik earnings.[44] By relieving the deflationary pressure from above, the atmosphere in which local decisions were made regarding the distribution of kolkhoz income was considerably relaxed. After 1961 incentive payments (bonuses) again became the vogue. Also, a more positive step on the part of the Khrushchev administration was to channel additional resources to the kolkhozes in order to increase individual incomes. Notwithstanding Khrushchev's often articulated opposition to further increases in prices beyond those that took place between 1953 and 1958, a decision was announced on June 1, 1962, which sharply raised both the procurement and the retail prices of livestock products. As far as farm costs were concerned, there were also savings to kolkhozes resulting from the reduction in 1961 of the prices of farm machinery, spare parts, fuel, building materials, and metals and metal products. Despite unfavorable weather conditions in 1962 and especially in 1963, payments per worker were more than a fifth above 1957 and more than a third above 1958, though the officially reported gross income of kolkhozes between 1958 and 1963 declined.[45] Although for 1964 no firm data are available, the increase reported in payment per man-day points to a higher income for kolkhozniks.[46] For 1965 an increase of 16 percent in payment to kolkhoz workers, including a distribution of 7 percent more grain over 1964, was reported.[47] A lower level of kolkhoznik earnings emerges from data given by Zaslavskaia, which are entirely in terms of percentages and apply only to able-bodied adult kolkhozniks.* This series appears to be inconsistent

* Zaslavskaia states that in 1964 the average annual income of an able-bodied kolkhoznik was equal to 53 percent of the annual earnings of a sovkhoz worker (*Raspredelenie,* p. 40). The income of a sovkhoz worker, according to the same source, was 69 percent of the wage of an industrial worker (p. 39). It is assumed that the reference is to the cash wage of an industrial worker. *Narodnoe khoziaistvo, 1964,* p. 555, gives the average monthly cash wage of workers in industry in 1964 as 98.7 rubles; of this,

with the one based on Venzher's data and official figures on average employment. The latter is preferred because of the wholly derivative character of the series obtained from Zaslavskaia's material.

In dealing with such national averages, large regional variations should not be overlooked. These are disclosed by the man-day rates for which data are available. The 1961–1963 average payment per man-day for various provinces of the RSFSR varied from 1.01 rubles in Gorkii province to 2.89 in Stavropol, where it was thus nearly three times larger.[48] There are also variations among raions and individual kolkhozes. Emel'-ianov, in a study of 118 kolkhozes in Briansk province in 1963, divided them into four groups, using the value of capital per 100 hectares of farmland as a criterion. He found that payment per man-day was trending upward with the increase in capital and varied from 1.01 rubles for the lowest group to 1.70 rubles for the highest. The average for the 118 kolkhozes amounted to 1.32 rubles.[49]

Although the number of kolkhoz workers considerably exceeds the number in sovkhozes, even after the numerous conversions of collectives into state farms, the state-farm sector has become increasingly more important since the 1950s as an employer and producer of farm products. The remuneration of labor is higher in sovkhozes than in kolkhozes, as we have seen, and the equalization of the two sectors became the goal of Soviet planners in 1966. The differing levels of well-being between kolkhozniks and sovkhoz workers recall, by historical analogy, the relatively superior position of state peasants over private serfs before and even after emancipation. The gap between the earnings of kolkhozniks and sovkhoz workers is indicated by Tables 55 and 57. Note the difference between the

---

69 percent comes to 68.1 rubles, and 53 percent of the latter amount is 36.1 rubles. This multiplied by 12 represents the annual payment in cash and kind to an able-bodied adult kolkhoznik in 1964. By applying Zaslavskaia's index to this figure, the series below of payments to able-bodied adult kolkhozniks is obtained.

Year	Index 1953=100	Rubles per year
1953	100	159.9
1954	120	191.9
1955	150	239.9
1956	158	252.6
1957	160	255.8
1958	182	291.0
1959	173	276.6
1960	168	268.6
1961	189	302.2
1962	221	353.4
1963	229	366.2
1964	271	433.2

two series of sovkhoz wage figures in Table 57. The larger figures in the last column are from an official statistical yearbook and apply to all state-farm enterprises, including special farms serving institutions, factories, and the like. The lower figures in the third column are derived from different sources and are for sovkhozes only. The inclusion in the first series of all state-farm enterprises may perhaps account for some of the difference; but there are also other unexplained factors. At any rate, it seems reasonable to assume that the two sets of figures delimit the range of sovkhoz wages. On this basis, a kolkhoznik in 1963 earned on the average 54–57 percent of the wages of a sovkhoz worker; in 1958 it was 48–54 percent. The fringe benefits are also smaller for kolkhozniks than for sovkhoz workers, but the returns from personal farming are larger and need to be larger to enable kolkhozniks to keep their heads above water.

The planned increase of 35–40 percent in the income of kolkhozniks during 1966–1970,[50] if it materializes, would markedly reduce but not close the gap, even if sovkhoz wages were to remain stationary. Assuming that the average annual earnings of kolkhozniks reached 500 rubles in 1965—a rather generous assumption—and that this amount will be increased by 40 percent to 700 rubles, the sovkhoz workers would still be ahead by 60–105 rubles. Part of this, perhaps even a large part, may be

Table 57. Annual average payment per worker in state farms, 1958–1964

Year	Total payments[a] (billion rubles)	Annual average employment[a] (thousand persons)	Payment per worker (rubles)	
			In sovkhozes[b]	In all state-farm enterprises
1958	2.2	3,835	574	637
1959	2.4	4,177	575	n.a.
1960	3.1	5,482	565	647
1961	4.2	6,571	639	n.a.
1962	5.2	6,893	754	n.a.
1963	5.4	7,109	760	805
1964	—	—	—	847

[a] Sovkhoz only, exclusive of other state-farm enterprises.
[b] Calculated.

Sources. Total payments, from Venzher, *Kolkhoznyi stroi na sovremennom etape*, p. 80. Average annual employment, from *Sel'skoe khoziaistvo, 1960*, p. 451; *Narodnoe khoziaistvo, 1962, Narodnoe khoziaistvo, 1963*. Payments per worker: for sovkhozes, calculated; for all state farm enterprises, *Narodnoe khoziaistvo, 1964*, p. 555.

traceable to the different composition and utilization of the labor force in kolkhozes and sovkhozes, and more time would be required to remedy the situation. What is perhaps more important, sovkhoz wages cannot be expected to stand still. The fact of the matter is that they too are low when compared to the average for all workers in the USSR (exclusive of kolkhozniks), especially industrial workers. The average sovkhoz wage in 1963 and 1965 was 77 percent of the average for all workers and 70–73 percent of the wages of industrial workers.[51] According to one authority, the linking of earnings in sovkhozes with usually high output goals that could not be fulfilled tended to depress sovkhoz wages.[52] This was particularly true of the economically weak sovkhozes, of which there are many. But wage levels suffered even in the stronger sovkhozes because it often happened that when the plan goals were fulfilled, entitling workers to higher earnings, they would be raised the next year, thus nullifying benefits as far as wages were concerned. Certainly sovkhoz workers should qualify for the increase set by the 1966–1970 plan of no less than 20 percent on the average for all workers.[53] An increase of such magnitude, let alone a larger one, would again widen the gap between kolkhozniks' earnings (even if these were increased by 40 percent) and those of sovkhoz workers.*

* Significant changes were made in the state-farm wage structure in 1966. To encourage early harvesting, a rule frequently violated in the USSR, with attendant heavy losses, special incentives were devised for mechanizers in sovkhozes and other state-farm enterprises. These incentives, in the form of percentage bonuses of the daily wage during the early days of mass harvest, were increased beginning June 1, 1966, from 50 to 100 percent for harvesting of small grains, pulses, corn for grain silage, sunflower seed, potatoes, and grass seed in the eastern regions (Siberia, Far East, and the new-lands regions of Kazakhstan, the Urals, and the Volga area). In all other regions this bonus was increased from 30 to 60 percent. The bonus for early harvesting of all other crops was increased from 30 and 15 percent to 60 and 30 percent for the corresponding regions. However, the period during which these higher wage rates could be applied was reduced from 15 to 10 days from the beginning of mass harvesting. I. N. Popov-Cherkasov, B. S. Turbin, and V. I. Buzykin, *Organizatsiia zarabotnoi platy rabochikh v sovkhozakh SSSR* (The Wage Structure of Workers in the Sovkhozes of the USSR; Moscow, 1964), p. 102; *Pravda* and *Sel'skaia zhizn'*, April 30, 1966. An important innovation is the establishment by the same decree of bonuses for the continuous service of mechanizers on a particular state farm, which are shown in the following tabulation.

Years of continuous service	Percent of annual wage paid as a bonus	
	Eastern region	Other
3–5	12	6
5–10	15	8
10–15	20	10
Over 15	25	15

The high turnover of mechanizers, a perennial evil, was responsible for this measure, the aim being to make it worthwhile for them to continue working for a long period on the same farm. The decree provided also for a general upward adjustment in the wages of the lower-paid categories of mechanizers on state farms.

In considering low average earnings, it should not be overlooked that kolkhozniks in the more efficient kolkhozes were better off than those in the economically weak kolkhozes. The reader may be reminded again that there were certain avenues of escape for poorly paid kolkhozniks. The oldest of these was the migration of kolkhoz peasants, especially the young ones, to the cities if there were no factories in the neighborhood, to join the ranks of industrial workers. The extent of such migration at midcentury was indicated by the head of the Komsomol, Pavlov, who stated at the May 1965 plenum that the number of persons of seventeen to nineteen years of age in rural communities "decreased during recent years by 6 million. In many kolkhozes the average age of the workers is fifty years." [54] To this was added in the 1950s and 1960s state employment through the conversion of kolkhozes into sovkhozes and the general expansion of the state-farm sector. Finally, kolkhozniks could, within limits varying with the twists of government policy, supplement their income by private farming. There are obstacles to the first method of betterment which may increase in the future because of the kolkhozniks' lack of industrial skills, a possible unforeseen reduction of the employment capacity of nonagricultural occupations, and the reluctance of kolkhoz managers to part with their workers, particularly the young ones. This is well illustrated by the dispute between the manager of the "new life" farm in Abramov's novel and an old kolkhoznik to whose son the manager refused to issue a document that would have enabled him to obtain employment in town. The escape to the sovkhoz payroll is also likely to be more limited in the future if the post-Khrushchev regime really means what it says about the continued coexistence of those two forms of agricultural organization. As for supplementing income by private farming, that will depend primarily on government policy, which under the Brezhnev-Kosygin leadership has become more liberal than during the latter part of the Khrushchev period. Whatever the future, the kolkhozniks in the mid-1960s remained at the bottom of the socialist totem pole, with earnings from socialized agriculture in 1963 equal to only 40 percent of the average wage for all workers and state employees (outside of collective farming) and 37 percent of the wages of industrial manual workers.

That the low remuneration of agricultural labor makes for low productivity and thus hurts the whole economy is generally admitted in the USSR. One of the consequences is that, although the agricultural labor force has been decreasing, it is still too large when compared with other industrial nations. In 1958 the number of workers in Soviet agriculture, including private farming, was over 30 million and in the United States 7.5 million, or less than a fourth. But the roughly estimated gross farm output of the Soviet Union in that very good year was only 62.5 percent of that in the United States (excluding Alaska and Hawaii).[55] In other words, gross output per agricultural worker in the Soviet Union averaged roughly six times less than for his American counterpart. Differences in climatic conditions, technology, the educational qualifications and skill of the labor force, and the type of farm organization are, of course, highly important in creating this disparity. But the adverse effect of low remuneration on the level of output cannot be gainsaid. This conception of the importance of labor in the economic process is strikingly confirmed by the author of *Capital,* the master himself. Marx often pointed out that the means of production, however perfect, merely represent piles of dead things. "Live labor must get hold of these things and resurrect them to life." [56]

Rewards and Penalties

In addition to wage payments for labor performed, kolkhozes provide fringe benefits pertaining to social security and other matters; these vary widely from kolkhoz to kolkhoz. Until 1964 it was up to the individual kolkhoz to establish its own pension system for the aged, disability compensation, aid to orphans, and the like. Actually many kolkhozes did not have any pensions, though they may have helped their aged members in other ways. The resulting insecurity, it was said, made parents "try to steer their children into employment anywhere but in a kolkhoz." [57] Some progress was made in social security in the late 1950s and early 1960s in the more efficient kolkhozes.[58]

But there was a considerable variability in the method and scope of social insurance. This was changed by legislation adopted in July 1964, which had a twofold purpose. First, it separated out the managerial and technical personnel in kolkhozes, such as chairmen, various specialists with college and high-school technical education, chief bookkeepers, tractor drivers, and other kolkhozniks working with mechanical equipment. They were brought in under the coverage of the national security system on October 1, 1964.[59] This has always been the case with sovkhoz labor and the MTS workers, who retained coverage even after their transfer to kolkhozes. All other kolkhozniks were brought in under a newly created system which began operation on January 1, 1965. It includes old-age pensions, disability compensation, pensions to families losing a breadwinner and unable to support themselves, and paid maternity leave for fifty-six days before birth and fifty-six days after birth. To finance the payment of these benefits, a centralized national fund was established to which kolkhozes make a major contribution by deducting a certain proportion, 3–4 percent of their income, and the state makes a smaller annual appropriation. In the RSFSR in 1965 the total cost of kolkhoz social security was estimated at over 400 million rubles, of which kolkhozes had to contribute 276 million rubles.[60]

Male kolkhozniks at the age of sixty-five are entitled to a pension after twenty-five years of work; for women the requirements are twenty years of work by the age of sixty. The amount of the pension is based on average earnings during a consecutive five-year period chosen by the applicant from the fifteen years preceding the date of application. The period credited toward a pension is reduced for failure to participate in kolkhoz work without a valid reason and for non-fulfillment of the required minima of workdays or man-days.[61] The pensions are set at 50 percent of monthly earnings up to 50 rubles and 25 percent of earnings exceeding 50 rubles a month. The minimum is fixed at 12 rubles per month and the maximum at 102 rubles per month, or the same as for sovkhoz workers under the national social-security system.[62] About 6.5 million kolkhozniks, or approximately two and a half times more than previously, were entitled to a pension in 1965, and its average size was 17 rubles.[63] Kolkhozes may establish or continue the existing higher pension rates, but at their own expense. How paltry the standard kolkhoz pensions are is revealed by a comparison with the minimum of 30 rubles under the national system.[64]

The fact that mechanizers, possessing somewhat greater skills, are included in the more advantageous national system must be particularly galling to rank-and-file kolkhozniks, an added token of discrimination engendered by the existence of a separate social-security system. Yet the 1964 law, for all its faults, is still a modest step toward greater security. This is illustrated by a survey of eight kolkhozes in Novgorod province in 1963; there was a total of 79 pensioners in seven kolkhozes and none in one. The average monthly pension was 8 rubles. After the social-security legislation was enacted, the number of pensioners increased to 491, or six times, including 54 pensioners in the kolkhoz that had none in 1963. The average monthly pension increased to 20.6 rubles.[65] Much is made of the fact that kolkhozniks individually do not contribute to the social-security fund but only kolkhozes as institutions, and these contributions are tax-free. But kolkhozniks, in theory at any rate, are legal owners of the kolkhoz, and the payments into the security fund, minus income tax, are presumably deductions from an income that belongs to them.

Unlike the situation in many other countries, the aged are encouraged by the 1964 legislation to continue working after they have reached the pensionable age. Such kolkhozniks are entitled to a full pension in addition to their earnings. If their earnings during a two-year period after the pension was set should exceed those of the period for which it was originally computed, the pension is correspondingly adjusted upward, according to article 17 of the law of July 15, 1964.[66] That the contribution of aged but healthy workers is often spurned by kolkhoz management was sharply criticized by Khrushchev at the January 1961 plenum, where he also insisted on bringing new blood into farm management. After condemning a bureaucratic and formalistic approach to the question of employment of aged workers and illustrating it by a specific case, Khrushchev remarked:

> One must, of course, not condemn people who now receive pensions —they are legally obtained. But look at some pensioners: one can hold a three-year old bull back by the tail (laughter and applause) but he has doomed himself to inactivity. He thinks he is no longer needed by society . . . It must be borne in mind that retiring on a pension is the final stage in a person's life. Aging people who are used to working, to being active, find it terribly hard when they are retired, especially at the beginning. They begin to feel that they have dropped out of the busy whirl of life, although they have worked all their lives and cannot imagine life without work. One must understand human psychology. Only idle folk can reconcile themselves to retiring on a pension before their time. One must, therefore, act sensibly toward people; one must not merely look at the date of birth but at the person himself, find out his capabilities, and give him an opportunity to work right to the end, to be in the ranks of the builders of communism. (Applause.) [67]

The dictum laid down by Khrushchev was that it is necessary "to combine the experienced with the young cadres."

Another fringe benefit is the establishment of clubs in a number of kolkhozes to serve as cultural and recreational centers. The clubs are also heavily used for party propaganda purposes and for farm extension and educational activities. Thus the club at Khutor Petrovskii in Stavropol province of the North Caucasus was the locus of the regional farm-extension courses organized during the winter of 1962. The Communists of the village, it was said, took an active part in all the operations of this club. One of the activities is an illustrated news bulletin put out jointly every ten days by the party organization and the club's board of directors. It is characteristically devoted to a review of the work record of kolkhozniks, praising the better farmers and reprimanding the laggards. A number of groups interested in various arts were organized, where club members are their own actors, lecturers, and leaders of recreational functions.[68] But there are clubs and clubs, ranging from model establishments, which the Soviets are proud to show foreign visitors, to those that the term club does not fit even by Soviet standards. "And just look at our club! It is simply a disgrace," a newspaper reporter was told on a state farm converted from a kolkhoz. He readily agreed, having already inspected a "hut, half ruined, damp, small, which is difficult to call a club" and which his companion, a farm official, refused to enter claiming with a mischievous smile that he carried no life insurance.[69] Not all kolkhoz clubs, to be sure, are like this. But neither are they like those that foreign visitors see in model kolkhozes. A Soviet author reviewing developments on the cultural front in kolkhozes stressed the progress achieved but acknowledged: "Frequently clubs and libraries are located in unsuitable quarters. Their material base is on the level of the initial years of the kolkhoz movement, which does not fit the needs and conditions of the contemporary life of kolkhozniks. Irrational expenditures of money from the indivisible funds occur because of a thoughtless, superficial approach toward the construction of cultural and educational institutions, without taking into account prospective development of kolkhozes." [70]

Judging from the Soviet press, the policy makers realize that cultural centers like clubs greatly help to retain or attract youth. An editorial in *Sel'skaia zhizn'* of March 17, 1965, characteristically entitled "More Care for the Welfare of the Rural Youth," referred to a letter from a kolkhoznik tractor driver who complained that in his kolkhoz a club, after six years, was still unfinished. "There is no place to spend one's leisure; the youth are running away from the kolkhoz." The number of kolkhoz clubs decreased from 32,116 at the end of 1950 to 24,022 at the end of 1964, but this was doubtless because of a change in reporting caused by the conversion of kolkhozes into state farms; yet many villages still lacked such facilities in the early 1960s. A compensating factor was the increased number of rural clubs and cultural centers under the jurisdiction of the Ministry of Culture of the USSR—these rose from 34,795 at the end of 1950 to 66,238 at the end of 1961.[71]

Another type of social service closely linked with farm employment and production is the provision of children's day nurseries and kindergartens. That this facilitates the increased participation of women in kolkhoz production has been fully acknowledged by Soviet sources. Khrushchev stressed at the December 1958 plenum the necessity of "freeing" women in kolkhozes from household duties of "low productivity," and to that end advocated the establishment of bakeries, laundries, and "in the near future" public canteens in addition to hospitals, schools, kindergartens, and nurseries.[72] The number of kindergartens and nurseries in rural areas increased during the 1930s and reached 12,000 in 1937, with 347,700 children enrolled and a staff of 24,100 persons. By 1940 a serious drop occurred: to 9,600, with an enrollment of 266,100 children and a staff of 20,200 persons. The fact that in urban institutions the upward trend continued during this period underscores the neglect and deterioration of this important service during the immediate prewar years. After a spurt during the war, caused by a still heavier burden on women workers, the downward movement continued until the 1950s, when a strong upward trend ensued. From 8,600 institutions with 210,700 children enrolled and staffs of 18,300 in 1950, the numbers increased to 22,700 institutions with 1,049,200 children and staffs of 76,800 in 1964.[73] No distinction is made here between kolkhoz and sovkhoz villages, but it is clear that many of them are lacking such facilities; and there is no doubt considerable variation in equipment and quality of service. This unevenness is characteristic to a certain extent even of the best establishments. Thus a nursery I visited in 1958 impressed me by its orderliness and cleanliness; to enter it, visitors were even required to don white coats. But, there were no screens in the windows and swarms of flies invaded the premises. Although there is wide scope for improvement, the growth of organized care of children of preschool age is probably a progressive step, even if one questions the official motives for it: the drawing of kolkhoz women more completely into the vortex of collective-farm production.

A wage structure differing from that for the rank-and-file kolkhoznik was adopted for managerial personnel and specialists employed in kolkhozes. Until 1940 there were no national standards.[74] They were promulgated by a decree of April 21, 1940, for the Asian regions of the USSR, extended by a series of decrees in 1940–41 to other regions,[75] and then further amended by a decree of April 19, 1948. In accordance with this legislation, the wages of a manager comprised (1) a flat number of workdays per month increasing with the size of the crop area of the kolkhoz, the numbers of communal livestock, and the length of the manager's service; (2) supplementary workdays credited to him as a bonus for the overfulfillment of production goals or, conversely, a reduction in the number of workdays for underfulfillment; (3) a specified cash payment varying with the annual money income of the kolkhoz, 70 percent of which was distributed in monthly installments and the balance at the end of the year. Thus, by using various indicators, the system was designed to stimulate the incentives of managers in boosting output and its marketable portion. The salaries of other officials and specialists, such as deputy chairmen, chief bookkeepers, agronomists, and the like, were set at 70 to 90 percent of the chairman's salary.

This salary scheme prevailed in many kolkhozes but some took advantage of a decree of March 6, 1956, which permitted modification of the standard provisions of the model charter. Some kolkhozes introduced straight money salaries for their officials; others made salary dependent on output, either on the quantities of various commodities produced or on the total production; still others related salaries to the size of total money income in the kolkhoz. Provisions often are included for upward and downward adjustment of salaries, depending upon the fulfillment or nonfulfillment of the production plans and, more rarely, on the reduction of production costs. Improvement and greater uniformity in the chaotic salary scale of agricultural specialists (agronomists, animal-husbandry specialists, veterinaries, and engineers) [76] was one of the important aims of a decree of April 12, 1962, dealing with the position of agricultural specialists.[77] It called for a monthly salary for senior specialists of 80 to 90 percent of the salary of a kolkhoz chairman, with a minimum of 80 rubles per month for specialists with more than two years' experience in their professions.

While concentrating on economic incentives, the noneconomic incentives used in varying degrees by the Soviet regime should not be neglected. Khrushchev put it in a nutshell in his speech at the January 1961 plenum: "You cannot get very far with the moral factor alone. [But] the moral factor reinforced by a good material stimulus is highly significant." [78] So the moral factor, that is, indoctrination, has been a much used weapon in the government's arsenal. Through "socialist competition" propaganda, the government has striven to organize competition for higher production goals among individual kolkhozniks, separate kolkhozes, and even whole agricultural regions. Special occasions, such as the national agricultural exposition held for a number of years in Moscow or a national holiday like the anniversary of the October Revolution, are employed for this purpose. Bulletin boards recording the performance of different workers have also helped to spur competition. Public pledges to Stalin by the collective farmers of a whole region, promising the achievement of certain goals, were widely employed because of their value in whipping up the citizenry. After Stalin's death, such pledges were addressed to the Central Committee of the party, to the Council of Ministers of the USSR, and to Comrade Khrushchev, as the first secretary of the Central Committee and chairman of the Council of Ministers. Often those responsible for organizing socialist competition and the participants adopted a "formal" attitude with little enthusiasm for the task, approaching it as just another campaign imposed from above that must be carried out and put up with. As for the pledges to the government, Khrushchev unmasked their often unrealistic and irresponsible character when he strongly criticized at the January 1961 plenum the failure of the pledgees, usually farm officials, to deliver on their promises.[79] Whatever the faults, there appears to be no weakening of the adherence to these methods for stimulating production.

Many awards of medals and honorary titles have also been made for superior performance by kolkhozniks and farm officials. Such decorations were numerous under Stalin in the late 1940s. In 1947, for example, 1,931 kolkhozniks and other workers in agriculture were awarded the honorary title of Hero of Socialist Labor; 4,348, the Order of Lenin; 12,500, the Order of Labor Red Banner; and more than 40,000, other decorations.[80] Special regulations prescribed in great detail the standard conditions that in 1948 and 1949 had governed the awarding of honors in kolkhozes on the basis of target yields of crops.[81] Prior to January 1, 1948, the awarding of medals as a rule entailed a number of privileges, such as free transportation on street cars, railroads, and steamers, some cash payments, reduced rents, and exemption from income tax. By a decree of September 10, 1947, all privileges except exemption from income tax were abolished.[82] Those who possess decorations usually are among those selected for managerial and administrative positions and for participation in such party and government meetings as special agricultural conferences, party congresses, the Supreme Soviet, and the like. In any event, the conspicuous display of medals by the awardees attest to their honorific value in Soviet society.

So far I have dealt with the proverbial carrot. What of the stick, the negative incentives of coercion? The ugly story of how force was used during the collectivization campaign, how millions of peasants were dispossessed, driven into exile and concentration camps, or put to death, and how millions perished from starvation has already been told. To the same period also belongs the draconian law of August 7, 1932, which prescribed the death penalty or, under extenuating circumstances, ten years' imprisonment as a punishment for theft of cooperative property, no matter how small the amount. The waste and devastation that the Stalinist terror left in its wake is well known. It was confirmed by the appearance in the magazine *Novyi mir* for November 1962 of Solzhenitsyn's "One Day in the Life of Ivan Denisovich," public revealing for the first time in the Soviet Union the misery of the concentration camps. The almost simultaneous publication in the magazine *Neva* for December 1962 of Ivan Stadnuk's "People Are Not Angels" described the horrors of collectivization, a subject theretofore avoided in the Soviet Union or referred to in mild or euphemistic terms. The coercive wartime legislation was abolished, but passport regulations still provide a deterrent to the kolkhozniks' mobility when the authorities are opposed to such a step. Fines and expulsion from the kolkhoz or dismissal from sovkhoz employment, entailing a loss of the private plot and expulsion from the party, are the other weapons in the arsenal of the authorities. But the emphasis after the Stalin regime, and especially in the 1960s, has been not on coercion but on positive economic incentives.

A curious re-emphasis on moral factors, on the farmer's professional pride in his work (what Veblen would have called the instinct of workmanship) and on an appeal to the individual's conscience, originated with a sixty-nine-year-old Ukrainian woman, Nadezhda Zaglada, who was the foreman of a small work unit in a kolkhoz and a "Hero of Socialist Labor." She wrote in the summer of 1962—whether on her own initiative or on orders from above—a piece for a Ukrainian paper, entitled "Take Pride in Being a Farmer," which was widely republished and editorialized in the Soviet press. Its message became a propaganda slogan during the last years of Khrushchev's regime, and Zaglada gained considerable prominence and new honors.[83] She deplored, with pungent wit and many examples, the nonobservance of some sound old rules in many kolkhozes: that a farmer should consider his calling an honor and take pride in his work; that he must obey the dictates of his conscience in standing up to what he knows are wrong orders and faulty farm practices; that kolkhozniks must exercise initiative without waiting for "directives" from above even in small matters, and that they must toil as conscientiously in collective fields as on their private plots. Zaglada did not underemphasize economic stimuli; quite to the contrary. She dwelt on the complementary character of the two sets of incentives and insisted that kolkhozniks should be helped by the kolkhozes to the mutual benefit of both. An illustration she gives is the annual mushroom and berry gathering by kolkhoz women, which is regarded by many kolkhoz chairmen as an evil because it disrupts farm work during the busy season. But Zaglada thought that collecting and selling mushrooms and berries, augmenting the food supply, was a good thing and that the kolkhoz management ought to facilitate the operation by providing means of transportation— but only to those women who worked well in the kolkhoz.

Zaglada also put her finger on the serious weakness in collective farm work stemming from the concern of each worker not to do more than his fellow kolkhoznik, especially when labor was performed on a group basis. If, for instance, a few workers are late, the others do not begin on time; if one sits down to rest, the others follow suit. Thus the work performance is actually brought down to the level of the marginal worker, unless the work tasks are individualized and clear responsibility and corresponding economic stimuli are established. This is why the Kremlin still clings to the system of payment by results and why Zaglada's propaganda, originating from the kolkhoz ranks and not from Moscow, was so welcome to Khrushchev. That this propaganda had much effect on the kolkhozniks, weary of so many years of exhortation, is problematical. When Brezhnev took over, he ignored Zaglada and this line and concentrated on economic incentives in agriculture.

The Problem of Consumer Goods

Before completing the discussion of this problem, it is necessary to focus attention once more on the old issue of the terms of exchange between agriculture and industry: on the prices, quality, and availability of goods manufactured in the countryside which determine the ultimate effectiveness of economic incentives in real or material terms. This raises the pivotal policy question of the heavy versus light industry, of textiles, footwear, and household goods versus atomic bombs and missiles. (There is a subsidiary question of the production by heavy industry of inputs needed by agriculture, such as machinery and fertilizer. But this was dealt with previously and will also be discussed in the next chapter.)

As far as the flow of consumer goods is concerned, not only the peasants but the city population—all consumers, in fact—have been vitally interested in improvement. But the kolkhoz farmer, with his low and fluctuating income, comprised the most neglected part, indeed the forgotten man, of the Soviet consuming public. The problem had been especially acute under Stalin, though successive reductions during 1948–1952 in the high wartime retail prices should not be lost sight of.[84] There is no question that after Stalin the Soviet economy became considerably more consumer-oriented. The output of consumer goods increased between 1952, the last year of the Stalin regime, and 1964, the last year under Khrushchev, 2.6 times according to official statistics. But the output of heavy industry, high to begin with, rose during the same period 3.6 times, and in 1964 it constituted 74.8 percent of the total output (compared to 69 percent in 1952).[85] The traditional "law of the priority of the growth of producer goods" remained at the center of Soviet economic policy until 1964. It is true, however, that Malenkov's pronouncements in 1953 could be interpreted as advocating at least equal if not greater priority for the development of light industry. That there were also some Soviet economists who held such views is indicated by a critical article published early in 1955 by Dimitri Shepilov, then editor of *Pravda*.[86]

The opposition that developed within the party hierarchy to a serious reorientation of industrial policy probably feared that, once the hegemony of the heavy industry was successfully challenged, even to a slight degree, more serious changes might follow. In any event, the challenge failed with the ousting of Malenkov from the premiership early in 1955 and the growing ascendency of Khrushchev. The top priority of heavy industry, its preferential development, was reasserted in official pronouncements and planning. Both the original (1956–1960) plan and its modified seven-year version (1959–1965) called for a continuation of a faster rate of growth for producer goods than for consumer goods. The targets set by the 1956–1960 plan were approximately for a 70 percent increase in the output of heavy industry and 60 percent in the output of consumer goods by the end of the five-year period.[87] Similarly, the targets of the 1959–1965 plan were for an 85–88 percent increase for heavy industry and a 62–65 percent increase for consumer goods.[88] The significance of the faster growth of production for heavy industry is accentuated by the fact that already in 1955 it constituted over 70 percent of total industrial output.[89]

Although state investment in light industry quadrupled between 1952 and 1964, it still constituted only 5.1 percent in the latter year, compared to 4.3 percent in the former.[90] The hegemony of heavy industry continued to block a real upsurge in production of consumer goods of reasonably decent quality and variety. The situation in the rural areas was aggravated by the poor distribution system and even higher retail prices than in the cities, where marketing was also inefficient. The rural population was receiving the short end of the growing but still thin stream of manufactured consumer goods. It is significant that sales of such goods per capita in 1963 amounted to 248 rubles in the cities but 89 rubles in rural areas.[91] The actual basket of goods bought by rural inhabitants was even smaller compared to that of citydwellers, because of higher prices in the countryside. Although additional purchases by peasants in the cities are not included in the above figures, there is little doubt that the farm population received considerably less than a proportionate share of the national output of manufactured goods.

The decentralization of the control of industry through the regional economic councils did not much help with the consumer-goods problem. An editorial in *Izvestiia* of September 2, 1964, after praising the sovnarkhozes of Latvia and Leningrad for their success on the consumer-goods front, continued: "It is a matter of regret that the leaders of some other sovnarkhozes have no genuine interest in the work of enterprises manufacturing consumer goods . . . Only this can explain why in some sovnarkhozes . . . production of consumer goods decreased." In July 1964 Khrushchev lamented the fact that when small local industry producing mainly consumer goods was transferred to the jurisdiction of the sovnarkhozes, with the expectation of technological improvement and increased output, production was actually reduced, with the manufacturing of some items completely discontinued. In Kirov oblast, for instance, the production of more than two hundred items for which, reportedly, there was a demand was eliminated over the course of two years.[92]

Although Khrushchev at first adhered to the fetishism of heavy industry—one only needs to recall his bitter denunciation of Malenkov in 1955—he began hinting, as the decade came to a close, of a switch to a less rigid stand, a stand more consistent with his championing of an improved standard of living and a welfare state. In a talk at the British Trade Fair in Moscow on May 20, 1961, which was not publicized in the USSR, Khrushchev was reported to have said: "Now we consider our heavy industry as built. So we are not going to give it priority. Light industry and heavy industry will develop at the same pace." [93] This sounded like a return to Malenkov's 1953 position. Whether Khrushchev meant precisely what the statement attributed to him implied, or whether, as is thought by some Western observers, he later modified his stand as a result of opposition in the Presidium, the fact remains that it did not become the official position. The twenty-year plan for building a "material-technical base of communism," embodied in the new party platform presented to the Twenty-second Party Congress in October 1961, again postulated a more rapid rate of growth for heavy industry—an increase of output by 1980 of 6.5 to 7 times, as compared with 5 to 5.2 times for light industry. Khrushchev himself affirmed the continuation of the leading role of heavy industry in the Soviet economic scheme. He quoted approvingly Lenin's dictum to the effect that "means of production [capital goods] are manufactured not for their own sake but only because they are increasingly required in the branches of industry manufacturing consumer goods." [94]

This qualification and the emphasis on "progressive" industries, such as the chemical industry, became important to Khrushchev, who apparently was seeking a way out of the straitjacket of the heavy-industry concentration supported by the industrial-military alliance in the Soviet bureaucracy. Thus at the February 1964 plenum Khrushchev, after making proper obeisance to the party's concern with the development of heavy industry, returned to his thesis that the party never considered this sector "an end in itself." [95] A detailed critical analysis of the orthodox Soviet doctrine on the interrelation of different sectors of the economy by A. A. Arzumanian appeared in the pages of *Pravda* shortly after Khrushchev's speech.[96] The prestigious position of the author as the director of the Institute of World Economics and International Relations of the Academy of Sciences, and the publication of his lengthy article in two successive issues of *Pravda*, made this analysis quite authoritative. Arzumanian directed his shafts against the "theoretical anachronisms" regarding the relationship of producer goods and consumer goods, anachronisms "rooted in the erroneous dogmas of Stalin." He was particularly critical of Soviet economists and policy makers for ignoring the role of personal consumption in the economic process and making an end in itself of producer goods, thus creating a serious imbalance between the two sectors of industry. Khrushchev had emphasized the new horizons opened for consumer goods by the progress of the chemical industry (synthetics and plastics) into which capital investment was heavily channeled, and Arzumanian considered this an important phase of a general "scientific-technological" revolution. It would make possible, as the American experience showed, the use of smaller amounts of capital (producer goods) and raw materials in the manufacturing processes, according to Arzumanian. It thus permits a greater concentration on the production of consumer goods.

This crucial theme had not been so boldly treated since the great economic debates of the 1920s. But, as had often happened in the past, it could have been just another evanescent theory, quickly disappearing without a trace. It is significant that Khrushchev returned to the theme several months later, shortly before his dismissal, at a closed meeting of the leadership called to discuss the prospective post-1965 plan. It is even more noteworthy that publicity was given to his apparently carefully edited remarks. After reiterating that the principal objective of the new plan must be "the further improvement of the standard of living of the population," Khrushchev observed: "If during the first Five-Year Plan periods and the postwar years we put the main emphasis on the development of the heavy industry . . . now when we have a powerful industry, when the defense of the country is properly secured, the party sets forth the objective of a more rapid development of the branches of industry producing consumer goods . . . At the present stage of communist construction, our objective is a further development of production of producer goods needed for increased output of consumer goods." [97]

He cautioned against overlooking the needs of capital accumulation and defense but repeated that the new plan must focus on the "accelerated production of consumer goods and increased welfare of the population." These were generalities, lacking the quantification that would give a clue to their implementation. But in conjunction with previous statements, it sounded as if Khrushchev really meant business; there was all the ring of a significant shift in industrial priorities. Whether a new deal for the Soviet consumer would have materialized if Khrushchev's leadership had continued, no one can tell. The above pronouncement was his last important published utterance, which led to speculation that his downfall was hastened by irritation among the top leaders over a supposed leak of views voiced at a presumably secret meeting.

An important aspect of the consumer-goods problem which preoccupied Khrushchev during the last year of his rule was that of inferior quality and lack of variety. These have consistently plagued the Soviet consumer and none more than the rural inhabitant.* The Soviet press and numerous official statements have long harped on this deficiency. Khrushchev specifically stressed the urgent need of paying attention to the quality of all goods, producer and consumer alike, in formulating the post-1965 plan. At the fateful September 1964 meeting he showed by examples that raising the quality of goods, leading to their greater longevity, is equivalent to increasing quantity.[98] In some instances, deterioration of the quality of manufactured goods results from the continuing pressure by planners for a reduction in production costs. This makes a cheap good of inferior quality (for example, cloth with a decreased percentage of wool) more advantageous to produce, meeting in this manner the reduced cost targets. In other, more numerous cases, such targets act as a powerful brake on the improvement of quality even when this requires only an insignificant increase of expenditures, no matter how advantageous and economical it may be for the consumer and for the whole economy. It seems curious that such an individualistic, one may say penny-wise pound-foolish, attitude could develop in an integrated collectivist economy. The question of quality will doubtless become more pressing as scarcities are reduced and the Soviet consumer becomes more discriminating. As Khrushchev described it: [99]

> We have already passed the time when any kind of a good would be sent to the store [by the factory] and the people would purchase it without being discriminative because there was not enough to choose from, much less than now. The customers bought anything that could be worn without looking too closely into quality, style, and color. Strictly speaking, formerly we did not have trade but actually rationed distribution without ration cards . . . The customer had no other

* Quality and variety of goods and services has never been a major problem in Western economies. Improvements over time, complementary to the increase in output, are taken for granted. The issue is not often brought out by economists, but Gottfried Haberler, in his presidential address to the American Economic Association in December 1963, had this to say: "The liberation of the economies of the industrial countries in Europe and elsewhere from the shackles of direct control released great energies which led to the spectacular rise in output and consumer satisfaction. I add 'consumer satisfaction' because improvements in quality and a great increase in the variety of products (including services such as increased opportunity to travel) surely are factors adding greatly to economic welfare while finding inadequate expression in output figures." "Integration and Growth of the World Economy in Historical Perspective," *American Economic Review*, 54:13–14 (March 1964).

choice. Suppose he needed a pair of pants; if the store did not have the size needed, he took whatever was available saying, all right, I will fix them up at home. Now the situation has changed. Our industry is manufacturing more consumer goods and, with the growth of the material and cultural levels of the population, the people become more discerning with regard to the goods they are being offered; they begin to examine them and select the best. And this is not a whim, not fault finding, but a quite normal phenomenon. The workers want to purchase footwear and clothing which are in style, in pretty colors, and conform to the season and fashion. This is a good thing.*

Another ingredient of this problem in the Soviet Union is inefficient marketing and inadequate service industries, particularly in the countryside. The consumer may not be able to obtain the goods he needs in state or cooperative stores (the country stores are usually of the latter type) not only because of insufficient output but also because of faulty

* A few days after Khrushchev's ouster, another condemnation of the methods of planning, producing, and distributing consumer goods appeared in an article in *Pravda* of October 18, 1964, entitled, "Unmarketable Goods: Where Do They Come From?" "While the demand for goods has changed, the planning of their manufacture has remained essentially as it was many years ago when goods were scarce. What does this lead to in practice? Let us take the textile industry. The output of fabrics is planned both in meters and in terms of money—on the basis of average prices and total amounts. As a result, quite frequently the leaders of combines and factories strive to manufacture more profitable and expensive fabrics to overfulfill the plan for the total amount, for profits, and for other indicators, and they care little whether the customer needs these fabrics or not. The same thing applies to the question of variety of products. The USSR Gosplan plans the output of fabrics 'in general.' But woolens alone comprise hundreds of articles. A specific type of raw material is required for each of them— hence each primary production cost is different. This circumstance is not being considered. The enterprises can arbitrarily select 'advantageous' or 'disadvantageous' products. This is why more than 70 percent out of fourteen types of half-woolen, even dyed fabrics for suits are represented by four articles and more than 80 percent out of ten types of teaseled coarse-cloth fabrics by three articles. In this way the plan for the total quantity is overfulfilled despite the fact that there is only a limited demand for expensive cloths. As a result of this, the stocks of woolens in factories and in the trade channels have more than trebled in the past five years. Shortcomings in planning constitute one of the main causes of the excessively slow improvement in the quality and assortment and of the piling up of surplus stocks of commodities in the warehouses and shops. The struggle for product quality, for an extensive variety of products and for the honor of the factory trademark, has not yet become an indisputable law in many plants. Substandard goods of outdated shapes and models continue to be manufactured. Last year the inspectorates for commodity quality rejected one fifth of the examined sewed products which had already left the enterprises, and one tenth of the footwear was rejected along with 17 percent of the knitted goods examined. About the same picture emerges from the checks that the inspectorates are now conducting."

distribution. Seasonal demand, the need for summer or winter clothing, for instance, or regional peculiarities of demand are disregarded, with a resulting overstocking of unsaleable goods and shortages of needed goods. Although much has been written about this in Soviet publications, little has been done to remedy the situation. Service industries were also repeatedly criticized for serious shortcomings.

Khrushchev gave the impression during his last years in office of coming to grips with the consumer-goods issue, though he had a long distance to travel toward a solution. The problem was inherited by his successors. From the outset the new leadership, especially Kosygin, manifested in their speeches a keen awareness of its importance. It is significantly reflected in the industrial reform inaugurated at the September 1965 plenum after considerable public discussion and debate among economists, led by Evsei Liberman. But the acid test of the intentions of the new administration was the crystallization of its program in the quantitative goals of the 1966–1970 plan, the preparation of which was started under Khrushchev but completed by his successors. It showed the continued predominance of heavy industry, even though its rate of growth was to be slowed down considerably: its output increased almost 60 percent during the period 1960–1965, but was planned at a 49–52 percent rise for 1966–1970. Conversely, the growth of light industry was to be

Table 58. Soviet production of selected consumer goods

Item	Unit	1960	1965	1970
Automobile	Thousands	138.8	201.2	700–800
Paper	Million tons	2.4	3.23	5.0–5.3
Cloth	Billion sq. meters	6,468	7,500	9,500–9,800
Shoes	Million pairs	419.3	486	610–630
Sugar (beet)	Million tons	6.4	8.9	9.8–10
Radios	Thousands	4,165	5,200	7,500–8,000
Television sets	Thousands	1,726	3,700	7,500–7,700
Refrigerators	Thousands	529.5	1,700	5,300–5,600
Motorcycles	Thousands	522.7	721	1,000–1,100
Furniture	Million rubles	1,116	1,800	2,600–2,800
Miscellaneous household goods	Billion rubles	—	9.0	15.5–16.5

Sources. For 1960, from *Promyshlennost' SSSR, 1964*, pp. 41–43, 411; for 1965 and 1970 from *Pravda*, February 20, 1966.

accelerated from a 35 percent increase in output in 1960–1965 to 42–46 percent in 1966–1970.[100] Data for some selected commodities are given in Table 58. If the plan is fulfilled, the gap in the pace of growth of the two sectors would considerably diminish. Yet the 1970 target for light industry is about 30 percent below that set by Khrushchev at the Twenty-second Party Congress in October 1961, while his 1970 goal for heavy industry was less than 10 percent below. Although the present 1970 target for light industry represents an important advance, it is still far from a breakthrough on the consumer-good front. And without a decisive breakthrough it will hardly be possible to achieve a solid industrial underpinning for a significant program of real economic incentives. This is essential to an increase in agricultural production. Such an increase would reciprocally exert a favorable impact on the consumer-goods industry by providing it with abundant and low-cost raw materials that would benefit the whole economy.

18

Mechanization and Electrification

Adding to the traditional factors of production—land and labor (labor requiring adequate economic incentives for an effective contribution)—mechanical power and machinery have become increasingly important in farm operations. They account for the major portion of the growing capital investment in modern agriculture. In the Soviet Union the process of agricultural mechanization largely paralleled that of collectivization but also antedated it. Although mechanization was a major Soviet objective, the Kremlin did not wait for its progress before collectivizing agriculture. The reader may be reminded of Stalin's dictum at the beginning of mass collectivization that the combination of simple implements and land in a kolkhoz ipso facto makes farming more efficient than in small individual units. Actually agricultural mechanization in Russia preceded not only collectivization, but even the Revolution—at any rate, as far as horse-drawn machinery was concerned. Although much is made by Soviet propaganda of the primitive farm equipment of prerevolutionary Russian agriculture, we know that the pace of technical progress was accelerated, especially during the decade preceding World War I. Not only were farm implements imported but factories were established in Russia itself which are still producing farm machinery—in Liubertsy near Moscow, Odessa, Elizavetgrad (now Kirovograd), and Rostov (the present Red Aksai). It is hardly conjectural to say that this technological progress would have continued in Russian agriculture after World War I, no matter what the regime, though the tempo and the cost might have been very different.

The Soviet government has always been alive to the importance of tractors both for increasing agricultural production, which was the immediate objective, and for the ultimate collectivization of agriculture. In 1923 a program was adopted for the manufacture of 3,400 tractors annually in a number of machinery building plants but lack of specialized equipment and high costs led to the abandonment of this operation by all but two of the plants: Red Putilovets (later named Kirov) in Leningrad, and the Kharkov Locomotive Works.[1] The chief source of tractors in the 1920s was not the domestic industry but imports from the United States. On October 1, 1928, of the 31,858 tractors on farms, 3,718 were of domestic manufacture and 28,140 were imported.[2] Of the 24,504 tractors on farms in 1927, kolkhozes and their associations owned 9,122, state farms owned 4,651, farm cooperatives owned 4,422, and the remaining 6,309 or 25.7 percent belonged to individual peasant farmers.[3] However, on October 3, 1926, the government prohibited further sale of tractors to individuals and in December 1928 barred their sale even to farm cooperatives; only kolkhozes and state farms could obtain tractors.[4]

As part of the industrialization program under the five-year plans, a new tractor industry was created with American technical assistance. Tractor plants were constructed in Stalingrad (now Volgograd), Kharkov, and Cheliabinsk. In 1932 importation of tractors was stopped even though increased domestic production was far from adequate to satisfy the expanded need for draft power. The capacity for manufacturing other farm implements was greatly expanded with the remodeling of the old and construction of new factories in Rostov, Gomel, Tashkent, and Dnepropetrovsk.

The creation of such a base for agricultural mechanization became the more necessary as the urgency of speeding up the pace increased because of the severe shortage of draft power caused by the collectivization crisis. It will be recalled that the number of horses decreased by more than one half in the early 1930s while the sown area, albeit with very low yields, increased by nearly 20 percent. Unlike the United States, therefore, the Soviets did not so much displace the horse with the tractor for economic reasons, but rather replaced it, trying frantically to bridge a critical gap in the supply of draft power. At the same time they began to use the tractor to control better the new collective farms which became greatly dependent upon it. Thus mechanization in Soviet hands was even more than a powerful lever for collectivization; it became a veritable lifeline to the regime, faced with a severe agrarian crisis (of its own making, to be sure) at the very time when it was bending every effort toward a speedy socialist industrialization.

Naturally, any method which by pooling tractors and other farm implements maximized their use was highly welcome. This became one function of the large state farms, but a more important part was played by a new unit, the machine-tractor stations, or MTS. State farms, following a spurt in the early 1930s when large grain and livestock sovkhozes were being organized, played a secondary role until the mid-1950s in the Soviet agricultural scheme. As far as the dominant sector of collective agriculture is concerned, the story of mechanization until the late 1950s is the story of the MTS, which together with the kolkhoz and the sovkhoz formed, during the course of three decades, the trinity of Soviet socialized agriculture.

The MTS in its origin was itself an offshoot of a sovkhoz. Its genesis, unlike that of the kolkhoz and sovkhoz, can be directly traced to the vision and organizational ability of one person, A. M. Markevich. As a manager of the Shevchenko state farm (named after the famous Ukrainian poet) near Odessa, Markevich, in 1927, undertook an experiment by assigning ten tractors with the necessary implements and operators to work, on a contractual basis, the land belonging to new settlers in neighboring villages who were short of draft power. One requirement of the contract was the voluntary pooling of labor and combining of the small, scattered holdings into large fields suitable for tractor operations. Here was a prototype of what became known as MTS. Note that collectivization, in the rather simple form of the TOZ and voluntary in nature, accompanied MTS from the start. The Markevich experiment proved successful,* and the number of tractors and acres involved was greatly increased during the following two years. Markevich called the new unit the inter-village machine-tractor station. He was the real pioneer both as an organizer and as a theoretician and advocate of the MTS idea in a little book which must be considered a classic.[5] Despite these services to the Soviet cause, Markevich perished in the early 1930s in the Stalin purge and his name was for a long time blacked out in Soviet literature. But MTS became the pillar of the collective farm system under Stalin whose attention it quickly attracted. He praised the Markevich experiment as early as the Fifteenth Party Congress in 1927.[6]

* A laudatory letter in *Izvestiia* of November 21, 1927, by peasants who benefited from the experiment is often quoted by Soviet sources. The signators declared that after witnessing the work of the tractors, they did not want to go back to their small individual plots and decided to socialize their farming on the basis of tractor power.

New MTS and, to a greater extent, smaller units called tractor columns or detachments, sprang up in 1928 organized by state farms, associations of kolkhozes, and agricultural cooperatives. On June 5, 1929, the announcement of a government program for the organization of 100 new MTS gave a further impetus and prestige to this institution.[7] At the same time a central agency—*Traktorotsentr*—was created in the form of a joint stock company or corporation to direct this work. The peasants who used the MTS services were supposed to contribute 25 percent of the cost of the new units by purchasing stock in the corporation. By 1930 there were 150 state-owned MTS and 479 cooperative MTS and tractor detachments.[8] By a decree of September 10, 1930, all cooperative MTS and tractor detachments were transferred to the Traktorotsentr. By the end of 1932 this agency was abolished and MTS came under the jurisdiction of the People's Commissariat of Agriculture of the USSR. The joint stock principle and contributions by the peasants were dropped and the MTS began to be financed entirely by the state, which was in turn the recipient of the revenue earned by these units for services performed. Thus complete state ownership and control of mechanization in kolkhozes was achieved.

Until the liquidation of the MTS, kolkhozes were not allowed to own tractors, combines, and other farm machinery, although during the war and early postwar years this rule, like many others, was not strictly adhered to. Some tractors which were evacuated from the war zone or "liberated" from the occupied regions apparently found their way into individual kolkhozes. However, by an edict of March 6, 1948, it was prohibited to sell or transfer tractors and tractor implements to the kolkhozes. Those that had tractors were obliged to sell them to MTS.[9]

Organizational Structure and Operations of MTS

The MTS had no land area of their own to farm and were wholly devoted to servicing kolkhozes, for a fee, with tractors and other machinery. Yet, important as the pooling principle was, the MTS was not just a farm-machinery, custom-work agency; it became a powerful arm of Soviet management and politico-economic control of collective agriculture as well as a highly effective instrument for state acquisition of large quantities of farm products. An MTS possessed a certain number of tractors and other machinery and a central headquarters with repair shops and other facilities. For operational purposes the MTS was usually divided into several tractor brigades, each consisting of three to five or more tractors with the necessary implements and personnel, headed by a brigadier or foreman. A tractor brigade was assigned work in one or several adjoining kolkhozes where it was supposed to cooperate with the kolkhoz field brigade. It had a staff of permanent and seasonal workers who operated and maintained the machinery, called mechanizers. They were recruited mostly from among the kolkhozniks and trained in special schools. The kolkhozes also provided all other labor necessary to assist with the field work of the tractors and combines, such as workers delivering fuel and water. The MTS employed various technicians: agronomists, engineers, bookkeepers, and other specialists. It was headed by a director or manager appointed by the Minister of Agriculture of the USSR, who alone had the legal power to dismiss him, though this apparently did not preclude frequent dismissals by lesser authorities.

The political aspect of the MTS is exemplified by the inclusion on the staff of a deputy director for political affairs whose functions were presumably similar to those of a political commissar in the Soviet armed forces. During the emergency periods of World War II and mass collectivization there were special political sections (politotdels) attached to MTS. In 1957, the last year before their liquidation was decreed, an MTS on the average had 78 tractors, employed over 330 workers (annual average), and serviced 10 kolkhozes with a sown area of 41,000 acres; but 8 percent of all MTS serviced 2–3 kolkhozes each, and 4.7 percent serviced 21–30 kolkhozes. At the two extremes, 1.1 percent serviced only one kolkhoz and 1.1 percent, 31 and more kolkhozes.[10] The number of MTS were increasing through 1954 but declined during the next three years, when they were affected by the numerous mergers of kolkhozes with sovkhozes. (See Table 59.)

The workday system for determining wages, discussed in the previous chapter, was applied to the MTS. While the salaries of administrative and technical personnel were paid by the state, wages of tractor brigade workers were paid partly by the state and partly by kolkhozes. The kolkhozes were responsible for distributing a guaranteed minimum of bread grain and cash per workday to tractor drivers and several other categories of workers in tractor brigades, and bonuses in kind to combine operators. Because of the difficulties experienced by kolkhozes during the Stalin era, the Malenkov-Khrushchev administration in 1953 assumed the responsibility for paying a higher guaranteed cash wage in addition to any cash distribution made by kolkhozes, which were usually small. In October 1956, with an improvement in the financial position of kolkhozes, the government began merely to supplement kolkhoz cash payments if they were below the guaranteed amount.[11] The grain minimum paid by the kolkhozes was first set at 3 kilograms (6.6 pounds) per workday. Beginning in 1947, however, this amount was distributed only if the goal for the yield was achieved on the plots worked by tractor brigades and the work

Table 59. Number of machine-tractor stations, principal equipment, and work done, selected years

	1932	1938	1940	1950	1954	1957
Total number of MTS	2,446	6,358	7,069	8,414	8,994	7,903
Total tractors (thousands)	74.8	394.0	435.0	482.0	649.0	601.0
Total tractor power (1,000 horsepower)	1,077.0	7,437.0	8,358.0	11,080.0	16,150.0	15,700.0
Total combines, grain (thousands)	2.2	127.2	153.0	173.0	265.0 [a]	321.0
Total trucks (thousands)	6.0	74.6	40.0	57.0	89.0	104.0 [b]
Area converted to plowing by tractors						
(million hectares)	20.5 [c]	206.2 [c]	227.3	318.2	563.0	570.7
(million acres)	50.7	509.5	561.7	786.3	1,391.2	1,410.2
Area harvested by combines						
(million hectares)	.08	39.9	41.7	50.0	89.0	79.3
(million acres)	.20	98.6	103.0	123.6	219.9	196.0
Average annual number of workers						
(thousands)	144.0	—	537.0	705.0	3,007.0 [d]	2,625.0

[a] Figure for 1953.
[b] Figure for 1956.
[c] Exclusive of threshing.
[d] During the last quarter of 1953 several categories of kolkhozniks who participated in the work of the tractor brigades were transferred to the permanent staffs of MTS; this raises the figure for 1954.

Sources. I. S. Malyshev, ed., *MTS vo vtoroi piatiletke* (Machine-Tractor Stations during the Second Five Year Plan; Moscow, 1939), p. 11; *Narodnoe khoziaistvo SSSR, 1956*, pp. 150–151; *Sel'skoe khoziaistvo SSSR, 1960*, p. 74.

of preparation for the next harvest was completed on time; otherwise the minimum was 2 kilograms (4.4 pounds) per workday.

Because of the usually high goals, the actual average grain minimum was nearer 2 than 3 kilograms. When this is compared with 2.3 kilograms per workday reported as distributed during the critical year 1932, and 2.4 and 4.0 kilograms reported for 1935 and 1937 respectively,[12] it seems really minimal. But remember that some kolkhozniks were receiving much less or nothing, especially under Stalin, and that the larger number of workdays earned by mechanizers was an important compensating factor. (A tractor driver earned from four to seven workdays, depending upon the kind of tractor operated, for performing the daily task.) [13] The guaranteed grain and cash wage, when properly distributed, provided at least a modicum of economic security for mechanizers, and in a number of cases during the post-Stalin period, considerably more. Also the kolkhozes were supposed to make up the difference between the guaranteed minimum and the amounts of cash and grain that they distributed per workday to their members generally. Products other than grain were distributed to tractor brigade workers in the same way as to other kolkhozniks.

In the autumn of 1953 a change was introduced by the Malenkov-Khrushchev administration in the method of collecting the bread grain designated for payment to mechanizers, apparently in order to make the supply more certain. Instead of delivering this grain to the MTS which then would distribute it to the workers, the kolkhoz was to deliver it to the state procurement agency together with the grain in payment for the work performed by the MTS. Procurement authorities provided the MTS with the grain needed for distribution among the mechanizers from their general stocks. Thus the MTS were freed from the vicissitudes of grain collection. The length of employment of tractor drivers and some other tractor brigade workers was increased in 1953 by making them permanent instead of seasonal employees and using them in the winter for such work as repairing tractors and farm machinery.

The guaranteed minimum grain-cash wage for mechanizers, on top of a greater number of workdays earned, made for a new stratification of workers based on technological skill which divided the village into a kind of a kolkhoz aristocracy and rank-and-file kolkhozniks. Following the liquidation of the MTS in 1958, the guaranteed minimum was abandoned. An interesting rural travelogue pointed out the adverse effect of the abolition of the guaranteed minimum on the "kolkhoz workers aristocracy," attributing to it the shortage of mechanizers. The travelogue quotes a party official as saying that the "work [of mechanizers] is not the easiest and they take it up only because of the high guaranteed wage.

They do not just simply become 'aristocratic workers.' "[14] The general guaranteed wage introduced in kolkhozes in 1966 should help to remedy the situation.

Frequent turnover of personnel in the MTS was a problem that constantly bedeviled the administration. Arrears in payment of wages, poor living conditions, and indiscriminate fining for excessive expenditure of fuel were frequently mentioned by Soviet sources as causes of dissatisfaction even before the abolition of the guaranteed wage offered another serious grievance. Often trained tractor drivers and combine operators were found working at other trades despite shortages of such personnel in MTS. Particularly the eastern regions—Siberia and Kazakhstan—experienced a chronic shortage of mechanizers and high turnover before and certainly after the new lands expansion campaign in the 1950s. Each year it was necessary to transfer personnel and machinery to these late harvest regions from sections where harvest was completed earlier.

A situation that contributed to the unrest among mechanizers, which was acknowledged by Soviet spokesmen themselves as harmful, was the encouragement and opportunity given by authorities to some individual tractor and combine operators to make high performance records, while little attention was paid to other workers. The result was that these so-called Stakhanovites greatly exceeded the performance of their fellow workers and consequently obtained much larger earnings. At the same time, the average productivity per worker remained low. As one writer put it: [15]

What is, then, the explanation of the abnormal situation in which the average daily amount of work per combine of many MTS and state farms is three to four times lower than that of the Stakhanovites working in the same units? One of the basic reasons for this is that the managers of the MTS did not observe the most important directive of the Communist Party and the government—that the strength of the Stakhanovite movement lies in its mass character. Often the managers, in striving to encourage high records of performance for individual workers, poorly direct the rank and file of combine operators, do not create the necessary organizational and technical conditions for efficient work with combines, do not provide the necessary assistance for the adoption of the Stakhanovite methods of increased productivity of labor, even though large numbers of combine operators are anxious to work in the Stakhanovite manner.

World War II with its huge army mobilization brought in its wake a deterioration in the skilled labor supply of the MTS, while the Red Army

451

found here a deposit of technical skill which it mined to advantage. This skilled manpower shortage in the MTS was not remedied during the early postwar years under Stalin when labor was mostly channeled into industry. Khrushchev admitted in his September 1953 report that "a large number of the most literate and cultured kolkhozniks have transferred to industry." The government, therefore, acted in 1953 to bring skilled workers as well as technicians to MTS and the farms. Various inducements were offered to those transferring to the MTS, including non-interest-bearing ten-year loans for building individual houses. This move acquired the status of an official mass campaign and a certain amount of party pressure was exercised especially on agronomists and other technicians engaged in office work in the cities. That the people transferred were often the expendable ones rather than those capable of rendering real assistance in farming was hinted by Khrushchev.[16] Conversely, there were a number of reports in the Soviet press that the transferred specialists were not always treated fairly at the local level and their training and skill was not adequately utilized. Shortages of mechanizers during the peak work periods continued to plague collective agriculture during the decade following the first Khrushchev reforms of 1953.

The Soviet government was faced with the problem of training on a mass scale peasants accustomed to traditional agriculture—with its reliance on animal, mostly horse, power—to operate the tractors and combines. Various kinds of schools and courses were established for these purposes, but the quality of training was often criticized. An editorial in the organ of the Soviet Department of Agriculture stated in 1939 that "it is not a secret that in many schools and courses the training of personnel is organized in an entirely unsatisfactory manner." [17] Fourteen years later, in his September 1953 report, Khrushchev described the pattern of training machinery operators as follows: "A fellow attends the course for two or three months, he is led around the machine a few times and then given a diploma—and presto, we have a tractor driver. In the spring this tractor driver somehow drives out into the field; if the tractor should stop, he will sit near it and wait until a mechanic arrives because he does not know what to do. That is why the work performance of tractors is low, their breakdowns frequent, and the quality of work poor."

To improve the training of machinery operators it was decided in September 1953 to establish a new type of agricultural machinery school similar to the trade schools set up for youth recruited for industry and transportation. The government soon had to concern itself with a serious deficiency in many of these schools: the lack of farms for practical training.[18] As part of the general educational reform of 1958 these schools were to be reorganized into "rural vocational-technical schools" with one- or two-year courses, admitting graduates of the eight-year rural schools.

Still another experiment was launched in 1962–63: the organization of on-the-job training during the fall-winter season for all rural adults, including nonfarm people, who could be drawn upon to help locally during the peak season, thus obviating the expense of bringing in outsiders.[19] In the virgin lands regions where the shortage of machinery operators was especially acute, 57,000 were brought in from other regions during the 1962 harvest season. It was also reported that despite the advance of mechanization 75 percent of all workers in sovkhozes and 85 percent in kolkhozes lacked any training or skill as operators.[20] Even though many of these workers, especially in kolkhozes, were women who only helped temporarily, the situation was clearly abnormal and called for intensification of various forms of training for the cadres of operators. Actually the number of operators trained declined from an annual average of 650,000 during 1951–55 to 597,000 during 1956–60, but was impressively stepped up to 810,000 during 1961–64.[21] The problem of keeping the operators on the farms continued to confound the government.[22] It has been aggravated by the fact that, as all Western observers agree, even in mechanized farm operations three or four workers are used in the Soviet Union where one worker would do the job in the West.

Each MTS was supposed to work out an annual "production-financial" plan specifying by quarters the various operations to be undertaken, their cost and timing. These MTS plans had to be coordinated with the centrally determined government directives and approved by the provincial agricultural authorities.[23] In March 1955, three years before the decision to liquidate MTS, a law was enacted by the government to relax and decentralize agricultural planning by giving the MTS and kolkhoz management greater freedom of action with respect to the type of work to be performed. But it remained a dead letter. The business relationship between an MTS and a kolkhoz was supposed to be on a contractual basis; conclusion of an annual agreement was required which specified in detail the kind and amount of work to be performed by an MTS and the time of its completion. Likewise the contribution that the kolkhoz was to make, such as the amount of labor to be assigned to help the MTS in its field work, was stated in the agreement. These agreements, which followed a standard form prescribed by the government, were in practice a mere formality, and their conclusion was often much delayed or entirely dispensed with.[24] Complaints of violations were frequently echoed in the Soviet press, especially regarding the timing of field work. This was crucial in view of the short Russian growing season and the adverse effect of delayed farm operations on crop yields.

Good and timely, or poor and delayed cultivation or harvesting of a kolkhoz field by an MTS often spelled the difference between good and poor crop yields, between success or failure of the kolkhoz to meet its production and income goals. Improvement of the low Russian yields was constantly harped upon by the government as a key objective of the MTS. Nevertheless, it was admitted by Soviet leadership that "our machine-tractor stations are little interested in improvement of yields, in good soil management, in timely seeding and harvesting." An important reason for this was the method used in evaluating the performance of the MTS, involving conversion of various operations by means of fixed coefficients into their equivalent in terms of plowing. This, coupled with the system of incentives for the MTS workers, led to the "chase after hectares," striving to do the type of work which would show the greatest number of hectares credited, irrespective of the quality, timeliness, or even need for the operation. "What good do the state and kolkhozes derive from such a fulfillment of their plan by MTS if it results in low yields?" asked Andreev. "The objective, after all, is not just to dig the soil a little but to create conditions for growing a good crop and to harvest it at the proper time with combines." [25] The practice of excessive plowing of the soil—which did not do any good and wasted labor and fuel, or actually caused harm—was often indulged in because it was profitable to the MTS. An amusing story was told in a Soviet literary magazine about diplomatic negotiations between a representative of an MTS and a kolkhoz manager in which the former tried to convince the latter of the need to replow a field.[26] In the end the kolkhoz manager reluctantly agreed to a compromise: the superfluous replowing of the field in exchange for a concession by the MTS.

The Soviet authorities recognized these deficiencies and were continuously groping for remedies. For instance, to penalize MTS for tardiness, the rate of payment for delayed work was reduced in 1947. But these problems apparently defied solution. A Soviet authority wrote at the end of 1957, almost on the eve of the liquidation of MTS: "In a number of MTS, in the race for fulfillment of the plan for tractor work, reckoned in plowing equivalent, the agreements with kolkhozes are violated, the work is frequently greatly delayed and of inferior quality, and sometimes tractor work is done which is unnecessary for increasing crop yields." [27]

Throughout the life span of MTS and continuing after their demise, reports of frequent breakdowns and stoppages of tractors and combines, inadequate supplies of spare parts, and lost time during the peak of the season appeared with monotonous regularity. The high cost of operation was another constant source of concern. Among the factors contributing to high costs, considerable prominence was given to wasteful use of fuel by tractors. This was caused by unsatisfactory adjustment of machines, wasted motion of tractors, lack of proper fueling equipment, and inadequate storage and transportation facilities. The importance attached to this problem stemmed from the fact that fuel was the largest element in the operating cost of tractor work. In 1937, for instance, together with lubricants, it accounted for 55.9 percent of the total expenditures of MTS as against 7.3 percent for wages, 9.9 percent for repair and overhauling of tractors and combines, 2.3 percent for repair of other machinery, and 15.3 percent for administrative and other expenses.[28] The figure for labor costs cited is low in that it does not include the contribution of kolkhozes to wages of tractor drivers and various helpers. The fact that a much larger number of workers are used in operation of farm machinery in the Soviet Union than in the West boosts these costs.

The degree of mechanization of farm work in the kolkhozes by MTS varied among different regions and different operations (see Table 60). Nearly complete mechanization was achieved by 1953 in plowing for all crops and in planting cotton and sugar beets. By 1957, the last year before the liquidation of MTS, sowing of grains, except corn, was also almost completely mechanized. But many other operations, such as harvesting of sugar beets and corn, planting and harvesting of potatoes, and scutching of flax fiber were much less mechanized. Also no progress was made after 1953 in mechanization of hay mowing. A shortage or absence of

Table 60. Percentage of mechanization of basic farm operations in kolkhozes, specified years

	1935	1940	1950	1953	1957
	Percent of total work				
Summer fallow plowing	57	83	92	97	98
Fall plowing	48	71	93	98	99
Planting					
Grains	20	56	73	91	96
Cotton	23	81	92	97	98
Sugar beets	43	93	92	95	97
Potatoes	0.3	4	5	25	49
Harvesting					
Total by tractor power	22	46	55	80	88
By combines only	7	43	51	78	87
Sugar beets by combines	—	—	2	6	57
Ensilaging	—	5	14	48	72

Source: *Narodnoe khoziaistvo, 1958,* p. 509.

necessary implements and faulty practices contributed to the imbalance in mechanization; 77 percent of all labor used in combine harvesting of grain was spent in gathering up of straw by manual labor. Similarly, hand loading and cleaning of sugar beets accounted for 85 percent of all labor used for combine harvesting of this crop, according to a Soviet study published in 1956.[29]

Among the field operations performed by the MTS, grain harvesting by combines has held a special place in the regime's interest. Stalin even devoted one of his infrequent speeches to the subject at the conference of the best combine operators held in Moscow in December 1935. Combine operators, even more than tractor drivers, represented the favored farm workers as far as earnings and status were concerned. They were made permanent employees of the MTS much before the tractor drivers. The attention focused on the combine is explained, in the first place, by the fact that delayed, inefficient harvesting with resulting large crop losses constituted one of the weakest spots in Soviet collective agriculture. Complete mechanization of the harvest was looked upon as the way out of such difficulties, though the results have often been disappointing because of the inefficient operation of combines. In the second place, grain can be shipped directly from the combine to the government procuring center. This may not only result in economies but also make for a more certain and promptly delivered supply. The combine in the USSR has had a persistent enemy in the abundant growth of weeds, which add much trash to the grain and on occasion clog the combines. I witnessed such an incident during one of my trips to the farm areas of the Soviet Union. Weeds are evidence of poor cultural practices: lack of proper crop rotation, particularly of summer fallow in the dryer regions, and lack of chemical weed-killers. Increased attention was paid to the weed problem in the mid-sixties.

When we move from the field to the farmstead, mechanization becomes still less advanced, particularly in the areas of farm transportation and animal husbandry. With respect to the first, it was surprising to find, on visiting Soviet collective and state farms in 1962 and 1963, how widely horses were used for transportation, though their number continuously declined from 15.3 million in 1954 to 7.9 million in 1965.* Yet the num-

---

* On the other hand, there was justified chiding in Soviet literature about the inadequate use of horses in farm operations and a tendency to rely on tractors in the northern regions with their small fields, and in mountainous regions where greater use of horse draft power would have been more economical. See "The Work of Horses in Spring Sowing," *Konnievodstvo,* 4: 32 (April 1956); For Better Utilization of Animal Draft Power in Kolkhozes," *Partiinaia zhizn',* 10: 32–34 (1957); A. Bugakov, *Sel'skaia zhizn',* June 16, 1966; G. Nechiporenko, *Sel'skaia zhizn',* August 10, 1966.

ber of new trucks provided annually for agriculture after increasing from 68,900 in 1953, to 125,300 in 1957, decreased to 63,000 in 1964. The shortage of transportation facilities is to a considerable extent responsible for the frequently reported failure of collective and state farms to claim from railway points promptly, or even at all, mineral fertilizer consigned to them; for the failure to cart manure to the fields and to move crops like sugar beets from the fields to the factories. The dismal state of rural roads, familiar to all who have had an opportunity to travel in the Russian countryside, especially their almost impassable condition in the autumn and spring, contributes to the problem. A gloomy analysis of the highway situation by a deputy of the Supreme Soviet of the USSR, V. Klauson, appeared in *Izvestiia* on July 28, 1966. At that time little was being done or planned to improve the situation, outside of the Baltic republics. Klauson comments that "poor roads is one of the causes of high transportation costs," and cites an official estimate of annual losses in excess of 3 billion rubles caused by "inadequate development of a [highway] transportation network in the country."

Of the specific farmstead operations, those connected with livestock production, particularly with the dairy industry, rank most important. Yet even the better farms I visited in 1963 were not adequately supplied with milking machines, though the number of such machines reportedly increased from a mere 8,000 in 1954 to 27,000 in 1959,[30] the last year for which such information is available. Such operations as feeding and watering of livestock and cleaning of barns are also little mechanized. The great amount of hand labor used in livestock operations clearly increases the cost of production of animal products.

To sum up, mechanization under the MTS system made the greatest strides in major field crops, though even here it was uneven. Little progress was achieved in vegetable and fruit crops, in animal husbandry, and in other farmstead operations.

The fiscal function performed by MTS was as an extractor of grain— and to a lesser extent of other crops—for the state in the form of payment in kind (*naturoplata*) for servicing kolkhozes. These payments in kind had begun to surpass compulsory deliveries as a means of grain procurement before World War II.[31] In 1937, payments in kind of kolkhozes were 11,233,900 tons of standard weight and compulsory deliveries, 10,169,100 tons. In 1933, payments in kind constituted 2,715,000 tons and compulsory deliveries 14,227,700 tons.[32] No detailed data are available for the postwar years, but it has been reported that in 1957 payments in kind accounted for more than 47 percent of the total grain procurements from kolkhozes and sovkhozes, 28–30 percent of potatoes, and 36 percent of sunflower seed.[33]

The rates at which payments in kind were fixed by the government during the Stalin period varied with the officially determined biological yields of the unharvested crops. Yields were easily overestimated to the advantage of the regime because the higher the estimate, the larger the payments in kind. Such a manipulation of yield figures and excessive charges for MTS service were confirmed by Khrushchev after Stalin's death.[34] The dependence of payments in kind on crop estimates also made difficult early planning by kolkhozes of the distribution of the crop. Kolkhozes serviced by MTS were in addition subject to compulsory deliveries, but at rates lower than for the farms which were not serviced. The rates for the latter were 15–25 percent higher.

One of the early Khrushchev reforms was the replacement in 1953 of the easily abused variable rates of payment in kind by fixed rates for different operations. A deduction of 10 percent was set for delayed work by MTS, unless the planned target of grain yields for the kolkhoz as a whole was reached. If the target was exceeded, 10 percent of the amount of grain actually harvested above the target was added to payments in kind.[35] It was later indirectly acknowledged by Khrushchev that the new rates were too high for some of the weaker kolkhozes and especially onerous in years of unfavorable climatic conditions. Considerable grain arrears had to be canceled in 1958, together with arrears in other types of procurements.[36]

Although much was said and written and many resolutions passed to make individual MTS financially self-sustaining (*khozraschet*) from the fees they charged, their capital and current expenditures continued to be financed by the government out of the national budget. Thus there was no direct relationship between the operations of an individual MTS and its financial status. But the fiscal importance of MTS as revenue producers was considerable. With high charges and an increasing volume of MTS operations caused by growing mechanization, payments in kind gained a leading position in grain procurement.

The Ascendancy and Demise of MTS

By the time World War II began the more than 7,000 MTS, comprising over 80 percent of the Soviet tractor inventory, were already a pivotal element of the collective farm system. But during the war the MTS took a severe beating. The Germans destroyed or captured 137,000 tractors, 49,000 combines, and many other implements.[37] Two of the three tractor plants, those in the battle zone of Stalingrad and Kharkov, were gutted. Another destructive factor was Stalin's scorched earth policy, the results of which have not been calculated, or at least not publicized by the Soviets. In the unoccupied zone MTS suffered from mobilization of tractors and experienced personnel, and especially from lack of replacement of worn-out machinery.

The recovery of MTS from the heavy war damage at first proceeded slowly but in time gained momentum. This is highlighted by the dynamics of output and delivery of tractors. Between mid-1945, when peacetime production was resumed, and 1948, some 106,000 tractors were produced, compared to 180,000 during 1937–40, and 393,000 during 1933–36. For the next four years, 1949–52, we have a figure of actual deliveries of tractors to MTS and state farms which amounted to 295,600.[38] There is probably some overlapping between the production figure for 1948 and deliveries figure for 1949; but it is safe to say that during the first seven and a half postwar years Soviet agriculture received 370,000 to 380,000 new tractors, the great majority of them destined for the MTS. If the figure for tractor inventory in MTS of 567,000 at the end of 1952 is correct, there must have been a large number of old worn-out tractors on the farms hardly suitable for efficient operation, especially with the rough handling to which they were usually subjected in the USSR.

The government was faced with serious difficulties after the war in recruiting and training the skilled labor force for MTS. Not only was there strong and successful competition from industry for the demobilized men, but the women who during the war replaced male mechanizers and constituted the core of MTS labor force were quitting en masse after hostilities ended. On January 1, 1947, women constituted only 17.4 percent of tractor drivers and two years later, 5 percent.[39]

Despite the relatively slow recovery and the many shortcomings, the MTS under Stalin seemed a solid and permanent feature of the Soviet agricultural scene. Yet some Soviet economists apparently favored a change. We learn about it secondhand from Stalin's curious last opus, *The Economic Problems of Socialism,* which appeared on the eve of the Eighteenth Party Congress in October 1952.[40] In one of the supplements to his work Stalin included a reply to "letters" by two economists, A. V. Sanina and V. G. Venzher, in which he criticized their proposal to sell MTS machinery to kolkhozes. (The proposal apparently was made in the course of a discussion in the Central Committee of a textbook on economics.) Stalin quotes what seems to have been the central argument of these economists: "It would be wrong to think that kolkhoz investments must only be made for cultural needs of the kolkhoz village, while the basic investments for purposes of agricultural production must be left to the state. Would it not be better to free the state from this burden in view of the ability of kolkhozes to completely assume it? The state will find a number of other fields for the investment of its resources needed to create an abundance of consumers goods."

Stalin, on the contrary, flatly denied the ability of kolkhozes to invest sufficiently to provide for the continuing technological progress required for the growth of production. He pointed out that such things as the replacement of hundreds of thousands of wheel tractors by track-laying tractors, or of tens of thousands of old combines by new models, and the development of new implements for various industrial crops would cost billions which could only be recouped in six to eight years. Kolkhozes could not take on such expenditures even if they were in the "millionaire" class; only the state could shoulder this burden. Of course, Stalin never admitted that the root cause of the financial plight of kolkhozes was his heavy exactions policy. But he was more realistic than his economist-correspondents, if they were correctly quoted, about the capacity of kolkhozes for capital accumulation. That under such conditions liquidation of MTS would be ruinous to kolkhozes and a setback to agricultural mechanization was Stalin's main objection to the proposal. He did not mention the control functions exercised by MTS, but it is reasonable to assume that they also weighed heavily with him. The fact that Stalin publicly raised the issue of liquidation of MTS at all is a clue that the "heresy" was not confined to two obscure economists.

Whatever heresy existed, it had at first no effect on Stalin's heirs who, on the contrary, proceeded to enhance the role of the MTS in their early reforms. The basic decree of the Central Committee of September 7, 1953, following Khrushchev's celebrated report which inaugurated post-Stalin agricultural reforms, declared that MTS "constitute the industrial material-technical base of collective farming and are at present the decisive force in the development of kolkhoz production and the most important props for direction of kolkhozes by the socialist state."

Among the various decisions taken in the autumn of 1953 to strengthen the MTS, two were particularly important organizationally. The rural administrative apparatus was reorganized to achieve closer cooperation between the party and MTS, to make the MTS the grass-roots instrument of Soviet control of collective farming. With this end in view, the *raizo* (the raion agricultural department), which was the local administrative organ on the government level, was abolished, and a responsible party official, a second secretary of the *raikom* (the raion party committee), was installed in each MTS in a supervisory capacity with a staff of party workers called instructors. The new party functionary was a much more powerful official than the deputy director for political affairs, whom he replaced, since he was accountable only to the first secretary of the raikom, the real boss of the district. Thus party authorities acquired a kind of direct pipeline into the operations of the MTS.

The second important decision was to transfer to the permanent staffs several categories of kolkhozniks, notably tractor drivers, who were employed only seasonally by the MTS, though kolkhozes continued to pay part of their wages. As a result, the number of MTS employees increased from an annual average of 833,000 in 1952 to over 3 million in 1954. This strengthened the rather loose control by the MTS of the farm labor force. To the other functions of MTS was later added the responsibility for carrying out procurements generally in which their share in the form of payments in kind increased in importance with the growing volume of the farmwork they performed.

Thus, all evidence during the early post-Stalin period indicated that MTS were there to stay. Yet a change was taking place in the Soviet agricultural structure which was bound to bring the question of the fate of MTS to the fore. This was the merger and enlargement of kolkhozes or their conversion into state farms. In the latter case, rather typical of the new lands regions, the MTS was absorbed into the new state farm unit along with the kolkhozes it formerly served. Even when mergers resulted in a preservation of the kolkhoz form, the great reduction in the number of farm units undermined the position of MTS.

While the kolkhozes were relatively small in size and numerous, a good case could be made, despite certain drawbacks, for possible economies through pooling tractors and other complex machinery as well as managerial and operating personnel in a central servicing unit like MTS. Likewise from the standpoint of political control of collective agriculture, there was logic in the creation of such an apparatus. But with the number of kolkhozes drastically decreasing, their size greatly increasing, and the management passing into the hands of specialists and technicians trusted by the party, the raison d'être of MTS became much more problematical. This is best demonstrated by the extreme case when, as a result of mergers, only a single large kolkhoz remained for an MTS to service. Here the existence of "two bosses on the land"—the wasteful duplication of management, aggravated by the often conflicting interests between MTS and kolkhozes—stands out. But this condition prevailed, to a lesser degree, wherever the merger of kolkhozes assumed significant dimensions.

That by 1957 the relationship between MTS and kolkhozes was disturbing the Soviet leadership was first spotlighted by a public "discussion" of agricultural organizational questions which was initiated in one of Moscow's literary magazines, *Oktiabr'*, in November 1957. The first discussant was a roving reporter by the name of Ivan Vinnichenko who, on the basis of personal observation while traveling in the southern regions of the USSR, reported a significant change in the climate of opinion of the agricultural bureaucracy and technocracy regarding the

MTS. He summed up his impressions following a visit to a raion in southern Ukraine, where the first MTS (Shevchenko) was organized: "No matter with whom I talked—the employees of MTS, kolkhoz managers, brigadiers of the tractor brigades, agronomists, party workers, and rank-and-file kolkhozniks—all these people, old and young, introverts and extroverts, adventurous and cautious, educated and half-literate—all agreed on one thing: it is no longer possible to tolerate two bosses on the land. The existing relationship between the MTS and kolkhozes must be changed."

What bothered these people, said Vinnichenko, was the familiar gamut of shortcomings in the MTS-kolkhoz dichotomy: the conflict of economic interests between the MTS and kolkhoz with respect to the kind of farm operations to be performed and the quality of work; the lack of incentives on the part of the MTS and its workers to strive for increased productivity; and the difficulties of planning and supervision. One instance reported by the author was that of a kolkhoz which badly needed tractors to help clear the snow from roads in order to be able to complete the plan for meat deliveries to the state. But the MTS could not help because such an operation was not within its plan of work, even though the machines were idle, just waiting for the sowing season. Its director pointed out that if the kolkhoz had asked for tractors ostensibly to cart manure, which is included in the plan of tractor operations, and then used them to clear the road, that would have been all right.

One kolkhoz manager analyzed the difficulty thus: "In the nature of things the kolkhoz is a customer [*zakazchik*] and the MTS a contractor [*podriadchik*]. But for some reason the contractor bosses the customer. Moreover, he [the contractor] also exercises, through the chief agronomist, state supervision over the quality of the very operations which he himself performs. And what legal value have the annual contractual agreements between MTS and kolkhozes? Hardly any . . . Just because the agreement is a 'typical' one providing, so to speak, for all eventualities, these mutual obligations have a purely formal character and actually neither of the parties is responsible for their fulfillment."

This ferment, according to Vinnichenko, led to a search for and adoption of improved forms of the MTS-kolkhoz relationship. An increasingly common practice was that of combining a tractor brigade with a kolkhoz (field crops) brigade into a unified team under a single command. This was not feasible where a tractor brigade operated with several field crop brigades in different kolkhozes. Another corrective practice used in some cases where an MTS serviced a single kolkhoz was for the two to operate under a joint manager, without, however, merging their identities and eliminating duplication of staffs. Then there was, of course, the conversion of kolkhozes into state farms. All these reforms had their limitations and were in fact half measures, Vinnichenko thought. A growing number of voices were heard in favor of a radical solution which five years earlier was branded by Stalin as heresy: the transfer of farm machinery to kolkhozes. A small step in this direction was taken when the rigid prohibition against ownership of tractors by kolkhozes was relented.

Perhaps if Vinnichenko had extended his observations to more northern regions with their smaller farms and to the many economically weak kolkhozes, he might have found the climate more favorable to the status quo. For as another discussant prophetically pointed out, Vinnichenko, though he presented differing points of view, looked upon the problem mainly "through the eyes of very large and very prosperous kolkhozes and perhaps through the eyes of weak MTS." There were other cautionary voices with respect to the many problems involved in the liquidation of MTS, relating to the supply of new machines, repair facilities, spare parts, and so forth.[41]

In retrospect Vinnichenko's article seems not merely a trial balloon or harbinger of change. For it was followed a month later by a cautious but highly significant declaration by Khrushchev himself in favor of a radical reform. Speaking before the Central Committee of the Ukrainian Party on December 26, 1957, he mentioned a "preliminary exchange of opinion" regarding the MTS. The gist of Khrushchev's statement was that the MTS had played an important part politically and organizationally in the development of collective farming but that times had changed: the kolkhozes had grown stronger and presumably could stand on their own feet. It riled Khrushchev that products procured by the state through payments for the services of MTS were considerably more expensive than those produced by state farms; this he attributed to the MTS's inefficient methods and excessive administrative expenses. "Consequently," he asked, "has not the time arrived to decide on the transfer of MTS machinery to some kolkhozes?" This reportedly brought a favorable response from the audience and Khrushchev proceeded to argue that "when the land and technology is in the hands of one boss [khoziain], all machines will doubtless be more efficiently utilized. Thus we shall allow even more for the initiative of kolkhozniks." [42] He then tried to dispel the doubts regarding financial aspects of the change. As to the MTS, they were to become essentially repair facilities for farm machinery and rental centers for machines which kolkhozes might require only sporadically. Thus in a few paragraphs Khrushchev clearly foreshadowed the approaching doom of the MTS. This was the most important agricultural institutional reform of the first post-Stalin decade.

That Khrushchev at the end of 1957 was determined to push the issue of liquidation—or, as it is officially termed, reorganization—of the MTS, became even clearer from his next speech. On January 22, 1958, at an agricultural conference in Belorussia, he repeated his thesis in a more extensive form. "Two bosses exist on the same land—kolkhoz and MTS—and where there are two bosses there cannot be good order. In modern farming everything depends on the work of the tractor and the combine. However, a kolkhoz must coordinate and clear with the MTS even such a question as to where to place the tractor. All this leads to irrational utilization of technology and hurts the interests of both the state and the kolkhoz. We frequently meet with such a phenomenon when an MTS services one or two kolkhozes and keeps a tremendous administrative staff. One asks, would it not be better to sell the machinery to the kolkhozes? It would seem that then the machines would work more efficiently, with greater productivity." [43] Khrushchev disclosed that a conference of party raikom secretaries, kolkhoz managers, and directors of MTS had been held by the Central Committee, and the consensus was that the question of MTS was ripe for a solution. He tried to reassure those comrades who feared that liquidation of MTS would lead to a diminution of the grain supply in the hands of the state: transfer of machinery to kolkhozes would result in increased production, he said, and ipso facto to an increased supply going to the state at a lower cost.

Despite the claim of widespread support, Khrushchev did not announce a firm decision in January 1958 but invoked the same procedure as was followed during the industrial reorganization a year earlier. His proposal for "reorganization" of the MTS and the sale of their machinery to kolkhozes was approved by the plenum of the Central Committee of the party on February 26, 1958.[44] For all practical purposes this was the end of the story. But several other steps were felt to be necessary by the Soviet leadership to formalize such an important change. First the theses, the essentials of Khrushchev's report to the plenum, were published in the Soviet press on March 1, 1958. This was followed by several weeks of so-called general public discussion (*vsenarodnoe obsuzhdenie*) of the problem in the press and at numerous meetings. At the end of March, Khrushchev presented the proposal on behalf of the government to the Supreme Soviet in a long introductory speech and wound up the discussion by another speech.[45] The proposal was then passed by the Supreme Soviet and became law.

This procedure had not affected the essentials of the proposed reform or the official case for it. These were determined by Khrushchev and his colleagues in the Presidium in consultation with selected functionaries and specialists, without a really serious public debate. But apparently there was significant opposition in some party circles to what seemed like degrading state, "all peoples," property to ideologically lower ranking kolkhoz-cooperative property. This had an important bearing on the doctrine of transition to communism, which the party's theorists visualized as supremacy of state property represented in agriculture by MTS and state farms. The doctrine postulated a corresponding escalation of the kolkhoz-cooperative property to the level of state property.

Khrushchev, in his speech to the Supreme Soviet on March 27, 1958, went to considerable pains to resolve this ideological difficulty. While accepting the differences between the two types of property and their ranking according to the degree of socialization, he denied the existence of any antithesis. Both types of property are socialist in character, he maintained, and "the road to communism lies in the evolution of state property as well as of kolkhoz-cooperative property." [46] Khrushchev also saw in the growth of the "indivisible funds"—representing the investments and assets of kolkhozes—and in the development of interkolkhoz enterprises additional important evidence of increased socialization and, accordingly, of progress in the transformation of the kolkhoz-cooperative property into an ideologically higher form. This process was aided to an important degree, according to him, by the contribution of socialist industry to agriculture, and by the state through training of cadres, financing of research, and various subsidies. The converse phenomenon of overinvestment in heavy industry at the expense of agriculture was not mentioned. Khrushchev summed up his case against the opposition by stating that the transfer of equipment from MTS to kolkhozes would lead

> to a more rational utilization of machinery and rising productivity of labor. As a result kolkhozes will produce more. This will make it possible to satisfy better the people's demand, to supply cities and industrial centers better, and thus raise the standard of living of the toilers. Does this contradict the goal of the construction of a communist society? No, it does not contradict but is fully consistent with it because it accelerates the movement of our country toward communism. The indivisible funds of kolkhozes will grow, the degree of socialization of kolkhoz production will increase, interkolkhoz relations will expand and this will facilitate further development of kolkhoz property and its transformation into state property.[47]

Khrushchev quickly disposed of those "people out of touch with reality" who were apprehensive about the weakening of the dominant role of the state as a result of the MTS reform. Such a weakening could not occur when the state, guided by the Communist Party, occupies the heights, commands powerful industry and nationalized land and retains all other levers of control over the economy of the country. He also rejected the idea of a wholesale conversion of kolkhozes into state farms, as advocated by some economists. This would have been appropriate if kolkhozes, as an organizational form, had exhausted the possibilities for further progress—a notion which Khrushchev categorically dismissed. It may be observed that while he was grappling with various ideological problems involved in the MTS issue, Khrushchev's motivation was essentially pragmatic, as may be gathered from the following statement: "Our party, in creating the MTS, has never sworn everlasting fealty to this form of production—technical servicing of kolkhozes—it never considered the development of MTS an end in itself." [48]

Khrushchev laid down two basic principles for the reform. One was the requirement of sale and not free transfer of machinery to kolkhozes, though it might be a sale on credit, with a varying repayment period, depending on the economic and financial capacity of the kolkhoz. New machinery as well as spare parts and fuel were to be purchased by kolkhozes from the state when necessary and not arbitrarily assigned from above (as was done with MTS, often leading to the accumulation of useless inventories). The other principle was the insistence on gradualism in the liquidation of MTS, so that weak kolkhozes which were not able to purchase machinery or use it effectively would not suffer. Khrushchev envisaged a period of two to three years or even longer as necessary to reorganize MTS in regions with weak kolkhozes. "One should not hurry with this," he said.[49]

The reform was formally adopted by the Supreme Soviet along the lines laid down by Khrushchev with the enactment on March 31, 1958, of a broad law entitled: "Concerning the Further Development of Kolkhoz Type of Organization (Order) and the Reorganization of Machine-Tractor Stations." [50] This was followed on April 20, 1958, by a decree of the Central Committee and the Council of Ministers with a similar title which dealt in greater detail with various aspects of the reform.[51] It provided that MTS machinery was to be sold to kolkhozes "on a voluntary basis upon their request, and only that which was in technically good working order." As a rule the implements assigned to the tractor brigade servicing a particular kolkhoz were to be sold to it. Special commissions in raions, chaired by the head of the *raiispolkom* (raion executive committee) and consisting of officials of various departments and chairmen of the kolkhozes concerned, were to determine pricing of machinery. The decree warns specifically against charging kolkhozes low prices but is silent about possible overpricing. To kolkhozes not able to pay cash, installment credit was extended up to two to three years with approval of raion authorities, and up to five years with approval of provincial authorities. No interest would be charged if payments were made on time.

The machine operators of the liquidated MTS were to continue working in the kolkhozes where they were presently employed. They were to be paid on the same basis as other kolkhozniks, provided that the remuneration, including monthly advances, "was not lower than that received in MTS for the same work task in accordance with the guaranteed minimum." Apparently this did not prove to be a strong enough mandate to maintain the guaranteed minimum wage for the operators. The government also "recommended" that kolkhozes employ specialists who formerly worked in MTS at a similar salary scale. Kitchen garden plots were to be allotted to the transferred operators and specialists, and credit was to be made available by the Agricultural Bank to kolkhozes for loans to these workers.

The process of liquidation of MTS proceeded at a rapid pace. At the beginning of 1958 there were 7,903 MTS, 82 less than the peak number at the beginning of 1954. By the end of 1958 the number had dwindled to 345, and during the next two years became a mere "corporal's guard" of 34 and then 23.[52] No MTS were listed by Soviet sources at the end of 1961.

While farm machinery quickly passed into the hands of kolkhozes, many MTS were consolidated and reorganized as Repair-Technical Stations (RTS). There were 2,900 RTS at the beginning of 1961, with an average annual labor force of less than 400,000.[53] As their name indicates, they were supposed to provide facilities for repairing or overhauling kolkhoz machinery, rent out some machines which kolkhozes did not possess, perform specialized services, and sell spare parts, implements, and other farm requisites.

The performance of the RTS and of the whole system of supplying agricultural requisites was soon adjudged unsatisfactory by the government, and a new reorganization was ordered on February 10, 1961. A new central supply agency, *Soiuzsel'khoztekhnika,* was created with whose local branches the RTS were merged.[54] Thus came to an end, after thirty years, the youngest of the trinity in the Soviet farm system: the MTS and its offshoot the RTS.

Mechanization without the MTS

How successful was the MTS reform in fulfilling the promises of greatly increased efficiency and productivity of collective farming which were held out by Khrushchev? Generally the performance of Soviet agriculture during the period following the MTS reform was bitterly disappointing to the Soviet rulers. For unlike the years 1954–58, marked by rapid growth of agricultural production, the early 1960s were characterized by stagnation or decline. This was a result of many factors, climatic, economic, and institutional. Among the institutional factors was the manner in which the MTS were liquidated.

The performance of tractors in quantitative terms, which may be used as an overall measure of the efficiency of mechanization, increased somewhat during the first years following the liquidation of MTS. The average volume of work per 15-horsepower tractor in terms of plowing equivalent in kolkhozes reached 538 hectares in 1961, compared with the peak when the MTS were in operation of 520 hectares in 1956, and 497 hectares in 1957. After 1961, however, a downward trend set in, and in 1964 the average was 487 hectares.[55]

Reports of idleness and inefficient utilization and maintenance of tractors and other machinery in kolkhozes did not abate, contrary to the optimistic expectations of a marked improvement. A law was enacted in December 1960 making poor and negligent care of machinery a criminal offense. A subsequent decree of the Council of Ministers of the USSR of November 30, 1961, while praising progressive farms, repeated the old complaints that "on many farms, tractors, combines, machinery, and other equipment are utilized unsatisfactorily; as a result many very important farm operations are not carried out on time and agrotechnical requirements are violated." [56] Management and technical personnel of a number of kolkhozes were censured for poor maintenance and repair and for prematurely writing off machinery, contrary to the official amortization standards. The decree also noted that the MTS wage scale of the mechanizers who became kolkhozniks—an incentive to efficient work— was not maintained in many kolkhozes, as was intended by the reform.

The Minister of Agriculture, V. V. Matskevich,* blamed the Khrushchev administration for most of the difficulties with the machinery repairs because it did away with the RTS which were supposed to have taken over the repair functions of the MTS. The difficulties began, according to Matskevich, when the government approved a proposal by a prosperous kolkhoz in Stavropol province to buy an RTS repair shop. The farm, which had sixty tractors, was not able to utilize the shop fully, while its neighbors were deprived of the RTS service and had to make repairs under primitive conditions. More than 3,500 repair shops were

---

* Matskevich was Minister of Agriculture of the USSR under Khrushchev from 1955 to 1960, when he was deposed and became head of the Tselinograd ispolkom (oblast executive committee) in the virgin lands area. He was restored to his former ministerial post by Khrushchev's successor in 1965.

sold to kolkhozes or transferred to sovkhozes and various other agencies. The largest of these enterprises were transferred to the jurisdiction of the industrial councils (*sovnarkhozes*), and a number of them were converted to industrial uses.[57]

It is difficult to understand why such a fragmentation was permitted by the Kremlin. Why, for instance, in the case of the Stavropol kolkhozes cited by Matskevich could not custom work be arranged? After all, while kolkhozes are supposed to be economically independent of each other, they are not hostile competitors, and are tightly controlled by the party-state apparatus. Why, it may be further asked, could not joint inter-kolkhoz repair shops, of which there were sixty-six at the end of 1964, be more widely used? This seems to be another illustration of the lack of flexibility in the functioning of the Soviet system which seriously impedes progress. At any rate, 26,000 farms used poorly equipped, unsatisfactory repair facilities in 1965, and 9,000 kolkhozes and sovkhozes had none. As for *sel'khoztekhnika,* an important function of which was to assist kolkhozes with repair of machinery, it was only able to do so in 1964 for 46 percent of the tractors, 38 percent of the trucks, and 26 percent of the grain combines in need of repair.[58]

The haste with which liquidation of MTS was carried out, contrary to Khrushchev's original thesis of gradualness, had unfavorable repercussions in many kolkhozes, particularly the smaller and economically weaker ones. Matskevich emphasized the financial plight of a number of kolkhozes caused by the speeding up of payment for the machinery bought from MTS. The basic legislation on liquidation of MTS provided that such payments could be made on an installment basis, depending on the economic position of kolkhozes. Managers of some of the more prosperous kolkhozes offered to complete payment within one year. The publicity and encouragement which this step received generated pressure on many kolkhozes which, though financially unable to pay as quickly, followed suit. The problem was accentuated by a rise in the prices of machinery and other productive inputs which kolkhozes now had to purchase. Prices of spare parts were raised 90 percent on January 1, 1959. The general result was a heavy drain on kolkhoz income and an adverse effect on remuneration of labor and on production.[59]

Mechanization of farm operations made further progress during the years following the liquidation of MTS, but as Table 61 indicates there were considerable disparities. In kolkhozes, 61 percent of the sugar beets was harvested by combines in 1964, but only 46 percent was mechanically loaded for shipment to factories or farms; 64 percent of the potatoes was planted but only 40 percent was harvested by machines; 60 percent of the hay was machine cut as compared with combine harvesting of 96

Table 61. Percentage of total crop production mechanized in kolkhozes and state farms in 1964

Operation	I Kolkhozes	II State farms	Average of I and II
Planting of potatoes	64	79	69
Cultivation			
Corn	96	97	96
Potatoes	79	89	83
Sugar beets	84	88	85
Vegetables	46	74	59
Cotton	80	88	82
Harvesting by combines			
Small grains	96	99	98
Corn (dry grain)	71	84	73
Sunflower seed	99.8	100	99.8
Sugar beets	61	46	58
Cleaning of grain	94	98	96
Digging of potatoes	40	66	48
Scutching of flax	57	66	58
Harvesting of silage crops	92	94	93
Mowing of hay	60	88	76
Stacking of hay and straw	39	68	53
Loading of threshed grain	74	93	82
Loading of harvested sugar beets	46	41	45

Source. *Narodnoe khoziaistvo, 1964,* p. 385.

percent of small grains and 71 percent of corn for grain. The progress of mechanization was much slower in animal husbandry. Only 18 percent of the cows were milked by machine in kolkhozes in 1964 (see Table 62).

Even when Soviet statistics record completely or nearly completely mechanized operations, such as in sowing and harvesting small grains or sunflowers, they are often deceptive. Such figures fail to disclose that one of the principal advantages of farm mechanization, the timeliness of farm operations, is lacking. This is particularly true of harvesting, where delay leads to large crop losses. Experiments have shown that harvesting grain twelve days after maturity results in a 13 percent loss; a delay of twenty days results in a loss of up to one third of the crop.[60] Yet dragging out the harvest for even longer periods was not uncommon. The reverse is the situation with sugar beets where early harvesting misses the period of the most intensive development of sugar in the beets. In experiments

Table 62. Percentage of livestock production mechanized in kolkhozes and state farms in 1964

Operation	I Kolkhozes	II State farms	Average of I and II
Milking	18	37	25
Water supply			
Cattle farms	53	47	51
Hog farms	67	68	68
Feeding			
Cattle farms	2	3	2
Hog farms	10	12	10
Cleaning of barns			
Cattle farms	7	8	7
Hog farms	10	14	11
Shearing of sheep (electric shears)	77	92	84

Source. *Narodnoe khoziaistvo, 1964*, p. 386.

in the Krasnodar province the harvesting of this crop in the beginning of August as compared with the end of the month, led to a loss of 5.9 centners of sugar per hectare, and harvesting at the beginning of August instead of the beginning of October resulted in a loss of 14.3 centners.[61] But harvesting had to begin early in order to enable the farms to bring the whole crop in before cold weather.

The principal reason for these timing deficiencies, as well as for the low rate of mechanization of a number of operations, was the inadequacy of the machine inventory, inadequacy in numbers and in the quality and character of the implements. While the gap between the actual inventories and requirements (given by Khrushchev at the March 1962 plenum and based on the assumption of performance of farm operations during optimum periods) was narrowing (see Table 63), it was still wide by 1965. In the Soviet Union in 1965 there were 359 acres of sown area and cultivated summer fallow per tractor, or five times as much as in the United States, with 72 acres per tractor.[62] (Actually the acreage per tractor was somewhat larger in the Soviet Union because the figure above did not include the area on which crops were winter killed, as is done in U.S. statistics.) The gap between the United States and the Soviet Union is even greater when a comparison is made on the basis of tractor power instead of numbers, converting for this purpose total tractor power into 15 hp tractor units. In 1965 there were 178 acres per unit in the Soviet

Table 63. Selected farm machinery inventories for specified years (in thousands)

End of year	Tractors	Grain combines	Motor trucks
1928	26.7	—	0.7
1932	148.5	14.5	14.2
1938	483.5	153.8	195.8
1940	531.0	182.0	228.0
1945	397.0	148.0	62.0
1950	595.0	211.0	283.0
1953	744.0	317.6	424.0
1958	1,001.0	502.0	700.0
1964	1,539.0	513.0	954.0
1970 (plan)	2,490.0	845.0	1,341.0
Requirements [a]	2,696.0	788.0	1,650.0

[a] For performance of farm operations during optimum periods as given by Khrushchev, *Pravda,* March 6, 1962.

Sources. *Sotsialisticheskoe sel'skoe khoziaistvo, 1939,* p. 17; *Sel'skoe khoziaistvo, 1960,* pp. 410, 413; *Narodnoe khoziaistvo, 1964,* p. 380; P. Kozhevnikov, "To Develop Agriculture on a Stable Material-Technical Base," *Ekonomika sel'skogo khoziaistva,* 6: 29 (June 1962).

Union and only 26 in the United States.[63] These figures, which could be duplicated for other implements, highlight the inadequacy of farm machinery inventories.

This inadequacy was even more marked during the years immediately following the liquidation of the MTS, at the beginning of the Seven-Year Plan (1959–65)—the years when delivery of tractors and other farm machinery to Soviet agriculture decreased. It was later brought out that during this period the amount of rolled metal allotted for manufacturing of farm machinery was "annually decreased by 20–40 percent, compared with 1957. Therefore some of the farm machinery factories turned to the manufacturing of other products." [64] The deficiencies in farm machinery were subsequently criticized by Khrushchev who blamed the bureaucracy for this.[65] But where was he, then at the zenith of his power? Why did he permit such a situation to develop? Khrushchev certainly disregarded the explanation given in several Soviet statistical yearbooks that the reduction was caused by conversion of plants for manufacturing of improved models.[66] Whatever the facts, the upward trend in deliveries of farm machinery was resumed in the 1960s but at a slower rate. Thus the deliveries of tractors in 1964 were 42 percent greater than in 1960; the rise between 1953 and 1957 was 95 percent. The number of combines delivered was 41 percent greater in 1964 than in 1960, but it more than tripled between 1953 and 1957. The number of trucks decreased slightly in 1964 compared to 1960; it was 80 percent greater in 1957 compared to 1953.

The relatively low priority given to the manufacturing of farm machinery is indicated by the lag in growth of output behind that of all machinery. While the average 1959–61 total machinery output was 35 percent above 1958, farm machinery output was 29 percent higher. Not until 1964 did the rate of growth become practically equal: 21 percent above 1958 for farm machinery and 23 percent for all machinery.[67] Despite domestic deficiency, the Soviet Union was exporting tractors and other farm machinery in this period. The number of tractors exported ranged from 5,400 in 1956 to 23,100 in 1963; [68] in 1964 and 1965 it was over 21,000.[69]

Quantitative inadequacy was aggravated by a qualitative inferiority of farm machinery and its inefficient use. One important indicator is that in the mid-1960s annual expenditures for repairs and technical maintenance of tractors constitute 25–30 percent of their cost.[70] But, as Lemeshev correctly points out, such high unproductive expenditures are not the whole story; equally important is the fact that they reflect frequent breakdowns and stoppages of machines, with a deleterious effect on the timeliness of farm operations and crop yields. The deficiency in quality and use are no doubt responsible for the tendency toward a short life span of farm machinery in the USSR, with a resulting increase in the amortization expense. At one time ten years was considered a proper minimum period of service for farm machinery; this was reduced to five years in the mid-1960s. In 1965, according to one Soviet authority, the life expectancy of farm implements in the USSR was only one quarter to one half that in the United States, and the normal cost of repairs three to four times higher.[71] Even taking into account the smaller amount of work per machine in the United States than in the USSR, there is still a marked discrepancy.[72]

A Soviet source blames negligent maintenance of machinery for this short life span, necessitating expensive overhauling; but it does not say anything about the basic deficiency of the machines. That some Soviet farm machinery performs poorly was observed by U.S. Department of Agriculture specialists in 1958 and 1963 with respect to sugar-beet harvesting machinery, where a considerable amount of manual labor had to be employed to complete cutting off the remaining tops of the beets, an operation which should have been done by the machine in the first place. A Soviet economist speaks of the large amount of labor used for "supplementary cleaning" of beet roots because of a lack of proper mechanical devices.[73] It is not clear whether this refers to the above-mentioned operation or to cleaning the dirt off the roots, which in the United States is done by a mechanical device in the sugar mills rather than on the farms. The Soviets also had great difficulties in developing satisfactory cotton pickers, but these had apparently been overcome by the mid-1960s.

Another problem has been the nature of the supply of machinery. Too often shortages of some items have been ignored while production continues of machines which many kolkhozes and sovkhozes refuse to acquire because they find them of little or no value. Standardization of spare parts leaves much to be desired. It was stated by Soviet specialists in 1965 that "frequent replacement of the models of a machine, requiring new spare parts, created an intolerable situation." [74] The shortage of spare parts sometimes has led to such an extreme as the purchase of a tractor by a kolkhoz when it merely needed a wheel for an otherwise good machine.[75] Another method used to obtain parts in short supply has been to remove them from other machines. New machines sometimes do not escape this fate either, as in the case reported in 1956 from Krasnoiarsk province where recently delivered self-propelled combines were used as a source for spare parts with the result that only skeletons were left of twenty new machines.[76]

Khrushchev criticized the Soviet farm machinery industry at the Twentieth Party Congress in February 1956 for the uniformity of the implements manufactured, for the failure to adapt them to different regional conditions, for using the same heavy track-laying tractors, the same combines for the vast steppes of the Kuban as for the small fields of the Baltic republics and other northwestern regions.[77] Having the northwestern regions in mind, Khrushchev demanded increased production of the lighter wheel tractors. Beginning in 1962 more machines of this than of the track-laying type were produced. In 1964, for instance, 186,300 wheel and 142,700 track-laying tractors were manufactured.[78] However, adjustments to fit varying regional conditions were not made for other types of machinery. Adjustments are needed also to meet requirements for new practices and programs. After the crop failure of 1963 a strong emphasis was placed on such practices as an increased use of mineral fertilizer, liming of acid soils, drainage of marshy land, irrigation, and stubble mulching in dry regions; these programs required a large number of new kinds of agricultural machines.

The government is cognizant of the dynamic character of modern technology with its stream of new implements and practices. To encourage the introduction of new machine models on the farms, the government decreed that they be sold during the first year of their production at prices covering the planned cost during the second year of manufacturing, when unit costs would normally go down. The profit rate was set at 3 percent and subsidies were to compensate the enterprises for losses incurred during the initial year of manufacture. Actually, no such subsidization took place, and in most cases new machines were sold at higher prices and a profit of 5 percent or considerably more was charged.[79]

In his March 5, 1962, speech Khrushchev criticized the setting of high prices for new models of farm machinery based on high costs during the early stages of production. However, the customary Soviet practice (prior to the economic reform of 1965) of evaluating the performance of an enterprise in terms of the gross value of output often led to a deliberate inflation of costs and selling prices of new machines.[80] For low prices would depress the gross value of the factory's output and the productivity of labor calculated on this basis—the two principal indicators by which the performance of the enterprise was judged. The picture is complicated by the fact that different factories project in their production plans widely varying costs for identical new models. Thus one factory planned a mass production cost for a new sugar-beet combine at 2,300 to 2,400 rubles, while another factory produced pilot models, which should be more expensive, at a cost of only 1,671 rubles.[81] Another example is that of three plants which in 1962 began manufacturing field bean reapers at a cost of 548, 950, and 1,161 rubles respectively.

The high prices of new types of farm machinery contribute to the tendency to retain old, worn-out machinery that breaks down frequently. This keeps repair costs high, adding to the financial burden on kolkhozes since they took over the functions of MTS.

Some improvements have been made in Soviet farm implements, of course, though there were many justifiable complaints about the slow pace.[82] Output of row crop tractors on wheels with low pressure tires has increased since the early 1950s; these are adaptable for transportation as well as for field work. The equipment of tractors and other implements with automatic attachment mechanisms made it possible to dispense with the labor of many thousands of workers (*stsepshchiki*) whose job it was to attach implements to tractors. Another important development is the shift to self-propelling combines, rising from an output of 24,000 out of a total of 43,100 in 1953 to 82,900 in 1963 when only the self-propelled model was produced.[83] These combines freed a considerable number of tractors for other operations during the harvest season.

Despite the many difficulties and high costs, mechanization made possible a great expansion of the crop acreage which was primarily responsible for the increase in Soviet agricultural production. The sown area in the pre–World War II territory of the USSR increased between 1928 and 1938 by more than 80 percent. In the enlarged postwar territory the total sown area increased by 45 percent between 1940 and the peak of 1963. But this period included the years of great war devastation and decline of acreage, and thus the subsequent rate of expansion was even larger: between 1945 and 1963 the acreage increased by more than 90 percent. This included the addition of more than 100 million acres of virgin land to the sown area in the eastern regions, which would have been impossible without the tractor.

Mechanization also made possible a decrease in the farm labor force, though it has been a slow and irregular process. The average annual number of workers employed in the socialist sector and directly involved in crop and livestock production decreased from 27.8 million in 1940 to 26.2 million in 1953, and then increased to 28.2 million in 1956. A downward trend ensued in 1957, and by 1964 the number of workers was down to 24.9 million, but the total had risen to 25.2 million by 1965 (which was the same figure as in 1962).[84] There is one category of farms which mechanization has not touched, though they produce about one third of the total output: the small private holdings of kolkozniks and others. The average annual number of persons working on such holdings increased from 3.1 million in 1959 to 3.7 million in 1964.[85] When these figures are added, the total average annual farm labor force engaged in crop and livestock production declined during this period only from 30 million to 28.9 million—or 3.7 percent. There was, then, no spectacular decline of farm labor in the wake of mechanization such as occurred in the United States, where total farm employment decreased continuously in the 1950s and early 1960s—from 10 million in 1949 to 6.1 million in 1964 and 5.6 million in 1965.[86]

The government's enthusiasm for overall ("complex" is the Soviet term) mechanization of farm operations has remained unabated. In adhering to this goal, the Soviet rulers have been motivated not only by concrete economic and technical considerations common to all advanced agricultural countries—such as reduction in labor requirements, lowering of production costs, lightening the burden of farm labor, and ensuring the timeliness and speed of farm operations—but also, it seems to me, by a peculiar ideological mystique. Mechanization like bigness is deemed by the Soviets an essential attribute of a socialist farm enterprise, contributing mightily to that Marxist desideratum, the erosion of the gap between agriculture and industry. To this must be added the very practical consideration of the political leverage over agriculture which mechanization affords. Thus agricultural mechanization has become for the Soviets an end in itself, surpassing the more mundane objectives of labor saving and cost reduction. True, these objectives have been stressed by Khrushchev and his successors, but mechanization has been pursued without regard for abundance of the farm labor supply or whether or not the machinery is economically profitable. A case in point is the questionable advantage of some tractor operations on the small fields of the central and north central regions.

Considerably stepped up mechanization was an important ingredient in the program of Khrushchev's successors for maximizing agricultural production embodied in the decisions of the May 1965 plenum and the directives for the 1966–70 plan. Record increases of agricultural machinery to be supplied to farms during 1966–70 were planned. They included 1,790,000 tractors compared with 1,093,000 supplied during 1961–65, and 747,500 during 1956–60. The number of trucks specified for delivery by the 1966–70 plan is 1.1 million compared with 363,000 and 484,000 respectively during the two preceding five-year periods. Similar figures for grain combines were 550,000; 384,400; and 388,600. Record increases were planned for other machinery as well. But despite the planned large increase, still greater progress will be necessary to attain adequate mechanization even by the relatively low Soviet standards.

The only significant organizational step in connection with farm mechanization after Khrushchev was the official blessing given at the May 1965 plenum to an expansion of specialized units having the necessary machinery and cadres to deal with various phases of reclamation and land improvement. Official action did not go beyond this; but voices began to be heard favoring restoration or partial restoration of the MTS. At the May 1965 plenum, Ia. N. Zarobian, First Secretary of the Party in Armenia, severely criticized, with the approval of the audience, the liquidation (he used the official term "reorganization") of the MTS. He noted the serious deterioration of repair facilities and the loss of skilled cadres of machine operators, which resulted in lowering the productivity of tractors. He pointed out that about 300 kolkhozes in Armenia were not able at the present stage to purchase farm machinery or acquire the needed repair facilities. This was characteristic of small, economically weak kolkhozes, and Zarobian thought there must be many thousands of them in the country in the same predicament. He stated that the leadership and agricultural experts in the Armenian republic gave much thought to the subject and concluded that "perhaps it is not expedient at present to restore the MTS, but there are other organizational forms which could help considerably to improve the use of technology." [87] The solution which Zarobian hesitatingly proposed was the creation of units similar to the MTS with which kolkhozes could contract for custom work on a purely commercial basis; then the machinery would be better utilized and maintained. There was no reaction to this idea by the national leadership, either positive or negative; thus the door was left open.

In the meantime, support for restored pooling of farm machinery came from another quarter, from those who advocated a much further extension of interkolkhoz cooperation. Thus the writer Bukovskii advanced the idea of restoring the MTS not as state enterprises with department interests of their own, which could and often did conflict with those of kolkhozes, but as interkolkhoz cooperative enterprises which would have the same interests and aspirations as kolkhozes.[88] This would be, in a sense, a return to the early forms of the MTS before their etatization which should avoid the dichotomy of two bosses on the land as was the case with the state-owned MTS.

Whether anything will be done along these lines it is impossible to tell. But the very fact that ideas such as those of Zarobian and Bukovskii have been permitted to circulate publicly is a visible indication of a ferment in this area. Thus, it seems fairly certain that the progress of agricultural mechanization will continue, but its organizational forms have not fully crystallized.

Electrification

Agricultural electrification for a number of years made slow progress in the Soviet Union despite Lenin's famous slogan that electrification plus cooperation is equivalent to socialism. A gloomy picture of rural electrification was painted by Brezhnev at the May 1965 plenum: "In recent years giant electric power plants were built in our country. At the same time 12 percent of collective farms do not have electric power even for lighting. Agriculture consumes only 4 percent of the power produced in our country, only 2 percent for production purposes." [89] The elimination of hand labor in many farmstead operations, in milking, for instance, and improvement in rural homemaking depend on the use of electricity, as American experience with rural electrification has demonstrated.

An important cause of the tardy development of electrification was that kolkhozes were barred from connecting with the state grid system during the Stalin period, leaving them to their own devices. This meant relying on small, mostly hydroelectric plants with low capacity, irregular service, and high cost of electric power.[90] The cost of generating power in small rural plants was six to ten times higher than in the large state plants.[91] The prohibition of access to the state grid was removed by 1954; yet most of the electric power consumed in kolkhozes continued to be generated by rural plants until 1962, when not quite half came from this source. Out of 7,438 million kilowatt-hours of power received by kolkhozes in 1964, two thirds, 4,879 million, were generated by state plants.[92] In 1959 more than a third of the kolkhozes still lacked electric power, but 94 percent of the kolkhozes were reported as having electricity by 1966.[93] There was a considerable gap in electrification between kolkhozes and sovkhozes. Electric power was available in 1953 to 88 percent of the sovkhozes. During the years 1956–57 the figure increased to 93 percent, and in 1958–59 to 96 percent of the growing number of sovkhozes.[94]

A new program for agricultural electrification was announced in a decree of February 21, 1961.[95] It provided that wherever possible kolkhozes and state farms connect with the existing or projected state power grids or with individual industrial power plants or with the power installations of the electrified railroads. In areas remote from central power plants, the decree called for construction of raion or interraion diesel power plants and hydroelectric power plants of increased capacity and, in individual cases, of steam turbine and gas turbine plants. In sparsely populated regions where the operation of interraion or raion power plants is not feasible, the construction of the most economical type of interkolkhoz or kolkhoz and state farm power plant was authorized. The state was to assume the cost of construction of the raion and interraion power plants supplying farm enterprises and also construction of high voltage transmission lines and branch plants when power was supplied by the state grid or power plants. Construction of kolkhoz and interkolkhoz power plants and low voltage transmission lines was to be undertaken by state construction agencies at the expense of the kolkhozes. The kolkhozes were also to pay for all electrical equipment and installations on the farms.

Despite ambitious plans of rural electrification, many kolkhozes found that it was not an easy matter to obtain electricity. A tale of woe was told in a press report from Kaluga oblast, near Moscow, of long promises to electrify villages. In 1963 half of the villages of six districts in this province had no electricity.[96] Rural electrification has been hampered by the shortage of electrical equipment on farms and by the high cost of electric energy for farm production use, even when supplied by the state. In the early 1960s industrial enterprises paid 0.5 to 1.2 kopecks per kilowatt-hour, whereas farm enterprises paid 1.9 kopecks. At that time a reduction in the charges for electric power for farms was advocated.[97] This was one of the measures recommended by Brezhnev at the May 1965 plenum; it was put into effect in 1966.

During the early 1960s rural electrification made considerable strides.

Consumption of electricity in agriculture increased from 9,970 million kilowatt-hours in 1960, to 11,978 million in 1961, and to 21 billion in 1965. But in the United States, with a considerably smaller agricultural population, consumption of electric power on farms in 1964 was estimated at 37.6 billion kilowatt-hours.[98] Further acceleration of rural electrification was one of the goals of the Brezhnev agricultural program presented at the May 1965 plenum, and considerable expansion no doubt will be achieved.

19

Expansion of Production

Khrushchev initiated a number of specific programs designed to foster expansion of various branches of agricultural production. In the 1950s the extensive approach—more acres under crops and more animals—was emphasized in practice; the intensive approach, increased yields per acre and production per animal, was stressed in the 1960s. Before turning to these programs it is well to bear in mind that besides obstacles of an institutional and socioeconomic character, which the Khrushchev administration tried to overcome, it was faced with an unfavorable climate. Because of the northern location of the country, and its continental climate, much of the country is unsuitable for farming. A short growing season and aridity hamper agriculture even in the more fertile regions. Modern science and technology can go a long way to overcome some of these problems by facilitating adaptation of crops to climatic conditions. Yet a disregard of such adaptations was rather characteristic of much of the Khrushchev expansion campaign. Moreover, many of the means he adopted were questionable. This will become apparent as the different elements of the programs are unfolded.

Grain Output

Khrushchev addressed himself first to the task of increasing the grain output, which was at the root of the agricultural production problem. Increasing grain output had the double objective of securing the national bread supply of a growing urbanized population and providing for an improvement of the diet, so basic for the promised higher standard of living. An improved diet presupposes increased consumption of animal products—and that means more grain to feed livestock.* The government also wanted more grain for exports and stocks. In 1953 the grain situation was unsatisfactory for these purposes. If the regime had any illusions about solving the grain problem, as suggested by Malenkov's statement in 1952, the repudiation of biological yields quickly dispelled them. It is true that the actual barn crop in 1952, though only 92 million tons, and not the 131 million reported by Malenkov, was the best of the postwar decade. But in 1953 grain production declined to 82.5 million tons, or about its customary level.

Curiously enough this return of the traditional grain problem was not reflected in the important September 1953 Khrushchev report. Several months later Khrushchev presented a new analysis of the problem and proposed remedies in a memorandum to the Presidium which remained unpublished until 1962.[1] This memorandum gives the best available statistical picture of the grain situation during the early post-Stalin period. The central thesis of the memorandum was that the grain problem actually had not been solved because production in 1953 failed to cover the increasing demand. Government grain procurements from the 1953 harvest declined considerably below the level of the preceding four years while requirements continued to grow with the rapidly rising urban population. A deficit resulted which made it necessary for the government to dip into stocks. A subsidiary difficulty pointed out by the memorandum was the disproportion which developed in the production and procurement of different grains. While wheat procurements were trending upwards in the early 1950s as a consequence of an increased wheat acreage, supplies of feed and "groats" grains (*krupiannye*) and of pulses were down. Khrushchev noted that this decline meant substitution of valuable wheat or rye for other grains in animal feed and industrial consumption (principally manufacture of alcohol). The memorandum estimated the total amount of grain needed for various requirements at 118 million

* It may be assumed that with an improvement of the diet some grain formerly used as food would be shifted to animal feeding. But the reduction in consumption of bread-stuffs is likely to be a slow process and the production of a pound of bread requires one sixth to one tenth as much grain as a pound of meat, particularly with the low feed efficiency prevailing in the Soviet Union.

tons in 1955–56, compared with reported production of 92 million in 1952 and some 80 million in 1950–51 and 1953.

Khrushchev admitted in the memorandum that the shortfalls of production resulting from the low yields, no longer inflated statistically by biological estimates, aggravated the heavy burden of high procurements on kolkhozes and left little to distribute among the peasants. This set in motion the familiar chain reaction of disincentives to kolkhozniks and spiraling adverse effects on production. The need of reducing procurements by 200–300 million poods (3.3–5 million metric tons) in order to break this vicious circle was clearly recognized by the memorandum, but the government could ill afford to spare such a substantial amount of grain. The way out of the dilemma, as the memorandum recognized, was a considerable expansion of grain production.

The Stalin regime had also projected a large increase in grain production, despite its more optimistic assessment of the situation. But the methods adopted by the Khrushchev and Stalin programs differed significantly. Stalin relied on improvement of yields; Khrushchev pinned his hopes primarily on the addition of many new acres to the sown area. Stalin did not seek the improvement of yields by such well-tested methods as increased application of chemical fertilizer, pesticides, and herbicides. This would have involved a sizable new investment in the chemical industry and considerable temporary imports from abroad of equipment or chemicals, or both. Neither was the wider use of such standard dry-farming practices as summer fallow and stubble mulching emphasized, nor improved plant varieties like hybrid corn introduced. The much touted "Stalin Grand Plan for Reconstruction of Nature" had as its principal ingredients only the Williams crop rotation system, emphasizing wide use of perennial grasses in rotation, coupled with afforestation of the dry steppes as a means of climatic control; and development of irrigation in the drier regions of the USSR, like the Volga basin, for growing high yielding grain. The grasses were supposed to have a soil improving effect and a beneficial influence on yields of successor crops; the Williams system permeated Soviet agricultural thinking and planning during the late Stalin era.

Khrushchev's adoption of a different road to an abundant grain supply was predicated upon a rejection of Stalin's "Grand Plan" as unrealistic. The irrigation program was shelved silently after Stalin's departure. In a published interview Khrushchev indicated that shortage of capital made necessary the slowing down or postponement of the development of this program.[2] In 1961 he actually lamented the fact that the extensive program of hydroelectric power development was not linked with irrigation which would have been highly beneficial to agricultural output.[3]

Only after the disastrous drought in 1963 was official attention focused again on expansion of irrigated grain farming.

Khrushchev's reaction to the Williams system was more explicitly negative. He saw in grasses an antagonist of grain and other crops, and the system became a favorite target for his attacks, which continued until the end of his regime. In 1954 he began storming against what he called the "mechanical stereotype" of crop rotation, that is, indiscriminate expansion of the acreage under grasses not only in the relatively humid regions to which they are well suited, but in the drier regions as well, where poor yields are obtained.[4] He pointed out that in the drier regions grasses tend to dry up the soil instead of improving its structure. One of the worst consequences, according to Khrushchev, of the wide extension of grasses was the displacement of higher yielding grains, particularly feed grains (oats, barley, and corn), thus aggravating the chronic shortage of feedstuffs.

But Khrushchev now envisaged the expansion of grain production on a vaster scale than the reverse shift from grasses to grains. He was in a hurry and also wanted to do it as cheaply as possible, without too heavy a capital outlay. This left no alternative but the traditional Russian way of expanding agricultural production: plowing up virgin land while it existed.

The Virgin Lands Campaign

The steppes east of the Volga and the Urals, with their large tracts of uncultivated level land, not requiring reclamation and suitable for power farming, seemed to offer the best possibilities. This area, including Siberia and the present Kazakhstan, had been the locus of an agricultural expansion since the closing decades of the nineteenth century. Particularly during the interlude between the Revolution of 1905 and the First World War the Stolypin-Krivoshein administration encouraged peasant colonization in the area. In the early 1930s, under Stalin, another rapid thrust forward took place, this time by mechanized large farming. It was followed by a temporary setback, but the upward trend was soon resumed. Between 1913 and 1940 the sown acreage in this eastern agricultural area increased from 63 million acres to 102.5 million. By 1953 another 16 million acres were added to crops.[5] The Khrushchev program set forth in the January 1954 memorandum and officially announced in March of that year, called for an area of about 32 million acres to be brought under cultivation in 1954 and 1955. In August 1954 the goal was revised upward to 69–74 million acres by 1956,[6] which was overfulfilled; 78 million more acres were planted to crops in this zone during 1954–56. During the following three years this acreage changed little, but in 1960–62 another 27 million acres were added, which increased the sown area in the eastern zone by about 90 percent, compared with 1953. More than half of the sown area in this zone was under spring wheat. As a result the spring wheat acreage in the USSR increased from about 75 million acres in 1953 to around 120–125 million acres in 1962–63. Thus from the purely quantitative standpoint of pushing extensive utilization of land resources, the virgin lands operation must be rated a success. But the coin had another side.

A great deal of this new acreage was actually virgin land (*tselina*); the rest was land that had been cultivated at one time but, after a long period of continuous cropping, had been left idle to regain fertility and reverted to sod (*zalezh'*). A considerable proportion of this area was pasture or hay land, so that bringing it under cultivation was not entirely a net gain. In general, since the colonizing and developing of this agricultural frontier began, much of the best farmland had already been brought under cultivation before the new drive for plowing virgin land started in 1954. Various types of black and chestnut soils predominate in the area of the new lands. But interspersed with these fertile soils are various alkaline soils which present a serious difficulty.[7] They often form a salt layer below the soil surface, some of which is likely to move upwards after several years of cultivation. The consensus of authorities on soil and agronomy is that such land should not be used for crop production without some reclamation. The new program was launched on such a scale and with such speed that careful selection of land proved difficult.[8] A decree of the Central Committee published as early as June 27, 1954, called attention to the "errors" in selecting the new land, the allocation of small scattered plots in some districts and use of land with alkaline soil, despite "the existence of large tracts of good fertile land." Yet one official labeled the opposition to the use of alkaline soils as "too academic." He praised an MTS director for "the correct conclusion that there is no reason to refuse to plow such plots; it is necessary only to develop a proper agrotechnique." [9]

Other physical difficulties were encountered, such as inadequate water supply on some of the newly organized farms. But of all the deficiencies and drawbacks that hamper farming in the virgin lands regions, none is more serious than the climate. Severe winters make the growing of winter (fall sown) grains impossible in most of the eastern areas. Efforts were made to introduce such crops; the last one was on the recommendation of Lysenko. But the Central Committee, in its decree of June 27, 1954, called for replacement of winter crops by spring wheat in these regions.

This is a disadvantage since spring wheat usually completes development under more severe temperatures and transpiration conditions than winter wheat, which matures earlier. Thus much of the eastern area does not have the "insurance" benefits of a more diversified crop pattern provided by winter crops in the Ukraine and North Caucasus. Even for a spring crop area, the growing period is short in the eastern regions, averaging between 120 and 130 days. Late frosts in the spring and early frosts in the autumn often damage the crops. But the most serious limiting factor is moisture. The annual precipitation is light, for the most part less than 16 inches and in some sections only about 10 inches. Strong winds in the winter blow the snow from the fields, removing a potential source of soil moisture. The greatest damage to crops is caused by spring and summer droughts. These are frequently aggravated by scorching, soil-blowing winds, turning from time to time into veritable dust storms. Conversely, the harvest period is often marked by inclement weather, complicating harvesting operations and making the drying of grain a major problem. Thus climatic conditions make the eastern regions a zone of low and highly variable crop yields, a zone of precarious farming. Another difficulty confronting farmers in this area is mass infestation of weeds, particularly of wild oats. A report from one district in Kazakhstan in 1961 stated that because of weeds a good yield of grain was cut in half after it was cleaned; a report from another district indicated that more than a third of the harvested grain was actually weeds.[10]

The Soviet leadership must have realized from previous experience that a large extension of acreage in this zone was a risky business. Malenkov's and Molotov's opposition to this venture, which was publicized by Khrushchev, became a part of the indictment of the "anti-party group." Their side of the story has not been told and we do not know how active their opposition really was. At any rate, it did not stop Khrushchev, though in 1954 he was still some distance from the pinnacle of power. As to the scientists and technicians who were drawn into the preliminary discussion of the project, it is reasonable to infer that some opposed it but their views were kept from the public. This inference is indirectly supported by the existence during the interwar period of an influential current of Russian agronomic thought, led by the academician N. I. Vavilov, which advocated a "northernization" of Soviet agriculture as a means of combatting the recurrent droughts. What the Vavilov school had in mind was a shift of many crops to the more northern regions with poorer soils but with more stable and normally higher yields, provided that proper fertilization, liming, and, in many areas, drainage were supplied.[11] This view could hardly have lost all its influence among the Soviet agronomic fraternity but the voices heard were only those of the supporters of Khrushchev's program, like Lysenko, whose report was attached to the January 1954 memorandum. In any event, Khrushchev was willing to take a gamble, banking, no doubt, on the "multiplier" of a large acreage which even with low yields was bound to result in a substantial accretion of the grain output. He figured that with one average harvest, two good harvests, and two poor harvests during a five year period, the undertaking would be worthwhile.[12] The fact that during the initial year 1954 good yields were obtained in the new lands regions no doubt contributed to the success of Khrushchev's gambit. But during the following years the results sharply deviated from expectations.

Official figures of grain yields were low. Of the three most important new lands regions represented in the tabulation below of the 1954–61 average yields of all grains, only West Siberia corresponded to the national average and the minimum goal set by Khrushchev in 1954 of 0.4 tons per acre, or 10 centners per hectare. Even these figures were lower than those for such traditional agricultural areas as the Ukraine and North Caucasus.

	Tons per acre	Centners per hectare
West Siberia	.42	10.4
Urals	.37	9.1
Tselinnyi Krai	.32	7.9
Ukraine	.59	14.7
North Caucasus	.55	13.5

And there is good reason to believe that the official Soviet statistics overstated the usable grain, particularly in the new lands regions. The figures represent grain coming straight from the bunker of the combine, containing a large proportion of water, weeds, and other trash which is likely to be greater in the new lands than in the traditional farm regions. Such grain requires extra drying and cleaning to make it usable. The general tendency to overreport crop yields is further confirmed by the campaign waged by the Kremlin against statistical falsification and hoodwinking.

Even more deleterious than the low yields in the new lands is the wide fluctuation from year to year (see Table 64). Here again the Tselinnyi Krai stands out, in some years producing barely enough grain for seed. The early 1960s was a particularly difficult period. A wet but cold 1960 season was followed by three successive dry years, climaxed by the catastrophic general drought of 1963. Despite a late spring 1964 was a good season over a large area of the new lands, however, and this materially contributed to the recovery of Soviet grain production.

Table 64. Total sown area, yield per acre, and production of all grain in virgin land regions, 1953–1960.

Year	Area (1,000 acres)	Yields (quintals per acre)	Production (1,000 tons)
1953	113,162	2.4	27,162
1954	98,902	3.8	37,555
1955	157,788	1.8	28,064
1956	145,087	4.4	63,646
1957	145,087 [a]	2.7	38,517
1958	172,238	3.4	58,853
1959	167,203	3.3	55,266
1960	172,826	3.4	59,178

[a] Assumed to be the same as 1956.

Sources. Acreage—*Narodnoe khoziaistvo, 1960,* pp. 394–395, except for 1954 and 1956 which are taken from *Posevnye ploshchadi,* I, 206–211; production—*Narodnoe khoziaistvo, 1960,* pp. 440–441.

It is well established that fluctuations of yields in the new lands regions are caused largely by the variation in precipitation. Changes in the annual amount of precipitation were found to have an important effect on yields, but even more important is precipitation during the vegetation period and especially during May-June. This is illustrated by records of the state farm KazTSIK extending over twenty-seven years.[13] In 1934, for instance, the annual precipitation was slightly above normal but seasonal precipitation was 29 percent above normal, and the yield of spring wheat was 82 percent above a long-time average. In 1935, with the annual and seasonal precipitation only a little over half of normal, the yield was 54 percent of normal. In 1954 annual and seasonal precipitation were respectively 3 and 9 percent above normal and the yield was 87 percent above. But in 1955, with annual precipitation 72 percent and seasonal precipitation 64 percent of normal, the yield was 54 percent. During the whole period of twenty-seven years, May-June precipitation was below normal in thirteen years and above in fourteen years. The average yield of spring wheat in the first group was 5.3 centners per hectare and in the second, 8.8 centners, an increase of 66 percent. In the below-normal group, seven years had very low precipitation during May-June, which brought the average yield down to 4.7 centners; six years in the above-normal group had heavy precipitation, raising the yield to 9.4 centners. Similar results were obtained during a twenty-year period at the Atbasarsk test plot, except that the level of yields was generally higher because of superior production practices.[14]

Herein lies a lesson. Yields have fluctuated primarily because of unfavorable weather. But a further adverse factor has been the production practices imported from another environment in the process of settlement of the new lands, practices not adapted to the area's severe climatic conditions.[15] The experience of some farms and experiment stations suggests that variation of yields can be mitigated to a certain extent and their general level elevated by improved production methods.* Heading the list of major obstacles to higher and more stable yields is the virtual single crop system of spring wheat adopted in the new lands. In Tselinnyi Krai small grains, predominantly wheat, occupied 75 percent of the acreage in 1953 and over 80 percent in 1960.[16] The situation was well summed up by a manager and a chief agronomist of a sovkhoz which had 33,000 hectares of wheat and 3,500 in other crops. From the very beginning of its existence, according to them, the sovkhoz had been a single crop enterprise. "Everything stems from this—the exhaustion of the soil, its infestation by pernicious weeds, and the displacement of other very effective grains. If to this is added the fact that not until 1959 did 1,200 hectares of summer fallow appear within our arable tract of 43,000 hectares (2.8 percent), it will show how we have neglected our land." [17] Similar diagnoses were made by other scientists and specialists.[18]

It was, of course, realized by Soviet agronomists at the very outset of the virgin lands campaign that continuous cropping—planting mostly spring wheat year in and year out—would result in weed infestation and deterioration of the productivity of the land. A guide to farming in the new lands published by the Ministries of Agriculture and of State Farms in 1955 recommended introduction, after an unstated initial period following the plowing up of virgin land, of regular rotation of wheat and other small grains with row crops, principally corn and summer fallow, the latter particularly on weedy land.[19] But regular crop rotation or fallowing has been little practiced in the eastern new lands regions. As was stated by the sovkhoz officials quoted above: "Really there is still no

* Here are a few examples. In the Atbasarsk seed test plot referred to above, the yield of grain during eight years with below-normal precipitation was a respectable figure of 0.39 tons per acre (equivalent to 14.4 bushels of wheat to the acre). The grain yield of the Lenin sovkhoz was reported approximately 0.4 tons per acre (15 bushels of wheat) during the especially difficult year of 1963. The seed farm of the Karabalyk Agricultural Experiment Station obtained in that year 0.31 tons of grain per acre (over 11 bushels of wheat) and twice as much during the preceding year. (V. Savostin, "Urgent Problems of Virgin Land Agriculture," *Partiinaia zhizn'*, November 1963, no. 22, pp. 27–32.) The severe drought had its effect on these farms too but it was much less detrimental than on most others, some of which were lucky to recoup the seed used.

crop rotation on the majority of virgin lands farms. And where it was introduced a few years ago, it is disregarded every year because plans for growing this or that crop are made without considering the crop rotation schemes." [20] The latter complaint has been a recurrent theme for many years. The pressure to obtain as large an output as possible immediately (that is, during a current season) and to fulfill or overfulfill the obligations to the state militates against summer fallow and regular crop rotation, since the tendency is to plant every year every available acre to grain.

The value of summer fallow in the dry regions in theory, however, was not disputed until the emergence of a new school of agronomic thought. It was represented by the Director of the Altaisk Institute of Agricultural Research in western Siberia, G. Nalivaiko, who opposed the traditional school, led by Baraev, the Director of the All-Union Research Institute of Grain Farming. The Nalivaiko school minimized the use of summer fallow in favor of corn and pulses in rotation with small grains.[21] This view was highly palatable to Khrushchev since it lent support for his favorite crop—corn, which he strongly pushed in the new lands as elsewhere. That Nalivaiko and not his opponent was invited to address the Twenty-second Party Congress in October 1961 was symptomatic of his standing with Khrushchev. At a subsequent agricultural conference in Tselinograd in Kazakhstan, Khrushchev showed that he was impressed by Nalivaiko's claim of achieving greater production per unit of arable land with hardly any fallow, as compared with Baraev's institute which had one third of the arable land in summer fallow.[22] While Khrushchev indicated that further testing and verification of claims of the opposing schools was necessary, his negative attitude toward fallowing was apparent. This tilted the balance against it, making it a target for attack in the early 1960s.

The proponents of the practice claim that in the dry regions it raises yields not only during the year immediately following fallow, but also over a period of years, and thus in the long run pays for itself. Opponents of fallow like Nalivaiko, in order to maximize production, rely on rotation of small grains with other crops such as corn, peas, and beans, with differing moisture and nutrient requirements. Row crops like corn, which require cultivation, are particularly favored by this school as a means of weed control. The 1963 crop fiasco created a more favorable atmosphere for the proponents of summer fallow. Also experience in the dry regions of the United States and western Canada strongly supports fallowing, even allowing for the much greater availability there of herbicides to control weeds. In fact, the proportion of summer fallow in the U.S.-Canadian dry zone of 50 percent of the arable land is much higher than the 15 to 20 percent usually recommended by authorities in the Soviet

Union, with variations from 10 or 12 to 25 percent. Certainly data of experiment stations and farms in the new lands leave no doubt that introduction of summer fallow results in increased production which is cumulative over a period of years. It has not been as conclusively demonstrated that alternative methods of crop rotation, minimizing or eliminating summer fallow, would increase aggregate output or result in larger money returns.

But there could hardly be any question that some further diversification of the crop pattern would be useful. One crop which seems well adapted to the new lands is barley. It has a short growing season, responds well to late planting (allowing ample time for the elimination of weeds), and is more drought-resistant than wheat—a combination of desirable qualities which is rare. Barley yields are not greatly different and sometimes higher than those of wheat.[23] This grain is much better adapted to the climatic conditions of the region than corn and requires less labor, which is important in this sparsely settled territory. It is a source of groats for human consumption and a valuable animal feed, especially for hogs; thus it would help the planned development of livestock production in the new lands. Barley acreage in the region did in fact increase between 1961 and 1962. Thus the barley area in Tselinnyi Krai more than doubled then, from 1,337,000 acres to 3,202,000.[24] Another highly drought-resistant grain which could be grown as an insurance crop under the precarious conditions of the new lands is millet. The different response of millet and wheat to drought conditions can be gauged from the fact that wheat seed requires more than twice as large a proportion of water to weight for growth as millet (55 and 25 percent respectively).

Among other special production practices advocated by Soviet specialists to raise crop yields in the new lands, a new role is assigned to stubble mulching in preference to the usual moldboard plowing. This is a form of tillage in which the plant residue is retained on the surface of the soil, protecting it from wind erosion, including retention of snow cover that provides an important source of moisture for the crops. The adoption of stubble mulching, however, is handicapped by a shortage of special implements required for this purpose. Considerable importance is also attached by a number of Soviet specialists to a later planting of crops like spring wheat than is considered optimal in traditional agricultural regions where early planting is emphasized.[25] The reasons for delaying planting (usually to the second half of May) are to minimize the effect on crops of the frequent May-June droughts, to allow more time to destroy weeds, and to take advantage of the usually more abundant mid-summer precipitation. But the idea of delayed planting was once challenged by some other specialists, notably by Lysenko, who stressed the danger of early frosts to the late maturing crop. This dilemma might be resolved by the practice of planting on each farm not just one variety of, say, wheat but a combination of early and late maturing varieties, to spread the risk of damage. Though Khrushchev's fertilizer program was designed primarily for humid regions, it may eventually also benefit crop yields in the new lands by providing phosphates which are claimed to be needed.

The above criticism of production practices in the new lands and suggestions for improvement, emanating from Soviet specialists, are confirmed by firsthand observation of American agriculturalists who accompanied Secretary Freeman during his visit to the USSR in 1963.

> In general, we believe that insufficient attention has been given to crop practices in the new lands region to conserve moisture, control weeds, reduce erosion and lower production costs. It is perhaps of some interest to note that the estimated 1958–62 average USSR spring wheat yield of 10 bushels per acre is about the same as the U.S. average in the late 1930's. Yields of spring wheat were also highly variable in the United States during the 1930's, averaging only about 4½ bushels per planted acre in the 1934 and 1936 drought years. Yields of wheat in the four major spring wheat states of the United States now average over 18 bushels per seeded acre, due in large part to increased fallowing of wheat land and better seeding and tillage methods. At the same time, labor and machinery costs have been substantially reduced.
>
> Methods of accumulating and conserving moisture and reducing wind erosion are needed, particularly in the new lands wheat region. Such methods are not now practiced to any substantial extent. Extremely wide variations in yields are likely to continue in the new lands areas unless more emphasis is given to developing systems of farming that will conserve and accumulate moisture. Soil damage from wind erosion could become serious. The use of summer fallow would probably mean somewhat lower total wheat production. But, as in similar areas in the United States and Canada, use of summer fallow, stubble mulching, or other appropriate moisture-conserving methods would seem likely in many areas to increase substantially the stability and efficiency of wheat production as well as the yield per planted acre. Increased use of herbicides also would appear likely to increase yields and reduce costs.[26]

Despite the fact that the yields in the new lands were considerably below the original expectations and fluctuated more widely, the area became the most important source of grain to the government. Grain procurements in the new lands trebled between 1949–53 and 1958–62 (see Table 65). Their share of national procurements increased from 30 percent before the expansion, to 46–68 percent during the years 1954–62, with the exception of one year, 1955, when the proportion was slightly above 30 percent. Notwithstanding lower yields, a larger proportion of grain could be procured in these sparsely settled regions of predominantly huge state farms than in the older regions of dense peasant population, requiring larger quantities of grain for human consumption and animal feeding. The new lands thus accounted for most of the increment in the government procured grain and performed a kind of insurance function in some years when weather conditions in traditional regions were unfavorable and yields low. But it is a precarious insurance.

What about the cost of this expansion? The picture is obscure because of lack of adequate data. All that Khrushchev and the Soviet statistical handbooks disclosed was that investment in new lands during 1954–62 over and above "the usual capital investment in those regions" amounted to 6.7 billion rubles or about 30 percent of the additional state investment in agriculture as a whole during this period. In return the government obtained additional revenue of 9.7 billion rubles in turnover taxes and profits on the increment of marketable grain alone (134.4 million tons) compared with the 1949–53 average. Thus the state is said to have obtained 3 billion rubles of net income (*chistyi dokhod*) and 4.7 billion

Table 65. Procurements of all grains in new lands regions, and total for USSR (1,000 metric tons)

Year	Procurements in new lands regions	Total USSR procurements	Percent new lands are of total USSR
1949–53 average	9,905	32,769	30.2
1954	17,824	34,601	51.5
1955	11,276	36,902	30.6
1956	36,800	54,107	68.0
1957	17,058	35,411	48.2
1958	32,709	56,608	57.8
1959	27,942	46,637	59.9
1960	29,057	46,736	62.2
1961	23,784	52,109	45.6
1962	27,100	56,600	47.9

Source. For 1949–53, *Narodnoe khoziaistvo, 1960*, pp. 442–443; *1961*, p. 375; *1962*, p. 293.

rubles of additional assets in sovkhozes and other organizations (production funds), which must represent added value in farm buildings, machinery, livestock, and so forth.[27] Similar cumulative data are also available for earlier periods, making it possible to arrange the statistics partly on an annual basis, as in Table 66.

Table 66. Investment and returns from agricultural expansion in virgin lands (billion rubles)

Year	Additional investment	Turnover tax and profits	Net income	Assets of sovkhozes, and so forth
1954–58 average	0.6	0.98	0.38	0.5
1959	0.6	1.3	0.7	0.6
1960	0.7	1.4	0.7	0.5
1961	0.9	1.0	0.1	0.8
1962	1.4	1.1	−0.3	0.4

Sources. Adapted with slight modification from Keith Bush, *The Profitability of the Virgin Lands,* Radio Liberty Research Paper, no. 2, 1964, p. 3 (compiled from *Narodnoe khoziaistvo, 1959* and volumes of the same annual for 1960–62; and Khrushchev's speech reported in *Pravda,* December 10, 1963).

These figures pose a host of questions and reservations. Why are state earnings only from additional marketable grain given and not from the 8.1 million tons of meat (liveweight), 23.8 million tons of milk, and 565,000 tons of wool?[28] Why did the growth of assets through 1961 keep pace with additional investment, while in 1962 there was a discrepancy of one billion rubles (as indicated in Table 66)? * What is the precise meaning of "usual capital investment in these regions"; specifically, does this include kolkhoz investments? This is pertinent since prior to and even for several years after the expansion campaign began, the kolkhoz continued to be the dominant type of farm organization, but eventually most of them were transformed into state farms. In the Tselinnyi Krai, for instance, the number of kolkhozes decreased from 412 in 1960 to 107

* Keith Bush, who calls attention to this discrepancy, comments that "this may be due in part to the 1961 revision of the prices of trucks, agricultural machinery and spare parts." (*The Profitability of the Virgin Lands,* p. 3.) It is curious that the figure of a gain of 4.7 billion rubles in assets during 1954–62 was given by Khrushchev, but was omitted by the 1962 statistical handbook, though similar figures were cited in previous handbooks.

in 1961.[29] Were all items which should have been charged to capital and other costs actually so charged? Doubts about this are cast by a number of reports of heavy financial losses of sovkhozes in the new lands regions.[30] Were such losses, which the state must make good, deducted from the profits reported on procured grain? There is also something amiss in the accounting or reporting procedure which does not provide for gradual depreciation of capital but pits the cumulative figure of total investment for a period of years against profits. Finally, ample profits may be more an impressive manifestation of the Soviet government's taxation and monopolistic price fixing powers than conclusive evidence that the decision to invest such large resources in the marginal new lands was wiser than an alternative course of investing in traditional agricultural regions. Traditional regions certainly had in their favor better climatic conditions and a saving in the expenditures involved in long-distance transportation and the settlement of hundreds of thousands of new workers.

An element which must be reflected in the grain cost structure in the new lands is the extra effort required to dry and clean the grain because of high moisture content and other dockage. The moisture content is increased when the harvest is delayed and extended. In the sovkhoz Sverdlov in Kustanai province in Kazakhstan, for example, when grain was harvested for a period of forty days, deduction on delivery of substandard grain with high moisture content reached 25 percent. Because of such deductions the average 1959–1960 production cost of grain delivered by new lands sovkhozes was 15 percent above the farm cost.[31] Provision of increased facilities for drying and cleaning of grain to improve its quality would result, too, in additional capital and current expenditures. Additional cost is also involved in the two-stage harvest operation—first windrowing grain and letting it dry and then combining it. This method was introduced following a visit to the United States by a Soviet agricultural delegation in 1955, and is designed to speed up the harvest by making an earlier start possible.

Besides economic costs there were also large human costs involved in the uprooting of hundreds of thousands, mostly young, workers who were pressured or induced to migrate to the new lands regions to work on the farms. The great hardships experienced by these settlers, accustomed though they were to austerity, was decried in the Soviet press from time to time and even commented upon by Khrushchev. At a conference in Tselinograd in November 1961, more than seven years after the beginning of the virgin lands campaign, Khrushchev read a letter he received from three tractor drivers of a state farm in that area: [32] "Now it is winter outside; white snow covers the ground and the dormitory where we are placed is cold. The stove smokes but does not give any warmth; the walls are not plastered, the doors are broken. The food in the canteen does not taste good; even potatoes are seldom served. And this on virgin lands where, if properly farmed, high yields of potatoes and vegetables could be obtained. As to mass cultural activities on our state farm, the less said the better. In our unit on the farm, there is no radio or books, and we learn about what is going on in the wide world from newspapers which appear occasionally." The writers of the letter said that they wanted to remain in the sovkhoz as permanent workers. But the manager peremptorily discharged them, presumably at the end of the season, because they were unmarried. They said: "It is insulting to hear such words. We did not go to virgin lands like birds flying to warm regions when cold weather sets in. What if we are single, should the virgin lands be a stepmother to us?"

In attempting to pass an objective judgment on the new-lands program, one must steer between the Scylla of total pessimism, and the Charybdis of excessive optimism. The project was neither a total failure as some believe, nor the unqualified success asserted by Khrushchev. It was not something brand new, but an acceleration, in many respects a harmful acceleration, of a historic trend. And it suffered greatly from neglect of proper production practices.

In the long run, the crucial factor is the Soviet capability to improve yields in the traditional agricultural regions through the fertilizer program and other means of intensifying agriculture, and to reduce production costs. Success achieved by these programs may well lead to a retreat in the marginal new lands. It is significant that Khrushchev himself suggested such a possibility of reduced acreage at a meeting with U.S. Secretary of Agriculture Freeman, in the summer of 1963. Contraction of sown acreage would probably also occur if a marked increase in summer fallowing were to take place, unless it were offset by additional virgin land brought under cultivation. Thus signs point to contraction, or at least stability, rather than to expansion of the sown area in the new lands, but not necessarily to reduced production.

Restructuring of the Crop Pattern. A Shift to Corn

Shortly after the new lands program was started, a restructuring of the crop pattern in the traditional agricultural regions was initiated by Khrushchev. The two programs were interrelated phases of the campaign for the expansion of farm output; the increased bread grain acreage in the new lands supposedly facilitated a shift to feed crops in the traditional regions, which was at the root of the restructuring of the crop pattern. The raison d'être for this program was the need to bolster the lagging feed supply that was the bottleneck in the expansion of livestock production sought by Khrushchev. Hence the pivotal role was assigned by him to corn, an excellent feed grain. Prior to 1955 corn was a minor crop in the Soviet Union and its acreage was small compared to such feed grains as oats and barley. Climatic conditions did not favor its extension beyond a limited area in the southern part of the country. Sections of the Caucasus and of southern Ukraine, and especially what is known now as the Moldavian Republic (Bessarabia) were the principal growing regions. But nowhere was it a major crop, except in Moldavia and Georgia (Gruziia) in the Caucasus, where corn is the second most important crop in terms of acreage after winter wheat, and is an essential ingredient of the local diet.

The insignificant role of corn was one of the striking differences between the crop economy of the Soviet Union and that of the United States. The fact that the Soviet Union is located much farther north than the corn belt of the United States, with a consequent short growing season, goes far to explain this difference. Furthermore, the semiarid and dry zones, including much of the black soil (*chernozem*), marked by an annual precipitation of less than 16 inches, are also more extensive in the Soviet Union than in the United States. Thus, over a large area of the Soviet Union, it is either too cold or too dry for successful corn culture.

This does not mean, of course, that the corn acreage could not be increased on a limited scale. In fact, there has long existed a lively interest in corn among Soviet agronomists and in official circles. It has been highly regarded as a feed crop as well as for its ability to withstand the frequent late spring and early summer droughts. Nevertheless, corn acreage not only did not increase but even contracted during the years 1951–1953, when it was lower than it had been in a smaller territory in 1928. Early in 1955, however, Khrushchev, who had long been known as a corn enthusiast, proposed a large expansion of the corn area with a goal of not less than 70 million acres by 1960, as compared with 8.6 million acres in 1953 and 10.6 million in 1954. His proposal was approved by the Central Committee of the Communist Party on January 31, 1955.[33] Khrushchev, inspired by the corn growing experience of the United States, saw in a large expansion of this high-yielding crop a speedy method of increasing the feed supply. He recognized that in many regions of the country corn would not mature for climatic reasons, but he advocated harvesting it before maturity at the milk-wax stage and using it for silage. Khrushchev also recommended that the ears and the stalks be ensilaged separately. The preserved ears of corn (concentrates) were to be fed to the hogs and horses and the preserved stalks (roughage) were to be used for cows and sheep. In this manner, the unfavorable climatic environment for mature corn grain was to be bypassed and a rapid increase in the available supply of feed for livestock achieved. The Soviet corn expansion program, as conceived by Khrushchev, differs significantly from the United States pattern where corn is grown primarily for grain. In the Soviet program, silage plays a much more prominent role than in the United States.

Khrushchev was greatly impressed by the progress made in corn production in the United States as a result of the introduction of hybrid varieties, and urged that a similar step be taken in the Soviet Union. To be sure, in the United States hybrid corn required many years of research and development. Similar research began also in the Soviet Union with promising results, but, according to the testimony of Soviet scholars, it was interfered with in the early 1930s by the vehement opposition of Lysenko and his school.[34] Thus, when Soviet agriculture was confronted with a corn expansion program, it was without the benefit of hybrid varieties. Another significant factor which contributed to high corn yields in the United States—the increased use of mineral and chemical fertilizer—was originally not even mentioned by Khrushchev. Corn was to be one of the beneficiaries of the expanded and accelerated fertilizer program of December 1963, however. The whole program had the earmarks of a crash project, undertaken without adequate preparation in terms of research, equipment, proper seed varieties, and knowledge of cultural practices. It resembled the indiscriminate enthusiasm of Soviet officialdom during the Stalin era for perennial grasses, inspired by the teaching of Williams.

During the first year of the new program the corn area quadrupled, expanding from 10.6 million acres in 1954 to 44 million acres in 1955. The planting of corn under Khrushchev's relentless pressure became a kind of a test of the politico-agronomic reliability of farm managers and local agricultural officials. Corn was, therefore, introduced into regions where it had never been grown before and expanded throughout the USSR—from the Black Sea littoral quite far northward, and from the Baltic to the Pacific. The total corn area reached its peak in 1962 with more than 90 million acres and declined slightly in 1963 to 85 million acres. But of this huge total in 1962 and 1963 only 17 million acres were under corn for dry grain comparable to the great bulk of the United States production; the rest was immature corn used mainly for silage and green forage. Most of the corn for grain is grown in the Ukraine, North Caucasus, and Moldavia. It was relatively easy to expand by fiat the corn acreage, principally at the expense of rye, winter wheat (in the Ukraine), oats, grasses, and summer fallow. But the production results proved disappointing. Thus, according to Soviet statistics, which are considered inflated, the 1959–1962 average yield of corn for dry grain was about 32 bushels to the acre and the 1954–58 average, 25.6 bushels. Corn yields in the United States were considerably higher and steadily increasing, from 39.4 bushels in 1954 to 61.8 bushels in 1961—and these on a much larger acreage.*

The output of corn silage—a much more important component of the Soviet crop—increased sharply, from 43 million tons in 1955 to a peak of 206 million in 1960—declining to 190 and 195 million tons during the next two years. The low yield of 12 to 15 tons or less per hectare was often criticized by Khrushchev, but he became even more concerned about the poor feeding quality of the Soviet corn silage, which in many regions contained too small a proportion of ears. He said in 1962 with reference to Belorussian agriculture: "Some of our farms obtain a large volume of green mass [corn], incur considerable expenditures for its transportation, but obtain little feed because corn is harvested without ears. Corn silage without ears is an inferior feedstuff . . . You talk about the tons of harvested corn but actually you were harvesting water. If the cows could talk, they would have come to the meeting and told the kolkhoz chairman, the sovhoz director, the secretary of the party raikom: why are you talking about the tons of feed obtained; you did not procure feed but water. There seems to be a lot of tonnage but nothing to eat." [35] Khrushchev demanded that in a northern region like Belorussia more ears of corn be produced; but the feasibility of this is questionable for climatic reasons. The situation may be more favorable in the southern regions, climatically somewhat more suitable to corn culture. Yet it is probable that a large proportion of the corn silage is of inferior quality.

Another consideration relevant to the assessment of the Soviet corn program is that of competition with other crops. As was already noted, the expansion of corn acreage took place for the most part through displacement of a number of crops. This was justified where high corn yields could be obtained. But the reverse was often true; in many areas the crops displaced were better adapted to the local climate and soil conditions than corn and might be more responsive to improved cultural methods. While expressing dissatisfaction with the low yields obtained in many cases, Khrushchev continued to extol corn as the "queen of the fields," which responds with high yields to those who learn how to grow

---

* During the five years ending in 1961 the United States corn acreage harvested for grain fluctuated between 58.7 million acres and 72.1 million. Acreage for corn silage fluctuated between 6.1 million acres to 7.2 million. Green forage corn acreage (hogging down, grazing, and forage) fluctuated between 1.6 and 2.8 million acres.

it properly. However, he admitted a shortage of implements needed in corn growing. This increased the seasonal pressure on farm manpower and often resulted in protracting the corn harvest period, with consequent delay in subsequent preparation of the soil and sowing of winter grain or in fall plowing for planting next year's spring crops—in both cases affecting adversely the yields of the crops following corn. Without abandoning the idea of the great superiority of corn, Khrushchev conceded, as time went on, the desirability of growing other feed crops where high corn yields could not be obtained. Such a diversification of the feed supply appears logical and inevitable in a large country with diverse climatic and soil conditions. But again Khrushchev singled out some feed crops like sugar beets, grown especially for feed (a rather strange selection), and forage legumes, particularly peas, as worthy companions of corn. Peas are particularly in this class as a source of protein, which is deficient in the Soviet animal feed supply.

But these crops were not serious rivals of corn which Khrushchev succeeded in enthroning. The corn area, which in 1953 was somewhat lower than in 1940, rose rapidly until 1956. This was true of mature corn (dry grain) and even more so of immature corn used for silage and green fodder, which was not significant enough to be reported prior to 1955 (Table 67). A setback followed during the next three years, but an

Table 67. Soviet corn area by types, specified years (1,000 acres)

Year	Grain	Milk wax stage	Other	Total
1913	5,377			5,377
1940	9,000			9,000
1953	8,611			8,611
1954	10,608			10,608
1955	15,261	7,252	21,760	44,273
1956	16,318	6,649	36,166	59,133
1957	8,045	6,363	30,742	45,150
1958	10,877	9,224	28,639	48,740
1959	8,765	12,758	33,862	55,385
1960	12,567	15,204	41,824	69,595
1961	17,655	14,838	30,902	63,395
1962	17,309	17,732	56,729	91,770
1963	17,300	9,400	57,800	84,500

Source. *Narodnoe khoziaistvo SSSR, 1960,* and volumes of the same annual for 1961–63.

upward trend was resumed during 1960–63 when new records were set. The performance in terms of yields and production was less encouraging. If we omit the very poor year 1963 and use the official 1958–62 average yield per acre of dry grain, we come up with over 33 bushels of corn. But the official figures are considered overestimated; the more realistic U.S. Department of Agriculture estimate is only about 25 bushels to the acre. In the United States the corresponding figure was 58.4 bushels; in 1963 it was 67.6, and in 1964 it was 62.1 bushels. Soviet corn yields are half or less of United States yields on an area about one third as large.

A more pragmatic and realistic approach to the corn problem came in the wake of the crop failure in 1963. It may be best described in the words of Khrushchev himself at the December 1963 plenum: [36]

> It must be carefully considered what is more advantageous to grow for grain in the dry regions of the Ukraine and some other republics, winter wheat or corn. What should be the approach here, which crop should have priority? Of course the one which gives more grain with the smallest expenditure of labor. Under certain conditions when kolkhozes and sovkhozes obtained wheat yields of 15–20 centners per hectare, and corn 40–50 and even 60 centners per hectare, it was necessary to strive for expansion of the corn acreage. Today, however, when there are available wonderful varieties of wheat . . . the situation has changed. If corn yields 40 centners per hectare and the same quantity of wheat is gathered by a kolkhoz, it is clear that it is more advantageous to grow wheat . . . Some may wonder what happened, why does Khrushchev, who advocates so strongly the introduction of corn, sound today as if he were beginning to retreat? This is not the situation, comrades. We also stress today that corn is a powerful crop, capable under favorable conditions of giving the highest grain yields, the largest quantity of nutritive silage feed in many regions. However, we have not sworn eternal fealty to any one particular crop, we do not plan to worship it. Priority must be given to output. That crop which under conditions existing in a certain zone gives the highest yields, and greater returns for the labor input, should become the leading crop on a farm. (Prolonged applause.) One should not be afraid to change the crop structure and, if necessary, reduce corn acreage in the dry zone in favor of the high yielding varieties of wheat, barley, peas, and sorghum.

At the February 1964 plenum Khrushchev continued in the vein of new realism: "Increased intensiveness of animal husbandry is unthinkable without obtaining high yields of forage crops and particularly corn and sugar beets [grown specifically for feed]. But distortions must not be tolerated. Some farms plant a large area to corn but obtain very low yields. They are not prepared for planting large acreages to this crop and cannot properly grow it. However, some officials *sometimes force kolkhozes* [emphasis added] to plant corn which they cannot grow properly." The statement speaks for itself and fully justifies the serious misgivings of some Western observers at the outset of the corn campaign.[37] The only further comment needed is to call attention to the fact that Khrushchev was washing his hands of the responsibility for forced planting of corn; and at the same time he blamed subordinate officials for Stalin's similar action regarding the excesses of forced collectivization in March 1930. Following Khrushchev's lead, others began to voice publicly their pent-up doubts and criticisms of the corn mania. One economist, for example, wrote: "The basic fault in planning corn production in a number of oblasts and raions was that their natural and economic conditions which exerted a decisive influence on the yields of this crop were not taken into account. For example, the proportion of corn in the grain acreage of the kolkhozes and sovkhozes of the Krasnodar and Stavropol provinces was approximately the same in raions where the yield was 30 to 40 centners per hectare as in those where it did not exceed 10 to 15 centners per hectare over a period of years. This caused serious economic losses to kolkhozes and sovkhozes." [38]

Toward the end of his regime Khrushchev gave yet another twist to his predilection for corn by associating it with a revived interest in irrigation following the 1963 drought. He concentrated on extolling the high yields of corn grown under irrigation. The removal of Khrushchev signaled the end of corn hegemony. But it is doubtful that the corn area will again shrink to the pre-Khrushchev level now that the Soviet farmers have acquired more know-how, the supply of fertilizer is increasing, and the removal of Lysenko opens new vistas in crop research and development of improved varieties.

The expansion of corn—the first and most important step in the restructuring of the corn pattern in the traditional regions toward a more intensive agriculture—involved displacement of certain crops. What were these crops and how reasonable was their displacement? The bread grain area (winter wheat and rye) was reduced in some important regions while spring wheat was expanded on the new lands. In the Ukraine the winter wheat acreage decreased from 22.3 million acres in 1953 to 17.1 million in 1961; in the North Caucasus winter wheat decreased from a high of 12.5 million acres in 1958 to 11.6 million in 1961. Winter wheat in these regions is much higher yielding than the spring wheat grown in the east. Rye, a sturdy winter grain, is a good insurance crop to fall back upon in years of generally poor harvests. But the rye area was reduced between 1953 and 1963 by one fourth, from 50 million acres to 37 million. The heavy risk incurred in drastically reducing the acreage under high-yielding winter wheat and so steady a crop as rye was fully revealed by the 1963 crop failure, which necessitated huge imports of grain in addition to restrictive domestic measures. The 1963–64 grain deficit would have been smaller if a larger acreage were devoted to bread grains in regions of high yields; making full use of such regions would have made it possible to build up over a period of years larger stocks for emergencies. Greater recognition of the importance of winter grains was shown during Khrushchev's last year in power and under his successor.[39]

Oats was another important grain downgraded in the course of the corn campaign and the restructuring of the crop pattern. By 1963 its acreage was reduced to only a little over one third of that ten years earlier. Khrushchev complained about the low yields of oats, but this was primarily the result of inadequate fertilization and other cultural methods. Oats actually is more suitable to the poor soils of the northern and central regions—where it is mostly grown—than many other crops, and certainly more suitable than corn.* Moreover, in the United States and in such a northern country as Sweden improvement in varieties of oats resulted in an upward trend in yields; this improvement should be possible in the Soviet Union too. An authoritative study published in 1959 by the Academy of Sciences of the USSR recommended increasing the oats acreage by 45–50 percent in RSFSR, 50–60 percent in Belorussia, and 2 to 2½ times in the Baltic republics to boost the animal feed supply.[40] In the Ukraine, only in the steppe and wooded steppe zones, where little oats is grown anyway, was some reduction recommended; expansion was suggested in the forest zone, with its podzolic soil.

The other traditional Russian feed grain, barley, fared better during the restructuring of the crop pattern. It is true that barley acreage for a number of years had been declining—28 million acres in 1940, compared to 24 million in 1953 and about the same in 1958. But by 1963, it had reached a high of over 50 million acres. We know that expansion in the new lands helped to boost this crop and its future seems to be secure.

Khrushchev's strongest campaign was directed against perennial grasses of the Williams system which he wished largely to replace by corn. His strictures against perennial grasses were originally limited to the dry regions. He said in 1954: "Clover, for instance, brings high yields of hay

* "It is generally known that on the strongly podzolized soils oats grow better than other grain crops" (P. M. Zemskii, *Razvitie i razmeshchenie zemledeliia*, Moscow, 1959, p. 115).

in the humid, non–black soil zone. Therefore it is necessary to encourage the growing of clover. It is necessary also to pay attention to alfalfa in those regions where the kolkhozes and sovkhozes obtain high yields of this crop." [41] Khrushchev then objected to the purely mechanical use of the Williams doctrine in all regions of the country. But by 1961 this important geographical distinction was forgotten, and perennial grasses and the Williams system became enemy number one, to be fought relentlessly wherever found.

Though there was a valid case against expansion of grasses in the dry regions, it did not hold in the humid regions. On the contrary, the introduction of a perennial grass like clover was historically a progressive step in twentieth century Russia as it was a century earlier in western Europe. It not only helped to increase the feed supply but to raise crop yields and production by breaking up the traditional three-field system and by increased fertilization. The fertilizing mission of clover is twofold: it enriches the soil with nitrogen fixed from the air and increases the quantity and improves the quality of manure by providing a good supply of hay for livestock.[42] This is particularly true when the crop area encroaches on hay land and pasture, as is the case in a number of regions of the USSR, and when an adequate supply of mineral fertilizer is unavailable. But Khrushchev, who presumably was well aware of these advantages, was willing to brush them aside in his wager on corn.

Khrushchev was not the first to criticize the Williams grass system. A strong warning against the dangers and fallacies of its indiscriminate application was early signaled by a venerable leader of Russian agronomic science, D. N. Prianishnikov, whose writings were often cited by Khrushchev.[43] Prianishnikov objected to a preponderance of grasses in every kind of rotation, as advocated by Williams, and to the inevitable reduction of the grain acreage, which later was also stressed by Khrushchev. Yet the anti-clover tendencies which became prominent during the late Khrushchev era, when all grasses came under a cloud,* were alien to Prianishnikov. On the contrary, he was anxious to increase the proportion of clover and other legumes in the acreage because of their important fertilizing function. More than a decade after Prianishnikov's 1937 attack, Williams' agronomic ideas were posthumously subjected to a critique in the pages of *Pravda* by no other than Lysenko.[44] Lysenko complained that inferior grass crops, which are common, did not have

---

* A vivid confirmation of this situation was supplied by an article of a kolkhoz manager from Kirov province who recalled how at one time clover plantings were hidden from well-traveled roads. For "who would want to be known as a malicious *travopol'-shchik* [an adherent of the grass system]?" asked the writer. (P. A. Prozorov, *Sel'skaia zhizn'*, December 9, 1964.)

the expected beneficial effect on soil and the yields of succeeding crops. At the same time, poor grass crops reduce agricultural output when grass is introduced at the expense of other crops. Especially harmful, from the economic standpoint, according to Lysenko, is the competition of low-yielding grass with the usually high-yielding winter wheat in regions where climatic conditions make its cultivation advantageous. This competition results from the insistence of Williams and his supporters that the land under perennial grasses be plowed only in the fall, when it is already too late to plant winter crops. Ironically enough, Lysenko, who did so much to stifle scientific criticism, chided Soviet research workers and agronomists for rigid, uncritical adherence to the Williams doctrines without taking into consideration various modifying circumstances.

Though public criticism of the Williams grass system antedated the Khrushchev regime, it was greatly intensified then. Yet despite Khrushchev's fulminations, perennial grasses gave way slowly. In 1953 their area was about 42 million acres, or more than a third above 1940; by 1958 it declined to around 35 million acres; but during the next three years it skyrocketed to a new high of nearly 48 million. By 1963 it dropped to less than 34 million acres, no doubt reflecting Khrushchev's continuous blasting. Since his departure, expansion of the area under perennial grasses in the humid northern and central regions seems to be again in the cards.

Khrushchev waged a long fight against another important element of the cropping system: summer fallow. The problem of summer fallow in the humid zone differs from that in the dry zone, which was discussed in the section on new lands: in the humid northern and central regions summer fallow is not needed to preserve and augment moisture supply in the soil. Here it is a survival of the three-field system. Khrushchev pointed out that its Russian name, *chistyi par* (literally "clean fallow"), is a misnomer. For more often than not the fallow actually becomes overgrown with vegetation and is used as pasture for livestock, which is contrary to all agronomic precepts. While Khrushchev's negative or ambivalent attitude on summer fallow in the dry regions was questionable, he was on sure ground in demanding a more productive utilization of land in humid regions by replacing fallow with suitable crops. Here Khrushchev's case becomes even stronger in view of the large area involved, 73 million acres in summer fallow in 1953. This area decreased to 59 million acres by 1958 and plummeted to 15.6 million by 1963.[45]

The extent of the reduction of summer fallow for different regions is indicated by its proportion in the total arable area (*pashnia*). In Belorussia it was 14.6 percent of the total in 1953 and 2.8 percent in 1961. Similar percentage figures for Lithuania were 13.9 and 4.7; for Latvia, 7.5

and 1.0; for the northwestern region, 15.3 and 4.3; and for the north central region, 7.7 and 3.4.[46] All these regions are in the humid zone. What mars this success is the decrease in the proportion of summer fallow in some of the dry regions like western Siberia, where it declined from 17.3 percent in 1953 to 0.8 in 1962; or the Volga region, with a decline from 18.5 to 2.5 percent in the same period.[47] Another qualification regarding Khrushchev's successful anti-fallow campaign in the humid zone is that the conversion of fallow to crops was not always economically effective because of a lack of resources to carry out the operation properly. In some instances crops were seeded on land which previously would have been used for fallow, but then were so poorly tended and harvested so late because of shortages of labor and machinery that the yields were meager. This is a common aspect of a rather general disparity observed also in the case of corn between the quick-paced drive for increased intensiveness of agriculture and the inadequacy of capital and labor inputs and managerial structure.

The restructuring of the crop pattern involved a sharp increase in the area under pulses (*zernobobovye*), principally field peas, largely as a result of de-emphasis on corn during the last years of Khrushchev's regime and a greater recognition of the desirability of a diversified feed supply. In the case of pulses there is the added advantage of a feedstuff which would help to overcome the protein deficiency. The area of pulses in 1953 was considerably smaller than in 1940, about 6 million and 8.6 million acres respectively; by 1958 it decreased to about 5 million acres but had risen to 26.7 million acres in 1963. Peas alone increased from 2.2 million acres in 1958 to 19.3 million in 1963. The yields of pulses, though officially reported as rising, were rather low. The highest yield before the 1963 crop failure was 12.2 centners per hectare, or 1,080 pounds per acre in 1962. Even if no downward adjustment is made in this official figure, as is usually done with other grain figures, it is considerably lower than the United States yields of dry field peas (cleaned), which amounted to 1,404 and 1,492 pounds per acre during 1962–63 and 1,548 pounds per acre in 1964.

What was the impact of Khrushchev's policy on the group of crops known as technical or industrial? Such major Soviet crops as cotton, sugar beets, sunflower seed, flax for fiber, hemp, and tobacco come under this category. Included also are a number of minor oilseed crops: flax grown for seed (*kudriash*), mustard seed, soy beans (limited to the far eastern territory), and others. These are highly valuable crops, occupying a relatively small acreage requiring large inputs of labor or capital, and are considered significant indicators of the degree of intensiveness of a country's agriculture. A considerable increase in the area under technical crops took place during the interwar period and was publicized by the Soviets with much pride. The recovery of these crops after the drastic decline of World War II was uneven. The acreages of sugar beets, sunflower seed, and yellow tobacco in 1953 were above 1940, while flax for fiber, hemp, and makhorka (a low-grade tobacco) were down. The cotton acreage in 1953 was considerably below 1940 because the unproductive acreage in the southern European part of the USSR had been abandoned. Judging from the relatively modest increase in procurement prices since 1953, technical crops were not as badly underpriced by the Stalin regime as grains and livestock products. Khrushchev's policy was to continue and accelerate the expansion of technical crops. Expansion continued through 1956; a decline in the area of oilseed crops brought down the 1957 aggregate area under technical crops, but in 1958 the upward trend was resumed. By 1963 this area reached 37 million acres, more than three times as large as in 1953; but it constituted only 6.6 percent of the total arable area compared to 6.1 percent in 1953, and 6.6 percent also in 1940. These ratios indicate that technical crops did just a little better than hold their own in the great expansion of sown area beginning in 1953.

This category of crops was favored by the government in the allocation of fertilizers, other agricultural chemicals, and irrigation facilities. This was true particularly of cotton and sugar beets grown for sugar, which received the lion's share of mineral fertilizer. In 1962 cotton occupied nearly 5.9 million acres of the more than 19 million acres of irrigated land; * but only a small area of sugar beets, 287,000 acres out of a total of 7.8 million, was grown under irrigation. Mechanization, however, was less adequate. Mechanized loading of beets shipped from the fields, for instance, accounted for only 39 percent of the crop; [48] mechanized cotton picking began to make strides only in 1964.

The level of yields, which is a true index of intensiveness, has been rather low for a number of these crops. Official figures indicate an in-

---

* Cotton is the only major Soviet crop grown entirely under irrigation in the Central Asiatic republics, mainly in the Uzbek republic and to a lesser extent in the Transcaucasus. In the 1930s the government decided to extend the cotton area west and north into southern European USSR. This acreage was wiped out during the German invasion, restored in the early 1950s, but abandoned in 1954. The new regions in the Ukraine, Crimea, North Caucasus, and lower Volga proved to be climatically unsuitable for cotton: the growing season is too short and the temperatures not high enough for maturing of the crop. The yields were low, the quality inferior (a considerable proportion was of the immature bollie kind), and the cost was high. Here is another example, antedating the Khrushchev period, of flouting climatic limitations. When I questioned Academician Vavilov during one of his visits to the United States in the 1930s about this cotton shift, the answer elicited was that it is a matter of *valiuta* (foreign exchange). The Soviet manufacturing industry relied heavily on foreign, mainly American cotton until it became largely self-sufficient in the 1930s.

crease in the average yield of sugar beets per acre from 6 metric tons during 1949–53 to 7 tons during 1954–58, but a decrease to 6.6 tons during 1959–62.[49] The average 1958–62 yield in the nonirrigated regions of the United States was between 13 and 17.5 metric tons to the acre, or more than double the Soviet yields. A substantial increase took place in the Russian yield of cotton from an average of 463 pounds of ginned cotton during 1949–53 to 595 pounds during 1954–58.* But after reaching a record yield of 653 pounds in 1959, it declined during the three successive years and only in 1963 had risen to 639 pounds.[50] Even these high yields are considerably below the 1000–1100 or more pounds obtained in the irrigated regions of the United States. An exception to the procession of low-yielding crops is sunflower, the principal Russian oilseed crop. A distinctly higher level of yields prevailed in the late 1950s and early 1960s than during previous years, chiefly as a result of the development and introduction of improved varieties with a considerably higher oil content. (This development represents primarily the work of the plant breeder Pustovoit and the Institute of Oilbearing Crops in Krasnodar with which he was connected.)

By 1964 the Soviets admitted to disappointment in the restructuring of the crop pattern because of the continued low yields. Even Khrushchev recognized toward the end that all was not well with corn, and this time it was not the fault of the farmer. The specific causes of the fiasco began to be publicly explained. An article in a scholarly economic monthly now dared to raise the issue of climatic limitations: "Considerable areas were planted to row crops in the southern regions suffering from insufficient moisture, and in the northern and eastern regions which have a short growing season and lack proper temperature conditions." [51] The author pointed out that despite the sensitivity of corn and sugar beets for feed to the quality of the soil and their responsiveness to fertilizers, the larger part of the increased acreages under these crops was on poor land and lacked adequate fertilization. He cited similar deficiencies in a number of other inputs. This brings us to the curx of the matter. Increased agricultural intensiveness for which the Khrushchev regime was striving involved two correlative facets: returns and inputs. The returns are in the form of higher crop yields per unit of land, a larger output of livestock products per animal, and greater output per worker or unit of invested capital. The Khrushchev administration had repeatedly demanded such gains; but it greatly neglected and underemphasized the need to provide larger, often technically different and more expensive, inputs. This dichotomy in the

---

* Soviet cotton statistics, unlike those in the United States, report only unginned or seed cotton. The proportion of ginned in the seed cotton is approximately one third, and the ratio used for conversion is 34 percent.

regime's conduct helped to torpedo the basic objective of Khrushchev's policy.

The Livestock Problem

The effort to expand grain production, to restructure the crop pattern, was intimately linked with the livestock problem, which has long been of great concern to the Soviet regime. A very considerable increase in the output of animal products and reduction of the excessive production costs is essential if the Russian diet is to be improved and the heavy predominance of starches reduced. Khrushchev made this general goal more explicit—and by the same token more difficult to attain—by his 1957 slogan of catching up by 1960 with the United States, which had a considerably higher per capita production of animal products. This goal required greatly increased supplies of feed grains (concentrates), especially since animal feedstuffs are not utilized efficiently in the USSR, and the severe climate and shortage of grazing land in many important agricultural regions like the Ukraine, or central black soil area, impose a long stall-feeding period.

Just as there are two parallel roads for expansion of crop production—increased acreage and yield per acre—so there are two avenues for expansion of livestock production: increased number of animals and greater production per animal. The USSR took the first and the easier of these two roads both in crops and in livestock expansion. An increase in livestock numbers seemed the more essential because the recurrent crises since World War I—the period of War Communism and the famine of the early 1920s, collectivization in the early 1930s, and World War II—brought in their wake heavy liquidation of livestock. Each period of liquidation was followed by building up of livestock numbers, but according to Soviet statisticians there were fewer cattle on January 1, 1954, than in 1916 and in 1929, before collectivization. The number of hogs and sheep in 1954, on the other hand, were at record levels. During the ensuing decade, cattle as well as other livestock numbers trended steadily upwards, with heavy gains in the socialist sector. But there was less improvement in meat and milk outputs, and the Soviet government on numerous occasions acknowledged the inadequate supply of these products in the face of the growing demand. Shortages in the cities were indicated from time to time in the early 1960s. The gap between the volume of livestock production in the United States and in the Soviet Union remained large, especially in meat production, despite Khrushchev's crusade. Soviet per capita meat and egg production in the early 1960s was less than 40 percent and that of milk about 75 percent of the output in the United States.[52]

The Kremlin made a fetish of large livestock numbers. A great many poorly fed cattle, with low milk and meat yields, were held on farms long after their useful lifespan and without sufficient regard to feed supply limitations. Large delivery quotas in terms of meat, which made heavy inroads on the herds of underweight cattle, further aggravated the situation. The most remarkable case was that of hogs. The total number of hogs increased from 23.3 million at the beginning of 1954 to 66.7 million in 1962, exceeding by 9.7 million the hog population of the United States. Yet Soviet pork production was only a little more than half that in the United States, and did not increase substantially, according to Soviet data, between 1957 and 1961.[53] In 1962 and 1963 pork production increased substantially because of higher prices and distress slaughter due to feed shortages.

Some light was thrown on the situation by Khrushchev with data on low feeding efficiency. He pointed out that while it takes five to six months to fatten hogs to the weight of 100 kilograms on American farms, it requires a year or even more to do so in the Soviet Union. In the United States 15 centners of pork per sow is produced during a year, compared to 4 centners in the Soviet Union. In the United States 200 eggs are obtained per hen and only 90 in the Soviet Union. Khrushchev declared that: "One can cite a number of other facts indicating that livestock production is carried out irrationally on a large number of our farms. We are fattening livestock for longer periods but do not get additional meat. An extra large amount of feed is used and labor and other expenditures are increased. As a result, production becomes more expensive and losses are incurred . . . Collective and state farms produce a small volume of animal products because on the one hand they do not have enough feed and, on the other hand, because the feed which they do possess is not used rationally." [54] There is a close relation between the low feeding efficiency pointed out by Khrushchev and shortages of feed. When the amount of feed is inadequate it merely keeps the animals alive, with little gain in weight and low milk production. This tends to prolong the unproductive feeding period for meat animals and increases the actual expenditure of feedstuffs. A relatively small increase of feed over the minimum would repay in a more than proportionately larger output. Another unfavorable aspect of the feed supply is its high seasonality. It was described as follows by a Soviet animal husbandry specialist: "It is assumed that meat and milk are produced mainly during the summer when the kolkhozes and the sovkhozes are really concerned with the fattening of livestock, are striving for a high milk output. In the winter, however, some farms are solely preoccupied with the problem of saving the herd, just to tide it over until grass appears." [55]

United States Department of Agriculture specialists found

> that livestock production in the USSR is relatively high-cost and inefficient. Particularly striking to the U.S. visitor is the large amount of labor involved in livestock production. This is due in part to their system of livestock production. On the state and collective farms visited most of the cattle are stall-fed throughout the year. Green feed, roots, tubers, and silage are fed. Feeding and cleaning of stalls usually is done by hand.
>
> On most of the farms visited—all of them probably considerably better than average—at least some of the cows are hand-milked. Even where milking machines are used, labor requirements remain high because of the labor required for other activities, such as feeding and caring for the cows and producing feed. Large quantities of green fodder are fed, adding greatly to labor needed in milk production.
>
> The heavy dependence on green fodder, silage, and root crops presents special problems in the attempt to achieve a rapid increase in livestock efficiency, because of large labor requirements and low levels of milk and meat production per animal.[56]

The extremely high cost of livestock products in the USSR is confirmed by the high ratios of their production costs to the procurement prices of feed grain per metric quintal in kolkhozes and sovkhozes, computed by Jasny and compared by him to similar ratios of livestock and corn prices in the United States.[57] (The ratios for the USSR are for 1958, and for the United States for the average of 1956–60. Higher ratios for sovkhozes were due to lower procurement prices paid by the government for the grain.)

	Kolkhozes	Sovkhozes	United States
Pigs	26	28.8	8.2
Cattle	18.6	23.0	9.7
Poultry	25.7	41.0	6.9
Milk	3.1	3.5	1.9

A similar conclusion emerges from Jasny's calculation of actual prices of feed grains and animal products in the USSR and some Western countries (See Table 68).

Procurement prices in 1962 did not cover the high production costs of livestock products. In 1960 average procurement prices (per quintal)

Table 68. Prices of feed grain and animal products, selected countries (per quintal) [a]

Country	Feed grains [b]	Pigs	Cattle	Poultry	Milk	Eggs
USSR						
kolkhozes	5.0	130.2	93.2	128.4	12.6	160.0
sovkhozes	3.5	100.7	80.6	143.6	12.4	102.0
United States	4.4	35.8	42.8	29.4 [c]	9.3	54.3
England and Wales	6.6	—	44.0	—	9.44	78.3
Netherlands	6.6	45.5	45.2	—	7.75	54.4
Denmark	6.7	—	32.8 [d]	—	5.42	48.5
West Germany	8.9	60.1	53.3	59.0	8.26	72.2

[a] For the USSR, mostly 1958 production costs in new rubles. For Western countries, dollar prices of 1956–60.

[b] All feed grains for the USSR, mostly maize for the other countries.

[c] Chickens.

[d] Young cows, first class, Copenhagen.

Source. Naum Jasny, "The Failure of the Soviet Animal Industry," *Soviet Studies,* 15: 207 (October 1963).

were below production costs: for milk, 14 percent below; cattle, 35 percent below; pigs, 33 percent; sheep, 2 percent; and eggs (price per thousand), 35 percent. Only for wool did the procurement price exceed production costs by 43 percent.[58] But these were averages for the country as a whole; actually in many kolkhozes the disparity in the price-cost structure were greater. On June 1, 1962, the government raised the procurement prices of livestock on the average by 35 percent. The procurement prices of cattle were raised by 41.9 percent, hogs by 28.7 percent, sheep by 15 percent, and poultry by 52.3 percent. For milk and eggs the seasonal lowering of prices in the summer was abandoned. Retail prices to consumers were raised correspondingly. These measures were expected to stimulate production. Though highly unpopular with consumers, to the point of rebellion in some places, the price increases were beneficial to the industry. Yet some kolkhozes still felt the price-cost squeeze.

In 1963–64 a new disaster befell the livestock industry when, as a result of the crop failure and an exceedingly short feed supply, heavy liquidation of pigs took place. The pig population plunged from the record figure of nearly 70 million in January 1963 to 40.7 million at the beginning of 1964; thus the steady increase since 1957 was wiped out in one year. The reduction between 1963 and 1964 was not as large in other livestock. Total cattle numbers decreased from 87 million to 85.4 million, but the reduction was in the young cattle population; the number of cows actually increased slightly, from 38 million to 38.3 million, as every effort was made to maintain the herd. Sheep and goats decreased at a higher rate than cattle but much less than pigs, from 146.4 million to 139.5 million. Recovery in the livestock industry ensued with a better harvest in 1964. By the beginning of 1965 the small loss of total cattle population was recouped, and the number of cows increased by 400,000, to 38.7 million; pigs increased to 52.8 million, which was still 17.2 million below 1963. Sheep and goats, however, continued to decline to a low of 130.6 million. This was probably a consequence of poor pasture and range conditions and the severe shortage of feed during the early months of 1964, which could not be offset during the latter part of the year.

Privately owned sheep and goats decreased at a higher rate, 14 percent between 1963 and 1965, compared with 10 percent for the socialist sector. The situation was diametrically opposite in the case of pigs, which declined between 1963 and 1964 in the private sector by 19 percent and in the socialist sector by 49 percent. Total cattle and cow herds were quite stable in both sectors. On the whole the private sector held out better than the socialist under the trying conditions of 1963, paricularly when allowance is made for the difference in government policy toward the two sectors. It should cause no surprise that, emulating their predecessors during previous livestock crises, Khrushchev's successors ordered the abandonment of the restrictionist policy toward the private sector pursued between 1956 and 1964. Prime Minister A. N. Kosygin formulated the new line as follows: "Attaching paramount importance to the development of socialized production in sovkhozes and kolkhozes, the party and the government at the same time deemed it necessary to lift the unreasonable and groundless restrictions on personal farming of the kolkhozniks, workers and salaried employees, to abolish the tax on persons possessing livestock within established norms, and to sell concentrates to [private] owners of livestock." [59] It is important to note that Kosygin, in announcing a more liberal policy toward private animal husbandry, reaffirmed the priority of the socialist sector, just as Khrushchev did on a similar occasion a decade earlier. The livestock problem, which seemed to Khrushchev so near to solution in 1957–58, was still bedeviling his successors in the mid-1960s. Meat production, which reached a record figure in 1963 because of distress slaughter and higher procurement prices, declined 20 percent in 1964, wiping out all gains made since 1958 when Khrushchev so confidently looked forward to catching up shortly with per capita consumption of the United States.

That the feed supply and its efficient utilization constitute the key underpinning of a growing livestock industry has been well recognized. There also seems to be a growing awareness in Soviet official circles of the corollary that extending livestock numbers without securing an adequate feed supply does not pay. Through the feed base the livestock problem is intimately bound with the solution of the grain problem which proved far more difficult than expected by the Kremlin in mid-1950. But grain, though a large part of the story, is not the whole story. There are other important feed crops like oilcake and potatoes. Oilcake production greatly increased judging from the fact that the factory output of vegetable oils nearly doubled between 1953 and 1963, amounting to 1,160,000 tons and 2,211,000 tons respectively.[60] Potatoes were deemphasized by Khrushchev as a feedstuff. Yet a large proportion was used for feed—39 percent in 1958–61 according to one source,[61] though not as large as in some western European countries.*

Toward the end of Khrushchev's regime greater interest was displayed in pastures and natural meadows as an important source of forage, especially in the northern and central parts of the country. Reports from various regions complained of the neglect and deterioration of such land, which was subject to swamping and was often overgrown with bushes and noxious weeds. The productivity of pastures and natural meadows was decreasing, said an editorial in *Sel'skaia zhizn'* of March 3, 1965. The output of hay from natural meadows, according to this source, was 40 percent less in 1964 than in 1940. This situation placed a heavier load on the sown area for animal feed. Soviet officials and specialists urged, and not for the first time, the improvement of pastures and natural meadows and greater mechanization to augment the quantity and quality of inexpensive green fodder and storable hay. This concern is understandable because roughage is of much greater importance in the Soviet feed supply than in that of the United States and will apparently continue to be so in the foreseeable future.[62]

While feed is the major limiting factor in the expansion of livestock output, it does not eclipse other aspects of management and operation. Foremost among these are: adequate economic incentives to workers, increasing mechanization and electrification, and specialization of farms.

---

* A disturbing fact is the downward trend in potato acreage since it reached a peak in 1957. It was stated that "due to low yields and an insufficient level of mechanization, growing of potatoes especially for feed is in many cases unprofitable." (S. A. Il'in, *Ekonomika proizvodstva kartofelia*, p. 13.) The author then proceeds to a disparaging comparison of potatoes with sugar beets as a feedstuff, which sounds like an echo of Khrushchev, the more so that in a footnote on the same page data are given on the importance of potatoes in the intensive feeding of pigs in various countries.

Specialization involves concentration on a particular type of livestock or poultry operation, as in the United States, instead of the Soviet pattern of scattering resources and raising animals of every kind irrespective of the diverse natural and economic conditions prevailing on different farms. A significant aspect of specialization in animal husbandry in the West is in dairy and beef cattle, while in the Soviet Union dual-purpose cattle predominate. Nonspecialized cattle was favored by Khrushchev as more economical under Russian conditions, and in the short run he was probably right for certain regions. But some Soviet specialists whom I met were convinced that greatly increased productivity of animals cannot be attained without such specialization.

This brings us to a more general problem of improvement of breeds as a means of increasing the productivity of animals. It is the consensus of American specialists that the Soviet breeding program, by scattering in many directions, did not get very far by the early 1960s, despite the possession of such a powerful technique as artificial insemination in which the Russians had done pioneer work. It is also essential for the success of an improved breeding program that the more productive animals, usually also the more demanding, be ensured an adequate and steady feed supply, free from sharp seasonal fluctuations characteristic of the USSR. Even granting higher feeding efficiency of improved breeds, that is, a lower amount of feed per unit of output, a better quality of feed would be needed. Thus the use of protein additives, vitamin and mineral supplements and processed mixed feeds, which are still in their infancy in the USSR, would acquire far greater importance with improved breeds than with the less demanding nondescript livestock population. Thus the analysis of the Soviet livestock problem highlights the fact that if not all roads lead to the feed supply, certainly most of them do.

20

State Farms

Two organizational forms have long characterized Russian agriculture. In the prerevolutionary period they were peasant farming and the estates; in the Soviet period and especially since collectivization they have been the collective farm or kolkhoz and the state farm or sovkhoz. Just as peasant farming served as a basis for the organization of kolkhozes, so the estates served as prototypes for the state farms. Many of the sovkhozes in the European part of the country were in fact organized on former estates, as I had occasion to note during my visits to the Russian countryside. Both the kolkhoz and the sovkhoz are officially regarded as socialist forms of organization but the sovkhoz is considered the more socialized of the two and therefore ideologically superior. The formal distinction between the collective and state farm is that between a supposedly cooperative type of organization and one owned and managed outright by the state; or, in Soviet terminology, between a kolkhoz-cooperative and an "all peoples" or national form of property. In practice this differentiation is so greatly diluted by the pervasive control of the state that it hardly exists. It is true that sovkhozes, just as factories in the Soviet Union, follow the classical model of "post office socialism": complete ownership and management by the state, which provides the necessary capital, hires labor and technical and managerial personnel, is responsible for the wage bill, and wields monopolistic control in the disposal of output. On the other hand, each kolkhoz, however great the subordination to the state, is responsible for its own wage bill and current expenses, and to a large extent for its own investment, depending upon its income. It also has a limited control over the disposal of its output, a part of which it may distribute to its members in payment for their work or sell on the free market—something a sovkhoz cannot do legally.

After the unsuccessful collectivist experiment of War Communism, state farming played a very modest role during the NEP period. An exception was sugar-beet growing where state farms continued the tradition of the former private estates as suppliers of raw material for the sugar industry. The first great spurt in the development of state farming took place during the grain and livestock crises of the late 1920s and early 1930s, when intensive collectivization of Russian agriculture and the sharpening of the conflict with the peasantry began. This was the time when huge mechanized grain and livestock state farms were organized. They were to utilize, in accordance with the Marxist dogma and the American experience, advantages of large scale mechanized farming, and to secure the food supply of the "socialist" industrial sector. The experience of the first great expansion of state farming in the 1930s was decidedly not a happy one for the Soviet rulers. Instead of showing an example of efficient management to the kolkhozes, the sovkhozes manifested the same evils—but often in an exaggerated form—that were characteristic of kolkhoz farming: delayed and protracted field work, weeds, and huge crop losses.

At the Seventeenth Party Congress in January 1934 Stalin pointed out "the great discrepancy" between the "enormous investments of the state" in the new large grain sovkhozes and the results of their operation. Although he had previously pushed for bigness, Stalin now began to attack giantism, attributing the unsatisfactory performance of these farms to the fact that they "are too unwieldy; the managers are not able to cope with the enormous sovkhozes; the farms are too specialized and they lack crop rotation, summer fallow, and livestock." It was necessary, according to Stalin, "to divide the sovkhozes and liquidate their excessive specialization," [1] objectives which the government had begun to pursue even earlier.* The length to which gigantomania had gone in official circles may be gauged from the statement of the then Commissar of Agri-

---

* A decree of November 27, 1931, for example, blasted the performance of the grain sovkhozes and ordered their subdivision. (Kilosanidze, *Vazhneishie resheniia*, 2nd ed., pp. 519–523.)

culture, Ia. A. Iakovlev, at the Sixteenth Party Congress in July 1930, to the effect that state farms of not tens of thousands but hundreds of thousands of hectares were needed. "The lowering of the quality of farming would be compensated by the increased sown area." [2] Not only was ordinary farm and soil management neglected in the chase for more and more acres, with consequent luxuriant growth of weeds and very low crop yields, but also the modern machine technology, on which so much was staked, was utilized most inefficiently. Another unfavorable factor was that so many of the state farms were started from scratch in the sparsely settled eastern and southern regions of the semiarid zone. Such farms were operated under difficult climatic conditions and had many organizational problems, such as recruitment of a labor force in the face of heavy turnover, construction of housing and roads, provision of water supply.[3]

It was not long before large livestock farms, of which there were more than 1000 at the end of 1931, also came under attack. A government decree of March 31, 1932, censured them for "Inefficiency and complete lack of organization of the process of production, entirely unsatisfactory care of animals, excessive mortality of young animals, high percentage of barrenness, and poor condition of the livestock." [4]

In the case of both grain and livestock farms, subdivision and diversification—the very reverse of the original stress on concentration and extreme specialization—was the policy adopted by the government in the mid-1930s. In addition to the subdivision of the large state farms there was still further deflation due to the transfer of a sizable area of their land to kolkhozes. The sown area of state farms declined from 34.9 million acres in 1933 to 30.7 million acres in 1938, and the ratio to total sown area decreased from 10.9 percent to 9.1 percent. Even in sugar beets, which had been the traditional state farm crop, their ratio to total acreage was reduced—from 8.3 percent in 1933 to 4.5 percent in 1938.[5] In animal husbandry, too, sovkhozes had a declining role. Their ratio of livestock numbers decreased between 1933 and 1937; for cattle from 10.7 to 7.3 percent, for hogs from 24.6 to 10.9 percent, and for sheep and goats from 16.2 to 10.5 percent. Only in the case of horses was there an increase, both absolute and relative to the total horse population (from 8.7 to 12.5 percent).[6]

Kolkhozes were clearly the predominant form of farm enterprise before World War II. The situation did not change greatly during the postwar period. By 1950, when recovery from the worst effects of the war may be assumed, there were 4,988 state farms, including those organized in the occupied regions. The number decreased in 1953 to 4,857; these accounted for 9.6 percent of the total sown area, or slightly more than in 1938.*

Important developments beginning in 1954 resulted in a new upsurge of the state farm sector. First among the causes of this upsurge was the great expansion in the new lands regions. This area has long been the locus classicus of large sovkhozes, mainly specializing in spring wheat. When in 1954 the government embarked on a crash program of bringing a large area under plow and had to make considerable investments in tractors and other machinery, the state farm appeared to be the logical means. An important consideration in favor of it was the fact that a larger proportion of its output would be available to the government than of kolkhoz output, with the normally larger kolkhoz population and food requirements. The upshot was the organization of several hundred new sovkhozes and enlargement of existing ones. While this brought state farms more to the fore, it did not constitute a radical departure from the past.

A departure was involved, however, in the conversion or consolidation of kolkhozes with state farms in the new lands regions, together with the MTS servicing them. Kolkhozes thus converted were largely those that did not possess sufficient manpower and equipment to expand greatly and rapidly without substantial assistance from the state. Once a precedent was established it was only a step to extend the practice to other regions when problems were encountered—and this is precisely what was done in the late 1950s when kolkhozes were weak and needed additional capital investment. Such was the situation with many kolkhozes in the former war zone. In the Uzbek Republic considerable conversion into state farms took place when substantial government aid was needed for irrigation construction. Some conversion also was resorted to when the government decided to organize specialized sovkhozes growing vegetables and potatoes in the vicinity of large cities.

The total number of state farms increased by about 6 percent between 1953 and 1955 and decreased slightly in 1956. Although the process of

* Khrushchev claimed in his speech of February 28, 1964 (*Pravda,* March 7, 1964) that Stalin, not long before his death, proposed to dissolve sovkhozes, because of their unprofitableness and need of subsidization, and to transfer the land to kolkhozes. The unprofitableness, as Khrushchev points out, was caused largely by low procurement prices of farm products. It is tempting to speculate that Stalin may have been aware of the reason why sovkhozes were in the red; but thought that so long as squeezing tactics were to be applied to the peasants in the form of low prices, the kolkhoz was the best instrument to carry out this policy. From Stalin's standpoint, it would have been logical to expand kolkhoz operations by doing away with sovkhozes rather than to continue subsidizing them.

Table 69. Principal indicators of the development of state farms, specified years (in thousands and percentages)

Indicators	1940	1953	1958	1962
Number of farms, end of year	4,159	4,857	6,002	8,570
Average annual number of all employees	1,373	1,844	3,835	6,893
Workers engaged in production	1,186	1,708	3,626	6,504
Tractors, end of year				
Physical units	74	90	279	554
In terms of 15-horsepower units	100	165	536	1,049
Grain combines, end of year	27	42	168	256
Trucks, end of year	21	40	140	299
All agricultural land				
Hectares	50,740	63,627	149,450	242,531
Acres	125,379	157,222	369,291	599,294
Sown area				
Hectares	11,559	15,155	52,451	86,678
Acres	28,562	37,448	129,606	214,181
Percentage of total sown area	7.7%	9.6%	26.8%	40.1%
Grain area				
Hectares	7,681	7,832	37,113	59,625
Acres	18,980	19,353	91,706	147,333
Percentage of total grain area	6.9%	7.3%	29.7%	43.9%
Livestock				
Numbers, end of year				
Cattle	2,462	3,404	8,217	20,973
Cows only	952	1,128	2,833	7,446
Hogs	1,910	3,502	8,127	16,771
Sheep	5,841	10,056	26,193	40,952
Ratio to total livestock numbers				
Cattle	4.5%	6.1%	11.6%	24.1%
Cows only	3.4	4.4	11.2	19.6
Hogs	6.9	10.5	16.7	24.0
Sheep	7.3	10.1	20.2	29.3

Sources. For 1940, *Sel'skoe khoziaistvo SSSR, 1960*, pp. 46–47; for 1953, 1958, and 1962, *Narodnoe khoziaistvo, 1962*, pp. 356–357.

plowing up virgin land was practically completed by 1956, the upward trend in the number of state farms was resumed in 1957, suggesting that conversion of kolkhozes became the principal factor in the growth of state farming. (No statistical data on conversion of kolkhozes were published.) During the period 1954–61 4,600 state farms were organized. Of this number, 3,856 were new (many of them converted kolkhozes), 434 were reorganized auxiliary farms of various state enterprises, and 310 were created as a result of subdivision of large farms. As against this, 516 small sovkhozes were consolidated with other farms, 615 were transferred as auxiliary farms to other state enterprises and institutions, and 45 were liquidated; the total of state farms eliminated was 1,176. Thus the net increase was 3,424.[7] A further net increase of 289 state farms was reported in 1962. As a result of the new expansion the sown area of state farms increased from 37 million acres in 1953 to 214 million acres in 1962, or from less than 10 percent of the total sown area to 40 percent. Livestock numbers on state farms also increased substantially (see Table 69).

The heaviest concentration of state farms was in the eastern regions, particularly in Kazakhstan and in the adjoining Ural, West Siberia, and Volga regions. The Ukraine, North Caucasus, and North Central regions were other important areas of state farm concentration (see Table 70). An increase in the number of state farms was reported for all regions between 1953 and 1961, but was especially spectacular in Kazakhstan, where it nearly quadrupled.

Both specialization and diversification have been stressed by the official policy with respect to state farms without apparently recognizing that the two may conflict. In reality there is a considerable degree of specialization in sovkhozes, as indicated by the following tabulation (figures as of January 1, 1963).[8]

	Number of Farms
Grain and seed	1,135
Sugar beets	277
Cotton	127
Fiber crops	8
Essential oils	26
Tobacco	29
Tea	32
Fruit and grapes	356
Fruit–berry and fruit–vegetable farms	277
Vegetables, potatoes, vegetable–dairy	589
Dairy and meat–dairy	3,170
Hogs	573
Sheep and karakul	772
Horses (stud farms)	67
Reindeer and fur-bearing animals	167
Poultry	443
Total	8,570

Table 70. Regional distribution of state farms, total number for specified years.

	1940	1953	1961
RSFSR	2,600	2,780	4,544
Northwestern	228	337	442
North Central	487	466	805
Volga-Viatka	81	61	109
Central Black Soil	251	268	330
Volga	391	432	544
North Caucasus	339	402	659
Ural	362	324	600
W. Siberia	267	278	527
E. Siberia	118	109	275
Far East	76	103	253
Ukraine	929	895	906
Donetsk-Dnepr	496	398	355
Southwestern	251	246	257
Southern	182	251	294
Moldavia	40	67	65
Belorussia	92	120	358
Lithuania	—	88	232
Latvia	—	82	162
Estonia	—	108	144
Georgia	76	98	162
Azerbaijan	50	52	119
Armenia	14	40	118
Kazakh	194	293	1,132
Uzbek	81	102	180
Turkmen	26	40	50
Tadjik	21	33	41
Kirgiz	36	59	68
Total USSR	4,159	4,857	8,281

Source. *Narodnoe khoziaistvo, 1961*, p. 449.

Except for oilseeds, every branch of Soviet agriculture seems to be represented in this tabulation. The largest number of farms is of the dairy and meat-dairy types, followed by grain farms (half of which are in Kazakhstan) and by other livestock farms. A considerable number of sovkhozes specialize in growing vegetables and potatoes; this was swelled by the organization of farms in the vicinity of large cities to help supply them with these products. In some cases the farms specialize in production of vegetables only; in others they combine the growing of vegetables with potatoes or dairy products or fruit. There are also sizable numbers of fruit and grape farms and those growing sugar beets and cotton.

A marked feature of state farming is the huge size of the farm unit, since it is supposed to embody the Marxist principle of the superiority of large-scale agricultural production. While the policy before World War II was to discourage giantism to some extent because of the painful experience during the early collectivization period, the reverse tendency prevailed during the postwar period. The size of the state farms manifested an upward trend, as will be seen from Table 71. In 1962 an average sovkhoz had 2.5 times as many employees as in 1940 and more than double that in 1953. It had over 25,000 acres of sown area in 1962, or more than triple the area of 1940 and 1953. These are, of course, average figures for all types of state farms, some growing highly intensive crops like cotton and tea on small acreages and others engaged in extensive grain and ranch farming in the eastern and southern steppes. As might be expected, there were considerable variations between farms of different types and regions. The average sown area, for instance, per grain sovkhoz was nearly 70,000 acres in 1962, more than double the average acreage of all state farms. The grain sovkhozes themselves had undergone

Table 71. The average size of state farms, specified years

Indicators	1940	1953	1958	1962 All state farms	1962 Grain state farms
Number of employees	330	380	639	825	933
Agricultural land					
1,000 hectares	12.2	13.1	24.9	28.3	47.7
1,000 acres	30.1	32.4	61.5	69.9	117.9
Sown area					
1,000 hectares	2.8	3.1	8.7	10.1	27.8
1,000 acres	6.9	7.7	21.5	25.0	68.7
Tractors in 15-horsepower units	24	34	90	124	308
Livestock numbers					
Cattle	592	701	1,370	2,447	3,564
Cows only	229	232	472	863	1,155
Hogs	459	721	1,355	1,956	2,725
Sheep	1,404	2,070	4,364	4,779	—

Sources. *Sel'skoe khoziaistvo SSSR, 1960*, p. 49; *Narodnoe khoziaistvo, 1962*, p. 359.

a vast enlargement compared with the 1930s: the average sown acreage in 1933 was 34,000 and in 1937 about 26,000 acres.[9] Another index of size is the way the population and the work force of a sovkhoz is spread out over a number of villages. The average spread per sovkhoz for the whole USSR on January 1, 1963, was 11.3 villages; this varied from 2.2 villages in Armenia to 17.3 in Lithuania.[10] Such scattering of the work force, with the prevailing poor country roads and inadequate transportation and means of communication, is not conducive to efficiency.

The cult of bigness in the 1950s had, if anything, even a greater sway in sovkhozes than in the merged kolkhozes. What was, therefore, said above regarding the management difficulties engendered by kolkhoz giantism applies equally to sovkhoz giantism. An early method of overcoming these difficulties in sovkhozes as in kolkhozes was to divide the large farm unit into several subdivisions: brigades in kolkhozes, branches (*otdelenie*) in sovkhozes. Such a scheme was prescribed for sovkhozes by a decree of November 27, 1931.[11] These branches when fully organized are actually farms in themselves with their own managers, personnel, and equipment. In fact, the impression a visitor to a typical large sovkhoz gets is that of a combination of producing units under central supervision with certain unified services, such as repair shops and supply service.

In the 1950s subdivision into branches was omitted in some of the new state farms. They resorted to the simpler device of a brigade which is essentially a labor gang, rather than a producing unit like the *otdelenie*. This practice was criticized by one authority as particularly inefficient and costly in livestock production, which the grain farms in the new lands regions were urged to develop as a sideline, a kind of second *tselina* (virgin land).[12] It meant concentration of large numbers of animals at the farmstead with consequent heavy expenditures for delivery of feed and hauling of manure for long distances, as well as difficulties in providing adequate water supply and conveniently located pasture. Other specialists pointed out that the remoteness of the fields from the state farm center would hinder timely field work and interfere with such operations as weeding, snow retention, and fertilization.[13] Yet some specialists opposed subdivision into branches because of the increased administrative expenses and the difficulty of providing decent living conditions for the workers in numerous small settlements. Others argued that the increased administrative expenses would be more than offset by other economies, and that good living conditions could be provided in smaller farm settlements. As was pointed out by one discussant, there is another alternative to the subdivision of sovkhozes into branches: the splitting of large sovkhozes themselves into smaller units.[14]

In any event, there were signs by the beginning of 1960 that Soviet officials and specialists, after a decade of gigantomania, again became aware that bigness is not synonymous with optimum size and that the problem needs further study. This was reflected in research and in Soviet economic literature. Khrushchev, who must bear the major responsibility for initiating farm giantism, mildly remonstrated against it on a few occasions. But at last he apparently realized that there exists the problem of the optimal size of the farm enterprise. He said in a speech in Kazakhstan in March 1961:

It is necessary that economists, basing themselves on the rich experience of our agriculture, work out recommendations regarding the size of socialist farm enterprises. It is very important to solve scientifically the question of the optimal size of the enterprise, what acreage, especially of arable land, it must have in order to be economically efficient and easily manageable. What is the acreage of arable land that requires subdivision into branches, what is the labor force and machinery required when growing different crops so that production of each crop and production as a whole should be profitable? It is necessary to provide the kind of recommendations for sovkhozes as well as their branches so that the size of the farm unit should not be a matter of accident, as sometimes happens. One sovkhoz may have 80,000 hectares of agricultural land, another 40,000–50,000, and a third, 10,000 hectares. Which is the correct one? It is not possible that the first, the second, and the third are equally advantageous under similar conditions. Apparently, in this respect, we have little economically tested data. I speak mainly about sovkhozes but this applies to kolkhozes . . . Making recommendations regarding the size of the farm enterprise requires serious analysis, calculation, and scientific substantiation.[15]

In September 1963 the All-Union Institute of Agricultural Economics and the Institute of Economics of the Academy of Science of the USSR, with the cooperation of a number of other research agencies, published a methodological guide which they developed for establishing an optimal sovkhoz size. This was defined as one permitting "the most rational and effective utilization of land, material, labor, and financial resources, thus maximizing production results in the interest of society." [16]

Actually, splitting up of sovkhozes began on a small scale even before Khrushchev's remarks in 1961. During the period 1954–60, over 170 sovkhozes were established in this manner.[17] The process was accelerated in 1961, the last year for which such data are available, when the number of new sovkhozes established through splitting increased by 138.[18] Such indicators of the average size of state farms as the number of workers, sown area, and number of livestock suggest further increases in subsequent years. Yet it is possible that some sovkhozes were below their optimal size, particularly because of conversion of a number of kolkhozes of the weaker type into state farms. At any rate, a much larger number of small sovkhozes were consolidated with others than split up during the years 1954–61, the figures being 516 and 310 respectively.[19] It is well to bear in mind that the Soviet concept of the optimal size of a farm unit is likely to remain larger than the similar American concept. Even if the splitting process were intensified, the farms in the Soviet Union would probably remain large by Western standards.

Apart from the ideological predilection, what are the principal pragmatic advantages of state farms from the Soviet standpoint? A glance at Table 72 reveals that a very important reason lies in the large and growing share of state farms in government procurements, particularly in procurements of grains and vegetables, where the proportion for state farms approaches one half. The expansion on virgin land and the establishment of specialized vegetable farms were obviously responsible for this expanding share. But in animal products too there was a substantial gain. Only in sugar beets, the original sovkhoz crop, did the proportion of total procurements remain low in 1962.

Another advantage of sovkhozes is lower labor requirements in production compared with kolkhozes. This is shown in Tables 73 and 74.

Table 72. The share of sovkhozes and other state enterprises in government procurements, specified years (percentages)

Product	1953	1958	1962
Grains	12	38	45
Cotton, unginned	4	13	18
Sugar beets	4	4	7
Potatoes	3	10	27
Vegetables	20	29	49
Livestock and poultry [a]	24	27	39
Milk	19	23	36
Eggs	13	24	34
Wool	16	28	36

[a] Including gain in weight in state feed lots.
Source. *Narodnoe khoziaistvo, 1962*, p. 240.

Table 73. Labor required to produce farm commodities in sovhozes and kolkhozes, 1960–1962 (man-days per centner)

Commodity	Kolkhozes			Sovkhozes		
	1960	1961	1962	1960	1961	1962
Small grains	0.9	0.8	0.7	0.26	0.29	0.26
Cotton, unginned	6.8	6.3	6.9	6.1	5.6	6.1
Sugar beets	0.4	0.4	0.4	0.4	0.4	0.4
Potatoes	0.8	0.7	0.9	0.7	0.7	0.8
Vegetables	2.1	2.1	2.1	1.2	1.3	1.2
Milk	2.6	2.7	2.7	1.8	1.8	1.8
Cattle [a]	14.7	14.6	14.3	8.2	8.4	8.5
Hogs [a]	16.6	15.2	14.5	7.1	7.1	7.0
Sheep [a]	11.3	10.4	10.2	6.6	6.3	6.9
Wool [a]	54.9	49.9	49.5	30.0	31.0	34.5

[a] Per centner of liveweight gain.
Source. *Narodnoe khoziaistvo, 1962,* p. 362.

Table 74. Ratio of labor required in production in sovkhozes (man-days per centner) to that required in kolkhozes

Commodity	1960	1961	1962
Small grains	28.9%	36.2%	37.1%
Cotton, unginned	89.7	88.9	88.4
Sugar beets	100.0	100.0	100.0
Potatoes	87.5	100.0	88.9
Vegetables	57.1	61.9	57.1
Milk	69.2	66.7	66.7
Cattle	55.8	57.5	59.4
Hogs	42.8	46.7	48.3
Sheep	58.4	60.6	67.6
Wool	54.6	62.1	69.7

Source. Calculated from Table 73.

Less labor was required in sovkhozes to produce every commodity except sugar beets, but the disparity was especially great for small grains, vegetables, and livestock products. As far as the effect on cost of production is concerned, this disparity in labor requirements is partly offset by lower

527

Chapter Twenty. State Farms

wages in kolkhozes than in sovkhozes.* The relatively higher wages partly explain the higher productivity of sovkhoz workers since they have greater incentive than the less well paid kolkhozniks. It cannot be overstressed, however, that greater economic incentives for workers in sovkhozes is a highly relative term—relative, that is, to the low level prevailing in kolkhozes. An average wage of more than 600 rubles for state farm workers compares favorably with less than 400 rubles of average earnings by kolkhozniks in collective farms; but it still lags considerably behind the average nonagricultural wage of more than 900 rubles which, with high prices, connotes a very low standard of living.† An additional source of income for workers in sovkhozes is provided by small private farming, but it is on an even more limited scale than in kolkhozes. Livestock ownership by sovkhoz workers particularly was a target for criticism by the Khrushchev administration after 1958. Soviet statistics do not give a breakdown between holdings of state farm workers and other workers and it is not possible, therefore, to judge how successful was this campaign.

Experimentation is going on within the prevailing piece wage system ‡ to stimulate productivity of sovkhoz workers by linking earnings

* That wages are lower in kolkhozes than in sovkhozes is confirmed by published Soviet statistics on cost of production in kolkhozes, for the calculation of which two alternative methods were used: actual payments to kolkhozniks and putative payments for the same amount of labor, using sovkhoz wage rates. The alternative production costs in rubles per metric ton of different commodities were as follows in 1962 (*Narodnoe khoziaistvo, 1962*, pp. 338–339).

	Actual payment	Payment based on sovkhoz wage rates
Small grains	37	44
Cotton, unginned	224	247
Sugar beets	16	19
Sunflower seed	30	33
Potatoes	38	48
Cattle, liveweight	834	1,014
Hogs, liveweight	1,146	1,347
Sheep, liveweight	512	571
Milk	129	156
Wool	2,504	2,748

† It is difficult to say whether the fringe benefits not included in the regular wage which theoretically should be the same for all employees of a certain grade, are smaller or greater for sovkhoz workers than for city workers. It is possible that on the better-managed farms, particularly where foodstuffs are sold to the workers at discount prices, they may be equal or even better than in the cities. But clearly this was not true in the virgin lands regions where on many farms housing and other living conditions for the new settlers were often wretched.

‡ The same procedure of setting up "norms" of performance or tasks as in kolkhozes is followed on state farms. But there is no intermediate step or workday unit. It is a straight cash wage system.

with output and by paying bonuses for exceeding planned goals. A method which has come into prominence and reminds one of the *zveno* is a kind of a contract with a group of workers who undertake not merely to perform certain operations like plowing or harvesting, but to produce a specified quantity of output; so many tons of sugar beets, for instance. For this purpose the group is supplied with resources, land, machinery, and seed, calculated as necessary to do the job. Under this system, called *akordnaia sistema,* the workers benefit financially from whatever economies they achieve and from exceeding the output goals set. The salaries of the managerial personnel also increase with increased annual deliveries or sales. Furthermore, the manager of a sovkhoz is guaranteed only 70 percent of his monthly salary while the remaining 30 percent is based on the extent of the fulfillment each month of the annual plan of deliveries to the state. If 10 percent of the annual plan is fulfilled during the month, the manager is entitled to 10 percent of that part of the annual salary which was withheld; if only 5 percent of the plan is fulfilled, he will receive only 5 percent of the amount withheld. There are also bonuses for exceeding the plans of deliveries and profits. An effort is being made to spur on individual workers and managers of sovkhozes, but it is limited by the wage fund allotted by the government to each state farm, which cannot be exceeded.

Another factor contributing to greater labor productivity in sovkhozes is the tighter discipline of a hired labor force. Sovkhoz workers can be ordered about, disciplined, and if necessary fired by the management much more easily than can kolkhozniks. It is symptomatic that the highly realistic scenes of sharp bargaining about work assignments between managers and workers described by writers like Abramov and Dorosh take place in kolkhozes not in sovkhozes. The tighter labor discipline is a point emphasized by the proponents of the sovkhoz form of organization who believe that, as one of them put it to me, "it is the only way to overcome completely the survival of the anarchy of small peasant farming," which, in the opinion of this school, exists in kolkhozes.

Labor productivity in sovkhozes is also raised by the larger supply of capital and machinery and other equipment in the state farm sector, into which government agricultural investments were primarily channeled. Such investments, as Table 75 indicates, rose sharply in 1954 when the plowing up of virgin land began and the upward trend continued without interruption through 1960. This is true of capital expenditures for production as well as for other purposes, such as housing and roads, designated as unproductive investment by the Soviets. The proportion of capital investment in sovkhozes to the total state investments in agriculture also increased almost continuously during this period and reached an all-record high of over 60 percent in 1960. That the sovkhozes are

Table 75. Government capital investment in state farms, 1929–1960

Calendar year	For production	Other	Total	Percent of state capital investments
	In million rubles at comparable prices			
1929–1932 [a]	326	100	426	41
1933–1937 [b]	313	99	412	30
1938–1941 [c]	230	52	282	32
1941–1945 [d]	68	9	77	24
1946–1950 [e]	640	110	750	28
1951	238	41	279	25
1952	196	47	243	23
1953	198	44	242	25
1954	370	110	480	27
1955	581	152	733	32
1956	624	147	771	32
1957	774	165	939	35
1958	883	191	1,074	40
1959	1,132	295	1,427	57
1960	1,475	409	1,884	61

[a] First Five Year Plan.
[b] Second Five Year Plan.
[c] 3½ years of the Third Five Year Plan (January 1938–July 1, 1941).
[d] July 1941–December 1945 (World War II).
[e] Fourth Five Year Plan.
Source. *Kapital'noe stroitel'stvo*, p. 167.

better equipped with machinery and implements than kolkhozes is substantiated by the Soviet estimate that at the end of 1962 their value was 4,289 million rubles in state farms, as against 3,871 million rubles in the collective farms (gross value without allowance for depreciation).[20] When these figures are related to the sown area, an even more favorable picture emerges for sovkhozes with their smaller acreage. In examining the distribution between collective and state farms of tractor power, the most important component of the machinery and implements class for which we have statistics in physical terms, we find again a more favorable situation in sovkhozes. The ratio of sown area to a 15-horsepower tractor unit in 1962 was 82.6 hectares (204 acres) in sovkhozes and 101.4 hectares (251 acres) in kolkhozes. The qualification which must be borne in mind in dealing with statistics of farm machinery—that not all tractors and other implements listed as being on farms are really in satisfactory operating condition—applies both to sovkhozes and to kolkhozes.

It is important to note that capital investment varies between different state farms with consequent effect on their productivity. The broad correlation is described by the Soviet economist Khalturin as follows: "The higher the capital stock supply per unit of arable land, the higher the gross production (in comparable prices) per unit of arable land; the greater the supply of machinery, the higher the productivity of labor in zones with comparable natural conditions."[21] The correlation between the supply of capital and productivity, measured by the value of produce delivered to the state, in 1960 in groups of sovkhozes in two Ukrainian provinces, Lugansk and Kharkov, is shown in the following tabulation (capital stock and value of produce in 10,000 rubles per 100 hectares of agricultural land).[22]

Capital stock		Number of sovkhozes	Value of produce
Lugansk			
Total	Average		
Up to 20.0	16.3	26.0	3.9
20.1 - 30.0	24.3	18.0	5.9
30.1 - 40.0	36.9	10.0	9.6
Kharkov			
Up to 20.0	17.7	10.0	6.2
20.1 - 30.0	25.0	16.0	8.2
30.1 - 40.0	34.3	15.0	11.3
Over 40.0	54.1	9.0	17.3

State farms have managerial problems, some of which are specific to them and others common to all Soviet enterprises. Certainly the problem of *blat*—maintaining good relations with officials at various levels, including supply agencies, the state bank, and neighboring farms, involving the principle of "you scratch my back and I'll scratch yours"—is as important in state farm management as in other enterprises. Blat is a means of escape from the rigidities and scarcities of the Soviet system. If a farm manager needs to buy quickly some deficient article such as a spare part for a tractor, or to have some foolish or even harmful bureaucratic regulation waived or overlooked, or to obtain a loan, he has to be prepared to pay for it by extending favors—in the case of state farms, usually illegally supplying produce such as butter and meat animals. This involves the risk of official wrath should the transaction be discovered, a risk intensified by the atmosphere of general distrust and official encouragement of universal reporting. This is the essence of blat, of which only an echo appears occasionally on the surface, but which is an essential ingredient of the Soviet system.

On the other hand, there is no lack of criticism of the stranglehold of rigidity, paternalism, and pettiness of bureaucratic control and interference in which the sovkhoz managers are caught. An article entitled "Liberate Us from Petty Paternalism" by a sovkhoz manager from the former Stalingrad province, published in the organ of the Ministry of Agriculture, voiced a number of such complaints.[23] The author complained of constant government interference in planning, despite the law passed in 1955 that production plans must be made essentially by the farms. He reported that his sovkhoz had set a goal of 60,000 head of poultry raised during the year (which was double what it was asked to do) and planned its operations accordingly. All of a sudden the farm was ordered to increase the goal to 140,000 head; all efforts to convince the authorities that this was not possible failed. Tens of thousands of young chicks were delivered but half of them perished because the farm was not equipped to take care of them. This was not the end of the story: the slaughterhouse too was overloaded and could not handle the poultry which the sovkhoz was able to raise and deliver. Another complaint touched on bureaucratic interference with the timing of farm operations, which is best left to the discretion of the farm management. An example was an order to complete sowings on all farms in three days irrespective of the different topographic and soil conditions (in some fields soil dries up more rapidly than in others).

The independent status of the principal specialists and technicians of the sovkhoz (agronomists, animal husbandry specialists, accountants, engineers, bookkeepers, veterinarians) was another grievance. The writer of the article suggested that the regional authorities should merely recommend specialists; the powers of appointment, dismissal, reward, and reprimand should be left to the manager. The possibility of abuse is ruled out because "it would be corrected, inasmuch as he [the manager] clears the decision of each more or less important question with the farm party committee and the labor (trade union) committee." This procedure suggests a further serious limitation of the manager's powers—this time from below. The author apparently had no quarrel with it. He was concerned, though, about the hamstringing of sovkhoz managers in the matter of expenditures. Though the investments and output are valued in millions of rubles, the manager was not authorized to spend more than 50 rubles (old money) in cash. Similarly with standard piece rates: he can scale them up or down by only 10 percent, whereas 30 percent is indicated by practice as the desirable deviation. Like so many other Soviet managers and specialists, the author was up in arms against the frequent meetings and conferences during the busy season; for instance, being called twenty times during the 20–25 days of harvest to conferences dealing with it in the raion center, 27 kilometers (15½ miles) from the sovkhoz. He also castigated that bane to farm managers, the "representative" (*upolnomochenyi*) of the raion or other authority who is sent out to the farm to push some operation or campaign—most often harvesting and procurements. Citing a recent example from his experience, the author wondered what earthly good the representative accomplishes by following the manager around "like a shadow," exhorting him to "harvest the grain more rapidly." The situation is even worse when the representative takes it upon himself to direct operations, ordering an idle combine into action not knowing that the reason for its idleness was unsatisfactory threshing, requiring some adjustment.

Such are the problems as seen through the eyes of one farm manager who pleads with the Soviet government for greater faith in sovkhoz managers and greater independence. The evidence and arguments adduced in the article can be easily multiplied.

Following the quest of sovkhov managers for greater independence was a similar movement among managers of state farm branches. They too are hamstrung by rules and regulations and by the need to obtain permission from sovkhoz managers for many small details of operation, with consequent waste of time and money.[24] This treatment of the state farm managerial personnel may seem the more surprising in that it includes an increasing number of trained specialists. The number of persons with higher and special secondary education in sovkhozes and other state farming enterprises increased from 31,000 on July 1, 1953, to 209,000 on December 1, 1962. Among these, employees with agricultural training increased from 27,000 to 147,000.[25] Yet there were serious complaints of frequent turnover among the managerial personnel because of removal for inefficiency. In Novgorod province half of the managers in forty-one sovkhozes were removed in the course of two years, and in only nine sovkhozes had the managers kept their posts for more than four years.[26] The turnover was no doubt intensified in 1963 when many sovkhoz managers, like their counterparts in kolkhozes, were involved in extensive changes in farm leadership.[27] Unfortunately removal of a sovkhoz manager for incompetence does not preclude his being entrusted with a responsible post in another sovkhoz, so long as his loyalty to the party is not questioned.

Another perennial problem that sovkhozes share with kolkhozes which has successfully resisted recurrent official attacks is the excessive number of administrative personnel. "Almost every tenth employee walks with a briefcase," wrote a sovkhoz specialist.[28] A state farm official in Amur province observed in 1963 that in a number of sovkhozes in his region, for every four or five workers engaged in production there was one employee supervising, keeping records, guarding, or providing some service. For all the 57 sovkhozes of the Amur province it was estimated that 15.4 percent of the employees were not engaged in production.[29] No doubt the huge size of the farms, the prevailing atmosphere of distrust, and inadequate incentives necessitate a large number of supervisory, record-keeping, and custodial employees.

Difficulties in the matter of production planning, also common with kolkhozes, stem from the imposition of plans from above and their frequent change. An additional and related difficulty is, in the words of a high official, that "Every year the sovkhozes function the first 2-3 months without a production-financial plan. Under the existing system of planning they cannot draw up in advance a production-financial plan for the new year until the accounts for the preceding year have been completed." [30]

In considering the future outlook for the sovkhoz type of farming, we must bear in mind one serious disadvantage which it has. The state must assume full financial responsibility for the operation of sovkhozes, while kolkhozes, in contrast, can be left largely to forage for themselves and still be held responsible for delivering their quotas of farm products to the government. The state must make it possible for the sovkhozes to meet their operating costs, above all their wage bill, and to provide the necessary capital. Whether it does so by direct subsidies from the state budget or by raising prices to the level of at least average production costs is a matter of financial procedure and not of basic principle.

Until the government is willing and ready to assume the same financial responsibility, in fair weather and in foul, for all collective farms (including the inefficient and unprofitable) just as it does for state farms, it must cling to the policy of coexistence of the two competing organizational types. This position was advocated by Khrushchev at the Twenty-second Party Congress in October 1961 and adopted in the new party platform.* It does not preclude continuing piecemeal conversion of kolkhozes or the development of a closer relationship between kolkhozes and sovkhozes on an administrative level, which will be dealt with in the following chapter.

---

* An important party official, D. S. Polianskii, upheld the coexistence line when he criticized at the January 1961 plenum the "incorrect" tendency of provincial leadership of "stubbornly insisting on petitioning" for conversion of all backward kolkhozes into sovkhozes. "Kolkhozes are still far from having exhausted their potentialities; they must and will develop simultaneously with sovkhozes. He who strives to convert them into sovkhozes in reality is trying to escape from the responsibility of strengthening kolkhozes, wants to achieve an easy life for himself" (*Pravda,* January 12, 1961).

In addition to sovkhozes or state farms proper, there are numerous small farms attached as auxiliary establishments to various state enterprises and institutions. There were periods in the past when such farms, then called orsy,* played a prominent role in supplying urban population with food, especially during the crises of 1918–21, the early 1930s, and World War II. Though considerable liquidation usually followed the end of these crises, still in 1953 there remained 114,064 such auxiliary farms with a sown area of 7.6 million acres and an average of 67 acres per farm. By 1962 the number of farms decreased to 96,288 but the total sown area increased considerably—to 20.1 million acres—and the average per farm to 209 acres.[31] Despite a substantial increase in acreage, these auxiliary farms accounted for less than 4 percent of the 1962 total sown area and are still quite small enterprises compared with sovkhozes and kolkhozes.

* Plural of ors, which is an abbreviation of *otdel rabochego snabzheniia*, department of supply for workers.

21

Administrative Control and Planning

The pervasive character of government control of agriculture, including day-to-day management decisions and the tensions manifested in successive agricultural crises, led to the creation of an elaborate administrative apparatus. Its complicated character has been accentuated by the fact that administration and supervision of agriculture, like nearly everything else in the Soviet Union, is exercised by two parallel and inter-related sets of organs: by regular government agencies and by the Communist Party bureaucracy. In practice, it is difficult to draw a functional line of demarcation between the party and the government except that most of the technicians, such as agronomists and livestock specialists, are employed by the government and not by the party. But no aspect of agriculture, however technical, is immune from party control and intervention.

The agricultural administrative machine has undergone numerous reorganizations. The federal or national Ministry of Agriculture (called the Commissariat of Agriculture until 1946), created at the end of 1929 during the period of mass collectivization, was alternately split and recombined. At the end of the Second World War it was split into three ministries (agriculture, technical crops, and animal husbandry) and rather speedily reconstituted into a single ministry. Subsequently (April 6, 1950) a new ministry was carved out to administer agriculture in the cotton growing regions, but after Stalin it was reabsorbed by the Ministry of Agriculture. It would not be profitable to pursue this checkered path in chronological detail. Rather it may be well to concentrate on the more recent models of administrative machinery representing broadly the two alternatives of administrative centralization and decentralization. In the first model, which prevailed up to the 1960s, there is one principal government agency in charge of most of the agricultural operations in the country: the Ministry of Agriculture of the USSR in Moscow. In the 1940s and 1950s the ministry was organized on functional as well as regional lines with separate bureaus or administrations in Moscow in charge of large regions consisting of several provinces and republics. The powers of these bureaus were curtailed to some extent in 1947 when the Chief Administration of Machine-Tractor Stations was established in the Ministry to unify the direction of the MTS, which previously devolved entirely on the regional bureaus.[1] Each republic, province (oblast or krai), and raion had a department of agriculture which was a branch of the respective republican, provincial, or raion administration. These departments were also subordinate to the central Ministry of Agriculture in Moscow.

The Ministry of Agriculture and its various subdivisions exercised control over kolkhozes largely through MTS, which came to play an even more important part as focal points of command during the early post-Stalin period. Most of the state farms until 1957 were under the jurisdiction not of the Ministry of Agriculture but of a separate Ministry of State Farms. Some of the more specialized sovkhozes were controlled by other ministries which existed at the time: sugar-beet sovkhozes by the Ministry of Food Industry, dairy sovkhozes by the Ministry of Meat and Dairy Industries, and cotton sovkhozes by the Ministry of Cotton Growing. Regional sovkhoz administrations, so-called trusts, were the local organs administering state farms.

State procurement of agricultural products was managed by a separate ministry of procurements of the USSR which operated directly through its agents in the various republics, provinces, and raions. The Gosplan (State Planning Commission) always played a central role in agricultural as in other forms of national planning. The Central Statistical Administration (which was at one time attached to the Gosplan but in 1949 was elevated to the status of an independent agency under the Council of Ministers) was responsible for collection and analysis of statistical data and for crop and livestock estimates.* In addition a council of kolkhoz affairs, consisting of a number of high party and government functionaries, was established by a decree of September 19, 1946, with broad powers to supervise and deal with various problems of collective farming during the reconstruction period following the war; little was revealed of its activities when it was dissolved by a decree of March 17, 1953.[2]

A further step toward concentration of authority in the Ministry of Agriculture was its merger in 1957 with the Ministry of State Farms which put most of the sovkhozes under the unified ministry in Moscow and its republic counterparts.[3] A few months earlier, in December 1956, the often criticized system for supplying kolkhozes, MTS, and sovkhozes with materials and equipment—which was dispersed among a number of departments—was unified under the Main Administration of Agricultural Supply (*Glavsel'snab*) in the Ministry of Agriculture.[4]

Less systematic information is available on the organization and functioning of the party organs in the agricultural realm before 1962, though there can be no doubt of their controlling voice in the administration of agricultural affairs. The central committees of the party in Moscow and in various republics, as well as the provincial party committees, had agricultural sections (*sel'skokhoziaistvennye otdely*). Little is disclosed about their operations, but presumably they functioned as a sort of general staff in the party direction of collectivized agriculture. So important was their work considered that when in the spring of 1939, on behalf of the politburo at the Eighteenth Party Congress, it was proposed to abolish the sections of the Central Committee and of the republican and provincial party committees dealing with various sectors of national economy, an exception was made for the agricultural sections and they were retained.

These party agencies and the local party bosses—the secretaries of the provincial and raion committees (obkoms and raikoms)—always wielded great power over agriculture, even though they had no government status. Their intervention was usually intensified and accelerated during what were deemed emergencies, such as a lagging harvest or procurement drive. In serious crises like collectivization or war, party and government bureaucracies were associated by creation of emergency organs such as

---

* The State Crop Estimating Inspection, headed by a chief inspector, was set up in 1947 as an agency attached first to the Gosplan and later to the Council of Ministers of the USSR. It was ultimately responsible for authoritative crop and livestock estimates, with the assistance of local agricultural authorities and the Central Statistical Administration. It was abolished after Stalin's death in 1953 and the Central Statistical Administration took over the task of crop and livestock estimation.

politotdels, the political sections of the MTS, which were abolished once the crisis passed. But the party was given a permanent official representation in the administration of the MTS following the decree of September 15, 1953. A second secretary of a raikom with a staff of subordinates was permanently assigned to each MTS.

On the national scene, during most of the Stalin era one of the members of the politbureau acted as a spokesman for the top leadership on agricultural matters and presumably served as a farm policy coordinator, though this was never publicly formalized. In the late 1930s and in the 1940s A. A. Andreev performed such a function. Late in 1949 Khrushchev was brought to Moscow from Kiev and, for reasons unknown, replaced Andreev. He immediately started a campaign for the larger brigade as against the small *zveno* in kolkhozes, favored by Andreev, and more importantly, for the enlargement and merger of kolkhozes. It appears that after Khrushchev had overreached himself by urging speedy resettlement of villages and creation of "agrotowns," he was replaced by Stalin as the "agriculturalist" in the politburo.* After Stalin's death Khrushchev again assumed direction of agricultural affairs, several years before his ascent to top leadership.

The Reorganization of 1961–1962

The great concentration of power in the Ministry of Agriculture in the 1950s was the swan song of our centralized model. Actually a step toward decentralization was taken as early as 1955 when the rigid planning procedure of Stalin days was modified by greater allowance for grass roots initiative and flexibility. (That it was not enforced is something else again; here we are concerned with principles.) The liquidation of the MTS in 1958, which unhinged the local control centers of the Ministry of Agriculture, may be viewed as a further step toward agricultural decentralization. That decentralization was in the air was also evidenced by the industrial reform of 1957. But probably the decisive motive for Khrushchev's decentralization of the agricultural control apparatus was the disappointing production results in 1959 and 1960, following several

* Perhaps the most tangible evidence of the eclipse of Khrushchev as an agricultural spokesman for Stalin was the fact that at the Nineteenth Party Congress in October 1952 Khrushchev did not deal with agriculture at all but served as a rapporteur of the proposed new party statutes. It is difficult to believe that Khrushchev would not have spoken about agriculture if he had a hand in directing it. Malenkov dealt with the agricultural problems as a general rapporteur for the Central Committee, which is a normal procedure. What is more suspicious is Malenkov's vigorous attack on Khrushchev's position on resettlement.

years of rapid agricultural growth which culminated in the bumper harvest of 1958. The harvest of 1958 encouraged Khrushchev to start his celebrated campaign to catch up with the United States in per capita consumption of animal products and to set high agricultural targets for the seven-year plan, 1959–1965. When by the end of 1960 the agricultural picture for a second successive year did not bear out Khrushchev's optimistic expectations, he started reorganizing.

The January 1961 plenum was devoted to a critical review of the agricultural situation by Khrushchev and others. The new organizational scheme was announced on February 21, 1961. The Ministry of Agriculture of the USSR was shorn of most of its functions and power. The reorganized Ministry corresponded functionally to a combination of the Agricultural Research Service, Extension Service, and Office of Information of the U.S. Department of Agriculture. Its twofold objective was to promote and administer agricultural research and education and to channel their results and achievements into practice, in order to raise agricultural productivity and reduce production costs. The low productivity of Soviet agriculture and high production costs worried Khrushchev, who was impatient about the gap between scientific progress and its application on the farm. It was the task of the reorganized ministry to narrow this gap.

As a result of the reorganization, the functions of the Gosplan and of the republican ministries of agriculture were expanded. And the supply setup for farm requisites (machinery, fuel, fertilizer) was again reorganized, following a repetition of familiar criticisms that insufficient attention was paid to the requirements of collective and state farms. It was again maintained that implements were sent to places where they were not needed, while farms that could use such equipment were left without it; and that in manufacturing little was done to adapt farm machinery to variable regional requirements. So a new high-ranking agency, the *Soiuzsel'khoztekhnika,* independent of the Ministry of Agriculture, was created directly under the Council of Ministers of the USSR, to take over the whole supply service including repairing and servicing of machinery. The agency, through its local branches, was authorized to take over the RTS as well as stores and warehouses distributing farm requisites.

A new State Committee of Procurements of the Council of Ministers of the USSR replaced the former Ministry of Procurements in directing government acquisition of farm products. What is more important, a beginning was made in connection with procurements to tighten the local machinery of government supervision of agriculture (which had loosened up some with the liquidation of the MTS) by the creation of a new institution of state procurement inspectors. They were endowed with wide powers of supervision over collective and state farms in the interest of successful procurements. It was their task to check on whether the management of farm implements complied with procurement contracts and to report noncompliance and shortcomings to raion, provincial, and republican authorities. In such cases the procurement inspectors also had the very important power to limit or stop government cash advances on procurements from the farms. The inspectors, further, had the mandate to participate in the planning by kolkhoz and sovkhoz management of "measures for increased production and sale to the state of agricultural products." The significance attached to the duties of the inspectors is revealed by the directive to the party and government authorities of the constituent republics to select for the posts "politically mature" and experienced people.[5]

The procurement inspectorate was a short-lived prelude to a more far-reaching reform of the administrative agricultural apparatus which veered again toward greater centralization. With another mediocre crop year in 1961 came further reorganization in 1962, characterized this time by a turnabout toward centralization and tightening of control over farms. This third model had as the lowest link in the chain of command a territorial collective production administration (*proizvodstvennoe upravlenie*) which supervised both the collective and state farms of its district and was supposed to give them technical assistance. Such a degree of integration was something new in the administration of Soviet agriculture on the local level. Approximately fifteen hundred district agencies of this kind replaced a much larger number of discontinued raion agricultural organizations. On the provincial level, the former general administrative agency—ispolkom—was also split up in most provinces in the fall of 1962 into an agricultural ispolkom and an industrial ispolkom. The district production administrations were subordinated to the agricultural provincial ispolkoms, and the latter to the newly organized republican ministries of production and procurement of farm products, which were the operational agencies in charge of agriculture in each republic. There was no such ministry in Moscow for the country as a whole, but a new All-Union Committee on Agriculture became the principal administrative agency under the Council of Ministers of the USSR dealing with all aspects of agriculture.

In addition to this general administrative structure a number of independent functional organs were continued from the previous period. Thus research, agricultural education, and extension work continued to be the responsibility of the Ministry of Agriculture of the USSR and of similar ministries organized in most of the republics. Planning was still the function of the Gosplan; supply services, of the *Soiuzsel'khoztekhnika* with its network of local branches; and procurement of farm products, of the State Committee on Procurement. When a new irrigation program was adopted in the fall of 1963, a committee was established in Moscow for central direction of irrigation and reclamation work.

On the party side another and perhaps the strongest attempt was made to regularize a continuous and not merely sporadic participation of party organs in day-to-day supervision of farming. A previous important attempt of this sort was the assignment in the fall of 1953 of second secretaries of the raikoms and staff of Communist "instructors," with broad functions, to each MTS. A hiatus developed with the liquidation of MTS which was offset to some extent by the growth of party organizations on the farms, headed usually by professionals. A new move to inject party organs into the administrative structure was initiated by Khrushchev in the fall of 1962. In accordance with what he termed the "production principle" of organization, party organs at almost every level of the hierarchical pyramid were split into those supervising agriculture and those responsible for industry, each headed by a high-ranking functionary. A party committee headed by a secretary was attached to each district production administration, taking over the functions of the abolished raikoms with respect to all rural affairs of the district. The local party control over industry was vested either in the city party committees (gorkom) or in special committees for enterprises located in rural areas. At the province level too there was a division of the party structure into parallel agricultural and industrial sectors. It will be recalled that the government apparatus at the province level (the obispolkom or kraiispolkom) was split on a similar basis. The division did not go so far as the republic level, where the single central committee and its presidium were retained. However, two separate bureaus—one for industry and another for agriculture—were organized under the presidium. Similar bureaus presumably operated at the highest level, the Central Committee of the Communist Party in Moscow.

Khrushchev's central motive in carrying out such an unusual bifurcation of party organs was to compel a concentration on agriculture, to pinpoint responsibility for it on a definite sector of the party bureaucracy. This was in contrast to the party habit of alternately focusing attention now on industry, now on agriculture, in order to cope with some emergency or try to meet some goal. The result of such sporadic "campaign" methods of dealing with problems (*kampaneishchina*) was, according to Khrushchev, a weakening of party leadership in the branch of the economy, be it industry or agriculture, which happened to be neglected at the time.[6]

The reorganization of the agricultural apparatus along the twin government and party lines no doubt attained Khrushchev's purpose to strengthen the party's role in administering agriculture and in tightening its grip over it. The dualism resulting from meshing of party and government officials in the same structure is not conducive to efficiency. But since this integration was a firm official line, no criticism appeared in published Soviet sources. Khrushchev, however, made an important qualification apropos the reorganization in his speech before the November 1962 plenum. "It must be firmly borne in mind that the most perfect structure of party organs and also of organs of [government] administration of industry and agriculture will not bring the desired results if it will not place in production management positions energetic, talented organizers who are thoroughly familiar with industrial or agricultural production and ready to display revolutionary zeal for the party's objectives." He said that such cadres were available. Yet in subsequent speeches he displayed dissatisfaction with the functioning of the new administrative apparatus, particularly with the local production administrations. In his speech of February 28, 1964, Khrushchev stated that "strictly speaking the new organs of administration of kolkhozes and sovkhozes employ in a number of cases old methods. The organizational forms changed, but the character of the work remains the same." [7] In various speeches in 1962 and 1963 he stressed that these agencies must try to help farmers solve their problems and teach them improved methods and practices, not merely order them around.

It is difficult to see why Khrushchev expected such a transformation from Soviet officialdom. Not a few of these officials were ill-prepared for their jobs, but because of their status and power and the need to simulate activity, they issued orders, often with detrimental results, regarding farm operations which should have been left to the discretion of farm managers. For years the Soviet press had been filled with reports of this tenor and, judging from an array of similar cases cited by Khrushchev in his speech of February 28, 1964, the reorganization of 1962 did not change the picture much. Once again we come up against a crucial failing of the agricultural operations: excessive regimentation and interference with managers of farm enterprises selected by the government itself. Lack of clear-cut rules detailing the functions and powers of the different echelons of farm officialdom and management is doubtless a factor encouraging such regimentation; but only partly so. Existence of such rules in the case of planning, as we shall see, has not helped much.

Planning

A special but basic problem with which the administrative agricultural apparatus must deal is that of planning. Here, as we know, a highly centralized model prevailed under Stalin. What was to be produced and to a large extent how it was to be produced, as well as the share of the state in the output, was specified in plans on a national scale from Moscow and then distributed downward on the geographic administrative ladder until an allotment or quota reached each kolkhoz, state farm, and MTS. The plans set forth the acreages to be devoted by a kolkhoz or sovkhoz to each crop, the expected yields per acre, the area to be plowed for summer fallow, the number of livestock to be raised, the quantities of farm products to be delivered to the government. The government also planned the distribution of important inputs of nonagricultural origin such as tractors, machinery, chemical fertilizer. No role except that of the executor was assigned to the management of farms under this system. There was of course, bargaining about plan goals between individual managers and authorities, but it was entirely informal. This rigidity of planning was accompanied by the insistence on certain stereotype farm practices and patterns generalized over a large territory. Some of these, like the use of grasses in crop rotation (Williams' system) were useful in some regions but not in others; yet no exception was made by the planners. Other practices, like Lysenko's yarovization treatment of seed, were largely or entirely fads.

Khrushchev, who aimed at maximizing farm output and lowering costs, recognized the deleterious effect on production of the highly centralized system of planning because of its inflexibility, the failure of local adaptation of farming to the widely varying regional conditions, and the risk of magnifying errors. As a result, a decree was issued on March 9, 1953, which sharply criticized centralization of planning and prescribed remedial measures.* Its essential features were: (1) Only government procurements were to be planned in Moscow under the direction of the Gosplan. This plan, following approval by the Council of Ministers of the USSR, would be relayed to each republic and province, and thence to individual farms in the same manner as previously. (2) Each farm was to draw up a production and financial plan meeting the procurement quotas and its own requirements. The farm's management would determine what crops it should grow, what animals it should raise, and what methods it should use. The decree "recommended" that the crop acreage and livestock plans

---

* A previous attempt at some planning decentralization but on a much more modest scale had been made in 1939. A decree of December 28, 1939, provided that the planned goal be set only for the total grain acreage and the winter grain acreage for each kolkhoz. The distribution of the total grain acreage between different crops was left to the discretion of kolkhozes, provided that state procurement goals were met. (*Vazhneishie resheniia*, 1938–1940, p. 23.) This slight concession to kolkhoz autonomy proved to be a dead letter.

drawn up by the executive boards (*pravlenie*) of kolkhozes be submitted for approval by their membership. What we know about the generally passive role of members in kolkhoz affairs suggests that this may not have been done. (3) Such plans were to be reviewed by the supervising authorities—originally the raiipolkom and beginning in 1962 the district production administration—which would make certain that they provided adequately for the fulfillment of the procurement goals, and, if necessary, "recommend" changes. What would happen if a kolkhoz management did not agree with the raiispolkom was not explicitly stated. Since no appeal procedure was indicated, the power of review of farm plans by supervising authorities carried by implication also the power of veto. As I heard one Soviet official explain, the authorities would not tolerate it if a kolkhoz in a cotton growing region, for instance, should not include enough cotton acreage in its production program.

From the approved plans of different farms the production plans of raions were drawn up. And so the process continued moving on the administrative escalator until it reached the Gosplan and the Council of Ministers of the USSR. On the basis of such data and with an eye on allocation of resources over the whole economy, the Gosplan would plan the inputs of farm machinery and fertilizer it deemed necessary.*

Such was the authoritative doctrine of planning. From the start, however, the provision that planning be initiated by the farm was honored by the bureaucracy more in its breach than in observance. For nearly a decade the press and official speeches criticized the erosion of planning initiative of farms, which was constantly flaunted by local officials who either changed arbitrarily or brushed aside the plans drawn up by the farm management. Sometimes they did not even wait for the plans to be drawn up, but simply imposed ready-made plans of their own. Because of insufficient knowledge of detailed conditions on various farms such command planning by authorities often resulted either in crop acreage goals that were beyond the capabilities of kolkhozes and sovkhozes, or in sowing wrong crops, or in goals that were too low. Khrushchev devoted a part of his speech on February 28, 1964, to violations of this kind in planning.

In this speech Khrushchev foreshadowed the appearance of a new decree on the subject. It was adopted on March 20, 1964, with a title that told the story: "Concerning the Facts of Gross Violations and Perversion in the Planning Practices of Kolkhoz and Sovkhoz Production." [8] After

---

* For additional details on material balances see Herbert S. Levine, "Centralized Planning of Supply in Soviet Industry," Comparison of the United States and Soviet Economics, Joint Economic Committee, U.S. Congress, Washington, D.C., 1959, pp. 162–164.

repeating in the preamble criticisms of the faulty planning methods made
by Khrushchev and others, the decree calls for a strict observance of the
previous planning regulation of March 9, 1955. It categorically and
specifically forbids central planning for collective and state farms except
for government procurements. The decree provides for a strict party
accountability, criminal prosecution, and civil liability for farm losses
of any official guilty of violating planning regulations. More important
than the stern language is the provision that specifies that in case of disagreement between a kolkhoz or sovkhoz and the production administration regarding planned goals for crop acreages, yields, and livestock, the
last word belongs to the farm management and not to the officials of
the production administration. This should mean that the authorities
were deprived of the veto power over plans drawn up by collective and
state farms.

The decree provides for another innovation in farm planning: a survey of kolkhozes and sovkhozes during 1964–1965 to determine their
specialization involving "the most effective combination of different
branches of production in accordance with natural and economic conditions." The determination of specialization was to be worked out jointly
by the government and party organs and the management, specialists,
and party activists of the farms. These studies would serve as a guide in
setting up, in the interest of more efficient production planning on farms,
state procurement goals for a five-year period, 1966–1970. The decree
further enjoins the production administration to consider in setting up
procurement goals for farms not only the problem of fulfillment of the
procurement plan but also the general economic growth and development
of each kolkhoz and sovkhoz, including "strict observance of the principle of material incentives of the workers." In the evaluation of results
of the work of collective and state farms and production administrations,
the criterion, according to the decree, should be not only the fulfillment
of the procurement plan but "first of all" the volume and cost of production and the conditions created for the potential growth of production.

Much of the skepticism regarding the planning autonomy of collective
and state farms stems from the fact that it was severely handicapped not
only by the lawlessness and arbitrariness of local authorities but also by
the Kremlin's own tactics of administrative interference and pressure.
For the habit persisted under Khrushchev to press from Moscow for
the planting of certain crops and for introduction on a wide scale of
standardized farm practices. An example of such imposed or "political"
crops is corn. Failure to pay homage to the "queen of the fields" by including a sizable corn acreage in the production program of a farm was
to court trouble for the management. It was better to face losses due to

low yields or even failure of the corn crop than to incur official wrath. If a kolkhoz management by chance forgot this unwritten law, it would be quickly corrected by its supervising guardians.

Corn was not the only case where policy objectives of the central government conflicted with the relative freedom of the farm management to formulate the production plans granted by the decree of March 9, 1955. There was the campaign against grasses (tame hay). It began in 1954–55 as a reaction to the Stalinist policy of insistence on universal introduction of grasses in rotation to improve the soil structure, in accordance with Williams' theory.* Khrushchev claimed that the new anti-grass campaign was directed against such a rotation practice only in the drier regions where the yields of grasses were low; it did not apply to the humid regions where the planting of grasses, particularly of forage legumes, such as clover, has long been considered beneficial. The campaign marked a transition from the traditional three-field crop rotation cycle (*trekhpolka*) to a more intensive, higher yield system.

Clover and other legume grasses are particularly important in the crop rotation scheme since they not only augment the animal feed supply but also are a source of fertilizer—directly, by enriching the soil through absorption of nitrogen from the air and indirectly by increasing the quantity and improving the quality of manure.[9] This is the more valuable when chemical fertilizers are in short supply. To complete the favorable picture, the soil-improving properties of clover and other perennial grasses must be reckoned with. Yet in 1961 Khrushchev, while combatting Williams' theories, extended his strictures also to grasses in the humid northern and central regions of the European USSR. Grasses, he said, must be replaced by higher yielding crops such as corn, sugar beets, and peas. But this phase of the anti-grass campaign seems to have been short-lived. The Minister of Agriculture, I. P. Volovchenko, qualified the doctrine on grasses at the February 1964 plenum: "Some workers had drawn incorrect conclusions from the entirely correct criticism of the grass rotation system; they generally diminished the attention to planting grasses. Some even are afraid to plant clover or alfalfa: 'One may suddenly become tagged as a *travopol'shchik*' [a devotee of a grass rotation system]. This is absolutely wrong. The abandonment of the grass rotation system does not signify that grasses should not be planted where it is feasible

* The favor in which grasses were held by farm management may be explained not only by the spell of Williams' theory but in some measure by the fact that they are not subject to government procurements. This was suggested by a reply given by a manager of a Siberian sovkhoz to Khrushchev, who wanted to know the reason for the importance attached to a particular grass crop. Said the manager: "The state does not acquire grass from me. If I should plant grain, it will be necessary to sell some of it to the state." (*Stroitel'stvo kommunizma*, 6: 189.)

and advantageous." [10] Volovchenko specified that the yields should be high—40 to 50 centners and more of hay per hectare, not the 8 to 10 centners which Khrushchev criticized. This represents a retreat to a more sensible policy.

Another target for Khrushchev's attack was summer fallow, which took out of production 73 million acres in 1953.* His objection at first centered on the use of summer fallow in the humid northern and north-central regions of the USSR where it was a remnant of the old three-field system consisting of a spring crop, usually oats; summer fallow; and a winter crop, rye. In these regions summer fallow could, for the most part, be advantageously replaced by some planted grass or root crop, augmenting the feed supply. This is precisely what happened in western Europe when potatoes [11] and clover were introduced in the eighteenth and early nineteenth centuries. The same process began in the late nineteenth century in Russian peasant agriculture, but it did not go far enough. Perhaps one reason for clinging to summer fallow is that often the area is used for grazing before it is plowed up and thus partly offsets the shortage of pasture. But if there is a considerable delay in plowing, the value of summer fallow is likely to diminish. Its purpose would also be defeated if the fallow was not kept clean of weeds by successive cultivation, as was, in fact, frequently the case in the USSR.

Khrushchev's advocacy of dispensing with summer fallow in the humid regions, unlike his opposition to grasses, had considerable merit and was fairly successful. The proportion of summer fallow to arable land decreased in Belorussia from 14.6 percent in 1953 to only 2.8 percent in 1962, in Lithuania from 13.9 percent to 4.7 percent, and in Latvia from 7.5 to 1 percent.[12] But in 1961 Khrushchev extended the doctrine of no summer fallow, or as little of it as possible, to dry regions as well, including the new lands territory. Yet this is precisely the zone where, as the experience not only of the Soviet Union but also of the United States and Canada teaches, summer fallow in generous proportions is necessary to maintain yields. This has been recognized by most Soviet scientists and specialists. Summer fallow in these areas was strongly advocated by so authoritative a body as the All-Union Grain Research Institute in Kazakhstan—headed by A. I. Baraev—which specialized in dry farming investigations.† Another school, however, appeared on the scene in the

---

* Summer fallow is arable land tilled late in summer or fall or in the spring but not planted; it is kept clean for a growing season in order to conserve moisture and control weeds.

† According to Baraev, "The increase of yields obtained during three to four years following summer fallow fully covers the loss of output during the year when the land

late 1950s which claimed that corn and other cultivated crops in rotation in the dry regions could replace summer fallow as well as perennial grasses without diminishing wheat yields. Moreover, it was argued that by bringing fallow land under cultivation the total output would be increased. The leading proponent of this school was A. G. Nalivaiko, the Director of the Altai Agricultural Research Institute in western Siberia.

With respect to summer fallow in the dry regions, as with grasses in the humid regions, the official policy turned a complete circle before a costly lesson was learned. There are other cases where the lesson has not been learned as yet. Such is the two-stage method of grain harvesting. In North America the two-stage method is employed in regions with a short harvesting season and grain with heavy moisture content. The method involves first windrowing the moist grain and after it dries, combining it. In this manner the short harvesting period is artificially extended, which is important for regions like Siberia and Kazakhstan where harvesting often coincides with inclement weather. But double-stage harvesting, which was adopted in the USSR in the mid-1950s from Canada, has not been confined to such regions; it was needlessly extended to areas with a long harvest period, where it serves no useful purpose. This again illustrates the continuous tendency in Soviet planning to generalize on a countrywide scale and standardize cultural practices and methods which may be valid and useful under some specific environmental conditions but not under others. Another tendency was to adopt and herald as the last word of science and technology methods which were already obsolete or on the wane in the West. The excessive enthusiasm for the check rowing (*kvadratnogniezdovoi*) method of planting crops is a case in point. On the other hand, practices well tested and found useful in the West failed to be supported by the Kremlin. A notable instance was

---

is under summer fallow and naturally does not produce a crop." (*Sel'skaia zhizn'*, February 13, 1964.) At his institute, spring wheat during the three dry years 1961–1963 averaged 7.6 centners per hectare without the use of fallow, 13.6 centners during the first year following fallow, 11.2 centners during the second year, and 10.8 centners during the third year. The increment of yields during the three years following summer fallow was 12.8 centners per hectare. This more than compensated for the loss of 7.6 centners because the land was not cropped one year. The difference was even greater on collective and state farms where the fields were not as clean of weeds as they were in the institute. In one sovkhoz in Tselinograd province spring wheat yielded 13.5 centners per hectare in 1963 after summer fallow and only 3.2 centners on land without it. In another sovkhoz during the dry year 1962 the yields were respectively 18 centners and 4.4 centners.

stubble mulching which is an important soil conservation measure * and, with summer fallow, constitute the alpha and omega of rational farming in dry regions. While some of the cobwebs and fads which characterized agricultural planning during the Stalin era were swept away, others took their place during the post-Stalin period.

The more specifically economic flaws in modern Soviet agricultural planning have been pinpointed as follows: [13] "though use of modern methods of economic analysis of the input-output type has been increasing in Soviet planning, the emphasis in agricultural planning apparently has been on broad directives, physical concepts, and accounting. The fact that no economic value is imputed to land in the USSR and no interest charge is made for capital no doubt handicaps economic planning and the efficient allocation of resources. In the United States and other Western countries, interest charges on investments vary with the productive life of the resource and the amount of risk involved. Under the Soviet system, cost comparisons among various types of investments exclude interest charges, and thus do not include an interest charge for the length of time required for the investment to be reflected in production."

One factor seriously hampering agricultural planning is weather. Adverse weather conditions played a major part in the agricultural stagnation which upset the plans for economic growth during the early 1960s. With Russia's generally short growing season and large subhumid area, weather variations are bound to cause fluctuations of crop yields. The risk of poor crops is accentuated by the shift of farming into the climatically more hazardous eastern and southern regions. Improved and specialized cultural practices, let alone irrigation, could help to neutralize unfavorable climatic influences, but this was precisely the weak point of Soviet planning, as we have seen.

Finally, a serious weakness underlying Soviet planning is insufficient public debate about projected plans and policies, and the total lack of opposition once plans are officially adopted. This, combined with inflexibility, increases the risk of multiplying costly errors which is inherent in central planning. Certainly some dubious, uneconomic, or even harmful practices were introduced through central planning. On the positive side of the balance sheet, of course, is the opportunity for speedy, useful innovations on a wide scale, exemplified by the tractor, the combine, arti-

---

* Stubble mulching is the tillage of the soil and treatment of crop residues in ways to leave plant materials within or on the soil surface to form a mulch. Mulches are generally used to help conserve moisture, control temperature, prevent surface compaction or crusting, reduce runoff and erosion, improve soil structure, or control weeds. (*Soil, The Yearbook of Agriculture, 1957*, U.S. Department of Agriculture, p. 763.)

ficial insemination, and a wide dissemination of a number of improved plant varieties.

Agricultural Research

The Soviet government has always been vitally interested in science as a means of expanding agricultural production, and to that end has promoted research. Unlike the situation in the United States, all research in the Soviet Union, including agricultural, is government-sponsored—conducted either at some research institution, an experiment station, or agricultural college. A highly important corollary is that political interference with research, while varying in intensity from period to period, has never been absent.

In the USSR there are two categories of agricultural research institutions: the national or all-union and the republican. On the national level the Ministry of Agriculture of the USSR has responsibility for coordinating and directing all research.[14] Within the ministry is the Lenin All-Union Academy of Agricultural Science, whose members are supposed to be outstanding scientists in the country. It is the planning body for science programs. Five of the republics have ministries of agriculture which are responsible for research on the republican level. In the other republics a department in the Ministry of Production and Procurements performs this function. The national research programs are carried out by thirty-four all-union institutes, such as those of Crops (plant industry), Plant Protection, Grain Crops, Sugar Beets, Mechanization, Soils, and Agricultural Economics. Each of these institutes has responsibility for all work in its field throughout the country and often has branches and substations where research is done in addition to the work at headquarters. For instance, the All-Union Institute of Crops in Leningrad has twenty plant-introduction stations throughout the USSR. Each republic has a number of research institutes and regional experiment stations concerned with local agricultural problems. The republic institutes specialize largely in applied research or service work, such as growing seed and testing varieties. They operate relatively large farms, and the sales receipts help to finance research. For example, the Krasnodar Agricultural Research Institute operates approximately 7,500 acres of land and receives 40 percent of the sales receipts from the farm products sold, in addition to a direct allotment of funds from the republic. A considerable part of the staff's time is spent in farming activities and in conferring with personnel on collective and state farms. There are also ninety-four higher agricultural educational institutions which, like land grant colleges in the United States, conduct research along with teaching.[15]

Political interference with research was most prominent in the 1930s and 1940s under Stalin. Social sciences, agricultural economics, and statistics were the first to experience severe mass purges, followed by biological and agricultural sciences, headed by genetics. In these purges perished such noted leaders of Russian agricultural science as N. E. Vavilov and N. M. Tulaikov, whose names have since been rehabilitated. The later Stalin period also witnessed the rise of Trofim Lysenko to virtual dictatorship over the biological and agricultural sciences. His campaign for a retreat from the position of modern genetic science to obsolete dogmas, like the inheritance of acquired characteristics, appealed ideologically to the Kremlin and was supported by it.[16]

After Stalin's death Lysenko's authority became greatly deflated and at one time it even seemed as if he might end in a total eclipse. Criticism of his theories was permitted in learned magazines, and in the spring of 1956 he was removed from the influential post of president of the Lenin Agricultural Academy, the top research coordinating body. But a new tide followed the ebb in his fortunes. Trenchant criticism of Lysenkoism in an unsigned article in the August 1958 issue of the Soviet Botanical Journal brought a dismissal of all but one member of the editorial board. Then in 1961 he was again appointed to the presidency of the Lenin Academy. He did not remain long in this post because of poor health, but his successor was one of his disciples and collaborators, Ol'shanskii. On a number of occasions Khrushchev went out of his way to praise Lysenko's work. A visit by Khrushchev and other high officials to Lysenko's experimental farm in Gorkii, near Moscow, was reported in the Soviet press as a tribute to the man. Yet Lysenko no longer possessed the power to command and discipline scientists who did not agree with him, even if they could not openly criticize him. Also somewhat of a throwback to Lysenkoism was a decree adopted on January 9, 1963, entitled "Concerning Measures for Further Development of Biological Science and Strengthening Its Connection with Practice," which bolstered Michurinist biology. The decree stated that, "It is necessary to develop more widely and deeply the Michurinist current in biological science." The name of Michurin—a practical plant breeder who worked particularly with fruit and who won Lenin's favor—was used to denote the Lysenkoist school.

In 1964 Khrushchev—apparently with the intent to stimulate the flow of ideas—adopted a more cautious approach than formerly toward taking sides in scientific controversies, including those among agricultural scientists. This was manifested at the February 1964 plenum with respect to serious differences between Lysenko and other scientists. After highly praising the results obtained by Lysenko on his experimental farm, Khrushchev remarked: "By presenting Lysenko's school as a model I do not mean to say that we cannot have other opinions in science regarding this question. The Central Committee of the Party is of the opinion that it is necessary to be tolerant of scientific controversies. Out of such debates and conflict of opinion, the truth is born; the best results are secured. But the latter must be tested and verified in practice." To further emphasize the reversal of the existing custom, he laid down the dictum that: "The Central Committee of the Party should not say that some one particular method should be used [in scientific research]. And I, as the first secretary of the Central Committee and the chairman of the Council of Ministers do not want and cannot say this. Why? Because there should be competition of the minds, of ideas, among scientists. The proposals of scientists should be verified in practice and the best should be introduced in kolkhozes and sovkhozes." [17]

The shortcomings in Soviet agricultural research, as it became unfettered from Lysenkoism, were exposed at an agricultural scientific conference in 1956 by a former Minister of Agriculture of the USSR, V. M. Matskevich, without mentioning Lysenko.[18]

The leaders of many scientific institutions, using as an excuse that they are busy with research work needed to meet present-day requirements of collective and state farm production, are therefore not concerning themselves with theoretical questions of agricultural and biological sciences. Frequently, however, behind the screen of this apparent scientific interest in production problems there is concealed an insufficient depth of scientific investigation and a tendency to extend, in a hackneyed fashion throughout the Soviet Union or to an entire republic, dubious achievements which, at best, are of limited and local significance only. The departments of biology, biochemistry, and genetics in many of the institutions and experiment stations have been liquidated or lead a sorry existence. Leaders of research institutions do not reckon with the fact that without an accumulation of necessary theoretical knowledge, without a certain "know-how," it is impossible under modern conditions successfully to solve purely practical problems posed by production. Even the largest research institutions specializing in various branches of agriculture and agricultural colleges do not devote enough attention to theoretical research, although they are the very ones which should be the first to do so . . .
In many scientific institutions serious violations of scientific methodology take place. Experiments are carried out without sufficient repli-

cation or observance of the necessary complex of agricultural technical methods and are not accompanied by controlled observations and studies. Such an important method of verification of experimental data as mathematical analysis is not practiced. Some research workers make serious errors in the interpretation of experimental data. There have been cases when, as a result of lack of control and complete in-attention to methodological problems on the part of the leaders of scientific institutes, publication of unreliable data became possible . . . A serious shortcoming, unfortunately still prevalent in the work of our scientific institutions and of some of our research workers, is an element of conceit (*zaznaistvo*). Often the root of this conceit is simply ignorance. A number of scientific workers, especially those who are most proud of their "remarkable" discoveries, producing a revolution in science, had not even acquired a sound knowledge of either their native or foreign literature dealing with the subject of the practices of socialist agriculture.

Even the blight of Lysenkoism could not wholly arrest progress; some work was continued by Soviet plant breeders on hybrid corn despite Lysenko's opposition. During the period following the conference and Matskevich's speech, further progress in agricultural research took place. The quality of research and the capability of scientists vary greatly within and among Soviet institutes. Such institutions as the All-Union (Vavilov) Institute of Crops, with its countrywide network of experiment stations, the Agrophysical Institute named after Ioffe, the All-Union Institute of Grain Crops in Kazakhstan, the Institute of Oilseed Crops, and the Agricultural Research Institute in Krasnodar rank high in the competence of their staffs and the character of their scientific work. Research work in agricultural economics, which languished for a long time, was resumed after 1956 with the organization of the All-Union Research Institute of Agricultural Economics in the Ministry of Agriculture of the USSR and by similar cooperating institutes in various republics. It was supported by the Institute of Economics of the Academy of Sciences of the USSR. However, concentration on supply and production to the almost total neglect of demand and marketing, and failure to use marginal analysis, continued to be weak points of Soviet economic research.

Agricultural research in the USSR has been greatly aided by the softening or abandonment of the cultural and scientific isolationism of Stalin's days and the re-establishment of scientific and technical contacts abroad. Khrushchev frequently sermonized, with supporting quotations from Lenin and specific examples, on the value and desirability of learning from the agricultural experience of capitalism before it is "buried" by communism. In line with this policy reciprocal exchange of technical agricultural delegations or missions with foreign countries were promoted. Because of the value attached by Khrushchev to American experience, such exchanges were especially numerous with the United States, in accordance with cultural exchange agreements concluded every two years beginning in 1958. Articles dealing with foreign experience regarding such problems as animal feeding, poultry raising, and soil conservation increasingly appeared in the Soviet press. And a comprehensive program of abstracting and translating foreign technical literature was initiated.

While Matskevich, in his 1956 speech quoted above, deplored the failure to grapple with theory and to undertake basic research, Khrushchev was concerned that agricultural science was not utilitarian or practical enough and, above all, that its achievements are far too slowly adopted in agriculture. His second charge suggests that, despite a plethora of specialists and technicians, the wide authority wielded by the government, and opportunities presented by central planning, the Kremlin has not solved the problem of speedy introduction of innovations and of effective extension work in collectivized agriculture.

Summary and Outlook

We have seen that the government's agrarian policy from the Emancipation in the 1860s to the Revolution of 1917 had a number of positive features, but that it was not able to end the historic contest for land beween peasant and landlord and to forestall the two agrarian revolutions of 1905 and 1917. Among the positive features of the agrarian policy were: the allotment of land to a majority of peasants upon emancipation; the commercialization of agriculture, facilitated by the growing network of railroads; the expansion of foreign trade, especially grain exports; and the development of a domestic market. Another positive feature was the extension of agriculture into the southern and eastern steppes, involving great expansion of valuable wheat production, compared with the more traditional rye. Parallel with this was the beginning of intensification in the western regions (sugar beets, flax, potatoes) and of cotton growing on a large scale in the irrigated regions of Central Asia and Transcaucasia.

On the negative side was the fact that certain groups of the peasant population were not allotted land or were allotted very little, less than they had cultivated as serfs. Even more serious was the heavy financial burden of redemption payments for land and taxes. Other negative features were: the ill-balanced character of many peasant holdings (lack of pasture, woodland, and so forth); the failure of the government until 1906 to combat the inefficiency of the scattered-strip system of farming and to undertake other measures to raise the low level of agricultural productivity; the retention until 1906 of civil disabilities interfering with the peasant's mobility; and the lack of effort to stamp out illiteracy in the village, which made of the peasantry a kind of a caste at the bottom of the social scale. The combined effect of these factors was growing rural poverty and distress, compounded by recurrent famines in years of crop failure. Most serious, therefore, was the stubborn refusal of the tsarist government to enact land redistribution in line with peasant aspirations, even when agrarian unrest reached a revolutionary boiling point in 1905. However, the peasant revolution of 1905–06, though abortive from the standpoint of satisfying the demands of the peasantry for expropriation of estate land, succeeded in channeling the energies of the government toward the removal of civil disabilities and toward various measures of agricultural improvement and rural education.

Land tenure under the mir, with its basic feature of successive redistributions, was a highly controversial policy issue in the nineteenth and early twentieth centuries, provoking sharply conflicting attitudes. The preservation of the mir up to 1906 was considered by its opponents a negative factor and they welcomed the government's effort under Stolypin to destroy it. The indictment of the mir as a barrier to technical progress is debatable; those who hold this view tend to identify the mir with scattered-strip farming, which is not peculiar to the mir or Russia. But what is not debatable is that mir tenure with its land divisions based on egalitarian principles contributed to the instability of land property relations in the countryside and was, ipso facto, a psychological and political threat to the continued existence of estate farming and even of peasant farming based on the principle of private property. Estate farming was retreating before small peasant agriculture prior to the revolution of 1905 as land was sold off to the peasants at high prices. Thus on the eve of the Revolution the peasants owned two thirds of the farmland of European Russia. The process was accelerated after 1905 with increased financial assistance from the government. But the stronger, the more viable sector of estate farming remained intact and played a highly important part in commercial agriculture before the First World War.

The Revolution of 1917 brought the historic contest between peasants and landlords to a close: with Lenin's blessing but contrary to Marxist principles, the estates were divided up. The peasant-landlord contest, however, was soon replaced by a new conflict between the Communist state and the peasants. The ideological bias of Marxism, especially Russian Marxism, against small peasant farming as a technological anachronism and a breeding ground for capitalism was no doubt a catalytic agent in stirring up such a conflict. But the immediate cause was the urgent need to feed and clothe the city workers and the Red Army, the strongholds of Communist power. Since the Soviet state could afford to pay but little for food and agricultural raw materials during the civil war, force was used to extract them from the unwilling small independent peasant producers. They, in turn, responded by drastically curtailing production and becoming more and more self-sufficient. During the first round of this struggle the peasants won a signal victory when the regime of War Communism was replaced in 1921 by the NEP, with the partial restoration of the market and other aspects of free enterprise in the village. But the victory was short-lived.

The recovery of agriculture and the nationalized industry from the ravages of war and revolution permitted the Soviet government under Stalin, goaded on by the Trotsky faction, to embark on an ambitious industrialization program. Hence more food and raw materials were needed to feed industrial workers and for export, in exchange for imported machinery. In the early stages, with the low efficiency of Soviet industrial operations and particularly with the overriding emphasis on the development of heavy industry, the available means of payment to the peasants was in the form of consumer goods which were high priced, often scarce, and of poor quality. At the same time, prices of agricultural products were kept by the government on a low level. Such unfavorable terms of trade obviously could not stimulate badly needed agricultural production but, on the contrary, did the reverse. Moreover, the growth of population and the fragmentation of small peasant farming, with its numerous scattered strips, was undermining efficiency. Yet the Soviet policy of discrimination against the more prosperous peasant farmers, the kulaks, who were feared as the advance guard of capitalist restoration, certainly did not discourage fragmentation.

In 1929 Stalin turned first gropingly and soon more decisively to collectivization of peasant agriculture as a solution to agricultural difficulties. Parallel with it was the expansion of the state farm sector. With the help of party cadres Stalin hoped to control the kolkhozes much more effectively than he could millions of independent peasant farmers. And a collective farm, with its large fields that could be cultivated with the aid of tractors, should be much more efficient than the small peasant holding fragmented into numerous scattered little strips.

The horrors of collectivization, with its millions of victims uprooted from the land, deported to concentration camps, shot, or starved to death, are well known. It was even admitted by Stalin to Churchill. The inefficiency and disorganizing effect on agricultural production of the new collective and state farms, particularly the mass slaughter of livestock, were no doubt very disappointing to the architects of the new farm system. The exceedingly rapid tempo of the forced collectivization early in 1930, combined with ruthless liquidation of kulaks (usually the best farmers), produced near chaos in the countryside. Stalin euphemistically called it "dizziness from success," but he was compelled to order a temporary strategic retreat. The Kremlin never faltered in its grip over the exactions of large quantities of grain and other farm products for the Soviet state, even at the cost of a terrible famine in 1932–33. Stalin said that the first commandment of collective farms was to deliver their quotas of grain to the government. There was much to be said for the celebrated simile of a leading member of the Trotsky opposition, Preobrazhenskii, who likened agriculture to a colony from which capital is siphoned off to the mother country—industry—in accordance with the familiar pattern of original capital accumulation in Karl Marx's *Capital*.

A new apparatus for exaction of farm products and for grass-roots control of collective farming was forged in the MTS. It was organized as a state agency for pooling tractors and machinery to perform, for payment in kind, various operations on several collective farms, which for a long time were not allowed to own such equipment. The heavy destruction of horses during the mass collectivization drive enhanced the importance of MTS as a source of power for agriculture and made of it a more effective instrument of Soviet control.

Stalin learned that force, indoctrination, and tractors were not enough to make peasants efficient producers; economic incentives were also essential. The result was not decollectivization but a kind of limited NEP in the mid-1930s. A sharply differentiated method of payment for labor in kolkhozes, resembling a piece rate system and resulting in a considerable inequality of income, was strongly emphasized. And a restricted free market and a limited private sector within the collective economy, based on "an acre and a cow" type of holding, were legalized. This private sector performed yeoman service in the recovery of the livestock industry that lost nearly half of the cattle during the collectivization drive, more than half of the hogs, and more than two thirds of the sheep. It contributed much to the food supply of the peasants themselves as well as of the city population, though at prices considerably higher than in state stores. Suffice it to say that the private market in the cities, where individuals and collective farms were selling their surpluses, accounted for one fifth of the total value of trade in foodstuffs in 1940.[1]

The private sector had to be tolerated or even encouraged by the regime when the kolkhozes were weak. But its attitude stiffened as the collective farming gained in strength in the late 1930s. For the private sector was, after all, ideologically a foreign body in the collective organism. What was equally or more important, the private sector competed with the collective economy for the labor and loyalty of the peasants. Since the peasants had to rely so much on their little private plots and few animals for a livelihood, they naturally gave more attention to them and to the private market (a time-consuming operation) than to tending collective fields and livestock under someone else's command. This, of course, affected adversely kolkhoz production, and a vicious circle developed. It could have been broken by economic means, by an increase in the low earnings of collective farmers in order to divert their energies to collective farm work. This would inevitably necessitate higher prices for farm products and a larger supply of consumer goods if an increase of the already existing considerable inflation were to be avoided. Since this method was not acceptable to the government, bent on the rapid growth of heavy industry, it began to apply restrictive measures against the private farm sector toward the end of the 1930s. It should be reiterated that this private sector was an appendix to the collective economy, that the old type of the independent peasant farmer had practically disappeared.

The Nazi invasion and the ensuing tight food supply interrupted this offensive against the private sector. During the war collective farming disintegrated in the large occupied zone and was quite disorganized in the unoccupied part. Agricultural production greatly declined and much of the farm equipment was destroyed. With the end of the war, the restoration of the collective farm system and its extension to the annexed territories became the objective of Soviet policy, together with recovery of agricultural production. Far greater importance, however, was attached by Soviet planners to the recovery and expansion of heavy industry, and resources were largely channeled in that direction. Thus state capital investment in heavy industry during the postwar years 1946–1950 (Fourth Five Year Plan) was 145.3 billion rubles (old); in light industry, 20.3 billion rubles; and in agriculture, 24.8 billion rubles—far below that of heavy industry even when the kolkhoz investment of 31.2 billion rubles out of their own resources is added.[2] Labor, especially young and skilled, was also attracted to industry.

Previous major wars, like the Crimean War of 1854–55, the Russo-Japanese War of 1904–05, and the First World War, resulted in a more or less radical shake-up of the agrarian structure which usually brought some concessions to the peasantry—but not the Second World War. Stalin's postwar agricultural policy was all stick and no carrot, as Khrushchev and a number of lesser lights in Soviet bureaucracy testified on numerous occasions. The value of economic incentives was forgotten, with some exceptions, such as cotton. Large procurements extracted by the government were at unchanged prices, despite a long spell of inflation, and were certainly below production costs. Little was left to remunerate peasants—the residual claimants to the kolkhoz income—for their labor. They reacted accordingly, trying to do as little as possible in the kolkhoz and as much as possible on their private plot and with their livestock, in order to eke out what was for the most part a meager wage even by Soviet standards. With such exploitation of the farm population and neglect of economic incentives, severe regimentation was necessary to maintain, let alone increase, production. One aspect of this command economy was the highly centralized, detailed, and rigid agricultural planning. In such planning much reliance was placed during the Stalin era on certain fads and pseudo-scientific panaceas (Lysenko's yarovization or Williams' universal grass-rotation system, for example). Another aspect was that the self-governing democratic character of the kolkhoz became a fiction and a formality because the authorities appointed and removed the "elective" officials at will.

The slow growth of agricultural production during the early postwar period was obfuscated by highly exaggerated crop statistics based on so-called biological yields. These were estimates of crops standing in the field before harvest, which did not reflect the officially admitted large harvesting losses and, in general, lent themselves to overestimation for fiscal or propaganda purposes. Such figures were repudiated after Stalin. The revised estimate of the total grain crop for 1933–37, for instance, is nearly a fourth less than the originally estimated biological crop. As for livestock, even official figures and statements did not conceal this weak spot in Soviet collective agriculture. The number of cattle on January 1, 1953, was less than in 1916 and in 1928 on the same territory. Production of butter in Siberia, the principal butter exporting region of Russia before the First World War, was less in 1952 than in 1913.

Increased agricultural production was essential for the improvement of the living standard in the USSR, for a better balanced, more palatable diet, for building up contingency food reserves and export surpluses. There was, moreover, the problem of the resumed rapid growth of population, 3 to 3½ million annually, following the demographic disaster of the war. But the Soviet Union was bedeviled by underproduction and scarcities. Whether Stalin fully realized the nature and scope of Soviet agricultural difficulties is immaterial. The significant thing is that Stalin could afford dilatory tactics in satisfying popular aspirations for a better life (which he himself defined in 1934 as the essence of socialism). His successors, not so well entrenched, could not adopt such tactics even if they wished, and Khrushchev, judging from his frequently reiterated utterances, was seriously concerned with the raising of living levels in the USSR. In view of this, agricultural reforms were inevitable once Stalin passed from the scene, and they came half a year later.

The post-Stalin changes in agricultural policy may justly be called Khrushchev reforms, for he predominated in the formation of agrarian policy long before reaching the zenith of political power, and they bear the imprint of his dynamic personality. A rapid upsurge, a maximization of agricultural production at the least possible cost was the end to which all changes were directed. In general, Khrushchev aimed to make the collective farm system more economical and therefore more viable. There was never any question of decollectivization like that which took place temporarily in a number of East European countries and persisted in Poland and Yugoslavia. But there were some concessions to the peasants. Increased economic incentives to farmers, larger investment of capital and labor input in agriculture, changes in the crop pattern, administrative and organizational changes, and intensification of agriculture, mainly through increased application of chemical fertilizer and to a lesser extent through irrigation, are the lines of Khrushchev's attack against agricultural underproduction.

The outstanding Khrushchev reforms in the area of economic incentives were: encouragement of the private sector through reduction of taxation; a substantial increase in the very low procurement prices of farm products, coupled with revamping and simplification of the price and procurement structure, in order to enable kolkhozes to pay their members more and increase their investment for productive as well as welfare and cultural purposes; and insistence on more frequent and regular payments to kolkhozniks instead of the annual lump-sum distribution. Ancillary to this was the device which only a minority of kolkhozes were able to adopt, a guaranteed cash wage with incentive bonuses to replace the prevailing cumbersome workday system of payments in cash and in kind. This would presumably modify the residual and uncertain character of the peasants' share in kolkhoz income.

The organizational and institutional changes included: the attempt, largely abortive, to decentralize agricultural planning and boost the initiative of kolkhoz management; the wholesale merger of kolkhozes into large, unwieldy units, which began under Khrushchev's direction during the last three years of the Stalin regime; absorption of kolkhozes by state farms (which forged ahead under Khrushchev and usually were assigned new or urgent tasks such as extension of farming on virgin land or an increase of the vegetable and potato supply in the cities); the liquidation of the machine-tractor stations, heretofore the pivotal point of the Soviet agrarian structure, and the sale of farm machinery to kolkhozes; successive reorganizations of the agricultural administrative apparatus with an ever firmer party control; and a partial unfettering of Soviet biological and agricultural sciences from the Lysenkoist grip. But the old habit, inherited from the Stalin era, of extending farm practices and crops to regions unsuitable for climatic and other reasons persisted.

With regard to the crop pattern, the Khrushchev policy centered on the expansion of some industrial crops like cotton and sugar beets, but principally on increased grain production, especially grain for feed. The inadequate feed supply was long recognized as a serious bottleneck in solving the livestock problem on which the improvement of Russian diet depends so much. However, since the successive poor harvests in the early 1960s, which caused heavy wheat imports during 1963–64, bread grains again gained importance. In dealing with the grain and other crop problems, Khrushchev's approach was that of changes and expansion of acreage. The regularly repeated cliché on the importance of increasing yields remained the official slogan, but Khrushchev did not rely on it, as Stalin had during the first postwar Five Year Plan of 1946–50. Specific expansion programs were developed for different crops and regions. The earliest and best known of these was the corn expansion program which boosted the corn area from about 9 million acres in 1953 to more than 60 million acres in 1962. This made corn a kind of universal crop, grown mainly for silage practically throughout the USSR, though not very successfully in most regions. There was also a drive to put under crops, mostly spring wheat, over 100 million acres of virgin and once cultivated land beyond the Volga and the Urals. These are marginal lands from a climatic standpoint—a short growing season, frequent droughts, inclement weather during harvest, and winters too severe to permit winter (fall sown) grain. The crop yields are low and unstable.

The fundamental objective of Khrushchev's policy of maximizing agricultural production at the least cost and essentially by collectivist methods remained intact, but there was much backing and filling, much zigzagging regarding its execution. Thus, Khrushchev's relatively liberal attitude toward the private sector changed—like Stalin's in the late 1930s—with the growing strength of the collective sector. Khrushchev, in fact, foreshadowed this in the celebrated September 1953 report. But he insisted, contrary to the inclination of the bureaucracy, on gradualism in the application of restrictions against the private sector which began in 1956. He was realistic enough to understand that the private sector must be tolerated when the general agricultural picture was not propitious and even began to look disastrous in 1963. After all, this sector with its preponderance of livestock products and high value crops, accounted for about one third of the estimated total Soviet agricultural production in the early 1960s and for about 40 percent of the kolkhozniks' total income in 1957–58, according to a Soviet sample survey. Khrushchev's zeal for economic incentives also cooled perceptibly in the late 1950s. He began to frown upon the relatively large earnings by members in some kolkhozes and urged that expansion of various communal and welfare services take precedence over the rise of individuals' earnings. This had, as he himself admitted later, an adverse effect on the kolkhozniks' incentives and on production. Consequently, in the 1960s a turnabout was made and the value of economic incentives again began to be stressed.

The increased grass-roots initiative in agricultural production planning provided by the law of March 9, 1955, which left only procurements to central planning, remained a dead letter for nearly a decade. It was nullified by the local bureaucracy by means of a loophole: the requirement of approval of such plans by local authorities, who often made arbitrary changes or did not even bother to wait for the planning proposals of farm management but imposed their own targets. Only in 1964 were definite steps taken to correct the situation by eliminating the loophole, leaving the last word in production planning (but not in procurements) to the farm management and threatening prosecution for illegal interference by the bureaucracy. Enforcement of this regulation is problematical in view of the persistent bureaucratic habit of meddling in farm affairs and the considerable degree of farm control and responsibility vested in 1962 in the newly organized regional production administrations. The creation of these agencies represented a new tightening of the administrative screws on kolkhozes four years after they were loosened by the liquidation of the machine-tractor stations.

There was some zigzagging in Khrushchev's policy regarding the crop pattern. The overriding emphasis on corn receded somewhat in the early 1960s as the importance of a more diversified feed crop pattern was recommended. Further de-emphasis took place in 1963–64 when priority was given in acreage programming to winter wheat over corn in regions suitable to the cultivation of the former. After the crop failure in 1963 Khrushchev's negative attitude also changed toward summer fallow, which was considered by most specialists essential in the semiarid (new lands) spring wheat regions to reduce risk of crop failure in these hazardous farm regions. Stubble mulching, another important dry farming practice and a preventive measure against soil erosion, gained increased attention. Finally, the taboo against grasses was lifted in the humid regions where their growing was considered advantageous by specialists.

Despite the various errors and blunders, Khrushchev's reforms paid off during the period 1953–58 in a substantial increase of production. Various indexes show a rise of roughly one third between 1953 and 1957 and about one half between 1953 and the bumper crop year 1958. This was the period of rising economic incentives and investment and of huge acreage expansion. Another important contributing factor to the large growth of production was the relatively favorable weather. In an upsurge of optimism in May 1957 Khrushchev made his famous prediction about catching up with the United States within a few years in per capita consumption of livestock products. The Seven Year Plan, 1959–65, projected a 70 percent increase in total agricultural production. But these sanguine expectations proved unrealistic. Actually most of this seven-year period was one of stagnation or slow growth. During 1959–62 agricultural production increased on the average by 4 percent compared with 1958,[3] according to Soviet figures, which include highly exaggerated grain production estimates. The U.S. Department of Agriculture index of estimated Soviet net agricultural production, which deflated the exaggerated grain figures, showed a decline of 3 percent in 1960 and 1963 and no change in 1961 and 1962, compared with 1958.[4] The decline would have been greater in 1963 were it not for the large increase in meat production caused by the heavy slaughter of animals, due to the short feed supply, and an excellent cotton crop in the irrigated central Asiatic regions.

Agriculture again became a retarding factor in Soviet economic growth. The crop failure in 1963 dramatized the weakness of Soviet agriculture, for it necessitated the adoption of many harsh measures. Among these were: restriction of bread consumption, manifested by the practical disappearance of white bread in the cities during the winter of 1963–64; the heavy liquidation of livestock, mainly hogs, the number of which declined by more than 40 percent between January 1963 and January 1964; and the reversal of Russia's traditional role of an important exporter of wheat and other grains to that of an importer of more than 10 million tons. This meant shipment of gold abroad instead of acquisition of foreign exchange. But while the unsatisfactory agricultural situation came into focus in 1963, it was already simmering during the preceding four years of lagging production which did not permit the accumulation of adequate grain reserves. In the light of this, the large exports during 1959–62 appear to have been a big gamble. Here again the situation was obscured beginning in 1958 by inflated grain statistics, which might have misled Khrushchev if he really trusted them. For on the basis of official Soviet crop figures ample stocks of bread grains (wheat and rye) should have existed which would have made heavy imports unnecessary.[5] Poor weather was a factor in this period, but it cannot be blamed for the crisis. The situation was aggravated by lagging economic incentives, inadequate—even though increasing—capital investment in agriculture, faulty farm practices, giantism, and regimentation of farm management. These economic and institutional factors are also responsible for the weak position of Soviet agriculture, notwithstanding a decade of Khrushchev reforms.

What can be said about the future? In evaluating the prospects of Soviet agriculture we must steer between the Scylla of excessive pessimism and the Charybdis of exaggerated optimism. Considerable weather fluctuations from year to year will, of course, continue. In fact, the nursery rhyme about the little girl can be applied to Russian weather: when it is good it is very, very good, but when it is bad it is horrid. However, the variations in yields and production may become less sharp if well-tested, improved farm practices and crop patterns are increasingly adopted.

Expansion of production will continue to be a major issue in the foreseeable future. It is true that the Soviet Union does not suffer from the kind of population pressure on land which bedevils so many underdeveloped countries. This is evident from the ratio of arable land to population (a crude measure, to be sure) which in the Soviet Union is over two acres per person, whereas in Asia it is less than an acre and in many other countries much less. The sad fact that the USSR had two demographic catastrophes during the collectivization campaign and again during the Second World War helped in this respect. But even with the continuation of the present fairly rapid growth of population (about 3.5 million annually) the Malthusian specter of a serious disparity between population and food supply is not inevitable in this scientific age in a country which is becoming as highly industrialized as the Soviet Union and which has so large an agricultural plant. But if "the devil of Malthus," to paraphrase a famous British economist,[6] remains chained in the USSR, the Soviet government still faces a serious food problem because of the increasing number of mouths to be fed and the strong desire for an improved diet.

Highly significant from this standpoint is the official recognition that land resources of the USSR are limited. Soviet agriculture reached its extensive frontier with the expansion on the new lands in the 1950s. This means that further increase of production must come not through extension of acreage, the traditional method in Russia, but through higher yields, through intensification. It remains to be seen to what extent the program in progress to greatly step up use of chemical fertilizers (including increased use of grain, to which little chemical fertilizer is applied) will be implemented, but it is reasonable to expect an increased use of fertilizer with an upward effect on yields.

A larger area under irrigation would also raise the output appreciably and is particularly important in a country like the USSR with its vast semiarid and dry zones. The significance of irrigation is also enhanced by the fact that chemical fertilizer, which cannot be used effectively in the dry farming areas, could be applied on irrigated land. This, incidentally, is the story of Soviet cotton, which is grown entirely under irrigation with heavy application of fertilizer. The Kremlin has been concerned with the highly ineffective utilization of the existing irrigation network; still, less attention is given to this method of raising yields than it deserves. The heavy capital investment required is no doubt a deterrent.

Increasing production by intensification, by raising the yields, is a more difficult process than expansion of acreage, especially when tractors are available for expansion. It should be remembered that crop yields in western Europe were not always as high as they are in the mid-twentieth century. In fact, they were quite low at the beginning of the nineteenth century, when planting of soil-enriching forage legumes, like clover, was in the initial stage and chemical fertilizers were unknown. Even if climatic conditions should prevent the USSR from reaching the high level of, say, Netherland's yields, there are potentialities for growth. Thus yields on seed test plots have been found to exceed by 42–88 percent average farm yields in the USSR.[7]

The exploitation of such potentialities will depend upon socioeconomic and institutional factors such as incentives to the farmers, the farmers' know-how, capital investment, and organization and management of farm enterprises. Yet a meaningful prediction related to these factors is exceedingly difficult because they are based on a complex array of interrelated political, ideological, sociological, and economic considerations. A few observations, however, are in order.

Speculation is tempting on the possibility of a radical solution of collectivization such as was attempted in the mid-1950s in other East European Communist countries. No such process has taken place in the Soviet Union since Stalin's temporary retreat from collectivization in 1930. The government has never given any indication of favoring retreat from the collectivist road beyond some temporary concessions to the private sector. It is symptomatic that decollectivization was reversed, after a short interval, in all the other Communist countries except Poland and Yugoslavia. Even in these two countries the Communist leadership is dedicated to the goal of agrarian collectivism which is influencing their policy toward individual peasant farming. It would seem that only a major politico-economic crisis in which the very fate of the Soviet regime was at stake could induce it to sanction decollectivization. In the past, wars provided such crises, but this is hardly conceivable in our atomic age when a major war would result in a global catastrophe and not a mere crisis. What would or could happen when the leadership passes to a different generation is anybody's guess. But it must be pointed out that the tractor makes decollectivization, in the sense of a division of kolkhoz land into viable small peasant holdings, a much more difficult problem than it was in the days of the horse. Besides, the implications of decollectivization for the food supply in an industrialized country are different from those in a predominantly agrarian economy, much of it self-sufficient. Perhaps some form of a really democratic producers cooperative which would secure the benefits of the scale of production may be a way out of the difficulty. But it is fair to add that historical experience with producers cooperatives, unlike other types of cooperatives, is not auspicious.

If the prospects of decollectivization in the Soviet Union appear dim, this cannot be said quite so categorically about the small private farming of the collectivized peasantry. Although ideologically this private sector is doomed, there is no schedule for its disappearance and it is not inconceivable that prior to its withering away it may again be revitalized.

Etatization of agriculture—conversion of kolkhozes into state farms— would seem to have better prospects than decollectivization. The advance already made along these lines was noted above, and the eventual coalescence of the two farm types is held up as the long run policy goal. It is also significant that there is a school of thought in the USSR, calling itself sovkhoznik, which believes that only in sovkhozes can the "anarchy," as they call it, of small peasant agriculture be completely eradicated and a proper labor discipline imposed. This school, which is not uninfluential, though it cannot publicly express itself while the party line emphasizes coexistence, would like to see the goal of coalescence advanced. In that case the government would have to assume responsibility for the wage and investment bills of all farms, not only of state farms as at present. State financial responsibility came to be the chief practical distinction between collective and state farms and doubtless the most serious obstacle to their complete consolidation. If and when the government is ready and willing to shoulder full responsibility for wages and investment, the coalescence of the two farm sectors is likely to come rapidly. But it must be emphasized that the farm units will be sovkhozes. A reverse transformation from state farms into kolkhozes does not seem to be within the realm of probability.

Further structural changes within the ambit of collective and state farm sectors and in the administrative apparatus and planning procedure may be expected. As in the past, some of them may be oriented toward greater initiative of farm management and others toward increased regimentation. Planning, pricing, and costs techniques are backward and in a state of flux. It is not unreasonable to expect that gradual penetration of Western concepts and methods of economic analysis might lead to improvement. An important organizational change, as the baleful effect of giantism penetrates the official mind, may be the splitting of the huge farm units into enterprises of more economical size.

It may be expected that substantial investment in agricultural research and training of specialists will continue, and that an improvement, albeit a slow one, will take place in the dissemination and adoption of scientific information on farms. If no new regression to Lysenkoism occurs, scientific development should augur well for agricultural progress in the USSR. And so does the reservoir of human capital provided by the now overwhelmingly literate peasantry, including an increasingly broader segment of educated people.

The biggest problem of all is that of economic incentives on which depend the well-being of the peasant population and its contribution to production. The crux of the matter here is future government policy regarding the old issue of priorities for heavy industry versus consumer goods. Unless the supply of consumer goods rises much more rapidly than it has lately, economic incentives in agriculture cannot be increased. The outlook seems favorable to an increased consumer orientation of industry and de-emphasis on producer goods, but this trend may not be sustained in the future. If not, agricultural production will suffer. The peasant, and especially the peasant woman, a very important component of the farm labor force, will concentrate on acre-and-a-cow farming or escape to the cities. Migration to cities is likely to be the choice of the most energetic, able, and younger elements of the peasant population. Also let us not forget that the economic incentive of the pay envelope in a kolkhoz or sovkhoz must compensate for the lacking psychological incentives formerly provided by ownership of land, which collective ownership and factorylike environment of the socialist farms cannot replace. It may be truly said on the basis of Soviet experience that when the magic touch of incentives is applied, agriculture prospers within the limitations imposed by the severe climate. But when there are no adequate rewards to farmers for their effort and when the decisions that should be made by farm management are dictated by party or government officials of questionable competence, agriculture withers like an undernourished plant.

To sum up the outlook: barring a basic change in the social order or a radical reorientation of Soviet economic policy away from the predominant emphasis on the growth of heavy industry and regimentation of farm management, agriculture is likely to continue to be something of a problem child of the Soviet economy. It may, therefore, continue to act as a brake on Soviet economic growth. But this does not rule out gradual, though irregular, progress which may be punctuated by more or less serious setbacks. Much will depend upon whether the trend toward increased economic incentives and capital investment in agriculture will be maintained. Weather will continue to play a major role in harvest fluctuation unless irrigation is developed to a much greater extent and a significant advance is made in adoption of improved cultural practices. Agriculture is often described as the Achilles' heel of Soviet economy. However, it is usually forgotten that "Achilles could, after all, walk upon his heel"; [8] likewise the Kremlin has been able to lean heavily on Russian agriculture.

As for the peasant, collectivization deprived him of the economic independence gained during the Revolution. His inferior status in Soviet society is perhaps epitomized in an old kolkhoznik's remark to a Soviet bureaucrat in Nikolai Zhdanov's fine short story "A Trip to the Homeland": "You, then, are the bosses, we—the producers." [9] But the Russian peasant has retained a keen awareness of his economic interest and a determination to act upon it even within the framework and limitations imposed by a collectivist society. It is not unreasonable, therefore, to foresee for the peasant some ascent on the economic ladder, aided by his increased education and by the impact of technology, which requires new farm skills.

Note on Abbreviations   *Notes*   *Index*

Note on Abbreviations

In this volume, Dr. Volin often uses abbreviated citations for standard Soviet statistical and other reference works. I list below many of the more important of them, together with the corresponding full references. For convenience, use is made here of these further abbreviations—Gosplan: Gosudarstvennaia Planovaia Komissiia (State Planning Commission); TSU: Tsentral'noe Statisticheskoe Upravlenie SSSR (Central Statistical Administration of the USSR); TSUNKHU: Tsentral'noe Upravlenie Narodno-khoziaistvennogo Ucheta (Central Administration of National Economic Accounting).

Kapital'noe stroitel'stvo: TSU, *Kapital'noe stroitel'stvo v SSSR* (Capital Construction in the USSR), Moscow, 1961.

Kontrol'nye tsifry, 1928–29: Gosplan, *Kontrol'nye tsifry narodnogo khoziaistva SSSR na 1928/1929 god* (Control Figures of the National Economy of the USSR for 1928–29), Moscow, 1929.*

Narodnoe khoziaistvo, 1956: TSU, *Narodnoe khoziaistvo SSSR v 1956 godu* (The National Economy of the USSR in 1956), Moscow, 1957.

Promyshlennost' SSSR, 1957: TSU, *Promyshlennost' SSSR* (Industry of the USSR), Moscow, 1957.

* Here and elsewhere reference is to one of a series, all of which are abbreviated correspondingly.

Sel'skoe khoziaistvo SSSR, 1935: Narodnyi Komissariat zemledeliia SSSR i Narodnyi Komissariat Sovkhozov, *Sel'skoe khoziaistvo SSSR, ezhegodnik, 1935* (Agriculture of the USSR: Statistical Annual, 1935), Moscow, 1936.

Sel'skoe khoziaistvo SSSR, 1960: TSU, *Sel'skoe khoziaistvo SSSR* (Agriculture of the USSR), Moscow, 1960.

Sotsialisticheskoe sel'skoe khoziaistvo: TSUNKHU, *Sotsialisticheskoe sel'skoe khoziaistvo SSSR* (Socialist Agriculture of the USSR), Moscow, 1939.

Sotsialisticheskoe stroitel'stvo, 1934: TSUNKHU, *Sotsialisticheskoe stroitel'stvo SSSR* (Socialist Construction of the USSR), Moscow, 1934.

SSSR v Tsifrakh, 1960: TSU, *SSSR v tsifrakh v 1960 godu* (USSR in Figures in 1960), Moscow, 1961.

Statisticheskii spravochnik SSSR za 1928g.: TSU, *Statisticheskii spravochnik SSSR za 1928g.* (Statistical Handbook of the USSR for 1928), Moscow, 1929.

Strana sovetov: TSU, *Strana sovetov za 50 let* (Country of the Soviets for 50 Years), Moscow, 1967.

SUR, 1917–1918: Sobranie uzakonenii i rasporiazhenii rabochego i krest'ianskogo pravitel'stva, 1917–1918 (Collected Laws and Decrees of the Workers' and Peasants' Government, 1917–1918).

SUR: Sobranie uzakonenii i rasporiazhenii raboche-krest'ianskogo pravitel'stva.

SPR, SSSR: Sobranie postanovlenii i rasporiazhenii pravitel'stva SSSR (Collected Laws and Decrees of the Workers' and Peasants' Government of the USSR).

SZR, SSSR: Sobranie zakonov i rasporiazhenii SSSR (Collected Laws and Decrees of the USSR).

Zhivotnovodstvo, 1916–1938: TSUNKHU, *Zhivotnovodstvo SSSR za 1916–1938* (Livestock Raising in the USSR for 1916–1938), Moscow, 1940.

Zhivotnovodstvo SSSR, 1959: TSU, Zhivotnovodstvo SSSR: Statisticheskii sbornik (Livestock Raising in the USSR: Statistical Handbook), Moscow, 1959.

A. B.

Notes

Introduction

1. *The Economic Development of France and Germany, 1815–1914* (Cambridge, Eng., 1921), p. 1.

1. Serfdom: Origins and Development

1. For a more detailed discussion of this controversy, see A. A. Kizevetter, "The Peasantry in Russian Scientific Historical Literature," *Krest'ianskaia Rossiia*, 5–6:28–37 (1923); S. F. Platonov, "Concerning the Period and the Measures Taken for Binding Peasants to the Land in Muscovite Russia," *Arkhiv istorii truda v Rossii*, III, 18–22 (1922); B. D. Grekov, *Krest'iane na Rusi s drevneishikh vremen do XVII veka* (Peasants in Russia from Ancient Times to the Seventeenth Century; Moscow-Leningrad, 1946), pp. 807–861. See also M. K. Liubavskii, "The Beginning of Peasant Servitude," *Velikaia reforma 19 fevralia* (The Great Reform of February 19), ed. A. K. Dzhivelegov, S. P. Mel'gunov, and V. I. Picheta (Moscow, 1911), I, 1–13; Iu. V. Got'e, "The Peasants in the Seventeenth Century," *ibid.*, I, 14–36.

2. A. S. Lappo-Danilevskii, "Essays on the History of the Development of the Principal Classes of Peasant Population in Russia," *Krest'ianskii stroi* (The Peasant Order; St. Petersburg, 1905), pp. 60–61, 72.

3. P. B. Struve, *Sotsial'naia i ekonomicheskaia istoriia Rossii* (Social and Economic History of Russia; Paris, 1952), pp. 124–125.

4. S. F. Platonov, *Ocherki po istorii smuty v Moskovskom gosudarstve XVI–XVII vv.* (Essays on the History of the Period of Troubles in the Moscow State in the Sixteenth and Seventeenth Centuries; St. Petersburg, 1899), p. 167.

5. L. V. Cherepnin, "The Class Struggle in 1682 in the South of the Moscow State," *Istoricheskie zapiski*, 1938, no. 4, pp. 41–75; I. A. Bulygin, "The Fleeing Peasants of the Riazan District during the Sixties of the Seventeenth Century," *ibid.*, 1953, no. 43, pp. 131–149; A. A. Novoselskii, "The Spread of the Servile System in the Southern Districts of the Muscovite State," *ibid.*, 1938, no. 4, pp. 21–40; "Concerning the Question of the Significance of *Urochnye* Years during the First Half of the Seventeenth Century," *Akademiku B. D. Grekovu: Sbornik statei* (A Collection of Essays in Honor of Academician B. D. Grekov; Moscow, 1952), pp. 178–183; "Concerning the Question of the Economic Condition of the Peasants who Fled to the South of the Moscow State during the First Half of the Seventeenth Century," *Istoricheskie zapiski*, 1945, no. 16, pp. 58–64; A. G. Man'kov, *Razvitie krepostnogo prava v Rossii vo vtoroi polovine XVII veka* (The Development of Serfdom in Russia during the Second Half of the Seventeenth Century; Moscow-Leningrad, 1962).

6. Grekov, *Krest'iane na Rusi*, p. 861.

7. M. P. Pogodin, "Should Boris Godunov be Considered the Founder of Serfdom?" *Russkaia beseda*, 4:117–172 (1858).

8. Platonov characterizes the state of historical material for the sixteenth century, which is so important for our subject, as follows: "The storms of the Period of Troubles and the famous Moscow fire of 1626 destroyed the Moscow archives and old materials to such an extent that the events of the sixteenth century have to be studied on the basis of accidental remnants and fragments." S. F. Platonov, *Ivan Groznyi* (Ivan the Terrible; Petrograd, 1923), pp. 5–6.

9. V. O. Kliuchevskii, "Origin of Serfdom," first published in 1885 in *Russkaia mysl'* and republished in *Opyty i issledovaniia* (Experiments and Investigations; Petrograd, 1919), pp. 184–267.

10. E. N. Kusheva, "Concerning the History of Slavery at the End of the Sixteenth and Beginning of the Seventeenth Centuries," *Istoricheskie zapiski*, 1945, no. 15, pp. 87, 94.

11. Kliuchevskii, in *Opyty*, pp. 245, 267.

12. F. I. Leontovich, *Krest'iane iugozapadnoi Rossii po litovskomu pravu XV i XVI stoletiia* (Peasants of Southwestern Russia According to the Lithuanian Law of the Fifteenth and Sixteenth Centuries; Kiev, 1863), pp. 3, 20. Quoted by P. B. Struve, *Sotsial'naia i ekonomicheskaia istoriia Rossii* (The Social and Economic History of Russia; Paris, 1952), p. 145, n. 22.

13. S. Veselovskii, Review of A. Iakovlev, *Kholopstvo i kholopy v Moskovskom gosudarstve XVII veka* (Slavery and Slaves in the Moscow State in the Seventeenth Century), *Istoricheskii zhurnal*, October–November 1944, p. 116.

14. A. Iakovlev, *Kholopstvo i kholopy* (Moscow, 1943), I, 36.

15. Kliuchevskii, in *Opyty*, pp. 232–233.

16. Paul N. Miliukov, "Krest'iane" (Peasants), in *Entsiklopedicheskii slovar'* (St. Petersburg, 1897), XVI, 659–725.

17. D. Ia. Samokvasov, *Arkhivnyi material* (Archive Material; Moscow, 1909), pp. 45–46.

18. Platonov, *Arkhiv istorii truda v Rossii*, III, 22.

19. Grekov, *Krest'iane na Rusi*, I, 861.

20. N. S. Chaev, "The Question of Seizing and Binding of Peasants in the Moscow State at the End of the Sixteenth Century," *Istoricheskie zapiski*, 1940, no. 6, p. 162.

21. I. I. Smirnov, "The Problem of Serfdom and Feudalism in Soviet Historical Literature," *Dvadtsat' piat' let istoricheskoi nauki v SSSR* (Twenty Five Years of Historical Science in the USSR; Moscow-Leningrad, 1942), pp. 94–100.

22. *Ibid.*, p. 95.

23. Grekov, *Krest'iane na Rusi*, p. 783; italics added.

24. M. A. Diakonov, *Ocherki obshchestvennogo i gosudarstvennogo stroia drevnei Rusi* (Essays in the Social and Political Order of Ancient Russia; 4th ed., St. Petersburg, 1912), pp. 355–357; A. S. Lappo-Danilevskii, *Krest'ianskii stroi*, I, 60; A. A. Novoselskii, *Votchinik i ego khoziaistvo v XVII veke* (The Feudal Landlord and his Estate in the Seventeenth Century; Moscow-Leningrad, 1929), p. 126.

25. Kliuchevskii, "The Poll Tax and Abolition of Slavery in Russia," *Opyty*, pp. 268–357; P. N. Miliukov, *Gosudarstvennoe khoziaistvo Rossii v pervoi chetverti XVIII stoletiia i reforma Petra Velikogo* (The State Economy of Russia during the First Quarter of the Eighteenth Century and the Reform of Peter the Great; 2nd ed., St. Petersburg, 1905), p. 471.

26. A. A. Kornilov, *Ocherki po istorii obshchestvennogo dvizheniia i krest'-ianskogo dela v Rossii* (Essays on the History of the Social Movement and the Peasant Question in Russia; St. Petersburg, 1905), p. 119.

27. A. V. Romanovich-Slavatinskii, *Dvorianstvo v Rossii ot nachala XVIII v. do otmeny krepostnogo prava* (The Gentry in Russia from the Beginning of the Eighteenth Century until the Abolition of Serfdom; St. Petersburg, 1870), p. 353.

28. V. O. Kliuchevskii, *Kurs Russkoi istorii* (A Course in Russian History; Moscow, 1919), I, 434.

29. P. G. Arkhangel'skii, *Ocherki po istorii zemel'nogo stroia Rossii* (Essays on the History of Land Tenure in Russia; Kazan, 1921), p. 59.

30. Peter Struve, *Krepostnoe khoziaistvo* (Serfdom; St. Petersburg, 1913), p. 44, quoting William Coxe, *Travels in Poland and Russia* (5th ed., 1802), III, 154. Transportation by horse or by hand-propelled barges greatly depended on the labor of quitrent-paying peasants. See Iu. G. Saushkin, "The Nature of the Old Industrial Center and the History of the Development of Its Economy," *Izvestiia vsesoiuznogo geograficheskogo obshchestva*, 78.2: 167 (1946).

31. M. I. Tugan-Baranovskii, *Russkaia fabrika* (The Russian Factory; 6th ed., Moscow, 1934), p. 40.

32. For instance, in seven estates of the Princes Vorontsov, one of the largest landholding families of nineteenth century Russia, quitrents increased from three to six times between 1801 and 1823. E. N. Indova, "The Peasantry of Vorontsovs' Estates in the Central Industrial Region," *Istoricheskie zapiski*, 1951, no. 38, p. 192.

33. Iu. I. Gerasimova asserts that in the 1840s this type of servitude was significant and mentions, on the basis of a study of archive material, particularly the province of Vitebsk. See "The Peasant Movement in Russia, 1844–1849," *Istoricheskie zapiski*, 1955, no. 50, pp. 224–268.

34. Struve, *Krepostnoe khoziaistvo*, p. 51; P. I. Liashchenko, *Ocherki agrarnoi evoliutsii Rossii* (Essays on the Agrarian Evolution of Russia; 4th ed., Leningrad, 1925), vol. I, ch. 4.

35. This problem aroused lively discussion in the rather extensive agricultural literature during the second quarter of the nineteenth century. See Liashchenko, *Ocherki agrarnoi evoliutsii Rossii*, pp. 116–118.

36. For a description of the landlords' venture into the industrial field, see Tugan-Baranovskii, *Russkaia fabrika*, ch. 3; also his "Serf Factory," *Velikaia reforma*, III, 139–154.

37. Tugan-Baranovskii, *Russkaia fabrika*, p. 89.

38. I. I. Ignatovich, "Serfs on the Eve of Emancipation," *Russkoe bogatstvo*, November 1900, pp. 28–29.

39. Romanovich-Slavatinskii, *Dvorianstvo v Rossii*, p. 314.

40. A serf of the Turgenevs studied medicine at the University of Berlin at the same time as the great writer I. S. Turgenev. See P. N. Sakulin, "The Serf Intelligentsia," *Velikaia reforma*, III, 15.

41. I. Engelmann, *Istoriia krepostnogo prava v Rossii* (History of Serfdom in Russia), translation from German, ed. A. A. Kizevetter (Moscow, 1900), p. 129.

42. V. I. Semevskii, *Krest'ianskii vopros v Rossii*, (The Peasant Question in Russia; St. Petersburg, 1888), I, 197; *Entsiklopedicheskii slovar'*, 7th ed., XXV, 485.

43. Arkhangels'kii, *Ocherki*, p. 64.

44. N. M. Druzhinin, *Gosudarstvennye krest'iane i reforma P. D. Kiseleva* (State Peasants and the Reform of P. D. Kiselev; Moscow-Leningrad, 1946), I, 313.

45. *Ibid.*, I, 26; S. A. Kniaz'kov, "Count P. D. Kiselev and the Reform of State Peasants," *Velikaia reforma*, II, 212–214.

46. Druzhinin, *Gosudarstvennye krest'iane*, I, 84–86.

47. It was not stopped completely, for the government of Alexander I, beset by budget deficits and inflation, embarked in 1810, as a remedial measure, on a sale of public land, including that inhabited by state peasants. The operation was not too successful and was discontinued in 1816 but in the course of it, more than 10,000 male souls passed into private ownership. *Ibid.*, I, 148–152.

48. *Ibid.*, I, 69.

49. A. S. Lykoshin, "Military Settlements," *Velikaia reforma*, II, 86–106.

50. Semevskii, *Krest'ianskii vopros*, II, 136.

51. Druzhinin, *Gosudarstvennye krest'iane*, I, 99

52. *Krest'ianskoe dvizhenie, 1827–1869* (The Peasant Movement), ed. E. A. Morokhovets (Moscow, 1931), I, 18–19.

53. I. I. Ignatovich, *Bor'ba krest'ian za osvobozhdenie* (The Struggle of the Peasants for Liberation; Leningrad, 1924), p. 7.

54. N. I. Firsov, "Peasant Uprisings Prior to the Nineteenth Century," *Velikaia reforma*, II, 69.

55. In addition to numerous articles in Soviet historical magazines dealing with peasant uprisings during serfdom, the following compilations of documents and monographs may be mentioned: P. K. Aliferenko, *Krest'ianskoe dvizhenie i krest'ianskii vopros v Rossii v 30–50kh godakh XVIII veka* (The Peasant Movement and the Peasant Question in Russia in the 1730s–1750s; Moscow, 1958); A. I. Linkov, *Ocherki istorii krest'ianskogo dvizheniia v Rossii v 1825–1861* (Essays in the History of the Peasant Movement in Russia, 1825–1861; Moscow, 1952); V. V. Mavrodin, *Krest'ianskaia voina v Rossii v 1773–1775 godakh: Vosstanie Pugacheva* (The Peasant War in Russia in 1773–1775: Pugachev's Uprising; Leningrad, 1961), vol. 1; E. A. Morokhovets, comp., *Krest'ianskoe dvizhenie, 1827–1869* (The Peasant Movement, 1827–1869; Moscow, 1931); S. B. Okun', ed., *Krest'ianskoe dvizhenie v Rossii v 1850–1856 gg. Sbornik dokumentov* (The Peasant Movement in Russia, 1850–1856: A Collection of Documents; Moscow, 1962); A. V. Predtechenskii, ed., *Krest'ianskoe dvizhenie v Rossii v 1826–1849 gg: Sbornik dokumentov* (The Peasant Movement in Russia, 1826–1849: A Collection of Documents; Moscow, 1961); K. B. Sivkov, *Ocherki po istorii krepostnogo khoziaistva i krest'ianskogo dvizheniia v Rossii v pervoi polovine XIX veka* (Essays on the History of Serf Economy and the Peasant Movement in Russia during the First Half of the Nineteenth Century; Moscow, 1951); I. I. Smirnov, *Vosstanie Bolotnikova, 1606–1607* (The Revolt of Bolotnikov, 1606–1607; Petrograd, 1924, and Leningrad, 1951); S. I. Tkhorzhevskii, *Narodnye volneniia pri pervykh Romanovykh* (The People's Uprisings under the First Romanov Tsars; Petrograd, 1924). See also A. A. Zimin, "Questions of Peasant War in Russia at the Beginning of the Seventeenth Century," *Voprosy istorii*, March 1958, pp. 97–113.

56. Smirnov, *Vosstanie Bolotnikova;* Zimin, in *Voprosy istorii*, March 1958, pp. 97–113.

57. Firsov, in *Velikaia reforma*, II, 45–46.

58. Miliukov, "Krest'iane" *Entsiklopedicheskii slovar'*.

59. S. I. Tkhorzhevskii, *Pugachevshchina v pomeshchichei Rossii: Vosstanie na pravoi storone Volgi v iiune-oktiabre 1774 goda* (The Pugachevshchina in The Landlords' Russia: The Revolt on the Right Bank of the Volga in June–October 1774; Moscow, 1930), p. 9. See also A. A. Kizevetter, "Pugachevshchina," in *Istoricheskie siluety, liudi i sobytiia* (Historical Silhouettes, People, and Events); Berlin 1931, pp. 55–92.

60. Pushkin was greatly interested in this episode and studied it closely. He used it as a theme for his historical novel *The Captain's Daughter,* from which the above quotation is taken, and also wrote a history of the Pugachev rebellion. See the comments by N. I. Firsov, in his notes to the eleventh volume of Pushkin's works, published by the Russian Academy of Sciences (Petrograd, 1914).

61. Eugene Tarle, *Napoleon's Invasion of Russia, 1812* (New York, 1942), pp. 250–255.

62. P. P. Maslov, *Agrarnyi vopros v Rossii* (The Agrarian Question in Russia; St. Petersburg, 1908), II, 26.

63. Semevskii, *Krest'ianskii vopros,* II, 585.

64. Herzen referred in his memoirs to an instance of this kind where peasants demanded a written statement from their master that he would not divulge the whipping.

65. Ignatovich, "Krest'ianskie volneniia" (Peasant Disturbances), *Velikaia reforma*, III, 46, 64.

66. I. N. Kuntikov, "The Peasant Movement in Russia during the Nineteenth Centry," *Voprosy istorii,* August 1957, pp. 143–153.

67. Ignatovich, in *Velikaia reforma*, III, 65.

68. Firsov, in *Velikaia reforma*, II, 64.

69. Ignatovich, in *Velikaia reforma*, III, 52.

70. Semevskii, *Krest'anskii vopros,* II, 57.

71. Firsov, in *Velikaia reforma*, II, 27.

72. Ignatovich, *Bor'ba krest'ian za osvobozhdenie*, pp. 16–17.

73. See N. V. Riazanovsky, *Russia and the West in the Teaching of the Slavophiles: A Study of Romantic Ideology* (Cambridge, Mass., 1952), pp. 136–140; V. Ulanov and V. P. Baturinskii, "Slavophiles and Westerners on Serfdom," *Velikaia reforma*, III, 175–204.

74. V. A. Rosenberg, "Censorship and Serfdom," *Velikaia reforma*, III, 103–105.

75. *Ibid.*, 225.

76. Baturinskii, "Westerners of the 1840s," *Velikaia reforma*, III, 201.

77. Semevskii, *Krestianskii vopros v Rossii,* II, 387.

78. For a detailed account of the Decembrist Movement, see Anatole G. Mazour, *The First Russian Revolution, 1825* (Berkeley, 1937); Thomas G. Masaryk, *The Spirit of Russia,* 2 vols. (London, 1919).

79. Ignatovich, *Bor'ba krest'ian za osvobozhdenie*, pp. 43–44.

80. Nestor Kotliarevskii, *Kanun osvobozhdeniia, 1855–1861* (On the Eve of Emancipation, 1855–1861; St. Petersburg, 1916), p. 113.

81. Alexander Herzen, *Sochineniia* (Works; St. Petersburg, 1906), V, 308.

82. I. Ivaniukov, *Padenie krepostnogo prava v Rossii* (The Downfall of Serfdom in Russia; St. Petersburg, 1882), pp. 103–104.

83. Kornilov, *Obshchestvennoe dvizhenie pri Alexandre II, 1855–1881: Istoricheskie ocherki* (The Social Movement under Alexander II, 1855–1881: Historical Essays; Moscow, 1909), p. 40.

84. Kornilov, *Krest'ianskaia reforma* (Peasant Reform; Moscow, 1905), p. 10.

85. *Ibid.*, p. 11.

86. Miliukov, *Ocherki po istorii Russkoi kultury* (Essays in the History of Russian Culture; St. Petersburg, 1896), pt. I, p. 200.

87. See Semevskii, *Krest'ianskii vopros,* I, 461; Semenov-T'ianshanskii, "Memoirs," *Vestnik Evropy,* February 1911; the statement of Prince Vasilchikov (a high official under Nicholas I), quoted in A. Popel'nitskii, "The Influence of

Peasant Ideology on the Course of Emancipation from Serfdom," *Sovremennyi mir,* 1916, no. 2, p. 19.

88. Popel'nitskii, in *Sovremennyi mir,* 1916, no. 2, pp. 19–36.

89. Struve, *Krepostnoe khoziaistvo,* pp. 137, 139–40.

90. K. A. Pazhitov, "Concerning the Role of Serf Labor in Industry prior to the Emancipation Reform," *Istoricheskie zapiski,* 1940, no. 7, pp. 236–245.

91. E. P. Trifiliev, *Ocherki iz istorii krepostnogo prava v Rossii: Tsarstvovanie Imperatora Pavla I* (Essays on the History of Serfdom in Russia: The Reign of Emperor Paul I; Kharkov, 1904), pp. 15–17.

92. *Ibid.,* pp. 293–300.

93. I. M. Kataeva, "Peasant Legislation under Emperors Paul I and Alexander I," *Velikaia reforma,* II, 70–78.

94. Tarle, *Napoleon's Invasion of Russia.*

95. Semevskii, *Krest'ianskii vopros,* II, 60–61.

96. Vasilenko, in *Velikaia reforma,* IV, 106.

2. Emancipation

1. See "Nikolai Alekseevich Miliutin," in A. A. Kizevetter, *Istoricheskie otkliki* (Historical Comments; Moscow, 1915), pp. 223–267.

2. The Russian literature on the subject is voluminous. For a competent and well-documented treatment by an American scholar, see G. T. Robinson, *Rural Russia Under the Old Regime* (New York, 1932), pp. 64–93.

3. V. I. Anisimov, "Land Allotments," in *Velikaia reforma* (Moscow, 1911), VI, 80. See also Iu. E. Ianson, *Opyt statisticheskogo issledovaniia krest'ianskikh platezhei i nalogov* (Attempt at a Statistical Investigation of Peasant Payments and Taxes; St. Petersburg, 1877), p. 134.

4. Anisimov, in *Velikaia reforma,* VI, 86.

5. *Ibid.,* pp. 92–93; P. I. Liashchenko, *Ocherki agrarnoi evoliutsii Rossii* (Essays on the Agrarian Evolution in Russia; 4th ed., Leningrad, 1925), I, 133–135.

6. P. I. Liashchenko, *Istoriia narodnogo khoziaistva SSSR* (The History of the National Economy of the USSR; Moscow, 1959), p. 321.

7. I. V. Chernyshev, *Sel'skoe khoziaistvo dovoennoi Rossii i SSSR* (Agriculture of Prewar Russia and the USSR; Moscow, 1926), p. 35.

8. Miliukov, *Istoriia Russkoi kultury* (History of Russian Culture; St. Petersburg, 1896), p. 205.

9. A. A. Kaufman, *Agrarnyi vopros v Rossii* (The Agrarian Question in Russia; 2nd ed., Moscow, 1919), p. 24.

10. Anisimov, in *Velikaia reforma,* VI, 91.

11. *Ibid.,* pp. 98–100.

12. L. V. Khodskii, *Zemlia i zemledelets* (The Land and the Cultivator; St. Petersburg, 1891), II, 241–243.

13. Kaufman, *Agrarnyi vopros v Rossii,* pp. 44–45.

14. A. A. Manuilov, *Pozemel'nyi vopros v Rossii* (The Land Question in Russia; Moscow, 1905), p. 35.

15. S. S. Sobolev, "Dokuchaev and the Problem of the Drought," a paper

read at Dokuchaev's anniversary meeting of the Academy of Science of the USSR; reported in *Sotsialisticheskoe zemledelie,* December 13, 1946.

16. A. I. Chuprov, *Krest'ianskii vopros* (The Peasant Question; Moscow, 1909), p. 180.

17. P. Kovanko, *Reforma 19-go fevralia 1861 goda i ee posledstviia s finansovoi tochki zreniia: Vykupnaia operatsiia, 1861–1907* (The Reform of February 19, 1861, and Its Consequences from a Financial Point of View: The Redemption Operation; Kiev, 1914), p. 199.

18. D. I. Shakhovskoi, "Redemption Payments," *Velikaia reforma,* VI, 107.

19. *Ibid.,* p. 114.

20. *Doklad vysochaishe uchrezhdennoi komissii dlia issledovaniia nyneshnego polozheniia sel'skogo khoziaistva i selskoi proizvoditel'nosti v Rossii. Prilozheniia 6* (The Report of the Commission Established by the Emperor to Investigate the Present Condition of Agriculture and Agricultural Productivity. Supplement 6; St. Petersburg, 1873), p. 197.

21. *Ibid.,* pp. 35–36.

22. A Lositskii, *Vykupnaia operatsiia* (The Redemption Operation; St. Petersburg, 1906), p. 16.

23. Kovanko, *Reforma 19-go fevralia 1861 goda,* p. 222.

24. *Ibid.,* p. 229.

25. Shakhovskoi, in *Velikaia reforma,* VI, 122; Kovanko, p. 337.

26. S. Iu. Witte, *Zapiska po krest'ianskomu delu* (A Memorandum on Peasant Affairs; St. Petersburg, 1904), p. 45.

27. Shakhovskoi, in *Velikaia reforma,* VI, 121.

28. Kovanko, p. 220.

29. A. V. Peshekhonov, "Economic Position of Peasantry during the Post-Reform Period," *Velikaia reforma,* VI, 218.

30. A. Finn-Enotaevskii, *Kapitalism v Rossii, 1890–1917 gg.* (Capitalism in Russia; 2nd ed., Moscow, 1925), I, 179; Schvanebach, *Nashe podatnoe delo* (Our Tax System; St. Petersburg, 1903); Peshekhonov, in *Velikaia reforma,* VI, 220–222; I. Kh. Ozerov, *Ekonomicheskaia Rossiia i ee finansovaia politika na iskhode XIX i v nachale XX veka* (The Russian Economy and Its Financial Policy at the End of the Nineteenth and the Beginning of the Twentieth Century; Moscow, 1905), pp. 17–18.

31. P. P. Migulin, *Reforma denezhnogo obrashcheniia v Rossii i promyshlennye krizisy* (The Reform of the Money System and the Industrial Crisis; Kharkov, 1902), p. 286.

32. *Zemlevladenie i zemledelie v Rossii i drugikh Evropeiskikh gosudarstvakh* (Land Tenure and Farming in Russia and other European Countries; 2nd ed., St. Petersburg, 1881), I, 506.

33. Manuilov, "The Reform of February 19 and Communal Land Tenure," *Velikaia reforma,* VI, 54–75.

34. I. M. Strakhovskii, in *Krest'ianskii stroi* (The Peasant Social Order; St. Petersburg, 1905), I, 387.

35. A. A. Leontiev, "Peasant Legislation Following the Reform," *Velikaia reforma,* VI, 158–199.

36. Strakhovskii, in *Krest'ianskii stroi*, pp. 409–410.

37. A. F. Meyendorf, *Krest'ianskii dvor* (The Peasant Household; St. Petersburg, 1909), pp. 6–9.

38. V. A. Maklakov, "The Agrarian Problem in Russia before the Revolution," *Russian Review*, 9.1:3–15 (January 1950). Reprinted in *The Making of Modern Europe*, II: *Waterloo to the Atomic Age*, ed. Herman Ausubel (New York, 1951), pp. 881–895.

3. *Land Hunger and the Agrarian Crisis*

1. *Nuzhdy derevni* (The Needs of the Village), a collection of articles based on reports of the local committees of the Witte Commission (2 vols., St. Petersburg, 1904), II, 555–556.

2. N. Brzheskii, *Ocherki agrarnogo byta krest'ian* (Essays on Peasant Life; St. Petersburg, 1908), I, 5.

3. A. A. Kaufman, *Zemlia i kul'tura* (The Land and Its Agricultural Technique; Moscow, 1906), p. 4.

4. A. I. Shingarev, *Vymiraiushchaia derevnia* (Dying Village, 2nd ed., St. Petersburg, 1907), p. 53.

5. *Nuzhdy derevni*, II, 563.

6. Much statistical evidence on the social and economic effects of crop failures during the prewar and early postwar periods was marshaled by the Russian statistician E. A. Cherevanin in *Vliianie neurozhaev na narodnoe khoziaistvo Rossii* (The Effect of Crop Failures on Russia's National Economy; pt. 1, Moscow, 1927), pp. 160–301.

7. L. M. Stanilovskii, "The Chronology of Famine Years during the Fourteen Centuries from the Standpoint of Meterology," *Problemy urozhaia* (The Problems of the Harvest; A. Chaianov, ed., Moscow, 1926), pp. 330–333.

8. Lenin, *Sochineniia*, V, 211–218, 231–251.

9. *Vliianie urozhaev i khlebnykh tsen na nekotorye storony narodnogo khoziaistva* (The Influence of Crops and Grain Prices on Some Aspects of National Economy; 2 vols., St. Petersburg, 1897).

10. V. F. Zaleskii, "Peasant Budgets in Connection with the Question of the Significance of High and Low Grain Prices," *Narodnoe khoziaistvo*, 1.2:182–200 (February 1900).

11. A. A. Kaufman, "The Crowded Land and the Law of Diminishing Returns," *Sbornik statei. Obshchina, pereselenie, statistika* (A Collection of Articles on the Mir, Migration, and Statistics; Moscow, 1915), p. 209.

12. A. I. Vasil'chikov, *Sel'skii byt i sel'skoe khoziaistvo v Rossii* (Rural Life and Agriculture in Russia; St. Petersburg, 1881), p. 99.

13. *Nuzhdy derevni*, I, 111.

14. V. Zaitsev, "The Influence of Crop Fluctuation on the National Growth of Population," in *Vliianie neurozhaev na narodnoe khoziaistvo Rossii* (The Influence of Crop Failures on the National Economy of Russia; V. G. Groman, ed.; Moscow, 1927), pt. 2, p. 25.

15. A. G. Rashin, *Formirovanie rabochego klassa v Rossii* (The Development of the Working Class in Russia; Moscow, 1958), p. 25.

16. *Ibid.,* p. 120.

17. Alexander Gerschenkron, *Economic Backwardness in Historical Perspective* (Cambridge, Mass., 1962), pp. 16–20.

18. V. V. Morachevskii, ed., *Agronomicheskaia pomoshch' v Rossii* (Agronomic Assistance in Russia; Petrograd, 1914), p. 34.

19. A. I. Chuprov, *Melkoe zemledelie i ego nuzhdy* (Small Farming and Its Needs; St. Petersburg, 1907), p. 138.

20. S. N. Prokopovich, *Mestnye liudi o nuzhdakh Rossii* (What Russia Needs According to the Local People; St. Petersburg, 1904), p. 54.

21. *Ibid.,* p. 54.

22. *Ibid.,* p. 59.

23. A. A. Manuilov, *Pozemel'nyi vopros v Rossii* (The Land Question in Russia; Moscow, 1905), p. 47.

24. Prokopovich, *Mestnye liudi,* p. 63.

25. Ibid., p. 116.

26. *Agronomicheskaia pomoshch' v Rossii,* p. 34.

27. *Ibid.,* p. 53.

28. A. I. Vasil'chikov, *Zemlevladenie i zemledelie v Rossii i drugikh Evropeiskikh stranakh* (Land Tenure and Farming in Russia and other European Countries; St. Petersburg, 1876), II, 651.

29. Chuprov devotes considerable attention to this incident in his *Krest'ianskii vopros* (The Peasant Question; Moscow, 1909), pp. 115–144, 154–161. His account is largely based on a book by a zemstvo agronomist, A. Zubrilin (one of the leading pioneers in this work), entitled *Sposoby uluchsheniia krest'ianskogo khoziaistva v nechernozemnoi polose* (Methods of Improving Peasant Farming of the Non-Black Soil Area; Moscow, 1901).

30. A. A. Bogolepov, "The Activity of the Zemstvo," *Krest'ianskaia Rossiia,* 8–9:99 (Prague, 1924).

31. D. N. Shipov, *Vospominaniia i dumy o perezhitom* (Reminiscences and Reflections on One's Past; Moscow, 1918), p. 131.

32. Kaufman, "The Crowded Land," *Sbornik statei,* pp. 187–210.

33. V. M. Obukhov, "The Trend of Grain Yields in European Russia during 1883–1915," *Vliianie neurozhaev na narodnoe khoziaistvo,* V. G. Groman, ed., part 1, p. 7.

34. A. A. Kaufman, *K agrarnomu voprosu* (Regarding the Agrarian Question; Petrograd, 1917), p. 37.

35. *Ibid.,* p. 13.

36. V. O. Kliuchevskii, *Kurs Russkoi istorii* (A Course in Russian History; Moscow, 1904), I, 24.

37. Manuilov, *Pozemel'nyi vopros v Rossii,* p. 40.

38. V. Bazhaev, "Land Leasing," *Polnaia entsiklopedia Russkogo sel'skogo khoziaistva* (A Complete Agricultural Encyclopedia; St. Petersburg, 1912), XII, 48; N. P. Oganovskii, *Ocherki po ekonomicheskoi geografii SSSR* (Essays on Economic Geography of USSR; Moscow, 1924), p. 107.

39. V. V. (Pseudonym of V. Vorontsov), "The Causes of Peasant Disturbances in 1905–06," *Vestnik Evropy,* January 1911, pp. 220–245.

40. N. N. Sukhanov, *Ocherki po ekonomii sel'skogo khoziaistva* (Essays on Agricultural Economics; Moscow, Petrograd, 1924), pp. 143–200.

41. M. Tugan-Baranovskii, "Land Question," in *Entsiklopedicheskii slovar' Granata* (Encyclopedia Granat; 7th ed.), XXI, 51–148.

42. A. A. Kaufman, *Agrarnyi vopros v Rossii* (The Agrarian Question in Russia; 2nd ed., Moscow, 1919), pp. 521–522.

43. P. I. Liashchenko, *Krest'ianskoe delo i poreformennaia zemle-ustroitel'naia politika* (Peasant Affairs and Post-Reform Land Tenure Policy); in *Izvestiia Tomskogo Universiteta* (Annals of the University of Tomsk; 1917), vol. LXVI, pt. 2, p. 3.

44. V. Gorin, *Krest'ianskoe dvizhenie za poltora veka* (Peasant Movement during a Century and a Half; Moscow, 1909), p. 87.

45. Manuilov, *Pozemel'nyi vopros v Rossii,* p. 33.

46. E. Iakushkin, *Obychnoe pravo* (Customary Law; Iaroslavl, 1875), I, 19.

47. Aleksandra Efimenko, *Issledovaniia narodnoi zhizni* (Studies of the Life of the People; Moscow, 1884), p. 142.

48. Iakushkin, *Obychnoe pravo,* p. 19.

49. Efimenko, *Issledovaniia narodnoi zhizni,* p. 142.

50. Manuilov, *Pozemel'nyi vopros v Rossii,* p. 35.

51. A. A. Chaianov, *Chto takoe agrarnyi vopros?* (What is the Agrarian Question?—Published by the League of Agrarian Reforms; Moscow, 1917), p. 34.

4. *The Mir*

1. *Sbornik materialov dlia izucheniia sel'skoi pozemel'noi obshchiny* (A Collection of Materials for the Study of the Rural Obshchina), ed. by V. A. Barykov, A. V. Polovtsev, and P. A. Sokolovskii (St. Petersburg, 1880), vol. I.

2. *Ibid.,* p. 136.

3. *Ibid.,* pp. 174–175.

4. A. A. Leontiev, *Krest'ianskoe pravo* (Peasant Law; St. Petersburg, 1909), p. 201.

5. This controversy took place in 1856 in the pages of two Russian magazines: *Russkii vestnik,* in which Chicherin wrote, and *Russkaia beseda,* in which Beliaev's critique appeared. For a review of the theories of the origin of the mir, see also A. A. Kizevetter, "The Peasantry in Russian Scholarly Historical Literature," *Krest'ianskaia Rossiia,* 7:28–37 (Prague, 1923).

6. A. A. Kaufman, *Sbornik statei. Obshchina, pereselenie, statistika* (A Collection of Articles on the Mir, Migration, and Statistics; Moscow, 1915), pp. 91, 122.

7. P. Ven'iaminov, *Krest'ianskaia obshchina* (The Peasant Obshchina; St. Petersburg, 1908), pp. 119–121. Based on material collected by K. P. Kocharovskii.

8. *Sbornik materialov dlia izucheniia sel'skoi pozemel'noi obshchiny,* pp. 163, 185.

9. Article on land tenure in the magazine *Sovremennik,* no. 9, 1857. Reproduced in N. G. Chernyshevskii, *Polnoe sobranie sochinenii* (Collected Works; St. Petersburg, 1906), III, 477–480.

10. Quoted by V. M. Chernov, *Marks i Engel's o krest'ianstve* (Marx and Engels on Peasantry; Moscow, 1906), p. 121.

11. Marx and Engels, *Sochineniia* (Works; V. Adoratskii, ed., Moscow, 1934), XXV, 261. See also A. L. Regel, *Kapital Karla Marksa v Rossii 1870-kh godov* (The Capital of Karl Marx in the 1870s; Moscow, 1939), p. 56.

12. *Iuridicheskii vestnik,* no. 10, October 1888.

13. Chernov, *Marks i Engel's o krest'ianstve,* p. 123; T. G. Masaryk, *The Spirit of Russia* (London, 1919), II, 809n.

14. Marx's letter was first published, with an introduction by B. I. Nikolaevskii, in *Materialy po istorii Russkoi revoliutsii* (Materials on the History of the Russian Revolution), bk. 2, (Berlin, 1923). It was republished, together with three original drafts and an introduction by Riazanov, in *Arckhiv K. Marksa i F. Engel'sa* (Archive of Karl Marx and F. Engels), bk. 1 (Moscow, 1924), pp. 28–286.

15. David Mitrany, *Marx against the Peasant* (Chapel Hill, 1951), p. 31.

16. Masaryk, *The Spirit of Russia,* II, 309.

17. N. Kablukov, *Ob usloviiakh razvitiia krest'ianskogo khoziaistva v Rossii* (Concerning the Conditions of Development of Peasant Agriculture in Russia; Moscow, 1899), p. 95.

18. A. A. Manuilov, *Ocherki po krest'ianskomu voprosu* (Essays on the Peasant Question; Moscow, 1905), pt. 1, p. 274.

19. *Nuzhdy derevni,* II, 198.

20. D. K. Mendeleev, *Raboty po sel'skomu khoziaistvu i lesovodstvu* (Studies Dealing with Agriculture and Forestry; Moscow, 1954), p. 571.

21. P. B. Struve, *Kriticheskie zametki k voprosu ob ekonomicheskom razvitii Rossii* (Critical Comments on the Economic Development of Russia; St. Petersburg, 1894); M. N. Tugan-Baranovskii, *Russkaia fabrika v proshlom i nastoiashchem* (The Russian Factory in the Past and Present; St. Petersburg, 1898); I. M. Hourwich, *The Economics of the Russian Village* (New York, 1892); Lenin (under the pseudonym of Vladimir Ilin), "Ot kakogo nasledstva my otkazyvaemsia?" (What Heritage Are We Rejecting?), *Sochineniia,* vol. 3; G. V. Plekhanov (Volgin), *Obosnovanie narodnichestva v trudakh g-na Vorontsova (V. V.)* (The Substantiation of *Narodnichestvo* in the Writings of Mr. Vorontsov, St. Petersburg, 1896).

22. V. Vorontsov (V. V.), *Progressivnye techeniia, v krest'ianskom khoziaistve* (Progressive Trends in Peasant Agriculture; St. Petersburg, 1892); N. Danielson (Nikolai-on), *Ocherki nashego poreformennogo obshchestvennogo khoziaistva* (Essays on our Post-Reform National Economy; St. Petersburg, 1893).

23. N. I. Stone, "Capitalism on Trial in Russia," *Political Science Quarterly,* 13.1:114 (March 1898).

24. *Sbornik materialov dlia izucheniia sel'skoi pozemel'noi obshchiny,* p. 175.

25. Interesting statistical material on this question was summarized by A. V. Chaianov in his *Organizatsiia krest'ianskogo khoziaistva* (The Organization of

Peasant Farming; Moscow, 1925). See also A. A. Kaufman, *Voprosy ekonomiki i statistiki krest'ianskogo khoziaistva* (Questions of Economics and Statistics of Peasant Farming; Moscow, 1918), p. 19.

26. A. Peshekhonov, "Dynamics of the Peasantry during the Revolution," *Zapiski Instituta izucheniia Rossii* (Prague), 1925, no. 2, pp. 3–11; S. N. Prokopovich, *Krest'ianskoe khoziaistvo* (Peasant Agriculture; Berlin, 1924), p. 171; A. A. Kaufman, *Voprosy ekonomki i statistiki,* p. 294.

27. P. N. Pershin, *Zemel'noe ustroistvo dorevoliutsionnoi derevni* (Land Tenure Arrangements in the Prerevolutionary Village; Moscow-Voronezh, 1928), p. 63.

28. B. D. Brutskus, *Agrarnyi vopros i agrarnaia politika* (The Agrarian Question and Agrarian Policy; Petrograd, 1922), pp. 61–62; George Pavlovsky, *Agricultural Russia on the Eve of the Revolution* (London, 1930), p. 83.

29. *Nuzhdy derevni,* II, 174.

5. The First Agrarian Revolution and Stolypin's Reform

1. V. Gorin, *Krest'ianskoe dvizhenie za poltora veka* (The Peasant Movement during a Century and a Half; Moscow, 1909), p. 29.

2. P. A. Zaionchkovskii, *Provedenie v zhizn' krest'ianskoi reformy v 1861 g.* (Implementation of the Peasant Reform of 1861; Moscow, 1958), pp. 62–63.

3. For curious official secret reports concerning this attitude, see S. N. Valk, in *Krasnyi arkhiv,* 45: 147–164 (1931).

4. *Sotsialism i politicheskaia bor'ba* (Socialism and the Political Struggle), pp. 12–13, cited in George Plekhanov, *Nashi raznoglasiia* (Our Controversies; Geneva, 1885), p. 2.

5. A. V. Shapkarin, ed., *Krest'ianskoe dvizhenie v Rossii v 1890–1900 gg., Sbornik dokumentov* (The Peasant Movement in Russia, 1890–1900, State Documents; Moscow, 1959), 750 pp. See particularly "The Chronicle of the Peasant Movement in Russia (1890–1900)," pp. 601–648.

6. See S. Dubrovskii's article in *Sel'skokhoziaistvennaia entsiklopediia* (Agricultural Encyclopedia; Moscow, 1932), I, 86–103; Imperatorskoe Vol'no-Ekonomicheskoe Obshchestvo: *Agrarnoe dvizhenie v Rossii 1905–06 gg.* (Imperial Free Economic Society: The Agrarian Movement in Russia, 1905–06; St. Petersburg, 1908); P. Maslov, *Agrarnyi vopros v Rossii* (The Agrarian Question in Russia; 2nd ed., Moscow, 1924), vol. 2.

7. Victor Chernov, *Rozhdenie revoliutsionnoi Rossii* (The Birth of Revolutionary Russia; Paris, 1934), p. 45.

8. See *Novyi entsiklopedicheskii slovar'* (The New Encyclopedia), XXIII, 322–323.

9. Lenin, *Sochineniia,* IV, 396; VIII, 206; VIII, 218.

10. *VKP(b) v rezolutsiiakh* (Resolutions of VKP, All Union Communist Party; 2 vols., 4th ed., Moscow, 1933), I, 76–77.

11. Speech at the session of May 19, 1906. Reprinted in *Agrarnyi vopros v pervoi gosudarstvennoi dume* (The Agrarian Question in the First Duma; Kiev, 1906), p. 56.

12. A. A. Kaufman, *Zemlia i kul'tura* (The Land and Agricultural Technique; Moscow, 1906), p. 27.

13. The draft of the law with commentaries was published in S. Dubrovskii, *Agrarnyi vopros v Sovete Ministrov 1906 g.* (The Agrarian Question in the Council of Ministers in 1906; Moscow, 1924), pp. 27–63.

14. *Agrarnyi vopros v Pervoi gosudarstvennoi dume*, pp. 28–30; *Pravitel'stvennyi vestnik*, June 19, 1906.

15. I. I. Vorontsov-Dashkov, *Zapiska ob unichtozhenii krest'ianskoi obshchiny* (A Memoir Concerning the Abolition of the Obshchina; Geneva, 1900).

16. S. Dubrovskii, "Concerning the Agrarian Question in the Revolution of 1905," in *Agrarnyi vopros v Sovete Ministrov*, pp. 18–19.

17. V. I. Gurko, *Features and Figures of the Past* (Stanford, Calif., 1939), p. 474.

18. B. D. Brutskus, *Agrarnyi vopros i agrarnaia politika* (The Agrarian Question and Agrarian Policy; Petrograd, 1922), p. 91.

19. *Ibid.*

20. G. T. Robinson, *Rural Russia under the Old Regime* (New York, 1932), p. 213.

21. N. P. Oganovskii, "Land Organization," *Novyi entsiklopedicheskii slovar'*, XVIII, 556.

22. Stenographic Reports of the Third State Duma, second session, 1908, pt. 1, pp. 2282, 2283.

23. P. N. Miliukov, "A Republic or a Monarch?" *Krest'ianskaia Rossiia*, 4:54 (Prague, 1923).

24. S. N. Prokopovich, *Agrarnyi krizis i meropriiatiia pravitel'stva* (The Agrarian Crisis and Government Measures; Moscow, 1912), pp. 218–219.

25. Lenin, *Sochineniia*, XVIII, 131.

26. P. N. Pershin, *Uchastkovoe zemlepol'zovanie v Rossii* (Consolidated Farms in Russia; Moscow, 1922), p. 7.

27. *Ibid.*

28. Robinson, *Rural Russia*, pp. 225–226.

29. V. V. Morachevskii, ed., *Agronomicheskaia pomoshch' v Rossii* (Agronomic Assistance in Russia; Petrograd, 1914), pp. 87, 101.

30. A. A. Leontiev, "Peasant Legislation after the Reform," *Velikaia reforma*, VI, 190–191.

31. *Aziatskaia Rossiia. Glavnoe upravlenie zemleustroistva i zemledeliia. Pereselencheskoe upravlenie* (Asiatic Russia; published by the Main Land and Agricultural Administration. Colonization Department; St. Petersburg, 1914), I, 492.

32. N. P. Oganovskii, *Ocherki po ekonomicheskoi geografii SSSR* (Essays on the Economic Geography of the USSR; Moscow, 1924), pp. 81–82. See also Brutskus, *Agrarnyi vopros*, pp. 115–116.

33. *Sbornik statistiko-ekonomicheskikh svedenii po sel'skomu khoziaistvu Rossii i nekotorykh inostrannykh gosudarstv 1907, 1914* (A Compilation of Statistical and Economic Data on Agriculture in Russia and Some Foreign Countries; St. Petersburg, 1907, 1914), I, 35; VII, 49, 55.

34. Brutskus, *Agrarnyi vopros,* p. 117.

35. P. I. Liashchenko, *Istoriia narodnogo khozzaistva SSSR* (The History of the National Economy of the USSR; Moscow, 1939), I, 625.

36. Stenographic Reports of the Second Duma (St. Petersburg, 1907), I, 735–36.

37. Brutskus, *Agrarnyi vopros,* p. 113.

38. A. A. Kaufman, *Agrarnyi vopros v Rossii* (The Agrarian Question in Russia; 2nd ed., Moscow, 1919), p. 121.

39. *Ibid.,* p. 114; N. P. Oganovskii, *Individualizatsiia krest'ianskogo zemlevladeniia* (The Individualization of Peasant Land Tenure; Moscow, 1917), p. 51.

40. See A. N. Chelintsev, "Estate Farming in Russia before the Revolution," *Zapiski instituta izucheniia Rossii,* 1:9–14 (Prague, 1925).

41. R. W. Goldsmith, "The Economic Growth of Tsarist Russia 1860–1913," *Economic Development and Cultural Change,* 9.3:448, 450 (April 1961). Includes wheat, rye, barley, oats, buckwheat, millet, peas, corn, sugar beets, tobacco, flax seed, flax fiber, hemp seed, and hemp fiber.

42. *Sbornik statistiko-ekonomicheskikh svedenii,* 1914, VII, 516–17; 1917, X, 532–33.

43. *Ibid.,* 1916, IX, 636; Liashchenko, *Istoriia narodnogo khoziaistva,* p. 578.

44. *Bol'shaia sovetskaia entsiklopediia,* XVIII, 776.

45. Vladimir Gsovski, *Soviet Civil Law* (Ann Arbor, 1948), I, 255; Samuel Kucherov, *Courts, Lawyers and Trials under the Last Three Tsars* (New York, 1953).

46. E. M. Kayden and A. N. Antsiferov, *Cooperative Movement in Russia during the War* (New Haven, 1929). These and other data on cooperatives are taken from this excellent study.

47. *Ibid.,* p. 265.

48. *Narodnoe khoziaistvo Rossii* (The National Economy of Russia; St. Petersburg, 1913).

49. The index was prepared under the direction of one of Russia's outstanding economists, D. N. Kondrat'ev, and was first published in 1926 in the *Ekonomicheskii biuleten' Kon'iukturnogo instituta* (Economic Bulletin of the Business Cycle Research Institute, 1926), V, 12–20, no. 2. It was reproduced by Alexander Gerschenkron in "The Rate of Industrial Growth in Russia since 1885," *The Tasks of Economic History, Supplement VII,* 1947, to *Journal of Economic History,* p. 146.

50. Alexander Gerschenkron, "Problems and Patterns of Russian Economic Development," in *The Transformation of Russian Society,* Cyril E. Black, ed. (Cambridge, Mass., 1960), pp. 42–72.

51. *Entsiklopediia sovetskogo eksporta* (The Encyclopedia of Soviet exports; Berlin, 1928), I, 202.

52. A. G. Rashin, *Formirovanie promyshlennogo proletariata v Rossii* (The Development of an Industrial Proletariat in Russia; Moscow, 1940), pp. 103–154.

53. A. Iu. Finn-Enotaevskii, *Sovremennoe khoziaistvo Rossii* (The Contemporary Economy of Russia; 2nd ed., Moscow, 1925), p. 159.

54. Liashchenko, *Istoriia narodnogo khoziaistva,* I, 579.

6. *World War I and the Revolution of 1917*

1. A. M. Antsiferov and others, *Russian Agriculture during the War* (New Haven, 1930), p. 117.

2. M. Philips Price, "Inside Russia in 1917. II—Village Revolution," reprinted in the *Manchester Guardian,* November 7, 1957.

3. Antsiferov, *Russian Agriculture during the War,* p. 121.

4. N. D. Kondrat'ev, *Rynok khlebov i ego regulirovanie vo vremia voiny i revoliutsii* (The Grain Market and Its Regulation during the War and the Revolution; Petrograd, 1922), p. 41. Kondrat'ev expresses some doubt that crop statistics during the war accurately reflected the magnitude of changes in estate and peasant acreages. But though there might have been some exaggeration, the existence of divergent tendencies is not questioned.

5. *Ibid.,* pp. 15, 47.

6. D. Lutokhin, "The Land Question in the Work of the Provisional Government," *Zapiski Instituta izucheniia Rossii* (Notes of the Institute for the Study of Russia; Prague), 1925, no. 2, p. 346.

7. *Ibid.*

8. *Ibid.,* p. 363.

9. *Ibid.,* pp. 349–350.

10. V. M. Chernov, *The Great Russian Revolution* (New Haven, 1936), p. 236.

11. *Ibid.* According to Chernov, "it was later consulted frequently by the legislators and agrarian organizers of the Bolshevik Revolution."

12. For a severe and often unfair criticism of the SRs and Chernov, particularly, on this score, see: O. H. Radkey, *The Agrarian Foes of Bolshevism. Promise and Default of the Russian Socialist Revolutionaries. February to October, 1917* (New York, 1958), pp. 325–334.

13. Chernov, *The Great Russian Revolution,* pp. 256–257.

14. A. Alaverdova, "Essays on the Agrarian Policy of the Provisional Government," *Sotsialisticheskoe khoziaistvo,* March 1925, no. 2, p. 174.

15. Lenin, *Sochineniia,* XXVI, 197–202.

16. "The Agrarian Movement," in *Sel'skokhoziaistvennaia entsiklopediia* (Agricultural Encyclopedia, V. P. Miliutin, ed., Moscow, 1932), I, 92; K. G. Kotel'nikov and V. L. Medvedev, *Krest'ianskoe dvizhenie v 1917 godu* (The Peasant Movement in 1917; Moscow, 1917), p. 4.

17. Chernov, *The Great Russian Revolution,* p. 260.

18. *Ibid.,* p. 261.

19. B. Ianov, "Agrarian Disorders," correspondence from Tambov province, *Russkie vedomosti,* September 21, 1917 (no. 215).

20. *Ibid.*

21. A. V. Shestakov, "Peasant Organizations in 1917," in *Agrarnaia revoliutsiia* (Agrarian Revolution; Moscow, 1928), II, 99; S. Dubrovskii, "The Provisional Government and the Peasantry," *ibid.,* p. 69.

22. For a statement of his position see Lenin, *Sochineniia,* IV, 102.

23. *Ibid.,* XX, 417.

24. For the official attitude of the Bolshevik Party, see *Vsesoiuznaia Kommunisticheskaia partiia (b) v rezolutsiiakh i resheniiakh s'ezdov, 1898–1933* (All-Union Communist Party in Resolutions and Decisions of Congresses, 1898–1933; Moscow, 1932–33), pt. 1–2.

25. *Sochineniia*, XXIV, 112, 51.

26. *Ibid.*, XXI, 112.

27. V. Miliutin, *Agrarnaia politika SSSR* (The Agrarian Policy of the USSR; 3rd ed., Moscow, 1929), p. 57. For the texts of the Land Decree and other early Soviet agrarian laws, see *Sbornik dekretov i postanovlenii po narodnomu komissariatu zemledeliia, 1917–1920 gg.* (Collection of Decrees and Regulations Dealing with the People's Commissariat of Agriculture, 1917–1920; Moscow, 1921). For English translations of many of these laws, see James Bunyan and H. H. Fisher, *The Bolshevik Revolution, 1917–1918; Documents and Materials* (Stanford, 1934); James Bunyan, *Intervention, Civil War and Communism in Russia, April–December 1918; Documents and Materials* (Baltimore, 1936).

28. Lenin, *Sochineniia*, XXII, 23.

29. S. P. Sereda, Soviet Commissar of Agriculture, quoted by I. I. Evtikhiev, *Zemel'noe pravo RSFSR* (The Land Law of the RSFSR; Moscow, 1923), p. 82.

30. *Izvestiia*, January 30, 1918. Republished in *Sbornik dekretov i postanovlenii po narodnomu khoziaistvu, 25 okt., 1917–25 okt., 1918* (Collection of Decrees and Regulations of National Economy, October 25, 1917–October 25, 1918; Moscow, 1918), pp. 491–494. For comments see D. S. Rosenblum, *Zemel'noe pravo* (2nd ed., Moscow, 1928), pp. 51–53.

31. V. Keller and I. Romanenko, *First Results of the Agrarian Reform* (Voronezh, 1922), p. 7; quoted by Rosenblum, *Zemel'noe pravo*, p. 54; V. Chernov, "Total Division in 1918," *Zapiski Instituta izucheniia Rossii* (Prague), 1925, no. 2, p. 91.

32. V. Kachinskii, *Ocherki agrarnoi revoliutsii na Ukraine* (Essays on the Agrarian Revolution in the Ukraine; Kharkov, 1922), I, 79–80.

33. Evtikhiev, *Zemel'oe pravo*, pp. 75–79.

34. Chernov, in *Zapiski Instituta izucheniia Rossii*, pp. 83–84.

35. I. A. Kirilov, *Ocherki zemleustroistva za tri goda revoliutsii, 1918–1920* (Essays on Land Organization during the Three Years of Revolution, 1918–1920; Petrograd, 1922), p. 58.

36. Chernov, in *Zapiski Instituta izucheniia Rossii*, pp. 86–89.

37. W. H. Chamberlin, *The Russian Revolution, 1917–1921* (2 vols., New York, 1935), I, 257.

38. Iakov Sadovskii, "How I Divided the Land," *Russkaia mysl'*, 9–12:340 (1923–24).

39. *Ibid.*

40. M. Kubanin, "The First Division of Land," in *Agrarnaia revoliutsiia*, II, 213–216, 222–224.

41. An excessively high proportion, more than 20 percent, of undistributed confiscated plow land and meadow is indicated by a statistical compilation for thirty-two provinces of European Russia, based on reports to the Commissariat of Agriculture as of November 1, 1918. It was published in *Agrarnaia politika*

Sovetskoi vlasti (1917–1918). Dokumenty i materialy (Agrarian Policy of the Soviet Government 1917–1918. Documents and Materials; Moscow, 1954), pp. 498–502. The compilers themselves acknowledged that the data are quite incomplete, since local authorities lacked precise information, and that actually a considerably larger area of confiscated land passed to the peasants by November 1918 (ibid., 536n146). The extent of distortion can be seen from the fact that, for example, in Pskov province 1,515,213 desiatinas out of 1,583,183 are shown as undistributed land. Such a preposterous figure should never have been permitted in a statistical table.

42. *Aziatskaia Rossiia* (Asiatic Russia; St. Petersburg, 1914), I, 572–573.

43. *Narodnoe khoziaistvo SSSR 1958*, p. 345. Data are given for the territory within the Soviet frontiers as of September 17, 1939.

44. V. Knipovich, "The Course and the Results of the Agrarian Policy in 1917–20," in *O zemle* (Concerning the Land; Petrograd, 1921), I, 23–24.

45. *Ibid.*, p. 29.

46. S. N. Prokopovich, *Ocherki khoziaistva Sovetskoi Rossii* (Essays in Economics of Soviet Russia; Berlin, 1923), p. 70.

47. A. L. Vainshtein, *Oblozhenie i platezhi krest'ianstva v dovoennoe i revoliutsionnoe vremia* (Taxation and Payments of the Peasantry during the Prewar and the Revolutionary Periods; Moscow, 1924); supplement table no. 2.

48. *Narodnoe khoziaistvo SSSR*, 1958, p. 345.

49. The figure of the gross income of the peasant population is a revision by Vainshtein of S. N. Prokopovich's well-known estimate for fifty provinces of European Russia for the year 1913, which was originally given as 5,595 million rubles. The fact that figures of rents and purchases are estimated for 1912 and that for peasant income is for 1913 should not cause a serious discrepancy. Note that the figures are merely rough approximations and that they are in gold rubles of the pre–World War I era when they were freely convertible into foreign currencies. One gold ruble equaled $0.50 U.S. currency.

50. A. Peshekhonov, "Dynamics of the Peasantry during the Revolution," *Zapiski Instituta izucheniia Rossii* (Prague), 1925, no. 2, pp. 13–15.

51. *Ibid.*, p. 16.

52. See the note by N. Vishnevskii on the reliability of statistical material in *Materialy po istorii agrarnoi revoliutsii v Rossii* (Materials on the History of Agrarian Revolution in Russia; Moscow, 1928), I, 56–61.

53. A. A. Kaufman, *Pervaia gosudarstvennaia duma* (The First State Duma; St. Petersburg, 1907), II, 117.

54. A. Khriashcheva, "Agriculture in 1921," *Sel'skoe i lesnoe khoziaistvo*, 1922, nos. 1–2, p. 208.

7. *War Communism*

1. P. B. Struve and others, *Russian Food Supply during the War* (New Haven, 1930), p. 111.

2. S. N. Prokopovich, *Ocherki khoziaistva Sovetskoi Rossii* (Essays on the Economics of Soviet Russia; Berlin, 1923), p. 112.

3. G. I. Krumin, ed., *Ekonomicheskaia politika SSSR* (Economic policy of the USSR; Moscow-Leningrad, 1928), p. 137.

4. Lenin, *Sochineniia*, XXIII, 525.

5. I. A. Gladkov, *Ocherki Sovetskoi ekonomiki, 1917–1920 gg.* (Essays in Soviet Economics; Moscow, 1956), pp. 194–201.

6. N. Orlov, *Prodovol'stvennaia rabota sovetskoi vlasti* (The Food-Supply Activities of the Soviet Government; Moscow, 1918), pp. 182–183.

7. M. Frumkin, in *Chetyre goda prodovol'stvennoi raboty. Stati i otchetnye materialy* (Four Years of Food Supply Work. Articles and Reports; Moscow, 1922), p. 69.

8. A. Sviderskii, in *Tri goda bor'by s golodom* (Three Years of Struggle with Famine; Moscow, 1920), pp. 8–9.

9. Orlov, *Prodovol'stvennaia rabota*, p. 399.

10. *SUR, 1917–1918*, no. 35, art. 468, pp. 437–439 (18 [5] May 1918); no. 38, art. 502, p. 476 (4 June [22 May] 1918). A supplementary decree of June 1, 1918, by the Food Commissariat, "Concerning the Rules of Delivery of Grain to the State."

11. Prokopovich, *Ocherki khoziaistva Sovetskoi Rossii*, p. 97.

12. *Izvestiia*, June 12, 1918; *SUR, 1917–1918*, no. 43, art. 524, pp. 522–524 (18 [5] June 1918), reprinted in *Agrarnaia politika Sovetskoi vlasti, 1917–1918. Dokumenty i materialy* (Agrarian Policy of the Soviet Government, 1917–1918. Documents and Materials; Moscow, 1954), pp. 177–180. See also S. Ronin, "The Bolshevik Struggle for the Organization of Kombedy," *Istorik Marksist*, 1932, nos. 26–27, p. 96; V. Bronshtein, "Committees of the Poor in RSFSR," *Istorik Marksist*, 1938, no. 69, pp. 76–96; A. I. Korolev, "The Legal Position of Kombedy in RSFSR," *Vestnik Leningradskogo Universiteta*, 1959, no. 23, pp. 95–109; V. R. Gerasimuk, "Kombedy of the Russian Federation in Figures," *Istoriia SSSR*, July–August 1960, pp. 120–125; T. Shepelev, "The Struggle for Bread in 1918–1919," *Krasnyi arkhiv*, 97:8–43 (1939). All these sources treat the subject from a Bolshevik point of view.

13. *Komitety bednoty Belorossii. Sbornik dokumentov i materialov* (The Committees of the Poor in Belorussia. A Collection of Documents and Materials; Minsk, 1958), p. 18.

14. *Ibid.*, pp. 193–194.

15. Lenin, *Sochineniia*, XXVIII, 279.

16. A. Shestakov, article on "Kombedy" in the *Bol'shaia Sovetskaia entsiklopediia*, XXXIII, 554–556.

17. V. Zaitsev, *Politika partii Bol'shevikov po otnosheniiu k krest'ianstvu v period ustanovleniia i uprochneniia Sovetskoi vlasti* (The Policy of the Bolshevik Party toward the Peasantry during the Period of Establishment and Consolidation of Soviet Power; Moscow, 1953), pp. 144–145.

18. Orlov, *Prodovol'stvennaia rabota*, pp. 375–376.

19. Gladkov, *Ocherki Sovetskoi ekonomiki*, p. 190.

20. *SUR, 1917–1918*, no. 57, art. 633, p. 690 (7 August 1918); *Izvestiia*, August 6, 1918; reprinted in *Agrarnaia politika Sovetskoi vlasti, 1917–1918*, pp. 190–191.

21. Prokopovich, *Ocherki khoziaistva Sovetskoi Rossii*, p. 99.

22. Article in *Bol'shaia Sovetskaia entsiklopediia,* 9th ed., XXXIV, 602.

23. Prokopovich, *Ocherki khoziaistva Sovetskoi Rossii,* p. 101.

24. *Ibid.,* p. 100; quoting *Vtoroi god bor'by s golodom* (The Second Year of Struggle against Hunger; Moscow, 1919), p. 19.

25. N. D. Kondrat'ev, *Rynok khlebov* (The Grain Market; Moscow, 1922), pp. 196–199.

26. V. P. Timoshenko, *Agricultural Russia and the Wheat Problem* (Stanford, 1932), p. 153; N. Vishnevskii, "Agriculture of the USSR during Ten Years of the Revolution," *Na ograrnom fronte,* 1927, nos. 11–12, pp. 127–132.

27. Timoshenko, *Agricultural Russia,* p. 157. The data are for the territory of the USSR as it existed prior to World War II, excluding Transcaucasia, Central Asia (Turkestan), and the Far East.

28. V. P. Nifontov, *Zhivotnovodstvo SSSR v tsifrakh* (Livestock Figures of the USSR; Moscow, 1932), p. 4.

29. Timoshenko, *Agricultural Russia,* p. 159.

30. G. I. Krumin, ed., *Ekonomicheskaia politika SSSR,* p. 137.

31. Lenin, *Sochineniia,* XXVII, 394.

32. *Ibid.,* XXVIII, 156.

33. *Ibid.,* p. 157; XXIX, 190.

34. Prokopovich, *Ocherki khoziaistva Sovetskoi Rossii,* p. 84.

35. *Agrarnaia politika Sovetskoi vlasti,* pp. 403–405.

36. Article 2 of the "Model Charter of a Commune," *Agrarnaia politika Sovetskoi vlasti,* p. 400.

37. *Ibid.,* pp. 399, 415–416, 407; "Instruction to Agricultural Departments Concerning the Allotment of Land to Agricultural Communes, Approved by the Commissariat of Agriculture."

38. *SUR, 1919,* no. 4, art. 43, pp. 49–61 (1 March 1919); *Izvestiia,* February 14, 1919; republished in *Agrarnaia politika Sovetskoi vlasti,* pp. 417–431.

39. *Sotsialisticheskie formy sel'skogo khoziastva v 1918–1919 gg.* (Socialist Types of Agriculture in 1918–1919); *Krasnyi arkhiv,* 96:35 (1939).

40. P. N. Pershin, *Uchastkovoe zemlepol'zovanie v Rossii* (Consolidated Farms in Russia; Moscow, 1922), pp. 42–43.

41. *Agrarnaia politika Sovetskoi vlasti,* pp. 462–470.

42. *Ibid.,* pp. 512–513.

43. "Socialist Forms of Agriculture in 1918–1919," *Krasnyi arkhiv,* 96:40 (1939).

44. Lenin, *Sochineniia,* XXX, 176; Kirilov, *Ocherki zemleustroistva,* pp. 52–60, 185–187.

45. "Socialist Forms of Agriculture in 1918–1919," *Krasnyi arkhiv,* 96:40 (1939).

46. Knipovich, *O zemle,* I, 36–42.

47. "Socialist Forms of Agriculture in 1918–1919," *Krasnyi arkhiv,* 96:40 (1939).

48. N. Osinskii (pseud. for Valerian Valerianovich Obolenskii), quoted by D. S. Rosenblum, *Zemel'noe pravo RSFSR* (Land Law of the RSFSR; Moscow, 1928), p. 89.

49. Lenin, *Sochineniia,* XXX, 176.

50. Knipovich, in *O zemle,* I, 42.

51. Orlov, *Prodovol'stvennaia rabota*, p. 372.

52. V. P. Miliutin, *Sotsialism i sel'skoe khoziaistvo* (Socialism and Agriculture; Moscow, 1919), p. 54.

53. S. P. Sereda, at the First All-Russian Congress of Agricultural Departments, Kombedy, and Communes, December 1918.

54. *SUR, 1917–1918,* no. 52, art. 593, pp. 619–620 (23 July 1918).

55. *Sel'skokhoziaistvennaia entsiklopediia* (Agricultural Encyclopedia; 3rd ed., Moscow, 1955), IV, 531.

56. *SUR, 1917–1918,* no. 72, art. 787, pp. 886–887 (10 October 1918); *Izvestiia,* October 9, 1918; republished in *Agrarnaia politika Sovetskoi vlasti,* p. 412.

57. *SUR, 1919,* no. 9, art. 87, pp. 113–114 (12 April 1919); *Izvestiia,* February 18, 1919; republished in *Agrarnaia politika Sovetskoi vlasti,* pp. 432–433.

58. *Agrarnaia politika Sovetskoi vlasti,* pp. 508–510.

59. Knipovich, in *O zemle,* I, 35.

60. Rosenblum, *Zemel'noe pravo,* p. 87.

61. Prokopovich, *Ocherki khoziaistva Sovetskoi Rossii,* citing a Report of the People's Commissariat of Agriculture to the Ninth All-Russian Congress of Soviets for 1921.

62. N. Osinskii, *Gosudarstvennoe regulirovanie krest'ianskogo khoziaistva* (State Regulation of Peasant Farming; Moscow, 1920), p. 9.

63. Rosenblum, *Zemel'noe pravo,* pp. 89–90.

64. N. Osinskii, *Gosudarstvennoe regulirovanie krest'ianskogo khoziaistva,* p. 9.

65. I. Teodorovich, *O gosudarstvennom regulirovanii krest'ianskogo khoziaistva* (Concerning State Regulation of Peasant Agriculture; Moscow, 1920), p. 8.

66. I. Teodorovich, *Vos'moi Vserossiiskii s'ezd Sovetov, Stenograficheskii otchet* (Eighth All-Russian Congress of Soviets, Stenographic Report; Moscow, 1921), p. 125.

67. Lenin, *Sochineniia,* XXXI, 472, 473.

68. Osinskii, in Stenographic Report of the Eighth Congress of Soviets, pp. 146–147.

69. *SUR, 1921,* no. 1, art. 9, pp. 7–9 (3 January 1921); Rosenblum, *Zemel'noe pravo,* pp. 91–95.

70. Stenographic Report of the Eighth Congress of Soviets, p. 200. Dallin later lived in the United States and became well known as the author of a number of works on the Soviet Union and Communism.

71. *Ibid.,* p. 201.

8. *The New Economic Policy*

1. V. G. Groman, "Grain Production and the Grain Export of Russia," *Entsiklopediia Sovetskogo eksporta* (Encyclopedia of Soviet Export), I, 175. The figures for Central Asia (Turkestan), Transcaucasia, and the Far East were not included. According to the estimate of the Central Statistical Office for the same territory, not accepted by the Gosplan, grain production in 1920 was 46 percent below

1909–13. See *Sbornik statisticheskikh svedenii po soiuzu SSR 1918–1923* (A Statistical Handbook for USSR, 1918–1923; Moscow, 1924), p. 131.

2. S. N. Prokopovich, *Ocherki khoziaistva Sovetskoi Rossii* (Essays in Economics of Soviet Russia; Berlin, 1923), p. 121.

3. Lenin, *Sochineniia,* XXXII, 151.

4. Paul A. Samuelson, *Economics: An Introductory Analysis* (4th ed., New York, 1958), pp. 181–182.

5. Prokopovich, *Ocherki khoziaistva Sovetskoi Rossii,* p. 119.

6. W. H. Chamberlin, *The Russian Revolution* (2 vols., New York, 1935), II, 431.

7. *Ibid.*

8. M. Frumkin, in *Chetyre goda prodovol'stvennoi raboty. Stat'i i otchetnye materialy* (Four Years of Food-Supply Work. Articles and Reports; Moscow, 1922), p. 70.

9. A. L. Vainshtein, *Oblozhenie i platezhi krest'ianstva v dovoennoe i revoliutsionnoe vremia* (Taxation and Payments of the Peasantry during the Prewar and Revolutionary Periods; Moscow, 1924), p. 72.

10. Chamberlin, *The Russian Revolution,* II, 436.

11. *Ibid.,* pp. 438–439.

12. Leonard Schapiro, *The Origin of the Communist Autocracy* (Cambridge, Mass., 1956), pp. 273–295.

13. Lenin, *Sochineniia,* XXXII, 111. This is said to be an unpublished draft of "theses on peasantry" made by Lenin during a meeting of the Politburo on February 8, 1921.

14. Two articles appeared in *Pravda* on February 17 and February 26, 1921, advocating the replacement of the requisitions by a tax in kind to increase peasant incentives to plant more. They did not, however, raise the question of legalization of free trading.

15. Lenin, *Sochineniia,* XXXII, 133.

16. Chamberlin, *The Russian Revolution,* II, 439–445; D. Fedotoff White, *The Growth of the Red Army* (Princeton, 1944), pp. 127–157; Schapiro, *The Origin of the Communist Autocracy,* pp. 296–305.

17. Lenin, *Sochineniia,* XXXII, 161, 164, 192.

18. *Ibid.,* XXXII, 321.

19. *Ibid.,* XXXII, 210.

20. *Ibid.,* XXXII, 196, 204.

21. N. N. Popov, ed. *Desiatyi s"ezd RKP(b), mart, 1921 g.* (The Tenth Congress of the Russian Communist Party, Bolshevik, March, 1921; Moscow, 1933), pp. 562–566; *Vsesoiuznaia Kommunisticheskaia Partiia(b) v rezoliutsiiakh i resheniiakh s'ezdov, konferentsii i plenumov Ts.K.* (All-Union Communist Party in Resolutions and Decisions of Congresses, Conferences and Plenary Meeting of the Central Committee; 4th ed., pt. 1; Moscow, 1936), pp. 397–398.

22. *Desiatyi s"ezd RKP(b),* pp. 434–437, 448–449.

23. *SUR, 1921,* no. 26, art. 147, pp. 153–154 (11 April 1921).

24. J. M. Keynes, *Economic Consequences of the Peace* (New York, 1920), p. 41.

25. *The Parliamentary Debates;* fifth series (March 22, 1921), vol. 139, p. 2511.

26. *VKP(b) v rezoliutsiiakh,* pp. 405–407.

27. Lenin, *Sochineniia, XXXII,* 386, 391, 412.

28. *SUR, 1922,* no. 13, art. 130, pp. 180–182 (12 March 1922).

29. *SUR, 1920,* no. 35, art. 170, pp. 152–154 (14 May 1920); *1920,* no. 52, art. 226, p. 230 (10 June 1920); *1920,* no. 90, art. 473, pp. 476–477 (26 November 1920); *1921,* no. 16, art. 103, p. 100 (15 March 1921).

30. D. S. Rosenblum, *Zemel'noe pravo RSFSR* (Land Law of RSFSR; Moscow, 1928), pp. 99–100.

31. *Zemel'nyi kodeks RSFSR s izmeneniiami po 1 ianvaria 1930 goda* (The Land Code of RSFSR with Changes up to January 1, 1930; Moscow, 1930), 80 pp. Generous excerpts from the code were translated in: Vladimir Gsovski, *Soviet Civil Law* (Ann Arbor, 1949), II, 463–470. For a further discussion of the Land Code of 1922 see Gsovski, *Soviet Civil Law,* I, 697–706; Rosenblum, *Zemel'noe pravo,* pp. 117–415.

32. *SUR, 1922,* no. 36, art. 426, pp. 576–580 (18 June 1922).

33. Gsovski, *Soviet Civil Law,* I, 698.

34. H. H. Fisher, *The Famine in Soviet Russia* (New York, 1927), pp. 497, 504.

35. Groman, "Grain Production and the Grain Export of Russia," *Entsiklopediia Sovetskogo eksporta,* I, 162–175.

36. M. M. Morgenshtern, *15 mesiatsev golodnogo fronta* (Fifteen Months of the Famine Front; Moscow, 1922), pp. 9–22.

37. Lenin, *Sochineniia, XXXII,* 418.

38. Morgenshtern, *15 mesiatsev golodnogo fronta.*

39. For a detailed account of the tortuous negotiations between ARA and the Soviet Government see Fisher, *The Famine in Soviet Russia,* pp. 28–70.

40. *Ibid.,* pp. 556–557 and 560. It should be pointed out that of the 61.6 million dollars spent by the ARA for relief, 11.4 million came from the gold funds of the Soviet Republics. In addition the Soviet government contributed to ARA in local currency, services, and facilities an amount estimated at nearly 14 million dollars. *Ibid.,* p. 553.

41. M. Kalinin, "A Year of Work," in *Itogi bor'by s golodom v 1921–22 gg.* (Results of Fighting Famine in 1921–22; Moscow, 1922), p. 5.

42. Fisher, *The Famine in Soviet Russia,* p. 398.

43. A. N. Kogan, "Anti-Soviet Activities of the ARA in Soviet Russia, 1921–1922," *Istoricheskie zapiski,* 1949, no. 29, pp. 3–32.

44. "The Basic Questions of Our Policy in the Village," *Na agrarnom fronte,* October 1925, p. 8.

45. "New Problems of Our Peasant Policy," *Pravda,* April 24, 1925.

46. Report at the Seventh Soviet Congress of the Moscow Province, in *Ekonomicheskaia zhizn',* April 14, 1925.

47. *SZR, SSSR, 1925,* no. 26, art. 183, pp. 327–330 (29 April 1925). Rosenblum, *Zemel'noe pravo,* pp. 192–195.

48. Lenin, *Sochineniia, XXVII,* 391–397.

49. Calvin B. Hoover, *The Economic Life of Soviet Russia* (New York, 1931), p. 225.

50. Vladimir P. Timoshenko, *Agricultural Russia and The Wheat Problem* (Stanford, 1932), pp. 163–173. The author discusses the organization of crop statistics in the USSR in the 1920s. For Gosplan's point of view, see S. G. Strumilin, *Statistiko-ekonomicheskie ocherki* (Statistical-Economic Essays; Moscow, 1958), pp. 329–337. Republished from *Planovoe khoziaistvo,* 1924, pp. 329–337.

51. Timoshenko, *Agricultural Russia,* pp. 181–182, giving estimates by Oganovskii and Gosplan for 1927 and 1928 respectively.

52. Estimates of gross agricultural production by the Gosplan, given by B. Gukhman, "Dynamics of Production," *Ekonomicheskoe obozrenie,* September 1929, p. 114. (The production year is October to September, so that 1927/1928 comprises crop production for 1927, and livestock production for October to September, 1927/1928.) Crop area from *Sotsialisticheskoe stroitel'stvo, 1934,* pp. 4–5.

53. *Sotsialisticheskoe stroitel'stvo, 1934,* pp. 176–177.

54. O. Auhagen, "Agrarverfassung und Landwirtschaft im Bezirk Odessa," *Berichte über Landwirtschaft,* 10:405–410 (n.s., no. 3, 1929); M. Wolf, "In the Steppe Ukraine," *Na agrarnom fronte,* October 1925, pp. 147–154; A. M. Bol'shakov, *Derevnia, 1917–1927* (The Village, 1917–1927; Moscow, 1927), pp. 43, 55.

55. A. Gaister, "The Leasing of Land," *Na agrarnom fronte,* June 1927, pp. 30–55; A. Azizian, "The Characteristic Features of Farms Leasing and Renting Land," *Na agrarnom fronte,* October 1927, pp. 37–52.

56. Commercial production for 1913 from *Kontrol'nye tsifry, 1925–26,* p. 72; for 1927–28, *ibid., 1928–29,* p. 226. See also I. I. Girkovich and I. N. Ozerov, "Agriculture and the Agricultural Market in 1926–27," *Ekonomicheskii biulleten' Kon'iunkturnogo instituta,* 1927, nos. 11–12, p. 52.

57. Girkovich and Ozerov, in *Ekonomicheskii biulleten',* p. 60. No adjustment has been made in the 1913 figures for postwar territorial changes but most of the important agricultural export regions were within the present territory of the USSR.

58. D. N. Kondrat'ev, *Rynok khlebov* (The Grain Market; Moscow, 1922), p. 15.

59. A. L. Vainshtein, "The Number and the Trend of Peasant Households in Prewar Russia," *Statisticheskoe obozrenie,* July 1929, pp. 9–19; *Statisticheskii spravochnik SSSR za 1928 g.,* p. 82.

60. K. Vorob'ev, "The Basic Socioeconomic Features of Peasant Farms in Various Producing Regions of the USSR," *Statisticheskoe obozrenie,* April 1929.

61. P. I. Liashchenko, *Russkoe zernovoe khoziaistvo v sisteme mirovogo khoziaistva* (Russian Grain Farming in the System of World Economy; Moscow, 1927), pp. 337–342; G. A. Studenskii, "Intensivity and Pseudo-Intensivity of Russian Peasant Agriculture," *Trudy Samarskogo sel'sko-khoziaistvennogo instituta* (Annals of the Samara Agricultural Institute; Samara, 1927), no. 4, pp. 45–81; A. Mikhailovskii, "The Balance of the Market Grain Supply," *Statisticheskoe obozrenie,* May 1930, p. 37.

62. *Kontrol'nye tsifry, 1929–30,* p. 443.

63. *Ibid.*

64. *Statisticheskii spravochnik SSSR za 1928 g.,* pp. 280–281.

65. *Biulleten' kon'iunkturnogo instituta,* October 1928, p. 16.

66. I. Vermenichev, A. Gaister, and G. Raevich, *710 khoziaistv Samarskoi derevni* (Seven Hundred and Ten Farms of the Samara Countryside; Moscow, 1928), p. 20.

67. *Kontrol'nye tsifry, 1928–29,* p. 218.

68. *Ibid.*

69. R. Belotserkovskii, "The Price Policy with Reference to Agricultural Raw Materials," *Ekonomicheskoe obozrenie,* January 1929, pp. 42–53.

70. *Biulleten' kon'iunkturnogo instituta,* October 1928, pp. 16–17.

71. E. A. Preobrazhenskii, *Novaia ekonomika* (The New Economics; 2nd ed., Moscow, 1926), p 123.

9. *Decline of the NEP and a New Offensive*

1. *Statisticheskii spravochnik SSSR 1927 g.,* pp. 78–83.

2. Lenin, *Sochineniia,* XXXI, 7–8.

3. D. N. Kondrat'ev, "Concerning the Question of Economic Stratification of the Village," *Puti sel'skogo khoziaistva,* May 1927, pp. 123–140.

4. *Vsesoiuznaia Kommunisticheskaia partiia(b) v resoliutsiiakh i resheniiakh s"ezdov konferentsii i plenumov TsK* (All-Union Communist Party, Resolutions and Decisions of the Congresses, Conferences, and Plenary Meetings of the Central Committee; Moscow, 1936), II, 216.

5. J. V. Stalin, *Leninism;* trans. Eden Paul and Cedar Paul (London, 1928), I, 247.

6. See Trotsky's speech at the Fifteenth Party Conference, November 1, 1926, *XV konferentsiia Vsesoiuznoi Kommunisticheskoi partii: Stenograficheskii otchet* (The Fifteenth Conference of the All-Union Communist Party: Stenographic Report; Moscow, 1927), p. 506.

7. E. A. Preobrazhenskii, "Economic Notes," *Bol'shevik,* August 31, 1926, pp. 15–16; see also his *Novaia ekonomika* (New Economics; 2nd ed., Moscow, 1926).

8. Preobrazhenskii, *Novaia ekonomika,* I, 279.

9. *Novaia ekonomika,* chap. 2. See the trenchant discussion of Preobrazhenskii's theory in Alexander Ehrlich, *The Soviet Industrialization Debate, 1924–1928* (Cambridge, Mass., 1960); also, Maurice Dobb, *Russian Economic Development since the Revolution* (London, 1928), pp. 59–68.

10. The replies to Bukharin and other critics are appended to the second edition of his *Novaia ekonomika,* pp. 249–335.

11. *Ibid.,* pp. 280, 281.

12. *Ekonomicheskaia zhizn',* December 29, 1925.

13. For a discussion of this point see Paul H. Douglas, "The Russian Economic Situation—Discussion," *American Economic Review,* Suppl. to 19.1:111–117 (March 1929).

14. Dobb, *Russian Economic Development,* pp. 264–265.

15. *VKP v rezoliutsiiakh,* II, 167.

16. *Ibid.*, p. 134.

17. *Ibid.*, p. 221.

18. Leon Trotsky, *The Real Situation in Russia;* Max Eastman, tr. (New York, 1928), pp. 68–69.

19. *SZR, SSSR, 1929.* For an analysis of these laws, see O. Auhagen, "Die Neueste Russische Agrargesetzeübung," *Berichte über Landwirtshaft,* 10:193 (n.s., no. 2, 1929).

20. Kalinin's report at the Sixteenth Party Conference, *Ekonomicheskaia zhizn',* April 30, 1929; also "Agricultural Tax," *Biulleten' ekonomicheskogo kabineta Prof. S. N. Prokopovicha,* May 1928, p. 58.

21. *VKP v rezoliutsiiakh,* II, 459.

22. M. Chernov, "The Basic Questions of New Grain Procurements," *Ekonomicheskoe obozrenie,* July 1929, p. 3. Chernov was one of the victims of Stalin's Great Purge.

23. See N. M. Vishnevskii, "Agricultural Production in 1928–29," *Ekonomicheskoe obozrenie,* December 1928, pp. 101–102; "Agricultural Production in 1929–30," *ibid.,* October 1929, pp. 99–106; *Kontrol'nye tsifry, 1928–29,* p. 218.

24. Stalin, *Sochineniia,* XII, 89–90; *Piatiletnii plan narodno-khoziaistvennogo stroitel'stva SSSR* (The Five Year Plan of National-Economic Development of the USSR; Moscow, 1929), vol. II, pt. 1, p. 270.

25. Stalin, *Leninism,* II, 108–109.

26. Stalin, *Sochineniia,* XI, 167.

27. *Ibid.,* XII, 52–59.

28. "Notes of an Economist," *Pravda,* September 30, 1928. See also Leonard Schapiro, *The Communist Party of the Soviet Union* (New York, 1960), pp. 368–369.

29. Stalin, *Sochineniia,* XI, 267, 302.

30. *Ibid.,* XI, 123–132, 267–286; XII, 42–59, 87–100.

31. *Ibid.,* XI, 129, 217.

32. *VKP v rezoliutsiiakh,* II, 335.

33. *Piatiletnii plan,* vol. II, pt. 1, pp. 336–337.

34. For a discussion of this struggle, see Schapiro, *The Communist Party of the Soviet Union,* chap. 20; R. V. Daniels, *The Conscience of the Revolution: Communist Opposition in Soviet Russia* (Cambridge, Mass., 1960), chap. 13.

10. *Collectivization and the Ordeal of the Peasants*

1. "A Year of Great Change" and "Concerning Questions of Agrarian Policy of the USSR," Stalin, *Sochineniia,* XII, 124–134, 141–172.

2. Stalin, *Sochineniia,* XII, 129–130.

3. *Ibid.,* pp. 155–156, 165.

4. *Ibid.,* p. 152. Stalin's italics.

5. *Ibid.,* p. 151.

6. *Ibid.,* pp. 169–170, 171

7. *Izvestiia,* July 4, 1929.

8. *Ibid.*, October 11, 1929.

9. *Ekonomicheskaia zhizn'*, September 1, 1929.

10. Calvin B. Hoover, *The Economic Life of Soviet Russia* (New York, 1931), p. 95.

11. *Ibid.*, p. 96.

12. Merle Fainsod, *Smolensk under Soviet Rule* (Cambridge, Mass., 1958), pp. 240–241.

13. *Ibid.*, p. 241.

14. *Ibid.*, p. 240.

15. *Ibid.*

16. *Ibid.*, p. 241.

17. *SZR, SSSR, 1929*, no. 5, art. 51, pp. 107–108 (30 January 1929). Reprinted in *Kollektivizatsiia sel'skogo khoziaistva* (Collectivization of Agriculture; Moscow, 1957), p. 108.

18. *VKP v resoliutsiiakh i resheniiakh s'ezdov konferentsii i plenumov TsK* (All-Union Communist Party in Resolutions and Decisions of Congresses, Conferences and Plenary Meeting of the Central Committee; Moscow, 1936), II, 383, 389.

19. *SZR, SSSR, 1929*, no. 75, art. 718 (December 1929); *Kollektivizatsiia sel'skogo khoziaistva*, pp. 240–241.

20. V. P. Danilov, ed., *Ocherki istorii kollektivizatsii sel'skogo khoziaistva v soiuznykh respublikakh* (Essays on Collectivization of Agriculture in the Federal Republics; Moscow, 1963), p. 34.

21. *SZR, SSSR, 1930*, no. 1, art. 1, p. 2 (1 January 1930); *Kollektivizatsiia sel'skogo khoziaistva*, pp. 254–255.

22. B. A. Abramov, "Concerning the Work of the Commission of the Politburo of the Central Committee about Wholesale Collectivization," *Voprosy istorii KPSS*, January 1964, p. 33.

23. Danilov, ed., *Ocherki*, p. 43.

24. *Pravda*, March 10, 1963.

25. See N. A. Ivnitskii, "Concerning the Initial Stage of Complete Collectivization (Fall of 1929–Spring of 1930)," *Voprosy istorii KPSS*, April 1962, pp. 55–71; Danilov, ed., *Ocherki*; Abramov, in *Voprosy istorii KPSS*, January 1964, pp. 32–43.

26. Abramov, in *Voprosy istorii KPSS*, January 1964, pp. 32–43.

27. *Vazhneishie resheniia po sel'skomu khoziaistvu* (The Most Important Decisions regarding Agriculture; V. V. Kilosanidze, comp.; Moscow, 1933), pp. 77–79.

28. *SZR, SSSR, 1930*, no. 9, art. 105, pp. 187–188 (24 February 1930); *Kollektivizatsiia sel'skogo khoziaistva*, p. 267.

29. Winston S. Churchill, *The Second World War* (Boston, 1950), IV, 498. For Churchill's account of Stalin's attitude related in conversation with Tito, see Fitzroy Maclean, *Escape to Adventure* (Boston, 1950), p. 364.

30. Hoover, *The Economic Life of Soviet Russia*, pp. 103–104.

31. *Ibid.*, pp. 105–106; John Scott, *Behind the Urals* (Cambridge, Mass., 1942), p. 174.

32. Fainsod, *Smolensk*, p. 246.

33. *Ibid.*, pp. 242–247.

34. Ibid., pp. 243, 246, 244–245; Danilov, *Ocherki*, p. 45.

35. Hoover, *The Economic Life of Soviet Russia*, p. 106.

36. Fainsod, *Smolensk*, p. 245.

37. *Ekonomicheskaia zhizn'*, January 31, 1930, "Kulakdom as a Class Must Be Exterminated"; and February 8, "The Kulak Is Not Surrendering Without a Fight."

38. Fainsod, *Smolensk*, pp. 246, 250.

39. *Pravda*, March 3, 1930.

40. Fainsod, *Smolensk*, p. 247.

41. "Concerning Distortions of the Party Line in the Collective Farm Movement," *Pravda*, March 16, 1930. Reprinted in *Vazhneishie resheniia*, pp. 80–82.

42. Fainsod, *Smolensk*, pp. 248, 263.

43. *Ibid.*, pp. 185–186.

44. *Istoriia Kommunisticheskoi Partii Sovetskogo Soiuza* (The History of the Communist Party of the Soviet Union; Moscow, 1962), pp. 443, 463.

45. "Social, Economic Planning in the Union of Socialist Soviet Republics," in *Report of the Delegation from the USSR to the World Social Economic Congress* (Amsterdam, August 23–29, 1931), p. 121.

46. *Sel'skoe khoziaistvo SSSR, 1935,* p. 215.

47. Danilov, *Ocherki*, pp. 38–39.

48. *Ekonomicheskaia zhizn'*, April 1, 1930.

49. *Pravda*, March 22, 1930.

50. *International Press Correspondence*, vol. 10, no. 17 (April 3, 1930).

51. *Ekonomicheskaia zhizn'*, January 5, 1930 (discussion of collective farm situation in the Lower Volga region).

52. *Ibid.*, January 5, 1930.

53. Markoosha Fischer, *My Lives in Russia* (New York, 1944), pp. 49–51.

54. Fainsod, *Smolensk*, pp. 251–253.

55. A. F. Zylko, "The Basic Landmarks of the Collective Movement of 1929–1930," *Na agrarnom fronte*, May 1930, p. 31.

56. *Vazhneishie resheniia*, 1933, p. 79.

57. Hoover, *The Economic Life of Soviet Russia*, p. 109.

58. Fainsod, *Smolensk*, p. 253.

59. Hoover, *The Economic Life of Soviet Russia*, pp. 108–109

60. *Ibid.*, p. 109.

61. Danilov, *Ocherki*, p. 45.

62. Ivnitskii, in *Voprosy istorii KPSS*, April 1962, p. 65.

63. Stalin, *Sochineniia*, XII, 188.

64. *Ibid.*, pp. 191–199.

65. *Istoriia Kommunisticheskoi Partii*, pp. 442–443.

66. *Vazhneishie resheniia*, 1933, pp. 80–82.

67. Stalin, *Sochineniia*, XII, 202–228.

68. Danilov, *Ocherki*, pp. 46–47.

69. Fischer, *My Lives in Russia*, pp. 49–51.

70. *Vazhneishie resheniia,* 1933, p. 91.

71. Fainsod, *Smolensk,* p. 258.

72. *Vazhneishie resheniia,* 1933, p. 91.

73. *Vazhneishie resheniia,* 1933, p. 88.

74. Fainsod, *Smolensk,* p. 258.

75. *Vazhneishie resheniia,* 1933, pp. 95–96.

76. *Ibid.,* p. 89.

77. Naum Jasny, *Socialized Agriculture of the USSR* (Stanford, 1949), pp. 539–541.

78. W. H. Chamberlin, *Russia's Iron Age* (Boston, 1934), p. 83.

79. Otto Schiller, *Die Krise der Socialistischen Landwirtschaft,* pp. 44–45, quoted by E. M. Kulischer, *Europe on the Move* (New York, 1948), p. 98.

80. Fainsod, *Smolensk,* pp. 259–262.

81. Chamberlin, *Russia's Iron Age,* pp. 88, 89.

82. Kulischer, *Europe on the Move,* pp. 97–98.

11. *Collectivized Agriculture in the Prewar Period*

1. Ia. A. Iakovlev, *Voprosy organizatsii sotsialisticheskogo sel'skogo khoziaistva* (Questions of the Organization of Socialist Agriculture; Moscow, 1933), p. 159.

2. The concluding remarks of V. M. Molotov at the third session of the Central Executive Committee of the USSR. *Ekonomicheskaia zhizn',* January 29, 1933.

3. B. Sheboldaev, "To Break up the Sabotage in Sowing and Grain Deliveries Organized by the Kulaks in Kuban," *Sotsialisticheskoe pereutroistvo,* June 1932, p. 4.

4. I. G. Naumchik, "The Strengthening of the Financial Power of Kolkhozes," *Sotsialisticheskaia rekonstruktsiia sel'skogo khoziaistva,* August 1935, p. 14.

5. K. Vorob'ev, "The Basic Socioeconomic Features of Peasant Farming by Regions in the USSR," *Statisticheskoe obozrenie,* April 1929, p. 7.

6. Merle Fainsod, *Smolensk under Soviet Rule* (Cambridge, Mass., 1958), pp. 266–267.

7. L. M. Kaganovich, in *Sotsialisticheskoe zemledelie,* July 14, 1932.

8. *Izvestiia,* August 6, 1937.

9. *Vazhneishie resheniia po sel'skomu khoziaistvu* (The Most Important Decisions Regarding Agriculture), V. V Kilosanidze, comp.; 2nd ed., Moscow, 1935), p. 437.

10. *Ibid.* (1933 ed.), pp. 172–174.

11. *Ibid.,* pp. 195–196.

12. Stalin, *Sochineniia,* XII, 222–224.

13. *Vazhneishie resheniia,* 1935, p. 169.

14. Reported by Kaganovich at the Seventeenth Party Congress. *Pravda,* February 12, 1934.

15. P. Fileev, *Zapiski nachal'nika politotdela* (Memoirs of a Politotdel Chief; Moscow, 1934); A. Krymskii, "Politotdels in the Machine-Tractor Stations, the First Stage of Work," *Sotsialisticheskoe zemledelie,* February 27, 1933.

16. *Sotsialisticheskoe zemledelie,* January 17, 1933.

17. *Vazhneishie resheniia* (1933), p. 258; also a decree of May 20, 1932, pp. 258–259.

18. *Ibid.,* pp. 258–259.

19. *Ibid.,* pp. 271–290.

20. *Ibid.* (1935), pp. 589–590.

21. Decrees of August 2 and 18, 1933, *Vazhneishie resheniia* (1935), pp. 446, 448–449.

22. Decrees of August 14 and November 5, 1933, *Vazhneishie resheniia* (1935), pp. 446–448.

23. Fainsod, *Smolensk,* pp. 262–263.

24. *Vtoroi vsesoiuznyi s'ezd kolkhoznikov-udarnikov: Stenograficheskii otchet* (The Second All-Union Congress of Shock Kolkhozniks: Stenographic Report; Moscow, 1935), pp. 225–232. An English translation of the charter will be found in Vladimir Gsovski, *Soviet Civil Law* (Ann Arbor, 1948), II, 441–462; L. S. Hubbard, *The Economics of Soviet Agriculture* (London, 1939), pp. 131–147. For a historical account and analysis of the charter, see A. P. Pavlov and others, *Kolkhoznoe pravo* (Kolkhoz Law; Moscow, 1939), pp. 118–132.

25. Iakovlev, Head of the Agricultural Section of the Central Committee, and V. M. Chernov, Minister of Agriculture, in *Vtoroi vsesoiuznyi s'ezd kolkhoznikov-udarnikov,* pp. 12–13, 226–227.

26. Pavlov, *Kolkhoznoe pravo,* pp. 114–115.

27. *Ibid.,* p. 342.

28. Decree of the Commissariat of Agriculture, June 15, 1933, approved by the Council of People's Commissars on June 20, 1933. *Vazhneishie resheniia* (1935), p. 444.

29. *Vazhneishie resheniia* (1935), p. 477.

30. Pavlov, *Kolkhoznoe pravo,* p. 89.

31. Alexander Gerschenkron, "The Soviet Indices of Industrial Production," *Review of Economic Statistics,* 29:217–226 (1947); Gregory Grossman, "Thirty Years of Soviet Industrialization," *Soviet Survey,* October–December 1958, pp. 15–21.

32. *Socialist Construction in the USSR: Statistical Abstract* (Moscow, 1936), p. 410.

33. Franklyn D. Holzman, "Soviet Inflationary Pressures, 1928–1957: Causes and Cures," *Quarterly Journal of Economics,* 74:167–188 (May 1960).

34. The estimates were arrived at by deducting government procurements of all kinds from the figures of commercial production. *Sel'skoe khoziaistvo SSSR, 1960,* pp. 86, 87, 93. A margin of error is involved in this procedure since published figures of procurements of a number of products are stated presumably not in physical units but in standard units, making allowance for deviations in quality from a typical standard prescribed by the state, such as a certain butter fat content in the case of milk. Figures for commercial production are in gross physical units.

35. Jerzy F. Karcz, *Soviet Agricultural Marketings and Prices* (Santa Monica, 1957), p. 34.

36. Lazar Volin, *A Survey of Soviet Russian Agriculture* (Washington, D.C., 1951), p. 188.

37. *Izvestiia,* September 21, 1933.

38. *SPR, SSSR, 1939,* no. 45, art. 357, p. 670 (9 August 1939).

39. *Slovar'-spravochnik po sotsial'no–ekonomicheskoi statistike* (A Reference Dictionary of Social-Economic Statistics; 2nd ed., Moscow, 1948), p. 201.

40. *Sbornik rukovodiashchikh materialov po kolkhoznomu stroitel'stvu* (Collection of Leading Materials on Kolkhoz Development; Moscow, 1948), p. 187.

41. For instance, the decree of May 28, 1939, referred to "the numerous facts of deliberate lowering of yields on collective farms and artificial decrease of the payments in kind to machine-tractor stations" based on such yields. It went on to flay the local officials: "This situation was permitted to develop unhindered by the local party, Komsomol, and Soviet organs and the opportunistic attitude of their leaders to the anti-state practice of Regional Commissions for Determining the Level of Yields of Collective Farms, was corrected only as a result of intervention of the Central Committee of the Communist Party and the Council of People's Commissars of the USSR." *SPR, SSSR, 1939,* no. 34, art. 236, pp. 498–516 (7 June 1939).

42. Khrushchev, *Stroitel'stvo kommunizma i razvitie sel'skogo khoziaistva v SSSR* (Moscow, 1960–64), I, 88.

43. See Naum Jasny, *The Socialized Agriculture of the USSR* (Stanford, 1949), pp. 659, 728; Lazar Volin, "Recent Developments in Soviet Agriculture," *Foreign Agriculture,* 1:23 (January 1937), and *A Survey of Soviet Russian Agriculture,* pp. vii–viii.

44. *Pravda* and *Izvestiia,* August 9, 1953.

45. *Ibid.,* September 15, 1953.

46. *Sotsialisticheskoe sel'skoe khoziaistvo,* p. 61; *Sel'skoe khoziaistvo SSSR, 1960,* p. 196.

47. *Narodnoe khoziaistvo, 1960,* p. 362.

48. *Comparisons of the United States and Soviet Economies,* Joint Economic Committee of the U.S. Congress (Washington, D.C., 1959), Pt. I, pp. 204, 205.

49. *Pravda* and *Izvestiia,* April 20, 1938.

50. *Sotsialisticheskoe sel'skoe khoziaistvo,* p. 126.

51. On the basis of a sevenfold increase in retail prices between 1928 and 1937 and 2.2 able-bodied workers per kolkhoz household. I. V. Sautin, ed., *Kolkhozy vo vtoroi Stalinskoi piatiletke* (Kolkhozes during the Second Stalinist Five-Year Plan; Moscow and Leningrad, 1939), pp. 2, 35.

52. Jasny, *Socialized Agriculture of the USSR,* p. 694.

53. Abram Bergson, *Soviet National Income and Product in 1937* (New York, 1953).

54. Abram Bergson, Hans Heyman, Jr., and Oleg Hoeffding, *Soviet National Income and Product, 1928–48: Revised Data* (Santa Monica, November 15, 1960), p. 6.

55. The year 1928 calculated by applying 74.8 percent given by Warren W. Eason in *Comparisons of the United States and Soviet Economies,* p. 89, to total population figure of 150.3 million at the beginning of 1928 given in *Statisticheskii*

spravochnik SSSR za 1928g., p. 2; 1937 calculated by applying 56.3 percent, given by Eason in an unpublished Columbia University dissertation, to total population figure of 163.8 million from *Narodnoe khoziaistvo, 1962*, p. 7.

56. Naum Jasny, *The Soviet Price System* (Stanford, 1951), p. 57.

57. Abram Bergson, *The Real National Income of Soviet Russia since 1928* (Cambridge, Mass., 1961), p. 118.

58. Jasny, *Socialized Agriculture of the USSR*, p. 694.

59. *Ibid.*

60. Sautin, *Kolkhozy vo vtoroi Stalinskoi piatiletke*, p. 110.

61. Cited by Jasny in *Soviet Price System*, p. 152. Data for 1937 from M. Nesmi, "Income of Kolkhozes and Kolkhozniks," *Planovoe khoziaistvo*, 1938, no. 9, pp. 73–107. Data for 1927–28 from *Piatiletnii plan narodno-khoziaistvennogo stroitel'stva* (Five-Year Plan for National Economic Construction; Moscow, 1930), vol. II, pt. 2, pp. 18–19, 74–75.

62. Stalin, *Sochineniia*, XIII, 356–357.

63. Sautin, *Kolkhozy vo vtoroi Stalinskoi piatiletke*, p. 36.

64. D. Rud, *Raspredelenie dokhodov v kolkhozakh* (Distribution of Income in Kolkhozes; Moscow, 1938), p. 28.

65. Sautin, *Kolkhozy vo vtoroi Stalinskoi piatiletke*, p. 35; *Narodnoe khoziaistvo, 1958*, p. 532; I. S. Malyshev, ed., *MTS vo vtoroi piatiletke* (The MTS during the Second Five-Year Plan; Moscow and Leningrad, 1939), p. 90.

66. Malyshev, *MTS vo vtoroi piatiletke*, p. 90.

67. Sautin, *Kolkhozy vo vtoroi Stalinskoi piatiletke*, pp. 62, 65–77.

68. *Pravda*, July 5, 1937; *Sotsialisticheskaia rekonstruktsiia sel'skogo khoziaistva*, January 1938.

69. *Izvestiia*, August 26, 1937.

70. *Ibid.*, September 1, 1937.

71. A. Karavaev, "Stalin's Law of Further Strengthening the Kolkhoz System," *Problemy ekonomiki*, April 1938, p. 47.

72. *Pravda* and *Izvestiia*, April 20, 1938.

73. *Pravda*, June 21, 1938.

74. *Sotsialisticheskoe zemledelie*, May 21, 1938.

75. *Izvestiia*, January 3, 1938.

76. Collectivized peasants were not supposed to have workhorses in their individual possession, although a small minority did. The great majority, when they needed horses for their own use, had to obtain permission—often with considerable difficulty and red tape—to hire the collectivized horses, or hire them from individual peasants.

77. *Sotsialisticheskoe zemledelie*, April 24, 1938.

78. Lead editorial in *Izvestiia*, April 21, 1938.

79. *Finansovyi i khoziaistvennyi biulleten'*, 1938, nos. 33–34.

80. *Sotsialisticheskoe zemledelie*, March 16, 1939.

81. *Vazhneishie resheniia* (1938–1940), pp. 41–47.

82. *Sotsialisticheskoe sel'skoe khoziaistvo 1939*, p. 73.

83. Calculated from *Zhivotnovodstvo SSSR 1959*, p. 26.

84. N. Maksimenko, "The Fate of Animal Husbandry in USSR," *Sotsialisti-*

cheskii vestnik, May 1950, pp. 94–96. The author, a refugee Russian agronomist, writes on the basis of firsthand observation and experience.

85. *Ibid.*

86. *Ibid.*

87. "Measures for the Development of Communal Livestock in the Kolkhozes," *Vazhneishie resheniia* (1938–1940), pp. 346–362.

88. *Sel'skoe khoziaistvo SSSR, 1960,* pp. 263, 264.

89. The basic legislation was promulgated in the decree of April 7, 1940, "On Changes in the Policy of Procurements and Purchases of Farm Products," supplemented by a number of other measures. *Vazhneishie resheniia* (1938–1940), pp. 557–562, 587–632.

12. Collectivized Agriculture and the War

1. I. G. Cherniavskii, *Voina i prodovol'stvie. Snabzhenie gorodskogo naseleniia v velikuiu otechestvennuiu voinu, 1941–1943* (War and the Food Supply. Supplying the Urban Population during the Great Fatherland War; Moscow, 1964), p. 16.

2. *Ibid.,* p. 18.

3. *Sotsialisticheskoe stroitel'stvo 1934,* p. 265; *1935,* p. 449; *1936,* p. 493.

4. A. Galitskii, "International Shipment in the USSR," *Planovoe khoziaistvo,* July 1938, p. 26.

5. Cherniavskii, *Voina,* p. 36.

6. N. A. Voznesenskii, *Voennaia ekonomika SSSR v period otechestvennoi voiny* (Moscow, 1948), p. 91; trans. as *The Economy of the USSR during World War II,* by Gregory Grossman (Washington, D.C., 1948).

7. Cherniavskii, p. 16.

8. A. N. Antsiferov and others, *Russian Agriculture during the War* (New Haven, 1930), p. 117.

9. G. I. Shigalin, *Narodnoe khoziaistvo SSSR v period velikoi otechestvennoi voiny* (The National Economy of the USSR during the Great Fatherland War; Moscow, 1960), pp. 189 and 212.

10. K. M. Shchegolev, "The Struggle of Kolkhoz Peasantry of Western Siberia in Supplying the Front and the Rear with Food," *Iz istorii rabochego klassa i krest'ianstva SSSR* (From the History of the Working Class and Peasantry in the USSR; M. I. Kim, ed., Moscow, 1959), pp. 232–233.

11. "A Summary Compilation of Kolkhoz Reports during the Fatherland War," *Istoricheskii arkhiv,* 1962, no. 6, p. 37. Separate figures are given for able-bodied men and women participating in collective farm work who were obliged to complete a minimum of workdays; but no segregation by sexes is indicated for those workers who were not obliged to complete such a minimum because of being drafted into the army or employed in industry. The figures cited are for men and women who were required to complete a minimum of workdays.

12. Iu. V. Arutiunian, *Sovetskoe krest'ianstvo v gody velikoi otechestvennoi voiny* (Soviet Peasantry during the Years of the Great Fatherland War; Moscow, 1963), p. 69.

13. Voznesenskii, *Voennaia ekonomika*, pp. 92–93.
14. Shigalin, *Narodnoe khoziaistvo*, p. 212.
15. *Istoricheskii arkhiv*, 1962, no. 6, p. 52.
16. Voznesenskii, *Voennaia ekonomika*, p. 93.
17. Arutiunian, *Sovetskoe krest'ianstvo*, p. 66.
18. Shigalin, *Narodnoe khoziaistvo*, p. 209.
19. M. A. Vyltsan, "The Kolkhoz System on the Eve of the Great Fatherland War," *Istoriia SSSR*, January 1962, p. 36.
20. Arutiunian, *Sovetskoe krest'ianstvo*, pp. 142–144.
21. *Sel'skoe khoziaistvo SSSR, 1960*, p. 263.
22. Arutiunian, p. 186.
23. Shchegolev, in *Iz istorii rabochego klassa i krest'ianstva*, p. 256.
24. Arutiunian, p. 149.
25. *Ibid.*, pp. 5 and 9.
26. *Vazhneishie resheniia* (1938–1946), pp. 341–343.
27. Voznesenskii, *Voennaia ekonomika*, pp. 94 and 95.
28. Arutiunian, *Sovetskoe krest'ianstvo*, p. 163.
29. *Ibid.*, p. 169.
30. Cherniavskii, *Voina i prodovol'stvie*, p. 16.
31. Voznesenskii, *Voennaia ekonomika*, p. 92.
32. Lazar Volin, "German Invasion and Russian Agriculture," *The Russian Review*, 3.1:79–80 (1943).
33. *Istoriia velikoi otechestvennoi voiny Sovetskogo Soiuza 1941–1945* (The History of the Great Fatherland War of the Soviet Union; Moscow, 1960), I, 412.
34. Calculated from *Narodnoe khoziaistvo*, 1960, p. 411.
35. E. S. Karnaukhova, *Kolkhoznoe proizvodstvo v gody otechestvennoi voiny* (Kolkhoz Production during the Fatherland War; Moscow, 1947), p. 105.
36. Arutiunian, *Sovetskoe krest'ianstvo*, p. 174.
37. Karnaukhova, p. 113.
38. Arutiunian, p. 175.
39. Karnaukhova, pp. 80–81.
40. Arutiunian, p. 170.
41. Karnaukhova, p. 85; Arutiunian, p. 170.
42. Arutiunian, p. 178. It was estimated that the quantity of concentrates fed per milk cow on state farms decreased from 5.8 centners in 1940 to 0.8 in 1943; while the amount of the succulent feed, mainly silage, increased from 15.2 centners to 16.5; and roughages from 22.2 centners to 27.3.
43. Arutiunian, p. 43.
44. *Ibid.*, pp. 182–183.
45. *Vazhneishie resheniia* (1938–46), pp. 494–495.
46. Arutiunian, p. 186.
47. *Ibid.*, pp. 203, 205.
48. *Ibid*, p. 192.
49. *Ibid.*, pp. 192–193.
50. *Ibid.*, p. 199.
51. *Ibid.*, p. 70.
52. *Narodnoe khoziaistvo, 1964*, pp. 124–125.

53. Ia. E. Chadaev, *Ekonomika SSSR v period velikoi otechestvennoi voiny 1941–1945 gg.* (Economics of the USSR during the Period of the Great Fatherland War, 1941–1945; Moscow, 1965), p. 282.

54. Arutiunian, p. 196.

55. *Ibid.*, p. 198. Differences in the territory covered may explain some of the discrepancy; but hardly a major part of it.

56. *Ibid.*, pp. 194, 69.

57. *SPR, SSSR, 1942,* no. 10, art. 154, p. 163 (31 December 1942); *Pravda,* December 7, 1942.

58. *SPR, SSSR, 1944,* no. 4, art. 52, pp. 102–104 (3 April 1944).

59. Report of K. I. Nikolaeva at the Twelfth Plenary Session of the Central Trade Union Council, March 11, 1944, *V pomoshch' fabrichno-zavodskim i mestnym kommitetam* (April 1944), p. 21.

60. *Izvestiia,* April 6, 1944. See also Pravda, April 7, 1944.

61. *Trud,* February 22, 1945.

62. The average potato crop during 1938–40 amounted to 47,891,000 metric tons. For vegetables a figure of 13,713,000 tons was given for 1940. It is territorially not comparable with that for potatoes because it includes the annexed areas. *Sel'skoe khoziaistvo SSSR, 1960,* pp. 201–202.

63. V. Ia. Ashanin, "Political Sections of MTS during the Great Fatherland War," *Voprosy istorii KPSS,* 1960, no. 6.

64. *Vazhneishie resheniia,* pp. 208–210.

65. *Ibid.*, pp. 310–311.

66. *Istoricheskii arkhiv,* June 1962, pp. 38–39, 42.

67. *Ibid.*, pp. 52, 67.

68. "Concerning the Supplementary Payment for Labor of Kolkhozniks for Raising the Yields of Crops and Productivity of Livestock in the Ukrainian SSR. A Decree of the Council of People's Commissars and of the Central Committee of VKP(b) of December 31, 1940," *Vazhneishie resheniia,* pp. 291–306, 210–229, 312–317. Similar legislation, taking account of local differences, was passed for other regions of the country.

69. Arutiunian, *Sovetskoe krest'ianstvo,* p. 72, quoting Ia. S. Vinokurov's dissertation.

70. Order of June 20, 1945, by Commissar of Agriculture A. A. Andreev. *Vazneishie resheniia,* pp. 315–316.

71. *Pravda,* April 17, 1942.

72. Arutiunian, p. 90.

73. A. Krymskii, in *Sotsialisticheskoe zemledelie,* May 3, 1942.

74. A. Khanchin, in *Volzhskaia kommuna,* December 3, 1942.

75. Arutiunian, p. 91.

76. *Ibid.* He gives the total number of workdays as 5332.6 million in 1942, 5535.4 million in 1943, and 7077 million in 1944.

77. A. P. Teriaeva, *Trud v kolkhozakh vo vremia velikoi otechestvennoi voiny* (Labor in Kolkhozes during the Great Fatherland War; Moscow, 1947), p. 21.

78. Chadaev, *Ekonomika SSSR,* p. 129.

79. *Eleventh Report to Congress on Lend-Lease Operations for the Period Ended July 31, 1943,* p. 28.

80. New York *Herald Tribune,* May 18, 1943.

81. Cherniavskii, *Voina i prodovol'stvie,* pp. 83–84.

82. Voznesenskii, *Voennaia ekonomika,* p. 123; Cherniavskii, p. 81.

83. Karl Brandt in collaboration with Otto Schiller and Franz Ahlgrimm, *Management of Agriculture and Food in the German-Occupied and Other Areas of Fortress Europe* (Stanford, 1953); Alexander Dallin, *German Rule in Russia, 1941–1945* (London, 1957).

84. Brandt, *Management of Agriculture,* p. 631.

85. Dallin, *German Rule in Russia,* pp. 322, 323.

86. Brandt, *Management of Agriculture,* p. 93; Dallin, *German Rule in Russia,* pp. 324–334.

87. The translation of the text will be found in Brandt, *Management of Agriculture,* pp. 665–670.

88. *Ibid.,* p. 99.

89. Dallin, *German Rule in Russia,* pp. 354–355.

90. Translated in Brandt, *Management of Agriculture,* pp. 670–671.

91. Alexander Werth, in the New York *Times,* August, 29, 1943.

92. Henry Shapiro, in the New York *Herald Tribune,* September 7, 1943.

93. Arutiunian, *Sovetskoe krest'ianstvo,* pp. 233–234.

94. *Ibid.,* pp. 142–143.

95. Brandt, pp. 135, 133, 147, 146.

13. *Postwar Recovery*

1. Juozas Audenas, "Agriculture in Bolshevik-Occupied Lithuania," *Monthly Bulletin of the International Peasant Union,* 3:21–26 (September–October 1952).

2. *Vazhneishie resheniia* (1938–1946), pp. 318–323.

3. *Pravda,* September 19, 1947; *Sotsialisticheskoe zemledelie,* November 22, 1947.

4. A decree of the Council of Ministers of the USSR, March 17, 1953, no. 818. *Zakonodatel'nye i vedomstvennye akty po sel'skomu khoziaistvu* (Legislation and Government Regulations Dealing with Agriculture; Moscow, 1957), I, 113.

5. *Vazhneishie resheniia,* (1938–1946), pp. 83–130; *Pravda,* February 28, 1947.

6. *Narodnoe khoziaistvo, 1959,* p. 314.

7. *Ibid., 1964,* p. 246.

8. *Ibid.,* p. 380.

9. *Ibid.,* p. 378.

10. *Promyshlennost' SSSR,* 1964, p. 142.

11. *Vazhneishie resheniia,* pp. 15, 35–36.

12. *Narodnoe khoziaistvo, 1960,* pp. 542, 546.

13. For the USSR, *Sel'skoe khoziaistvo, SSSR, 1960,* p. 409; for the United States, P. E. Strickler and C. A. Hines, *Numbers of Selected Machines on Farms with Related Data,* U.S. Department of Agriculture, Statistical Bulletin no. 258 (Washington, D.C., 1960), p. 12.

14. *Promyshlennost' SSSR, 1964,* p. 279.

15. M. Moiseev, "Economic Links of Industry and Agriculture," *Voprosy ekonomiki,* July 1958, p. 20.

16. G. Gaponenko, "The Economic Basis of the New Purchase Prices for Farm Products," *Planovoe khoziaistvo,* November 1958, p. 33.

17. Moiseev, p. 20.

18. Franklyn D. Holzman, "Soviet Inflationary Pressures," *Quarterly Journal of Economics,* 74:168–169 (May 1960).

19. Janet Chapman, *Real Wages in Soviet Russia since 1928* (Cambridge Mass., 1963), p. 81. The index for 1948 was 306, or 280, depending upon whether 1937 or 1948 weights were used. For 1952, similar figures were 240 and 217 respectively (1937=100).

20. Holzman, pp. 168–169.

21. *Sovetskaia torgovlia* (Moscow, 1956), p. 180.

22. *Sel'skoe khoziaistvo SSSR, 1960,* p. 118; *Sovetskaia torgovlia,* pp. 19, 179.

23. Khrushchev, *Stroitel'stvo kommunizma,* VIII, 466.

24. Khrushchev made a statement in 1958 that, "The total payments in kind and cash on the basis of workdays earned [by kolkhozniks] increased in comparable prices [purchasing prices] from 47.5 billion rubles in 1952 to 83.8 billion rubles in 1957." *Plenum tsentral'nogo komiteta Kommunisticheskoi Partii Sovetskogo Soiuza, 15–19 Dekabria 1958 g. Stenograficheskii otchet* (Stenographic Report of the Plenary Meeting of the Central Committee of the Communist Party of the Soviet Union; Moscow, 1958, p. 62. The number of kolkhozniks who shared this total is not given, but for 1950 and 1953 there are available figures of the average annual number who worked in kolkhozes, derived by averaging monthly figures of kolkhoz employment, irrespective of the number of days worked by a kolkhoznik. It was 27.6 million in 1950 and 25.6 million in 1953 (*Sel'skoe khoziaistvo SSSR, 1960,* p. 450). In 1953 a number of kolkhozniks were transferred to the permanent staffs of the MTS which increased the labor force of these units from 700,000 in 1950, to 1.2 million in 1953. Also some kolkhozes were converted into state farms. In view of these changes it would seem that the 1952 average figure of kolkhoz workers should be higher than in 1953 and is assumed to be 26 million. By dividing 47.5 billion rubles by 26 million workers, the figure of 1820 rubles is obtained as the average earnings of a kolkhoznik in 1952.

25. *Narodnoe khoziaistvo, 1964,* p. 555.

26. Calculated from S. S. Sergeev, *Voprosy ekonomiko-statisticheskogo analiza kolkhoznogo proizvodstva* (Problems of the Economic and Statistical Analysis of Kolkhoz Production; Moscow, 1956), pp. 369, 373.

27. Former Minister of Finance Zverev in *Pravda* and *Izvestiia,* August 6, 1953; present Minister of Finance V. Garbuzov in *Finansy i kredit SSSR,* September 1953, pp. 9–15.

28. "The Crimes of the Stalin Era," special report to the Twentieth Congress of the Communist Party, February 1956; translated in *The New Leader,* July 16, 1956, section 2.

29. *Pravda and Izvestiia,* October 24, 1948.

30. J. S. Joffe, "Russian Contribution to Soil Science," in *Soviet Science,* arranged by Conway Zirkle and H. A. Meyerhoff (Washington, D.C., 1952), p. 63.

31. R. Y. Bailey and W. M. Nixon, "Rotations for Problem Fields," in *Grass. Yearbook of Agriculture 1948* (U.S. Department of Agriculture, Washington, D.C., 1948), p. 195.

32. The conflict between Prianishnikov and Williams is described by Joffe in ·*Soviet Science*, pp. 64–65. This conflict was often used by Khrushchev in his attacks on the Williams school.

33. D. N. Prianishnikov, *Azot v zhizni rastenii i v zemledelii SSSR* (Nitrogen in the Life of Plants and in Agriculture of the USSR; Moscow-Leningrad, 1945), p. 136.

34. Lazar Volin, *A Survey of Soviet Russian Agriculture* (Washington, D.C., 1951), p. 89.

35. T. D. Lysenko, "Concerning the Agronomic Teaching of V. R. Williams," *Pravda*, July 15, 1950.

36. For a discusison of the drought problem in the Soviet Union, see N. M. Tulaikov, "Agriculture in the Dry Regions of the USSR," *Economic Geography*, 1930.

37. *Vazhneishie resheniia* (1938–1946), pp. 329–341; Volin, "Effects of the Drought and Purge on the Agriculture of the Soviet Union," *Foreign Agriculture*, 3:175–196 (May 1939).

38. *Pravda*, October 24, 1948.

39. A. Paramonov, "Concerning the Question of Tree-Shelterbelts in the USSR," *Journal of the Institute for the Study of the Histroy and Culture of the USSR*, 3:81–85 (Munich; July–September 1955).

40. For a succinct account of the episode, see E. Buchholz, "Meinungsverschiedenheiten ueber einige theoretische Grundlagen des feldschuetzenden Waldanbaus zwischen T. D. Lyssenko und W. N. Sukatschew," *Zeitschrift für Weltforstwirtschaft*, 15.6:225–230 (December 1952).

41. V. Koldanov, in *Sel'skoe khoziaistvo*, November 16, 1954; see also E. Chekmenev, in *Izvestiia*, May 12, 1949; *Pravda*, April 11, 1952; A. Ponomarev, in *Sel'skoe khoziaistvo*, September 2, 1953.

42. Ponomarev, in *Sel'skoe khoziaistvo*, September 2, 1953.

43. *Kolkhoznoe proizvodstvo*, November 1952, pp. 4–8.

44. *Sel'skoe khoziaistvo SSSR, 1960*, p. 260.

45. I. Burdashvili, "Concerning Irrigation Management," *Sotsialicheskoe sel'skoe khoziaistvo*, August 1939, pp. 100–105.

46. *Izvestiia*, May 23, 1932; A. Mironov, "Irrigation of the Trans-Volga Area and Combatting the Drought," *Planovoe khoziaistvo*, August–September 1934, pp. 121–138.

47. *Izvestiia*, January 28, 1934.

48. *Ibid.*, August 22 and 31, and September 12, and 21, 1950.

49. E. Alekseevskii, *Kommunist Ukrainy*, December 1963, pp. 9–16.

50. It was originally published in *Bol'shevik*, 1952, no. 18, pp. 1–50; *Pravda*, October 5, 1952. English translations: "Economic Problems of Socialism in the USSR," *Supplement to the Current Digest of the Soviet Press* (New York, October 18, 1952); Stalin, *Economic Problems of Socialism in the USSR* (Moscow, 1952).

51. G. M. Malenkov, "Report to the Nineteenth Party Congress on the Work of the Central Committee of the CPSU(b)" (Moscow, 1952), pp. 65–66.

52. Khrushchev, in *Stroitel'stvo kommunizma*, I, 88.

53. Norman M. Kaplan and Richard H. Moorsteen, "An Index of Soviet Industrial Output," *American Economic Review*, 50:296 (June 1960); *Narodnoe khoziaistvo SSSR v 1958 godu*, p. 135.

54. Khrushchev's report, *Pravda* and *Izvestiia*, September 15, 1953.

55. Merle Fainsod, "Khrushchev's Russia," *The Australian Outlook*, December 1963, p. 238.

14. *Khrushchev: The Agrarian Leader and Reformer*

1. Khrushchev, *Stroitel'stvo kommunizma*, IV, 304.

2. D. H. Robertson, "A Word for the Devil," *Economica*, 3.9:203–208 (November 1923).

3. *Pravda*, July 10, 1953.

4. *Ibid.*, August 6, 1953.

5. *Izvestiia*, August 9, 1953.

6. *Ibid.*

7. Isaac Deutscher, *The Prophet Armed. Trotsky, 1879–1921* (New York and London, 1954), pp. 8–12. There was evidence that labor conditions on his father's farm helped to arouse a socially critical attitude on the part of young Trotsky.

8. Khrushchev, *Stroitel'stvo kommunizma*, I, 77.

9. *Sel'skaia zhizn'*, August 8, 1964.

10. *Pravda* and *Izvestiia*, October 2, 1964.

11. *Pravda*, September 3, 1964.

12. Khrushchev, *Stroitel'stvo kommunizma*, II, 419.

13. See Robert W. Campbell, "Marx, Kantorovich, and Novozhilov: *Stoimost'* versus Reality," *Slavic Review*, 20.4:402–418 (October 1961).

14. Khrushchev, *Stroitel'stvo kommunizma*, VI, 322–324.

15. *Ibid.*, II, 450.

16. *Ibid.*, III, 440.

17. Khrushchev, *Stroitel'stvo kommunizma*, IV, 36–43.

18. *Plenum tsentral'nogo komiteta kommunisticheskoi Partii Sovetskogo Soiuza. Stenograficheskii otchet* (Stenographic Report of the Plenary Meeting of the Central Committee of the Communist Party of the Soviet Union; Moscow, 1965). It is interesting to note that, unlike such meetings in Khrushchev's days, this one was not enlarged to include experts, farm managers, and outstanding farmers.

19. For a detailed analysis, see Lazar Volin and Harry Walters, "Soviet Grain Imports," ERS-Foreign 135, U.S. Department of Agriculture, September 1965.

15. *Capital Investment and Land*

1. Theodore W. Schultz, *Transforming Traditional Agriculture* (New Haven, 1964).

2. *Finansovyi i khoziaistvennyi biulleten'*, (1938), nos. 33–34, p. 1.

3. *Zakonodatel'nye i vedomstvennye akty po sel'skomu khoziaistvu* (Legislative and Administrative Measures Regarding Agriculture; Moscow, 1957), I, 135.

4. M. Sidel'nikov, *Dolgosrochnoe kreditovanie kolkhozov* (Long-Term Loans to Kolkhozes; Moscow, 1963), p. 7.

5. Khrushchev, *Stroitel'stvo kommunizma*, III, 407–408.

6. *Ibid.*, VI, 433.

7. *Sel'skoe khoziaistvo SSSR, 1960*, p. 92.

8. *Narodnoe khoziaistvo,.1964*, p. 776.

9. P. N. Pershin, ed., *Nedelimye fondy kolkhozov* (The Indivisible Funds of Kolkhozes; Moscow, 1960), p. 109; S. Bylkov, "The System of Replenishment of Indivisible Funds Needs to be Improved," *Voprosy ekonomiki*, June 1961, p. 141.

10. A. S. Murav'ev and S. M. Tsys, *Ekonomika i organizatsiia proizvodstva v sotsialisticheskikh selskokhoziaistvennykh predpriiatiiakh s osnovami buchgalterskogo ucheta* (Economics and Organization of Agricultural Enterprises with Basic Elements of Accounting; Moscow, 1964), p. 653.

11. *Narodnoe khoziaistvo, 1960*, p. 851; *1962*, p. 644; *1964*, p. 776.

12. *Ekonomika sel'skokhoziaistvennykh predpriiatii* (The Economics of Organization of Agricultural Enterprises; Moscow, 1965), p. 315.

13. V. Nikitskii, "Capital Investment of Kolkhozes and Long-Term Credits," *Den'gi i kredit*, July 1964, pp. 15–19.

14. S. Nosyrev, "Long-Term Credit and the Strengthening of the Economy of Kolkhozes," *Den'gi i kredit*, June 1965, p. 34.

15. *Narodnoe khoziaistvo, 1964*, p. 776.

16. Nosyrev, in *Den'gi i kredit*, pp. 34–35.

17. *Ibid.*, pp. 35–36.

18. *Ibid.*, pp. 36–37; K. Karpov and T. Mitiushkin, "Problems in the Improvement of Credit in Agriculture," *Voprosy ekonomiki*, January 1966, pp. 57–58.

19. Khrushchev, *Stroitel'stvo kommunizma* VI, 427; *Narodnoe khoziaistvo, 1963*, p. 332.

20. *Plenum tsentral'nogo komiteta Kommunisticheskoi Partii Sovetskogo Soiuza, 24–26 marta, 1965 g. Stenograficheskii otchet* (Plenum of the Central Committee of the Communist Party, March 24–25, 1965. Stenographic Report; Moscow, 1965), p. 128.

21. M. Terent'ev, "The Success of the Leninist Methods of Managing Agriculture," *Voprosy ekonomiki*, April 1965, p. 8.

22. S. S. Sergeev, *Voprosy ekonomiko-statisticheskogo analiza kolkhoznogo proizvodstva* (The Problems of Economico-Statistical Analysis of Kolkhoz Production; Moscow, 1956), p. 801; D. Alladatov, "Material-Technical Base of Kolkhozes and Its Role in the Growth of Agricultural Production. Based on Materials of the Turkmen SSR," in M. F. Makarova, M. F. Kovaleva, and S. A. Ignatov, eds., *Ispol'zovanie material'nykh i trudovykh resursov kolkhozov i povyshenie blagosostoianiia kolkhoznikov na sovremennom etape* (Use of the Material and Labor Resources of Kolkhozes and the Increased Well-being of Kolkhozniks at the Present Stage; Moscow, 1962), pp. 77–78.

23. Terent'ev, in *Voprosy ekonomiki*, p. 9.

24. *Ibid.*

25. See a collection of essays entitled *Ekonomicheskaia effektivnost' kapital'-nykh vlozhenii v sel'skoe khoziaistvo* (The Economic Effectiveness of Capital Investment in Agriculture; Moscow, 1962), 364 pp.

26. Gregory Grossman, "Scarce Capital and Soviet Doctrine," *Quarterly Journal of Economics,* 67: 312 (August 1953). Grossman provides a valuable analysis and reviews the literature dealing with the problem during the Stalin era.

27. V. S. Nemchinov, "Socialist Management and Planning of Production," *Kommunist,* May 1964, pp. 74–87; especially p. 85. See also N. G. Karotamm, *Ekonomicheskaia effektivnost' kapital'nykh vlozhenii v sotsialisticheskom sel'skom khoziaistve* (Economic Effectiveness of Capital Investment in Agriculture; Moscow, 1961), pp. 38–68; V. Belkin and I. Birman, "Independence of an Enterprise and Economic Stimuli," *Izvestiia,* December 4, 1964.

28. Khrushchev, *Stroitel'stvo kommunizma,* VI, 160–161.

29. V. Ushakov, "Credit, Enterprise, Profit," *Izvestiia,* October 6, 1964.

30. L. Braginskii, "Some Questions of Planning Capital Investment in Kolkhozes," *Voprosy ekonomiki,* February 1964, pp. 133–138.

31. J. K. Galbraith, *Economic Development in Perspective* (Cambridge, Mass., 1960), p. 9.

32. *Soviet Agriculture Today* (U.S. Dept. of Agriculture, Washington, D.C., 1964), p. 73.

33. Chauncy D. Harris, "Soviet Agricultural Resources Reappraised," *Journal of Farm Economics,* 38: 262, 264 (1956).

34. G. T. Selianinov, "Specialization of Agricultural Regions According to the Climatic Principle," *Rastenievodstvo SSSR* (pt. 1; Leningrad and Moscow, 1933), I, 10.

35. N. Baranov and N. Mikhailov, "The Application of Mineral Fertilizers Taking into Account the Special Features of Crops and Regions," *Ekonomika sel'skogo khoziaistva,* November 1963, pp. 29–30.

36. P. M. Zemskii, *Razvitie i razmeshchenie zemledeliia po prirodnokhoziaistvennym zonam SSSR* (The Development and Location of Agriculture in Different Natural-Economic Regions of the USSR; Moscow, 1959), p. 266.

37. A. V. Peterburgskii, "Fertilizer and Yields," *Izvestiia Timiriazevskoi sel'skokhoziaistvennoi akademii,* 1965, no. 3, pp. 8–9.

38. Zemskii, p. 254.

39. D. N. Prianishnikov, *Azot v zhizni rastenii i v zemledelii SSSR* (Nitrogen in the Plant Life and Agriculture of the USSR; Moscow and Leningrad, 1945), p. 174; see also Frank B. Morrison, *Feeds and Feeding* (21st ed.; Ithaca, 1949), p. 639.

40. *Statistisches Jahrbuch über Ernahrung Landwirtschaft und Forsten der Bundesrepublik Deutschland, 1963* (Hamburg, Berlin, 1964), p. 67.

41. Prianishnikov, *Moskovskaia sel'skokhoziaistvennaia akademiia imeni Timiriazeva. Trudy* (Annals of the Moscow Timiriazev Agricultural Academy; Issue 30, Moscow, 1945), p. 10; F. Matskevich, "For a Further Growth of Agricultural Production," *Ekonomika sel'skogo khoziaistva,* January 1957, pp. 10–11; N. Sapozhnikov, "Problems of the Agricultural System in the Northwestern Zone," *Ekonomika sel'skogo khoziaistva,* January 1957, p. 29.

42. Prianishnikov, "Some Wartime Agricultural Problems in the Soviet Union," *Foreign Agriculture,* 9: 146–150 (U. S. Department of Agriculture, Washington, D.C., October 1945).

43. T. D. Lysenko, "Concerning the Utilization of Winter Crops in the Non-Black Soil Area," *Sel'skoe khoziaistvo,* July 31, 1954.

44. V. D. Pannikov, "For a Many-Sided and Rational Chemicalization of Agriculture," *Zemledelie,* January 1964, p. 5; P. Naidin and I. Gunar, *Pravda,* February 24, 1965; Peterburgskii, in *Izvestiia Timiriazevskoi Sel'skokhoziaistvennoi akademii,* 3:15.

45. *Izvestiia,* March 21, 1939.

46. Naidin and Gunar, in *Pravda,* February 24, 1965.

47. *Ibid.;* I. P. Volovchenko, "Report at the February 1964 Plenum of the Central Committee," *Pravda,* February 15, 1964.

48. S. G. Kolesnev, "Concerning Urgent Measures for Raising the Level of Agriculture in the USSR," *Izvestiia Timiriazevskoi sel'skokhoziaistvennoi akademii,* 1965, no. 2, pp. 6–7.

49. P. Belousov and N. Tetrakov, "Economic Stimulation of Production and Use of Chemical Fertilizer," *Voprosy ekonomiki,* November 1965, pp. 144–146.

50. K. Obolenskii, "Economic Problems of Fertilizer Application," *Ekonomika sel'skogo khoziaistva,* June 1964, p. 21.

51. *Ibid.,* p. 23.

52. O. Kedrov-Zikhman, *Sotsialisticheskoe zemledelie,* June 6, 1948; A. Vladimirov, *ibid.,* May 10, 1949; N. Baranov, "Chemicalization of Agricultural Production," *Ekonomika sel'skogo khoziaistva* (December 1962), p. 51; Naidin and Gunar, in *Pravda,* February 24, 1965.

53. Obolenskii, *Ekonomika sel'skogo khoziaistva,* June 1964, p. 22.

54. V. M. Borisov and others, in *Izvestiia,* November 17, 1963.

55. Khrushchev, *Stroitel'stvo kommunizma,* VIII, 273; A. N. Kosygin, in *Pravda,* December 10, 1964.

56. *Pravda,* February 21, 1966.

57. G. Gaponenko, "The Basic Problems of the Development of Agriculture during the New Five-Year Plan Period," *Planovoe khoziaistvo,* March 1966, p. 4.

58. *Sel'skaia zhizn',* February 11, 1964.

59. *Sel'skoe khoziaistvo SSSR,* 1960, p. 193.

60. *Minerals Yearbook 1963* (U. S. Department of Interior, Bureau of Mines, Washington, D.C., 1964), II, 323.

61. *Soil. The Yearbook of Agriculture 1957* (The United States Department of Agriculture, Washington, D.C.), p. 244.

62. *Crop Research in the Soviet Union.* Report of Technical Study Group (U.S. Department of Agriculture, Washington, D.C., 1959), p. 16.

63. *SSSR v tsifrakh, 1965,* p. 57; Khrushchev, *Stroitel'stvo kommunizma,* VIII, 273.

64. *Izvestiia,* May 23, 1932.

65. *Ibid.,* January 28, 1934.

66. Khrushchev, *Stroitel'stvo kommunizma,* II, 294; VI, 46–47.

67. *Ibid.,* VIII, 199, 202–203.

68. *Ibid.,* 199–200.

69. *Sel'skaia zhizn',* February 12, 1964; March 27, 1965.

70. E. E. Alekseievskii, *Pravda,* February 28, 1965.

71. Alekseievskii, *Sel'skaia zhizn',* February 12, 1964.

72. *Ibid.;* V. Kulikov, in *Izvestiia,* February 23, 1965.

73. Kulikov, in *Izvestiia,* February 23, 1965.

74. Alekseievskii, in *Sel'skaia zhizn',* February 12, 1964.

75. *Izvestiia,* March 27, 1965.

76. *Irrigation in the Soviet Union. Report of the U.S. Delegation* (U.S. Department of the Interior, Bureau of Reclamation, Washington, D.C., 1964), p. 8.

77. Alekseievskii, in *Sel'skaia zhizn',* February 12, 1964.

78. S. S. Sobolev, *Zashchita pochv ot erozii* (The Protection of the Soil against Erosion; Moscow, 1961), p. 3, 4.

79. A. I. Baraev, "The Protection of the Soil against Wind Erosion in Virgin Lands Regions," *Vestnik sel'skokhoziaistvennoi nauki,* December 1963, p. 7; D. A. Zykov, "Soil Erosion in Kazakhstan and Measures for Controlling it," *Vestnik Akademii nauk Kazakhskoi SSR,* January 1964, pp. 3–4.

80. Baraev, p. 7.

81. Sobolev, "The Problems of Controlling Soil Erosion," *Zemledelie,* August, 1963, p. 18.

82. I. P. Volovchenko, "To Organize Proper Conservation of Soils against Erosion," *Vestnik sel'skokhoziaistvennoi nauki,* December 1963, p. 2.

83. Sobolev, in *Zemledelie,* August 1963, p. 18.

84. The speech of the Minister of Agriculture and some of the papers delivered were published in *Vestnik sel'skokhoziaistvennoi nauki,* December 1963.

85. *Pravda,* February 15, 1964.

86. The problem of rent in agriculture stirred up considerable discussion among Soviet economists, primarily in connection with procurement prices. See N. A. Tsagolov, ed., *Zemel'naia renta v sotsialisticheskom sel'skom khoziaistve* (Land Rent in Socialized Agriculture; Moscow, 1959) (papers delivered at a conference on rent held at Moscow University, September 1958); A. V. Bolgov, *Differentsial'naia zemel'naia renta v usloviiakh sotsializma* (Differential Land Rent under Socialism; Moscow, 1963); P. A. Timokhin and S. D. Cheremyshkin, "The Question of Determining the Size of Differential Rent and Its Role in the Development of Kolkhoz Production," *Vsesoiuznyi nauchno-issledovatel'skii institut ekonomiki sel'skogo khoziaistva. Doklady i soobshcheniia,* 19: 5–16 (Moscow, 1963); "Problems of Political Economy; Differential Rent" (a discussion by a number of economists), *Ekonomicheskaia gazeta,* April 14, 1965, pp. 5–6.

16. *Incentives and Procurements*

1. *Sel'skaia zhizn',* May 19, 1966.

2. This negative conception is strongly challenged by Theodore W. Schultz in his *Transforming Traditional Agriculture* (New Haven, 1964).

3. G. Gaponenko and M. Gorodskii, *O novoi sisteme zagotovok sel'skokhoziai-*

stvennykh produktov v kolkhozakh (Concerning the New System of Procurement of Agricultural Products in Kolkhozes; Moscow, 1959), p. 52; V. L. Shtipel'man, *Tsenoobrazovanie kolkhoznykh produktov v SSSR* (Pricing of Kolkhoz Products in the USSR; Leningrad, 1959), p. 25.

4. Gaponenko and Gorodskii, p. 38.

5. A. A. Vasiliev, *Kolkhoznaia torgovlia: Zagotovki sel'skokhoziaistvennykh produktov i syr'ia* (Kolkhoz Trade: Procurements of Agricultural Products and Raw Materials; Moscow, 1960), p. 44.

6. Shtipel'man, p. 32.

7. Beginning with the 1956 crop, premiums were set at 50 percent of the average procurement price on unginned cotton delivered to the state, (a) in excess of the procurement plan and (b) in excess of 23 centners of short staple and 20 centners of long staple per hectare of the actually planted area, irrespective of the plan. These price premiums were abolished in 1958. Decree of the Central Committee of the Communist Party and Council of Ministers of the USSR, August 11, 1956, no. 1136, in *Zakonodatel'nye i vedomstvennye akty po sel'skomu khoziaistvu* (Moscow, 1958), II, 428.

8. Gaponenko and Gorodskii, *O novoi sisteme*, p. 74.

9. Shtipel'man, p. 52.

10. Cited by Khrushchev in *Pravda,* June 21, 1958.

11. *Ibid.*

12. *Izvestiia,* June 5, 1957.

13. *Pravda,* June 20, 1958; July 1, 1958.

14. Gaponenko and Gorodoskii, *O novoi sisteme,* p. 63.

15. *Ibid.,* p. 69.

16. V. Matskevich, "Economic Problems in the Further Development of Agriculture," *Voprosy ekonomiki,* June 1965, pp. 4–5.

17. A. N. Malafeev, *Istoriia tsenoobrazovaniia v SSSR, 1917–1963 gg.* (History of Prices in the USSR, 1917–1963; Moscow, 1964), p. 267.

18. *Ibid.; Sel'skoe khoziaistvo SSSR, 1960,* p. 117; *Narodnoe khoziaistvo, 1960,* p. 716.

19. V. G. Venzher, "Institut ekonomiki Akademii nauk SSSR," *Izderzhki proizvodstva i sebestoimost' produktsii v kolkhozakh* (Expenditures and Costs of Kolkhoz Production; Moscow, 1960), p. 22; M. L. Terent'ev, *Sebestoimost' kolkhoznoi produktsii* (Kolkhoz Production Costs; Moscow, 1957), pp. 5–11.

20. L. N. Litoshenko, "The Geographical Distribution of the Cost of Production of the Most Important Field Crops," *Statisticheskoe obozrenie,* October 1928, pp. 16–28; "Output, Expenses, and Cost of Production in Individual Farming," *ibid.,* May 1930, pp. 50–70.

21. Venzher, *Izderzhki,* p. 25.

22. Terent'ev, *Sebestoimost',* p. 22.

23. N. S. Lagutin, "The Level and Structure of Income of the Agricultural Population," in M. Ia. Lemeshev, ed., *Ekonomicheskoe obosnovanie struktury sel'skokhoziaistvennogo proizvodstva* (The Economics of the Structure of Agricultural Production; Moscow, 1965), p. 260.

24. V. G. Venzher, *Kolkhoznyi stroi na novom etape* (Kolkhozes at a New Stage of Development; [Moscow], 1966), pp. 237–238.

25. The 1964 publication of the All-Union Scientific Research Institute of Agricultural Economics of the Ministry of Agriculture of the USSR cites as officially approved in 1963 only the actual payments method of cost calculation. *Voprosy ratsional'noi organizatsii i ekonomiki sel'skokhoziaistvennogo proizvodstva. Metodiki i rekomendatsii* (Questions of Rational Organization and the Economics of Agricultural Production. Methodologies and Recommendations; Moscow, 1964), pp. 329–330. In a textbook for agricultural technical schools, also published in 1964, it was stated that the method of cost calculation based on sovkhoz wage rates is used for comparative or other scientific purposes, when a period of years or several kolkhozes were involved. A. S. Murav'ev and S. M. Tsys, *Ekonomika i organizatsiia proizvodstva v sotsialisticheskikh sel'skokhoziaistvennyhk predpriiatiiakh* (The Economics and Organization of Production in Socialist Agricultural Enterprises; Moscow, 1964), p. 609.

26. Venzher, *Kolkhoznyi stroi*, p. 175.

27. G. Khudokormov, "Price Determination and Differentiation of Procurement Prices Depending on Variation of the Natural-Economic Conditions," *Tseny i tsenoobrazovanie na sel'skokhoziaistvennye produkty* (Prices of Agricultural Products and Their Determination, M. M. Sokolov, ed.; [Moscow], 1966), p. 51; A. Emelianov, "Conditions for Formation of Costs and Prices of Agricultural Products under Socialism," *ibid.*, p. 32.

28. E. Triapkina, "Concerning Differentiation of Purchase Prices by Zones," *Voprosy ekonomiki,* July 1961, pp. 143–148.

29. *Pravda,* February 1, 1961.

30. *Sel'skaia zhizn',* February 26, 1961.

31. Joseph S. Berliner, "The Informal Organization of the Soviet Firm," *Quarterly Journal of Economics,* August 1952.

32. *Sel'skaia zhizn',* June 14, 1961.

33. L. Korniets, "The New System of Procurements: An Important Lever for Further Growth in Agricultural Production," *Ekonomika sel'skogo khoziaistva,* July 1961, pp. 25–35.

34. *Pravda,* January 22, 1961.

35. *Ibid.*

36. *Plenum, 24–26 Marta, 1965 g.,* pp. 9–10.

37. Venzher, *Kolkhoznyi stroi*, pp. 181, 182, 196, 197.

38. Khrushchev, in *Sel'skaia zhizn',* August 15, 1964.

39. *Ibid.*

40. *Sel'skaia zhizn',* August 5, 1964.

41. E. Stratanovich, in *Sel'skaia zhizn',* May 9, 1963.

42. For USSR, *Mukomol'no-elevatornaia promyshlennost',* September 1963, p. 9; for the United States, U.S. Department of Agriculture, Statistical Reporting Service, *Stocks of Grains in All Positions* (January 24, 1964), p. 11. The figure of 5,471,230,000 bushels given as capacity of off-farm grain storage facilities was converted to metric tons on the basis of 60 pounds to a bushel. The United

621

States figure excludes rather substantial temporary or specialized storage capacity, such as CCC bins, mothball ships under government control used to store grains, warehouses used to store only rice, peanuts, and so forth.

43. V. Kuchinskii, in *Sel'skaia zhizn'*, August 21, 1963.

44. V. Antonov, in *Izvestiia*, July 7, 1964.

45. *Pravda*, December 29, 1959.

46. *Ibid.*, February 1, 1961.

47. Venzher, *Kolkhoznyi stroi*, p. 82.

48. Korniets, in *Ekonomika sel'skogo khoziaistva*, July 1961.

49. *Narodnoe khoziaistvo, 1961*, pp. 382–383; *ibid.*, 1964, p. 361.

50. V. Khlebnikov, "Concerning Further Strengthening of the Kolkhoz Economy," *Voprosy ekonomiki*, July 1962, pp. 53–54. All costs and prices are for live-weight gain. Costs are calculated on the basis of sovkhoz wage rates.

51. *Sel'skaia zhizn'*, June 16, 1962.

52. R. Gumerov, "Improvement of Prices of Kolkhoz Production and Strengthening of the Economic Accounting in Kolkhozes," *Finansy SSSR*, August 1965, pp. 8–9.

53. *Ibid.*

54. N. Gusev, "To Strengthen the Economy of Kolkhozes and Sovkhozes," *Ekonomika sel'skogo khoziaistva*, June 1965, p. 11.

55. Gumerov, p. 10; B. Savel'ev, "The New System of Procurements of Agricultural Products," *Ekonomika sel'skogo khoziaistva*, June 1965, p. 23.

56. Gusev, p. 12.

57. *Ibid.*, p. 14.

58. Gumerov, p. 12.

59. *Ibid.*, p. 2.

60. Savel'ev, pp. 24–25.

61. Gumerov, p. 12.

62. D. Gale Johnson, "What Is Potential for Expanded East-West Farm Trade," *Foreign Agriculture*, 4. 24:8 (June 13, 1966).

63. Gumerov, p. 13.

17. *Income and Consumer Goods*

1. I. A. Koniukov, *Ocherki o pervykh etapakh razvitiia kollektivnogo zemledeliia* (Essays on the First Stages of Development of Collective Agriculture; Moscow, 1949), pp. 169–170.

2. A decree of the Collegium of the Commissariat of Agriculture of the USSR, February 28, 1933, "Concerning Standard Work Norms," *Vazhneishie resheniia*, pp. 442–443.

3. T. I. Zaslavskaia, *Printsip material'noi zainteresovannosti i oplata truda v kolkhozakh* (The Principle of Material Interest and Payment for Labor in Kolkhozes; Moscow, 1958), p. 28; A. P. Larionov, "The Questions of Norms and Pricing of Work in Kolkhozes," *Sotsialisticheskoe sel'skoe khoziaistvo*, October 1947, pp. 32–39.

4. Section 16 of the Decree of the Council of Ministers of the USSR, April 19, 1948, no. 1259, *O merakh po uluchsheniiu organizatsii, povysheniiu proizvoditel'-nosti i uporiadocheniiu oplaty truda v kolkhozakh* (Concerning Measures for Improvement of the Organization, Increase of Productivity and Improvement of the Methods of Payment of Labor in Kolkhozes; (Moscow, 1948).

5. A. P. Larionov, *Normirovanie i tarifikatsiia truda v kolkhozakh i sovkhozakh* (The Setting of Standard Work Tasks and Their Valuation in Kolkhozes and Sovkhozes; Moscow, 1961), pp. 14–15; Zaslavskaia, *Printsip material'noi zaintereso-vannosti,* p. 16.

6. Zaslavskaia, *Printsip material'noi zainteresovannosti,* p. 17.

7. Larionov, *Normirovanie,* p. 15.

8. Zaslavskaia, *Printsip material'noi zainteresovannosti,* p. 30.

9. New sets of standard norms to guide kolkhozes were developed in recent years by various research institutions and government agencies, such as that prepared jointly by the Ministry of Agriculture of the Belorussian Republic and the Institute of Economics of the Belorussian Academy of Sciences (*Spravochnik po normirovaniiu truda v kolkhozakh;* A Handbook for Setting Work Tasks in Kolkhozes; Minsk, 1960). In working out standard norms this document took into consideration such factors as the length of the tractor run, the character of the soil, the yields of crops, the machinery used, and so forth.

10. I. V. Sautin, *Kolkhozy vo vtoroi Stalinskoi piatiletke* (Kolkhozes during the Second Stalin Five Year Plan Period; Moscow, 1939), p. 54.

11. Larionov, in *Sotsialisticheskoe sel'skoe khoziaistvo,* October 1947, pp. 35–36.

12. *Ibid.,* p. 34.

13. K. Orlovskii, "To Exchange More Widely the Experience in Labor Payment in Kolkhozes," *Pravda,* March 21, 1957.

14. A. Kraeva, "The Questions of Association of Personal and Social Interests in Kolkhozes," *Voprosy ekonomiki,* August 1961, pp. 72–79; G. Palienko and A. Mushtaleva, "Bonus Payments for Labor in Kolkhozes," *Kolkhoznoe proiz-vodstvo,* May 1961, p. 15.

15. V. I. Voropaev and P. P. Belichenko, *Dopolnitel'naia oplata truda v kolkhozakh* (Supplementary Payments for Labor in Kolkhozes; Moscow, 1962), p. 33.

16. Valentin Ovechkin, "The Difficult Spring," *Novyi mir,* September 1956, p. 121.

17. Lidiia Obukhova, *Pravda,* April 15, 1956.

18. A decree "Concerning the Harvesting and Procurements of Agricultural Products," *Pravda,* August 1, 1940.

19. *Pravda* and *Izvestiia,* March 10, 1956.

20. L. Shikhanovich, in *Sel'skaia zhizn',* June 17, 1961.

21. T. I. Zaslavskaia, *Raspredelenie po trudu v kolkhozakh* (Distribution According to Labor Performed in Kolkhozes; Moscow, 1966), pp. 140–142.

22. S. Karataev, in *Sel'skoe khoziaistvo,* July 20, 1957.

23. N. Popadiushkin, *Sel'skoe khoziaistvo,* July 15, 1955.

24. Khrushchev, *Stroitel'stvo kommunizma,* III, 423.

25. Zaslavskaia, *Raspredelenie,* p. 151.

26. Voropaev and Belichenko, *Dopolnitel'naia oplata truda,* p. 12.

27. Figure given during an interview of a visiting U.S. Department of Agriculture team of livestock specialists with the staff of the All-Union Research Institute of Agricultural Economics in Moscow.

28. Zaslavskaia, "The Economic Conditions for Adoption of a Money Wage for Kolkhozniks," *Voprosy ekonomiki,* November 1959, pp. 58–70.

29. T. Zaslavskaia and M. Mikhailov, "To Raise the Level of Research on the Problem of Economic Incentives," *Kommunist,* 1961, no. 9, pp. 106–111.

30. Orlovskii, "Collectives—a School of Communism for Peasantry," *Kommunist,* 1961, no. 11, pp. 103–113; "Workday or Money Wage," *Sel'skaia zhizn',* June 10, 1961.

31. I. Sokolov, "Advances and Supplementary Payments for Labor in Kolkhozes," *Bloknot agitatora,* December 1956, pp. 8–19.

32. *Plenum, 24–26 marta, 1965 g.,* p. 30.

33. *Ibid.,* p. 40.

34. *Pravda,* March 30, 1966; April 6, 1966.

35. *Sel'skaia zhizn',* May 18, 1966.

36. *Pravda,* April 20, 1938.

37. Sautin, *Kolkhozy,* p. 36.

38. Zaslavskaia, *Raspredelenie.*

39. V. Khlebnikov, "Concerning the Further Strengthening of the Kolkhoz Economy," *Voprosy ekonomiki,* July 1963, p. 50.

40. Kraeva, *Voprosy ekonomiki,* August 1961, p. 77.

41. *Pravda* and *Izvestiia,* May 24, 1957.

42. *Pravda,* December 23, 1959.

43. Khrushchev, *Stroitel'stvo kommunizma,* IV, 375.

44. *Ibid.,* VI, 433.

45. *SSSR v tsifrakh, 1965,* p. 92. While the gross income of all kolkhozes decreased from 13.6 billion rubles in 1958, to 12.5 billion in 1963, it increased from 11.1 to 12 billion rubles for the smaller number of kolkhozes which existed in 1958 and still remained at the end of 1965.

46. Zaslavskaia, *Raspredelenie,* p. 46.

47. *Pravda,* February 3, 1966. It was not stated whether the figures refer to total payments or averages per kolkhoz worker.

48. A. M. Emel'ianov, *Metodologicheskie problemy nakopleniia i rentabel'nosti v kolkhozakh* (Methodological Problems of Capital Accumulation and Profitability in Kolkhozes; Moscow, 1965), p. 99.

49. *Ibid.,* p. 62.

50. *Pravda,* February 20, 1966.

51. *Narodnoe khoziaistvo, 1964,* pp. 554–555; *SSSR v tsifrakh, 1965,* p. 126.

52. Emel'ianov, *Metodologicheskie problemy,* pp. 48–49.

53. *Pravda,* February 20, 1966.

54. Pavlov, *Plenum, 24–26 Marta 1965 g. Stenograficheskii otchet,* p. 162.

55. The figure of the Soviet agricultural labor force in 1958 is derived by adding to 27.3 million, given as the average annual number of those employed directly in socialized agriculture, 3 million estimated as engaged in private farming in 1959. *Sel'skoe khoziaistvo. Statisticheskii sbornik,* 1960, p. 450. It is assumed

that there was no substantial difference in this respect between 1959 and 1958. Figure for U. S. farm labor force is from *Agricultural Statistics, 1965,* Department of Agriculture, Washington, D.C., 1965, p. 445. Total farm output is from *The World Agricultural Situation 1961,* U. S. Department of Agriculture, Washington, D.C., p. 2. The output figures at world market prices were 16,550 million dollars and 26,475 million dollars for the Soviet Union and the United States respectively.

56. Quoted by Emel'ianov, *Metodologicheskie problemy,* p. 49, from the 1955 Russian edition of *Capital,* I, 190.

57. Orlovskii, in *Kommunist,* 1961, no. 11, p. 113.

58. Khrushchev gave several examples in his speech before the Supreme Soviet. *Sel'skaia zhizn',* July 14, 1964.

59. *Sel'skaia zhizn',* July 28, 1964.

60. P. Smyslov, "To Utilize Correctly the Kolkhozniks' Social Security Fund," *Finansy SSSR,* November 1965, p. 30.

61. Iu. Borzenkov, "Concerning the Period of Work Entitling Kolkhozniks to a Pension," *Ekonomika sel'skogo khoziaistva,* March 1966, p. 65.

62. *Sel'skaia zhizn',* July 16, 1964.

63. G. Sarkisian, "Raising the Living Level of Kolkhozniks," *Ekonomika sel'-skogo khoziaistva,* December 1964, p. 13.

64. *Spravochnik po usloviiam truda rabotnikov sel'skogo khoziaistva RSFSR* (Handbook on Labor in Agriculture of the RSFSR; Moscow, 1966), p. 298.

65. Sarkisian.

66. *Sel'skaia zhizn',* July 16, 1964.

67. Khrushchev, *Stroitel'stvo kommunizma,* IV, 370.

68. M. Kirimov, "They Can Work and They Can Rest," *Kolkhoznoe proiz-vodstvo,* November 1962, p. 41.

69. Valentin Belousov, in *Sel'skaia zhizn',* June 16, 1961

70. A. Evdokimov, "The Growth of Cultural and Service Construction in Kolkhozes," *Ekonomika sel'skogo khoziaistva,* November 1960, p. 79.

71. *Narodnoe khoziaistvo, 1964,* p. 715.

72. Khrushchev, *Stroitel'stvo kommunizma,* III, 407.

73. *Narodnoe khoziaistvo, 1964,* p. 677.

74. A. T. Ashcheulov and A. T. Bocharov, *Oplata truda rukovodiashchikh rabotnikov, spetsialistov i mekhanizatorov kolkhozov* (Remuneration of Managerial and Technical Personnel and Mechanizers in Kolkhozes; Moscow, 1962), p. 11.

75. *Vashneishie resheniia* (1938–46), pp. 288–289.

76. See S. Kireev, in *Sel'skaia zhizn',* May 20, 1961.

77. *Sel'skaia zhizn',* April 19, 1962.

78. Khrushchev, *Stroitel'stvo kommunizma,* IV, 349.

79. *Ibid.,* IV, 362.

80. I. Laptev, "Socialist Competition and Labor Discipline in Kolkhozes," *Pravda,* June 24, 1948; I. Benediktov, "Soviet Peasantry, Led by J. V. Stalin Heads for New Victories," *USSR Information Bulletin,* December 21, 1948, p. 768.

81. *Izvestiia,* April 25, 1948.

82. *Vedomosti Verkhovnogo Soveta SSSR,* November 30, 1947.

83. The Zaglada article was republished on the first page of *Sel'skaia zhizn'* for August 26, 1962, in the columns usually reserved for a lead editorial. Newspaper reporters sought her out for interviews and Khrushchev congratulated her on her seventieth anniversary when she was decorated with the order of "Labor Red Banner." *Sel'skaia zhizn',* September 10, 1962.

84. The index of nonagricultural retail prices decreased by 38 and 43 percent by April 1, 1952, and 1953 respectively, compared with the last quarter of 1947, the peak period. A. N. Malafeev, *Istoriia tsenoobrazovaniia v SSSR, 1917–1963* (The History of Prices in the USSR; Moscow, 1964), p. 405.

85. *Narodnoe khoziaistvo, 1964,* pp. 124–125; *ibid.,* 1962, p. 435; *Promyshlennost' SSSR 1964,* p. 37.

86. *Pravda,* January 24, 1955.

87. *Pravda* and *Izvestiia,* January 15, 1956.

88. *Narodnoe khoziaistvo, 1960,* p. 209.

89. *Promyshlennost' SSSR, 1957,* p. 13.

90. *Narodnoe khoziaistvo, 1962,* p. 435; *ibid., 1964,* p. 515.

91. *Sovetskaia torgovlia* (Moscow 1964), p. 49.

92. *Izvestiia,* September 23, 1964.

93. New York *Times,* May 21, 1961.

94. *Pravda* and *Izvestiia,* October 19, 1961.

95. Khrushchev, *Stroitel'stvo kommunizma,* VIII, 451.

96. Arzumanian, in *Pravda,* February 24 and 25. The second article is particularly germane for our discussion.

97. *Izvestiia,* October 2, 1964.

98. *Ibid.*

99. *Pravda* and *Izvestiia,* July 15, 1964.

100. *Pravda,* February 20, 1966.

18. *Mechanization and Electrification*

1. The historical account of mechanization and MTS is based mainly on the following sources: V. Venzher, "The Development of Machine-Tractor Stations," *Sotsialisticheskoe sel'skoe khoziaistvo,* November 1947, pp. 16–17; V. Khalturin, "USSR—the Country with the Largest and Mechanized Farms," *Mashinno-traktornaia stantsiia,* November 1947, p. 2; B. Likhter, "The History of the Creation of MTS," *Istoricheskii zhurnal,* August–September 1943, pp. 58–63; P. I. Denisenko, "From the History of Machine-Tractor Detachments and the First Machine-Tractor Station," *Istoricheskie zapiski,* 1954, no. 48, pp. 248–263; M. Gorshkov, "The Decisive Power in Development of Collective Farm Production," *Ekonomika sel'skogo khoziaistva,* August 1957, pp. 90–99.

2. *Statisticheskii spravochnik,* 1928, p. 292.

3. *Narodnoe khoziaistvo, 1932,* p. 145.

4. Likhter, p. 59.

5. A. M. Markevich, *Mezhselennye mashino-traktornye stantsii* (Inter-Village Machine-Tractor Stations; Moscow, 1929).

6. *XV S"ezd VKP(b), stenograficheskii otchet* (The Stenographic Report of the All-Union Communist Party (b); Moscow, 1928).

7. *SPR, SSSR, 1929,* no. 39, art. 353, pp. 742–744 (29 June 1929).

8. *Sotsialisticheskoe stroitel'stvo 1934,* p. 155.

9. "Legal Consultation on Kolkhoz Problems," *Sotsialisticheskoe zemledelie,* March 27, 1948.

10. *Narodnoe khoziaistvo, 1958,* pp. 512–513; *Narodnoe khoziaistvo, 1956,* pp. 150, 510.

11. A decree of August 23, 1956, "Concerning the Compensation of Tractor Drivers and other Mechanizers of MTS," *Sbornik zakonodatel'nykh i vedomstvennykh aktov po sel'skomu khoziaistvu* (A Collection of Legislative and Administrative Acts Pertaining to Agriculture; Moscow, 1957), I, 382–384; a decree of September 21, 1953, "Concerning the Further Improvement of the Work of Machine-Tractor Stations," *ibid.,* II, 6–9; see also instructions on the subject by the Ministry of Agriculture of the USSR and the Ministry of Procurements of the USSR of July 2–6, 1954, *ibid.,* II, 166–169.

12. I. V. Sautin, *Kolkhozy vo vtoroi Stalinskoi piatiletke* (Kolkhozes during the Second Stalin Five-Year Plan Period; Moscow, 1939), p. 110.

13. *V. pomoshch' izuchaiushchim ekonomiku MTS* (In Aid to Those Studying the Economics of MTS; Moscow, 1956), p. 234.

14. K. Bukovskii, "On the River and in the Steppes. Two Small Trips on the River Voron," *Oktiabr',* June 1966, pp. 167, 176.

15. M. Gorshkov, "The Economic Effectiveness of Harvesting with Combines and the Utilization of Combines in MTS," *Sotsialisticheskoe sel'skoe khoziaistvo,* May 1947, p. 26.

16. *Pravda,* December 4, 1953.

17. *Sotsialisticheskoe zemledelie,* June 26, 1939.

18. N. Krushinin, "Concerning the Rural Vocational-Technical School," *Sel'skoe khoziaistvo,* November 19, 1958.

19. Edict of the Bureau for RSFSR of the Central Committee of the Communist Party, *Sel'skaia zhizn',* September 19, 1962; G. Zelenko, State Committee on Professional-Technical Education of the Council of Ministers of the USSR, *Pravda,* January 10, 1963.

20. Zelenko, in *Pravda,* January 10, 1963.

21. *Narodnoe khoziaistvo, 1961,* p. 590; *1963,* p. 496; *1964,* p. 570.

22. "Trained Machine Operators Decline Work in Agriculture," *Radio Liberty Dispatches,* July 17, 1964.

23. A decree "Concerning the Work of Machine-Tractor Stations," January 13, 1939, *Sotsialisticheskoe zemledelie,* January 14, 1939.

24. A. A. Andreev, *Izvestiia,* March 7, 1947; I. A. Benediktov, *Sotsialisticheskoe zemledelie,* January 1, 1950.

25. Andreev, *Izvestiia,* March 7, 1947.

26. P. Katsev, "Notes of a Director of an MTS," *Novyi mir,* September 1956, p. 7.

27. Gorshkov, "The Decisive Force in the Development of Kolkhoz Production," *Ekonomika sel'skogo khoziaistva,* August 1957, pp. 90–99.

28. I. S. Malyshev, ed., *MTS vo vtoroi piatiletke* (Moscow and Leningrad, 1939), p. 117. See also K. Chebotarev, "For the Economy of Petroleum Products in Agriculture," *Planovoe khoziaistvo*, February 1939, pp. 141–149; K. Lomako, "Organization of the Petroleum Supply in MTS and Measures against Waste," *Mashinno-traktornaia stantsiia*, April–May 1946, pp. 38–42.

29. P. S. Kuchumov, *Kompleksnaia mekhanizatsiia sel'skokhoziaistvennogo proizvodstva* (Total Mechanization of Agricultural Production; Moscow, 1956), p. 6.

30. *Sel'skoe khoziaistvo SSSR, 1960*, p. 426.

31. M. Moiseev, "Payments in Kind for the Work of MTS and Its Significance for Strengthening the Economic Links between Town and Country," *Kommunist*, July 1954, p. 50.

32. Sautin, *Kolkhozy vo vtoroi Stalinskoi piatiletke*, p. 95.

33. Roy D. Laird, Darwin E. Sharp, and Ruth Sturtevant, *The Rise and Fall of the MTS as an Instrument of Soviet Rule* (Lawrence, Kansas, 1960), p. 58, citing Benediktov, in *Izvestiia*, December 27, 1957.

34. Khrushchev, *Stroitel'stvo kommunizma*, I, 88.

35. Moiseev, in *Kommunist*, p. 49.

36. Khrushchev, *Stroitel'stvo kommunizma*, III, 232. For the decrees dealing with this subject see *Pravda*, June 20, 1958, and July 1, 1958.

37. G. Shrabshtein, "MTS during the Postwar Period," *Mashinno-traktornaia stantsiia*, November 1947, p. 15.

38. *Promyshlennost' SSSR, 1964*, p. 279; *Sel'skoe khoziaistvo SSSR, 1960*, p. 419.

39. Iu. V. Arutiunian, *Mekhanizatory sel'skogo khoziaistva SSSR v 1929–57 gg.* (Mechanizers in the Agriculture of the USSR in 1929–57; Moscow, 1960), pp. 114–115.

40. It appeared originally in *Bol'shevik*, September 1952, pp. 1–50. English translations: "Economic Problems of Socialism in the USSR," *Supplement to the Current Digest of the Soviet Press* (New York, October 18, 1952); J. Stalin, *Economic Problems of Socialism in the USSR* (Moscow; Foreign Language Publishing House, 1952). All quotations from Stalin's article are my own translations from the Russian original.

41. P. Gvozdkov, "The Exciting Questions," *Oktiabr'*, December 1957, p. 185.

42. Khrushchev, *Stroitel'stvo kommunizma*, II, 499–500.

43. *Ibid.*, pp. 520–525.

44. *Sel'skoe khoziaistvo*, February 28, 1958.

45. Khrushchev, *Stroitel'stvo kommunizma*, III, 91–153.

46. *Ibid.*, p. 119.

47. *Ibid.*, pp. 127–128.

48. *Ibid.*, p. 106.

49. *Ibid.*, p. 132.

50. *Pravda*, April 1, 1958.

51. *Sel'skoe khoziaistvo*, April 20, 1958.

52. *Sel'skoe khoziaistvo SSSR, 1960*, p. 41; *Narodnoe khoziaistvo, 1961*, p. 291.

53. *Narodnoe khoziaistvo, 1960*, pp. 361, 521.

54. Their labor force was recorded in employment data among different non-

agricultural occupations: in industry, transportation, and so forth. *Ibid., 1961,* p. 568.

55. *Ibid., 1958,* p. 505; *1962,* p. 325; *1964,* p. 384.

56. *Sbornik reshenii po sel'skomu khoziaistvu* (A Collection of Decrees Dealing with Agriculture; Moscow, 1963), pp. 534–544.

57. V. Matskevich, "Economic Problems of Further Development of Agriculture," *Voprosy ekonomiki,* June 1965, pp. 5–6.

58. P. Kozhevnikov, "To Develop Agriculture on a Stable Material-Technical Base," *Ekonomika sel'skogo khoziaistva,* June 1965, p. 30.

59. Matskevich. *Ekonomika sel'skogo khoziaistva,* June 1965, p. 5; G. S. Lisichkin, *Plan i rynok* (The Plan and the Market; Moscow, 1966), p. 62.

60. M. Ia. Lemeshev, ed. *Ekonomicheskoe obosnovanie struktury sel'skokhoziaistvennogo proizvodstva* (The Economic Justification of the Structure of Agricultural Production; Moscow, 1965), p. 182.

61. *Ibid.,* p. 181.

62. *Changes in Farm Production and Efficiency,* U. S. Department of Agriculture, Statistical Bulletin no. 233, revised June 1966, p. 17; *SSSR v tsifrakh, 1965,* pp. 71–72.

63. *Changes in Farm Production,* p. 26; *Narodnoe khoziaistvo, 1964,* p. 382; *SSSR v tsifrakh, 1965,* pp. 71–72.

64. M. Terent'ev, "The Triumph of Leninist Principles of Leadership in Agriculture," *Voprosy ekonomiki,* April 1965, p. 8.

65. Khrushchev, *Stroitel'stvo kommunizma,* VI, 424–426; A. A. Ezhevskii, *Plenum, 24–26 marta, 1965 g.,* p. 149–150.

66. *Narodnoe khoziaistvo, 1959,* p. 422; *1960,* p. 491.

67. *Ibid., 1964,* p. 182.

68. *Soviet Foreign Agricultural Trade* (ERS-Foreign 120, Economic Research Service, U.S. Department of Agriculture, March 1965), p. 10.

69. *Vneshniaia torgovlia SSSR za 1964 god. Statisticheskii obzor.* (Foreign Trade of the USSR for 1964. A Statistical Review; Moscow, 1965), p. 25; *1965,* p. 26.

70. Lemeshev, *Ekonomicheskoe obosnovanie,* p. 186.

71. V. Antoshkevich, "The Life of Machines and Amortization in Agriculture," *Voprosy ekonomiki,* November 1965, pp. 64–65.

72. A. Bugakov, "The Life of Tractors," *Sel'skaia zhizn',* August 6, 1966. A concrete example was given by another Soviet source. A kolkhoz in the Lipetsk oblast, considered to be one of the best in the raion, had twenty-six tractors in the spring of 1966, only four of which had been in service longer than five years; the others were only two or three years old. Instead of the supposed life of a tractor being eight years, in this kolkhoz it was not more than four to five years, and even less. This raises production costs.

73. Lemeshev, p. 184.

74. Iu. Popov and E. Kogan, in *Sel'skaia zhizn',* July 7, 1965.

75. V. Burnashev and others, in *Sel'skoe khoziaistvo,* August 9, 1959.

76. V. Evsukova, in *Sel'skoe khoziaistvo,* August 19, 1956.

77. Khrushchev, *Stroitel'stvo kommunizma*, II, 204; *Izvestiia*, February 15, 1956.

78. *Narodnoe khoziaistvo, 1964*, p. 187.

79. M. Gabrieli, "Price and the Effectiveness of the New Agricultural Technology," *Voprosy ekonomiki*, July 1963, pp. 59–69.

80. *Ibid.*, p. 58.

81. *Ibid.*, p. 62.

82. Ezhevskii, "Mechanization—the Main Force in the Development of Agriculture," *Ekonomika sel'skogo khoziaistva*, September 1963, pp. 11–19.

83. *Promyshlennost' SSSR, 1964*, pp. 280–281.

84. *Narodnoe khoziaistvo, 1964*, p. 419; *Soviet Agriculture Today*, p. 28.

85. *Sel'skoe khoziaistvo SSSR, 1960*, p. 450; *Narodnoe khoziaistvo, 1964*, p. 419.

86. *Changes in Farm Production*, 1966, p. 34. These figures included farm operators, unpaid family workers, and hired workers.

87. *Plenum 24–26 marta, 1965 g.*, pp. 217–218.

88. K. Bukovskii, "Porechno-stepnye," *Oktiabr'*, June 1966, p. 175.

89. *Plenum 24–26 marta, 1965 g.*, p. 22.

90. Khrushchev, *Stroitel'stvo kommunizma*, IV, 53–54; A Mel'nikov, "Some Questions of the Economics of Electrification of Agriculture of RSFSR," *Voprosy ekonomiki*, June 1961, pp. 148–152; see also S. Shchurov, "Electrification and Technical Progress in Agriculture," *Voprosy ekonomiki*, May 1961, pp. 27–35; P. Bogdashkin, "The Prospects of Electrification of Agriculture of the USSR," *Ekonomika sel'skogo khoziaistva*, November 1961, pp. 31–40; Bogdashkin, "Electrification of Agriculture—the High Tempo," *ibid.*, July 1966, pp. 16–24.

91. Lemeshev, *Ekonomicheskoe obosnovanie*, p. 189.

92. *Narodnoe khoziaistvo, 1964*, p. 387.

93. *Sel'skoe khoziaistvo SSSR, 1960*, p. 428; Bogdashkin, "Electrification of Agriculture—the High Tempo," *Ekonomika sel'skogo khoziaistva*, July 1966, p. 1.

94. *Sel'skoe khoziaistvo SSSR, 1960*, p. 428.

95. *Sbornik reshenii po sel'skomu khoziaistvu*, 1963, pp. 458–462.

96. V. Iambaev, *Sel'skaia zhizn'*, August 10, 1963.

97. Mel'nikov, in *Voprosy ekonomiki*, June 1961, p. 151.

98. Estimated by the Federal Power Commission, Washington, D.C.

19. *Expansion of Production*

1. Khrushchev, "Methods of Solving the Grain Problem," *Stroitel'stvo kommunizma*, I, 85–100.

2. Khrushchev, *Stroitel'stvo kommunizma*, I, 365

3. *Pravda*, January 22, 1961.

4. *Pravda*, March 21, 1954.

5. *Sel'skoe khoziaistvo SSSR, 1960*, p. 224.

6. *Pravda* and *Izvestiia*, March 21, 1954; August 17, 1954.

7. K. P. Gorshenin, "Concerning the Cultivation of Virgin and Long Uncultivated Lands in Siberia," *Pochvovedenie*, April 1954, pp. 1–10.

8. *Sovkhoznaia gazeta,* September 8, 1954.

9. G. A. Aniskin, "Virgin Lands of Siberia—A Reserve of Increased Grain Production," *Zemledelie,* April 1954, pp. 3–9.

10. *Kazakhstanskaia pravda,* October 6, 1961; *Sel'skaia zhizn',* October 7, 1961.

11. N. I. Vavilov, N. V. Kovalev, and N. S. Pereverzev, *Rastenievodstvo SSSR* (Leningrad and Moscow, 1933), vol. I, pt. 1, pp. x–xi.

12. *Sel'skoe khoziaistvo,* February 15, 1956.

13. S. S. Sdobnikov, *Voprosy zemledeliia v Tselinnom Krae* (Moscow, 1964), p. 20.

14. *Ibid.,* p. 25.

15. A. I. Baraev, "Important Problems of the Virgin Lands Agriculture," *Zemledelie,* January 1964, p. 45.

16. Sdobnikov, *Voprosy zemledeliia,* p. 56.

17. K. Kiiko and P. Shcherba, *Sel'skaia zhizn',* October 7, 1961.

18. Baraev, "Important Problems of Virgin Land Agriculture," *Zemledelie,* January 1964, p. 52; Sdobnikov, *Voprosy zemledeliia,* p. 36.

19. *Sel'skoe khoziaistvo,* May 24, 1955.

20. Kiiko and Shcherba, in *Sel'skaia zhizn',* October 7, 1961.

21. See Nalivaiko's article entitled "The Row Crop System—a Key to Abundance," *Izvestiia,* December 20, 1961; and his speech at the Twenty-second Congress of the Communist Party, *Pravda,* October 28, 1961.

22. *Izvestiia,* November 25, 1961.

23. N. Nazartsev, "It is Necessary To Plant More Millet and Barley on Virgin Lands," *Kolkhozno-sovkhoznoe proizvodstvo,* April 1964, p. 44; Sdobnikov, *Voprosy zemledeliia,* pp. 61–62.

24. Sdobnikov, *Voprosy zemledeliia,* p. 62.

25. Sh. Khairullin, in *Sel'skaia zhizn,* February 21, 1964; Baraev, in *Izvestiia,* November 17, 1963.

26. *Soviet Agriculture Today,* Foreign Agricultural Economic Report no. 13, U.S. Department of Agriculture (Washington, D.C., 1963), p. 16.

27. *Narodnoe khoziaistvo, 1962,* p. 293; Khrushchev, in *Pravda,* December 10, 1963.

28. *Narodnoe khoziaistvo, 1962,* p. 293.

29. *Narodnoe khoziaistvo, 1960,* p. 500.

30. Keith Bush, *The Profitability of the Virgin Lands,* Radio Liberty Research Paper, no. 2 (New York, 1964), pp. 6–7.

31. V. Semenov, "New Lands Sovkhozes—a Large Source of Socialist Capital Accumulation," *Finansy SSSR,* February 1962, pp. 31, 32.

32. *Pravda* and *Izvestiia,* November 25, 1961.

33. *Ibid.,* February 3, 2, 1955.

34. P. A. Baranov, N. P. Dubinin, and M. I. Khadzhinov, "Problems of Hybrid Corn," *Botanicheskii zhurnal,* April 1955, p. 183.

35. Khrushchev, *Stroitel'stvo kommunizma,* VI, 317–318.

36. *Pravda,* December 10, 1963.

37. I expressed my doubts about corn expansion in "Khrushchev's Economic Neo-Stalinism," *The American Slavic and East European Review,* 14. 4: 462–463

(December 1955); "Soviet Agricultural Policy after Stalin: Results and Prospects," *Journal of Farm Economics*, 38: 285 (May 1956).

38. M. Lemeshev, "Some Questions about the Economic Basis of Intensive Agriculture," *Voprosy ekonomiki*, February 1964, p. 20.

39. *Pravda*, December 10, 1964.

40. P. M. Zemskii, *Razvitie i razmeshchenie zemledeliia* (Moscow, 1959), p. 118.

41. Khrushchev, *Stroitel'stvo kommunizma*, I, 242.

42. J. H. Clapham, *The Economic Development of France and Germany, 1815–1914* (Cambridge, 1921), p. 402.

43. D. N. Prianishnikov, "Grass System of Rotation and Agricultural Chemistry," *Khimizatsiia sotsialisticheskogo zemledeliia*, September 1937. Reprinted in D. N. Prianishnikov, *Izbrannye sochineniia* (Moscow, 1963), III, 194–205.

44. *Pravda*, July 15, 1950.

45. *SSSR v tsifrakh*, 1963, p. 98.

46. *Narodnoe khoziaistvo, 1961*, p. 250; *Narodnoe khoziaistvo RSFSR, 1962*, p. 178.

47. *Narodnoe khoziaistvo RSFSR, 1962*, p. 178.

48. *Narodnoe khoziaistvo, 1962*, pp. 300, 326.

49. *Ibid.*, pp. 282–283.

50. *Ibid.*, p. 281; *SSSR v tsifrakh, 1963*, p. 103.

51. Lemeshev, in *Voprosy ekonomiki*, February 1964, p. 16.

52. *Soviet Agriculture Today*, p. 20.

53. H. E. Walters, *Agriculture in the United States and the Soviet Union*. United States Department of Agriculture. ERS-Foreign-53 (Washington, D.C., 1963), pp. 17–18.

54. *Pravda*, April 24, 1964.

55. B. Karkulov, in *Sel'skaia zhizn'*, February 23, 1965.

56. *Soviet Agriculture Today*, p. 22.

57. Naum Jasny, "The Failure of the Soviet Animal Industry. I," *Soviet Studies*, 15.2:205 (October 1963).

58. V. Khlebnikov, "Concerning a Further Strengthening of the Economy of Kolkhozes," *Voprosy ekonomiki*, July 1962, p. 53.

59. *Izvestiia*, December 10, 1964.

60. *Promyshlennost' SSSR, 1964*, p. 443.

61. S. A. Ilin, *Ekonomika proizvodstva kartofelia* (Moscow, 1963), p. 12.

62. This is indicated by feed rations recommended by V. Nemchinov to achieve "sufficiently high norms of livestock productivity." In "Economic Problems of the Development of Animal Husbandry," *Voprosy ekonomiki*, February 1955, p. 18.

20. State Farms

1. *Sotsialisticheskoe zemledelie*, January 28, 1934.

2. *Ekonomicheskaia zhizn'*, July 12, 1930.

3. *Stroitel'stvo sotsialisticheskikh krupnykh zernovykh khoziaistv*, (Proceed-

ings of the First Conference of Managers of State Farms; Moscow 1931); A. Kara-vaev, "The Liquidation of Seasonal Labor in the Grain Farms," *Sotsialisticheskaia rekonstruktsiia sel'skogo khoziaistva*, no. 3, 1936, pp. 197–210; T. Kuznetsova, "Cost of Production in Grain State Farms," *Planovoe khoziaistvo*, 1937, no. 2, pp. 70–90; W. Ladejinsky, "Soviet State Farms," *Political Science Quarterly*, 53: 60–62, 207–232 (1938).

4. Kilosanidze, *Vazhneishie resheniia po sel'skomu khoziaistvu* (2nd ed., 1935), p. 511.

5. *Posevnye ploshchadi*, 1938, p. 21.

6. *Zhivotnovodstvo, 1916–1938.*

7. *Narodnoe khoziaistvo, 1961*, p. 448.

8. *Narodnoe khoziaistvo, 1962*, pp. 354–355.

9. *Sel'skoe khoziaistvo* (Ezhegodnik, 1935), p. 782, for 1933; *Sotsialistichoshoe sel'skoe khoziaistvo, 1939*, p. 30, for 1937.

10. *Narodnoe khoziaistvo, 1962*, p. 353.

11. Kilosanidze, *Vazhneishie resheniia* (2nd ed.), pp. 509–510.

12. A. Pak, "What Is Worrying Sovkhoz Workers," *Sel'skaia zhizn'*, September 22, 1960.

13. A. Zhukov and A. Kukhovarenko, "Are Branches Necessary in Virgin Land Sovkhozes?" *Sel'skaia zhizn'*, October 3, 1960.

14. A. Eliashvili, "In Such Sovkhozes Branches Are Superfluous," *Sel'skaia zhizn'*, October 30, 1960.

15. Khrushchev, *Stroitel'stvo kommunizma*, V, 297.

16. "The Methodology of Establishing the Optimal Size of Sovkhozes and Its Farm Subdivisions," *Ekonomika sel'skogo khoziaistva*, 1963, no. 9, p. 89.

17. *Narodnoe khoziaistvo, 1960*, p. 538.

18. *Narodnoe khoziaistvo, 1961*, p. 448.

19. *Ibid.*

20. *Narodnoe khoziaistvo, 1962*, p. 242.

21. V. Khalturin, "The Influence of the Growth of Capital Stock of Sovkhozes on the Effectiveness of Its Utilization," *Planovoe khoziaistvo*, 1962, no. 11, pp. 53–60.

22. Iu. N. Pakhomov, *Nekotorye voprosy sovershenstvovaniia sovkhoznogo proizvodstva*, 1963, pp. 6–7.

23. V. Bagdasarian, *Sel'skoe khoziaistvo*, December 17, 1959. See also A. Kuzmin, *Sel'skaia zhizn'*, May 20, 1961.

24. A lively discussion of the subject began in the pages of *Sel'skaia zhizn'* with an article in the issue of December 23, 1962, by P. Avlasovich.

25. *Narodnoe khoziaistvo, 1962*, p. 370.

26. G. I. Vorob'ev, "Further Development of Kolkhoz and Sovkhoz Production in the Northwest of RSFSR," *Sel'skoe khoziaistvo severozapadnoi zony*, 1960, no. 4, pp. 10–20.

27. L. I. Maksimov, Minister of Production and Procurements of Agricultural Products of RSFSR, in *Pravda*, February 11, 1964.

28. V. Iambaev, *Sel'skaia zhizn'*, September 22, 1962.

29. P. Morozov, *Sel'skaia zhizn'*, February 26, 1963.

30. B. N. Dvoretskii, *Kazakhstanskaia pravda,* February 13, 1964.

31. *Narodnoe khoziaistvo, 1962,* pp. 356–357.

21. *Administrative Control and Planning*

1. A. A. Ruskol, *Dogovornye otnosheniia MTS s kolkhozami* (Moscow, 1948), p. 12.

2. V. A. Boldyrev, *Sbornik zakonodatel'nykh i vedomstvennykh aktov po sel'skomu khoziaistvu,* v. 1, p. 113.

3. *Sel'skoe khoziaistvo,* May 31, 1957.

4. G. Sitnikov, *Sel'skoe khoziaistvo,* December 23, 1956. It is also worth noting that the Minister of Agriculture in the late 1950s, the aggressive and articulate V. Matskevich, was simultaneously vice chairman of the Gosplan, heading its agricultural department.

5. Decree of February 25, 1961, no. 175. *Sbornik reshenii po sel'skomu khoziaistvu,* 1963, pp. 462–469.

6. Khrushchev, *Stroitel'stvo kommunizma,* VII, 164, 167.

7. *Ibid.,* pp. 333–334; *Pravda,* March 7, 1964.

8. *Pravda,* March 24, 1964.

9. D. N. Prianishnikov, *Sevooborot i ego znachenie v pod'eme urozhainosti.* Reprinted in *Zemledelie,* 1962, no. 11, pp. 34–50; *Chastnoe zemledelie* (Moscow and Leningrad, 1929), pp. 664–673.

10. *Pravda,* February 11, 1964.

11. William L. Langer, "Europe's Initial Population Pressure," *American Historical Review,* 69: 1–17 (October 1963).

12. *Narodnoe khoziaistvo, 1962,* p. 250.

13. *Soviet Agriculture Today,* Foreign Agricultural Economic Report no. 13, U.S. Department of Agriculture, Washington, D.C., December 1963, p. 48.

14. The ensuing discussion is adapted from *Soviet Agriculture Today,* pp. 62–63.

15. For supplementary reading on controls in Soviet agriculture see: Merle Fainsod, *How Russia is Ruled* (revised ed., Cambridge, Mass., 1963), chapter 16, pp. 526–576.

16. For literature on Lysenkoism, see Lazar Volin, *A Survey of Soviet Russian Agriculture* (Washington, D.C., 1951), p. 101.

17. *Pravda,* February 15, 1964.

18. *Sel'skoe khoziaistvo,* June 22, 1956.

Summary and Outlook

1. *Narodnoe khoziaistvo, 1958,* p. 707.

2. *Ibid.,* pp. 622, 631.

3. *Narodnoe khoziaistvo, 1962,* p. 227

4. U.S. Department of Agriculture, *The 1964 Eastern Europe Agricultural Situation*, p. 3.

5. *Ibid.*, pp. 9–13.

6. D. H. Robertson, "A Word for the Devil," *Economica*, 3.9:203–208 (1923).

7. M. A. Ol'shanskii, *Stenograficheskii otchet. XXII S'ezda Kommunisticheskoi Partii Sovetskogo Soiuza*, vol. 2, p. 541.

8. Peter Wiles, "The Soviet Economy Outpaces the West," *Foreign Affairs*, 31: 566–580 (July 1953).

9. *Literaturnaia Moskva, Sbornik vtoroi* (Moscow 1956), pp. 404–414.

Index

Abramov, F. A., "One Day in the New Life," 377
Administration, agricultural: organization of, 536–537; 1961–1962 reorganization of, 539–542. *See also* Collective farms; Machine Tractor Stations; Planning
Alekseevskii, E. E., 372, 373
Alexander II, 5, 40. *See also* Emancipation
American Relief Association (ARA), 174–175
Andreev, A. A., 268, 291, 303, 454, 539
Antonov, A. S., 164
Artel, 153, 215. *See also* Collective farms
Arutiunian, Iu. V., 278, 279, 284
Arzumanian, A. A., 438–439

Bakunin, M., 82, 86
Baraev, A. I., 548–549
Barshchina, 16, 17–18
Bazhaev, V., 67
Beliaev, I. D., 80
Belinsky, V., 30
Bergson, A., 257, 258

Biological yield, adopted as crop measure, 253, 323, 329
Bolotnikov, I., 23
Brandt, K., 299–300
Brezhnev, L., on irrigation, 373; on malpractices in procurements, 392; on money wage to kolkhozniks, 415, 416; on rural electrification, 478, 479
Bukharin, N., and agrarian policies under NEP, 176–177, 178, 190; on capital accumulation, 193; purge of, 199, 262; on tempo of industrialization, 200
Bukovskii, K., 478
Bunge, N. Kh., 53

Capital investment, in agriculture: by collective farms, 266, 347–350, 352–353; by government, in collective farms, 347, 348, 349, 350–352; by government, in state farms, 350–351, 529, 531; and government loans to collective farms, 354–356; inadequacy of, 355–359; and irrigation, 370–372; and virgin lands program, 493–494

637

II, 458–459; 1958 abolition of, 459–460, 462–466; 1953 reorganization of, 460–461; liquidation of machinery of, 466–467, 469. *See also* Collective farms; Mechanization; Repair Technical Stations; *Soiuzsel'khoztekhnika*

Machinery, farm, 455–456, 469, 471–475

Makhno, N. I., 164

Malenkov, G., and repudiation of "biological yield" measurement for crops, 255, 329; on agrarian situation, 322–323, 329–330; industrialization policies of, 330, 436; opposition of to virgin lands campaign, 486

Man-day, *see* Earnings, farm; Procurements

Manorial serfs (*dvorovye*), 16, 18–19

Manuilov, A. A.: on educational policy of tsarist government, 65; on leasing, 73; on intensity of production and redistribution of land, 76, 92; on the mir, 85

Markevich, A. M., and prototype of Machine Tractor Stations, 446

Marx, K., on the mir, 83, 84; on modern technology and industrialization, 192; on large-scale farming, 203; Marxists, prerevolutionary: rejection by of the mir, 86–88; on economic differentiation in the Russian village, 89; agrarian program of during 1905 revolution, 98–99. *See also* Lenin; Mir

Maslov, S. L., 124

Matskevich, V. V.: on impact of liquidation of MTS, 468–469; on Soviet agricultural research, 553–554, 555

Mechanization: prerevolutionary increase of, 111, 444–445; under NEP, 182; impact of World War II on, 277–278, 306–307; Soviet policy on, 445; levels achieved, 455–457, 469–470; post-MTS achievements in, 469–471; and crop expansion, 475–476; and decline of farm labor force, 476; 1965 plan for, 477. *See also* Machine Tractor Stations; Machinery, farm

Mendeleev, D., 86, 367

Mensheviks, agrarian proposals of, 159

Mesiachnina, 18

Michurin, I. V., 552. *See also* Lysenko

Mikhailovskii, N. K., 84

Miliukov, P. N.: on origins of serfdom, 10; on emancipation, 35; on Stolypin's land reforms, 106; speech of in the Duma (Nov., 1916), 118

Miliutin, N., 41

Mir: role of in emancipation settlement, 52–54, 55, 79–81; land holdings of (1905), 77; organization of, 78–79; post-emancipation ideological debates on, 78, 82–86, 86–88, 89–90; farming methods in, 78–79, 89–92; debate over origins of, 79–80, 82; incidence of repartitioning on, 79, 80–82, 88, 92; Marx and Engels on, 83–84, 85; opposition to, 86–93; and population growth, 92; pro-mir policy of government (pre-1905), 92–93; impact of Stolypin's reforms on, 102–108; as model for land distribution of *1918*, 130

Molotov, V. M., 223, 244, 268; on peasant productivity after collectivization, 236; opposition of to virgin lands campaign, 486

Nalivaiko, A. G., 549

Narodnik, *see* Populism

Nashi raznoglasiia (G. Plekhanov), 88

Nemchinov, V. S., 357

New Economic Policy (NEP): adoption of, 166–167; provisions of, 167–168; agricultural recovery under, 169, 175–184; and the "scissors" crisis, 184–187; ideological opposition to, 189–190; debate over future agrarian policy, 193–195; wane of, 196–197

Nicholas I, 38

Novoselskii, A. A., 13

Obrok, 16

Oganovskii, N. P., 92, 105, 110

Ogarev, N., 32

Ol'shanskii, M., 337, 552

Orlovskii, K., 414–415

Ors (otdel rabochego snabzheniia), auxiliary farms, 555

Osinskii, N. (V. V.), 157, 158, 253–254

Otrub, 106

Ownership of land: under emancipation settlement, 54, 55, 77, 78; by the peasantry through purchases of gentry lands, 70, 109–110; by gentry, 70–71, 132–133; structure of as of *1905*, 70–71, 96; structure of as of *1916*, 132–133; Stolypin reforms and, 103–105, 106; socialization of, proclaimed, 128–129, 153; 1917–1919 redistribution of, 130–133, 135–137; by state, reaffirmed under NEP, 170; and peasant tenure under NEP, 170–172; and peasant tenure under collective farm system, 245

Panferov, F., 377

Panin, Count N., 41

RUSSIAN RESEARCH CENTER STUDIES

* Out of print.
† Publications of the Harvard Project on the Soviet Social System.
‡ Published jointly with the Center for International Affairs, Harvard University.